**CORE TAX ANNUALS**
# Inheritance Tax

# CORE TAX ANNUALS
# Inheritance Tax 2010/11

**Mark McLaughlin** CTA (Fellow) ATT TEP

**Toby Harris** LLB CTA TEP

and

**Iris Wünschmann-Lyall** MA (Cantab) TEP

*Series General Editor:* Mark McLaughlin CTA (Fellow) ATT TEP

Bloomsbury Professional

**Bloomsbury Professional Ltd, Maxwelton House, 41–43 Boltro Road, Haywards Heath, West Sussex, RH16 1BJ**

© Bloomsbury Professional Ltd 2010

All rights reserved. No part of this publication may be reproduced in any material form (including photocopying or storing it in any medium by electronic means and whether or not transiently or incidentally to some other use of this publication) without the written permission of the copyright owner except in accordance with the provisions of the Copyright, Designs and Patents Act 1988 or under the terms of a licence issued by the Copyright Licensing Agency Ltd, Saffron House, 6-10 Kirby Street, London EC1N 8TS. Applications for the copyright owner's written permission to reproduce any part of this publication should be addressed to the publisher.

Warning: The doing of an unauthorised act in relation to a copyright work may result in both a civil claim for damages and criminal prosecution.

Crown copyright material is reproduced with the permission of the Controller of HMSO and the Queen's Printer for Scotland. Any European material in this work which has been reproduced from EUR-lex, the official European Communities legislation website, is European Communities copyright.

A CIP Catalogue record for this book is available from the British Library.

ISBN: 978 1 84766 516 4

Typeset by Phoenix Photosetting, Chatham, Kent
Printed in the UK by CPI William Clowes Beccles NR34 7TL

# Preface

Welcome to the *Inheritance Tax Annual 2010/11*. It is the fifth year of this title in the Core Tax Annuals series, now published by Bloomsbury Professional. I hope that existing readers will continue to find the Core Tax Annuals a useful and constantly improving resource, and that new readers will agree that the authors have achieved their goal of producing a very helpful, user-friendly, practical guide for practitioners and others.

For yet another year, the publishers have continued their policy of pricing the *Inheritance Tax Annual 2010/11* and the other Core Tax Annuals at an affordable and highly competitive level. Tax books have always generally tended to be relatively expensive in the past, but the publishers have hopefully made the Core Tax Annuals affordable for all practitioners.

The inheritance tax landscape has not drastically changed as the result of a change of Government in 2010. Nevertheless, there have been some legislative changes, as well as various cases and changes of practice. As in previous years, the emphasis in this book, and in the Core Tax Annuals generally, is on concentrating the content on day-to-day tax issues that are most frequently encountered, rather than on subjects that are probably peripheral to the majority of readers. This means that the content may not be as comprehensive as annuals produced by other tax publishers, but I hope readers will agree that this is worthwhile in terms of making the annuals easier to digest and more practical. The intention remains to provide short, concise paragraphs written in plain English, punctuated by plenty of worked examples.

It has been a pleasure as always working my two co-authors on the IHT Annual, Toby Harris and Iris Wünschmann-Lyall. Both are very experienced and talented experts in their field, are very professional people to work with, and are very nice people as well.

My thanks as always to my wife Sharon and my children Shaun and Hayley for all their love, not to mention their unlimited forbearance!

Many thanks to Sarah Blair of Bloomsbury Professional, for her help, encouragement, support and understanding in this book, and in all the writing projects with which I am involved.

Thank you to Heather Saward for her help and considerable patience, and to everyone else at Bloomsbury Professional who has been involved in the Core Tax Annuals.

*Preface*

Last but not least, thanks to you, the reader, for picking up and reading this book. I hope that you find it a useful source of reference.

*Mark McLaughlin*
*Manchester, August 2010*

# Contents

| | |
|---|---|
| *Preface* | *v* |
| *Table of statutes* | *xi* |
| *Table of statutory instruments* | *xxi* |
| *Table of cases* | *xxiii* |
| *Abbreviations and references* | *xxxi* |

| | |
|---|---|
| **Chapter 1 Inheritance tax: introduction** | **1** |
| Background | 1 |
| Who is liable? | 1 |
| Domicile | 1 |
| What is chargeable to IHT? | 5 |
| Cumulation and the IHT threshold | 5 |
| Rates of IHT | 6 |
| Transfers of value | 7 |
| Potentially exempt transfers | 8 |
| Chargeable lifetime transfers | 8 |
| IHT on death | 9 |
| Excluded property | 9 |
| Exemptions—summary | 11 |
| Taper relief: outline | 14 |
| Quick succession relief: outline | 14 |
| Double taxation relief | 15 |
| Transfers of value by close companies | 16 |
| **Chapter 2 Lifetime transfers** | **18** |
| Introduction | 18 |
| Exempt lifetime transfers | 18 |
| Potentially exempt transfers | 20 |
| Chargeable lifetime transfers | 25 |
| Valuing lifetime transfers | 27 |
| Gifts with reservation | 28 |
| Associated operations | 29 |
| Calculating IHT | 30 |
| Reporting chargeable lifetime transfers | 33 |
| **Chapter 3 IHT on death** | **35** |
| Introduction | 35 |
| Estate on death | 37 |
| Liabilities | 40 |
| Rules for amount or value of liability | 43 |
| Asset valuations: outline | 45 |

Contents

|  |  |
|---|---|
| Related property: introduction | 46 |
| Calculating iht on the death estate | 46 |
| Chargeable and exempt estate | 50 |

**Chapter 4 Valuation of assets** — 62
| General | 62 |
| Related property | 64 |
| Particular assets | 68 |

**Chapter 5 Gifts with reservation of benefit** — 80
| Outline | 80 |
| Scope and effect of the GWR rules | 81 |
| Exceptions and exclusions from charge | 94 |
| GWR and double IHT relief | 100 |
| GWR and 'shearing' arrangements | 101 |

**Chapter 6 Compliance** — 102
| Liability and incidence of tax | 102 |
| Accounts and returns | 102 |
| Excepted estates | 116 |
| Particular compliance points | 120 |
| Payment of IHT | 121 |
| Penalties | 124 |
| Record keeping | 137 |
| Determinations and appeals | 137 |

**Chapter 7 Trusts: interest in possession** — 144
| IHT treatment | 144 |
| IPDI | 148 |
| Disposal of interest in possession | 151 |
| Termination of interest in possession | 153 |
| Reversionary and purchased interests | 158 |
| Transitional provisions, 2006–2008 | 162 |
| Excluded property trusts | 167 |
| Insurance policy trusts | 171 |

**Chapter 8 Relevant property trusts** — 176
| Types of discretionary or relevant property trusts | 176 |
| The relevant property IHT regime | 187 |
| Transfers into trust: the entry charge | 188 |
| The proportionate or 'exit' charge during the first ten years | 195 |
| The periodic or 'ten-year' charge | 206 |
| The impact of APR and BPR | 222 |
| The special charge under section 70 | *225* |

*Contents*

**Chapter 9 Exemptions and excluded property**    **231**
    Introduction    231
    Lifetime exemptions    233
    Dispositions which are not transfers of value    236
    General exemptions    239
    Death exemption    243
    Excluded property    244

**Chapter 10 Reliefs – General**    **250**
    Introduction    250
    Taper relief    251
    Quick succession relief    253
    Related property relief    255
    Transfers within seven years before death    257
    Post-death reliefs    260
    Double taxation relief    264
    Double charges relief    265
    Woodlands relief    266
    Heritage property    268

**Chapter 11 Business property relief and agricultural property relief**    **271**
    Scope of business property relief    271
    Conditions    279
    Valuation, excepted assets    285
    Scope of agricultural property relief    288
    Conditions for APR    294
    Loss of BPR and APR    301

**Chapter 12 Lifetime planning**    **306**
    Use all the reliefs    306
    Outright gifts    313
    Disabled trusts    317
    Protected gifts without trusts    320
    Traditional protected gifts    322

**Chapter 13 Wills and estate planning**    **327**
    The nil rate band    327
    Deferral of tax using spouse relief    333
    BPR, APR and woodlands relief    338
    Exempt gifts on death    344
    Policy trusts    348
    Post-death variations    348

**Chapter 14 Transferable nil rate bands**    **356**
    Background    356

*Contents*

| | |
|---|---|
| Outline of the rules | 357 |
| Calculating the unused nil rate band | 358 |
| Transfer claims | 361 |
| Clawback of nil rate band | 363 |
| Deaths before 25 July 1986 | 369 |
| Practical issues | 370 |
| Planning issues | 373 |
| Other issues | 380 |

**Chapter 15 The family home** — **382**
Introduction — 382
Lifetime planning — 389
Will planning — 396

**Chapter 16 Pre-owned assets** — **411**
Introduction — 411
The pre-owned assets charge on land — 413
The pre-owned assets charge on chattels — 415
Pre-owned assets charge on intangible property comprised in settlor-interested settlements — 417
Scope of the pre-owned assets legislation — 418
Calculation of tax charge in relation to land — 419
Calculation of tax charge in relation to chattels — 420
Calculation of tax charge in relation to intangible property — 422
Valuation problems — 423
Excluded transactions — 424
Exemptions — 425
Residence and/or domicile of taxpayer — 430
'Opting out' of the pre-owned assets charge — 430
Remedial action in relation to existing arrangements — 431

*Index* — *435*

# Table of statutes

[*All references are to paragraph numbers*]

**A**
Administration of Estates Act 1925 ... 3.1, 6.33
s 46 .................................................. 3.1

**B**
Banking Act 1987 ............................... 9.35
Blank Bonds and Trusts Act 1696 ...... 4.19

**C**
Civil Partnership Act 2004 .............. 1.20, 9.17
Sch 4
para 7–12 ................................... 3.1

**D**
Data Protection Act 1998 ................... 8.3
Diplomatic Privileges Act 1964
s 2(1) ............................................. 9.37
Domicile and Matrimonial Proceedings Act 1973 ................. 1.6

**E**
Enduring Powers of Attorney Act 1985
s 3(5) ............................................. 6.38

**F**
Finance Act 1894 ............................... 1.1
Finance Act 1975 ............................ 1.1, 11.42
Finance Act 1982
s 96 ................................................. 9.35
Finance Act 1986 ............................... 1.1
s 102 ...................... 2.11, 2.20, 4.13, 4.27, 5.1, 5.5, 5.14, 12.19, 12.21, 13.16
(1) .......................................... 5.5, 15.30
(a) .......................................... 5.4, 5.5
(b) .................. 5.4, 5.5, 5.28, 15.17
(3) ...................... 3.3, 4.3, 5.7, 5.11, 5.14, 5.19
(4) ...................... 2.12, 2.20, 5.1, 5.11, 5.14
(5) .................................. 5.2, 5.15, 5.25
(d)–(i) ................................... 16.22
(5A) .................... 5.9, 5.15, 5.26, 7.6, 15.8
(5B), (5C) ................... 5.9, 5.15, 5.26
102A ......................... 2.20, 5.1, 5.11, 5.12, 5.13, 5.14, 15.6, 15.7, 16.22

Finance Act 1986 – *contd*
s 102A(2) ....................................... 5.12
(3) ............................. 5.12, 5.13, 15.6
(4)(a), (b) ............................ 5.12
(5) ............... 5.12, 5.13, 15.6, 15.7
102B ........................ 2.20, 5.1, 5.11, 5.14, 15.20, 16.22
(1) ............................................ 15.18
(3)(a), (b) ....................... 5.14, 15.19
(4) ....................... 5.14, 15.19, 15.20, 15.21, 16.18, 16.22
102C ........................ 2.20, 5.1, 5.11, 5.15
(2) ............................................ 5.15
(3) ................... 5.15, 15.23, 16.22
(6) .................................. 5.14, 15.18
(7) ............................................ 5.11
102ZA ..................... 4.27, 5.19, 5.20, 7.7, 7.9, 13.14, 13.15, 13.16, 15.30
(1)(b)(ii) .................................. 7.25
(2) ........................ 2.11, 5.19, 13.15
103 ....................... 2.12, 3.10, 3.16, 10.23, 12.9, 13.2, 13.4, 13.5, 14.25, 15.47, 15.51
(1) ............................. 13.3, 13.4, **13.6**
(a) ...................................... 15.46
(4) ............................................ 3.10
(5) ............................................ 2.12
(7) ............................................ 3.11
104 ........................... 4.27, 5.8, 5.36
(1)(c) ........................................ 3.11
106 .................................................. 5.23
Sch 19
para 46 ..................................... 2.8
Sch 20 ..................................... 2.20, 5.1, 7.7
para 2 ........................................ 5.16
(2)(b) ................................... 5.17
(4)–(7) ................................. 5.17
3 ......................................... 5.16, 5.17
4 ......................................... 5.16, 5.17
4A ........................................... 5.20
5 .............................................. 5.20
(1) .......................................... 5.18
6(1)(a) ................. 5.29, 15.17, 16.23
(b) ................. 5.15, 5.30, 15.23, 16.22
(c) .......................................... 5.5
8(1A)(a), (b) ......................... 5.23
(2)(a), (b) ......................... 5.23

## Table of statutes

Finance Act 1986 – *contd*
  Sch 20 – *contd*
    para 8(3) ..................................... 5.23
        (b) .................................. 5.23
        (5) .................................. 5.23
    7 ..................................................... 5.22
Finance Act 1998 ............................... 10.30
Finance Act 1999 ........................ 5.11, 5.14
Finance Act 2002 ........................ 7.23, 9.18
Finance Act 2003 .......................... 5.9, 8.1
  s 43(1) ............................................ 15.50
  185 ..................................................... 7.6
  Sch 4
    para 1 .......................................... 15.50
Finance Act 2004 ................. 8.1, 16.2, 16.8
  s 84 .......................................... 5.3, 16.1
  Sch 15 ................................... 16.1, 16.16
    para 1 .................................. 16.9, 16.12
    3 ..................................................... 16.4
      (1) .............................................. 16.3
      (2) ................................... 15.6, 16.5
      (3) .............................................. 16.6
      (4) .............................................. 15.6
    4 ................................................... 16.14
      (1) .............................................. 5.30
    6 ..................................................... 16.7
      (2) .............................................. 16.9
      (3) ............................................ 16.10
    7 ................................................... 16.15
      (1) .............................................. 5.30
    8 ................................................... 16.12
    9 ................................................... 16.16
    10 ................................................. 16.18
      (1)(a) ....................................... 15.16
        (c) .......................................... 15.8
      (2)(c) ....................................... 16.13
    11 ................................................. 16.19
      (1) ............................................ 16.20
      (4) ............................................ 15.10
      (5) ....................... 5.3, 5.14, 16.21,
                                   16.22
        (a) ................ 16.6, 16.11, 16.23
        (c) ......................................... 15.21
        (d) ............... 5.30, 15.22, 16.23
      (9) .............................................. 7.15
      (11)–(13) ..................................... 7.15
    12 ...................................... 16.19, 16.27
    13 ...................................... 16.19, 16.25
    15 ................................................. 16.17
    21 ......................................... 5.3, 16.28
    22 ................................................. 16.28
    23 ................................................. 16.28
      (3) ............................................ 16.28
  Sch 29 ............................................... 7.40
    para 13(c) ...................................... 7.40
    15(1)(c) ......................................... 7.40

Finance Act 2005 .............................. 9.17
Finance Act 2006 ............. 5.9, 5.19, 5.35, 6.1,
                        7.9, 7.10, 7.15, 7.24,
                        7.31, 7.36, 7.37, 7.38,
                        7.40, 7.42, 8.1, 8.5,
                        8.17, 8.22, 8.24, 8.27,
                        8.31, 8.32, 8.61, 8.65,
                        8.71, 9.16, 9.39, 10.5,
                        11.4, 11.6, 11.51, 12.1,
                        12.3, 12.5, 12.8, 12.10,
                        12.13, 12.19, 12.23,
                        12.25, 12.26, 12.28,
                        12.29, 13.13, 13.21,
                        13.50, 15.40, 15.42
  s 80 .................................................. 7.15
    (1) ................................................. 7.35
    (4) ................................................. 7.35
      (b) ............................................ 7.35
  89 .................................................... 7.19
  156 .................................................... 7.7
  Sch 20 .............................................. 7.19
    para 3 .................................. 8.12, 8.25
      (3) .............................................. 8.25
    13 ................................................... 7.20
    14, 15 ............................................ 7.12
    16 ................................................... 7.16
Finance Act 2007 .................. 2.23, 6.45, 7.40,
                        14.1, 16.28
  s 4 ................................................... 14.22
  Sch 24 ..................... 6.36, 6.37, 6.38, 14.14
    para 1 ........................................... 14.14
      (1) .............................................. 6.36
    1A ............................................ 6.36, 14.14
    4C .................................................. 6.38
    6 ..................................................... 6.38
    9 ..................................................... 6.39
      (3) .............................................. 6.41
    10 ................................................... 6.39
      (3), (4) ....................................... 6.41
    11 ........................................... 6.39, 6.42
    12 ........................................... 6.39, 6.42
    14 ................................................... 6.47
    18(3) ............................................... 6.48
Finance Act 2008 ............ 6.36, 6.38, 8.1, 8.72,
                        9.17, 13.6, 13.7, 13.8,
                        13.17, 14.1, 14.11, 14.12,
                        14.15, 14.16, 14.20, 15.26
  s 10 .................................................. 13.1
  24 .................................................... 7.34
  25 .................................................... 7.34
  91 .................................................... 7.40
  Pt 7 (ss 113–139) ................................. 6.3
  s 113 .................................................. 6.3
  115–117 ............................................ 6.3
  122, 123 ......................................... 6.36
  140 ......................................... 7.8, 7.10

*Table of statutes*

| Finance Act 2008 – *contd* | | Income Tax (Earnings and Pensions) | |
|---|---|---|---|
| Sch 4................................................ | 13.1 | Act 2003 | |
| para 10(2)–(5) ........................ | 14.16 | s 181 ............................................. | 16.15 |
| 11 ..................................... | 14.16 | Sch 2............................................. | 9.24 |
| Sch 7................................................ | 7.34 | Income Tax (Trading and Other | |
| Sch 28.............................................. | 7.40 | Income) Act 2005 | |
| Sch 36.............................................. | 6.3 | s 461 ............................................. | 16.16 |
| Sch 37.................................... | 6.3, 6.51 | 624 ................................... | 12.18, 16.16 |
| Sch 39.............................................. | 6.3 | 625 ............................................. | 16.12 |
| Sch 40.......................... 6.3, 6.36, 6.37, 14.14 | | (1) ......................................... | 16.12 |
| para 1(4) ................................ | 6.36 | 629 ............................................. | 12.18 |
| 5..................................... | 6.38 | 703(1) ......................................... | 9.32 |
| 9, 10................................. | 6.39 | 727 ............................................. | 16.30 |
| 11 ..................................... | 6.39 | Inheritance Tax Act 1984 ........ 1.1, 6.53, 16.27 | |
| (3)..................................... | 6.42 | s 1 ............................................... | 1.1, 4.1 |
| Finance Act 2009 .......................... 8.48, 10.24 | | 2 ................................................. | 1.9, 1.16 |
| s 96 ............................................... | 6.3 | (1) ......................................... | 1.27, 2.1, 2.14 |
| 101(1) ..................................... | 6.46 | 3 ................................................. | 8.2 |
| 105 ......................................... | 6.50 | (1) ......................................... | 1.14, 2.7, 2.21, 4.2 |
| 106 .................................... | 6.36, 6.49 | (2) ......................................... | 1.14, 1.19, 2.17, 9.6, 9.28 |
| 107 ......................................... | 6.36 | (3) ......................................... | 7.40 |
| Sch 48.............................................. | 6.3 | (4) ......................................... | 3.3 |
| Sch 50.............................................. | 6.51 | 3A ......................... 1.15, 2.10, 7.25, 8.2, 9.2 | |
| Sch 53.............................................. | 6.46 | (1) ......................................... | 2.7 |
| Sch 55.............................................. | 6.50 | (1A)........................................ 2.7, 2.8, 5.19 | |
| Sch 56.............................................. | 6.49 | (c)(iii) ............................. | 2.8 |
| Finance Act 2010 .................... 7.12, 7.18, 9.19 | | (2) ......................................... | 2.12 |
| s 8 ........................................ 1.10, 2.23, 14.1, 14.22 | | (3), (3A)................................ | 2.8 |
| 52 ........................................... 7.24, 8.15 | | (4) ......................................... | 5.27, 15.16 |
| 53 ........................................... 7.22, 7.25, 7.26, 7.32, 8.15, 9.6 | | (5) ......................................... | 2.1, 2.5 |
| (2)(a) ..................................... | 7.25 | (6) ......................................... | 2.9 |
| (8) ......................................... | 7.25 | (6A)........................................ | 2.9, 7.25 |
| Sch 7................................................ | 1.20 | (7) ......................................... | 2.9 |
| Financial Services and Markets Act 2000 | | 4 ................................................. | 13.46 |
| s 236 ............................................ | 9.31 | (1) ......................................... 1.9, 1.17, 3.1, 3.2, 3.21 | |
| 243 ............................................ | 9.31 | (2) ......................................... | 3.7 |
| | | 5(1) ......................................... 4.3, 9.6, 9.28 | |
| **H** | | (a)(i), (ii) ............................. | 7.25 |
| Housing Act 1996 ........................ | 9.21 | (b)......................................... | 1.19 |
| Housing Associations Act 1985 ......... | 9.21 | (1A) ....................................... | 7.24 |
| | | (1B)........................... 3.2, 7.25, 7.26, 9.6 | |
| **I** | | (2) ......................................... | 4.3 |
| Income and Corporation Taxes Act 1988 | | (3) ......................................... | 2.17 |
| s 615 ............................................ | 7.40 | (5) ......................... 1.17, 2.17, 3.9, 3.12 | |
| (3) ......................................... | 1.20, 3.5 | 6 ................................................. 9.6, 9.28, 9.29 | |
| Sch 9................................................ | 9.24 | (1) ......................... 1.2, 1.18, 3.5, 5.32, 7.33, 9.39 | |
| Income Tax Act 2007 | | (1A) ....................................... | 3.5, 9.31 |
| s 403 ............................................ | 6.46 | (2) ......................................... | 1.8, 1.18, 9.30 |
| 497 ......................................... | 8.59 | (3) ......................................... | 1.8, 1.18, 9.32 |
| 720–730 ................................. | 16.16 | (4) ......................................... | 9.33 |
| 1005 ....................................... | 11.4 | 7 ................................. 1.10, 2.23, 3.21, 10.1 | |

*Table of statutes*

Inheritance Tax Act 1984 – *contd*
| | |
|---|---|
| s 7(1) | 12.8 |
| (2) | 1.11 |
| (4) | 1.21, 8.19, 10.2 |
| (5) | 1.22, 10.3 |
| 8 | 1.10, 14.22 |
| 8A | 3.22, 9.17, 14.1, 14.2, 14.16, 15.27 |
| (1) | 14.3 |
| (2) | 14.3, 14.9 |
| (3) | 14.3, 14.4, 14.5, 14.7 |
| (4) | 14.3, 14.9, 14.9 |
| (5) | 14.3, 14.4 |
| (6) | 14.4 |
| 8B | 3.22, 14.1, 14.2, 14.5, 15.27 |
| (1)(b) | 14.5 |
| (2) | 14.6 |
| (3) | 14.5 |
| (4) | 14.6 |
| 8C | 3.22, 14.1, 14.2, 14.8, 14.16, 15.27 |
| (1) | 14.8 |
| (2), (3) | 14.9 |
| (4), (5) | 14.10 |
| 10 | 1.14, 2.4, 3.3, 7.11, 7.22, 7.23, 7.25, 15.16 |
| 11 | 1.14, 1.20, 2.4, 3.3, 7.11, 9.3, 9.12, 15.16, 16.18 |
| (3) | 15.16 |
| 12 | 1.14, 2.4, 3.3, 9.3, 9.12 |
| 13 | 2.4, 3.3, 9.3, 9.12 |
| 14, 15 | 1.14, 2.4, 3.3 |
| 16 | 2.4, 3.3, 8.10 |
| 17 | 2.4, 3.3, 13.46 |
| (a) | 13.46 |
| 18 | 1.20, 2.3, 2.25, 3.5, 5.9, 5.25, 5.26, 6.11, 9.4, 9.16, 13.42, 14.1, 14.28, 15.26, 15.29, 15.42 |
| (2) | 1.6, 9.17 |
| (3) | 9.16 |
| 19 | 1.20, 2.3, 4.10, 6.11, 9.2, 12.25, 16.18 |
| (1) | 9.7 |
| (3)(b) | 8.17 |
| (3A) | 2.13 |
| (5) | 3.4, 5.1, 5.27 |
| 20 | 1.20, 2.3, 5.25, 6.11, 9.2, 9.8, 12.25, 16.18 |
| (3) | 3.4 |

Inheritance Tax Act 1984 – *contd*
| | |
|---|---|
| s 21 | 1.20, 2.3, 4.10, 5.1, 6.9, 6.10, 6.11, 6.12, 6.38, 7.28, 8.16, 8.50, 9.2, 9.9, 12.1, 12.2, 12.6, 12.17, 12.25, 13.37, 15.15 |
| (1)(b) | 6.13 |
| (2) | 2.5, 4.12, 9.10 |
| (3) | 2.5 |
| (5) | 3.4, 5.27 |
| 22 | 1.20, 2.3, 5.25, 6.11, 9.2, 9.11 |
| (4) | 9.11 |
| (6) | 3.4 |
| 23 | 1.20, 2.3, 3.5, 5.25, 9.4, 9.18 |
| (2) | 9.19, 13.31 |
| (4) | 9.19 |
| (6) | 9.18 |
| 24 | 1.20, 2.3, 5.25, 9.4, 9.20 |
| 24A | 1.20, 2.3, 5.25, 9.4, 9.21 |
| 25 | 1.20, 2.3, 5.25, 9.4, 9.22 |
| 26 | 1.20, 5.25 |
| 27 | 1.20, 2.3, 5.25, 9.4, 13.32 |
| 28 | 1.20, 2.3, 5.25, 9.4, 9.24 |
| (1)(b) | 9.24 |
| (2) | 9.25 |
| 29A | 3.4 |
| 30 | 2.3, 9.4, 9.23, 10.1, 10.27, 14.9 |
| (3BA) | 13.36 |
| 31 | 2.3, 9.4, 9.23, 10.27, 13.32 |
| 32 | 2.3, 9.4, 9.23, 10.27, 14.9, 14.10 |
| 33 | 2.3, 9.4, 9.23 |
| (5) | 13.32 |
| 34 | 2.3, 9.4, 9.23 |
| 35 | 2.3, 9.4, 9.23 |
| 35A | 9.23 |
| 36 | 3.25 |
| 37 | 3.25, 3.26 |
| 38 | 3.25, 3.33 |
| (6) | 3.26 |
| 39 | 3.25 |
| 39A | 3.27, 3.27, 3.28, 12.1, 13.25, 13.27 |
| (2) | 3.27 |
| (4) | 3.27 |
| (6) | 14.28 |

## Table of statutes

Inheritance Tax Act 1984 – *contd*
- s 40 .................................................... 3.25, 3.29
- 41 ........................................................ 3.25, 3.35
  - (1)(a) ............................................... 3.36
  - (b) ................................................... 3.36, 3.37
- 42 ........................................................ 3.25
  - (1) .................................................... 3.26
  - (2) .................................................... 3.26, 3.36
- 43 ........................................................ 6.16
  - (1)(a) ............................................... 7.5
  - (2) .................................................... 15.43
    - (a) ................................................. 15.24
    - (b) ................................................. 6.16
  - (3) .................................................... 7.32, 15.24, 15.32
  - (4) .................................................... 4.26
- 46 ........................................................ 4.26
  - (5) .................................................... 8.21
- s 46A .................................................. 7.36, 7.37, 12.25
- s 46B ................................................... 7.37
  - (1) .................................................... 8.21
- 47 ........................................................ 4.26
- 47A ..................................................... 7.23
- 48 ........................................................ 9.39
  - (1) .................................................... 1.18, 7.32, 9.38
    - (a) ................................................. 9.39
  - (3) .................................................... 1.18, 3.5, 5.35, 7.33, 9.29, 9.39
  - (3A) .................................................. 1.18, 3.5
  - (3B) .................................................. 1.18, 3.5, 5.35, 7.26, 7.34, 9.39
  - (3C) .................................................. 5.35
  - (4) .................................................... 1.8
- 49 ........................................................ 7.1, 11.47
  - (1) .................................................... 3.2, 4.8, 4.25, 7.10
  - (1A) .................................................. 2.8, 3.2, 4.25, 7.10, 7.25
  - (2) .................................................... 4.25
- 49A ..................................................... 2.25, 3.2, 7.9, 13.17, 13.20, 15.29
  - (1)(d) ............................................... 6.7
- 49B ..................................................... 2.25, 3.2, 6.7
- 49C ..................................................... 2.25, 6.7, 7.27
- 49D ..................................................... 2.25, 6.7, 7.27, 12.23
- 49E ..................................................... 2.25, 6.7, 7.29, 12.23
- 50(5) ................................................... 15.30
- 51(1) ................................................... 7.11
  - (1A) .................................................. 2.11, 7.25, 8.22
  - (1B) .................................................. 2.11, 8.22
  - (2) .................................................... 7.11
- 52 ........................................................ 2.9, 7.11, 7.12, 7.13, 7.15, 7.20, 7.25, 7.27, 8.23
  - (1) .................................................... 1.9, 8.23, 13.49
  - (2) .................................................... 8.23
  - (2A) .................................................. 7.25, 8.23

Inheritance Tax Act 1984 – *contd*
- s 52(3A) ............................................... 7.25
- 53 ........................................................ 7.12, 7.14
  - (1A) .................................................. 2.11, 8.23
  - (2A) .................................................. 7.27
  - (4) .................................................... 7.15
  - (5), (6) ............................................. 7.13, 7.14
  - (7), (8) ............................................. 7.13
- 54 ........................................................ 7.14
  - (2B) .................................................. 7.21
  - (4) .................................................... 3.7
- 54A ..................................................... 7.16
- 54B ..................................................... 7.16
- 55A ..................................................... 7.23
- 57 ........................................................ 1.20, 2.25, 12.1
  - (3) .................................................... 6.7
  - (4) .................................................... 7.17
- 57A(1A) .............................................. 7.25
- 58(1) ................................................... 9.24
  - (d) ................................................... 7.40
  - (f) .................................................... 8.43
- 62 ........................................................ 8.29
  - (2) .................................................... 8.34
- 63 ........................................................ 8.12
- 64 ........................................................ 2.22, 8.27, 8.38, 8.60, 13.48
- 65 ........................................................ 8.12, 8.27
  - (1) .................................................... 8.12
  - (4) .................................................... 8.12
- 66 ........................................................ 8.27, 8.38, 8.60
  - (3) .................................................... 8.60
  - (4) .................................................... 8.40, 8.59
  - (5)(a) ............................................... 8.51
- 67 ........................................................ 8.27, 8.38, 8.60
  - (1) .................................................... 8.50
  - (2) .................................................... 8.50
    - (a), (b) ........................................... 8.60
  - (3) .................................................... 8.53
    - (b) ................................................. 8.59
  - (4)(b) ............................................... 8.54
  - (5) .................................................... 8.54
- 68 ........................................................ 8.27
  - (1) .................................................... 8.26, 14.33
  - (2) .................................................... 8.37
  - (3) .................................................... 8.37
    - (b) ................................................. 8.12, 8.37
  - (4) .................................................... 8.26, 8.28
  - (5) .................................................... 8.30
  - (6) .................................................... 8.26, 8.28, 8.40
- 69 ........................................................ 8.27
  - (2)(b) ............................................... 8.12
  - (4) .................................................... 8.12
- 70 ........................................................ 8.6, 8.74, 8.68, 8.69, 8.70, 8.71
  - (7) .................................................... 8.6, 8.74, 8.68
- 71 ........................................................ 2.8, 8.5, 8.9

## Table of statutes

| Inheritance Tax Act 1984 – *contd* | |
|---|---|
| s 71(1)(a) | 8.16 |
| (1A) | 8.25 |
| (1B) | 8.17 |
| 71A | 2.11, 2.25, 3.2, 6.7, 7.12, 7.20, 7.31, 7.38, 8.5, 8.9, 8.17, 8.22, 8.71, 13.20 |
| (4)(a) | 8.6 |
| 71B | 8.71 |
| 71C | 6.7, 7.31 |
| 71D | 2.11, 7.12, 7.20, 7.31, 7.38, 8.5, 8.19 |
| (1)–(5) | 8.19 |
| (7) | 8.8 |
| 71E | 8.10, 8.71 |
| 71F | 8.27, 8.71 |
| (5) | 8.31 |
| 71G(1)(b) | 8.71 |
| 79 | 13.48 |
| 80 | 7.35 |
| (1) | 8.17 |
| (2) | 7.35 |
| 81A | 2.8, 7.24 |
| (1), (2) | 7.24 |
| 82 | 9.29 |
| 86 | 1.20 |
| (1) | 9.24 |
| (3) | 9.24 |
| 89 | 2.8, 2.25, 12.11 |
| (2) | 12.15 |
| (4) | 12.13 |
| (5), (6) | 12.12 |
| 89A | 2.8, 2.25, 12.13, 12.14 |
| (4) | 12.15 |
| 89B | 2.25, 3.2, 12.15 |
| (1)(a) | 12.13, 12.14 |
| (b) | 2.8 |
| (c) | 2.8, 12.13, 12.14, 12.16 |
| (d) | 2.8 |
| 91 | 4.3 |
| 92 | 3.8 |
| 94 | 1.16, 1.27, 2.14, 6.4 |
| (1) | 2.8 |
| (2) | 1.27 |
| (4) | 1.28 |
| (5) | 1.28, 2.19 |
| 95 | 2.14 |
| 96 | 2.14 |
| 97 | 2.14 |
| 98 | 1.16, 1.28 |
| (1) | 2.19, 3.17 |
| (3) | 2.8, 2.19 |
| 100(1A) | 7.25 |
| 101(1A) | 7.25 |

| Inheritance Tax Act 1984 – *contd* | |
|---|---|
| s 102(3) | 3.3 |
| (4) | 2.12 |
| 103 | 11.7 |
| (3) | 11.1 |
| (4) | 3.10 |
| 105 | 11.1, 11.50 |
| (1)(a) | 11.1 |
| (b) | 11.5 |
| (bb) | 11.4 |
| (cc) | 11.5, 11.50 |
| (d) | 8.62, 11.6 |
| (e) | 11.6 |
| (1ZA) | 11.4 |
| (3) | 11.1, 11.10, 11.12, 11.13, 11.14, 11.23 |
| (4) | 11.23 |
| (b) | 11.16 |
| 106 | 5.23, 11.5, 11.9 |
| (1)(a) | 11.7 |
| 107 | 11.5, 11.9, 11.12 |
| (1)(a) | 11.9 |
| (4) | 11.9 |
| 108, 109 | 11.5 |
| 110 | 11.7, 11.21 |
| 111 | 11.23 |
| 112 | 11.9, 11.22, 11.23 |
| (2)(b) | 11.23 |
| (4) | 11.23 |
| 113 | 11.49 |
| 113A | 8.65, 11.45, 12.5 |
| (1) | 11.51 |
| (3A)(a) | 11.50 |
| (b) | 11.49, 11.50 |
| 115 | 11.26 |
| (2) | 10.24, 11.28 |
| (3) | 11.45, 11.47 |
| 116 | 11.29 |
| 117 | 11.25, 11.26, 11.36, 11.37, 13.22 |
| 117A | 11.39 |
| 117B | 11.40 |
| 118 | 11.39, 11.40 |
| (3) | 11.40 |
| 120 | 13.21, 13.22 |
| (1)(a) | 11.38 |
| 122 | 8.62 |
| (1)(b) | 8.62 |
| 124 | 11.49 |
| 124A | 8.65, 11.45 |
| (1) | 11.51 |
| 125 | 3.6, 10.1 |
| (1) | 10.24 |
| 126 | 10.1 |
| 127 | 10.1, 13.23 |
| 128 | 10.1 |

## Table of statutes

Inheritance Tax Act 1984 – *contd*
| | |
|---|---|
| s 129 | 10.1 |
| 130 | 10.1 |
| (2) | 10.25 |
| 131 | 2.16, 10.1, 10.8 |
| 132 | 2.16, 10.1, 10.11 |
| 133–140 | 2.16, 10.1 |
| 141 | 1.23, 3.7, 3.23, 4.26, 10.1, 10.4 |
| (3) | 10.5 |
| 142 | 3.27, 3.38, 5.31, 11.3, 13.29, 13.38, 13.39, 13.40, 13.41, 13.42, 13.43, 13.44, 13.46, 13.47, 14.25, 15.25, 15.45 |
| (1)(b) | 13.43 |
| (2) | 13.45 |
| (2A) | 13.44 |
| (3) | 13.41, 13.42 |
| 143 | 8.72, 13.47, 14.32 |
| 144 | 7.9, 8.6, 8.72, 13.47, 13.48, 13.50, 13.51, 13.50, 14.23, 14.25, 15.34, 15.40 |
| (1) | 13.48, 13.50 |
| (a) | 13.48 |
| (1A) | 13.50 |
| (2) | 13.50 |
| (4) | 13.51 |
| 147(10) | 14.10 |
| 151A | 3.22 |
| 151B | 3.22, 14.11, 14.12 |
| 151BA | 14.2 |
| (5)–(7) | 14.11 |
| (8)–(12) | 14.12 |
| 151C | 3.22 |
| 152 | 1.20, 3.5 |
| 153 | 3.5, 9.34 |
| 154 | 1.20, 3.5, 9.5, 9.26 |
| 155 | 3.5 |
| (1) | 9.33 |
| 157 | 1.18, 1.20, 3.5, 9.35 |
| 158 | 1.25, 3.24, 10.20 |
| (6) | 1.8, 1.25 |
| 159 | 1.26, 3.24, 10.20, 10.22 |
| (3), (4) | 1.26 |
| (7) | 1.26 |
| 160 | 2.17, 3.17, 4.1, 4.6, 4.11, 4.13, 4.14, 4.29, 6.14, 6.22, 11.41, 16.17 |
| 161 | 3.18, 4.4, 10.1, 10.6, 10.10 |
| (2) | 4.4 |

Inheritance Tax Act 1984 – *contd*
| | |
|---|---|
| s 161(3) | 4.5, 4.6 |
| (4) | 4.6, 4.7 |
| (5) | 4.7 |
| 162(1) | 3.12, 3.13 |
| (2), (3) | 3.13 |
| (4) | 2.17, 3.13, 3.15 |
| (5) | 3.13 |
| 163 | 4.1 |
| 166 | 4.28 |
| 167 | 13.37 |
| (1) | 4.10 |
| (2)(a) | 4.10 |
| (3), (4) | 4.10 |
| 168 | 4.16 |
| 171 | 1.17, 3.17 |
| (1), (2) | 3.17 |
| 172 | 1.17, 3.14 |
| 173 | 3.15 |
| 174(1) | 3.9 |
| 175 | 3.15 |
| 176 | 3.18, 4.8, 10.6 |
| (3) | 10.6 |
| (4) | 3.18 |
| (5) | 10.7 |
| 177 | 11.42 |
| 178 | 10.1, 10.14 |
| 179 | 10.14 |
| 180 | 10.14 |
| (1) | 10.15 |
| 181–189 | 10.14 |
| 190 | 10.1, 10.17 |
| 191 | 10.17 |
| (2), (3) | 10.17 |
| 192 | 10.17 |
| 193 | 10.17 |
| 194 | 10.17 |
| 195 | 10.17 |
| 196 | 10.17 |
| 197 | 10.17 |
| 197A | 10.17 |
| 198 | 10.17 |
| 199(1) | 6.25 |
| 200(1) | 7.42 |
| (a), (b) | 3.21 |
| 201 | 7.42 |
| (1)(b) | 7.42 |
| 202 | 1.27, 6.4 |
| (2) | 1.28 |
| 204 | 6.26 |
| 207 | 6.36 |
| 208 | 6.26 |
| 211 | 6.33 |
| (1)–(3) | 3.26 |
| 216 | 6.36, 13.6 |
| (3A) | 6.15 |

## Table of statutes

| Inheritance Tax Act 1984 – *contd* | |
|---|---|
| s 216(6)(a) | 6.43 |
| (c) | 2.25 |
| 217 | 6.45 |
| 218 | 6.2, 6.43 |
| 219 | 6.51 |
| 219A | 6.51, 13.42 |
| 220 | 6.51 |
| 222 | 6.53 |
| 223 | 6.60 |
| 226(3A) | 6.27 |
| 227 | 6.29, 6.46 |
| (1C) | 6.28 |
| 228 | 6.28, 6.29 |
| 229 | 6.46 |
| 233(1)(b) | 6.46 |
| 234(2) | 6.30 |
| 237(1) | 6.32 |
| (3C) | 6.32 |
| 239 | 14.2, 14.13 |
| (4) | 14.13 |
| 241 | 10.7 |
| 242 | 14.2 |
| 245(2) | 6.43 |
| (7) | 6.43 |
| 245A | 6.43 |
| 247 | 6.44 |
| (1) | 14.14 |
| (2) | 14.14 |
| 248(1) | 6.45 |
| 256 | 6.36, 14.14 |
| 262 | 3.15 |
| 263 | 2.5, 4.12 |
| (2) | 4.12 |
| 266(3) | 2.24 |
| 267 | 1.3, 1.7, 7.34, 10.21, 16.27 |
| (1) | 10.19 |
| (b) | 7.34 |
| (2) | 1.8, 1.25 |
| (3) | 1.8 |
| 267A | 11.3 |
| 268 | 2.5, 2.21, 4.12, 5.17 |
| (2) | 2.22 |
| (3) | 2.22 |
| 271A | 3.5 |
| 272 | 2.21, 14.2 |
| 274 | 4.17 |
| Sch 1 | 1.10, 2.23, 3.21, 14.22 |
| Sch 2 | 14.10 |
| Sch 3 | 1.20, 2.3, 9.22, 9.23 |
| Sch 4 | 1.20, 2.3 |
| Sch 6 para 2 | 14.30 |

### L

| Law of Property Act 1925 | |
|---|---|
| s 30 | 4.24 |
| 149(3) | 5.13 |
| 184 | **3.7** |
| Law Reform (Succession) Act 1995 | 6.36 |
| Limited Liability Partnerships Act 2000 | 11.3 |

### M

| Mental Health Act 1983 | 12.12 |
|---|---|
| Mental Capacity Act 2005 | 6.11 |
| s 12 | 6.10 |
| 66(3) | 6.10 |
| Sch 4 | 6.10 |

### P

| Perpetuities and Accumulations Act 2009 | 8.3 |
|---|---|

### S

| Social Security Contributions and Benefits Act 1992 | |
|---|---|
| s 64 | 12.12 |
| 67(1), (2) | 12.12 |
| 71 | 12.12 |

### T

| Taxation of Chargeable Gains Act 1992 | |
|---|---|
| s 2(4) | 12.8 |
| 62(6) | 13.45 |
| 71 | 8.5 |
| 72 | 7.15 |
| (1)(b) | 7.15 |
| 73 | 7.15 |
| 77 | 8.1, 12.18, 16.16 |
| 86 | 16.16 |
| 126 | 11.9 |
| 165 | 8.1, 12.5, 12.6 |
| 169B | 8.1, 12.6 |
| 222 | 15.17 |
| 225 | 7.15, 15.30, 15.37, 15.39 |
| 260 | 8.1, 8.4, 8.12 |
| (2)(a) | 8.12 |
| (da) | 8.6 |
| 272(3) | 4.14 |
| (5) | 4.15 |
| 274 | 4.17, 4.30, 6.51, 14.15 |
| Taxes Management Act 1970 | |
| s 49A | 6.59 |
| 49C | 6.59 |
| 49E | 6.59 |
| Tribunals, Courts and Enforcement Act 2007 | 6.54 |

# Table of statutes

Trustee Act 1925
  s 31 .................................... 6.16, 7.10, 7.27,
                                  8.16, 8.24, 11.51
  32 ....................................... 6.16, 8.6, 8.8
  49 ................................................. 11.51
Trusts of Land and Appointment of
  Trustees Act 1996 ....................... 15.36
  s 12 .......................................... 15.36, 15.37

Trusts of Land and Appointment of
  Trustees Act 1996 – *contd*
  s 13 .......................................... 15.36, 15.37
  (7) ............................................ 15.36, 15.37
  14 ................................................... 4.24
  22(1) ............................................. 15.37

# Table of statutory instruments

[*All references are to paragraph numbers*]

Charge to Income Tax by Reference to Enjoyment of Property Previously Owned Regulations, SI 2005/724....... 5.3, 15.10, 16.17, 16.24
reg 3................................................ 16.15
4................................................ 16.30
5................................. 12.9, 15.16, 16.24
6................................................ 5.3, 5.37

**D**

Double Taxation Relief (Estate Duty) (France) Order 1963, SI 1963/1319 ................................. 10.21
Double Taxation Relief (Estate Duty) (India) Order 1956, SI 1956/998............................................ 10.21
Double Taxation Relief (Estate Duty) (Italy) Order 1968, SI 1968/304. 10.21
Double Taxation Relief (Ireland) Order 1978, SI 1978/1107.......... 10.21
Double Taxation Relief (Pakistan) Order 1975, SI 1957/1522.......... 10.21
Double Taxation Relief (South Africa) Order 1979, SI 1979/576............ 10.21
Double Taxation Relief (Switzerland) Order 1957, SI 1957/426............ 10.21
Double Taxation Relief (Taxes on Estates of Deceased Persons and Inheritances and on Gifts) (Netherlands) Order 1980, SI 1980/706 .................................... 10.21
Double Taxation Relief (Taxes on Estates of Deceased Persons and Inheritances and on Gifts) (Netherlands) Order 1996, SI 1996/730 .................................... 10.21
Double Taxation Relief (Taxes on Estates of Deceased Persons and Inheritances and on Gifts) (Sweden) Order 1981, SI 1981/840............................................ 10.21
Double Taxation Relief (Taxes on Estates of Deceased Persons and Inheritances and on Gifts) (Sweden) Order 1989 1989/986. 10.21
Double Taxation Relief (Taxes on Estates of Deceased Persons and Inheritances) (Switzerland) Order 1994, SI 1994/3214.......... 10.21

Double Taxation Relief (USA) Order 1979, SI 1979/1454.................... 10.21

**F**

Family Provision (Intestate Succession) Order 2009, SI 2009/135............................................ 3.1
Finance Act 2008, Schedule 40 (Appointed Day, Transitional Provisions and Consequential Amendments) Order 2009, SI 2009/571 ..................................... 6.36
Finance Act 2009, Schedule 51 (Time Limits for Assessments, Claims, etc.) (Appointed Days and Transitional Provisions) Order 2010, SI 2010/867
reg 2................................................ 10.7
Finance Act 2009, Section 96 and Schedule 48 (Appointed Day, Savings and Consequential Amendments) Order 2009, SI 2009/3054 ................................... 6.3

**H**

Housing (Northern Ireland) Order 1981, SI 1981/156 (NI 3)........... 9.21

**I**

Inheritance Tax (Delivery of Accounts) (Excepted Estates) (Amendment) Regulations 2006, SI 2006/2141 .................... 6.17
Inheritance Tax (Delivery of Accounts) (Excepted Estates) Regulations 2004, SI 2004/2543......................................... 6.17, 6.19
reg 4(6).......................................... 6.18
Inheritance Tax (Delivery of Accounts) (Excepted Settlements) Regulations 2008, SI 2008/606.................... 6.4, 6.6, 6.7, 6.9
reg 4.............................................. 8.38
(5).............................................. 6.4
Inheritance Tax (Delivery of Accounts) (Excepted Transfers and Excepted Terminations) Regulations 2002, SI 2002/1731.......................................... 2.25

## Table of statutory instruments

| | |
|---|---|
| Inheritance Tax (Delivery of Accounts) (Excepted Transfers and Excepted Terminations) Regulations 2008, SI 2008/605 | 6.4, 6.6, 6.7, 6.9 |
| reg 4, 5 | 2.25 |
| Inheritance Tax (Double Charges Relief) Regulations 1987, SI 1987/1130 | 2.20, 4.27, 5.2, 5.8, 5.36, 10.1, 10.23 |
| reg 5 | 5.36 |
| (3)(a) | 5.8, 5.36 |
| (b) | 5.36 |
| (4) | 5.37 |
| 6 | 3.11 |
| 9 | 5.37 |
| Inheritance Tax (Double Charges Relief) Regulations 2005, SI 2005/3441 | 5.37, 15.10, 10.1, 16.29 |

**S**

| | |
|---|---|
| Special Commissioners (Jurisdiction and Procedure) Regulations 1994, SI 1994/1811 | |
| reg 21 | 6.61 |

**T**

| | |
|---|---|
| Tribunal Procedure (First-tier Tribunal) (Tax Chamber) Rules 2009, SI 2009/273 | 6.61 |
| r 10 | 6.61 |
| 23 | 6.54 |

# Table of cases

[*All references are to paragraph numbers*]

**A**

Abacus Trust Co (Isle of Man) Ltd v NSPCC; sub nom Abacus Trust Co (Isle of Man) Ltd v National Society for the Prevention of Cruelty to Children [2001] STC 1344, [2002] BTC 178, [2001] WTLR 953, (2000-01) 3 ITELR 846, [2001] STI 1225, (2001) 98(35) LSG 37, Ch D .................................................................... 12.8, 23.9

Allnutt v Wilding; sub nom Strain (Deceased), Re; Allnutt v Allnutt [2007] EWCA Civ 412, [2007] BTC 8003, [2007] WTLR 941, (2006-07) 9 ITELR 806, CA .............. 12.8

Antrobus (No 2), Re [2005] Lands Tribunal DET/47/2004 ..................... 6.52, 11.25, 11.33, 11.34, 11.46, 13.36

Antrobus, Re. *See* Lloyds TSB v IRC.

Application to Vary the Undertakings of A, Re [2005] STC (SCD) 103, [2005] WTLR 1, [2004] STI 2502, (2004) 148 SJLB 1432, Sp Comm .............................................. 10.30

Arkwright (Williams Personal Representative) v IC; sub nom IRC v Arkwright [2004] EWHC 1720 (Ch), [2005] 1 WLR 1411, [2004] STC 1323, [2005] RVR 266, 76 TC 788, [2004] BTC 8082, [2004] WTLR 855, [2004] STI 1724, (2004) 101(31) LSG 26, Ch D ........................................................................................................... 4.6

Arnander (Executors of McKenna Deceased) v HMRC [2006] STC (SCD) 800, [2007] WTLR 51, [2006] STI 2460 ........................................................... 11.27, 11.28, 11.33, 13.36

Arnold, Sir Malcom (deceased), Re; Day v Harris and Others (2010) unreported .......... 13.6

Atkinson (Executor) v Revenue and Customs Comrs [2010] UKFTT 108 (TC), FTT (Tax) ............................................................................................................ 11.30, 11.37

Atkinson (Inspector of Taxes) v Dancer; Mannion (Inspector of Taxes) v Johnston [1988] STC 758, 61 TC 598, [1988] BTC 364, (1988) 85(17) LSG 50, Ch D ..................... 11.7

**B**

Baird's Executors v IRC [1991] 1 EGLR 201, 1991 SLT (Lands Tr) 9, Lands Tr (Scot) . 11.42
Barclays Bank Trust Co v IRC [1998] STC (SCD) 125 ..................................................... 11.23
Barty-King v Ministry of Defence [1979] 2 All ER 80, [1979] STC 218, QBD ............... 9.26
Beckman v IRC [2000] STC (SCD) 59, [2003] WTLR 773, [2000] STI 162, Sp Comm. 11.2
Bedford (Duke) (Deceased), Re; sub nom Russell v Bedford [1960] 1 WLR 1331, [1960] 3 All ER 756, (1960) 39 ATC 340, [1960] TR 327, (1960) 104 SJ 1058, Ch D ........ 13.35
Benham's Will Trusts, Re; sub nom Lockhart v Harker [1995] STC 210, [1995] STI 186, Ch D ...................................................................................................... 3.37, 3.38, 6.1
Bennett v IRC [1995] STC 54, [1995] STI 13, Ch D ................................................. 6.13, 9.9, 12.1
Bhatt v Bhatt and [2009] EWHC 734, [2009] All ER (D) 58 (Apr) ................................... 13.2
Blackwell v Blackwell; sub nom Blackwell, Re [1929] AC 318, 67 ALR 336, HL .......... 7.5
Bower v HMRC; sub nom HMRC v Bower; Bower (Deceased), Re [2008] EWHC 3105 (Ch), [2009] STC 510, [2009] STI 188, Ch D ................................................... 4.13, 12.26
Brander (Representative of Earl of Balfour deceased) v HMRC [2009] TC 00069 ......... 11.12
Brown's Executors v IRC [1996] STC (SCD) 277, Sp Comm ........................................ 11.2, 11.6
Buccleuch v IRC. *See* Duke of Buccleuch v IRC
Bull v Bull [1955] 1 QB 234, [1955] 2 WLR 78, [1955] 1 All ER 253, (1955) 99 SJ 60, CA ............................................................................................................................ 15.35
Burden v United Kingdom (13378/05) [2008] STC 1305, [2008] 2 FLR 787, [2008] 2 FCR 244, (2008) 47 EHRR 38, 24 BHRC 709, [2008] BTC 8099, 10 ITL Rep 772, [2008] WTLR 1129, [2008] Fam Law 628, [2008] 18 EG 126 (CS), (2008) 158 NLJ 672, ECHR .................................................................................... 9.17, 14.1, 15.27
Burkinyoung v IRC [1995] STC (SCD) 29, Sp Comm ....................................................... 11.11

xxiii

*Table of cases*

**C**

| | |
|---|---|
| Cairns v Revenue and Customs Comrs; sub nom Revenue and Customs Comrs v Cairns [2009] UKFTT 67 (TC), [2009] STC (SCD) 479, [2009] WTLR 793, [2009] STI 1801, Sp Comm | 6.3, 6.15 |
| Cancer Research Campaign v Ernest Brown & Co [1997] STC 1425, [1998] PNLR 592, Ch D | 13.28, 15.4 |
| Carr-Glynn v Frearsons [1999] Ch 326, [1999] 2 WLR 1046, [1998] 4 All ER 225, [1999] 1 FLR 8, [1998] 3 FCR 487. [1999] PNLR 13, [1998] Fam Law 739, [1998] EG 128 (CS), (1998) 148 NLJ 1487, [1998] NPC 136, CA (Civ Div) | 15.5 |
| Caton's Administrators v Couch. *See* Couch (Inspector of Taxes) v Administrators of the Estate of Caton | |
| Charkham (Deceased) v IRC [2000] RVR 7, Lands Tr | 4.21 |
| Clark v HMRC [2005] STC (SCD) 823, [2005] WTLR 1465, [2005] STI 1758n Comm | 11.1 |
| Cleaver (Deceased), Re; sub nom Cleaver v Insley [1981] 1 WLR 939, [1981] 2 All ER 1018, (1981) 125 SJ 445, Ch D | 7.5 |
| Clore (Deceased) (No 2), Re; sub nom Official Solicitor v Clore [1984] STC 609, Ch D | 1.5 |
| Cole (A Bankrupt), Re; sub nom ex p Trustee v Cole [1964] Ch 175, [1963] 3 WLR 621 [1963] 3 All ER 433. (1963) 107 SJ 664, CA | 5.4 |
| Corbally-Stourton v HMRC [2008] STC (SCD) 907, Sp Comm | 6.3 |
| Couch (Inspector of Taxes) v Administrators of the Estate of Caton; sub nom: Administrators of the Estate of Caton v Couch (Inspector of Taxes); Caton's Administrators v Couch (Inspector of Taxes) [1997] STC 970, 70 TC 10, [1997] BTC 360, (1997) 94(30) LSG 29, CA (Civ Div); affirming [1996] STC 201, Ch D; reversing [1995] STC (SCD) 34, Sp Comm | 11.19 |
| Courthope, Re (1928) 7 ATC 538 | 11.20 |
| Curnock v IRC [2003] STC (SCD) 283, [2003] WTLR 955, [2003] STI 1052, Sp Comm. | 12.6 |
| Customs and Excise Comrs v Lord Fisher; sub nom Lord Fisher DSC v Customs and Excise Comrs [1981] 2 All ER 147, [1981] STC 238, QBD | 11.14 |
| CVC/Opportunity Equity Partners Ltd v Demarco Almeida 2002] UKPC 16, [2002] BCC 684, [2002] 2 BCLC 108, PC (CI) | 11.20 |
| Cyganik v Agulian; sub nom Agulian v Cyganik [2006] EWCA Civ 129, [2006] 1 FCR 406, [2006] WTLR 565, (2005-06) 8 ITELR 762, CA | 1.5 |

**D**

| | |
|---|---|
| Daniels v Thompson [2004] EWCA Civ 307, [2004] PNLR 33, [2004] WTLR 511, (2004) 148 SJLB 386, CA (Civ Div) | 15.5 |
| Davies v Revenue and Customs Comrs [2009] UKFTT 138 (TC), [2009] WTLR 1151, [2009] STI 2095, FTT (Tax) | 7.5 |
| Denekamp v Pearce (Inspector of Taxes) [1998] STC 1120, 71 TC 213, [1998] BTC 413, Ch D | 11.20 |
| Dixon v IRC [2002] STC (SCD) 53, [2002] WTLR 175, [2002] STI 43, Sp Comm | 11.29 |
| Duke of Buccleuch v Inland Revenue Comrs; sub nom Duke Devonshire's Trustees v IRC [1967] 1 AC 506, [1967] 2 WLR 207, [1967] 1 All ER 129, [1967] RVR 25, [1967] RVR 42, (1966) 45 ATC 472, [1966] TR 393, (1967) 111 SJ 18, HL | 4.3, 11.41 |

**E**

| | |
|---|---|
| Ellesmere (Earl) v IRC [1918] 2 KB 735, KBD | 11.41 |
| Executors of Marquess of Hertford v IRC. *See* Ninth Marquess of Hertford (executors of Eighth Marquess of Hertford) v IRC | |
| Executors of Mrs Mary Dugan-Chapman v HMRC (2008) SpC 666 | 11.9 |
| Executors of Patch deceased [2007] SpC 600 | 7.1, 7.11, 13.49 |

**F**

| | |
|---|---|
| Farmer v IRC [1999] STC (SCD) 321, Sp Comm | 11.12 |
| Faulkner v IRC [2001] STC (SCD) 112, [2001] WTLR 1295, [2001] STI 943, Sp Comm | 7.5, 15.43 |

Fetherstonaugh (formerly Finch) v IRC; sub nom Finch v IRC [1985] Ch 1, [1984] 3
WLR 212, [1984] STC 261, (1984) 81 LSG 1443, (1984) 128 SJ 302, CA ............  11.6
Frankland v IRC [1997] STC 1450, [1997] BTC 8045, CA................................... 7.9, 13.48, 14.23
Fryer v Revenue and Customs Comrs [2010] UKFTT 87 (TC), FTT (Tax)..................... 7.40
Furness v IRC [1999] STC (SCD) 232, Sp Comm......................................................... 11.11
Futter v Futter; Futter (No ) Life Interest Settlement, Re [2010] EWHC 449 (Ch), [2010]
Pens LR 145, [2010] WTLR 609, [2010] STI 1442, Ch D.......................................... 12.8

**G**
Gartside v Inland Revenue Comrs; sub nom Gartside's Will Trusts, Re [1968] AC 553,
[1968] 2 WLR 277, [1968] 1 All ER 121, (1967) 46 ATC 323, [1967] TR 309,
(1967) 111 SJ 982, HL.............................................................................................. 7.5
Genovese v HMRC [2009] SpC 741................................................................................... 7.34
Gorham v British Telecommunications Plc [2000] 1 WLR 2129, [2000] 4 All ER 867,
[2001] Lloyd's Rep IR 531, [2000] Lloyd's Rep PN 897, [2001] PNLR 2, [2000]
Pens LR 293, (2000) 97(38) LSG 44, (2000) 144 SJLB 251, CA.............................. 15.3
Gray v Inland Revenue Comrs; sub nom Executors of Lady Fox v IRC; Lady Fox's
Executors v IRC [1994] STC 360, [1994] 38 EG 156, [1994] RVR 129, [1994] STI
208, [1994] EG 32 (CS), [1994] NPC 15, CA .............................................. 4.3, 11.41, 11.43

**H**
Hall (Hall's Executors) v IRC [1997] STC (SCD) 126 ..................................................... 11.11
Hardcastle v IRC [2000] STC (SCD) 532, [2001] WTLR 91, [2000] STI 1520, Sp
Comm......................................................................................................................... 11.2
Harding (executors of Loveday) v IRC [1997] STC (SCD) 321 ...................................... 13.47
Harrold v Inland Revenue Comrs [1996] STC (SCD) 195, [1996] EG 70 (CS), Sp
Comm................................................................................................................ 11.30, 11.37
Hastings-Bass (Deceased), Re; sub nom Hastings-Bass Trustees v IRC [1975] Ch 25,
[1974] 2 WLR 904, [1974] 2 All ER 193, [1974] STC 211, [1974] TR 87, (1974)
118 SJ 422, CA ................................................................................................ 10.13, 12.8
Hawkings-Byass v Sassen (Inspector of Taxes) [1996] STC (SCD) 319, Sp Comm ........ 11.20
Henwood v Barlow Clowes International Ltd (In Liquidation) [2008] EWCA Civ 577,
[2008] BPIR.778, [2008] NPC 61, CA ..................................................................... 1.4
HMRC v Bower. *See* Bower v HMRC
HMRC v Khawaja [2008] EWHC 1687 (Ch), [2009] 1 WLR 398, [2009] Bus LR 134,
[2008] STC 2880, [2008] STI 1748, (2008) 158 NLJ 1076, Ch D............................ 6.3
Hertford (Marquess), Executors of v IRC [2004] SpC 00444 .......................................... 11.23
Higginson's Executors v IRC [2002] STC (SCD) 483 ..................................... 11.32, 11.45, 13.21
Holland v IRC [2003] STC (SCD) 43, [2003] WTLR 207, [2003] STI 62, (2003) 147
SJLB 267, Sp Comm................................................................................................ 9.17, 14.1
Holmes v McMullan; sub nom Ratcliffe (Deceased), Re [1999] STC 262, [1999] BTC
8017, (1999) 96(11) LSG 70, Ch D .................................................................... 3.37, 3.38, 6.1
Howarth's Executors v IRC [1997] STC (SCD) 162....................................................... 6.31
Hughes v Richards (t/a Colin Richards & Co) [2004] EWCA Civ 266, [2004] PNLR 35,
(2004) 148 SJLB 353, CA ....................................................................................... 15.3
Hurlingham Estates Ltd v Wilde & Partners [1997] 1 Lloyd's Rep 525, [1997] STC 627,
[1997] BTC 240, (1997) 147 NLJ 453, Ch D .......................................................... 15.2

**I**
Ingram v IRC [2000] 1 AC 293, [1999] 2 WLR 90, [1999] 1 All ER 297, [1999] STC 37,
[1999] L & TR 85, [1998] BTC 8047, [1998] EG 181 (CS), (1999) 96(3) LSG 33,
(1999) 143 SJLB 52, [1998] NPC 160, HL; reversing [1997] 4 All ER 395, [1997]
STC 1234, [1997] BTC 8009, (1997) 94(34) LSG 29, (1997) 141 SJLB 204, [1997]
NPC 129, CA ................................................................................... 5.11, 5.12, 15.7,
16.1

*Table of cases*

IRC v Crossman [1937] AC 26, [1936] 1 All ER 762, 15 ATC 94, 105 LJKB 450, 80 Sol Jo 485, 154 LT 570, 52 TLR 415, HL .................................................................. 11.18
IRC v Eversden; sub nom IRC v Greenstock's Executors; Essex (Somerset's Executors) v IRC [2003] EWCA Civ 668, [2003] STC 822, 75 TC 340, [2003] BTC 8028, [2003] WTLR 893, [2003] STI 989, (2003) 100(27) LSG 38, (2003) 147 SJLB 594, CA; affirming [2002] EWHC 1360 (Ch), [2002] STC 1109, [2002] BTC 8035, [2002] WTLR 1013, [2002] STI 1008, (2002) 99(36) LSG 40, [2002] NPC 96, Ch D ........ 5.9, 5.26, 7.6, 15.8, 16.1
IRC v George; sub nom Stedman's Executors v IRC; George v IRC [2003] EWCA Civ 1763, [2004] STC 147, 75 TC 735, [2004] BTC 8003, [2004] WTLR 75, [2003] STI 2276, (2004) 101(3) LSG 34, CA .............................................................................. 11.11
IRC v Lloyds Private Banking Ltd [1998] STC 559, [1999] 1 FLR 147, [1998] 2 FCR 41, [1998] BTC 8020, [1999] Fam Law 309, (1998) 95(19) LSG 23, (1998) 142 SJLB 164, Ch D ............................................................................................ 7.2, 15.24, 15.43
IRC v Mallender. *See* Mallender v IRC

**J**

Jones v IRC [1997] STC 358, [1997] BTC 8003, [1997] EG 21 (CS), [1997] NPC 26, Ch D ........................................................................................................................... 10.17
Judge (Walden's Personal Representative) v HMRC [2005] STC (SCD) 863, [2005] WTLR 1311, (2006-07) 9 ITELR 21, [2005] STI 1800, Sp Comm .......... 7.3, 7.6, 7.9, 13.27, 15.32, 15.34, 15.38, 15.44

**L**

Lau v HMRC [2009] SpC 740 ................................................................................ 13.43
Lillingston (Deceased), Re; Sub Nom Pembery v Pembery [1952] 2 All ER 184, [1952] 1 TLR 1622, [1952] WN 338, (1952) 96 SJ 462. Ch D ............................................ 5.4
Lloyds TSB Bank Plc (Personal Representative of Antrobus (Deceased)) v IRC [2002] STC (SCD) 468, [2002] WTLR 1435, [2002] STI 1398, (2002) 146 SJLB 249m Sp Comm 249 ........................................................................... 11.33, 11.41, 11.42, 31.21, 13.35
Lloyds TSB Private Banking Plc (Personal Representative of Antrobus (Deceased)) v Twiddy [2006] 1 EGLR 157, [2006] RVR 138, [2005] WTLR 1535, Lands Tr ........ 11.45, 11.42, 13.35

**M**

McArthur's Executors v HMRC; sub nom McArthur (Deceased), Re [2008] STC (SCD) 1100, [2008] WTLR 1185, Sp Comm ....................................................................... 11.18
McCall v HMRC [2009] NICA 12, [2008] STC (SCD) 752, [2008] WTLR 865, [2008] STI 1256, Sp Comm ................................................................. 6.52, 11.1, 11.14, 11.28
McDowall's Executors v Inland Revenue Comrs [2004] STC (SCD) 22, [2004] WTLR 221, [2004] STI 146, Sp Comm ................................................................................ 9.10
McGregor (Inspector of Taxes) v Adcock [1977] 1 WLR 864, [1977] 3 All ER 65, [1977] STC 206, (1977) 242 EG 289, 51 TC 692, [1977] TR 23, Ch D .............................. 11.7
McKelvey v HMRC; sub nom McKelvey Deceased), Re [2008] STC (SCD) 944, [2008] WTLR 1407, [2008] STI 1752, (2008) SPC 694, Sp Comm ...................... 2.4, 9.12, 15.16
Mallender v IRC; sub nom IRC v Mallender [2001] STC 514, [2001] BTC 8013, [2001] WTLR 459, [2001] STI 548, [2001] NPC 62, Ch D .................................................. 11.2
Mannion (Inspector of Taxes) v Johnston. *See* Atkinson (Inspector of Taxes) v Dancer
Marquess of Linlithgow v Comrs for Her Majesty's Revenue and Customs [2010] CSIH 19, [2010] STI 1278, 2010 GWD 11-206, IH (Ex Div) ........................................... 6.4, 12.6
Martin v IRC [1995] STC (SCD) 5, Sp Comm ........................................................ 11.11
Melville v IRC [2001] EWCA Civ 1247, [2002] 1 WLR 407, [2001] STC 1271, 74 TC 372, [2001] BTC 8039, [2001] WTLR 887, (2001-02) 4 ITELR 231, [2001] STI 1106, (2001) 98(37) LSG 39, [2001] NPC 132, CA ................................................ 7.23

# Table of cases

Merrett v Babb [2001] EWCA Civ 214, [2001] QB 1174, [2001] 3 WLR 1, [2001] BLR 483, (2001) 3 TCLR 15, 80 Con LR 43, [2001] Lloyd's Rep PN 468, [2001] PNLR 29, [2001] 1 EGLR 145, [2001] 8 EG 167 (CS), (2001) 98(13) LSG 41, (2001) 145 SJLB 75, CA .................................................................................................................. 15.4
Mettoy Pension Trustees Ltd v Evans [1990] 1 WLR 1587, [1991] 2 All ER 513, Ch D . 10.13

## N

Nadin v IRC [1997] STC (SCD) 107 .......................................................................... 6.12
Nelson Dance Family Settlement Trustees v HMRC; sub nom HMRC v Nelson Dance Family Settlement Trustees [2009] EWHC 71 (Ch), [2009] BTC 8003, [2009] STI 260, [2009] NPC 11, Ch D ...................................................... 11.1, 11.2, 11.7, 11.14, 11.24
Ninth Marquess of Hertford (executors of Eighth Marquess of Hertford) v IRC [2005] STC (SCD) 177 ....................................................................................................... 11.20

## O

O'Neill & O'Neill's Executors v CIR, SpC [1998] SSCD 110 ........................................ 4.19
Oakes v Commissioner of Stamp Duties of New South Wales [1954] AC 57, [1953] 3 WLR 1127, [1953] 2 All ER 1563, 47 R & IT 141, (1953) 32 ATC 476, [1953] TR 453, (1953) 97 SJ 874, PC (Aus) ................................................................................ 5.21
Ogden v Trustees of the RHS Griffiths 2003 Settlement [2008] EWHC 118 (Ch), [2009] 2 WLR 394, [2008] 2 All ER 655, [2008] STC 776, [2009] BTC 8027, [2008] WTLR 685, [2008] STI 250, Ch D ..................................................................... 10.13, 12.8
Oxley v Hiscock; sub nom Hiscock v Oxley [2004] EWCA Civ 546, [2005] Fam 211, [2004] 3 WLR 715, [2004] 3 All ER 703, [2004] 2 FLR 669, [2004] 2 FCR 295, [2004] WTLR 709, (2003-04) 6 ITELR 1091, [2004] Fam Law 569, [2004] 20 EG 166 (CS), (2004) 101(21) LSG 35, (2004) 148 SJLB 571, [2004] NPC 70, [2004] 2 P & CR DG14, CA ........................................................................................................ 4.3

## P

Pearson v Inland Revenue Comrs; sub nom Pilkington Trustees v IRC [1981] AC 753, [1980] 2 WLR 872, [1980] 2 All ER 479, [1980] STC 318, [1980] TR 177, (1980) 124 SJ 377, HL ............................................................................................................. 7.5
Pepper (Inspector of Taxes) v Daffurn [1993] STC 466, [1993] 41 EG 184, 66 TC 68, [1993] EG 122 (CS), (1993) 90(32) LSG 40, Ch D ................................................... 11.7
Phillips v Burrows (Inspector of Taxes) (Set Aside) [2000] STC (SCD) 112, [2000] STI 168, Sp Comm ........................................................................................................... 6.61
Phillips v HMRC [2006] STC (SCD) 639, [2006] WTLR 1281, [2006] STI 2094, Sp Comm ....................................................................................................................... 11.13
Phizackerley v HMRC [2007] STC (SCD) 328, [2007] WTLR 745, [2007] STI 559, (2007) SpC 591, Sp Comm ................................................... 2.4, 3.10, 13.2, 13.5, 13.6, 13.7, 14.25, 15.47
Phoenix Office Supplies Ltd v Larvin; Phoenix Office Supplies Ltd, Re [2002] EWCA Civ 1740, [2003] BCC 11, [2003] 1 BCLC 76, (2003) 100(5) LSG 29, CA ............. 11.20
Pitt v Holt [2010] EWHC 45 (Ch), [2010] STC 901, [2010] BTC 235, [2010] WTLR 269, [2010] STI 1443, Ch D ........................................................................................ 10.13, 12.8
Powell v IRC [1997] STC (SCD) 181 ............................................................................. 11.11
Prosser v IRC DET/1/2000 ....................................................................... 4.23, 6.21, 6.38

## R

R v IRC, ex p Bishopp; sub nom IRC v Pricewaterhouse Coopers; IRC v Ernst & Young; R v Inland Revenue Comrs, ex p Allan [1999] STC 531, (1999) 11 Admin LR 575, 72 TC 322, [1999] BTC 158, [1999] COD 354, (1999) 149 NLJ 682, [1999] NPC 50, QBD .................................................................................................................. 11.3
Ratcliffe, Re, Holmes v McMullan. *See* Holmes v McMullan; sub nom Ratcliffe (Deceased), Re

*Table of cases*

Richards (t/a Colin Richards & Co) v Hughes; sub nom Hughes v Richards (t/a Colin Richards & Co) [2004] EWCA Civ 266, [2004] PNLR 35, (2004) 148 SJLB 353, CA (Civ Div) .................................................................................................... 15.5
Robertson v IRC (No 1) [2002] STC (SCD) 182, [2002] WTLR 885; [2002] STI 766, Sp Comm .................................................................................................... 6.15, 6.38
Robertson v IRC (No 2) [2002] STC (SCD) 242, [2002] WTLR 907; [2002] S.T.I. 899, Sp Comm .................................................................................................... 6.15, 6.38, 6.61
Rose (Deceased), Re; sub nom Rose v IRC [1952] Ch 499; [1952] 1 All ER 1217, [1952] 1 TLR 1577, (1952) 31 ATC 138, [1952] TR 175, CA ............................................... 12.6
Rosser v IRC [2003] STC (SCD) 311, [2003] WTLR 1057, [2003] STI 1152, Sp Comm .................................................................................................... 11.30, 11.34, 12.7
Royal Society for the Prevention of Cruelty to Animals v Sharp [2010] EWHC 268 (Ch), Ch D, [2010] STC 975, [2010] WTLR 855 .................................................................. 13.28
Russell v IRC [1988] 1 WLR 834, [1988] 2 All ER 405, [1988] STC 195, (1988) 132 SJ 659, Ch D .................................................................................................... 13.41, 13.46
Rysaffe Trustee Co (CI) Ltd v Inland Revenue Comrs; sub nom Rysaffe Trustee Co (CI) Ltd v Customs and Excise Comrs; Customs and Excise Comrs v Rysaffe Trustee Co (CI) Ltd [2003] EWCA Civ 356, [2003] STC 536, [2003] BTC 8021, [2003] WTLR 481, (2002-03) 5 ITELR 706, [2003] STI 452, (2003) 100(22) LSG 31, (2003) 147 SJLB 388, [2003] NPC 39, CA .................................................................. 2.22, 5.17, 8.47, 8.62

**S**

St Barbe Green v Inland Revenue Comrs; sub nom Green v IRC [2005] EWHC 14 (Ch), [2005] 1 WLR 1772, [2005] STC 288, [2005] BPIR 1218, [2005] BTC 8003, [2005] WTLR 75, [2005] STI 106, (2005) 102(7) LSG 26, [2005] NPC 6, Ch D ............... 3.9
Sansom v Peay (Inspector of Taxes) [1976] 1 WLR 1073, [1976] 3 All ER 375, [1976] STC 494, 52 TC 1, [1976] TR 205, (1976) 120 SJ 571, Ch D ...................................... 15.39
Scott, Re, Scott v Scott [1916] 2 Ch 268, 85 LJ Ch 528, 60 Sol Jo 478, 114 LT 1114 .... 13.35
Sieff v Fox; sub nom Bedford Estates, Re [2005] EWHC 1312 (Ch), [2005] 1 WLR 3811, [2005] 3 All ER 693, [2005] BTC 452, [2005] WTLR 891, (2005-06) 8 ITELR 93, [2005] NPC 80, Ch D .................................................................................................... 10.13, 12.8
Sillars v IRC [2004] STC (SCD) 180, [2004] WTLR 591, [2004] STI 900, (2004) 148 SJLB 536, [2004] SSCD 180, Sp Comm ....................................................................... 4.19
Smallwood v HMRC [2009] EWHC 777 .................................................................................................... 7.34
Smith v HMRC [2007] EWHC 2304 (Ch), [2008] STC 1649, 78 TC 819, [2007] BTC 8010, [2008] WTLR 147, [2007] STI 2560, (2007) 157 NLJ 1506, Ch D ............... 2.5, 4.12, 7.30, 12.26, 12.26
Smith v HMRC [2008] SpC 680 .................................................................................................... 6.3
Smith v HMRC [2009] SpC 742 .................................................................................................... 3.21, 7.5
Snowden (Deceased), Re [1979] Ch 528, [1979] 2 WLR 654, [1979] 2 All ER 172, (1979) 123 SJ 323, Ch D .................................................................................................... 7.5
Sokoya v HMRC [2008] EWHC 2132 (Ch), [2008] STC 3332, [2008] BTC 635, [2008] STI 1641, Ch D .................................................................................................... 6.3
Stack v Dowden; sub nom Dowden v Stack [2007] UKHL 17, [2007] 2 AC 432, [2007] 2 WLR 831, [2007] 2 All ER 929, [2007] 1 FLR 1858, [2007] 2 FCR 280, [2007] BPIR 913, [2008] 2 P & CR 4, [2007] WTLR 1053, (2006-07) 9 ITELR 815, [2007] Fam Law 593, [2007] 18 EG 153 (CS), (2007) 157 NLJ 634, (2007) 151 SJLB 575, [2007] NPC 47, [2007] 2 P & CR DG11, HL .................................................................. 4.3
Starke (Brown's Executors) v IRC [1996] 1 All ER 622, [1995] 1 WLR 1439, 139 Sol Jo LB 128, [1995] STC 689, [1996] 1 EGLR 157, [1996] 16 EG 115, [1995] 23 LS Gaz R 32, CA .................................................................................................... 11.30
Stedman's Executors v IRC. *See* IRC v George.
Stevenson (Inspector of Taxes) v Wishart [1987] 1 WLR 1204, [1987] 2 All ER 428, [1987] STC 266, [1987] 1 FTLR 69, 59 TC 740, (1987) 84 LSG 1575, (1987) 131 SJ 744, CA .................................................................................................... 6.12
Stoneham, Re; Sub Nom Stoneham v Stoneham [1919] 1 Ch 149, Ch D ........................ 5.4

*Table of cases*

**T**
Taylor v HMRC; Taylor v HMRC [2008] STC (SCD) 1159, [2008] STI 1993, [2008] SpC 704, Sp Comm.................................................................................................... 4.19, 6.23
Thomas v Lord Advocate; sub nom Thomas v IRC, 1953 S.C. 151; 1953 S.L.T 119, 46 R & IT 484, (1953) 32 ATC 18, [1953] TR 19, IH (2 Div) ........................................... 6.4

**U**
Udny v Udny (1866-69) L.R 1 Sc 441, (1869) 7 M (HL) 89, HL ..................................... 1.4

**V**
Vinton v Fladgate Fielder (A Firm) [2010] EWHC 904 (Ch), Ch D................................ 11.9, 15.5

**W**
Wade v Baylis [2010] EWCA Civ 257, CA (Civ Div) ...................................................... 4.3
Wells (Personal Representative of Glowacki (Deceased)) v HMRC [2008] STC (SCD) 188, [2007] WTLR 1863, [2007] STI 2232, Sp Comm........................................... 6.61, 13.46
Weston v IRC [2000] STC 1064, [2000] BTC 8041, [2001] WTLR 1217, [2000] STI 1635, (2001) 98(2) LSG 41, [2000] NPC 126, Ch D............................................... 11.11
White v Jones [1995] 2 AC 207, [1995] 2 WLR 187, [1995] 1 All ER 691, [1995] 3 FCR 51, (1995) 145 NLJ 251, (1995) 139 SJLB 83, [1995] NPC 31, HL................ 15.2, 15.3, 15.5
Wight v IRC (1982) 264 EG 935, [1984] RVR 163, Lands Tr ......................................... 4.21
Williams v HMRC [2005] STC (SCD) 782, [2005] WTLR 1421, [2005] STI 1682, Spc Comm........................................................................................................................ 11.26, 11.35
Wolff v Wolff [2004] EWHC 2110 (Ch), [2004] STC 1633, [2009] BTC 8017, [2004] WTLR 1349, [2004] STI 2068, [2004] NPC 135, Ch D........................................... 13.2
Woodhall v IRC [2000] STC (SCD) 558, [2001] WTLR 475, [2000] STI 1653, Sp Comm........................................................................................................................ 7.5, 15.43

# Abbreviations and references

| | |
|---|---|
| A&M | accumulation and maintenance trust |
| APR | agricultural property relief |
| BMT | bereaved minor trust |
| BPR | business property relief |
| CA | Court of Appeal |
| CGT | capital gains tax |
| CIOT | Chartered Institute of Taxation |
| CTT | capital transfer tax |
| 18/25 | age 18-to-25 trust |
| EPA | enduring power of attorney |
| FA | Finance Act |
| FSMA 2000 | Financial Services and Markets Act 2000 |
| GAAR | General Anti-avoidance Rule |
| GWR | gifts with reservation |
| HMRC | Her Majesty's Revenue and Customs |
| ICTA 1988 | Income and Corporation Taxes Act 1988 |
| IHT | inheritance tax |
| IHTA 1984 | Inheritance Tax Act 1984 |
| IHTM | Inheritance Tax Manual |
| IPDI | immediate post-death interest |
| IRA | Inland Revenue Affidavit |
| IRC | Inland Revenue Commissioners |
| ITA 2007 | Income Tax Act 2007 |
| ITEPA 2003 | Income Tax (Earnings and Pensions) Act 2003 |
| ITTOIA 2005 | Income Tax (Trading and Other Income) Act 2005 |
| LPA | lasting power of attorney |
| LPA 1925 | Law of Property Act 1925 |
| MCA 2005 | Mental Capacity Act 2005 |
| PET | potentially exempt transfer |
| POAT | pre-owned asset tax |
| QSR | quick succession relief |
| reg | regulation |
| s | section |
| Sch | Schedule |
| SDLT | stamp duty land tax |

*Abbreviations and references*

| | |
|---|---|
| SI | Statutory Instrument |
| SP | HMRC Statement of Practice |
| SSCBA | Social Security Contributions and Benefits Act 1992 |
| STEP | Society of Trusts and Estates Practitioners |
| TA 1925 | Taxes Act 1925 |
| TCGA 1992 | Taxation of Chargeable Gains Act 1992 |
| TLATA 1996 | Trusts of Land and Appointment of Trustees Act 1996 |
| TSI | transitional serial interest |

*Chapter 1*

# Inheritance tax: introduction

## BACKGROUND

**1.1** Inheritance tax (IHT) replaced the previous regime of capital transfer tax (CTT) in *Finance Act 1986*, with effect from 18 March 1986. CTT in turn replaced estate duty, which was originally introduced in *Finance Act 1894* and applied to deaths occurring up to and including on 12 March 1975, prior to its repeal in *Finance Act 1975*. The IHT regime continued the basic framework and administrative provisions of CTT, whilst following the estate duty principle of only charging tax on lifetime gifts made within seven years of the donor's death. The primary IHT legislation is contained in the *Inheritance Tax Act 1984* (*IHTA 1984*), as amended by subsequent Finance Acts.

IHT is a tax on chargeable transfers (*IHTA 1984, s 1*). It applies to chargeable transfers made by an individual during lifetime, and on the value of his estate on death, subject to various exemptions, exclusions and reliefs. IHT also applies to certain chargeable events relating to settled property. This chapter provides a brief introduction to the IHT system, the main principles of which are expanded upon in subsequent chapters. Unless otherwise stated, all statutory references are to *IHTA 1984*.

## WHO IS LIABLE?

**1.2** Individuals domiciled in the UK are liable to IHT on chargeable worldwide property. Non-UK domiciled individuals are also liable to IHT, but only on chargeable UK property (*s 6(1)*).

## DOMICILE

### Introduction

**1.3** As a general rule, an individual is domiciled in the country (or state) considered his permanent home. There are three different types of domicile:

**1.4** *Inheritance tax: introduction*

domicile of origin, domicile of dependence and domicile of choice. It should be noted that both a domicile of origin and a domicile of dependence are acquired by operation of law rather than by choice.

In addition to the general law concerning domicile, there is also a 'deemed domicile' rule for IHT purposes (*s 267*). Domicile is to be distinguished from residence but residence can be a factor determining domicile, especially deemed domicile, so knowledge of the rules as to residence becomes important. It does not help the practitioner that we presently have no statutory test of residence, being forced to rely on guidance in HMRC6, which replaced booklet IR20, although it is understood that a statutory residence test has been under consideration.

## Domicile of origin

**1.4** A person's domicile of origin is acquired at birth (normally that of the child's father). This remains the person's domicile until it is replaced by a domicile of dependence or a domicile of choice. A domicile of origin can revive when a domicile of choice is lost (see, for example, *Henwood v Barlow Clowes International Ltd (in liquidation) and others* [2008] EWCA 577). A person's domicile of origin is his father's domicile at the time of his birth unless he was illegitimate or his father died before he was born. In those cases, his domicile of origin will be his mother's domicile. This will often be the country in which he was born, but need not be so.

A domicile of origin will only be displaced if a person acquires a domicile of choice or a domicile of dependence. It will revive if, for example, a domicile of choice is abandoned, unless immediately replaced by a new domicile of choice (*Udny v Udny* (1869) LR 1 Sc & Div 441, HL).

## Domicile of choice

**1.5** A domicile of choice is acquired by an intention to settle permanently, and actual physical presence. Thus, it will not be acquired if the intention is conditional, or by going to work in another country unless there is a definite intention to remain permanently when the work has ceased. A domicile of choice can be lost by leaving the country without any definite intention of returning. A new domicile of choice will be acquired if a person moves to another country with the intention of settling there permanently. If a domicile of choice is lost and a new one is not acquired, the person's domicile of origin will revive. A person seeking to establish that a domicile of origin has been lost and a domicile of choice acquired, or that a domicile of choice has been replaced, must establish the change with very clear proof. HMRC consider that personal declarations are generally given a low weight when considering this proof as a whole and, if a domicile of choice cannot be established clearly, then the person's current domicile does not change (IHTM13022).

Case law has underlined the potential difficulties faced by those wishing to shed a domicile of origin in favour of a domicile of choice (see *Re Clore (No 2)* [1984] STC 609, and subsequently *Cyganik v Agulian* [2006] EWCA Civ 129). Domicile is essentially a concept of general law rather than tax law, and a detailed consideration of the principles involved is outside the scope of this book.

## Domicile of dependence

**1.6** The domicile of a minor initially follows that of the person on whom he is dependent. A domicile of dependence only affects children under 16 and persons of unsound mind. However, prior to 1 January 1974, a married woman acquired her husband's domicile on marriage, and her domicile changed with his. This rule was abolished by the *Domicile and Matrimonial Proceedings Act 1973*. For women who were married before 1 January 1974, their domicile of dependence was reclassified as a domicile of choice on 1 January 1974. However, this rule has no relevance to women married on or after 1 January 1974, and a woman can have a different domicile than that of her husband.

For transfers between spouses, it is important to know the domicile of both spouses. If the transferor spouse is domiciled in the UK but their spouse is domiciled abroad, the spouse exemption is limited to £55,000 (*s 18(2)*).

## IHT and domicile

**1.7** For IHT purposes, a person can be *deemed* to be domiciled in the UK if either of the following two rules apply, even though he is domiciled elsewhere under general law (*s 267*):

- *The 'three-year' rule* – A person is treated as domiciled in the UK if he or she was domiciled in the UK at any time in the three years immediately preceding the time at which the question of his domicile is to be decided;

**Example 1.1—The 'three-year' rule**

Christine is aged 40, and had been resident and domiciled in England all her life. She leaves the UK on 31 March 2007 and settles in Spain permanently, acquiring a domicile of choice in Spain under general law.

Christine will cease to be domiciled in the UK for IHT purposes under the 'three-year' rule on 1 April 2010. However, she will not lose her deemed domicile under the '17 out of 20' rule (see below) until she has been non-resident in the UK for three tax years and the fourth has begun. Her three years of non-residence would be 2007/08, 2008/09 and 2009/10. She will lose her deemed domicile under the latter rule on 6 April 2010 (ie at the start of the 2010/11 tax year).

**1.8** *Inheritance tax: introduction*

Care may be needed in some cases, as it may be unclear when an individual has actually abandoned his or her domicile in one territory in favour of another, for the purposes of determining when the three-year period begins and ends.

**Example 1.2—In two minds**

Davor, who was born in Croatia, came to live in England at a very early age and established a domicile of choice. Some years later, his lawyers found it difficult to establish whether he had acquired a new domicile of choice in France as soon as he left England. The lawyers used a Latin tag for this situation: *sine animo revertendi* (loosely translated as: 'I really haven't yet made up my mind whether or not to return to England').

The lawyers came to the conclusion that Davor had probably retained his domicile of choice in England whilst he made up his mind. On that basis, any delay on his part could postpone the start of the relevant three-year period, because he would not lose his domicile in England straightaway.

- *The '17 out of 20' rule* – A person will be deemed domiciled in the UK when he has been resident for 17 out of the 20 years of assessment ending with the present one (income tax rules generally apply for the purposes of determining residence in the UK for any particular tax year). This rule is the most relevant to someone who has come from abroad to live in the UK.

**Example 1.3—The '17 out of 20' rule**

Joseph came to the UK to stay on 1 May 1994. The Inland Revenue (as it then was) considered him to be UK resident for the tax year 1994/95 (ie Joseph was resident in the UK for more than six months in that tax year). He remains resident in the UK for 1995/96 and all later tax years up to and including 2009/10.

The tax year 2010/11 is the seventeenth tax year. If Joseph remains resident in the UK during 2010/11, he becomes deemed domiciled in the UK. A transfer of foreign situs assets by Joseph would then be caught for IHT purposes, unless exempt or potentially exempt.

**1.8** However, there are exceptions to the application of the 'deemed domicile' rule. The rule does not apply to the following:

- specified government securities in the beneficial ownership of persons neither domiciled nor ordinarily resident in the UK (*ss 6(2), 48(4)*);

- certain types of savings by persons domiciled in the Channel Islands or the Isle of Man (*s 6(3)*);
- certain pre-CTT double taxation agreements still in force by virtue of *s 158(6)*. Those agreements contain their own rules for domicile and for resolving the issue where both countries claim domicile (*s 267(2)*);
- for the purposes of deciding whether property settled before 10 December 1974 is excluded property (*s 267(3)*).

With regard to the third bullet point above, HMRC accept that domicile issues exclude deemed domicile when considering the double tax agreements with France, Italy, India and Pakistan. However, if domicile under general law is in Italy, India or Pakistan, the deemed domicile rules can apply to chargeable lifetime transfers (IHTM13024).

## WHAT IS CHARGEABLE TO IHT?

**1.9** IHT is a direct tax on transfers of capital (eg gifts) made on or after 18 March 1986. It is broadly a cumulative tax charge on the following:

- the value transferred by a chargeable transfer made by an individual during his lifetime within the preceding seven-year period (ie broadly the loss to the donor), and on the value of his estate on death. A 'chargeable transfer' is any 'transfer of value' (see below) made by an individual, other than an exempt transfer (*s 2*); and
- certain events relating to settlements (eg gifts to a discretionary trust).

The IHT charge on death (and in respect of certain settled property) is brought into charge by deeming a transfer of value to have been made immediately before death, equal to the value of the person's estate (and value of the settled property, if appropriate) (*ss 4(1), 52(1)*). The IHT legislation specifically precludes certain property from charge (see below).

## CUMULATION AND THE IHT THRESHOLD

**1.10** Chargeable transfers within the seven-year period ending with the date of the latest chargeable transfer are cumulated, for the purposes of determining the IHT rate (*s 7*). Where chargeable lifetime transfers and the individual's death estate do not exceed the IHT threshold (or 'nil rate band', as it is more commonly known) there is no IHT liability.

The nil rate band can normally be expected to increase annually by reference to the retail prices index. The increase in the retail prices index in September

**1.11** *Inheritance tax: introduction*

in each year is to apply to the rates of chargeable transfers made on or after 6 April in the following year (*s 8*). However, Parliament may determine the nil rate band otherwise than by reference to the retail prices index, and in recent Finance Acts have done so. The nil rate band for the current and recent years is as follows (*Sch 1*):

### Table 1.1—The 'nil rate band'

| *Transfer of value* | *Threshold* £ |
|---|---|
| 2008/09 | 312,000 |
| 2009/10 | 325,000 |
| 2010/11 | 325,000 |

The nil rate band for 2010/11 was originally set at £350,000 by *Finance Act 2007*, but it was subsequently announced in the Pre-Budget Report 2009 that the 2010/11 nil rate band would be set at its 2009/10 level of £325,000. This 'freezing' of the nil rate band was subsequently enacted in *Finance Act 2010, s 8*. In addition, the normal indexing of the nil rate band was disapplied for the tax years 2011/12 to 2014/15 inclusive.

## RATES OF IHT

### Lifetime

**1.11** Chargeable lifetime transfers are charged at half of the rate on death (s 7(2)). The 'death rate' of IHT for 2010/11 is 40%, and, therefore, chargeable lifetime transfers above the nil rate band are charged at 20%.

### Death

**1.12** Transfers made within seven years of death are charged at the rate on death, subject to taper relief for transfers made between three and seven years from death.

### Grossing-up

**1.13** IHT is based on the loss in value of the donor's estate as the result of a chargeable transfer. If the donor also pays the IHT on a gift, that payment results in a further loss to his estate. The tax must, therefore, be taken into account in the transfer of value. The gift (net of IHT) must be 'grossed-up' to determine the actual chargeable transfer.

### Example 1.4—Lifetime transfers

Mr A transfers £129,000 to a discretionary trust on 1 May 2010, £219,000 on 31 December 2010 and a further £35,000 on 1 February 2011. He bears the tax and he has made no other chargeable transfers. His IHT position is as follows:

|  | £ | £ | £ |
|---|---:|---:|---:|
| Gift on 1 May 2010 |  | 129,000 |  |
| Deduct annual exemption |  |  |  |
| –2009/10 | 3,000 |  |  |
| –2010/11 | 3,000 | 6,000 |  |
|  |  | 123,000 |  |
| Covered by nil rate band of £325,000 |  |  |  |
| Gift on 31 December 2010 |  | 219,000 |  |
| (Note: Annual exemption already used for 2010/11) |  |  |  |
| Cumulative net transfers |  | £342,000 |  |
| Tax thereon |  |  |  |
| 0–325,000 |  | 0 |  |
| 325,001–342,000 (£17,000 × ¼) |  | 4,250 |  |
| Tax on gift |  | £4,250 |  |
| Gift on 1 February 2011 |  |  |  |
|  | Gross | Tax | Net |
| Cumulative totals | 346,250 | 4,250 | 342,000 |
| Add Latest net transfer of £35,000 | 43,750 | 8,750 | 35,000 |
|  | £390,000 | £13,000 | £377,000 |
| Tax on £377,000 |  |  |  |
| 0–325,000 |  |  |  |
| 325,001–377,000 (£52,000 × ¼) |  | 13,000 |  |
|  |  | 13,000 |  |
| Deduct tax on previous transfers |  | 4,250 |  |
| Tax on latest gift |  | £8,750 |  |

## TRANSFERS OF VALUE

**1.14** A transfer of value is a disposition by a person resulting in the value of his estate immediately after the disposition being less than it would be but for the disposition. The amount by which his estate is reduced is the measure of the transfer of value (*s 3(1)*). This is sometimes referred to as the 'loss to the donor' principle.

However, the transfer of 'excluded property' (see below) does not count (*s 3(2)*). In addition, some 'dispositions' (eg gifts or transfers) are not treated as transfers of value, where certain conditions are satisfied. These can include gifts without gratuitous intent (*s 10*), transfers for family maintenance (*s 11*), dispositions which are allowable for income tax or corporation tax purposes (*s 12*) and waivers of remuneration and dividends (*ss 14, 15*).

## POTENTIALLY EXEMPT TRANSFERS

**1.15** Most types of gifts made during lifetime are potentially exempt transfers (PETs). A PET is broadly a lifetime transfer of value that satisfies the following conditions (*s 3A*):

- it is made by an individual on or after 18 March 1986;
- the transfer would otherwise be a chargeable transfer;
- before 22 March 2006, if it is either a gift to another individual or a gift into an accumulation and maintenance trust or a disabled person's trust;
- from 22 March 2006, if the transfer of value is made to another individual, a disabled person's trust or a 'bereaved minor's' trust on the ending of an 'immediate post-death interest' (see **Chapter 7**), ie lifetime gifts into the vast majority of trusts do not qualify as PETs from that date.

A PET made more than seven years before death becomes an exempt transfer. On the other hand, a PET becomes a chargeable transfer if made within seven years of death.

## CHARGEABLE LIFETIME TRANSFERS

**1.16** A lifetime transfer is broadly a disposition (eg a gift) made by a person resulting in a reduction in the value of the person's estate. A chargeable transfer is a transfer of value by an individual, other than an exempt transfer (*s 2*). As mentioned, most lifetime transfers are PETs, which are assumed will prove to be exempt when made, and which only become chargeable if the transferor dies within seven years of making them. A lifetime transfer that does not qualify as a PET will, therefore, be immediately chargeable to IHT. Examples include:

- transfers to a company;
- gifts to a discretionary trust; or

- lifetime gifts to an interest in possession settlement created since 22 March 2006.

Other transfers of value prevented from being PETs include transfers by a close company, and deemed dispositions on the alteration of share rights or capital of close companies (*ss 94, 98*).

With regard to lifetime transfers in general, see **Chapter 2**.

## IHT ON DEATH

**1.17** IHT is charged on the deceased's estate as if, immediately before his death, he had made a transfer of value. The value transferred is deemed to equal the value of his estate immediately before death (*s 4(1)*). The estate for IHT purposes includes the value of all property to which the deceased was beneficially entitled, certain interests in possession in settled property (see **Chapter 7**) and any gifts with reservation of benefit (see **Chapter 5**), but not excluded property.

Changes in the value of the estate caused by the death may be taken into account (*s 171*). Liabilities of the deceased may generally be deducted if imposed under a legal obligation, or if incurred for valuable consideration (*s 5(5)*), together with reasonable funeral expenses (*s 172*).

The amount of IHT chargeable on the death estate is subject to any IHT reliefs and exemptions to which the deceased's estate may be entitled (eg business or agricultural property relief, or the spouse or civil partner exemption), and depends on the total chargeable lifetime transfers and potentially exempt transfers made within the seven years before death.

With regard to IHT on death generally, see **Chapter 3**.

## EXCLUDED PROPERTY

**1.18** Some types of property are outside the scope of IHT. Such property is known as 'excluded property', and includes the following:

- Property situated abroad (and investments in an authorised unit trust or open ended investment company) if the beneficial owner is a non-UK domiciled person (*s 6(1)*).

- Settled property situated outside the UK, if the settlor was non-UK domiciled when the settlement was made (*s 48(3)*). However, if a UK-domiciled person acquires an interest in possession in the settled

**1.19** *Inheritance tax: introduction*

- property from 5 December 2005 for valuable consideration, that interest is not excluded property.
- Settled property (situated abroad or not) consisting of investments in an authorised unit trust or open ended investment company, if the settlor was non-UK domiciled when the settlement was made (*s 48(3A)*). However, if a UK-domiciled person acquires an interest in possession in settled property from 5 December 2005 for valuable consideration, that interest is not excluded property (*s 48(3B)*).
- A 'reversionary interest' (ie a future interest under a settlement) subject to certain anti-avoidance provisions (eg if the interest has previously been acquired for valuable consideration; see *s 48(1)*).
- Certain government securities owned by persons not domiciled or ordinarily resident in the UK (*s 6(2)*).
- National Savings certificates, war savings certificates, premium savings bonds or deposits with the National Savings Bank or a trustee savings bank of persons domiciled in the Channel Islands or Isle of Man (*s 6(3)*).

There is also an exclusion from the death estate in respect of foreign (ie non-sterling) currency bank accounts of a person who was not domiciled, resident or ordinarily resident in the UK immediately prior to death (*s 157*). In addition, certain other types of property are left out of account for IHT purposes, by concession:

- decorations for valour, if never transferred for consideration in money or money's worth (ESC F19); and
- certain compensation for World War II claims (see ESC F20).

## Settled property

**1.19** The excluded property legislation refers to the settlor's domicile when the settlement was made. HMRC take the view that, in the case of added property, a further settlement was made when that property was transferred. If the settlor was domiciled in the UK at that point, the property will not be excluded property. HMRC's Inheritance Tax Manual gives the following example (IHTM04272):

**Example 1.5—Foreign settled property**

S, when domiciled abroad, creates a settlement of Spanish realty. Later he acquires a UK domicile and then adds some Australian property to the settlement.

*Inheritance tax: introduction* **1.20**

The Spanish property is excluded property because of S's overseas domicile when he settled that property. However, the Australian property is not excluded property as S had a UK domicile when he added that property to the settlement.

---

IHT is not charged on lifetime transfers of excluded property. Nor does excluded property form part of a person's estate on death (*ss 3(2), 5(1)(b)*). However, excluded property is taken into account when measuring the loss in value of a person's estate following a transfer of non-excluded property.

## EXEMPTIONS—SUMMARY

**1.20** The following types of property are exempt and, therefore, outside the IHT charge:

- **Transfers between spouses** (*s 18*)

  There is a complete exemption for all transfers (ie lifetime and on death) between UK-domiciled spouses. However, where the transferor spouse is UK domiciled but the transferee spouse is foreign domiciled, the exemption is restricted to a cumulative total of £55,000 (IHTM11033). If the non-domiciled spouse subsequently becomes UK domiciled, unfortunately any preceding transfers to them are still subject to the £55,000 restriction. Following the *Civil Partnership Act 2004*, same-sex couples who enter into a civil relationship are given parity of tax treatment with married couples. Remember that a gift to a non-UK domiciled spouse that is within the gift with reservation rules may not be protected by spouse relief and may eventually prove to be chargeable.

- **Annual exemption** (*s 19*)

  Lifetime transfers of a value up to £3,000 per tax year are completely exempt from IHT. Any unused part of the exemption may be carried forward for one tax year only, and deducted after the annual exemption has been fully used in that later year. If the value of the gift or transfer exceeds the annual exemption, the excess will either be a potentially exempt transfer or an immediately chargeable transfer.

- **Small gifts to same person** (*s 20*)

  Lifetime gifts in a tax year with a total value not exceeding £250 to any one person are exempt from IHT. If the total value of gifts to that person exceeds £250 in the tax year, the exemption is completely lost, eg it cannot be set against part of a larger gift. The gifts must be outright. For example, they cannot be gifts of premiums on a life policy that has been written in trust (although the exemption for normal expenditure out of income in *s 21* might well apply (see below)).

**1.20** *Inheritance tax: introduction*

- **Normal expenditure out of income** (*s 21*)

  The exemption applies to lifetime gifts which:

  (a) form part of the normal expenditure of the person making it;

  (b) were made out of income (taking one year with another); and

  (c) left the donor with sufficient income to maintain their normal standard of living.

  Unlike other lifetime exemptions (eg the annual exemption), the normal expenditure out of income exemption is not subject to an upper maximum, and is only restricted to the extent of the donor's gifts, which satisfy the above conditions. Evidence is crucial to support claims to this relief.

- **Gifts in consideration of marriage or civil partnership** (*ss 22, 57*)

  Marriage gifts are exempt within certain limits. The amount of the exemption depends on the donor's relationship to the bride, groom or civil partner. Gifts of up to £5,000 by a parent of a party to a marriage or civil partnership are exempt. In the case of gifts by a grandparent or remoter ancestor, or by one party to the marriage or civil partnership to the other, the exemption limit is £2,500. For marriage gifts made by any other person, the upper limit is £1,000. These exemptions apply per marriage. The gifts must be made on or shortly before the marriage or civil partnership, and must become fully effective on the event taking place. Gifts in excess of the above exempt limits are chargeable to IHT, but only to the extent of the excess.

- **Gifts to charities** (*s 23*)

  Gifts to charities are exempt from IHT, if certain conditions are satisfied. For periods prior to changes included in *Finance Act 2010*, it is necessary for the charity to be established in the UK. However, a new statutory definition of a charity was introduced (*FA 2010, Sch 7*), which includes a four-stage test to determine if an organisation is eligible for UK charity tax reliefs. This includes a jurisdiction condition, which broadly allows the organisation to be located in the UK or an EU member state or specified country (of which Iceland and Norway were expected to be included). The *Finance Act 2010* changes as they apply for IHT purposes are to be applied by Treasury order. The IHT charity exemption is relevant to outright gifts to charity or to certain charitable trusts, and applies to lifetime gifts or transfers on death with no upper limit. Practitioners should also note the current debate concerning the 'fit and proper person' test which, if introduced as proposed, could deprive some organisations of their charitable status.

- **Gifts to political parties** (*s 24*)

  Gifts to qualifying political parties are exempt transfers for IHT purposes without limit.

*Inheritance tax: introduction* **1.20**

- **Gifts to housing associations** (*s 24A*)

  Gifts of UK land and buildings to a registered housing association or registered social landlord are exempt without upper limit.

- **Gifts for national purposes** (*s 25, Sch 3*)

  An unlimited exemption applies to qualifying gifts to those bodies designated in *IHTA 1984, Sch 3*.

- **Gifts for public benefit** (*s 26*) (repealed)

  Gifts within certain specified categories to bodies not established for profit were exempt from IHT if the Board so directed. This exemption was repealed for gifts made from 17 March 1998.

- **Maintenance funds for historic buildings, etc** (*s 27, Sch 4*)

  Transfers (during lifetime or on death) into settlement for the maintenance, repair or preservation of historic buildings and assets of outstanding scenic, historic or scientific interest, etc are exempt subject to certain conditions, where HMRC so direct (under *IHTA 1984, Sch 4*). The exemption must be claimed within two years after the date of the transfer concerned, or within such longer period as HMRC may allow.

- **Employee trusts** (*s 28*)

  Transfers, by an individual, of shares or securities in a company to 'trusts for the benefit of employees' of the company (within *IHTA 1984, s 86*) are exempt from IHT, if certain conditions are satisfied.

- **Other exemptions**

  – Annuities payable on a person's death under a registered pension scheme, a qualifying non-UK pension scheme or to a 'section 615 scheme' (ie a superannuation fund within *ICTA 1988, s 615(3)*) or, prior to 6 April 2006, either a retirement annuity contract or a personal pension scheme to a spouse or dependant, where a capital sum might at the deceased's option have become payable instead to his personal representatives (*s 152*).

  – 'Killed in war' exemption (ie broadly property of a member of the armed services (or certain associated services) passing on death caused by injury or disease received or aggravated whilst on active service (*s 154*)).

  – Foreign currency bank accounts held on the death of an individual not resident, ordinarily resident or domiciled in the UK (*s 157*) (see **1.18**).

Aside from the above exemptions, it should be noted that certain dispositions do not represent transfers of value for IHT purposes, such as dispositions not intended to confer gratuitous benefit (*s 10*) and dispositions for the maintenance of family (*s 11*); see **9.12**.

**1.21** *Inheritance tax: introduction*

## TAPER RELIEF: OUTLINE

**1.21** IHT on all lifetime transfers (chargeable lifetime transfers and PETs) made within seven years before death is subject to a potential reduction for taper relief, if the lifetime transfer was made more than three years before death. Note that the relief reduces the IHT that would otherwise be payable on a transfer, and not the value of the transfer itself.

Tax on chargeable lifetime transfers is calculated at lifetime rates. If the transferor dies within seven years the tax is recomputed at full death rates, subject to taper relief where the death is more than three years after the gift. However, taper relief cannot reduce the tax payable below that originally charged.

In addition, IHT at full death rates is calculated at the time of death on any PETs made within seven years prior to death, subject to the availability of taper relief. The value of the transfer stays the same for taper relief purposes, but the full rate(s) of IHT charged are reduced to a percentage of those rates on the following scale (*s 7(4)*):

### Table 1.2—Taper relief rates

| Transfer: | | |
|---|---|---|
| | 3–4 years before death: rate reduced to: | 80% |
| | 4–5 years before death: | 60% |
| | 5–6 years before death: | 40% |
| | 6–7 years before death: | 20% |

**1.22** However, if IHT on a chargeable lifetime transfer is recalculated on death with taper relief and produces a lower tax figure than the tax originally calculated at lifetime rates, the original figure stands (*s 7(5)*). In other words, no IHT repayments result from the application of taper relief. See **Chapter 10**.

## QUICK SUCCESSION RELIEF: OUTLINE

**1.23** Quick succession relief (QSR) is available on the death of an individual whose estate has increased in value as the result of a chargeable transfer (ie during lifetime or a transfer on death) made within five years before his death (*s 141*). If the conditions for QSR are satisfied, the tax charge on the later transfer is calculated in the normal way. The relief is then given by reducing the IHT on death by a percentage of the tax attributable to the net increase (see below) in the deceased's estate from the original transfer. It is not necessary for the asset in question to be retained. The percentage varies according to the length of time between the dates of transfer and death, as follows:

### Table 1.3—Quick succession relief

| Period between transfer and death | Relief percentage |
|---|---|
| One year or less | 100% |
| 1–2 years | 80% |
| 2–3 years | 60% |
| 3–4 years | 40% |
| 4–5 years | 20% |

The earlier transfer can be, for example, a failed PET on which IHT becomes payable. The same rates of quick succession relief apply to successive IHT charges within five years on trust property with an interest in possession. See **Chapter 10**.

Note one practical point in calculating QSR, the reference above to 'the net increase'. If, on the earlier death, the tax on the transfer was actually paid by the residue of the estate, that affects the amount of relief. Gifts of UK assets will be 'tax free', in the sense that tax is borne by residue, unless the will provides to the contrary. In such a case, what the beneficiary gets is the full value of the gift, so his estate is increased by the full amount, and on death soon after the full amount features in the calculation of QSR.

Suppose however that the gift was of foreign property; or the will put the burden of tax on the gift itself: in that case what the beneficiary inherits is effectively less, and QSR is reduced accordingly.

## DOUBLE TAXATION RELIEF

**1.24**   Where IHT is chargeable in the UK and tax of a similar nature (or which is chargeable by reference to death or lifetime gifts) is charged in another territory on the same property, double taxation relief may be available.

### Treaty relief

**1.25**   Relief is given if the UK has a double taxation agreement with the overseas territory containing provisions to eliminate the double taxation chargeable by reference to death or lifetime gifts (*s 158*).

A person can be deemed domiciled in the UK for IHT purposes even though he is domiciled elsewhere under general law (ie under the '17 out of the 20' tax years rule, or if domiciled in the UK within the previous three years (see **1.7** above)). That person may also be domiciled elsewhere under the domestic

**1.26** *Inheritance tax: introduction*

law of another state. The 'deemed domicile' IHT rule does not apply in all cases, such as where certain pre-CTT double taxation agreements are still in force (ie by virtue of *s 158(6);* see *s 267(2)*). Those agreements contain their own rules for domicile and for resolving the issue where both countries claim domicile. HMRC accept that domicile issues exclude deemed domicile when considering the double tax agreements with France, Italy, India and Pakistan, although if domicile under general law is in Italy, India or Pakistan, the deemed domicile rules can apply to chargeable lifetime transfers (IHTM13024).

## Unilateral relief

**1.26** Where relief is not provided under a double tax agreement, credit is available against UK tax for tax suffered in an overseas territory, on the same property (*s 159*). Unilateral relief may also be claimed if it provides greater relief than by applying treaty relief (*s 159(7)*).

If the property is situated in the overseas territory and not in the UK, credit is available on the whole amount of overseas tax. However, if the overseas tax exceeds the UK tax, the excess is not repayable. A measure of relief is also available if the property is situated as follows (*s 159(3)*):

- in a third territory; or
- both in the UK and the overseas territory (ie due to different laws on the situs of assets in the UK and that territory).

Relief similarly applies if tax is imposed in two or more overseas territories if the property is situated as follows (*s 159(4)*):

- neither in the UK nor those territories; or
- both in the UK and in each of those territories.

## TRANSFERS OF VALUE BY CLOSE COMPANIES

**1.27** Anti-avoidance rules apply to transfers of value (eg sales at undervalue) by close companies. Only individuals can make a chargeable transfer for IHT purposes (*s 2(1)*). However, if a close company makes a transfer of value, the transfer is apportioned between the participators in that company (*s 94*). Each participator is deemed to have made an immediately chargeable transfer of value (ie not a PET) equal to the amount so apportioned. The company is primarily liable to pay any IHT liability arising (*s 202*).

However, if the participator's estate increases as a result of the transfer, that increase may be deducted from the amount so apportioned. The balance reflects the net decrease in value of the person's estate. Therefore, a transfer of value to a participator with a 100% interest in the close company should not normally result in an overall decrease in the value of his estate.

A transfer of value is not apportioned to participators in the following circumstances (*s 94(2)*):

- if the amount is liable to income tax (or corporation tax) in the recipient's hands, eg as employment income or dividend income of the individual; or
- the participator is not domiciled in the UK, and the relevant asset is situated abroad.

**1.28** If the participator has less than 5% of the transfer apportioned to him, the transfer is not added to his cumulative total of transfers for IHT purposes (*s 94(4)*), and no IHT liability attaches to that person in respect of the transfer. However, the tax is calculated by reference to his IHT position at that time, although he cannot be held liable to pay the IHT if the company is in default (*s 202(2)*). The annual IHT exemption may be deducted (if not already used elsewhere) from the value of any amount apportioned (*s 94(5)*).

The IHT anti-avoidance rules for close companies also include provisions relating to alterations in unquoted share capital, loan capital or rights attaching to its unquoted shares or debentures. Participators to whom those provisions apply are broadly treated as having made a disposition for IHT purposes, which is not a PET (*s 98*).

*Chapter 2*

# Lifetime transfers

## INTRODUCTION

**2.1** IHT is a tax on 'chargeable transfers' made on or after 18 March 1986 during an individual's lifetime, and on the value of the death estate. A 'chargeable transfer' is any transfer of value made by an individual, other than an exempt transfer (*IHTA 1984, s 2(1)*). All statutory references in this chapter are to *IHTA 1984*, unless otherwise stated.

A 'potentially exempt transfer' (PET) becomes an exempt transfer seven years after the date of the gift. It is assumed that a PET will become an exempt transfer when the gift is made (*s 3A(5)*). An outright lifetime gift to another individual (or a disabled trust, or a trust for bereaved minors in certain limited circumstances; see **1.15**) is a PET, which therefore only becomes chargeable to IHT if the donor dies within seven years of making the gift.

However, transfers to a company and gifts to a relevant property trust (ie a discretionary trust and, from 22 March 2006, an interest in possession and accumulation and maintenance trust) are immediately chargeable lifetime transfers. IHT at the lifetime rate may become due (subject to any reliefs and exemptions) if the total value of those gifts exceeds the taxable IHT threshold or 'nil rate band' (ie £325,000 for 2010/11).

## EXEMPT LIFETIME TRANSFERS

**2.2** In addition to PETs made more than seven years before the donor's death, certain lifetime transfers are exempt from IHT. For further information on IHT exemptions generally, see **1.20** and **Chapter 9**.

**2.3** *Lifetime* exemptions are summarised below:

- Gifts between spouses or civil partners (restricted to a cumulative total of £55,000 where the transferee is domiciled outside the UK) (*s 18*).

*Lifetime transfers* **2.4**

- Annual exemption for gifts not exceeding £3,000 in any tax year. If the total value of gifts in one tax year is less than £3,000, the excess can be carried forward to the next tax year, but no further (*s 19*).

- Small gifts in any tax year up to a total of £250 per donee, to as many recipients as the donor wishes (*s 20*).

- Normal expenditure out of income is exempt with no upper limit, if certain conditions are satisfied (broadly that the gifts are part of the donor's usual expenditure, were made out of income, and left the donor with sufficient income to maintain his normal standard of living (*s 21*)).

- Wedding or civil partnership gifts within certain limits (ie £5,000 if the donor is a parent of a party to the marriage or civil partnership, £2,500 if the donor is a remoter ancestor or is one of the parties to the marriage or civil partnership, or £1,000 for any other donor) (*s 22*).

- Gifts to charities or registered clubs (*s 23*).

- Gifts to qualifying parliamentary political parties (*s 24*).

- Gifts to registered housing associations (*s 24A*).

- Gifts for national purposes (eg the National Gallery, National Museums and the National Trust) (*s 25, Sch 3*).

- Transfers to maintenance funds for historic buildings, where HMRC so direct upon making a claim (*s 27, Sch 4*).

- Transfers of shares or securities by an individual to an employee trust, subject to certain conditions (*s 28*).

- Transfers of national heritage property may be exempt from IHT where certain conditions are satisfied, ie 'conditionally exempt transfers' (*ss 30–35*).

## Dispositions that are not transfers of value

**2.4** In addition, certain 'dispositions' (eg gifts, payments or actions, such as the waiver of salary or dividends if certain conditions are satisfied) are not treated as transfers of value, and are, therefore, not taken into account for IHT purposes (*ss 10–17*) (see **Chapter 9**). This includes dispositions which are not intended to confer a gratuitous benefit on anyone (*s 10*), and payments for the maintenance of certain family members, eg current or ex-spouse or civil partner, the donor's children (including adopted children and stepchildren) who are under 18 for their education and training and relatives who are dependent due to old age or infirmity (*s 11*); as to the latter category of disposition, see *R McKelvey (personal representative of D V McKelvey) v HMRC* [2008] SSCD 944 (SpC 694), discussed at **15.16**.

**2.5** *Lifetime transfers*

'Maintenance' for the above purposes usually means making periodic payments rather than lump sum provision: see *Phizackerley v HMRC* [2007] WTLR 745.

## POTENTIALLY EXEMPT TRANSFERS

### Definition and scope

**2.5** A PET is a transfer of value made by an individual (as opposed to a 'person', which has a wider meaning, including a company), which would otherwise be a chargeable transfer. A PET made seven years or more before the transferor's death is exempt; any other PET is a chargeable transfer.

A PET is treated as exempt whilst the donor is alive, and in the seven-year period following the transfer it is assumed that the PET will become exempt (*s 3A(5)*).

In the case of a life insurance policy taken out or varied (since 26 March 1974) for the benefit of someone else, if an annuity was also taken out (before, at the same time or after the policy), then unless the taxpayer can show that the purchase of the annuity and the taking out of the policy were not associated operations (within *s 268*), a transfer of value is treated as having taken place in taking the policy out for someone else, which can qualify as a PET (*s 263*).

This form of IHT planning (known as 'back-to-back arrangements') is otherwise intended to benefit from the 'normal expenditure' exemption, although anti-avoidance provisions can deny the exemption (*s 21(2), (3)*). HMRC practice is not to treat arrangements as associated operations (and not to disqualify the premiums from the normal expenditure exemption) if it can be shown that the life policy was issued on 'normal' terms. This means that full evidence of health must have been obtained, and that the terms on which the policy was issued would have been the same even if the annuity had not been bought (*SP E4*). For back-to-back life policy arrangements involving husband and wife (or civil partners), full medical evidence should be obtained in respect of both parties (*Smith v Revenue and Customs Commissioners* [2008] STC 1649).

### Transfers before 22 March 2006

**2.6** Before 22 March 2006, gifts qualified as PETs if made by an individual to:

- another individual (or to an interest in possession trust for another individual);
- an accumulation and maintenance trust; or
- the trustees of a trust for the disabled.

*Lifetime transfers* **2.8**

## Transfers from 22 March 2006

**2.7** From 22 March 2006, gifts to an accumulation and maintenance trust are not PETs, ie they are immediately chargeable transfers instead (*s 3A(1)–(1A)*). Gifts to interest in possession trusts are discussed below.

A 'transfer of value' is a disposition made by a person resulting in the value of his estate immediately afterwards being less than it otherwise would be; the difference is the value transferred. The measure of the transfer is, therefore, the reduction in the transferor's estate (*s 3(1)*). A gift to another individual is a PET to the extent that the value transferred becomes comprised in that individual's estate, or to the extent that the transfer results in an increase in his estate (eg the forgiveness of a loan to another individual).

**2.8** A gift to a disabled trust is a PET to the extent that it becomes settled property within *s 89* ('Trusts for disabled persons') (*s 3A(3), (3A)*). A disabled person's interest within *s 89A* ('Self-settlement by person expected to lead to disability') is a qualifying interest in possession (ie within *s 49(1A)*), so the gift is a non-event for IHT purposes as it is treated as remaining part of the settlor's estate (*s 89B(1)(b)*). The same applies to an interest in possession to which a person with a condition expected to lead to disability is beneficially entitled (*s 89B(1)(d)*). An interest in possession to which the disabled person became entitled on or after 22 March 2006 is also a qualifying interest in possession (*s 89B(1)(c)*). A gift to such a settlement by another individual therefore constitutes a PET, as representing a gift to another individual within *s 3A(1A)* (IHTM42805).

In addition, a gift into a 'bereaved minor's' trust is a PET if made on the ending of an 'immediate post-death interest' (*s 3A(1A)(c)(iii)*) (see **Chapter 7**). Prior to 22 March 2006, a lifetime gift to an accumulation and maintenance trust was also a PET, if it became settled property within *s 71* ('Accumulation and maintenance trusts').

Certain transfers of value are specifically prevented from being PETs, ie transfers by a close company (*s 94(1)*), the deemed disposition on an alteration in the capital or share rights of close companies (*s 98(3)*), the release of a life interest between 18 March 1986 and 16 March 1987 (see IHTM04063), and a transfer to the extent to which the property transferred consists of woodlands subject to a deferred estate duty charge (*FA 1986, Sch 19, para 46*).

If a reversionary interest (ie a future trust interest) in relevant property has been purchased for money or money's worth, or is held by the settlor or spouse or civil partner, a deemed disposal arises for IHT purposes when the reversionary interest ends and entitlement to an interest in possession begins. The resulting IHT charge is based on the value of the reversionary interest immediately before it ended. A gift of such a reversionary interest is prevented from being

**2.9** *Lifetime transfers*

a PET. This rule applies to reversionary interests arising from 9 December 2009 (*s 81A*), but does not affect interests in possession outside the 'relevant property' regime, such as a disabled person's interest.

## Deemed PETs

**2.9** An exception to the general rule that occasions of IHT charge (ie where tax is charged as if a transfer of value had been made) are excluded from being PETs applies to charges under *s 52* ('Charge on termination of an interest in possession') (*s 3A(6)–(7)*). This exception relates to transfers of value from 17 March 1987. The release of a life interest is a PET in the circumstances outlined below.

However, there is an exception from PET treatment in respect of an IHT charge under *s 52*, where a UK-domiciled person purchased the interest in possession at arm's length. Such an IHT charge is prevented from being a PET (ie it is immediately chargeable), if the person's beneficial entitlement to the interest arose on or after 9 December 2009 (*s 3A(6A)*).

### Before 22 March 2006

**2.10** The disposal or release of an individual's beneficial entitlement to an interest in possession in settled property by gift before 22 March 2006 is a PET in the following cases (*s 3A*):

- another individual becomes beneficially entitled to the property in question, or to an interest in possession in that property; or
- the property is settled on accumulation and maintenance trusts or trusts for the disabled; or
- the value of another individual's estate is increased.

### From 22 March 2006

**2.11** An interest in possession created before 22 March 2006 and disposed of or released by gift to someone else from that date is a PET as above, unless the rules for bereaved minors (*s 71A*) or 'Age 18-to-25 trusts' (*s 71D*) applied to the trust property in which the interest subsisted immediately before that disposal (*ss 51(1B), 53(1A)*).

If an individual has an interest in trust property, which remains comprised in his estate for IHT purposes (eg a 'transitional serial interest'), if that interest is later terminated or gifted but he continues to enjoy the property thereafter, the rules regarding 'gifts with reservation' (in *FA 1986, s 102*) apply. The individual is treated for the purposes of those anti-avoidance provisions as having made a gift of the interest terminated or given away (*FA 1986, s 102ZA(2)*).

*Lifetime transfers* **2.13**

In the case of an interest created on or after 22 March 2006, a subsequent disposal or release of the life interest by gift is a PET if it is an 'immediate post-death interest', a 'disabled person's interest' or a 'transitional serial interest' *(s 51(1A))*. For further information on interests in possession generally, see **Chapter 7**.

**2.12** Certain transfers are treated as if they were PETs, ie the lifetime cessation of a benefit in 'gift with reservation' property *(FA 1986, s 102(4))* (see **2.20**), and the discharge or reduction of a debt subject to abatement (see below).

The release of a life interest between 18 March 1986 and 16 March 1987 cannot be a PET and is, therefore, an immediately chargeable transfer. This is because a transfer of value was originally prevented (by *s 3A(2)*) from being a PET if it resulted in settled property becoming comprised in an individual's estate, or in an increase in the value of settled property already comprised in the estate.

A further deemed PET arises on the discharge, or reduction, of a debt subject to abatement under *FA 1986, s 103* ('Treatment of certain debts and incumbrances') on or after 18 March 1986 *(FA 1986, s 103(5))*.

## Implications of PETs

**2.13** As indicated at **2.1** above, it is assumed that a PET will become an exempt transfer when made. Prior to death, it is, therefore, only necessary to notify HMRC Inheritance Tax of the transfer if it is relevant to the application of the annual IHT exemption in respect of an immediately chargeable transfer (see below). However, the PET is not cumulated with the immediately chargeable transfer. A PET becomes an exempt transfer if the donor survives seven years after the date of the gift, but is otherwise chargeable to IHT if the donor dies within that seven-year period.

If an individual dies within seven years, the earlier PET becomes chargeable to IHT at the date of that gift. For the purposes of allocating the annual exemption, a chargeable PET is deemed to have been made later than any non-PET made in the same tax year *(s 19(3A))*. However, HMRC practice (see below) is to allocate the annual exemption to transfers of value in chronological order.

For example, if an individual makes a PET (eg a gift to a sibling) earlier in the same tax year than a chargeable lifetime transfer (eg a gift to a discretionary trust), HMRC guidance (at IHTM14043) indicates that where tax is otherwise payable on the two transfers made on different days in the same tax year, the exemption should be applied to the earlier transfer, and that this would be the case irrespective of whether the transfers were PETs or chargeable when made.

If a PET becomes chargeable, IHT is calculated at the death rates applicable at the time of death, subject to taper relief. In addition, the transfer is cumulated with the death estate, and will also affect the individual's cumulative total of chargeable transfers (see **Example 2.1**).

## 2.13 Lifetime transfers

### Example 2.1—Death within seven years of a PET

Mr Smith dies on 30 April 2010, having made the following lifetime gifts:

| | | | £ |
|---|---|---|---|
| 1 June 2007 | – | Cash gift to daughter | 150,000 |
| 6 April 2009 | – | Cash gift to discretionary trust | 263,000 |

*Lifetime IHT position of gifts*

The IHT position on making the lifetime gifts is that the cash gift to Mr Smith's daughter on 1 June 2007 is a PET, which is not cumulated but uses his annual exemptions of £6,000 (ie £3,000 for 2007/08, plus £3,000 unused exemption brought forward from 2006/07). The creation of the discretionary trust on 6 April 2009 was an immediately chargeable transfer, but the amount chargeable to IHT of £257,000 (ie £263,000 less £3,000 annual exemptions for 2009/10 and 2008/09) was less than the nil rate band, so no IHT was payable.

*IHT position of lifetime gifts on death*

(a) On the gift to Mr Smith's daughter:

| | £ |
|---|---|
| Gift to daughter | 150,000 |
| Less: annual exemption ( × 2) | (6,000) |
| | 144,000 |
| Less: nil rate band (2010/11) | (144,000) |
| | Nil |

(b) On creation of the discretionary trust:

| | £ |
|---|---|
| Cash gift to trust | 263,000 |
| Less: annual exemption ( × 2) | (6,000) |
| | 257,000 |
| Less: nil rate band remaining (£325,000 – £144,000) | (181,000) |
| | 76,000 |
| IHT @ 40% | £30,400 |

Taper relief is not in point, as the gift was within three years of Mr Smith's death.

*Lifetime transfers* **2.14**

## CHARGEABLE LIFETIME TRANSFERS

**2.14** A chargeable lifetime transfer is a transfer of value made by an individual, which is not unconditionally or potentially exempt (*s 2(1)*). Hence this includes the following:

- transfers into relevant property trusts, such as discretionary trusts (and, for example, terminations of pre-22 March 2006 interests in possession in favour of such trusts, and (from 22 March 2006) lifetime gifts into most interest in possession trusts); and

- transfers by close companies, which can be charged on the shareholders (*ss 94–97*).

In addition, see **2.8** above for transfers of value that are chargeable on the basis that they cannot be treated as PETs.

A chargeable lifetime transfer is aggregated with other such transfers over a seven-year period, following which they fall out of the cumulative total. Business property relief and agricultural property relief may reduce the value of the gift, if the relief conditions are satisfied at the date of transfer (see **Chapter 11**). The rate of IHT is determined by reference to this total. Tax is charged (at half the rate at death) on the transfer as the highest part of the cumulative total, to the extent that it exceeds the nil rate band, after deducting any available reliefs and exemptions.

Where the transferor bears the IHT liability, the tax represents a further loss in the value of his estate, and the transfer must, therefore, be grossed-up to arrive at the overall amount of the chargeable transfer.

---

**Example 2.2—Cumulation of chargeable lifetime transfers**

Martin made the following lifetime gifts (after exemptions and reliefs):

|  |  |  | £ |
|---|---|---|---|
| 1 June 2001 | – | Discretionary trust | 50,000 |
| 6 April 2004 | – | Discretionary trust | 85,000 |
| 31 December 2008 | – | Gift to daughter (PET) | 100,000 |
| 6 April 2010 | – | Discretionary trust | 340,000 |

The transfer to the discretionary trust in 2001 was made more than seven years before the transfer in 2010, but the transfer in 2004 is taken into account. The PET in 2008 is ignored when calculating lifetime tax on the chargeable transfer in 2010. If Martin agrees to pay the tax on his lifetime gifts, his IHT position is as follows:

**2.15** *Lifetime transfers*

*6 April 2004 – Discretionary trust £85,000*

The transfer (although cumulated with the earlier transfer on 1 June 2001) is covered by the nil rate band.

*6 April 2010 – Discretionary trust £340,000*

The transfer is cumulated with the earlier transfer on 6 April 2004. However, it is not cumulated with the transfer on 1 June 2001 (ie more than seven years ago). Nor is it cumulated with the gift to Martin's daughter on 31 December 2008 (ie a PET when made).

The IHT position is, therefore, as follows:

|  | £ |
|---|---:|
| IHT: | |
| £240,000 (ie £325,000 – £85,000) × nil | NIL |
| £100,000 × ¼ (ie grossed-up) | 25,000 |
|  | £25,000 |

The gross value of the transfer is £340,000 + £25,000 = £365,000

**2.15** Additional IHT becomes chargeable at the 'death rate' (40% for 2010/11) in respect of immediately chargeable lifetime transfers made within seven years from the death of the transferor. The gift is cumulated with immediately chargeable gifts and PETs in the preceding seven years. The resulting IHT (as recalculated at the full death rate) is compared with the lifetime tax paid (if any), for the purposes of calculating any additional liability. However, if the recomputed figure is lower than the IHT paid at the time of transfer, no additional tax is payable, but the difference is not repaid.

**Example 2.3—Chargeable lifetime transfers: position on death**

Continuing the above example, suppose that Martin died on 5 October 2010. The additional IHT on death would be as follows (after reliefs and exemptions):

*6 April 2004 – Discretionary trust £85,000*

The transfer (cumulated with the earlier transfer on 1 June 2001) remains covered by the nil rate band.

*31 December 2008 – Gift to daughter £100,000*

The 'failed' PET is cumulated with the discretionary trust transfer on 6 April 2004 (but not the gift on 1 June 2001, which falls out of charge). The cumulative total (ie £100,000 + £85,000 = £185,000) is covered by the IHT nil rate band.

*6 April 2010 – Discretionary trust £340,000*

The transfer is cumulated with the transfers on 6 April 2004 and 31 December 2008. The additional IHT on the gross value of the transfer (ie £365,000) is calculated as follows (NB: the donee is liable for the additional IHT liability):

|  | £ |
|---|---|
| IHT: |  |
| £140,000 (ie £325,000 – £185,000) × nil | NIL |
| £225,000 × 40% (no taper relief) | 90,000 |
|  | 90,000 |
| Less: IHT paid at lifetime rates | (25,000) |
| Additional IHT due (payable by trustees) | 65,000 |

**2.16** The calculation of additional tax on death may be affected by considerations such as the following, which are discussed in subsequent chapters:

- The availability of relief for business and agricultural property (see **Chapter 11**).
- The availability of other reliefs. For example, a reduction in additional IHT on death may be claimed (ie by the person liable for the tax) if the value of an asset has fallen between the date of gift and the date of the transferor's death (or an earlier qualifying sale of the gifted property) (*IHTA 1984, ss 131–140* 'Transfers within seven years before death') (see **Chapter 10**).
- Whether the 'gifts with reservation' anti-avoidance rules apply (see **2.20** below).

## VALUING LIFETIME TRANSFERS

### General

**2.17** The general rule is that assets are valued for IHT purposes at the price they might reasonably be expected to fetch if sold in the open market at the time of transfer (*s 160*).

However, the value of a lifetime gift is measured by the reduction in value of the transferor's estate as a result of the transfer (but normally without taking into account the value of any excluded property ceasing to form part of the estate (*s 3(2)*)). The value of the gift will often equal the loss to the estate, but not always. For example, the loss to the estate of a 51% shareholder in a private company who makes a lifetime gift of 2% is greater than the value of the 2% gift; it is the value of the shareholder's loss of control in the company.

**2.18** *Lifetime transfers*

Liabilities are taken into account in valuing the estate at the date of transfer, if imposed by law or to the extent of being incurred for consideration in money or money's worth (*s 5(3), (5)*). A liability attaching to a particular asset will generally reduce the value of that asset (*s 162(4)*).

## Valuing PETs

**2.18** If property becomes comprised in another individual's estate, or becomes qualifying settled property, the value transferred by a PET is generally calculated by reference to the loss to the transferor's estate. There is no 'grossing-up' because the transferor is not liable for the tax on a PET. The loss to the transferor's estate will often (but not always) be the same as the increase in value of the transferee's estate. For example, the forgiveness of a loan should result in a loss to the estate and corresponding increase, whereas the omission to exercise a right may not (IHTM04066).

## Valuing transfers by close companies

**2.19** In the case of a close company transfer of value (see **1.27**), IHT is charged as if each individual participator had made a transfer of the amount apportioned to them by reference to their rights and interests in the company immediately before the transfer. The transfer is based upon the net amount apportioned to each participator after taking account of any corresponding increase in that participator's estate following the transfer. The annual exemption specifically applies to these transfers if not otherwise used elsewhere (*s 94(5)*), and the spouse or civil partner exemption is also available to the extent that the estate of the spouse or civil partner of a participator is increased (IHTM04068).

Alterations to a close company's unquoted share or loan capital (eg a subscription for valuable shares at par by an individual), or any rights attaching to its unquoted shares or debentures, are also treated as dispositions made by the participators (*s 98(1)*), which are apportioned among the participators in the same way as a transfer by a close company. The disposition is specifically prohibited from being treated as a PET (*s 98(3)*).

## GIFTS WITH RESERVATION

**2.20** The 'gifts with reservation' (GWR) anti-avoidance provisions (*FA 1986, ss 102–102C, Sch 20*) apply to lifetime gifts in certain circumstances. The rules are designed to prevent 'cake and eat it' situations, whereby an individual gifts an asset but continues to have the use or enjoyment of it. As mentioned, most lifetime gifts to individuals are PETs if not otherwise exempt, which only become chargeable if the transferor dies within seven years of the transfer. Without the GWR rules, if the transferor survived the transfer by seven years, the

*Lifetime transfers* **2.21**

PET would become an exempt transfer, even though for all practical purposes the transferor may have continued to enjoy the gifted asset until their death.

The effect of the GWR rules is broadly to ensure that the property subject to GWR is treated as forming part of the donor's death estate. If the benefit is ended during his lifetime, the donor is treated as having made a PET at that time (*FA 1986, s 102(4)*), which becomes a chargeable transfer on death within the following seven years. However, because the PET is not actual but deemed (ie because there is no actual transfer of value when the GWR ceases) the annual exemption is not available to offset against it. The property transferred by the PET is valued on the basis of the loss to the transferor's estate (IHTM04073).

In the absence of provisions to the contrary, IHT could become chargeable on the initial lifetime transfer, and on the value of the relevant asset when the reservation ceased (eg upon death). However, the GWR rules are supplemented by regulations designed to prevent a double tax charge arising (*Inheritance Tax (Double Charges Relief) Regulations, SI 1987/1130*). For further information on the GWR rules, see **Chapter 5**).

## ASSOCIATED OPERATIONS

**2.21** As mentioned, a transfer of value is any disposition made by a person as a result of which the value of his estate immediately after the disposition is less than it would be but for the disposition; and the amount by which it is less is the value transferred by the transfer (*s 3(1)*). A 'disposition' is defined (by *s 272*) to include a disposition effected by associated operations.

The 'associated operations' provision is a further anti-avoidance rule, which provides for transactions to be treated as gifts whether made directly or indirectly and made by way of two or more linked operations (*s 268*). Where this rule applies, the combined effect on the value of the transferor's estate will be taken into account and treated as made at the time of the last transfer. The provision applies to transactions affecting the same property or a series of linked transactions, which need not be effected by the same person. The following example is taken from HMRC's Inheritance Tax Manual (at IHTM14821):

**Example 2.4—Associated operations**

'T has a 100% shareholding in ABC Ltd. At 11 June 2001 it is valued at £100,000. T transfers:

- a 33% holding to S on 11 June 01
- a 33% holding to S on 12 June 01 and
- a 34% holding to R on 13 June 01

29

### 2.22 Lifetime transfers

Following T's death in August 2001, the loss to the estate on each transfer is individually valued at:

- £43,000
- £26,000, and
- £17,000 respectively.

A total of £86,000.

The total of the individual transfers for inheritance tax is only £86,000 but T had effectively given away £100,000 worth of assets.

The legislation at *IHTA 1984, s 268* counters this in certain circumstances so that you can look at the overall effect of several events through the concept of "associated operations".'

**2.22** However, case law has effectively restricted the scope of the associated operations rule in certain situations (see below).

The omission to exercise a right can be an 'operation' treated as an associated operation for these purposes. The value of a transfer made through associated operations is normally the overall loss to the transferor's estate, measured at the time of the last operation. However, if any of the earlier operations was also a transfer of value by the transferor, the value transferred by the earlier operation(s) (to the extent that the spouse or civil partner exemption is not available) is deducted from the overall amount (*s 268(3)*).

The associated operations rule does not apply to associate the grant of a lease for full consideration in money or money's worth, with any operation effected more than three years after the grant (*s 268(2)*).

With regard to the creation of settlements, in *Rysaffe Trustee Co (CI) Ltd v IRC* [2003] STC 536, the Court of Appeal held that as a matter of general law five separate discretionary settlements created on different dates (ie to maximise the availability of nil rate bands) on very similar terms constituted separate settlements for the purposes of the ten-year anniversary charge (under *s 64*). The court rejected HMRC's contention of only a single settlement, existing by associated operations. The settlor had intended separate settlements. Hence each settlement was eligible for its own nil rate band, as each settlement had been created by a 'disposition'.

## CALCULATING IHT

**2.23** The IHT rates for chargeable lifetime transfers for 2010/11 are shown in **Table 2.1** below (*s 7, Sch 1*). The IHT threshold (or 'nil rate band') for

*Lifetime transfers* **2.23**

2010/11 was originally set at £350,000 by *FA 2007*, but was subsequently changed to its 2009/10 level of £325,000 in *FA 2010, s 8*, which also set the nil rate band at that level for 2011/12 to 2014/15 inclusive.

**Table 2.1—Chargeable lifetime transfers after 5 April 2010: Tax on gross transfers**

| *Gross taxable transfers* £ | *Gross Cumulative totals* £ | *Rate* |
|---|---|---|
| First 325,000 | 0–325,000 | NIL |
| Above 325,000 | | 20% for each £ over 325,000 |

**Grossing-up of net lifetime transfers**

| *Net transfers* £ | *Tax payable thereon* £ | |
|---|---|---|
| First 325,000 | | NIL |
| Above 325,000 | 25% (or 1/4) for each £ over 325,000 | |

No IHT is payable if the chargeable transfers or failed PETs do not exceed the IHT threshold. If a transfer has become chargeable because of death, the IHT threshold and rate at the date of death is used to calculate the tax due. If there has been a change in the IHT rate bands, the new rates are used to calculate the tax on a subsequent transfer. The cumulative totals of chargeable transfers may need to be restated where IHT is included, before this calculation can be made.

Chargeable transfers of value are cumulated; the IHT rate will depend on the total value of any such transfers made within the seven-year period ending with the latest transfer. After seven years, these transfers drop out of the cumulative total.

## The '14-year backward shadow'

It may be necessary to look back at transfers made more than seven years before the date of death, up to a maximum of 14 years. For example, if a PET was made (say) six years and 11 months before death, the period 13 years and 11 months prior to the death will need to be reviewed. However, the only transfers more than seven years before death which need to be considered are immediately chargeable ones.

## 2.24 Lifetime transfers

### Example 2.5—Cumulation of lifetime gifts

Mr Jones died on 1 December 2010, having made gifts (after reliefs and exemptions) of £100,000 to his daughter on 5 April 1999, £150,000 to a discretionary trust on 5 April 2002 and £263,000 to his son on 31 December 2008. The additional IHT liabilities arising on Mr Jones' death are:

*5 April 1999 – Gift to daughter £100,000*

The gift to Mr Jones' daughter was a PET made more than seven years before death, which, therefore, became exempt. The gift is not cumulated with later gifts.

*5 April 2002 – Transfer to discretionary trust £150,000*

The gift to the discretionary trust was an immediately chargeable transfer, but no IHT was payable as the gross value was within Mr Jones' available nil rate band (£242,000 for 2001/02). The gift was also made more than seven years before death, and no tax is payable on that event.

*31 December 2008 – Gift to son £263,000*

The gift to Mr Jones' son was a PET made within seven years of death, which, therefore, becomes chargeable. The gift to the discretionary trust is cumulated, even though made more than seven years before death.

|  | £ |
|---|---|
| 5 April 2002 | 150,000 |
| Nil rate band remaining: £325,000 – £150,000 = £175,000 | |
| IHT: | |
| £175,000 × nil | NIL |
| £88,000 × 40% | 35,200 |
| | £35,200 |

No taper relief (ie death within three years of gift).

**2.24** Taper relief is applied if appropriate (eg if a PET becomes chargeable, which was made more than three years before the date of death). See **Chapter 10**.

If more than one chargeable transfer is made on the same day and their order affects the transfer values, they are treated as made in the order which results in the lowest value chargeable. Therefore, if two chargeable gifts are made on the same day, with tax being paid by the donor on one gift (ie such that 'grossing-up' applies) and by the donee on the other gift, the gift by the donor is treated as having been made first in order to ensure grossing-up at a lower rate. This rule applies to lifetime gifts, but not to transfers on death (*s 266(3)*).

## REPORTING CHARGEABLE LIFETIME TRANSFERS

**2.25** Chargeable lifetime transfers are reportable on an Account for Inheritance Tax (form IHT100), which must be submitted within 12 months from the end of the month of transfer (or three months after the person became liable, if later) (*s 216(6)(c)*; see **Chapter 6**). However, there are exceptions from the requirement for an IHT100 account, normally in the following circumstances:

- gifts or chargeable transfers made by an individual which are wholly exempt (eg gifts to a UK-domiciled spouse within *s 18*);
- gifts or chargeable transfers of value (ie actual, not deemed) made by an individual as follows:
    - for transfers of cash or quoted shares or securities – if the value transferred, together with the value of any chargeable transfers made by the transferor in the preceding seven years, does not exceed the IHT threshold (note that if any other assets are included in the transfer, it cannot be excepted under this test); or
    - for transfers of other assets – if the value transferred, together with the value of any chargeable transfers made by the transferor in the preceding seven years, does not exceed 80% of the IHT threshold, and the value transferred by the transfer of value giving rise to the chargeable transfer (excluding business or agricultural property relief) does not exceed that IHT threshold less the value of chargeable transfers in the previous seven years (the *Inheritance Tax (Delivery of Accounts) (Excepted Transfers and Excepted Terminations) Regulations, SI 2008/605, reg 4*).

    For chargeable lifetime transfers before 6 April 2007, the exception limits are as follows:
    - total chargeable transfers in any one tax year not exceeding £10,000; and
    - the cumulative total in the ten years preceding the transfer not exceeding £40,000 (the *Inheritance Tax (Delivery of Accounts) (Excepted Transfers and Excepted Terminations) Regulations, SI 2002/1731*);
- 'excepted terminations' of interests in possession in the settled property of a specified trust. A 'specified trust' for these purposes is one in which

## 2.25 Lifetime transfers

the person's beneficial entitlement arose before 22 March 2006, or trusts for bereaved minors (within *s 71A*), or 'immediate post-death interests' (within *s 49A*), or trusts for the disabled (within *ss 89* or *89A*), or a disabled person's interest (within *s 89B*) or 'transitional serial interests' (within *ss 49B–49E*). A termination is excepted in any of the following cases:

– it is wholly covered by an exemption made available by the life tenant to the trustees (eg if no chargeable transfers have been made personally); or

– the interest related to cash or quoted shares or securities, and the value transferred by the termination, together with the value of any chargeable transfers made by the transferor in the preceding seven years, does not exceed the IHT threshold; or

– the value transferred by the termination, together with the value of any chargeable transfers made by the transferor in the preceding seven years, does not exceed 80% of the IHT threshold and the value transferred by the termination (excluding business or agricultural property relief) does not exceed that IHT threshold less the value of chargeable transfers in the previous seven years (*SI 2008/605, reg 5*).

Terminations of an interest in possession before 6 April 2007 are excepted broadly if the life tenant has given the trustees notice informing them of an exemption (ie the annual or marriage or civil partnership exemption), and that exemption covers the whole transfer (*s 57*).

For general guidance on the completion of form IHT100, see 'When to use form IHT 100' in HMRC Booklet IHT110 *How to fill in form IHT100*, which is available via HMRC's website (www.hmrc.gov.uk/cto/forms/iht110_1.pdf).

As indicated at **2.1** above, a PET is not immediately chargeable, and, therefore, does not need to be reported on form IHT100 when it is made.

*Chapter 3*

# IHT on death

## INTRODUCTION

**3.1** A person is treated as making a notional transfer of value of the whole estate immediately before his death, and IHT is charged accordingly; *IHTA 1984, s 4(1)* (unless otherwise stated, all statutory references in this chapter are to *IHTA 1984*). The tax charged on the estate depends on the aggregate chargeable lifetime transfers and potentially exempt transfers (PETs) in the seven years preceding death. The estate generally consists of all the property to which the individual was beneficially entitled, less excluded property and liabilities.

The IHT liability will also depend upon the identity of the legatees of the net estate, ie whether the recipient is a chargeable person (eg a son or daughter), or an exempt person (eg a UK-domiciled spouse, or a qualifying charity).

If an individual dies without leaving a will, or if the will is invalid (eg if it is not signed by the testator or testatrix, or witnessed by at least two witnesses who were present when the will was signed), the estate is subject to distribution in accordance with the laws of intestacy (see below).

**Table 3.1—The distribution of intestate estates**

The distribution of intestate estates is governed by the *Administration of Estates Act 1925, s 46*. The following applies in respect of deaths on or after 1 February 2009 (not applicable in Scotland).

**Spouse or civil partner and issue survive:**

*Spouse or civil partner receives*
All personal chattels; £250,000 absolutely (or the entire interest where this is less); life interest in one half of residue (if any).

*Issue receives*
One half of residue (if any) on statutory trusts plus the other half of residue on statutory trusts upon the death of the spouse.

## 3.1 IHT on death

**Spouse or civil partner survives without issue:**

| *Spouse or civil partner receives* | *Residuary estate to* |
|---|---|
| All personal chattels; £450,000 absolutely (or entire estate where this is less); one half of residue (if any) absolutely. | The deceased's parents. If no parent survives: on trust for the deceased's brothers and sisters of the whole blood and the issue of any such deceased brother or sister. |

The above fixed sums of £250,000 and £450,000 apply for deaths on or after 1 February 2009 (*The Family Provision (Intestate Succession) Order, SI 2009/135*). Previously, the fixed sums were £125,000 and £200,000 respectively.

**Spouse or civil partner survives but no issue, parents, brothers or sisters or their issue:**

Whole estate to surviving spouse or civil partner.

**No spouse or civil partner survives:**

Estate held for the following in order given with no class beneficiaries participating unless all those in a prior class have predeceased. Statutory trusts may apply except under (b) and (e):

(a) Issue of deceased.
(b) Parents.
(c) Brothers and sisters and the issue of deceased brother or sister.
(d) Half-brothers and half-sisters and issue of any such deceased.
(e) Grandparents.
(f) Uncles and aunts and issue of any deceased uncle or aunt.
(g) Half-brothers and half-sisters of deceased's parents and issue of any deceased half-uncle or half-aunt.
(h) The Crown, the Duchy of Lancaster or the Duke of Cornwall.

Note: The *Administration of Estates Act 1925* was extended (by the *Civil Partnership Act 2004, Sch 4, paras 7–12*) to include the remaining surviving civil partner, who effectively acquires the same rights as a spouse in cases of intestacy.

The devolution of estates on intestacy is now subject to review by the Law Commission. Ideas being considered include provision for 'partners' who currently receive nothing as of right, even though they may have been living together in an intimate relationship for many years.

## ESTATE ON DEATH

### General

**3.2** A person on death (after 17 March 1986) is treated as having made a transfer of value equal to the value of his estate immediately before death (*s 4(1)*). A person's estate consists of the following:

- *free estate* – the aggregate of all property to which the deceased was beneficially entitled, but without taking into account any excluded property; and
- *settled property* – certain settled property in which the deceased was beneficially entitled to an interest in possession (see below).

An interest in possession in settled property to which the deceased originally became beneficially entitled before 22 March 2006 forms part of the estate (*s 49(1)*). In addition, an interest in possession to which the deceased was beneficially entitled on or after 22 March 2006 is included in the death estate if it falls within one of the following categories (*s 49(1A)*):

- an 'immediate post-death interest' (ie within *s 49A*);
- a 'disabled person's interest' (as defined in *s 89B*); or
- a 'transitional serial interest' (as defined in *s 49B*).

In addition, if an interest in possession is purchased by a UK-domiciled person at arm's length on or after 9 December 2009, the interest forms part of that person's estate (*s 5(1B)*).

However, interests in property to which the rules on trusts for 'bereaved minors' (*s 71A*) apply do not form part of the deceased's estate. See **Chapter 7**.

**3.3** Gifts with reservation (GWR) form part of the death estate by being treated as property to which the deceased was beneficially entitled (*FA 1986, s 102(3)*).

The IHT charge on death is a 'deeming' provision, ie it creates a transfer of value. In addition to exemptions which are only intended to apply to lifetime transfers (eg the annual and small gifts exemptions), HMRC do not consider that relief applies under provisions by which certain dispositions are not treated as transfers of value (*ss 10–17*), eg dispositions not intended to confer

**3.4** *IHT on death*

a gratuitous benefit, or for the maintenance of family members (see **9.12**). This is on the footing that the rules apply to actual dispositions, and therefore cannot apply to a charge which is based on a deemed transfer (eg death), unless the legislation specifically applies the provisions to the deemed transfer concerned (IHTM04042).

However, other types of IHT relief are available unless specifically excluded by statute (*s 3(4)*), such as business and agricultural property relief if the relevant conditions are satisfied (see **Chapter 11**). Various exemptions and exclusions from IHT also apply on death (see **3.4**), and certain liabilities may be deducted in determining the net estate (see **3.9**).

## Exemptions and exclusions

**3.4** Exemptions from IHT were summarised at **1.20** and are covered in **Chapter 9**. They are generally available on death, unless expressly excluded. As mentioned at **3.3** above, certain exemptions relate to lifetime transfers only, and cannot therefore be claimed on death. These include the annual exemption (*s 19(5)*), together with the exemptions for small gifts (*s 20(3)*), normal expenditure out of income (*s 21(5)*) and gifts in consideration of marriage (*s 22(6)*).

An exemption may be subject to restriction if an exempt beneficiary (eg the surviving spouse or civil partner) settles any claim against the deceased's estate otherwise than out of the deceased's transfer on death, where the claim is not a deductible liability for IHT purposes (*s 29A*). Thus, for example, if the surviving spouse directly settles a claim against the estate by the deceased's mistress, it is treated as a chargeable legacy (and not an allowable estate liability). The spouse exemption is restricted to the net benefit. This restriction removes the advantage of the spouse settling the claim out of her exempt share. The rule applies to deaths occurring after 26 July 1989.

**3.5** Some exemptions (eg the spouse or civil partner exemption in *s 18*, or the charity exemption in *s 23*) are available as a result of death. In addition, certain categories of estate property can be left out of the IHT account on death:

- Cash options under approved pension schemes – where under a registered pension scheme, a 'qualifying non-UK pension scheme' (within *s 271A*) or a '*s 615(3)* scheme' (ie a superannuation fund within *ICTA 1988, s 615(3)*) (or prior to 6 April 2006, either a retirement annuity contract or a personal pension scheme) an annuity becomes payable on a person's death to a spouse, surviving civil partner or dependant of that person, and a capital sum might at the deceased's option have become payable instead to his personal representatives, the deceased is not to be treated as having been beneficially entitled to that sum, with the result that it escapes liability to IHT (*s 152*).

*IHT on death* **3.7**

- Overseas pensions – the value of certain pensions payable to the deceased by former colonial governments is not included in the death estate (*s 153*).

- No IHT is payable on the death of a person from a wound, accident or disease sustained or aggravated whilst on active service, if certified by the Defence Council or the Secretary of State (*s 154*).

- Emoluments and tangible moveable property of visiting armed forces members and certain allied headquarters staff are excluded property for IHT purposes (*s 155*).

- The balances of any qualifying non-sterling accounts are excluded if the deceased was not domiciled, resident or ordinarily resident in the UK immediately before his death (*s 157*). This exclusion relates to banks and the Post Office, and includes the Bank of England (IHTM04380).

Offshore (and certain UK) property is excluded property for IHT purposes if the beneficial owner was domiciled outside the UK (*s 6(1), (1A)*). A similar rule applies to settled property, if the settlor was non-UK domiciled when the settlement was made (*s 48(3), (3A)*). However, if the interest in possession was acquired by a UK-domiciled person (from 5 December 2005) for valuable consideration, that interest is not excluded property (*s 48(3B)*). For further information on excluded property and exempt transfers, see **1.18** and **Chapter 9**.

## Woodlands relief

**3.6** A specific relief is available for transfers of woodlands on death (*s 125*), to take account of the fact that trees may take several generations to grow. If the relief is available, an election may be made to exclude the value of UK trees or underwood (but not the land itself) from the value transferred by the chargeable transfer on the deceased's death. IHT is instead payable when the trees are disposed of (ie by sale or gift), other than to the disposer's spouse or civil partner. In that case, tax is charged on a subsequent death in the usual way, unless another election is made to defer the tax.

In effect, the relief is a deferral of the IHT otherwise due on death. For further commentary on woodlands relief, see **Chapter 10**. However, if the woodlands form part of a business, business property relief may be available if the conditions for that relief are satisfied, see **Chapter 11**.

## Survivorship and the 'commorientes' rule

**3.7** The rule as to commorientes (in the *Law of Property Act 1925, s 184*) provides as follows (note this rule does not extend to Scotland):

### 3.8 *IHT on death*

'In all cases where ... two or more persons have died in circumstances rendering it uncertain which of them survived the other or others, such deaths, shall ... for all purposes affecting the title to property, be presumed to have occurred in order of seniority, and accordingly the younger shall be deemed to have survived the elder.'

This rule could give rise to a double (or multiple) IHT charges on death (subject to 'quick succession relief' (*s 141*) if there was a chargeable transfer – see **Chapter 10**). However, for IHT purposes, where it cannot be known which of two or more persons who have died survived the other or others, they shall be presumed to have died at the same instant. Therefore, the estate of the younger is not swollen (*ss 4(2), 54(4)*). In some cases, the interaction of this rule and *LPA 1925, s 184* can result in the estate of an elder spouse or civil partner escaping IHT on both deaths (see IHTM12197, which also points out that the treatment of simultaneous deaths in Scotland and Northern Ireland is different).

**3.8**   Double (or multiple) IHT charges may also arise on successive deaths (ie deaths which are not (or are not treated as) simultaneous but follow within a short period of each other, where it is ascertainable which person survived the other even if only for a relatively short time).

However, if under the terms of the will (or otherwise), property is held for any person ('Beneficiary A') on condition that he survives another for a specified period of not more than six months, and another beneficiary ('Beneficiary B') becomes entitled to property by reason of the survivorship condition (ie the original beneficiary has not complied with that condition), the IHT payable is the same as if that other beneficiary had taken the property direct, without the intervention of the survivorship condition. Beneficiary B is therefore deemed to have become entitled from the beginning of the survivorship period (*s 92*).

## LIABILITIES

### General

**3.9**   A liability may be taken into account in valuing a person's estate (unless otherwise provided by tax law) if it is legally enforceable and is:

- imposed by law (eg income tax and capital gains tax up to the date of death, and IHT liabilities in respect of chargeable lifetime transfers discharged by the deceased's personal representatives); or
- incurred for a consideration in money or money's worth (*s 5(5)*).
- For example, if executors claim the deduction of a liability incurred shortly before death, HMRC may be interested to know the whereabouts

of the money obtained by the deceased as a result of entering into the liability. If the money cannot be traced and there is no evidence that it has been given away, a deduction may be denied.

A deduction is given in the deceased's estate in certain circumstances where income tax liabilities arise as a result of death (ie involving offshore funds and deeply discounted securities (*s 174(1)*)).

Mortgages or secured loans can be deducted from the property they are charged against. If the mortgage is for more than the value of the property, the excess can generally be deducted from the deceased's other assets (see 'How to value the debts and liabilities of someone who has died' at www.hmrc.gov.uk/inheritancetax/how-to-value-estate/debts.htm#2 under 'Types of debts and liabilities – working out the value'), but where a person with liabilities in excess of his assets is tenant for life of a fund his personal indebtedness cannot offset the value of the trust fund (*St Barbe Green v Inland Revenue Commissioners* [2005] EWHC 14 (Ch)).

**3.10** Gaming debts are not an allowable deduction, because the debt cannot be enforced. However, betting through a 'totaliser' run by the Racecourse and Betting Control Board is not considered to be gaming or wagering. A debt due to an agent who has laid such a debt on the deceased's behalf can therefore be deducted (IHTM28130).

An anti-avoidance rule in *FA 1986, s 103* ('Treatment of certain debts and encumbrances') restricts debts incurred or created by the deceased on or after 18 March 1986 when determining the value of an estate immediately before death, to the extent that:

- the money borrowed originally derived from the deceased; or
- the money was borrowed from a person who had previously received property derived from the deceased (eg an interest in a property is gifted from Miss X to Mr Y, who takes out a loan secured on the property and lends the proceeds back to Miss X, who dies more than seven years after the original gift of the property interest).

However, this restriction does not apply if it can be demonstrated that:

- the original disposition by the deceased was not a transfer of value; and
- the property was not subject to associated operations (*s 103(4)*).

This anti-avoidance rule can affect estate planning (eg 'debt' or 'charge' arrangements), as illustrated in *Phizackerley v HMRC* [2007] STC SCD 328.

A disallowance of the debt may result in a double IHT charge.

## 3.11 IHT on death

**Example 3.1—Effect of *FA 1986, s 103***

On 1 January 2008, Adam gifts cash of £50,000 to Bob. On 6 April 2008, Bob lends £50,000 to Adam. On 1 December 2010, Adam dies.

The cash gift from Adam to Bob is a PET which becomes chargeable as the result of Adam's death. In addition, Adam's estate includes the £50,000 gifted back to him, but a deduction for the debt of £50,000 is denied under *FA 1986, s 103*, leading to a potential double IHT charge.

**3.11** However, relief is given in such circumstances (*FA 1986, s 104(1) (c)*; *Inheritance Tax (Double Charges Relief) Regulations (SI 1987/1130), reg 6*). The effect is broadly that whichever of the two transfers results in the higher overall IHT liability remains chargeable and the value transferred by the other is reduced (ie either the gift is taxed and the debt allowed, or the debt is disallowed and the gift reduced).

No debts or premiums in respect of life assurance policies are allowable unless the policy proceeds form part of the estate (*FA 1986, s 103(7)*).

## Guarantee debts

**3.12** A guarantee debt (ie a promise to pay the debts of a borrower if he is unable to repay those debts) to which the deceased agreed to act as guarantor may be deductible from the death estate if the loan remained outstanding at the time of death. However, before allowing a deduction, HMRC may seek to establish whether consideration was given for the debt (*s 5(5)*). This will generally be the case with commercial loan arrangements, but possibly not in family situations (eg where a parent gratuitously agrees to guarantee a child's bank borrowings). In addition, HMRC may consider the financial resources of the borrower at the date of death, as a liability is only taken into account to the extent that reimbursement cannot reasonably be expected (*s 162(1)*).

HMRC may regard the giving of the guarantee as a lifetime transfer by the deceased. For example, if the borrower is a 'man of straw' with no financial resources, the outstanding liability will be deductible in full, but the guarantee may be a lifetime transfer up to the full amount of the liability.

Even if there is no outstanding liability at the date of the guarantor's death, HMRC consider that lifetime transfers may nevertheless arise if the guarantee was made within seven years of death and the guarantee was called in and paid within that time, depending on the borrower's financial position when the guarantee was given (IHTM28356–7).

## RULES FOR AMOUNT OR VALUE OF LIABILITY

### General

**3.13** The normal rules for determining the amount or value of liabilities are summarised below:

- A liability for which there is a right to reimbursement is taken into account only to the extent that reimbursement cannot reasonably be obtained (*s 162(1)*).

- If a liability will be discharged after the time at which it is to be taken into account, it must be valued when it is taken into account (ie at its discounted value (*s 162(2)*)) – but see below.

- In valuing the transferor's estate immediately after the transfer, his IHT liability is computed as follows (*s 162(3)*):
   (i) without making any allowance for the fact that the tax will not be due immediately; and
   (ii) as if any tax recovered otherwise than from the transferor were paid in discharge of a liability for which the transferor had a right to reimbursement.

- A liability which is an encumbrance on estate property must (as far as possible) be taken to reduce the value of that property (*s 162(4)*).

- A liability due to a person not resident in the UK which neither falls to be discharged in the UK nor is an encumbrance on UK property must, as far as possible, be taken to reduce the value of property outside the UK (*s 162(5)*).

For the purposes of business and agricultural property relief (see **Chapter 11**), securing a debt on qualifying property usually has the effect of reducing the amount on which relief would otherwise be available. Debt should therefore be secured on non-qualifying property, if possible.

### Funeral expenses

**3.14** In determining the value of a person's estate immediately before his death, deductions can be made as below:

- reasonable funeral expenses (*s 172*), including the cost of a tombstone or gravestone (SP 7/87) and flowers (IHTM10372);

- reasonable amount for mourning for the family and servants (ESC F1). However, in its Technical Note 'Withdrawal of extra statutory

### 3.15 *IHT on death*

concessions' dated 9 December 2009, HMRC stated that this concession would be withdrawn from 9 December 2010, but added: 'We believe that it may not in fact be a concession at all, rather a statement of what HMRC considers reasonable.' This would seem to imply that *s 172* already provides scope for a possible deduction, without the need for the concession.

What is 'reasonable' broadly depends on the living standards of the deceased during his lifetime.

## Other expenses

**3.15** Further principles for determining the deductibility of expenses in certain circumstances are summarised below:

- Costs of administering the UK estate (eg probate fees, estate agent or valuation fees) cannot be deducted for IHT purposes, as they arise after death.
- However, a deduction is allowed for the additional expenses incurred by the deceased's personal representatives in administering or realising property situated abroad. The allowance is deducted from the value of the property, up to a maximum of 5% of the property value (*s 173*).
- A deduction is not normally allowable for professional fees in respect of work carried out after the date of death. However, there is an exception for post-death work undertaken in connection with tax repayments included as an asset of the estate. In that case, a deduction may be claimed for fees not exceeding 10% of the repayment (IHTM28040).
- Provisions apply to charge IHT in the case of dispositions which are transfers of value made for partial consideration in money or money's worth and the transferor makes a payment more than one year after the disposition. The effect is that any chargeable part of each payment is treated as a separate transfer of value at the time it is made (*s 262*). If the transferor dies while there are still outstanding liabilities the personal representatives have to complete the remaining payments (*s 175*). However, a deduction is only given for the non-gratuitous part of the remaining payments (IHTM14874).

A liability that represents an encumbrance on property (eg a mortgage) should be deducted from the value of that property as far as possible (*s 162(4)*). A potential planning point in this regard is, therefore, that debt should be secured against non-business or agricultural property (ie where possible and practical), in preference to property qualifying for, say, 100% business or agricultural property relief.

*IHT on death* **3.17**

## Schedule IHT419

**3.16** The IHT account of the estate on death (form IHT400) includes a supplementary form (Schedule IHT419 'Debts owed by the deceased') if the deceased's personal representatives are claiming a reduction in the estate for the following types of debt:

- money spent on the deceased's behalf (eg by a close friend or relative), which is to be repaid out of the estate;
- loans (including overdrafts) and liabilities (eg from close friends and relatives);
- liabilities related to an insurance policy and/or an investment bond (ie where its value is not fully reflected elsewhere in the form IHT400);
- guarantee debts; or
- if the deceased borrowed money and made a gift to the same person, such that a deduction for the debt may be restricted (*FA 1986, s 103*).

The purpose of the form is to provide HMRC with further information in support of the deductions claimed elsewhere on form IHT400, to establish whether a deduction is due. For example, if a loan was made to the deceased by a friend or family member, was it legally enforceable or made for consideration in money or money's worth? The answer to this question will help to determine the extent of any deduction for the liability.

## ASSET VALUATIONS: OUTLINE

**3.17** The asset valuation rule is broadly that the death estate is valued based on a deemed transfer of value immediately before the deceased's death. The value of assets comprised in a person's estate is generally their open market value immediately before death (*s 160*).

Changes in estate value caused by death are taken into account when valuing the estate (*s 171(1)*). The changes to be taken into account can include:

- an addition to the property in the estate (eg the proceeds from a life policy);
- an increase in the value of any estate property; and
- a decrease in any estate property, other than a decrease resulting from an alteration in the capital or share rights of a close company (*s 98(1)*).

However, *s 171* does not apply to the termination on the death of any interest or the passing of any interest by survivorship (*s 171(2)*). An open market valuation of assets applies instead.

**3.18** *IHT on death*

For the purposes of valuing a person's estate, certain items of property may be taken together, even if held under separate titles (and irrespective of whether all the various parts of the estate are chargeable to tax). This principle mainly applies to valuations of unquoted shares, interests in land, undivided property interests and 'sets' of assets such as antique chairs. For further guidance on the valuation of specific types of asset, see **Chapter 4**.

## RELATED PROPERTY: INTRODUCTION

**3.18** A particular rule deals with the valuation of property in an estate if other property exists which is related to it (*s 161*). It is intended to cover situations such as if a set of assets (eg antique chairs) is divided through an exempt transfer (eg a gift to the spouse), thereby reducing the value of the assets retained. The rule applies to both lifetime transfers and to deemed transfers on death.

'Related property' is broadly property included in the estate of a spouse or civil partner, or in certain cases property belonging to a charity or one of the political, national or public bodies to which exempt transfers may be made. For more detailed commentary on the related property rules, see **Chapter 4**.

Relief is potentially available broadly if related property is sold by a legatee or the deceased's personal representatives to an unconnected person within three years of death for less than the related property valuation on death. If the relief conditions are satisfied, a claim may be made by the deceased's personal representatives to recalculate the tax at death based on the value of the asset concerned, without reference to the related property (*s 176*). The relief only applies if the sale price (after adjusting for any change in circumstances) is less than the amount at which the property concerned was originally valued (*s 176(4)*). For more detailed commentary on the relief for sales of related property, see **Chapter 10**.

## CALCULATING IHT ON THE DEATH ESTATE

### General

**3.19** IHT on the death estate is calculated as follows:

### Lifetime transfers

**3.20** IHT on chargeable lifetime transfers is calculated at lifetime rates (see **Chapter 2**). If the transferor dies within seven years, the tax is recomputed at full death rates, subject to taper relief (see **Chapter 10**) where the death is

*IHT on death* **3.21**

more than three years after the gift. Taper relief cannot reduce the tax payable below that originally charged.

Tax at full death rates is calculated at the time of death on any PETs made within seven years prior to death, subject to the availability of taper relief. As PETs are assumed to be exempt transfers when made, no lifetime IHT would have been paid, and the PET did not enter into the transferor's cumulative total at that time. Upon the transferor's death within seven years of the PET, it becomes a chargeable transfer at the actual date of the gift.

When computing the tax on PETs which become chargeable, any chargeable transfers made within seven years of the PET must be cumulated, even if they were made more than seven years before death. If the PET was made before a chargeable lifetime transfer, the tax on that transfer may need recalculating, and the transferor's cumulative total will need to be revised.

## The death estate

**3.21** The deceased's estate is taken into account based on a notional transfer of value equal to its value immediately before death (*s 4(1)*).

IHT on death is charged according to the thresholds and 'death rate' as shown in the table below (*s 7, Sch 1*).

**Table 3.2—Transfers on death after 5 April 2010**

**Tax on transfers:**

| *Gross taxable transfers* £ | *Gross cumulative totals* £ | *Rate* |
|---|---|---|
| First 325,000 | 0–325,000 | NIL |
| Above 325,000 | | 40% for each £ over 325,000 |

**Grossing-up of specific transfers on death which do not bear their own tax**

| *Net transfers* £ | *Tax payable thereon* £ |
|---|---|
| First 325,000 | NIL |
| Above 325,000 | 2/3 for each £ over 325,000 |

The personal representatives are assessed to IHT on the deceased's free estate (*s 200(1)(a)*). If the deceased had an interest in possession in settled property which is deemed to form part of his estate on death (see **3.2**), the settlement

## 3.22 IHT on death

trustees are liable to IHT in respect of the trust property (*s 200(1)(b)*). Hence, the IHT calculated must be apportioned between the free estate and the settled property.

**Example 3.2—Free estate and settled property**

Mr Edwards died on 10 June 2010. His free estate consisted of net chargeable assets amounting to £273,000. In addition, he had a life interest in a trust originally created in 1997, which was worth £640,000. IHT on death is calculated as follows:

|  | £ |
|---|---|
| Free estate | 273,000 |
| Settled property | 640,000 |
| Chargeable to IHT | 913,000 |

IHT:
(£913,000 − £325,000) × 40% = £235,200

The IHT is apportioned and payable as follows:

Personal representatives:

$\dfrac{£273,000}{£913,000} \times £235,200$     70,328

Trustees:

$\dfrac{£640,000}{£913,000} \times £235,200$     164,872

£235,200

Alternatively, an average 'estate rate' of IHT can be calculated and applied to the free estate and settled property, ie £235,200/£913,000 × 100 = 25.76%.

The application of these rules was seen in *Smith and others v HMRC* [2009] SpC 742, where it was found that a settlement existed of money in an account. Whilst the executors were not liable to tax in respect of the fund itself, there was an adjustment to the overall liability that affected the estate in their hands. The case is considered at **7.5**.

## Transferable nil rate band

**3.22** The nil rate band of a spouse or civil partner may be wholly or partly unused on their death. Prior to the introduction of the facility to transfer unused nil rate bands, if all the deceased's assets were left to their UK-domiciled

*IHT on death* **3.23**

surviving spouse, the spouse IHT exemption may have resulted in the loss of the deceased spouse's nil rate band.

However, on the death of the surviving spouse (or civil partner) since 9 October 2007, a claim can be made for the unused proportion of the nil rate band from the earlier death to be added to the survivor's own nil rate band, so that a larger nil rate amount is available against their estate for IHT purposes. The nil rate band to be transferred is expressed as a percentage (not exceeding 100%, as the limit is one additional nil rate band, even if there was more than one former spouse) of the amount unused from the earlier death. The nil rate band that applies on the death of the surviving spouse is increased by that percentage (*s 8A*).

A claim to transfer unused nil rate band must be made by the survivor's personal representatives, within two years from the end of the month in which the survivor dies or (if later) within three months of the personal representatives first acting as such, although HMRC may allow a longer period at their discretion. In the absence of a claim by the personal representatives, a late claim may be made by any person liable to IHT on the survivor's death, subject to HMRC's agreement (*s 8B*).

There are potentially complicated rules for dealing with the transfer of the nil rate band and the calculation of IHT when certain IHT and capital transfer tax deferred charges (ie on heritage assts and woodlands) are triggered, where the deferred IHT is calculated by reference to the earlier deceased spouse (*s 8C*). There are also complex rules to determine the amount of nil rate band to be applied in calculating IHT where a dependant who inherits an alternatively secured pension fund dies or ceases to be a dependant (*ss 151A–151C*).

Further information on transferable nil rate bands is available via the HMRC website (www.hmrc.gov.uk/inheritancetax/intro/transfer-threshold.htm). The subject is also covered in **Chapter 14**.

## Quick succession relief

**3.23** Relief for successive charges (or 'Quick succession relief': see **Chapter 10**) applies if the value of the deceased's chargeable estate for IHT purposes was increased by a previous transfer (either during lifetime or on death) made within five years before his death (*s 141*).

Quick succession relief reduces the total IHT chargeable on death by a percentage of the tax attributable to the net increase in the deceased's estate resulting from the previous transfer. The relief percentage depends on the length of time between the two occasions. The apportionment of IHT payable between the free estate and settled property is of the tax as reduced by the relief. Note also the commentary on the relief at **1.23**.

**3.24** *IHT on death*

## Double tax relief

**3.24** Property situated abroad may be liable to IHT and also to a similar tax imposed by another country or state. Double tax relief is available for all or part of the overseas tax. Relief may be given under the terms of a double tax agreement with another territory (*s 158*). Otherwise, unilateral relief is given for the tax paid in the overseas territory against the IHT due on the same foreign property, up to the amount of overseas tax paid on those assets (*s 159*). See **Chapter 10**.

## CHARGEABLE AND EXEMPT ESTATE

### Introduction

**3.25** The deceased's estate may be wholly exempt, partly exempt or wholly chargeable to IHT, depending on whether the beneficiaries under a will or intestacy are wholly or partly exempt. If a transfer on death is only partially exempt (eg because the deceased leaves part of his estate to his spouse or to charity), it is necessary to have provisions (*ss 36–42*) to determine the extent and the impact of IHT liabilities on that part of the estate which is not exempt. The rules can apply to lifetime transfers (eg gifting interests in an asset to exempt and non-exempt beneficiaries), but are more common and of greater relevance in relation to transfers on death.

### Terminology

**3.26** The value of the estate is divided for IHT purposes into 'specific' and 'residuary' gifts. A 'gift' in this context is the benefit of any disposition or rule of law by which any property becomes the property of any person or applicable for any purpose.

- A *specific gift* is any gift other than a gift of residue or a share of residue (*s 42(1)*), such as the deceased's residence, company shares or personal effects. Certain liabilities are also treated as specific gifts for these purposes (*s 38(6)*).

- A *residuary gift* is the balance of the estate after all specific gifts have been made.

- A specific gift may '*bear its own tax*', ie IHT comes out of the gift itself so that the beneficiary gets the property less the tax on it, or the IHT attributable to the gift falls upon the beneficiary (*ss 42(2), 211(3)*). A specific gift bears its own tax if the deceased's will so states (*s 211(2)*). Otherwise, a specific gift of UK property is 'tax free' (see below), but a specific gift of non-UK property bears its own tax (*s 211(1)*). Other property bearing its own tax includes joint property passing by survivorship, nominated property, 'gift with reservation' property and any other property which does not vest in the deceased's personal representatives (IHTM26126).

- Alternatively, the gift may be *'tax free'* (ie the beneficiary gets the full value of the gift, without reduction for the IHT on the gift, and the IHT is paid out of residue).

The value of a specific gift will normally be a specified sum (eg £50,000 cash) or the market value of a particular asset. However, the partial exemption rules may produce a value of the gift when calculating the IHT due which is different from the specified sum or value of that asset.

If the total value of the specific gifts exceeds the total value of the estate, the specific gifts may need to be reduced so that their total value equals the value of the estate, by a process of 'abatement' (*s 37*). For example, if an individual's estate is worth £400,000 and in his will he gifts £200,000 to charity, £200,000 to his daughter (bearing its own tax) and £400,000 to his wife, abatement will apply. The legacies total £800,000, but the estate is only worth £400,000, so each legacy is reduced by one-half.

## Interaction with business and agricultural property relief

**3.27** If an estate includes property attracting business property relief (BPR) or agricultural property relief (APR) (see **Chapter 11**), special rules apply for the purposes of valuing specific and residuary gifts if part of the estate is exempt. If the business or agricultural property is given by a specific gift, its value is reduced by BPR or APR (*s 39A(2)*).

However, if any residuary gifts (after 17 March 1986) include business or agricultural assets, any specific gifts of non-business or non-agricultural assets (eg cash gifts to chargeable parties) will be entitled to a due proportion of business or agricultural property relief (*s 39A*). The value of such specific gifts is the 'appropriate proportion' of their value, which is calculated as follows (*s 39A(4)*):

| | | |
|---|---|---|
| Estate (after BPR/APR) | less | Specific gifts of business or agricultural property (net of BPR/APR) |
| Estate (before BPR/APR) | less | Specific gifts of business or agricultural property (before BPR/APR) |

Settled property is excluded from the *s 39A* calculation (see HMRC examples at IHTM26110 and IHTM26158).

The above rule presents a potential pitfall, as BPR or APR is effectively wasted if given against exempt legacies, possibly resulting in a higher overall IHT liability.

**3.28** *IHT on death*

**Example 3.3—*IHTA 1984, s 39A***

Richard died on 5 June 2010. His estate of £1,250,000 consists of shares in an unquoted trading company worth £700,000 and other assets worth £550,000.

His will leaves cash and some of the other (non-business) assets of £400,000 to his spouse, with the residue to his son and daughter.

The value of Richard's estate (net of BPR) is £550,000. The 'appropriate proportion' (see above) of the spouse's exempt legacy is:

$$£400,000 \times \frac{£550,000}{£1,250,000} = £176,000$$

The non-exempt residue (ie the chargeable free estate) is (£550,000 – £176,000) = £374,000

The loss of BPR (or APR) such as in the above circumstances can be avoided by ensuring that specific gifts of business and agricultural assets which attract 100% relief are made to chargeable parties (possibly in addition to the nil rate band if appropriate, although for surviving spouses (or civil partners) who have died since 9 October 2007, it may alternatively be possible to transfer unused nil rate band from the first spouse to die). If the deceased's will does not provide for such specific legacies, it may be possible to vary the dispositions in the will using a deed of variation within two years of the deceased's death, and to include a statement in the deed that it is to apply for IHT purposes (*s 142*).

## Partly exempt gifts

**3.28** The calculation of IHT where gifts are partly chargeable and partly exempt is potentially complex. HMRC's Inheritance Tax Manual (at IHTM26071 onwards) sets out a five-step process for applying the partly exempt transfer rules in the correct order. Alternatively, a grossing calculator is available via the HMRC website (www.hmrc.gov.uk/cto/g_up.pdf), which will calculate the chargeable estate in most circumstances, if the estate is partially exempt from IHT and there are tax-free legacies.

The five-step process mentioned is summarised in the table below.

**Table 3.3—Partly exempt transfer rules: HMRC's five-step process**

**Step 1 – Value legacies**

Set out the starting values of specific gifts.

*IHT on death* **3.30**

### Step 2 – Abatement (if applicable)

If the total value of specific gifts exceeds the value of the free estate, consider abatement.

### Step 3 – BPR/APR (if applicable)

The value of specific gifts may need to be reduced if business and/or agricultural property relief has been allowed (*s 39A*).

### Step 4 – Grossing-up

The values of any chargeable specific gifts which do not bear their own tax are 'grossed-up' (see **3.29**).

### Step 5 – Calculate residue

The total value of specific gifts (exempt and chargeable) is compared with the value of the free estate (after any business and/or agricultural property relief). If the free estate exceeds the specific gifts, the balance is the value of the residue. However, if specific gifts exceed the free estate, there is no residue, and abatement may apply.

# Grossing-up

**3.29** The process of calculating the chargeable part of the deceased's estate when specific tax-free gifts are made to a chargeable beneficiary and the estate is partly exempt is termed 'grossing-up'. It is therefore important to recognise which gifts bear their own tax and which do not (see **3.26**).

For the purposes of grossing-up, if the deceased's estate on death includes property under different title (eg free estate and settled property), the property chargeable under each title is considered separately and in isolation (*s 40*).

## Simple grossing

**3.30** 'Simple' (or 'single') grossing applies only if the specific chargeable gifts are all tax free and the residue is wholly exempt. The specific gift is a net transfer which must be grossed-up.

---

**Example 3.4—Simple grossing (no lifetime gifts)**

Daphne died on 6 May 2010. Her free estate is valued at £950,000. In her will, Daphne leaves £450,000 free of tax to her son, and the residue to her husband.

### 3.31 *IHT on death*

She made no lifetime transfers in the seven years preceding her death. The grossing calculation is as follows:

|  | £ |
|---|---|
| Chargeable tax-free gift | 450,000 |
| IHT on gift: | 83,333 |
| Value of estate (after IHT): £950,000 − £83,333 | 866,667 |
| The net estate is divided: | |
| Son | 450,000 |
| Husband (£500,000 − £83,333) | 416,667 |
|  | 866,667 |

**3.31** The above result can be checked by calculating IHT on the grossed-up tax-free gift, ie (£450,000 + £83,333) = £533,333 − £325,000 = £208,333 × 40% = £83,333.

If lifetime gifts have been made in the previous seven years but their total is less than the IHT nil rate band, those gifts are deducted and the remaining nil rate band is used in the grossing calculation.

### Example 3.5—Simple grossing (lifetime gifts below nil rate band)

The facts are as in **Example 3.4** above, except that Daphne made a PET of £150,000 on 24 December 2007. The grossing calculation becomes:

|  | £ |
|---|---|
| IHT on gift: £450,000 − (£325,000 − £150,000) × ⅔ | 183,333 |
| Value of estate (after IHT): £950,000 − £183,333 | 766,667 |
| The net estate is divided: | |
| Son | 450,000 |
| Husband (£500,000 − £183,333) | 316,667 |
|  | 766,667 |

*IHT on death* **3.33**

**3.32** If lifetime gifts made in the previous seven years exceed the nil rate band, the chargeable specific tax-free gifts are grossed-up by the fraction 5/3.

**Example 3.6—Simple grossing (lifetime gifts above nil rate band)**

The facts are as in **Example 3.4** above, except that Daphne made a PET of £400,000 on 24 December 2007. The grossing calculation becomes:

|  | £ |
|---|---:|
| £450,000 × 5/3 | 750,000 |
|  |  |
| IHT on gift: |  |
| £750,000 × 40% | 300,000 |
|  |  |
| Value of estate (after IHT): |  |
| £950,000 − £300,000 | 650,000 |
|  |  |
| The net estate is divided: |  |
| Son | 450,000 |
| Husband (£500,000 − £300,000) | 200,000 |
|  | 650,000 |

## Double grossing

**3.33** What if the residue is partly exempt and partly chargeable, or there are tax-bearing legacies? The tax-free legacies must be grossed-up using a procedure (in *s 38*) commonly referred to as 'double grossing-up'. This procedure is described in HMRC's Inheritance Tax Manual as 'The four stages' (see IHTM26152 onwards), upon which the following summary is based.

**Table 3.4—'Double grossing' stages – Summary**

**Stage 1 – Grossing-up**

Gross-up chargeable specific tax-free legacies, as if they were the only chargeable free estate.

**Stage 2 – Calculate IHT rate**

Using the gross value from Stage 1, calculate the chargeable free estate (ie including any specific chargeable gifts bearing their own tax). Add the value of any exempt specific gifts.

### 3.34  IHT on death

The initial value of the residue is the difference between the resulting total and the overall value of the estate for IHT purposes.

The value of the chargeable part of the residue is then determined (ie the total residue less the exempt residue).

The chargeable free estate for these purposes is the total of the chargeable specific gifts and chargeable residue. Calculate the tax on the chargeable free estate, to arrive at the estate rate.

**Stage 3 – Re-gross at estate rate**

Gross-up the chargeable specific tax-free gifts by the estate rate found in Stage 2.

**Stage 4 – Calculate IHT on chargeable estate**

Calculate the chargeable estate (ie the total of all chargeable specific tax-free gifts (Stage 3) and the total value of any chargeable specific gifts bearing their own tax).

Find the total value of all specific gifts (ie including any exempt specific gifts).

Find the value of the residue (ie the value of the estate for IHT purposes, less total specific gifts).

The chargeable residue is the total residue, less the exempt residue.

Calculate the IHT on the chargeable estate (ie the total of the chargeable specific gifts and the chargeable part of residue).

**3.34** The following is a relatively straightforward example of the double grossing procedure for a free estate (ie no settled property, or joint property passing by survivorship) in which there is no business or agricultural property.

**Example 3.7—Double grossing**

Joe died on 30 April 2010, leaving a free estate of £1,500,000, comprising cash and investments. He made no lifetime gifts and had no other chargeable property such as trust interests.

In his will, Joe left £500,000 to his son tax free, and the residue equally between his wife (exempt) and daughter (chargeable). The IHT payable on Joe's death and the distribution of his estate is set out below.

*IHT on death* **3.34**

**Stage 1 – Grossing-up**

Gross-up the chargeable specific tax-free legacy (using the available nil rate band):

£325,000 × Nil

£175,000 × ⅔ = £116,666

The gross value is £500,000 + £116,666 = £616,666

**Stage 2 – Calculate IHT rate**

Calculate the chargeable free estate, the IHT thereon and the estate rate:

|  | £ |
|---|---|
| Total free estate | 1,500,000 |
| Less: gross specific legacy | (616,666) |
| Value of residue | 883,334 |
| Less: exempt residue (1/2) | (441,667) |
| Chargeable residue | 441,667 |
| Chargeable free estate (£616,666 + £441,667) | 1,058,333 |

IHT thereon:

£325,000 × Nil

£733,333 × 40% = £293,333

The estate rate is:

$$\frac{£293,333}{£1,058,333} \times 100\% = 27.7165\%$$

**Stage 3 – Re-gross at estate rate**

Gross-up the chargeable specific tax-free gift by the estate rate found in Stage 2:

$$100 \times \frac{£500,000}{100 - 27.7165} = £691,721$$

**Stage 4 – Calculate IHT on chargeable estate**

Calculate the chargeable estate:

### 3.34 IHT on death

|  | £ |
|---|---:|
| Total free estate | 1,500,000 |
| Less: gross specific legacy | (691,721) |
| Value of residue | 808,279 |
| Less: exempt residue (1/2) | (404,140) |
| Chargeable residue | 404,139 |
| | |
| Chargeable free estate (£691,721 + £404,139) | 1,095,860 |

Calculate IHT on the chargeable estate:

£325,000 × Nil

£770,860 × 40% = £308,344

**Summary**

Estate rate: $\dfrac{£308,344}{£1,095,860} \times 100\% = 28.1372\%$

Tax on gross legacy (£691,721 × 28.1372%) = £194,631

Tax on chargeable residue

(£404,139 × 28.1372%) = £113,713

Residue:

|  | £ |
|---|---:|
| Total free estate | 1,500,000 |
| Less: gross legacy (£500,000 + £194,631) | (694,631) |
| Value of residue | 805,369 |
| Less: exempt residue (1/2) | (402,685) |
| Chargeable residue | 402,684 |

Division of free estate:

|  | £ |
|---|---:|
| Legacy to son | 500,000 |
| Residue to wife | 402,685 |
| Residue to daughter (£402,684 − £113,713) | 288,971 |
| IHT | 308,344 |
| Total estate | £1,500,000 |

*IHT on death* **3.37**

A more complicated example of the 'double grossing' procedures (ie featuring the interaction with BPR (see **3.27**)) and settled property is featured in the Inheritance Tax Manual at IHTM26158.

## Allocating the burden of tax

**3.35** Having calculated the IHT in double grossing situations involving chargeable and exempt proportions, there are provisions to determine how the tax should be borne by the beneficiaries (*s 41*). The rules expressly override the terms of the will or other disposition. They provide that no tax falls on any exempt specific gifts (or any exempt part of a specific gift), and that no tax attributable to the value of residue should fall on an exempt share of that residue.

**3.36** The burden of tax can broadly be summarised as follows:

- Chargeable specific gifts bearing own tax – the tax is deducted from the gift (*s 42(2)*).

- Exempt specific gifts – the gift is made without deduction of tax (*s 41(a)*).

- Chargeable specific tax-free gifts – the gift is made without deduction of tax (HMRC's view is that the tax is paid out of residue, even if it is wholly or partly exempt; see IHTM26203).

- Residue is dealt with as follows:
    - the tax on tax-free specific gifts (see above) is deducted from the whole residue;
    - the balance is divided according to the terms of the will or other disposition;
    - the tax on any chargeable part of the residue is borne by that part (*s 41(b)*), despite any provisions to the contrary in the will.

### *Re Benham's Will Trust* and *Re Ratcliffe*

**3.37** The interpretation of wills in which the residuary estate is divided between gifts to exempt and chargeable beneficiaries was considered in *Re Benham's Will Trust* [1995] STC 210 and *Re Ratcliffe, Holmes v McMullan* [1999] STC 262.

The question of meaning concerns the proper construction of the following common type of clause in wills:

'I give devise and bequeath all my real and personal estate whatsoever and wheresoever not hereby otherwise disposed of unto my Trustees upon trust to sell and convert the same into money with power at their absolute discretion

## 3.38 IHT on death

to postpone any such sale and conversion for so long as they shall think fit without being answerable for any loss and after payment thereout of my debts and funeral and testamentary expenses to stand possessed of the residue as to one half part thereof for my children in equal shares absolutely and as to the remainder of my estate upon trust for the following charities …'

Should such a clause be interpreted as meaning that the children should receive their residuary share of the estate subject to IHT, thereby receiving less than the charities? Prior to *Re Benham* this was widely assumed to be the proper construction. The alternative construction (ie that the IHT should be paid and then the residue split) was disregarded, as it is prohibited (by *s 41(b)*) and therefore could not be effected. *Re Benham* held that there was a third construction which was not so prohibited (ie that the non-exempt beneficiary's share should be grossed-up so that after his share bore the IHT, he would receive an equal sum to the exempt beneficiary), albeit that this would result in more IHT being payable.

**3.38**   Subsequently, in *Re Ratcliffe* [1999] STC 262, it was held that on a proper construction of the common will clause, the non-exempt beneficiaries receive their share subject to IHT and without grossing-up. Thus, in the case of wills drafted in accordance with *Re Ratcliffe*, the proper IHT treatment would be to calculate the residuary estate, deduct the exempt beneficiary's share, and calculate IHT on the balance.

---

### Example 3.8—'*Ratcliffe*' will clause

Alice died on 30 June 2010, leaving an estate worth £800,000. She had made no lifetime transfers. In her will (which is drafted in accordance with *Re Ratcliffe*), Alice leaves her estate equally to her husband Albert and her daughter Beatrice.

IHT on Alice's estate is calculated as follows:

|  | £ |
|---|---:|
| Residuary free estate | 800,000 |
| Less: exempt residue (1/2) | (400,000) |
| Chargeable residue | 400,000 |
| IHT on chargeable estate: |  |
| £325,000 × Nil |  |
| £75,000 × 40% | 30,000 |
|  |  |
| Division of estate: |  |
| Albert | £400,000 |
| Beatrice (£400,000 − £30,000) | £370,000 |

The Inheritance Tax Manual (at IHTM26131) states that grossing-up in accordance with *Re Benham* is 'very rare', but acknowledges (at IHTM26172) that 'It is perfectly possible, though to date unusual, for you to come across wills deliberately drafted to achieve a *Re Benham* result'.

Clearly, it would be better to avoid such doubt by reviewing and clarifying wills, or possibly by rectifying the will following the testator's death by way of a variation (*s 142*).

*Chapter 4*

# Valuation of assets

## GENERAL

**4.1**  IHT is charged on the value transferred by a chargeable transfer; *s 1*. (Unless otherwise stated, all statutory references are to *IHTA 1984*.) As a general rule, the value of property for IHT purposes is the 'open market value', ie the price which the property might reasonably be expected to fetch if sold in the open market at that time. The price is not reduced on the basis that selling the property on the hypothetical open market at the same time would flood the market (*s 160*), and assumes a willing seller and a willing buyer, and sometimes a special buyer. A 'special buyer' is a person prepared to pay more for an asset than anyone else (eg a 49% shareholder in a company wishing to acquire a further 2% of the company's shares to assume a controlling interest would probably be willing to pay more for those shares than another person acquiring the 2% holding in isolation).

A restriction or fetter on the freedom to dispose of property (eg a provision in a partnership agreement stating that a deceased's partnership interest passes on death to the retiring partners without cost) can reduce the value of a person's estate. However, the property is valued ignoring restrictions unless certain conditions are satisfied, eg the contract was made after 26 March 1974 and consideration was given in money or money's worth (*s 163*). Thus, a stipulation in a testator's will that the grounds of his house are 'never to be sold for building land but always kept with the house' cannot restrict the value of that land if, at the date of death, it has 'hope value'. This is because the testator has received nothing as consideration for the restriction. It would be different if, for example, the testator had given the National Trust covenants over the land for the benefit of some property belonging to the Trust.

Other valuation principles also need to be considered for IHT purposes, which are considered below.

## The 'loss to estate' principle

**4.2**  The value transferred by a transfer of value is the amount by which a person's estate is reduced as a result (*s 3(1)*). This value will not necessarily be the actual value of an asset.

## Example 4.1—Loss in value of estate

ABC Ltd has 100,000 issued ordinary £1 shares. The shares (shown as a percentage of the company's overall issued share capital) are valued as follows:

51%–75% = £25 per share

26%–50% = £14 per share

25% or less = £8 per share

Mr Scott owns 60,000 shares (ie 60% of the shares). He makes a gift of 20,000 shares to his daughter. The transfer of value for IHT purposes is as follows:

|  | £ |
|---|---|
| Before (60,000 × £25) | 1,500,000 |
| After (40,000 × £14) | (560,000) |
| Value transferred | £940,000 |

Note that although the value of 20,000 shares in isolation is £160,000 (ie 20,000 × £8), for IHT purposes the reduction in Mr Scott's estate is higher as the result of losing his controlling interest in the company.

## The 'estate concept'

**4.3** A person's estate consists of all the property to which he is beneficially entitled (but not excluded property) (*s 5(1)*). The estate generally also includes property over which a person has a general power (*s 5(2)*), together with certain settled property in which the person is beneficially entitled to an interest in possession (see **3.2** and **Chapter 7**).

A beneficial interest in the net assets of an unadministered residuary estate also forms part of the estate (*s 91*), together with property subject to a 'gift with reservation' (*FA 1986, s 102(3)*).

## Example 4.2—Estate assets

On Mr Johnson's death, his free estate included 2,000 ordinary £1 shares in XYZ Ltd, representing 20% of the company's issued share capital. He was also a life tenant under a will trust created on his wife's death in April 2005. The trustees held a further 6,000 ordinary shares in the company.

In valuing Mr Johnson's estate for IHT purposes, it is necessary to value 8,000 shares in XYZ Ltd, out of the company's issued share capital of 10,000 ordinary shares.

**4.4** *Valuation of assets*

There is case law authority for the treatment of valuing property together (*Gray (surviving executor of Lady Fox) v IRC* [1994] STC 360), and for dividing estates into 'natural' or appropriate units (*Buccleuch v IRC* [1967] 1 AC 506) if doing so results in higher valuations.

When considering the value of land or buildings, the Valuation Office Agency will normally divide the estate so as to provide the highest value. HMRC's Shares & Assets Valuation may similarly decide how to divide certain other assets (eg wine collections) for estate valuation purposes (IHTM09715).

A person other than the sole legal owner of an asset such as land and buildings may claim to have a beneficial interest in that asset. Alternatively, property may be registered in joint names (eg unmarried co-habitants), but one of the parties may have a greater beneficial interest than the other, perhaps having contributed a larger proportion of the purchase price. In such cases, the asset may be treated as owned by the parties in accordance with their respective beneficial shares. This principle is derived from two non-tax cases, *Oxley v Hiscock* [2004] EWCA Civ 546, [2005] Fam 211 and *Stack v Dowden* [2007] 2 All ER 929. However, HMRC consider that the onus is upon the non-legal owner to demonstrate that they have any interest in the property, as if the claimant was presenting their case to a court of law (IHT & Trusts Newsletter– December 2007).

In *Wade v Baylis* [2010] EWCA Civ 257, a couple commenced living together as man and wife in 1982, but separated in 2005. Following the split, Mr Wade claimed a 50% beneficial interest in the property, even though he had been removed from the deeds in 1986 at his own request. He had apparently made no contribution to the capital cost of the property, and contributed little to the mortgage repayments, although he had worked for free in a business run by Ms Baylis. The Court of Appeal dismissed Mr Wade's appeal against an earlier decision that Ms Baylis was the sole beneficial owner of the property in question.

There are specific IHT valuation rules, such as for quoted shares and life assurance policies, and also in the case of property that is related to property in the estate of a spouse or civil partner or the property of a charity.

# RELATED PROPERTY

## Rule of valuation

**4.4** The value of 'related property' must be taken into account when valuing a person's estate if this results in a higher valuation (*s 161*). This rule applies to lifetime and death transfers, and prevents the division of an asset into less valuable parts by means of exempt transfers to reduce overall IHT liabilities.

Property is broadly 'related' for these purposes if it is:

- in the spouse's or civil partner's estate; or
- is (or was during the preceding five years) the property of a charity (or a qualifying political, national or public body, to which exempt transfers may be made) as the result of an exempt transfer (after 15 April 1976) by the individual, spouse or civil partner (*s 161(2)*).

The transferor's property and the related property are combined and valued as a single unit. The combined value of the estate property and related property is then apportioned to the estate property in the proportion that its value in isolation bears to the separate values when added together.

The related property rules are mostly used in practice to value transfers of unquoted shares and jointly owned property.

## How does the rule apply?

**4.5** In the case of jointly owned property, the value of the combined unit is apportioned between the property in the individual's estate and the related property according to their separate values (*s 161(3)*). This general rule also applies for valuing other assets (but see below for a special rule in respect of shareholdings).

---

**Example 4.3—Related property (land)**

Husband owns land worth £15,000 and his wife owns adjoining land worth £25,000.

The combined value is £80,000.

The related property value of the husband's land is:

$$\frac{15,000}{15,000 + 25,000} \times £80,000 = £30,000$$

---

**4.6** Should the value of jointly owned property be discounted to take into account the rights of the co-owner? The Inheritance Tax Manual (at IHTM04045) states the following:

'It is often said that in order to sell either half share, the co-operation of the other joint owner is required and so a discount should be allowed to compensate for the uncertainty involved. Whilst in reality this may be true, for IHT purposes the statute imposes the hypothesis that the deceased

**4.7** *Valuation of assets*

is beneficially entitled to the whole and it is the whole that is valued in accordance with Section 160 IHTA 1984. If tax is only chargeable on a fractional share (because, say, the other share is exempt) it is the arithmetic proportion that is taxed and not the value of the share involved.'

In the context of real, heritable or leasehold property, the Inheritance Tax Manual (at IHTM09739) also comments as follows:

'The related property rules apply because the interests of the spouses/civil partners are together worth more than the sum of their separate interests – the separate interests would normally be subject to a discount for joint ownership. The interests of the husband and wife, or civil partners, will normally be identical and will extend to the whole of the land and property so the value of the deceased/transferor's interest will be the appropriate proportion of the entirety value.'

However, in *Arkwright and another (Personal Representatives of Williams, deceased) v IRC* [2004] STC 1323, Mr and Mrs W owned a freehold property as tenants in common. On Mr W's death, HMRC determined that IHT was due on 50% of the property's agreed open market value. The personal representatives appealed, contending that Mr W's interest should be valued at less than 50% of the vacant possession value, because his widow had the right to occupy the property and not have it sold without her consent.

The Special Commissioner accepted this contention and allowed the appeal in principle, holding that the value of Mrs W's interest should be determined in accordance with *s 161(3)* (ie on the basis that both shares in the property were related, and that their values should therefore be aggregated). The Court of Appeal subsequently held that the Commissioner was entitled to conclude that the value of the deceased's interest in the property was not inevitably a mathematical one-half of the vacant possession value, rejecting HMRC's argument that *s 161(4)* applied to treat the land as 'units' and that the valuation ratio was one-half. However, the court considered that the value of Mr W's interest was a question for the Lands Tribunal to determine. The appeal was subsequently settled by agreement.

However, HMRC subsequently stated (in *Revenue & Customs Brief 71/07*) that, following legal advice, they would apply *s 161(4)* when valuing shares of land as related property in cases received after publication of that Brief (27 November 2007) and would consider litigation in 'appropriate cases', but that any existing cases would be dealt with on the basis of the Special Commissioners' decision in the *Arkwright* case as it relates to the interpretation of *s 161(4)*.

**4.7** A 'special' rule applies for the purposes of valuing shares and other securities of the same class (*s 161(4), (5)*). In that case, the apportionment of the combined value is based on the number of shares, not the value of the different holdings.

### Example 4.4—Related property (shares)

On the husband's death on 31 October 2010, the share capital of a private company was held as follows:

Issued share capital – 10,000 shares

| | | |
|---|---|---|
| Husband | 4,000 | 40% |
| Wife | 4,000 | 40% |
| Others (employees) | 2,000 | 20% |
| | 10,000 | 100% |

The value of an 80% holding is £80,000, while the value of a 40% holding is £24,000. In his will, the husband left his 4,000 shares to his daughter.

The related property rules apply to aggregate the shares of:

| | |
|---|---|
| Husband | 4,000 |
| Wife | 4,000 |
| Related property | 8,000 shares |

Chargeable transfer on legacy to daughter:

| | |
|---|---|
| IHT value of 8,000 shares (80%) | £80,000 |
| IHT value attributed to legacy of husband's shares | $\dfrac{4,000}{8,000} \times £80,000 = £40,000$ |

This special rule applies not only to shares of the same class, but also to stock, debentures and other 'fungible' property, ie that which is capable of being divided into units of an identical nature, such as unit trusts or bottles of wine of the same vintage. In the case of lifetime transfers, both the 'loss to estate' principle and the 'related property' rule apply in arriving at the value transferred (ie the related property rules are used to calculate the 'before' and 'after' estate values).

## Related property relief

**4.8** If related property is sold to an unconnected person within three years of death for less than the related property valuation, a claim may generally be made to recalculate the tax at death without reference to the related property (*s 176*). The claim may be made by the deceased's personal representatives, or by persons in whom the property vested immediately after the death. Relief is also available if the property was valued with other property in the estate (eg

**4.9** *Valuation of assets*

if the deceased held property absolutely, together with property subject to an interest in possession (ie within *s 49(1)*), or a 'gift with reservation' of which the deceased was the donor). See **Chapter 10**.

Note that related property relief does not substitute the value of the property at the date of sale. The valuation date is immediately before the death.

## PARTICULAR ASSETS

**4.9** Certain assets have their own valuation rules. Some of the more common assets and situations are listed below. A list of specific types of property is contained in the Inheritance Tax Manual (at IHTM09702), together with references to detailed instructions elsewhere in the manual on how to value them.

## Life policies

### Lifetime transfers

**4.10** The lifetime gift of a life policy or annuity (ie by assignment or declaration of trust) from one person to another constitutes a transfer of value (*s 167(1)*). The value transferred is broadly the greater of the premiums paid (less any proceeds received under the policy or annuity contract prior to the transfer, eg on a partial surrender) and the open market value of the policy (ie normally its surrender value).

The above valuation rule does not apply to transfers of value on death (*s 167(2)(a)*) (see below). In addition, term assurance policies are excluded if the sum assured becomes payable only if the life assured dies before the expiry of a specified term (or before the expiry of a specified term *and* during the life of a specified person). However, if the specified term ends, or can be extended to end, more than three years after the policy is made and if neither the life assured nor the specified person dies within the specified term, then the premiums must be payable during at least two-thirds of that term and at yearly or shorter intervals, and the premiums payable in any one period of 12 months must not be more than twice the premiums payable in any other 12-month period (*s 167(3)*) for this exclusion to apply.

A separate rule applies for the purpose of valuing unit-linked policies. This broadly provides for a reduction in the value of the policy if the value of the units has fallen since the date of their allocation (*s 167(4)*; see IHTM20244).

A policy taken out for another person is also a transfer of value, normally based on the amount of the first premium, and on any subsequent premiums. If premiums are paid on a policy owned by somebody else, the amount of each premium is a separate transfer of value, subject to any exemptions due (eg the annual exemption (*s 19*) or the normal expenditure out of income exemption (*s 21*)).

## Transfers on death

**4.11** The proceeds of a policy taken out on the person's own life or for his own benefit, which are payable on death to the deceased's personal representatives are taken into account as part of the estate, based on the policy's open market value (*s 160*). The open market value will be the amount for which the policy could be sold, and might exceed its surrender value (IHTM20231).

If the proceeds from the life policy are payable to someone other than the life assured, and if that beneficial owner dies before the life assured, there will be a transfer on their death based on the value of the life policy.

## 'Back-to-back' arrangements

**4.12** A special anti-avoidance rule applies to cover circumstances in which an individual (who may be in poor health) purchases one or more annuities to enable him to take out one or more life policies written in trust for someone other than the life assured, and where the annuity payments feed the premiums for the life policy. If the life policy was taken out (or varied) since 26 March 1974 and the two events are associated operations, the IHT exemption for normal expenditure out of income does not apply (*ss 263, 21(2)*).

In addition, unless it can be shown that the purchase of the annuity and the taking out of the life insurance policy are not 'associated operations' (as defined in *s 268*), the purchaser of the annuity is treated as having made a transfer of value when the policy became vested in the other person. The amount of the transfer of value is the lower of the following:

- the cost of the annuity and any premiums (or other consideration) paid on or before the transfer; and

- the value of the greatest benefit capable of being conferred by the policy, calculated as if that time was the transfer date (*s 263(2)*).

However, HMRC Inheritance Tax should be prepared to accept that the two contracts are not 'associated operations' if the life policy is shown to have been underwritten on the basis of medical evidence without reference to the annuity (Statement of Practice E4; see IHTM20375). The easiest way to demonstrate that the two contracts were not 'associated' would be to take up the annuity and the policy with separate, unconnected life offices. If the same life office is used, the policy should be issued and the premiums fixed on the basis of full medical evidence.

**4.13** *Valuation of assets*

In the case of joint life assurance policies (eg between husband and wife) full medical evidence is required in respect of both lives assured. In *Smith v Revenue and Customs Commissioners* [2008] STC 1649, it was held that Statement of Practice E4 did not apply to a joint life policy, where a medical report had not been obtained in respect of the wife's health. The Court upheld the earlier decision of the Special Commissioner that the purchase of the annuity and making of the life assurance policy were associated operations.

## Discounted gift schemes

**4.13** A discounted gift scheme broadly involves the gift of a bond, subject to retained rights such as withdrawals or successively maturing reversions. The retained rights are such that the 'gift with reservation' anti-avoidance rules (*FA 1986, s 102*) do not apply. The gift of the bond is a transfer of value, based on the difference between the amount invested in the bond and the open market value of the retained rights (*s 160*).

In May 2007, HMRC issued a Technical Note concerning the valuation and other issues relating to discounted gift schemes, which stated HMRC's view, *inter alia*, that if the settlor was uninsurable for any reason at the date of gift the open market value of the retained rights would be nominal, and the gift would be close to the whole amount invested. HMRC also stated that settlors older than 90 years of age would be considered uninsurable (www.hmrc.gov.uk/cto/dgs-tech-note.pdf).

However, in *Bower v Revenue and Customs Commissioners*, a 90-year old lady in relatively poor health took out a life annuity policy. She paid a premium of £73,000, and the policy was issued to a settlement she created, subject to the reserved right to a 5% life annuity. Mrs Bower died five months later. HMRC valued the reserved right at only £250, whereas the insurance company had valued the rights at £7,800. Her executors appealed. The Special Commissioner ([2008] SpC 665) considered that the open market value of the reserved rights to the annuity was £4,200. HMRC appealed.

In *Business Brief 23/08*, HMRC stated an intention to appeal to the High Court against the decision in the above case, and indicated that in the meantime new cases would continue to be dealt with in accordance with the May 2007 Technical Note mentioned above. Subsequently, the Court allowed HMRC's appeal ([2009] STC 510), on the grounds that the Commissioner was erroneous in law in concluding that he was required or entitled to assume hypothetical speculators or to indicate the price that the hypothetical buyer was assumed to have paid.

HMRC subsequently issued Revenue & Customs Brief 21/09 (dated 2 April 2009), confirming that cases would be dealt with in accordance with its technical note issued in 2007. The Brief also stated that '... there is nothing in the Inheritance Tax legislation which allows any withdrawals actually taken between the gift date and the date of death of the settlor to be offset against the sum invested'.

## Quoted shares and securities

**4.14** Quoted investments must be valued based on the general rule regarding open market value in *s 160*. In practice, the lower of two valuations is applied using the following methods, based on capital gains tax valuation rules (*TCGA 1992, s 272(3)*), upon which their value for IHT purposes is ascertained:

- The 'quarter-up' method, ie the lower closing Stock Exchange price plus one-quarter of the difference between the lower and higher closing prices (this can normally be obtained, for example, from a *Financial Times* or similar periodical for the day following the valuation date).

**Example 4.5—'Quarter-up' method**

James owned 5,000 shares in Widgets plc at the date of his death. Their price range on that date was 110–122 pence. The valuation would be:

$$110 + \frac{1}{4}(122 - 110) = \underline{113 \text{ pence}}$$

The value of 5,000 shares would therefore be 5,000 × 113p = £5,650.

- Mid-price between the highest and lowest recorded bargains for the day of valuation. This is sometimes referred to as the 'average bargain' rule.

If the transfer takes place on a day that the Stock Exchange is closed, the market value can be ascertained by reference to the previous day or the following day, and the lower valuation is taken.

If shares are transferred 'ex-dividend' (ie broadly dividends declared but not yet paid at the date of valuation), the right to the dividend represents an asset of the estate, which should therefore be taken into account unless the right to receive it is transferred.

These valuation rules can be applied both to lifetime transfers and for the purposes of valuing the death estate.

A special rule currently applies to holdings in Bradford & Bingley, where a right to compensation may exist but cannot easily be valued. HMRC indicated

**4.15** *Valuation of assets*

on their website on 24 September 2009 (www.hmrc.gov.uk/inheritancetax/solicitors-advisers/bb-shares.htm) that for the purposes of completing IHT accounts the right to receive that compensation may be disregarded where, as is common, the actual shareholding is 1,000 shares or fewer. For larger shareholdings, contact the Shares and Assets Valuation helpline on 0115 974 2222.

## Unit trusts

**4.15** The market value of unit trusts is the buying price, being the lower of two published values (ie the buying and selling price) for the date in question, or on the last previous business day if the transfer does not take place on a business day (*TCGA 1992, s 272(5)*).

## Unquoted shares and securities

**4.16** Unlike for quoted shares and securities, there is normally no ascertainable or readily available value for unquoted shares and securities. The valuation of unquoted shares and securities is based on the price that they might reasonably be expected to fetch when sold in the open market if any prospective purchaser possessed all the information that might reasonably be required (*s 168*).

Valuations may take into account relevant factors such as the size of the company and shareholding, its activities and profit levels, asset backing and dividend history. The IHT value is generally subject to negotiation with HMRC Shares and Assets Valuation, a specialist office. If a valuation cannot be agreed, it will be subject to appeal before the Tax Tribunal.

**4.17** In practice, it is not always necessary for a full and formal valuation to be agreed with HMRC Shares and Assets Valuation (eg if the share value is likely to be well within the transferor's available nil rate band, or if the shares qualify for 100% business or agricultural property relief (see **Chapter 11**)). In the latter case, if HMRC agree that full relief is due, this is not an indication that the share value has been accepted (NB in those circumstances, the value has not been 'ascertained' for IHT purposes, and, therefore cannot be relied upon in any subsequent CGT computations (*TCGA 1992, s 274*)). It should be noted that such share transfers are subject to the same reporting requirements as other types of assets, and that a reasonable valuation should still be advanced.

## Joint property

**4.18** Jointly owned property can be held either as 'joint tenants' or as 'tenants in common'. Ownership will be as joint tenants (in equal or identical interests) unless the owners declare otherwise. The interest of a joint owner passes upon death by survivorship to the remaining owner. However, joint tenancies can be severed, with the owners holding the asset as tenants in common. An important consequence of ownership as tenants in common is that the interest or share of any owner passes on death under their will or, if there is no will, under the rules of intestacy.

Under Scots law, the two main categories of joint ownership are 'common property' (ie joint owners have separate title to a specific share, which transmits separately by survivorship, or by will or intestacy) and the joint property rights of trustees and partners (which accrues on death to the survivors) (see IHTM15091).

## Money accounts

**4.19** Joint money account holders (eg with banks, building societies, etc) are normally regarded as beneficially entitled to the proportion of the account attributable to their contributions. In addition, HMRC accept that, as a general rule, if one individual places money in a joint account with another as joint tenants and retains the right to withdraw the whole of it, there will not be a lifetime transfer when the money is paid into that account (although there may be a transfer on a later withdrawal of funds for the other joint owner) (IHTM15042–3).

However, care should be taken when one or more beneficial interests in joint accounts are gifted to other individuals (particularly if those individuals are not exempt beneficiaries), to avoid the whole account being included in the transferor's estate (*O'Neill & O'Neill's Executors v CIR*, SpC [1998] SSCD 110; *Sillars v IRC* [2004] SSCD 180). In *Taylor and another v Revenue and Customs Commissioners* [2008] SSCD 1159, the deceased was held to have a general power enabling her to dispose of the whole of two joint accounts. This was on the grounds (among other reasons) that there was no evidence that the other joint account holder was to benefit from the accounts on the particular facts of the case, and that the deceased was able to dispose of the whole balance in those accounts.

Under Scots law, where bank or building society accounts are held in joint names, the special or survivorship destination does not by itself pass the ownership of the money in the account to the survivor. An account with a bank or building society is not a document of title (ie it is not a deed of trust in terms of the *Blank Bonds and Trusts Act 1696*). It is a contract between the bank and the customer. The question of the ownership of the funds in the account therefore falls to be determined according to the ordinary principles of ownership. The individual who deposited funds in the account remains the owner, unless a transfer of ownership has occurred. This applies to all bank

**4.20** *Valuation of assets*

or building society accounts governed by Scots Law, and therefore applies to taxpayers living in England, Wales and Northern Ireland with an account governed by Scots Law (IHTM15054).

## Land

**4.20** If joint tenants (see above) purchase land with the help of a mortgage, unless there is an agreement to the contrary, their beneficial interests will generally equate to their respective shares of the mortgage. In addition, as indicated on the death of a joint owner of property (eg the family home) the survivor takes absolutely and by operation of law. Hence, it is impossible to make testamentary or lifetime dispositions to third parties.

If the beneficial interests in land vary from the legal title, in the absence of a gift HMRC will require evidence of the parties' beneficial ownership (IHTM15044). See **4.3** above.

In the case of a tenancy in common, disposals of interests in the property during lifetime or by will are possible. A tenant in common of an interest in the family home would entitle that co-owner to occupy the whole property. On the transfer of an interest by a tenant in common (eg on death), that person's share could be eligible for a discount of between 10–15%, although the level of discount will be subject to the Land Tribunal's agreement. However, in the case of property held by spouses or civil partners (whether as joint tenants or tenants in common, albeit that joint property passing by survivorship may be subject to the spouse exemption in any event), HMRC may seek to challenge any discount claimed, based on the related property provisions (see **4.6** above).

**4.21** In *Wight v IRC* 264 *Estates Gazette* 935, the value of an interest in a dwelling house owned as tenants in common in equal shares was held by the Lands Tribunal to be its vacant possession value less a discount of 15% to reflect the restricted demand for this type of interest.

In *Charkham v IRC* [2000] RVR 7, an individual held minority interests in a number of investment properties. The Revenue considered that the value should be discounted overall by between 10–15%. The taxpayer appealed. The Lands Tribunal held that there should be a single discount on each property, and that the appropriate discount should be 15% on some properties, and 20% or 22.5% on others. However, these larger discounts are exceptional: see below.

**4.22** HMRC made their view of development value very clear in their IHT Newsletter of 28 April 2006. The potential for development value must be accounted for where an estate contains land or buildings. The personal representatives should take all appropriate steps to disclose the value that the land may expect to achieve if sold on the open market and that must take account of any feature that may make it attractive to a builder or developer, for example a large garden or access to other land.

The personal representatives should consider all the evidence available when completing the IHT account. It is not enough just to obtain a professional valuation. If further information then comes to light, for example on advice about marketing the property, and if that later advice casts some doubt on the original valuation, the extra information should be disclosed.

**4.23** It may happen that after the personal representatives have lodged form IHT400 based on the situation as they saw it as at the date of death, new information will come to light during the administration of the estate and before winding up the estate. If that affects the value as at the date of death, HMRC Inheritance Tax would expect to be notified as quickly as possible. Where it is clear that reasonable and adequate steps have not been taken to ascertain the open market value based on all the information that was available, the personal representatives may be liable to penalties.

That does not mean that the full development value is taxable. In *Prosser v IRC* DET/1/2000 it was realised that a house enjoyed a garden big enough to serve as an extra building plot. The district valuer suggested a figure as at the date of death of 80% of the value that the plot would have with planning consent, allowing for the fact that no application for planning permission had yet been made. That was considered to be wrong. The Lands Tribunal held that, at the date of death, there was a 50% chance of obtaining planning permission and that a speculator, in the absence of permission, would not offer 80% of the development value but would offer only 25%.

**4.24** The Valuation Office Agency (VOA) generally applies discounts when valuing an undivided half-share interest in accordance with the table below (Valuation Office Agency Inheritance Tax Manual, Ch 1B, Practice Note 2, para 9.7, which can be viewed online at: www.voa.gov.uk/instructions/chapters/inheritance_tax_ch_1b/pnotes/frame.htm):

**Table 4.1—Discounts re undivided half-share interest in land**

| | | |
|---|---|---|
| (a) | where the other co-owner(s) is (are) not in occupation and the purpose behind the trust no longer exists | 10% |
| (b) | where the other co-owner(s) is (are) not in occupation but they have a right to occupy and the purpose behind the trust still exists | 15% |
| (c) | where the other co-owner(s) is (are) in occupation | 15% |

**4.25** *Valuation of assets*

The VOA Inheritance Tax Manual also indicates that a discount may be appropriate even for a majority share (Ch 1B, Practice Note 2, para 10.9):

> 'When valuing a minority share a larger discount than 10% may be appropriate in cases where
>
> **i** it is felt unlikely that a potential purchaser would seek an order for sale (under Section 14 TLATA 1996 or Section 30 LPA 1925) or, there is evidence that the majority of the share owners under a trust of land would oppose an application for an order for sale by a minority shareholder, and
>
> **ii** it is felt that there is potential for dispute concerning how the property is managed,
>
> However, the discount should not normally exceed 20%.'

The guidance goes onto state:

> 'Clearly even a majority share has disadvantages compared with ownership of the entirety. There will be circumstances however, where a discount of less than 10% share should be considered –.e.g. where it is known the co-owner(s) is/are keen to place the entirety interest on the market, or in cases involving large majority shares, such as a share of over 90% in a high value property ...'

The extent of any discount will therefore depend on the circumstances of each case.

The law of special or survivorship destination in Scotland provides that if an asset is purchased jointly under which there is a contractual agreement that on death the property passes to the survivor and they have paid equally for the asset, the survivor will be entitled to the whole on the death of the first to die. If the price was not provided equally, the donor can revoke the survivorship destination by will. If one party provided the whole property, he retains ownership unless there is indication of intention to make an immediate gift to the joint owner (see IHTM15050).

## Settled property

**4.25** The value of settled property in which an individual has an 'interest in possession' generally forms part of the estate on death, if he became beneficially entitled to it before 22 March 2006, or alternatively if he became beneficially entitled to an 'immediate post-death interest', a 'disabled person's interest' or a 'transitional serial interest' on or after that date (*s 49(1), (1A)*) (see **Chapter 7**).

If an interest in possession falls within the above categories, the individual is effectively treated as the absolute owner of that property, or the relevant proportion of it. The value of the life interest for IHT purposes is the value of the settlement property in which the individual's life interest subsisted. An exception to this rule applies if the interest in possession is acquired for money or money's worth, ie the extent (if any) to which the giving of consideration is a transfer of value falls to be determined without regard to this particular valuation rule (*s 49(2)*).

**4.26** The lifetime cessation of the above interests in possession is usually a PET, which becomes chargeable on the individual's death within seven years. If an immediate IHT charge arose at lifetime rates (eg if the settled property went into a discretionary trust) further IHT may become due at the rate on death, upon the individual's death within seven years.

Scots law has always had a unified system of law and equity and therefore does not recognise the principles of legal and beneficial estates (ie it does not recognise that the beneficiary could have real rights in trust property). Specific IHT legislation therefore applies in respect of proper life-rents (*ss 43(4), 46, 47*) (see IHTM16072).

If the individual's estate was increased by an earlier chargeable transfer of the settled property within the previous five years, 'quick succession relief' is available (**Chapter 10**). The IHT charged on death is reduced by a percentage of the tax charged on the earlier transfer (*s 141*).

# Gifts with reservation

**4.27** Property may fall to be treated as forming part of a donor's estate for IHT purposes if the 'gifts with reservation' (GWR) rules apply (see **Chapter 5**). For example, a parent may transfer his home into joint ownership with his adult daughter, but continue living there. Unless the parent pays rent for his continued occupation or his daughter takes up co-occupation, there is a GWR.

A gift caught by the GWR rules at the individual's death is treated as part of the donor's estate, and is liable to IHT accordingly. In addition, where the gift was made within seven years prior to the transferor's death, or the reservation ended within that period, there is a further chargeable transfer in respect of the same gift. However, there are regulations to eliminate this double tax charge (*FA 1986, ss 102, 104; IHT (Double Charges Relief) Regulations, SI 1987/1130*), which effectively determine the value of the gift to be taken into account on the donor's death.

The lifetime termination of an interest in possession falling within the categories mentioned in **4.25** above is treated as a gift for GWR purposes. If the individual retains use or enjoyment of the settled property after their interest has ended, it therefore remains part of their estate under the GWR rules as if they owned the property outright (*FA 1986, s 102ZA*).

**4.28** *Valuation of assets*

## Other assets

## Debts

**4.28** It is generally assumed that the right to receive a sum due under any obligation will be paid in full (ie the face value of the debt is included in the creditor's estate), unless that recovery is impossible or not reasonably practicable (eg if the debtor is insolvent). It may be possible to include a reduced value on the death estate if either title to the debt or the amount due is in doubt. However, if a reduced figure is used, HMRC Inheritance Tax will probably require an explanation, including how that amount has been calculated and any evidence in support of the reduced amount shown. No allowance is made if the recovery is in doubt because of any act or omission by the creditor (eg failing to enforce collection) (*s 166*). The amount to be included in the death estate also includes interest due up to the date of death. If some or all of the debt has been written off, that amount is treated as a gift.

If the lender waives a loan (voluntarily and not for consideration), HMRC will generally expect the debt release to be effected by a deed before allowing a reduction in the lender's estate, clearly indicating that it is intended as a deed by the parties involved. The deed must be validly executed (usually by signature) by those persons. However, in Scotland the release of a debt does not need to be effected by deed (IHTM19110).

## Household goods and personal effects

**4.29** Household and personal goods are subject to the 'market value' rule (*s 160*), ie 'the price which might reasonably be expected to fetch if sold in the open market ...'

In its *IHT Newsletter* (December 2004), Inland Revenue Capital Taxes (as it then was) stated:

> '... we will be paying particularly close attention to the values included for household and personal goods. In appropriate cases we will open an enquiry and ask you for further information to satisfy ourselves that all of the goods have been included and that they have been valued on the statutory basis.'

HMRC may seek to impose a penalty if the value of household or personal goods as returned for IHT purposes is estimated inaccurately, or if incorrect information is not corrected within a reasonable time. If preparing an IHT account (ie on form IHT400 or IHT100), which includes the value of household and personal goods, it would therefore clearly be advisable to provide the fullest information possible in the circumstances. This should also reduce the possibility of enquiry by HMRC Inheritance Tax. In particular, references in the account to the valuation being made 'for probate purposes' or for 'IHT purposes' should be avoided.

Note that HMRC Inheritance Tax do not accept that the value of jointly owned household goods should be discounted as a matter of course, where the related property provisions (see **4.4** above) do not apply. The Inheritance Tax Manual states (at IHTM21043):

> 'Whereas we allow a discount as a matter of course for jointly owned land, we do not do so automatically for jointly owned chattels as the discount is to reflect problems with disposing of less than a full share and, for chattels, the circumstances in which a sale could be obtained may vary.'

## Values 'ascertained'

**4.30** As explained in the *Capital Gains Tax Annual 2010/11* (Bloomsbury Professional), and as indicated at **4.17** above, if IHT was chargeable on the value of a person's estate immediately before death and the value of an asset as part of that asset has been 'ascertained' for IHT purposes, that value is taken to be the market value for CGT purposes at the date of death (*TCGA 1992, s 274*). However, where a value has been ascertained solely for the purpose of ascertaining the amount of transferable nil rate band between spouses or civil partners (see **Chapter 14**), that value will not apply for capital gains tax purposes.

## Valuation of liabilities; guarantees

**4.31** It was noted at **3.9** that a liability may be taken into account to reduce the chargeable estate only to the extent that it was incurred for money's worth and is enforceable. One area of regular difficulty is the valuation of a guarantee given by the deceased that has not been called upon at the date of death. HMRC strongly resist allowance of the full value guaranteed. For HMRC guidance on the calculation of allowable deductions for guarantee debts, see IHTM28355. The negotiation of that valuation generally involves considering:

- what security has been given by the deceased to support the guarantee;
- the likelihood that the guarantee will be called upon; and
- the amount by which the original debtor will default, such that the guarantor must make it good.

This is unsatisfactory: from the point of view of the guarantor because an obligation has been assumed that no doubt restricts his freedom to deal with certain assets because they support the guarantee. It will often be better, from a tax point of view, simply to provide the money rather than a guarantee; but in family situations the donor/lender may be reluctant to do that.

*Chapter 5*

# Gifts with reservation of benefit

## OUTLINE

**5.1** An individual who gives away property on or after 18 March 1986 makes a 'gift with reservation' (GWR) broadly if:

- the recipient does not immediately enjoy pssession of the property; or
- the donor continues to enjoy, or benefits from, the property gifted.

As indicated at **2.20**, the GWR rules (*FA 1986, ss 102–102C, Sch 20*) are anti-avoidance provisions designed to prevent 'cake and eat it' situations in which an individual makes a lifetime gift of an asset (which they hope to survive by at least seven years), but continues to have the use or enjoyment of it.

Property subject to the GWR rules on the individual's death is treated as part of the donor's estate, and charged to IHT accordingly. If the reservation ends during the individual's lifetime, the gift is generally treated as a PET at that time, which is subject to IHT upon death within seven years (*FA 1986, s 102(4)*). The annual exemption cannot be used against the value of the 'deemed' PET (*s 19(5)*). In addition, the 'normal expenditure out of income' exemption (*s 21*) does not prevent a gift being chargeable under the GWR rules (IHTM14319).

**5.2** If the transferor pays a full market rent for continued enjoyment or benefit of the property, the gift is not treated as a GWR. In addition, a gift which is an exempt transfer (eg a straightforward transfer to a UK-domiciled spouse or civil partner, or transfers subject to the small gift or marriage gift exemptions) cannot be a GWR (*FA 1986, s 102(5)*).

Special rules apply if an individual disposes of an interest in land by gift (on or after 9 March 1999), where the donor or his spouse enjoys a 'significant right of interest', or is party to a 'significant arrangement' in relation to the land. In such cases, the gifted interest in the land is treated as a GWR, unless certain specific exceptions apply (see **5.10ff**).

Relief is available in certain circumstances where a double IHT charge would otherwise arise in respect of the same property (ie where the original gift was

*Gifts with reservation of benefit* **5.4**

immediately chargeable), or as the result of a PET becoming chargeable within seven years of death, where that property is also included in the death estate for IHT purposes because it was a GWR *(Inheritance Tax (Double Charges Relief) Regulations (SI 1987/1130))* (see **5.36** below).

## Pre-owned assets

**5.3** The 'pre-owned assets' income tax charge (or the 'charge to income tax on benefits received by former owner of property', to be precise) was introduced (by *FA 2004, s 84*, and *Sch 15*, and underpinned by subsequent Treasury Regulations) in response to certain IHT planning arrangements. The charge operates for 2005/06 and subsequent years, but applies with retroactive effect to 18 March 1986.

It should be noted that there is no 'pre-owned assets tax' charge if the GWR provisions apply *(FA 2004, Sch 15, para 11(5))*, or if an election is made (under *FA 2004, Sch 15, para 21*) to effectively 'opt out' of the income tax charge and into the GWR rules for IHT purposes. A double IHT charge could arise if an election is made and the taxpayer dies within seven years of the original gift (ie both on the original transfer that must now be aggregated with the death estate, and on the property subject to the reservation). Double charge regulations *(Charge to Income Tax by Reference to Enjoyment of Property Previously Owned Regulations (SI 2005/724))* therefore prevent a double liability (ie on the original gift and the GWR); the higher amount of tax is charged *(SI 2005/724, reg 6)*.

For further commentary on pre-owned assets, see **Chapter 16**.

## SCOPE AND EFFECT OF THE GWR RULES

## Scope of GWR rules

**5.4** The GWR provisions are anti-avoidance rules designed to stop taxpayers decreasing the value of their IHT estates by making gifts whilst leaving their overall circumstances effectively unchanged. The rules apply to gifts of property on or after 18 March 1986 by an individual ('the donor') if:

- possession and enjoyment of the property is not assumed ('bona fide' as the legislation puts it) by the recipient of the gift ('the donee') at or before the beginning of the 'relevant period' (see below); and/or
- at any time in the relevant period the property is not enjoyed to the entire exclusion, or virtually to the entire exclusion, of the donor and of any benefit to him by contract or otherwise *(FA 1986, s 102(1)(a), (b))*.

**5.5** *Gifts with reservation of benefit*

The requirement that the donee must assume 'bona fide' possession and enjoyment of the gifted property to prevent a GWR means that the beneficial interest in the gifted property must be duly transferred, and the donee must have had actual enjoyment of that property (eg through physical occupation, or the receipt of income generated therefrom), instead of just the legal right of enjoyment.

Chattel gifts are usually perfected by the delivery of the item to the donee. Several cases examine what constitutes a valid gift, and from these we may perhaps see what amounts to the assumption of possession and enjoyment of the thing given. In *re Cole (a bankrupt)* [1964] Ch 175 as between husband and wife, the gift of such chattels as remained in the house was not a gift by delivery. The gift, in *re Lillingston* [1952] 2 All ER 184, of a key to a box was the gift of the contents of that box. Where the claimant had lived in a house where some furniture was situated, and there was a verbal gift of the furniture, that amounted to a valid gift because the donee lived there: *re Stoneham* [1919] 1 Ch 149. A gift of a chattel to a person living in the same house may be challenged, on the ground that the donor can still use it. Only special circumstances, such as the fact that the item is stored in the attic and the donor is too frail to have access to it, will displace the GWR argument.

**5.5** The 'relevant period' is the period ending on the date of the individual's death and beginning seven years before that date, or (if later) on the date of the gift *(FA 1986, s 102(1))*. For example, if the donor makes a gift eight years before his death (which satisfies condition *(a)* or *(b)* in *s 102*), the relevant period is seven years before his death. However, if the gift was made four years prior to death, the relevant period is four years. Note that the GWR rules can apply if the donor derives a benefit 'at any time' during the relevant period.

The Inheritance Tax Manual (at IHTM14333) indicates that 'virtually' intends to take gifts outside the reservation of benefit rules if the donor's benefit is 'insignificant' in relation to the gifted property. The requirement that the gifted property must be enjoyed to the exclusion of any benefit to the donor 'by contract or otherwise' is considered by HMRC to be a separate requirement to the 'virtually' test, and applies to a benefit obtained by the donor through 'associated operations' *(FA 1986, Sch 20, para 6(1)(c))*. See **2.21**.

The scope of the GWR rules was extended in 1999 and again in 2003, to counteract IHT avoidance arrangements designed to exploit loopholes in the provisions in connection with interests in land and the spouse exemption. Those provisions are considered later in this chapter.

## 'Property' and 'gift'

**5.6** To determine whether a gift is subject to the GWR rules, it is first necessary to ascertain the property given away. For example, if Mr X gave his

*Gifts with reservation of benefit* **5.7**

home to Miss Y (his daughter) in 1998, and Miss Y decided to lease the house back to Mr X at a nominal rent, the 'property' would be the house, and the reserved benefit (subject to the GWR rules) would be the lease.

It was previously possible to make arrangements for gifts of an interest in land whilst continuing to enjoy a benefit from it. However, changes to the GWR rules were introduced (with effect from 9 March 1999) with the intention of blocking such arrangements (see **5.12**).

The GWR rules apply to 'gifts', which can include sales at undervalue. HMRC's view is that a sale for less than full value arising from a 'bad bargain' is not necessarily a gift with reservation. However, where the GWR provisions do apply to a sale at undervalue, they only apply in respect of the undervalue proportion (IHTM14316). It is possible to reach the alternative conclusion that any element of undervalue is sufficient for the entire property to be 'caught' under the GWR rules. However, taxpayers and their advisers will no doubt wish to apply HMRC's more generous view.

**Example 5.1—GWR: sales at undervalue**

Henry sold his home to his daughter Daphne on 1 September 1998 for £10,000, when the value of the property was £100,000. Henry continued living at the house rent free until his death on 15 June 2010, when the property had increased in value to £500,000.

Henry's sale of the property to Daphne at undervalue is a GWR. The value of the property disposed of by way of 'gift' is 90% of the value of the whole property. Therefore, 90% of its death value is treated for GWR purposes as property to which Henry was beneficially entitled, ie £500,000 × 90% = £450,000.

# Effect of GWR rules

**5.7** Without the GWR rules, if an individual could make a PET of property and survive at least seven years, the property would fall outside his estate and he could continue to enjoy or benefit from the gifted asset with impunity for IHT purposes.

The GWR rules therefore provide that if property subject to a reservation would not otherwise form part of the donor's estate immediately before his death, it will be treated as such *(FA 1986, s 102(3))*. The gift is deemed for IHT purposes to be property to which the individual was beneficially entitled immediately before his death, and is therefore ineffective to reduce the value of his IHT estate. However, this GWR treatment does not apply to excluded property (IHTM04072). See **5.32**.

**5.8** *Gifts with reservation of benefit*

---

**Example 5.2—'Caught' by GWR rules (1)**

On 5 September 2002, Derek gave his house and its contents to his grandson Gerald, but continued to live in it with his wife Fiona, paying no rent. The house and contents were valued at £400,000 (after annual exemptions).

On 3 July 2010, Derek died leaving his estate of £400,000 by way of a specific legacy of £200,000 to Fiona, with residue to his granddaughter Hannah. The value of the house at that time was £600,000.

*5 September 2002 – Gift*

Derek's original gift of the house to Gerald is a PET. However, the property is subject to the GWR rules.

*3 July 2010 – Death*

Derek's gift of the house to Gerald on 5 September 2002 is a PET which has become exempt, because it was made more than seven years before Derek's death.

However, the GWR rules apply to treat the house as forming part of Derek's death estate. IHT is charged on the value of the house on death. The chargeable estate is therefore £800,000 (ie the house worth £600,000, plus his other chargeable estate of £200,000 (the other £200,000 passing to his wife is exempt)).

|  | £ |
|---|---|
| Chargeable transfer | 800,000 |
| IHT thereon: |  |
| £325,000 × nil | NIL |
| £475,000 × 40% | 190,000 |
|  | 190,000 |

---

**5.8** In the above example, the original gift of the property was a PET made more than seven years before Derek's death. Had the gift been a chargeable PET made within seven years before his death, a double IHT charge would arise (ie on the original gift, and on the property forming part of Derek's estate under the GWR rules).

Special rules therefore apply to prevent double taxation in such circumstances (*FA 1986, s 104*; *Inheritance Tax (Double Charges Relief) Regulations, SI 1987/1130*). The rules as they apply to a GWR are discussed at **5.36** below.

*Gifts with reservation of benefit* **5.8**

## Example 5.3—'Caught' by GWR rules (2)

The facts are as in **Example 5.2**, except that the date of the GWR is 5 September 2007.

*5 September 2007 – Gift*

Derek's original gift of the house to Gerald (see previous example) is a PET. The property is subject to the GWR rules.

*3 July 2010 – Death*

Derek's gift of the house to Gerald on 5 September 2007 is a PET which becomes chargeable, because it was made within seven years of Derek's death. The house also forms part of Derek's death estate, so it is necessary to consider the double charges relief regulations.

*Calculation (a) – Ignore PET and charge house in death estate*

5 September 2007 – gift ignored: IHT = nil.

3 July 2010 – tax on chargeable death estate of £800,000 = £190,000

*Calculation (b) – Charge PET and ignore house in death estate*

5 September 2007 – IHT on £400,000:

|  | £ |
| --- | --- |
| IHT thereon: | |
| £325,000 × nil | NIL |
| £75,000 × 40% | 30,000 |
| | 30,000 |

3 July 2010 – tax on chargeable death estate of £200,000 (no nil rate band available):

£200,000 × 40% = £80,000

Total IHT (£30,000 + £80,000) = £110,000

## Conclusion

A higher amount of IHT is payable on calculation (a) by charging the house as part of Derek's death estate. This amount (£190,000) is therefore charged, and the second IHT charge (£110,000) is reduced to nil (*SI 1987/1130, reg 5(3)(a)*).

**5.9** *Gifts with reservation of benefit*

## GWR and spouse exemption

**5.9** As mentioned at **5.1** above, certain exempt transfers (eg to a spouse or civil partner) cannot generally be a GWR. However, legislation was introduced in *Finance Act 2003* (inserting *FA 1986, ss 102(5A)–(5C)* into the GWR rules) to block '*Eversden* schemes' resulting from the Court of Appeal's decision in *IRC v Eversden (exors of Greenstock, decd)* [2003] EWCA Civ 668.

In that case, a married woman (W) settled a 5% interest in the family home she owned for herself absolutely. The other 95% was settled on an interest in possession trust to benefit her husband (H) for life, following which the trust fund would be held on discretionary trusts for a class of beneficiaries including W. They continued to occupy the property until H's death four years later. The property was sold a year later, and a replacement property was bought together with an investment bond. The interests held by W and the settlement remained unchanged. W died five years later. The Court of Appeal held that the original gift of the property was an exempt transfer between spouses under *IHTA 1984, s 18*.

The effect of the GWR rules (following *FA 2003*) is that the donor is treated as making a gift when the life interest of their spouse or civil partner terminates. This means that if the donor subsequently occupies or enjoys a benefit from the settled property, the gift is one to which the reservation of benefit rules apply. For example, the rules affect a husband making a gift to a trust under which his wife takes an initial interest in possession, which is subsequently terminated in favour of a discretionary trust in which the husband is a potential beneficiary. However, following changes to the IHT treatment of interest in possession trusts introduced in *FA 2006*, the anti-avoidance rules are only of likely relevance to interests in possession before 22 March 2006 (see **Chapter 7**).

## Gifts of interests in land

**5.10** As indicated at **5.6**, previously (ie prior to 9 March 1999) it was possible to make arrangements for gifts of an interest in land whilst continuing to enjoy a benefit from it.

### Ingram schemes

**5.11** A 'loophole' in the GWR rules at that time was highlighted in *Ingram (Executors of Lady Ingram's Estate) v IRC* [1997] STC 1234. In that case, Lady Ingram gifted to her children the freehold interest in a property, subject to a leasehold interest which she retained. The leasehold interest was created by the conveyance of the property to a nominee, followed by the grant of a lease to Lady Ingram for 20 years. The purpose was to enable Lady Ingram to

*Gifts with reservation of benefit* **5.12**

continue occupying the property by reason of the lease, without making a gift of the freehold subject to the GWR provisions.

The House of Lords held that Lady Ingram had made an effective gift of the freehold reversion, in which no benefit had been reserved. She had simply gifted one property interest in which she reserved no benefit, and retained (or 'carved out') another interest which entitled her to remain in residence.

Following the decision by the House of Lords in Lady Ingram's favour, changes to the GWR rules were quickly introduced by *FA 1999* with the intention of countering the effects of that decision (*FA 1986, ss 102A–102C*). The provisions apply to gifts of interests in land from 9 March 1999. It should be noted that pre-9 March 1999 *Ingram* schemes considered effective for IHT purposes are subject to a pre-owned assets income tax charge (see **5.3**). In addition, the general GWR provisions (*FA 1986, s 102(3), (4)*) discussed earlier are still capable of applying to 'straightforward' gifts of land (*s 102C(7)*).

## The 'interests in land' rules – FA 1986, s 102A

**5.12** The GWR rules for gifts of interests in land (from 9 March 1999) provide that if the donor or spouse (or civil partner) enjoys a 'significant right or interest', or is 'party to a significant arrangement' in relation to the land during the 'relevant period' (as defined in **5.5**), the gifted land interest is a GWR. A right, interest or arrangement is 'significant' only if it entitles or enables the donor to occupy all or part of the land, or to enjoy some right in relation to all or part of it, otherwise than for full consideration in money or money's worth (*FA 1986, s 102A(2), (3)*). Thus, no GWR arises if, for example, a donor gifts the freehold interest in a house to another individual (a PET) but retains, or is immediately granted, a lease at a full rent.

There are exceptions from the GWR rule if the right, interest or arrangement (as appropriate) is not 'significant', ie:

- it does not and cannot prevent the enjoyment of the land to the entire exclusion, or virtually to the entire exclusion, of the donor (*FA 1986, s 102A(4)(a)*); or

- it does not entitle or enable the donor to occupy all or part of the land immediately after the disposal, but would do so but for the interest disposed of (*FA 1986, s 102A(4)(b)*);

- the right or interest was granted or acquired before the seven-year period ending with the date of gift (*FA 1986, s 102A(5)*).

An example of the second exception above is where the donor gifts a 20-year rent-free leasehold interest and retains the freehold reversion, as those rights

**5.13** *Gifts with reservation of benefit*

do not entitle or enable the donor to occupy the land immediately after the disposal, but would do so but for the interest disposed of.

The third exception above means that a *Lady Ingram* type scheme is not caught by *FA 1986, s 102A* as a 'significant right or interest' if there is a gap of at least seven years between the creation of the lease and the gift of the freehold reversion. However, note that the exception does not preclude a 'significant arrangement' in relation to the land from being a GWR.

## Reversionary lease schemes

**5.13** IHT avoidance arrangements involving reversionary leases in land originally came into being before 9 March 1999. The 'reversionary lease scheme' typically involves a donor granting a long lease for (say) 999 years to the proposed donee. The lease would not commence until a future date (ie normally beyond the donor's life expectancy, but less than 21 years to avoid problems under the *Law of Property Act 1925, s 149(3)*). To fall within the GWR exception in *FA 1986, s 102A(5)* mentioned above, a gap of at least seven years would need to be left between the date of purchase of the land and the date of the grant of the lease.

HMRC have indicated (in the Inheritance Tax Manual at IHTM14360) that such schemes '... had previously escaped the GWR provisions' before 9 March 1999, although reversionary lease schemes were one of the targets of the 'pre-owned assets' income tax provisions covered in **Chapter 16**. HMRC's 'Income tax and pre-owned assets guidance' states (at section 5, Appendix 1) (www.hmrc.gov.uk/poa/poa_guidance5.htm#9):

> 'Such schemes entered into before 9 March 1999 are not gifts with reservation of benefit so long as the lease contains no terms that are beneficial to the donor ... and the income tax charge will apply.'

At the time of writing, IHTM14360 indicates that HMRC consider that *FA 1986, s 102A* catches reversionary lease schemes from 9 March 1999, on the basis that the donor's occupation (even though acquired more than seven years before creation of the lease) is a 'significant right in relation to the land' within *FA 1986, s 102A(3)*. A right, interest or arrangement is considered to be 'significant' if it entitles or enables the donor to occupy all or part of the land, otherwise than for full consideration in money or money's worth. IHTM14360 gives instructions that such schemes should be referred to the HMRC's Technical Group.

However, in its pre-owned assets guidance, HMRC appear to contradict this approach, stating: '... HMRC now consider that where the freehold interest was acquired more than 7 years before the gift, the continued occupation by the donor would not be a significant right, and therefore contrary to its

*Gifts with reservation of benefit* **5.15**

previously held view, section 102A cannot apply to the gift because of section 102A(5)'.

HMRC amended their pre-owned assets guidance in respect of reversionary lease schemes on 29 January 2007, whereas (at the time of writing) IHTM14360 has not been amended since that date. HMRC's position as stated in their pre-owned assets guidance is therefore assumed to prevail. On that basis, although a GWR charge would not apply, a charge to income tax will apply unless the donor elects into the GWR provisions.

## 'Share of interest in land' – FA 1986, s 102B

**5.14** The GWR rules were extended in *FA 1999* to cover gifts of an undivided share of an interest in land (from 9 March 1999), such as where a sole freeholder gifts a half interest to another individual (*FA 1986, s 102B*). The share disposed of is a GWR (*FA 1986, s 102(3)* and *(4)*).

There are exceptions from this GWR rule if:

- the donor does not occupy the land (*FA 1986, s 102B(3)(a)*); or
- the donor occupies the land to the exclusion of the donee for full consideration in money or money's worth (eg a full market rent) (*FA 1986, s 102B(3)(b)*); or
- both donor and donee occupy the land, and the donor receives no (or negligible) benefit from the donee in connection with the gift (*FA 1986, s 102B(4)*).

The third exception above means that if, for example, a father gifts an interest in the property to his daughter who lives with him and shares the property outgoings, there is no GWR (NB: the daughter should not contribute in any way to the father's share of the household upkeep and expenses). There is also an exemption from the 'pre-owned assets' income tax charge in these circumstances (*FA 2004, Sch 15, para 11(5)*), see **Chapter 16**. If *FA 1986, s 102B* applies, the other GWR rules (*FA 1986, ss 102* and *102A*) do not (*FA 1986, s 102C(6)*).

## Other points – FA 1986, s 102C

**5.15** Supplemental rules (*FA 1986, s 102C*) linking the interests in land rules with the general GWR rules provide that exempt gifts (listed at **5.25**) fall outside both sets of rules (*FA 1986, s 102C(2)*).

In addition, the donor's occupation of land is expressly disregarded if certain conditions are all satisfied (*FA 1986, s 102C(3)*, and *Sch 20, para 6(1)(b)*):

**5.16** *Gifts with reservation of benefit*

- it results from unforeseen changes in circumstances of the donor since the gift (eg a sudden serious illness, but not merely getting old); and
- the donor is unable to maintain himself through old age, infirmity, etc; and
- it represents a reasonable provision by the donee for the donor's care and maintenance; and
- the donee is a relative of the donor or his spouse.

The exception for exempt transfers to spouses or civil partners in *FA 1986, s 102(5)* is applied to the GWR land rules *(FA 1986, s 102C(2))*. However, the spouse exemption is limited in its application for GWR purposes *(FA 1986, s 102(5A)–(5C))* (see **5.9**).

## 'Tracing' GWRs

**5.16** There are complicated GWR rules dealing with situations whereby the donee does not retain the gifted property until the donor's death or until the benefit ends, eg the property is sold, exchanged or otherwise disposed of *(FA 1986, Sch 20, paras 2–4)*.

For GWR purposes, it is necessary to determine whether the original subject matter of the gift can be traced and substituted. These rules (entitled 'substitutions and accretions') prevent what might otherwise be simple IHT avoidance. For example, a mother may give Property A to her daughter, who may exchange it for Property B, and allow her mother to live there rent free. The tracing rules mean that the mother has reserved a benefit by occupying Property B.

**5.17** The tracing rules do not apply to absolute gifts of cash *(FA 1986, Sch 20, para 2(2)(b))*. However, HMRC consider that if individual A gives £100,000 cash to B which B uses to purchase A's residence (worth £100,000), with A remaining in occupation rent free until his death, this constitutes a GWR of the residence, under the 'associated operations' rules in *IHTA 1984, s 268* (see **2.21**) (see the example given at IHTM14372). Whilst the scope of the associated operations rules was effectively diminished by the Court of Appeal in *Rysaffe Trustee Co (CI) Ltd v IRC* [2003] STC 536, this nevertheless remains a point that HMRC appear to take.

The GWR provisions only apply to the property originally given. Thus if, for example, individual C gives land to individual D, and individual D builds a house on that land, if the GWR rules are in point they apply only to the extent of the gifted land, though interesting valuation issues may arise where the development has increased the value of the subject matter of the gift.

If the donee gifts the relevant property to someone else or voluntarily disposes of it for less than full consideration (other than back to the donor), the donee is treated as continuing to have possession and enjoyment of the property (*FA 1986, Sch 20, para 2(4), (5)*). If the gifted property was shares or debentures, any bonus and rights issues are generally treated as comprised in the gift (*FA 1986, Sch 20, para 2(6), (7)*), subject to a deduction for consideration paid by the donee for the shares in valuing the property comprised in the gift (*FA 1986, Sch 20, para 3*).

If the donee predeceases the donor, or dies before the benefit ends, then unless the property is settled by will or intestacy, the GWR rules apply as if he had not died, and the actions of his personal representatives are treated as his own. Any property taken under the donee's will or intestacy is treated as a gift made by him on death (*FA 1986, Sch 20, para 4*).

## Settled gifts and GWR

**5.18** The GWR rules also potentially apply to settled property. However, a pre-18 March 1986 settlement is not subject to the rules (even if it would have been caught if made after 17 March 1986), unless further gifts into settlement are made after that date, in which case the GWR provisions will only apply to the property settled by those further gifts (IHTM14311).

If a donor makes a gift by way of settlement, the type of property is immaterial. The property comprised in the settlement needs to be considered instead. The normal 'tracing' rules described above do not apply to a gift of settled property, although the GWR rules potentially apply instead to the settled property at the date of the donor's death (or when the GWR ceased), unless it is unrelated to the original gifted property (*FA 1986, Sch 20, para 5(1)*) (see **5.20**).

The donor should be excluded from being a beneficiary. In addition, if there is a settlement power to add beneficiaries, any argument by HMRC that the GWR rules apply can be avoided if the trustees are expressly prevented from adding the donor as a beneficiary.

If the donor creates a discretionary settlement in which the donor's spouse or civil partner (but not the donor himself) is a potential beneficiary, this is not, of itself, a GWR. However, a trust distribution to the spouse or civil partner may be a GWR, if the donor can share in the benefit of that distribution. The GWR rules can apply not only if the donor is a beneficiary of the settlement, but also if a gift is made into trust for others, to the extent that the donor's beneficial interest is not completely lost, or if the property can revert back to the donor.

## Interests in possession and GWR

**5.19** GWR rules dealing with the lifetime termination of interests in possession were introduced by *FA 2006* (*FA 1986, s 102ZA*). The rules apply to:

**5.20** *Gifts with reservation of benefit*

- pre-22 March 2006 interests in possession; or
- a post-21 March 2006 interest in possession which is an immediate post-death interest, disabled person's interest or a transitional serial interest (for further discussion, see **Chapter 7**).

The GWR rules apply to gifts, whereas the lifetime termination of an interest in possession is a transfer of value. The effect of these rules is that the lifetime termination of the interest is treated as a gift of the settled property (*FA 1986, s 102ZA(2)*). See **13.16**. If the individual retains use of the settled property after their interest in possession has ended, the property remains part of their estate under the GWR rules as if they owned it outright.

The creation of a life interest trust on or after 22 March 2006 is not normally a potentially exempt transfer (*s 3A(1A)*), with the trust entering the 'relevant property' regime as for discretionary trusts. If the trust is settlor-interested, there is arguably no GWR on the value of the settled property upon the settlor's death under *s 102(3)*. This is on the basis that the settlor has given away the remainder interest in which no benefit is reserved, but there is no gift of the right to receive the income because the donor has always had it (see *Trust Taxation* by Emma Chamberlain and Chris Whitehouse (Sweet & Maxwell)).

### 'Tracing' the settled GWR

**5.20** There are also 'tracing' provisions under which the GWR rules may apply if the property subject to the deemed gift continues to be settled property immediately thereafter and is replaced by other assets; or if all or part of the settled property ceases to be settled while the reservation still exists; or if gifted property is not settled directly by the donor but subsequently becomes settled by the donee. In the latter case, the period between the original gift and settlement by the donee is subject to the normal tracing rules, but from the date of settlement by the donee, the tracing rules for settled property apply instead (*FA 1986, Sch 20, para 5*).

On the lifetime termination of an interest in possession to which *FA 1986, s 102ZA* applies (see **5.19**), if the property continues to be settled, the individual's deemed gift for GWR purposes is the settled property at the material time, or property representing or derived from it. However, accumulated trust income arising after that time is not treated as derived from that settled property (*FA 1986, Sch 20, para 4A*).

### Settlor as trustee and GWR

**5.21** A trustee's duties are of a fiduciary nature (ie to safeguard the interests of the beneficiaries). Thus, as a matter of trust law, and for GWR purposes,

*Gifts with reservation of benefit* **5.23**

there is normally no objection to the donor (or spouse or civil partner) being one of the trustees (IHTM14394). In addition, a donor can receive reasonable remuneration for his duties as a trustee without constituting a GWR. This is despite the decision in *Oakes v Comr of Stamp Duties of New South Wales* [1954] AC 57, an Australian case in which it was held that remuneration paid to the settlor as trustee was a benefit.

If company shares are settled and the settlor is a trustee and also a paid director of that company, the gift does not, of itself, constitute a GWR. There is a possible GWR argument if the settlor settles shares onto a trust and *then* obtains a paid position as director or employee of the company. In this situation, the settlor should obtain no more than reasonable remuneration for the work done. HMRC accept that the continuation of reasonable commercial remuneration arrangements entered into before the gift does not of itself constitute a reservation, provided that the benefits were in no way linked to or affected by the gift. However, a new remuneration package may be challenged as a GWR 'by contract or otherwise' if the gift was taken into account as part of the arrangements (IHTM14395).

## Insurance policies

**5.22** There are also GWR rules specifically in respect of insurance policies, which can apply if there is a gift relating to a policy of insurance on the life of the donor, the spouse or civil partner or joint lives, where the resulting benefits to the donee vary according to benefits of the donor, spouse or civil partner. If those GWR provisions apply, the property comprised in a gift relating to the insurance policy is treated as a reserved benefit for the donor (*FA 1986, Sch 20, para 7*).

Note that this rule can apply to policies from which the donor's spouse (or civil partner) can benefit. This is an exception to the general rule that property from which the donor's spouse (but not the donor) can benefit or enjoy is not, of itself, a GWR.

If an insurance policy is taken out for another person, the date of gift is the date on which the insurance contract is taken out. Gifts made before 18 March 1986 are not subject to the GWR rules, but HMRC consider that such gifts may be caught if the policy is significantly varied on or after that date (IHTM14433).

## Agricultural and business property

**5.23** The availability of business property relief (BPR) or agricultural property relief (APR) (see **Chapter 11**) on gifts charged as a GWR depends on whether the property is qualifying business or agricultural property (eg land or buildings) or qualifying shares or securities in a company (NB: if the shares

**5.24** *Gifts with reservation of benefit*

or securities subject to the GWR charge do not qualify for APR, they may qualify for BPR instead).

For the purposes of establishing entitlement to BPR or APR in terms of the minimum period of ownership requirement (*ss 106, 117*), ownership by the transferor before the GWR is treated as ownership by the donee (*FA 1986, Sch 20, para 8(2)(a)*), and occupation by the transferor (ie before and after the GWR) is treated as occupation by the donee (*para 8(2)(b)*). The question whether BPR or APR is available (and, in the case of APR, at what rate) is determined on the basis that a notional transfer of value had been made by the donee (*FA 1986, Sch 20, para 8(1A)(b)*). As to the availability of APR for shares or securities in farming companies, see below.

HMRC will consider whether the relief conditions were satisfied at the date of gift (and by reference to the donor's ownership history), and also when the GWR charge arises, ie on the death of the donor, or when the benefit ceases (IHTM25381, IHTM24200).

For shares or securities in farming companies, if the GWR rules apply the availability of APR is subject to separate requirements (*FA 1986, Sch 20, para 8(3)*). These are, broadly, that the shares or securities qualified for relief when the GWR was made, the donee has retained ownership of the shares between the dates of the gift and GWR charge, and that the shares or securities qualify for relief on the basis of a notional transfer of value by the donee.

The conditions for APR (or BPR) in respect of shares or securities must be satisfied at the time of gift, and also when the GWR charge arises (*FA 1986, Sch 20, para 8(1A)(b)*). In addition, as mentioned the donee must retain ownership of the shares between the date of gift and the date of the GWR charge (*FA 1986, Sch 20, para 8(3)(b)*). The rate of BPR on shares or securities is generally determined on the basis that they remained in the donor's ownership, ie as if the gift had never been made (*para 8(1A)(a)*). The normal requirement that the donee must retain the gifted property until the time of the GWR charge is subject to tracing provisions, as discussed above, unless the gifted property is shares or securities (see IHTM24206).

If the donee dies prior to the GWR charge, the donee's personal representatives or beneficiaries of the GWR property are treated as the donee for the above purposes (*para 8(5)*).

# EXCEPTIONS AND EXCLUSIONS FROM CHARGE

## Gifts made before 18 March 1986

**5.24** The GWR rules do not apply to gifts before 18 March 1986, even if there is a reservation of benefit after then. For example, a pre-18 March 1986

*Gifts with reservation of benefit* **5.27**

discretionary trust which would have been caught by the GWR provisions had it been made after 17 March 1986 will escape the GWR charge, unless further gifts into trust are made after that date (in which case the GWR rules will apply to those later gifts).

## Gifts which are exempt transfers

**5.25** The GWR rules do not apply to certain exempt transfers (*FA 1986, s 102(5)*). The exemptions are listed below (all references are to *IHTA 1984*):

- transfers between spouses or civil partners (but see below) (*s 18*);
- small gifts (*s 20*);
- gifts in consideration of marriage or civil partnership (*s 22*);
- gifts to charities (*s 23*);
- gifts to political parties (*s 24*);
- gifts to registered housing associations or registered social landlords (from 14 March 1989) (*s 24A*);
- gifts for national purposes etc (*s 25*);
- gifts for public benefit (although this relief has now been repealed) (*s 26*);
- maintenance funds for historic buildings (*s 27*); and
- employee trusts (*s 28*).

**5.26** Before changes to the GWR rules were introduced (*FA 1986, ss 102(5A)–(5C)*), arrangements were possible to take advantage of the exception from the GWR provisions for exempt gifts between spouses. *Eversden* schemes (such as outlined at **5.9**) used the spouse exemption (*IHTA 1984, s 18*) to avoid a GWR on the gift of an asset to a trust. Such schemes were blocked (with effect for disposals from 20 June 2003), and pre-existing schemes are potentially subject to an income tax charge under the pre-owned assets regime (see **Chapter 16**).

Whilst the GWR rules do not apply to a gift (eg to a discretionary trust) in which a benefit is reserved by the donor's spouse or civil partner (ie as a potential beneficiary), if enjoyment of the gift is effectively shared by the donor (eg if distributions from the discretionary trust are paid into a joint bank account of the donor and spouse/civil partner), the GWR provisions will need to be considered.

**5.27** It should be noted that the following categories of exempt gift can fall within the GWR rules:

**5.28** *Gifts with reservation of benefit*

- PETs made more than seven years before the donor's death (*IHTA 1984, s 3A(4)*);
- the £3,000 annual exemption (*IHTA 1984, s 19(5)*); and
- the normal gifts out of income exemption (*IHTA 1984, s 21(5)*).

For example, if there is a GWR and the reservation ceases with the gift becoming a PET, there can be no £3,000 exemption when the reservation thus ends, as *s 19(5)* effectively precludes the annual exemption from applying to the deemed transfer when the reservation ends (IHTM14343). This exclusion seems logical, because the gifted property passed to the actual donee at the time it was actually made, not when the reservation ceased.

## De minimis exceptions

**5.28** As indicated at **5.4**, one of the conditions to avoid a GWR is that the gifted property must be enjoyed by the donee to the entire exclusion or virtually to the entire exclusion of the donor (*FA 1986, s 102(1)(b)*). There is no definition of 'virtually' in the legislation. However, in HMRC's view, the expression 'virtually to the entire exclusion' covers cases in which the benefit to the donor is 'insignificant' in relation to the gifted property. Examples of situations in which HMRC consider that the donor can benefit to some extent without the GWR rules applying are illustrated in Revenue Interpretation 55, and are reproduced below:

**Table 5.1—GWR:** *de minimis* **exceptions (RI 55)**

- a house which becomes the donee's residence but where the donor subsequently:
  - stays, in the absence of the donee, for not more than two weeks each year; or
  - stays with the donee for less than one month each year;
- social visits, excluding overnight stays made by a donor as a guest of the donee, to a house which he had given away. The extent of the social visits should be no greater than the visits which the donor might be expected to make to the donee's house in the absence of any gift by the donor;
- a temporary stay for some short-term purpose in a house the donor had previously given away, for example:
  - while the donor convalesces after medical treatment;
  - while the donor looks after a donee convalescing after medical treatment;
  - while the donor's own home is being redecorated;

- visits to a house for domestic reasons, for example babysitting by the donor for the donee's children;
- a house together with a library of books which the donor visits less than five times in any year to consult or borrow a book;
- a motor car which the donee uses to give occasional (ie less than three times a month) lifts to the donor;
- land which the donor uses to walk his dogs or for horse riding provided this does not restrict the donee's use of the land.

The above guidance warns taxpayers that if a benefit escalates into something more significant, the GWR provisions may apply (eg a house in which the donor then stays most weekends, or for a month or more each year).

## Full consideration

**5.29** If the donor gives full consideration in money or money's worth there should normally be no reservation. There is a specific rule to this effect for land and chattels. Its effect is that the retention of a benefit by the donor is disregarded if the donor is in actual occupation or actual enjoyment and pays full consideration in money or money's worth (*FA 1986, Sch 20, para 6(1)(a)*), eg a 'commercial lease' pursuant to which the donor pays a full arm's-length rent for the lease or tenancy retained.

Full consideration is required throughout the period, and regular rent reviews should take place to ensure that this condition is satisfied. HMRC accept that 'full' consideration falling within 'normal' valuation tolerances will be acceptable (Revenue Interpretation 55), although there is no statement of what is regarded as 'normal' in this context.

Note that the above GWR exception applies to land and chattels. Care should be taken with other assets. The Inheritance Tax Manual (at IHTM14336) cites an example in which A, who is a partner, withdraws capital from his partnership capital account and gives it to B. B then lends the partnership an equivalent cash sum. HMRC consider that this is a GWR, and state that even though A may pay B a commercial rate of interest for the loan, this payment will not prevent the loan being a reservation.

**5.30** To reduce the possibility of a GWR challenge by HMRC, the 'full consideration' should be negotiated at arm's length between parties with separate professional advisers in accordance with normal commercial criteria at the time. HMRC guidance on the meaning of 'full consideration' can also be found in Revenue Interpretation 55 (see **5.28**), and specific examples are included in the Inheritance Tax Manual (at IHTM14341). There is a similar full consideration let-out from the pre-owned assets income tax charge (see

**5.31** *Gifts with reservation of benefit*

**Chapter 16**) in relation to land and chattels, but not intangible property (*FA 2004, Sch 15, paras 4(1), 7(1)*).

The donor's occupation of gifted land is not a GWR if it represents reasonable provision for an infirm relative, if certain conditions are all satisfied (*FA 1986, Sch 20, para 6(1)(b)*) (see **5.15**). There is also an exemption from a pre-owned assets income tax charge in those circumstances (*FA 2004, Sch 15, para 11(5)(d)*).

## Instruments of variation (IHTA 1984, s 142)

**5.31** The GWR rules cannot apply to a disposition which is subject to a variation by the beneficiary (ie within *IHTA 1984, s 142*). The variation is treated for IHT purposes as having been made by the deceased person whose estate is the subject of the variation, not the persons entitled under his will.

For example, if Mr B died leaving property under his will to Mrs B, and within two years Mrs B varied the will (ie by an instrument of variation within *s 142*) so that the property became settled on a discretionary trust for Mrs B and her adult children, the discretionary trust is treated for IHT purposes as having been made by the deceased, Mr B. Therefore, the GWR rules cannot bite.

## Non-UK assets of non-UK domiciliary

**5.32** The 'excluded property' of a non-UK-domiciled person (see **1.18**) is not subject to the GWR rules.

---

**Example 5.4—GWR exception: excluded property**

James was born and domiciled in New Zealand. In 1999, he gave away an investment property portfolio in Wellington to his daughter Mary. The lettings income was shared equally between them. James died in 2008, still domiciled in New Zealand.

The gifted property was subject to a reservation at James' death. However, it was situated outside the UK, and James remained domiciled outside the UK throughout. The property is therefore excluded property (*IHTA 1984, s 6(1)*), and the GWR charging provisions do not apply.

---

However, HMRC's view (as stated in the Inheritance Tax Manual at IHTM14318) appears to be that if the donor makes the gift and subsequently becomes UK domiciled, there may be a GWR claim on death, or alternatively if the reservation ceased in the donor's lifetime, a deemed PET may be treated as being made.

## Gifts with reservation of benefit 5.34

**5.33** A popular IHT planning point has been that if a non-UK domiciliary held assets abroad, those assets could be gifted into trust if there was any possibility of the individual becoming actually or deemed domiciled in the UK (eg settling the non-UK situs assets on discretionary trust with the settlor as a possible beneficiary), in order to continue benefiting from excluded property status. It was commonly thought that the GWR rules could not apply, because the excluded property rules prevailed. However, guidance in the Inheritance Tax Manual has created some uncertainty on this issue. IHTM14396 states the following:

> 'If the settlor was domiciled outside the UK at the time a settlement was made, any foreign property within that settlement is excluded property and is not brought into charge for inheritance tax purposes.'

> 'Foreign property settled by a settlor with foreign domicile remains excluded property if the reservation continues **up to the settlor's death**, even though the domicile may have changed between those dates.'

**5.34** However, the guidance then goes on to provide the following example:

> '*Example*
>
> The donor, who is domiciled in Australia, puts foreign property into a discretionary trust under which he is a potential beneficiary. He dies five years later domiciled in the UK and without having released the reservation.
>
> The property is subject to a reservation and is therefore deemed to be part of the donor's death estate.
>
> Refer any cases where this is the situation to Litigation.'

On the face of it, the example appears to contradict the preceding comments. However, it could perhaps be interpreted in such a way that although the property forms part of the donor's death estate (so as potentially to affect the valuation of another asset in the estate), an IHT charge is nevertheless excluded, on the basis that the excluded property provisions override the GWR rules.

In addition, whilst the cessation of a reservation in an 'excluded property settlement' was commonly thought not to constitute a deemed PET if an individual who was non-UK domiciled when the settlement was made subsequently became UK domiciled, IHTM14396 also states:

> '*Reservation ceasing during lifetime*
>
> However, had the donor in the above example attained UK domicile after the gift and then released the reservation during his lifetime, it is arguable that the release would have been a PET, chargeable on the death within seven years. In effect, the property ceased to be excluded property at the time the reservation was released. The release would thus have triggered a charge which would not have arisen had the release not been made.

**5.35** *Gifts with reservation of benefit*

Refer any case where you consider that there is such a charge, or any enquiries about the possibility of a charge, to Litigation.'

**5.35** It therefore seems that there is still some uncertainty (at least from HMRC's perspective), in which case it seems possible that the interaction of the GWR and excluded property rules may be the subject of litigation in the future. One possible explanation for the apparent contradiction in HMRC's guidance is that changes were made in anticipation of a potential overhaul of the tax laws affecting domicile. However, what is not in dispute is that assets which are added to an excluded property trust after the settlor has become UK domiciled will not themselves be excluded property (Revenue Interpretation 166).

An anti-avoidance rule was introduced in *Finance Act 2006* to counteract 'deathbed' IHT planning. This planning broadly involved an individual purchasing an interest in a pre-existing settlement created by a non-UK domiciled individual. Prior to 5 December 2005, a purchased interest in settled property was not precluded from being 'excluded property'. However, from that date the exemption in *IHTA 1984, s 48(3)* is removed if the interest in excluded trust property has been purchased by a UK-domiciled individual (*IHTA 1984, s 48(3B)–(3C)*).

## GWR AND DOUBLE IHT RELIEF

**5.36** As indicated at **5.2** above, the GWR rules give rise to the possibility of a double IHT charge in respect of the same property. However, there are provisions (*FA 1986, s 104*; the *Inheritance Tax (Double Charges Relief) Regulations, SI 1987/1130*) which provide for relief in those circumstances.

The regulations provide for the avoidance of a double charge in the following circumstances involving a GWR (*SI 1987/1130, reg 5*):

- an individual makes a gift caught by the GWR rules (which may be a PET or a chargeable lifetime transfer) and the property is (by reason of the GWR rules) also subject to a deemed transfer which is chargeable as a result of the transferor's death; or

- facts as above, except that the donor's benefit ends before death (ie a deemed PET under the GWR rules), which becomes chargeable on the donor's death within seven years.

In both cases, two calculations are performed as a consequence of the death:

- charging the GWR in the death estate, and ignoring the lifetime transfer (*reg 5(3)(a)*); or

- charging the lifetime transfer and ignoring the GWR (*reg 5(3)(b)*).

*Gifts with reservation of benefit* **5.38**

**5.37** Whichever transfer produces the higher amount of tax remains chargeable. In addition, provision is made for credit to be given for any lifetime tax already paid (*reg 5(4)*). See the example (**Example 5.3**) at **5.8**. In addition, the regulations include a schedule with worked examples of the double IHT relief rules as they apply to GWRs, although the examples do not prevail over the rules as stated in the regulations (*SI 1987/1130, reg 9*).

As indicated at **5.3**, the 'pre-owned assets' income tax legislation (see **Chapter 16**) also provides a measure of relief from IHT in certain very specific circumstances, where the taxpayer elects for those provisions not to apply and if two IHT charges otherwise arise on the same underlying asset value (*Charge to Income Tax by Reference to Enjoyment of Property Previously Owned Regulations, SI 2005/724, reg 6*). The double charges relief provisions effectively retain the charge on the transfer that produces the higher overall amount of IHT, and reduce the other transfer to nil.

Further provisions (*Inheritance Tax (Double Charges) Regulations, SI 2005/3441*) were designed to deal with the double charges that may arise for taxpayers who decide to dismantle a 'double trust' arrangement and return to the position they were in previously. Once again, IHT is charged on the transfer producing the greater amount of tax, with the other transfer being reduced to nil.

## GWR AND 'SHEARING' ARRANGEMENTS

**5.38** There is always a fine line to be drawn between 'shearing' and GWR. At its simplest, shearing has been described thus: if Alan owns three assets and gives two of them away, he does not reserve a benefit out of the third; he simply does not give it away.

In the context of more subtle schemes it has been suggested that it may be possible to separate capital from income, such as by a settlement in which the settlor retains a right to income but excludes himself from the possibility of benefiting from the capital. It is suggested that such a trust might invest in let property and that the settlor might receive the income stream. HMRC may consider this to be fairly aggressive tax planning: the draftsman should issue the client with a 'health warning'.

*Chapter 6*

# Compliance

## LIABILITY AND INCIDENCE OF TAX

**6.1** The difference between 'liability' and 'incidence' is similar to the difference between legal and equitable interests. Liability is the duty to pay the tax, from the assets that lie to hand. It concerns the relationship between HMRC and the accounting party. Incidence is the allocation of the burden of the tax between beneficiaries. An executor or trustee will be concerned with the rules as to incidence when administering an estate where, for example, the residue passes partly to children and partly to charity. He is liable for the tax but must apply the rules of incidence to ensure that, subject to the terms of the will and to the rules in *Re Benham's Will Trust* [1995] STC 210 and *Re Ratcliffe* [1999] STC 262, the tax is actually suffered by the children. For analysis of these decisions, see **3.37–3.38**. *Finance Act 2006* threw up some anomalies in this area: see 'A sting in the tail' at the end of **Chapter 7**.

## ACCOUNTS AND RETURNS

### Recent developments: the forms

**6.2** The main control documents:

- IHT100, the account for the lifetime transfer of value, and
- IHT400, which replaced IHT200, the HMRC Account for IHT beyond death,

are supplemented by administrative forms that apply in situations, especially on death, where an estate is of substantial size but where no tax is in fact chargeable. The forms are updated regularly, several forms having changed in the last year, so always use the most recent version, downloading from the HMRC website at www.hmrc.gov.uk. Note, however, that the simplest, free, version of *Adobe Acrobat* is 'not man enough' for the task, because you cannot save the forms mid-way through completing them and return to the task later. You must have everything ready and complete each form, correctly, in one go or start all over

*Compliance* **6.3**

again. Really, to use the website forms to best advantage, practitioners must purchase *Adobe Acrobat 9 Pro* or similar editing software: this is a fault of the website and puts smaller firms to an expense that they could well do without.

The IHT400 series takes account of common practices such as the gift of personal effects to charity, which this year is dealt with in form IHT408, which is actually a 'one-off' variation of the dispositions of the estate and as such should be read in conjunction with any other variation contemplated by the personal representatives. Extra information, which was hitherto set out in a supplemental sheet, can now fit into pages 15 and 16 of form IHT400.

Form IHT407, formerly IHT409, Household and personal goods, looks more user friendly than its predecessor but its proper completion will be much more demanding than most families will expect or enjoy.

The duty of notification on creation of offshore trusts stipulated by *s 218* should not be overlooked. Those concerned with the creation of such trusts, except barristers, must inform HMRC within three months. A letter is usually enough.

## Recent developments: a new look at compliance

**6.3** Following consultation, legislation was introduced in *Finance Act 2008, Pt 7* and *Schs 36, 37, 39* and *40*. *Finance Act 2009, s 96* and *Sch 48* extend the rules as to information and inspection powers to IHT. By *The Finance Act 2009, Section 96 and Schedule 48 (Appointed Day, Savings and Consequential Amendments) Order 2009 SI 2009/3054* this applies from 1 April 2010: see CH20150; and for a useful summary of commencement dates see the links there set out.

The general scope of the legislation is to amend the rules on record keeping and the information and inspection powers. The general thrust of the compliance checks is to reassure the majority who do comply that the system is fair and to ensure that taxpayers know what their obligations are in relation to registration for tax.

Taxpayers should understand what records are needed in order to calculate the tax due and, in the context of the administration of estates, the preparation of proper executorship accounts must come high on the list. The checks are also intended to find out where people do not understand the law and put that right; and to eradicate weaknesses in the systems and processes which are used by taxpayers, correcting mistakes and discouraging people from non-compliance.

The checks are also intended to expose deliberate understatement of tax. The whole approach is informed by what HMRC perceive to be the risk involved. On the one hand, as for example with valuation of chattels, the risk may

## 6.3 Compliance

only involve a small amount of tax each time, but errors may be widespread. Alternatively, there may be segmental risk where, for example, taxpayers in a particular category or holding a particular type of asset may exhibit behaviour leading to risk which can be addressed through work with representative bodies or trade organisations.

The new basis includes the following features:

- flexibility according to the way taxpayers behave;
- going easy on the compliant majority;
- cracking down on the minority who deliberately understate their tax;
- greater clarity and consistency across the various taxes;
- clear definitions of HMRC powers and safeguards against inappropriate use.

To some extent, none of this is all that new. The 'old' rules have not lacked teeth, as the following (non-IHT) cases show.

For example, HMRC were able to use existing legislation very effectively against the taxpayer in *Smith v HMRC* [2008] SpC 680, where the Inspector examined private bank accounts to trace credit card expenditure of £47,500 and other unexplained transfers of £410,000 from companies controlled by the taxpayer. He extrapolated backwards into (more than six) earlier years to estimate the full level of under-disclosure of tax.

In *Sokoya v HMRC* [2008] ChD STC 3332, the taxpayer complained unsuccessfully from the decision of the Special Commissioner against a request from HMRC for documents to check 'nil' entries in his return. The burden of proof to be satisfied by HMRC is not that of the criminal courts: see *HMRC v Khawaja* [2008] ChD STC 2880. The Inspector need not be clairvoyant, so the inclusion of a round sum as a loss is not sufficient notice that the taxpayer has been using a tax scheme to create an artificial loss, such that time runs against HMRC in discovering it: *Corbally-Stourton v Revenue and Customs Commissioners* [2008] STC (SCD) 907 (SpC 692).

Note, however, that the First-tier Tribunal can take a robust and practical line, as it did in *Cairns v Revenue & Customs* [2009] TC00008, an investigation into the estate of a former Chief Examiner with the Estate Duty Office. The deceased's house was in extremely poor condition and had been valued shortly before death at about £400,000. The personal representative adopted that figure in IHT200, not considering it necessary to revalue, since on sale the price achieved would very likely be substituted anyway. Following sale for £600,000, which was then agreed to be the value at date of death, HMRC pressed for penalties for delivery of an incorrect account. Fraud was not alleged; instead

HMRC alleged negligence on the basis that the personal representative should have obtained another valuation.

Not so, held the Tribunal. The account was not negligently delivered. The value specified should have been shown as provisional but that was a mere technical error which had no consequence whatsoever. There was no loss to the public purse because in fact IHT had been overpaid and was later repaid. Any finding of negligence would have been the merest technicality. A proportionate approach would have been a nominal penalty.

A detailed consideration of the legislation, which appears at *Finance Act 2008, ss 113, 115–117* and *Schs 36–37* is beyond the scope of this book, but is included in Chapter 1 of *Capital Gains Tax Annual 2010/11* (Bloomsbury Professional). In practical terms, help is being rolled out to practitioners by HMRC in the form of 'checklists' for various taxes. These follow a format that identifies significant areas of risk and suggests procedures to eliminate errors from returns. New checklists are trialled by practitioners, and the professional organisations are involved in the form and content of the checklists. Slavish adherence to each element of the list would no doubt greatly increase the time spent on compliance and the resultant cost to the client. However, examples of checklists so far released tend to show a practical approach; what many practitioners do anyway, almost without stopping to notice. Compliance with the methodical approach advocated by the checklists will be evidence of taking reasonable care to complete returns.

## Lifetime transfers

**6.4** The requirement to deliver an account of a lifetime transfer is not sufficiently well known, though HMRC have issued a reminder to the public. It is discussed at **2.25**. No account is needed of a PET but a chargeable transfer must be reported even though, being made in lifetime, seven years may elapse before the death of the transferor.

Where the transfer is immediately chargeable and not exempt from reporting under the rules described below, the account is to be delivered by the transferor. If he does not pay the IHT by the due date, other persons become liable such as donees, trustees and beneficiaries under settlements, though they do not have to deliver the account themselves. In the rare cases where a close company makes a transfer of value, it becomes liable for IHT on it, but need not deliver an account. IHT is charged as if the participators in the company had made the transfer: see *IHTA 1984, ss 94* and *202* and the commentary at **1.27** (all subsequent statutory references are to *IHTA 1984*, unless otherwise stated).

*Finance Act 2006* greatly increased the number of transactions that will be chargeable transfers, even though no immediate tax results. The present level of disclosure was revised and reduced by the *Inheritance Tax (Delivery*

### 6.5 Compliance

*of Accounts) (Excepted Transfers and Excepted Terminations) Regulations 2008 (SI 2008/605)* and the *Inheritance Tax (Delivery of Accounts) (Excepted Settlements) Regulations 2008 (SI 2008/606)*, which are discussed below.

The changes caught many taxpayers out but not (see *Marquess of Linlithgow and Earl of Hopetoun v HMRC* [2010] CSIH 19) those who acted promptly (or with prescience). That case turned on the effective date of a transfer of land under Scots law. Two transfer documents to an accumulation and maintenance trust, dispositions, were executed on 15 March 2006, so just days before the changes; but not recorded in the Register of Sasines until October and November of that year. An attempt by HMRC to treat the transfers of value as chargeable failed: Following the estate duty case of *Thomas v Lord Advocate* [1953] SC 151, the date of transfer was that of the disposition, not registration.

## Excepted transfers and terminations

**6.5** The regulations as to excepted transfers and excepted terminations came into force on 6 April 2008 and, in relation to the transactions covered by the regulations, removed the obligation to deliver an account unless HMRC served a notice requiring one. There is now a duty:

- on trustees to file an account in respect of failed PETs; and
- on trustees and others to file an account on the termination of a settlement which would have been a PET, but fails under the seven-year rule; and
- to file a return where the parties thought that the transfer was excepted within the new rules and it turns out not to be.

## Excepted transfers

**6.6** An excepted transfer under the new rules must be one by an individual and must be an actual transfer, not a deemed transfer. There are two categories.

### (a) Fixed-value transfers

Where the transfer is either cash or quoted shares or securities the transfer will be excepted if the value transferred, together with values of chargeable transfers by that transferor in the preceding seven years, do not exceed the current nil rate band.

### (b) Transfers of uncertain value

Where the transfer includes assets other than cash or quoted shares or securities the transfer is exempt where:

- its value, together with other transfers by that transferor in the preceding seven years do not exceed 80% of the nil-rate band; and
- the value transferred by this particular transfer does not exceed the nil rate band after deducting the value of all the previous chargeable transfers.

For this purpose neither BPR nor APR is to be taken into account, so to be excepted the entire value must be within the limits prescribed.

### Example 6.1—Gift of a share in a flat

Louis wishes to give his grandchildren a one-third interest in a flat in London which is let. The flat is worth £660,000. He settles the interest, which might seem to be a gift of £220,000 but for the loss to estate rule. Before the transfer his estate includes the full value; after, he has 67%, which should be discounted, say 15%, and is therefore worth £375,870. The loss to his estate is £284,130.

At a time when the nil rate band is £325,000 and the reduction is to 80%, the limit above which the transfer must be reported is £260,000. Louis' transfer must be reported; it is not £220,000, which would have been within the limit, but £284,130. Even the availability of two annual exemptions would not help here.

### Example 6.2—Generous grandfather

Harry, having used his annual exemptions, set up a series of small discretionary trusts totalling £39,500 in the years 2003–2007. Some were of cash, some of assets that have since been valued within the amounts shown. All of that was below the old filing threshold. In November 2010, he proposes to settle another £270,000 in cash and quoted securities and as before he will by then have used his annual exemption. This will bring his cumulative total to £309,500, which would have been well over the limit under the old rules.

Under the 2008 Regulations the relevant limit will be the nil rate band, ie £325,000, of which Harry still has £285,500 unused. Harry need not file an IHT100.

## Excepted terminations

**6.7** The rules as to excepted terminations apply only to 'specified' trusts, ie

- interest in possession trusts that existed before 22 March 2006;
- trusts for bereaved minors under *s 71A*;

6.8 *Compliance*

- IPDI trusts within *s 49A(1)(d)*;
- disabled persons trusts; or
- TSI trusts within *ss 49B–49E*.

The termination of an interest in possession in a trust can be a chargeable transfer, but it need not be reported in one of three circumstances described below.

## (a) Small or exempt transfers

The transfer may be small, for example within the annual exemption, and the life tenant may have served notice under *s 57(3)* that an exemption is available. If the amount of the transfer is within the specified exemption, there is no need for a return.

## (b) Nil rate band: fixed-value fund

Where the trust property is cash or quoted securities and the value of the fund in respect of which the termination takes place, and the value of transfers by the tenant for life of any other kind together are within the nil rate band, there is no need for an account.

## (c) Variable value funds

Where the trust fund does not consist wholly of cash or quoted securities there is still no need to file a return if the value of the 'termination fund' and of previous chargeable transfers by the life tenant in the previous seven years do not exceed 80% of the nil rate band.

As with the rules for excepted settlements, these termination rules take no account of APR or of BPR. The 2008 Regulations replaced those made in 2002 in relation to lifetime transfers made on or after 6 April 2007.

# Excepted settlements

**6.8** The rules as to excepted settlements reduce the filing requirements in respect of pilot trusts and small settlements. There is no need to file a return in respect of a pilot trust, ie a settlement made to UK trustees who stay in the UK of cash of £1,000 or less where there are no related settlements.

Apart from such pilot trusts the regulations have removed the obligation to file a return in respect of:

*Compliance* **6.9**

- UK trusts (which remain in the UK); by
- settlors domiciled in the UK at the time the settlement is made; who
- remain domiciled here until either the chargeable event or the death of the settlor whichever first happens; where
- there are no related settlements; and
- one of the following conditions are met.

*Extra condition 1*: from the ten-year charge. The trust is excepted where the value in the trust is not more than 80% of the nil rate band (disregarding liabilities or reliefs such as APR or BPR).

*Extra condition 2*: from the exit charge in the first ten years of the trust. The language of the *Inheritance Tax (Delivery of Accounts) (Excepted Transfers and Excepted Terminations) Regulations 2008 (SI 2008/605), reg 4(5)* is somewhat obscure, which is hardly surprising in anything dealing with the taxation of relevant property trusts, but it concerns the value that is transferred by the notional chargeable transfer which is one element of calculating the exit charge in the first ten years of the relevant property trust. For a transfer to be excepted, the calculation of value disregards liabilities or reliefs such as APR and BPR. On an exit charge in the first ten years of a relevant property trust, there is no need for a return if the value released from the trust does not exceed 80% of the nil rate band.

*Extra condition 3*: from an exit charge after the first ten-year anniversary. There is no need to file a return if the value of the transfer does not exceed 80% of the nil rate band.

*Extra condition 4*: from an exit charge from an 18-to-25 trust. There is no need for a return where the chargeable transfer is within 80% of the nil rate band.

## A trap for unwary trustees

**6.9** There is one circumstance that could easily catch trustees out. It is described in IHTM06130 and arises on the death of a transferor. Trustees may have received sums which are well within the nil rate band and may have appointed funds out, again well within the levels that are now exempt from reporting. If this is the only chargeable transfer made by the settlor, there is no problem, but if the settlor had made other transfers, such as PETs, in the seven years before death those PETs will fail on his death and there will be a 'knock-on' effect on the trust because, when seen in the context of the failed PETs, the transfers that were previously exempt from reporting must now be shown in an account. Depending on the value there might not be any extra tax to pay, but the return must be filed.

## 6.9 Compliance

**Example 6.3—Death affecting prior transactions**

Jessica gave her daughter Celia a plot of land in 2006. This was a PET, so no return was made. There was some prospect that Celia could get planning permission on the land, but she and her mother assumed that the value of the gift was £60,000. On 1 July 2009 (which is a date that is covered by the new regulations) Jessica settled £235,000 being partly cash and partly quoted securities. Seen in isolation that was an 'excepted transfer' and there was no need to report it.

On 15 May 2010, the trustees advanced £80,000 to John, a beneficiary, to help him buy a house. The settlement had been within the nil rate band on creation so there would be no exit charge under normal principles. At the time of the appointment the nil rate band is £325,000. Applying the new filing rules, 80% of that is £260,000 so an appointment that could conceivably give rise to an exit charge need not be reported under the new rules because in this example the original fund, at £235,000, is well within the reporting limits.

Jessica dies on 6 August 2010, so the PET to Celia fails. That triggers a review of the tax charges on the settlement. The effect will depend on the value finally agreed for the transfer of the land. If the value is, as claimed, £60,000, the notional aggregate of chargeable transfers goes up to £295,000. That is still within the nil rate band, so there will be no exit charge on the appointment made by the trustees, but the figures now exceed the limits in the new regulations so the trustees will have to deliver an account.

Greater difficulties will arise if it transpires that the likelihood of planning permission was so great at the time of the gift that the true value of the land was much more than £60,000. A significant increase in the valuation of the gift of the land could easily bring the tax rates applicable to the trust up to the level where an exit charge would be due on the £80,000 that was advanced to John.

Practitioners should read the detailed and useful draft guidance, with further illustrations, inserted into the IHT Manual at IHTM06100 to IHTM06130. See for example the detailed guidance on discounted gift schemes and their valuation at IHTM06105: where the discount turns out to have been claimed at too high a level, a duty to file may arise on discovery within six months.

Settlors sometimes try to get around the chargeable transfer rules using the *s 21* 'normal expenditure out of income' exemption. Under the 2008 Regulations, there is no duty to file a return if the transfers are covered by the rules as to the nil rate band; but if greater the transfers are assumed for this purpose to be chargeable, and reportable, because HMRC have not been satisfied that the exemption applies. It may do, but it must be 'shown' to; see IHTM06106.

*Compliance* **6.10**

Discovery and catch-up: a taxpayer may have thought that a transfer was outside the filing rules and realise the error later. If so, he has six months to put things right.

## Transfers on death and failed PETs

**6.10** **Chapter 1** explained how a lifetime transfer might become chargeable if death occurred within seven years, what is termed a failed PET. The primary duty to complete returns rests with the personal representatives, who owe a duty of care to complete the return to the best of their knowledge and belief, subject to a test of reasonableness. HMRC's 'Inheritance Tax: Customer Guide' contains guidance to encourage consistency between HMRC's approach to the penalty legislation for IHT (www.hmrc.gov.uk/cto/customerguide/page22.htm).

---

**Example 6.4—Accounting for a gift (and illustration of some rules)**

Joe died on 17 May 2009, leaving his estate to his daughter Emma. He had made simple, outright, cash lifetime gifts as follows:

| | |
|---|---|
| *1*: January 2002 | £20,000 to Emma |
| *2*: June 2002 | £16,000 to his son Philip |
| *3*: December 2002 | £3,000 between his grandchildren |
| *4*: December 2003 | £3,000 as before |
| *5*: December 2004 | £3,000 as before |
| *6*: May 2005 | £10,000 to the National Trust |
| *7*: December 2005 | £3,000 as before |
| *8*: December 2006 | £3,000 as before |
| *9*: May 2007 | £20,000 to Philip |
| *10*: December 2008 | £3,000 as before |

Under an enduring power of attorney in standard form (made earlier, whilst that was still possible before the changes to LPAs on 1 October 2007), Philip continued the pattern of gifts at Christmas and also made, on behalf of his father, gifts as follows:

| | |
|---|---|
| *11*: January 2008 | £15,000 (personal effects to Emma) |
| *12*: May 2009 | £25,000 between grandchildren |

The executors can claim relief under *s 21* (ie normal expenditure out of income) for all the Christmas gifts up to 2006. *Gift 1* is more than seven years before death and out of the reckoning. The writers have seen an attempt by HMRC to argue that a gift, even though made outside the seven-year period, may none

**6.11** *Compliance*

the less absorb the annual exemption for that year, leaving less to set against gifts that do fall within the seven-year period; but so far have seen no authority, in case law or statute, to support that view.

*Gift 2* enjoys, on the basis for which the writers contend, £6,000 of annual exemption, so is a failed PET of £10,000 net. It is set against the nil rate band. *Gift 6* is to a charity and exempt. *Gift 9* benefits from two annual exemptions, leaving £14,000 to go against the nil rate band.

Of the gifts under the power of attorney, those at Christmas are probably exempt both under *s 21* and because they were habitual and therefore reasonable for the attorney to continue. *Gift 11* may also have been reasonable within the terms of the power, if Joe was moving into a nursing home and the alternative was to sell the chattels.

*Gift 12* fails in every sense. It goes beyond what is reasonable under a power, unless there was specific authority, and (as it turns out) half the cheques were in fact still unpresented at the date of death and thus, not effective gifts.

---

There was a rush to complete enduring powers of attorney (EPAs) under the transitional rules by the end of September 2007 so as to escape the cost and registration requirements for lasting powers of attorney (LPAs) as now required under *Mental Capacity Act 2005*: see *MCA 2005, s 66(3)* and *Sch 4*. The processes concerning LPAs have now settled down considerably, reducing the cost. Until recently, the delays originally experienced seemed to be resolved but anecdotal evidence suggests that delays of up to 14 weeks in achieving registration are now being experienced. The power of an attorney under an LPA is more closely defined than used to be the case under an EPA: see *MCA 2005, s 12*, which provides that there is no general power to make gifts but that, subject to any express limitation in the power, the attorney may make gifts on customary occasions to persons related to or connected with the donor, including the grantee of the power; and may make certain charitable gifts. 'Customary occasion' means births, birthdays, marriage, formation of civil partnership or any other customary occasion, which allows cultural flexibility.

## Reporting lifetime transfers after death: the duty of care

**6.11** Personal representatives should enquire into the history of lifetime transfers by the deceased. How far they should pry depends on the circumstances. Having established the extent of the property remaining in the estate at death, executors should call for back statements on bank and similar accounts to check the pattern of withdrawals. They should make enquiries of relatives, professional advisors and close business colleagues. If, in the course of those enquiries, their suspicions are raised that gifts may have been made that were not disclosed by other papers of the deceased, their enquiries should

*Compliance* **6.11**

continue until they are reasonably sure that they have identified the gifts made by the deceased.

A particular problem concerns the date and nature of the gifts. In relation to 'old' gifts, their date will be material, perhaps to show that a gift was made more than seven years before death. Equally, a gift may have been made out of property that was at that time held jointly with some other person who has since died. The gift may therefore have been of only one half or some other fraction of the property given away.

Lifetime gifts may qualify for exemption under *ss 18, 19, 20, 21, 22* or *23* and following. New form IHT403 replaced form D3a and suggests a checklist of information that should be supplied. Where it is correctly completed it can save an enquiry into the return. The difficulty, which has been noted before, lies in page 6 of IHT403, which attempts to help the personal representative to claim relief under *s 21* by setting out columns for each tax year prior to the death to show the available income so that gifts may be allocated to tax years and set against the relevant income. If the deceased died on 5 April, the form works fine; but if on any other day in the year an extra column may be needed, if the deceased made gifts on a regular basis – as is implied by reliance in *s 21* anyway. As an alternative for the practitioner's own use, the following (partly completed) table may be prepared as a spreadsheet to help to calculate the amount of nil rate band available after the lifetime gifts have been brought into account on death.

---

**Example 6.5—Checking lifetime gifts**

Susan French died on 17 December 2009 having made the following lifetime gifts:

- June or July in each year: £2,000 to her niece;
- September 2002: 12,000 to her godson;
- February 2003: £10,000 to a niece;
- May 2004: £5,000 to her nephew;
- September 2005: £4,000 to a friend;
- December 2009: £1,000 (effected by her attorney, also named as her executor in her will) to each of five beneficiaries named in her will, 'to save trouble'; three of the cheques remained uncashed at the date of death.

Her income was steady, at about £30,000 per annum after tax. She lived frugally, taking a holiday (cost £3,000) only in alternate years. Her living expenses were £15,000 per annum in the 'non-holiday years'. The table, which

**6.11** *Compliance*

should be created as a spreadsheet, can be used to sort the gifts and to claim the reliefs before completing IHT400. Note that gifts that are clearly exempt need not be set out in IHT400 itself but this form ensures that none are forgotten.

| Period | Income* See note below | Gifts | Annual Exemption | s 21 Claim | Other Claims | Chargeable |
|---|---|---|---|---|---|---|
| Part year 18.12.2002 – 5.4.2003 | 4,375 | 10,000 | 6,000 | | | 4,000 |
| Year to 5.4.2004 | 12,000 | 2,000; | | 2,000 | | |
| Year to 5.4.2005 | 15,000 | 7,000 | 5,000 | 2,000 | | |
| Year to 5.4.2006 | 12,000 | 6,000 | 3,000 | 2,000 | | 1,000 |
| Year to 5.4.2007 | 15,000 | | | | | |
| Year to 5.4.2008 | 12,000 | | | | | |
| Year to 5.4.2009 | 15,000 | | | | | |
| Part year 6.4.2009 –17.12.2009 | 8,500 | None** | | | | |
| Total chargeable | | | | | | 5,000 |
| NRB unused | | | | | | 320,000 |

\* For this purpose 'income' means disposable income, so a preliminary filter or table is needed to establish the sum each year or part year that was truly available to fund gifts.

The table is an example of the situation where there are actually eight periods for consideration, as noted above. The nil rate band at date of death was £325,000. The regular gifts form part of a pattern and are exempt under s 21. The isolated gift of £12,000 in September 2002 falls entirely out of account, with the result that the annual exemption is still available for that year, and for the previous year. Therefore, the gift in February 2003 of £10,000 may be reduced by two annual exemptions leaving only £4,000 to be set against the nil rate band.

\*\*Gifts by attorneys should be examined with care. Cheques uncashed at death are not effective gifts anyway: their value is still part of the estate at death. An attorney may not make gifts over and beyond the limits set out in *Mental Capacity Act 2005*: seasonal gifts are permitted up to reasonable limits but merely accelerating bequests does not fall within that category. The value must be added back to the estate.

All of this is, it must be said, a counsel of perfection. In real life (or more properly real death) there may be formidable obstructions to the proper performance by the personal representatives of their duties. Family may be secretive, especially where one sibling knows that she has received more by way of lifetime gifts than the others. Chattels taken from the residence to avoid burglary during the funeral may somehow not be returned to be included in the inventory or probate valuation (if indeed there is one). All of this will place an extra burden on the executor who is concerned to take 'reasonable care' so as to avoid penalties.

## Normal expenditure out of income

**6.12** Claims under *s 21* (normal expenditure out of income) meet resistance from HMRC where the evidence is, frankly, thin. The taxpayer must show that:

- the gift was made of part of normal expenditure;
- it was made out of income; and
- the transferor was left with enough to live on.

Note that form IHT403 ('Gifts and other transfers of value') includes nursing home fees as an expense to be met out of income. This is consistent with the decision in *Nadin v IRC* [1997] STC (SCD) 107, but takes no account of the views expressed in *Stevenson (Inspector of Taxes) v Wishart* [1987] STC 266, where nursing home fees were substantial. The issue causes regular difficulty and is discussed at **1.20**, **2.3** and **9.8–9.9**.

It is not necessary to set gifts against the annual exemption in priority in making an *s 21* claim: thus, in the example above, where Susan made a gift in May 2004 that used up the annual exemption for that year, but she could make gifts in the following year of £3,000 and still have available £15,000 (more or less) to set against gifts in respect of which an *s 21* claim was made.

**6.13** To satisfy the test as to normal expenditure there must be:

- regularity;
- a pattern of gifts; or
- a commitment to make regular gifts; and preferably all three.

The scope for 'overs and shorts' under *s 21(1)(b)* is interpreted narrowly by HMRC. They will to some extent allow 'storing up' of income ready to make gifts but resist claims to relief based on bringing forward income from an earlier year that was not used up on gifts unless there is evidence of intention to make particular gifts. They strongly resist a claim based on averages which relies on bringing back into a year the income of a later period. The legal authority for this resistance is unclear: the legislation only requires the taxpayer to show 'that (taking one year with another) [the gift] was made out of [the taxpayer's]

**6.14** *Compliance*

income'. The leading case on the allowability of exemption under *s 21* is *Bennett v IRC* [1995] STC 54 and repays careful reading: it is more generous to the taxpayer than generally realised. Each case will turn on its own facts and on the quality of records: sadly for the executors, these are seldom complete or even available.

## Personal effects

**6.14** Another area of difficulty is personal effects, where HMRC consider that there may previously have been insufficient disclosure. The true value to be shown is governed by the market value rule in *s 160*. There is no such thing as 'probate value': the value to be disclosed is 'the price which the property might reasonably be expected to fetch if sold in the open market' at the date of death. That is the gross selling price, not the net. Here, in particular, the latest form IHT407, which replaced D10, asks much more searching questions than the forms that accompanied IHT200, even down to the registration number of the deceased's car; whether chattels that have been sold were purchased by relatives; and how the value of other chattels was arrived at.

## Estimates

**6.15** There is statutory authority in *s 216(3A)* for the use of estimates. The personal representatives must make very full enquiries but, if unable to arrive at the exact value, must:

- say that they have made full enquiries;
- supply a provisional estimate of the value; and
- undertake to deliver a further account as soon as the value is ascertained.

For an example of litigation on these issues and on the costs of the litigation itself, see *Robertson v CIR* [2002] STC (SCD) 182 and *Robertson v CIR (No 2)* [2002] SSCD 242. For a case that highlighted the duty, see *Cairns v Revenue & Customs* [2009] UKFTT 67 (TC) TC00008, noted at **6.3** above.

## EXCEPTED ESTATES

## Bare trusts

**6.16** Following *FA 2006*, there was a resurgence in the popularity of bare trusts, since these were outside the scope of the relevant property regime. As usual, some advisers went to the limit of what might be considered to be a bare trust. Perhaps in response to this, HMRC revealed that they were considering one analysis of such trusts where there was, either expressly or by implication, a duty on the trustees to accumulate the income. Such arrangements might be substantive trusts and caught by *FA 2006*. A second issue was whether the power of advancement under *Trustee Act 1925, s 32* might be used to make settled advances, which would again allow ongoing trusts of precisely the kind eschewed by *FA 2006*.

This suggestion provoked uproar among professional advisers, who considered it to be wrong in law. If such trusts are substantive trusts, their creation is a chargeable transfer and much else follows. Some of the argument turns on the effect *s 43(2)(b)* and its reference to accumulations. There is perceived to be inconsistency between the established treatment of bare trusts for income tax (see, for example, TSEM1031) and as proposed for IHT. Cautious advisers will therefore exclude *TA 1925, s 31* to weaken the suggestion that there is a substantive trust. The argument that where trustees have active duties there is a substantive trust sits ill with, for example, the position of unit trusts, where the trustees are active and which are nevertheless bare trusts.

The issue now seems to have been resolved. A bare trust of capital for a minor beneficiary is not settled property and thus cannot be relevant property. HMRC have commented:

> 'We confirm that our view is that where assets are held on an absolute trust (ie a bare trust) for a minor the assets so held will not be settled property within the meaning of section 43 IHTA 1984 and that this will be the case whether or not the provisions of section 31 Trustee Act 1925 have been excluded.'

## Transfers on death

**6.17** There are now three categories of excepted estate, see *Inheritance Tax (Delivery of Accounts) (Excepted Estates) Regulations 2004 (SI 2004/2543)*. Many practitioners fail to take advantage of the regulations, using form IHT400 (previously IHT200) where it is not needed. This is not encouraged by HMRC, because it just makes for unnecessary work that yields no tax. The reporting levels were increased by *Inheritance Tax (Delivery of Accounts) (Excepted Estates) (Amendment) Regulations 2006 (SI 2006/2141)* with effect from 1 September 2006.

## Category One: small estates: the traditional form

**6.18** The conditions are:

(1) The deceased, UK domiciled, died on or after 1 September 2006.

(2) The estate relates to property in the following categories:

- it passes under the will of the deceased or on his intestacy;

**6.19** *Compliance*

- it passes under nomination taking effect on death;
- it is contained in one settlement only in which the deceased had an interest in possession; or
- it was joint property and passes by survivorship (or in Scotland by survivorship in a special destination).

(3) Of the property passing on death:
- no more than £100,000 was situated overseas; and
- no more than £150,000 was trust property.

(4) In the seven years before death the deceased made transfers which, before deduction of business or agricultural relief, did not exceed £150,000.

(5) The whole estate, including certain categories of transfer, did not exceed the IHT threshold. Note that for this purpose the relevant threshold is the 'old' one in the period from 6 April to 6 August.

The categories of transfers referred to in this last condition are two. 'Specified transfers' are defined in *SI 2004/2543, reg 4(6)* to mean chargeable transfers in the seven years up to death consisting only of:

- cash;
- personal chattels or moveable property;
- quoted shares or securities; or
- interest in land (with qualifications).

The same regulations define 'specified exempt transfers' as those made in the seven years up to death which are exempt under one of the following headings:

- transfers between spouses;
- charities;
- political parties;
- gifts to housing association;
- gifts to maintenance funds for historic buildings;
- employee trusts.

## Category Two: estates: spouse/charity exemption

**6.19** *SI 2004/2543* created a new category of excepted estate of a gross value of up to £1 million where, after spouse or charity exemption, the estate was still within the IHT threshold. To comply with this category the following conditions must be satisfied.

(1) UK domicile, death on or after 6 April 2004.
(2) The estate to include only property passing:
- by will or on intestacy;
- under a nomination taking effect on death;
- under a single settlement of which the deceased was tenant for life; or
- joint property passing by survivorship or in Scotland by survivorship in a special destination.

(3) The estate included:
- not more than £100,000 foreign property;
- not more than £150,000 of settled property but ignoring settled property that on death passes to a spouse or to charity; and
- that in the seven years leading up to death the deceased did not make chargeable transfers other than specified transfers not exceeding £150,000 before deduction of business or agricultural relief.

(4) The estate did not exceed £1,000,000, including within that figure:
- the gross value of the estate;
- the value transferred by specified transfers;
- the value transferred by specified exempt transfers.

(5) Applying the formula A − (B + C), the total does not exceed the IHT threshold. For this purpose:
- A is the aggregate of the estate, specified transfers and the specified exempt transfers.
- B is the total value transferred on death that qualifies for exemption as passing to a spouse or charity, but subject to qualification of that rule in relation to Scotland. C is the total liabilities of the estate.

## Category Three: small foreign estates

**6.20** This category of estate is one where the deceased was never domiciled or deemed to be domiciled in the UK and the estate in the UK comprises only cash or quoted shares or securities with a total value not exceeding £150,000. Remember to state the value of worldwide estate. If below the IHT threshold, domicile is less likely to be examined in detail; there is no point.

### 6.21 *Compliance*

The personal representatives of an excepted estate are not entirely excused from supplying information. In all such cases they must complete the short form IHT205. This may in any event serve a separate function by offering some protection to beneficiaries, especially charities, because without IHT205 there might actually be no formal inventory of the estate.

## PARTICULAR COMPLIANCE POINTS
### Development value of land

**6.21** Cases such as *Prosser v IRC* (DET/1/2000) have shown that the value of land for IHT must take some, but not full, account of 'hope' value. In that particular case a plot of garden ground, in respect of which planning permission was eventually obtained, was held to be worth 25% of its ultimate value for probate purposes. The IHT Newsletter of 28 April 2006 stressed that development value must be accounted for, and that the value of a house should reflect any feature that makes it attractive to a builder or developer. If new information comes to light that enhances the value, the personal representatives should declare it, on pain of penalties for failure to do so.

Note that HMRC do now take the point that, if an asset is sold relatively soon after the death for substantially more than probate value, the personal representatives may have failed in their duty of disclosure and penalties may result. Back in the 1970s, when the return was an 'Inland Revenue Affidavit' (IRA) rather than a mere account, it was routine to get a proper 'Red Book' valuation of land before completing the IRA; that practice fell into abeyance but we may be returning to it.

### Annuities

**6.22** There will seldom be any residual value of an annuity, but where payments do continue after death, as where the annuitant dies before the end of the guaranteed period, the right to the income stream must be valued. Whilst personal representatives may value as they think fit, many will want to make use of the HMRC calculator on their website, giving a reasonable estimate of the value under *s 160*; see www.hmrc.gov.uk/cto/forms/g_annuity.pdf

### Joint property

**6.23** Property owned as joint tenants passes to the survivor by the *ius accrescendi*, without the need for a grant of representation. That does not mean, however, that no IHT is due. If the surviving joint owner is neither the spouse nor the civil partner, the value may be taxable. Form IHT400 will be appropriate, with form IHT404 annexed.

The deceased may have opened an account jointly with a child, perhaps for convenience through frailty or failing intellect. Payment of money into such an account is not necessarily a gift of half to the child: but the withdrawal of funds by the child for her own purposes will usually be a transfer for IHT and should be brought into account. HMRC explained, in IHT Newsletter for December 2006, that they look critically at accounts opened shortly before death. See also *Taylor v HMRC* [2008] SpC 704, noted at **4.19**.

## PAYMENT OF IHT

**6.24** In the past, most IHT was payable by reference to death. The position has probably changed somewhat following the rules introduced by *FA 2006*, which caused many settlements to migrate from the regime under which most transfers were exempt into the 'mainstream' regime of exit charges and periodic charges. It remains to be seen whether taxpayers, as in the past, will order their affairs so as to avoid the 'mainstream' charges.

### Lifetime transfers

**6.25** Hitherto most transfers, by number and possibly by value, have been PETs, so that tax on them would arise only if they failed. The 'top-up' charge that arises on the failure of a PET is charged, see *s 199(1)*, on:

- the transferor;
- the transferee whose estate is increased by the transfer;
- the recipient of the property in whom it is vested, whether for his own benefit or not, at any time after the transfer;
- anyone enjoying an interest in possession in the transfer;
- anyone for whose benefit the property or its income is applied where the property has become settled.

**6.26** First in line is the person liable but, if he does not pay the tax, *s 204* makes the personal representatives liable. That can cause a real problem for executors, who may not know the full facts. HMRC indicated, in a letter dated 13 March 1991 to the Law Society, that they will not normally pursue personal representatives who have made the fullest enquiries that are reasonably practicable to discover lifetime transfers and have done all they can to make full disclosure and have obtained the certificate of discharge and have distributed the estate before a chargeable transfer comes to light.

There is a special rule for woodlands: see *s 208*.

*6.27 Compliance*

## Due date: lifetime transfers

**6.27** This is normally six months from the end of the month in which the transfer takes place. In relation to failed PETs, it is six months after the month in which the death occurred: see *s 226(3A)*, but with special rules where a lifetime transfer is made between 5 April and October in any year.

## Payment by instalments

**6.28** The tax may be paid by ten equal yearly instalments on 'qualifying property' where certain conditions apply. 'Qualifying property' means:

- land;
- shares or securities within *s 228*; or
- business or an interest in a business.

The conditions are:

- the transfer is made on death; or,
- the tax is being paid by the person who benefits from the transfer; or
- the transfer comes within the settled property regime, which will be more common in future, and either the tax is being borne by the beneficiary or the property is staying in the settlement.

That would seem to exclude the transfers currently under discussion, arising on failed PETs but actually the instalment option is available, see *s 227(1C)*, where:

- the property was owned by the transferee from the date of the transfer to the death of the transferor (or if earlier of a transferee); or
- the charge arises under clawback of APR or BPR following the death of the transferor.

## 'Section 228' shares

**6.29** Four categories of shares or securities of a company qualify for the instalment option:

- shares giving control;
- unquoted shares where at least 20% of the tax chargeable on the value transferred is tax for which the person paying the tax attributable is liable

in the same capacity and is tax attributable to the value of the shares or securities or other tax qualifying for instalment relief under *s 227*;

- unquoted shares where the tax cannot be paid without undue hardship; and

- other shares neither giving control nor unquoted but where the value of the transfer is over £20,000 and the shares are at least 10% of the nominal value of all the shares in the company at that time, or they are ordinary shares and their nominal value is at least 10% of the nominal value of all the ordinary shares of the company at that time.

## Interest

**6.30** Interest is added to each instalment, running from the date at which the instalment is payable except, see *s 234(2)*, for special rules for certain securities dealing companies.

## Loss of the instalment option

**6.31** Curiously, payment of more than the instalment currently due can cause the loss of the instalment option. If it suits the taxpayer to pay extra at any time, the extra should be sent under cover of a separate letter as money to be put on deposit pending the due date for payment. The right to pay by instalment belongs to the beneficiary, who can claim against an executor or trustee who pays the money too early.

The executor is in a difficulty both ways, because if he releases property to the beneficiary in advance of payment of the tax he remains liable: see *Howarth's Executors v IRC* [1997] STC (SCD) 162, where a lawyer was fixed with liability for tax on property that he had released to the beneficiaries who subsequently let him down.

## The Inland Revenue charge

**6.32** Where tax charged on the value of a chargeable transfer is unpaid *s 237(1)* imposes a charge in favour of HMRC on the relevant property. It is known by statute as the 'Inland Revenue charge', see *s 237(1)*, rather than the 'HMRC charge'. The rules were updated by *s 237(3C)* in relation to certain specialised forms of charge.

## Payment of IHT on death

**6.33** The personal representatives are liable and the tax is treated as part of the administration expenses of the estate. The *Administration of Estates*

**6.34** *Compliance*

*Act 1925* sets out the order in which the tax is charged against the assets in the estate. That rule is limited by *s 211* to the value of property in the UK that vests in the personal representatives of the deceased and was not comprised in a settlement immediately before the death. There are rules for recovery of tax where property is vested in another person.

## IHT direct payment scheme

**6.34** Since 31 March 2003 and by arrangement between HMRC and certain financial institutions, it has been possible for personal representatives to access funds in the name of the deceased before the grant of representation issues. This is a great help because tax must be paid 'up front' on all property except what qualifies for the instalment option. Where, for example, a dispute about the will prevents the issue of a grant of representation, this facility still allows the tax to be paid, stopping interest from running.

The scheme is voluntary, so check with the financial institution whether they participate. Sadly, not all banks do. It applies only to accounts in the sole name of the deceased and, if the deceased has several accounts, the institution will not release more than the net value (ie after setting off overdrafts or credit card liabilities). The number of the account must be nominated on the form. Use form IHT423 for each financial institution from which the personal representatives wish to take money to pay the tax.

## Acceptance of property in lieu of tax

**6.35** This is a specialist topic, but in outline it is possible to offer heritage property in satisfaction of tax liabilities. It must be of outstanding quality. The procedure is protracted, but it does secure for the nation valuable objects that might otherwise have been sold to overseas buyers to pay tax. As an incentive, the taxpayer receives a credit that slightly exceeds the net of tax commercial value of the item. This is known somewhat archaically as the 'douceur' (under a tax law rewrite it would perhaps become 'cashback').

## PENALTIES

## A new (and tougher) approach

**6.36** Another part of the consultation on the modernising of powers, deterrents and safeguards was the reform of penalties. Whereas other aspects of the modernisation did not specifically concern IHT, as was noted at **6.3** above, IHT is included in *Finance Act 2008, ss 122–123* and *Sch 40*. The intention of the new legislation was described during the HMRC consultation

*Compliance* **6.36**

as being to influence behaviour, to be effective and to be fair. There are five areas of concern:

- incorrect returns;
- failure to notify a new taxable activity;
- late filing and late payment;
- record keeping and information powers failures; and
- other regulatory failures.

The legislation in *Finance Act 2008* is not the end of this particular story. It concerns failure to notify and understatement and does not fully address the issue of the failure to submit returns at all. The structure of the legislation is to amend *Finance Act 2007, Sch 24. Finance Act 2008, Sch 40, para 1(4)* extends the existing schedule of taxes affected so as to include for IHT purposes accounts under *IHTA 1984, ss 216* and *207*, information or documents required by *IHTA 1984, s 256* and statements or declarations in connection with deductions, exemptions or reliefs. Beyond that, draft legislation that was the subject of further consultation was included in *Finance Act 2009, s 106* to impose penalties for late filing and, as a separate matter in *Finance Act 2009, s 107*, to penalise late payment of tax.

In IHT situations, there is often shared responsibility for information gathering. The most obvious example concerns lifetime gifts.

The penalty rules for inaccuracies generally apply for IHT purposes in respect of the following (*see The Finance Act 2008, Schedule 40 (Appointed Day, Transitional Provisions and Consequential Amendments) Order 2009 SI 2009/571*):

- documents relating to periods commencing from 1 April 2009, for which the filing date is on or after 1 April 2010; and
- relevant documents produced under regulations under *s 256* ('Regulations about accounts etc' ), where the date of death is on or after 1 April 2009.

The examples that follow are framed as if the new rules applied to them.

---

**Example 6.6—A difficult estate to administer**

Philip had led a long and colourful life. A liaison with a nurse whilst he was at medical school produced a daughter, Alice. He paid for her upkeep for a few years before leaving the UK to practise medicine in Africa, where his first marriage brought him a son, Brian, and daughter, Celia. That marriage ended in divorce and in middle age he returned to the UK to work as a shop fitter

## 6.36 *Compliance*

in the pharmaceutical industry, specialising mainly in transactions that were settled in cash. The length and bitterness of his divorce was exacerbated (or perhaps caused) by a relationship with Dorothy, with whom Philip lived until his death.

Philip's will was prepared whilst he was still in Africa and named two of his then colleagues as executors. The terms of the will were affected by the *Law Reform (Succession) Act 1995*, in that they took effect as if the former wife had died on the date of decree absolute, but the rest of the will was still valid and made no provision for Dorothy.

In his last years, Philip sought some reconciliation with each of his children, in particular Alice who had followed him into the medical profession and who (she said) cared for him in his latter years. His mental powers were failing; he signed an enduring power of attorney in favour of Alice. By the time of his death serious difficulties had arisen between Alice, Brian, Celia and Dorothy. The estate was complicated, involving assets in Africa and in the UK and serious issues arose as to whether certain gifts had or had not been made and whether, at the time of gifts, Philip had had capacity to make them.

The executors in Africa face very significant difficulties in discharging their obligation under *IHTA 1984, s 216* to deliver an account that specifies all the appropriate property and its value.

This situation is addressed by *paragraph 1A* inserted into *Finance Act 2007, Sch 24*. Most of the schedule centres on the obligations of a person identified in *para 1(1)* of the schedule as P. The penalties in *para 1A* concern a different person, T, and address the situation where the inaccuracy in the return made by P is attributable to false information that is deliberately supplied, either directly or indirectly to T or where T deliberately withholds information from P.

The inaccuracy is one which results in:

- an understatement by P of the liability to tax; or
- a false or inflated statement of a loss (which would not normally apply to IHT though debts at death have a similar effect); or
- a false or inflated claim to repayment of tax.

Thus, in the example of Philip the obligations would be shared by the executors and the family and if, for example, it transpired that Philip had made a substantial gift to Alice which Alice kept quiet about, the burden would lie on Alice.

## Degrees of culpability

**6.37** *Finance Act 2007, Sch 24* had already set out the new classifications, but the wording is tidied up by the amendments in *Finance Act 2008, Sch 40*.

Penalties may arise if 'reasonable care' has not been taken in preparing an IHT account or excepted estate return, or if any inaccuracy is discovered but reasonable steps are not taken to inform HMRC about it. HMRC consider that personal representatives will have taken reasonable care in the following circumstances (see HMRC Inheritance Tax and Trusts Newsletter, April 2009):

- The PRs follow the guidance provided about filling in forms such as the IHT400 and IHT205/207/C5.
- They make suitable enquiries of asset holders and other people (as suggested in the guidance) to establish the extent of the deceased's estate.
- They ensure correct instructions are given to valuers when valuing assets.
- They seek advice about anything of which they are unsure.
- They follow up inconsistencies in information they receive from asset holders, valuers and other people.
- They identify any estimated values included on the form.

If the PRs leave the account or return to an agent, they are nevertheless required to check the entries carefully. Merely signing a form completed by an agent is not reasonable care.

The penalty regime identifies three categories of behaviour that can give rise to penalties for an inaccuracy in an account or return:

- The lowest level of culpability, described as 'careless', is where the taxpayer fails to take reasonable care in completing the return.
- The 'middle' level of culpability is 'deliberate but not concealed' where the return is wrong and it results from the deliberate action of the taxpayer, but the taxpayer makes no arrangements to conceal the inaccuracy.
- Finally, the most serious level of wrongdoing is that which is 'deliberate and concealed' where the taxpayer has deliberately sent in a wrong return and deliberately tries to conceal the parts of the return that are wrong, for example by submitting false eviden ce in support of false figures.

When it turns out that a return was inaccurate, the taxpayer will be treated as careless, even though he may not have been at the time of the return if he

**6.38** *Compliance*

discovers the inaccuracy some time later and does not take reasonable steps to inform HMRC.

In this summary of the law, the word 'return' has been used but the rules apply in the much wider context of documents that, whether or not returns, fix the liability to tax.

## The level of penalties

**6.38** These maximum levels were established by *Finance Act 2007, Sch 24*, but their scope is extended by *Finance Act 2008*:

- The 30% rate: a penalty of 30% of the potential lost revenue applies where the taxpayer was careless.
- The 70% rate: a penalty of 70% applies where the action of the taxpayer was deliberate but not concealed.
- The 100% rate: a penalty of 100% applies where the action of the taxpayer was deliberate and concealed. This can apply in two circumstances. Under *Finance Act 2007, Sch 24, para 4(C)* the full penalty could apply to 'deliberate and concealed action'. That penalty still stands but is extended to cover 'third party' acts such as might apply to the family of Philip in **Example 6.6** above. The collection of tax lost through third-party inaccuracy is extended by *Finance Act 2008, Sch 40, para 5*, so that it includes any inaccuracy that results from the supply of false information or the withholding of information.

The penalty regime in *Finance Act 2007, Sch 24* did not previously apply to IHT, so specialists in that area of practice may not have become familiar with the scheme of that schedule. In a situation where there are various errors, such as could easily apply in the administration of an estate, careless inaccuracies are corrected before deliberate inaccuracies; and deliberate but not concealed inaccuracies are corrected before deliberate and concealed inaccuracies. In calculating the lost tax, account is taken of any overstatement in any document given by the taxpayer that relates to the same tax period.

---

**Example 6.7—Too casual an approach to compliance**

Henry, a widower whose late wife had used her nil rate band, died on 24 April 2010, leaving a house, a share in an investment partnership and personal effects. There were no liabilities, Henry having taken out funeral costs insurance. His son John as sole executor knew that Henry had always used his annual exemption and was aware of lump-sum gifts of £70,000. John completed IHT400 thus:

|  |  £ |
| --- | --- |
| house | 313,000 |
| partnership share | 100,000 |
| personal effects | 12,000 |
| gifts | 70,000 |
|  | 495,000 |
| less nil rate band | 325,000 |
| taxable | 170,000 |
| tax liability | 68,000 |

John had been in a hurry to get a grant of probate, anxious to catch the property market before his father's house fell in value. He did not get a professional valuation. He did not use the 'estimates' box in the return. He thought he knew property prices in the area. Actually, it turned out that an area of land to the side of the house had realistic prospect of development and that, if sold separately, with the benefit of planning permission, it might realise £100,000 without taking any value off the house. Applying the valuation rule in *Prosser v IRC*, this added £25,000 to the estate and £10,000 to the tax liability.

It also transpired that the investment partnership had made certain losses in respect of which it was entitled to a refund of tax, so £20,000 would be added to the value of the estate when the returns were settled. John told HMRC as soon as he had the right figures. No business relief was available in respect of the investment partnership, so this added £8,000 to the eventual liability.

John knew that his father had given his sister, Sarah, the family yacht, some eight or nine years before his death. It had then been worth £30,000. John had not the slightest interest in sailing and had never been concerned with the arrangement between his father and his sister, and assumed that the gift need not be disclosed because it was outside the seven-year period. He did know that his father continued to sail with his daughter, but it never occurred to him that that might constitute a reservation of benefit out of the gift within *Revenue Interpretation 55*. Sarah complained occasionally that she had to bear all the costs of running the boat whilst her work as a matrimonial lawyer prevented her from taking time off to sail, whereas her father in retirement made extensive use of the vessel. When the reservation of benefit point was raised in correspondence on another aspect of the estate, John immediately realised that there was a problem and disclosed the gift.

John was less forthcoming about the cheques that he had signed in his capacity as attorney for his father. For the last four years of his father's life, acting under an enduring power of attorney which had not been registered despite his father's failing powers, John had regularly drawn off £1,000 per month into a separate account and had used the money towards the cost of

**6.38** *Compliance*

his children's education. He thought that the gifts would be covered by *IHTA 1984, s 21* relief for normal and reasonable expenditure of the deceased, even though the gifts went well beyond what John had power to make under (what was then) *Enduring Powers of Attorney Act 1985, s 3(5)*. It was only when HMRC called for copy bank statements that the £48,000 of gifts were discovered and even then John offered a number of implausible reasons that the sums should not be taxable. Adding them back to the estate increased the tax liability by £19,200.

The valuation error was careless. It was held in *Robertson v CIR* [2002] STC (SCD) 182 that a material understatement of value did not trigger penalties, but in that case the executor had indicated in the return that the value was an estimate and was therefore, in *Robertson v CIR (Number 2)* [2002] SSCD 242, able to recover handsomely from HMRC. In the present case, a penalty of up to £3,000 arises because the error is not simply the difference between one person's view of a value and that of another; there is a fundamental error in the basis of valuation which would have been avoided if John had been in less of a hurry and had obtained a proper valuation in the first place.

The restatement of value of the partnership interest probably does not attract a penalty at all. John showed the value of the partnership as he understood it at the date of death, and it is only after some negotiation with another branch of HMRC that the tax refund materialises. John has disclosed the change as soon as aware of it, so it is simply a case of paying the tax and interest, but not a penalty.

John did not disclose the reservation of benefit in connection with the boat, which was careless because he should have thought about the issue and the form of the return contains ample prompts on the issue. Sarah has made no secret of the fact that her father has had some benefit from the boat that he has given away, so she is not to blame. Tax is chargeable subject to negotiation as to value, remembering the option of HMRC to treat the gift as a chargeable transfer or to treat it as part of the estate at death. Where an asset falls in value, HMRC will probably prefer to treat the gift as a failed PET and tax the value at the time of the gift. On that basis, there is extra tax of £12,000 to find and the penalty could be another £4,000, subject as below.

In relation to the school fees, John's action is deliberate and concealed, so the penalty (subject to the observations below) is 100% of the tax: an extra £19,200.

*Finance Act 2007, Sch 24, para 6* requires an initial calculation of the careless inaccuracies, here the £10,000 on the valuation issue and possibly the £8,000 in respect of the business. Next in gravity comes the £12,000 on the boat and finally the £19,200 on the school fees. As to mitigation, see below.

## Reduction in penalties for disclosure

**6.39** The scheme of *Finance Act 2007, Sch 24, para 9* is to set bands of penalties and to allow some reduction within the band but, which is an important departure from previous practice, not total reduction in the more serious cases. *Paragraphs 9* to *12* of *Sch 24* are updated by *Finance Act 2008, Sch 40 paras 9 to 11*. There are reductions in penalties where a person, including a third party, discloses inaccuracy in a tax document. This may be by simply telling HMRC about the situation; or giving HMRC reasonable help to quantify the inaccuracy; or giving HMRC access to records to enable the inaccuracy to be corrected.

Where the disclosure is made by the taxpayer at a time when he has no reason to believe that HMRC have discovered or are about to discover the inaccuracy, that disclosure is classified as 'un-prompted'. The effect of this is that an un-prompted disclosure of a careless error can reduce the penalty to nil. Applying the example of John's estate, the revaluation of the business following the obtaining of the tax refund, if disclosed promptly, may avoid a penalty entirely.

## Mitigation of 30% penalties

**6.40** Where the disclosure is prompted, a careless error, attracting a penalty of 30%, may be reduced, but not below 15%. The error by John in valuing his father's house was careless. If he notified HMRC as soon as he discovered that the property was significantly more valuable than he thought, that might be treated as an unprompted disclosure. However, the mechanism of valuation in deceased estates relies on disclosure which in turn includes answering the question whether the property is to be offered for sale. The value of the property is routinely referred to the Valuation Office. If it is known that a property is to be sold within a reasonably short time of the death, then it is quite common for the gross sale proceeds to be taken as the value at the date of death. There is scope for arguing that John, in **Example 6.7** above, merely put forward an opinion of the value of the property that turned out to be wrong and that he was, in effect, disclosing as part of the estate whatever price would eventually be received on sale, on the basis that the sale price would be substituted for the valuation. However, that is a weak argument and by his carelessness John has certainly risked a penalty of at least £1,500.

## Mitigation of 70% penalties

**6.41** Where the action of the taxpayer was deliberate but not concealed the starting point for penalties is 70% but it may be reduced, see *Finance Act 2007, Sch 24, para 10(3)*, down to a minimum of 20%. The mitigation will depend on the 'quality' of the disclosure, which is defined by *Finance Act 2007, Sch 24, para 9(3)* as including timing, nature and extent.

**6.42** *Compliance*

In the case of Henry's estate in the example above the failure to disclose the gift with reservation was careless, but it was not actually concealed. It was not unprompted. It arose only from the detailed correspondence on the administration of the estate. Had John volunteered details of the gift, the penalty could have been reduced to 20% but under *Finance Act 2007, Sch 24, para 10(4)* a penalty that is otherwise chargeable at 70% cannot be reduced below 35%. On the face of it, therefore, John is at risk of a penalty of £4,200 in respect of the boat.

## Mitigation of 100% penalties

**6.42** Similar, but sharper rules apply to errors that fall into the 100% regime. Where disclosure is unprompted the minimum penalty is 30%, but where the disclosure arises only after HMRC have raised questions the penalty cannot be less than 50%. In relation to the undisclosed, unauthorised transfers to pay school fees from Henry's estate John has done nothing much to help HMRC. He did finally supply copies of his father's bank statements, but only after he had been asked a couple of times. He attempted to 'explain away' the payments. He will be lucky to escape with a penalty of much less than £18,000.

There is facility for 'special reduction' of a penalty in *Finance Act 2007, Sch 24, para 11* if HMRC think it right to reduce a penalty because of 'special circumstances', but that does not include inability to pay, nor the fact that the increased liability of one taxpayer may reduce the liability of another.

There is a 100% cap on penalties, introduced by *Finance Act 2008, Sch 40, para 11(3)* which inserts the limitation into *Finance Act 2007, Sch 24, para 12*. This is necessary where, for example, a penalty could be charged against both the taxpayer and a third party. Thus, in the example of Henry's estate if Sarah had kept quiet about her father's use of the boat and John had been careless about the issue of reservation of benefit, a penalty could apply to both of them but either way it would not exceed 100% of the tax in issue.

## Failure to file

**6.43** A penalty of £100 applies for failure to deliver an account on time, and is now regularly claimed (*s 245(2)*). A further penalty of not more than £60 per day may be claimed, though this is much less common. This is per day of default running from the day on which the failure to deliver the account has been declared as a default, either by a court or by the Special Commissioners. The daily charge runs up to the day on which the account is delivered. Usually, HMRC will give notice of an action to seek penalties so the taxpayer has one last chance to comply.

The penalty is not imposed where the taxpayer can show reasonable excuse. The procedure involves the simple completion of a form setting out the circumstances, but the penalty will be charged unless the taxpayer delivers the account without unreasonable delay after the excuse has ceased: see *s 245(7)*. The mere fact that the estate is complicated is not itself a factor: there must be some other element.

---

**Example 6.8—Late filing of return**

Josiah's estate comprised his many business interests, investments and properties, all in the UK. His will appointed as executors his daughter, who had worked in the businesses with her father; and his friend, who was qualified as a registered trust and estate practitioner. Josiah died on 1 September 2009 and the normal filing date under *IHTA 1984, s 216(6)(a)* for form IHT400 was therefore 12 months from the end of the 'death month' ie 30 September 2010.

The account was late. It seemed for a time that, by a codicil, Josiah's estranged wife might be appointed executrix, but the difficulty was resolved by 7 May 2010 without her having to act. Had she become an executrix, she could have argued, under the 'three-month' rule in *s 216(6)(a)*, that time did not run against her until appointed, but: (a) she did not act anyway; and (b) the executors as a body are jointly liable for penalties, so the daughter and friend had no excuse. The size and complication of the estate are not excuses *per se*: the daughter knew all about the assets and the TEP had the specialist knowledge to deal with the account.

---

Where the failure relates to non-resident trustees the risk is perceived to be higher and the penalties greater. The rules as to disclosure are in *s 218* and failure to make a return may trigger a penalty of up to £300 plus £60 per day of default (*s 245A*).

Penalties will not be claimed from a deceased person who had not been compliant, but that in no way exonerates delinquent personal representatives. HMRC Enquiry Manual, at EM1395 confirms this: 'Where an error or failure offence has occurred after the date of death in respect of the deceased's estate and this offence is attributable to the personal representatives you should seek to impose a penalty on the personal representatives.' The Compliance Handbook, at CH402000 adds:

> 'If a penalty assessment, raised prior to a person's death, remains under appeal then negotiations to conclude any appeal must continue with personal representatives.'

# Incorrect returns

**6.44** The penalties for failure to make returns are modest by comparison with those where incorrect information is supplied. Under *s 247(4)*, any person

**6.45** *Compliance*

assisting in the production of an account that he knows to be incorrect is liable to a penalty of up to £3,000. The person who actually makes the return wrongly may be liable for a penalty of up to 100% of the tax in issue, where the inaccuracy is both deliberate and concealed. If that person makes the return, but is not himself liable for the tax he may still be liable to a penalty of up to £3,000.

As an historic guide, errors were prevalent in completing form D4 (joint property). About 10% of forms IHT200 merited detailed examination. Form D10 (chattels) was often a fruitful source of enquiry for HMRC. These forms have been replaced by IHT404, IHT400 and IHT407 respectively, but the pattern of enquiry is likely to continue.

**6.45** It is in the nature of probate work that the full story does not emerge immediately. That is recognised, see **6.15** above, in the provisions for the use of estimates. It is also recognised by HMRC in connection with the delivery of an account which turns out to be wrong. Errors must be put right without 'unreasonable delay': see *ss 217* and *248(1)*. If not, the person liable to deliver the account suffers the same penalty as someone who delivers an account negligently. Correction may be made on form C4 but, if there are a number of small changes and the overall value is not significant, the changes can be dealt with by correspondence.

As a rule of thumb Inland Revenue Capital Taxes, as they then were, at their Open Day in 2000, suggested that penalties could be avoided by putting errors right quickly. 'Quickly' means within six months in relation to accounts and within 30 days in relation to other information and documents. Where an error arises which, on correction, generates £1,000 or more of tax, the error should be notified immediately.

The pre-*FA 2007* rules as to calculation and mitigation of penalties allow practitioners to negotiate mitigation of the penalty by up to 30% for disclosure, up to 40% for cooperation and up to 40% in respect of seriousness (ie size and gravity), but all that changes for inaccuracies in returns for periods covered by the new rules described in this chapter.

## Interest

**6.46** Traditionally, probate lawyers never worried much about interest on IHT. It was regarded as a normal expense of administration and the work would be done as and when the lawyer got round to it. Until the changes in *Finance Act 2009, s 100, s 101(1)* and *Sch 53* the level at which interest was charged on IHT was less than the charge in respect of other taxes. That helped advisers, but personal representatives and beneficiaries are much less tolerant of this easygoing attitude on the part of lawyers now. Clients are aware of the due dates and expect lawyers to administer estates more promptly to mitigate the burden of interest. It can be avoided by the use of the direct payment scheme mentioned at **6.34** above. Under *Finance Act 2009, s 101(1)* the rate applies to any tax, so the rate of interest for IHT is aligned with that for other taxes and will track Bank of England Base Rate. The new rules also set the late payment start dates for certain IHT instalments (ie under *IHTA 1984, ss 227, 229*). In consultation the professional bodies argued that the same rate should apply to repayments as to late payments, but the government have rejected that idea.

Interest is inevitable where payment of the tax itself is made by instalments. Where tax and interest arise on death, *s 233(1)(b)* charges interest from the end of six months beginning with the end of the month in which the death occurred. There are special rules in relation to specialised forms of property. Interest charged by HMRC is not allowable as a deduction in calculating any income profits or losses for any tax purposes.

That, however, is different from the situation where the executors have taken out a loan specifically in order to pay IHT (ie where they have not used the direct payment scheme). Where a specific loan account is taken out (not merely an overdraft) the interest for the first year may be deductible in calculating the income tax liability of the executors (*ITA 2007, s 403*). This facility relates only to the initial loan to fund the tax payable before a grant of representation can issue and does not relate to any further loans taken out by the personal representatives at any other time.

## Suspension of penalties

**6.47** The new penalty regime will include an 'enabling' facility to encourage better compliance, where the error in a return is careless, but results from a faulty procedure or misunderstanding on the part of the taxpayer that can be put right. Penalties can be suspended where, by notice under *Finance Act 2007, Sch 24, para 14*, HMRC specify the action to be taken and the period for which it must be taken. This is unlikely to apply to family members who act as executor.

## Shifting the blame onto the adviser

**6.48** It has long been the complaint of taxpayers that 'I left it to the accountant/solicitor/adviser to get the forms right.' The prevalent reluctance of taxpayers either to pay tax or to give sufficient time to form filling suggests that sometimes such a complaint is unjustified, but *Finance Act 2007, Sch 24, para 18(3)* only exonerates the taxpayer who can show that he took reasonable care to avoid inaccuracy or unreasonable failure.

*6.49 Compliance*

## Penalties for late payment

**6.49** *Finance Act 2009, s 106, Sch 56* introduces a more sophisticated penalty regime to tackle the issue of late payment. No doubt it will mainly affect 'ordinary' taxpayers more than trusts and estates, but the regime will be tougher. Where, as for IHT, the obligation to file is occasional rather than annual, the regime will provide:

- 5% of the tax penalty one month after the filing date;
- 5% more at six months;
- 5% more at 12 months; but
- suspension where the taxpayer agrees an arrangement for time to pay (though that does not apply to IHT, being inappropriate).

For a tax on capital, where there may be little liquidity, these are serious amounts of extra money to find.

## Penalties for late filing

**6.50** *Finance Act 2009, s 105, Sch 55* applies penalties simply for late filing, something that has hitherto been almost routine in probate work. For IHT the new rules will be:

- £100 straight after the due date;
- £10 for each day that the failure to submit a return continues, for up to 90 days (but only if HMRC 'decide' that the penalty should be payable and issue a notice to that effect;
- 5% of the tax due (or £300, if greater) for prolonged failure (ie at six months);
- 5% more (or £300, if greater) at 12 months;
- 70% of the tax due where a person fails to submit a return for over 12 months and has deliberately withheld information that HMRC need to assess the tax due; and
- 100% where there has been concealment.

The latter two tax-based penalties are subject to potential reduction for disclosure. It remains to be seen how the new regime will work. Not all families are full of impatient, needy or grasping relatives; some are capable of finer feelings. It is not uncommon for family to be so affected by bereavement that there is a delay before the formalities of probate are even approached, let alone tackled. Where the estate is complex, these new penalties in effect force the family to begin the task of gathering information with what may feel like unseemly haste.

# RECORD KEEPING

**6.51** The absence of records can be a major headache for personal representatives. Specific instances have already been described at **6.8** where the executors have a duty to notify HMRC of events of which they have had no personal knowledge before taking office. It is of course good practice for any person who has an estate that may on his death become taxable to maintain personal records of gifts etc in a form that will be intelligible to the personal representatives. That has become more important as many more transfers have been treated as chargeable since 22 March 2006.

Capital taxation long enjoyed a separate and more relaxed compliance regime than now applies, for example under self-assessment. However, the information-gathering powers of HMRC are just as strict as the corresponding provisions under self-assessment. There is power to require information under *s 219*, to call for documents under *s 219A* and to inspect property under *s 220*.

Practitioners will usually keep probate and trust files for a very long time. In relation to trusts the papers will be kept because of the ongoing nature of the matter and because of the record-keeping requirements under self-assessment. In relation to estates, it is not uncommon that queries will arise some time later, for example where assets have been appropriated to beneficiaries *in specie* and where the probate value has not been notified to the beneficiary or, if it has, the beneficiary has lost the record. The value for tax purposes at which the beneficiary acquired the asset will normally be its probate value under the rule in *TCGA 1992, s 274* (where the value was 'ascertained' for IHT).

*Finance Act 2008, Sch 37* contains new obligations as to record keeping, but they do not affect IHT. There were proposals for this in the recent consultation but the professions doubted the validity of a proposal for documents to be kept for two years from the date of preparation of returns because (a) the time limit did not sit easily with others; and (b) most papers were retained anyway, so there was no need to legislate. Budget Note 89 to the Budget 2009 confirmed that in the light of these comments the government will not pursue the idea of special record-keeping requirements for IHT, so we are left with the more general rules in *Finance Act 2009, Sch 50*.

# DETERMINATIONS AND APPEALS

## Procedure

**6.52** In practice, the issue of a Notice of Determination will rarely come as a surprise to the taxpayer. After the usual examination of a return and correspondence about matters such as value, a disagreement as to treatment will

**6.53** *Compliance*

arise where the positions of HMRC and the taxpayer are so far apart that they cannot be reconciled. There is a review procedure, under which the taxpayer may ask for the HMRC file to be passed to a separate officer to consider the issues in dispute: see **6.59** below. This can result in agreement without formal proceedings, so it should be tried.

**Example 6.9—Progress of a dispute with HMRC (I)**

John Davis was an engineer working in the Middle and Far East. At the age of 45 he returned to his native East Anglia and purchased a smallholding. Adjoining the house were a range of farm buildings and 50 acres of land which he put to profitable use. He kept sheep and poultry. In later life he discontinued the poultry operation because it was no longer profitable. Age and infirmity eventually forced him to take on help with the flock, which he sold to a neighbour who continued to graze them on his land on an arrangement which, if it had been reduced to writing, would have been more like a partnership or contracting agreement than a tenancy or licence. Those farm buildings that had not fallen into disrepair were used partly by his grandson for the repairing of vehicles but otherwise for the management of what remained of the farming business. There was some development value on part of the land.

Following his death his executors claimed that the house, buildings and land were a farm and that agricultural relief should be available on the entirety. Mindful of the recent decision in *McCall v Revenue and Customs Commissioners* [2008] STC (SCD) 752, it was agreed that no business relief would be available, but the claim to agricultural relief was pursued.

HMRC quoted *Re Antrobus (No 2)* [2005] Lands Tribunal DET/47/2004: buildings used for car repairs are not occupied for the purposes of agriculture. They were willing to allow agricultural relief on the land, and on one of the farm buildings, but not on the house, nor on the remainder of the property because, in affect, the deceased had given up farming some years before he died. His residence was merely a house with land rather than a farm. Correspondence ensued: see below.

## The form of the notice

**6.53** There is some latitude: it can include:

- the date of the transfer;
- the value transferred;
- the value of any property to which the value transferred relates;
- the transferor;

*Compliance* **6.57**

- the tax chargeable;
- the person liable to tax or part of it;
- the amount that anyone has overpaid tax and the date from which that overpaid tax carries interest;
- 'any other matter that appears to the Board to be relevant for the purposes of [*IHTA 1984*]'.

The notice specifies a time limit for appeal and the way in which the appeal can be made. Essentially, this makes the taxpayer decide exactly what to appeal against and why. That appeal is covered by *s 222* and must be made within 30 days by notice in writing given to the Board. Since 1 April 2009, appeals have normally proceeded to the Lower-tier Tax Tribunal.

**6.54** Under the new appeals process introduced by the *Tribunals, Courts and Enforcement Act 2007* there is a primary filter in *rule 23* under which all cases must be allocated to a category, viz:

- default paper;
- basic;
- standard; or
- complex.

## The treatment of a 'default paper' appeal

**6.55** Within this category will come late returns and fixed percentage surcharges for late payment, so may affect few IHT situations. There will be a statement of the case, which can include a request for an oral hearing; a reply, which likewise could request a hearing; possibly listing for hearing but otherwise consideration of the papers and a decision.

## The treatment of a 'basic' appeal

**6.56** 'Basic' will include appeals: from penalties; from information notices; for leave to appeal late; to postpone payment of tax pending appeal; or to close an enquiry; so again not really affecting many IHT situations. These will just be listed for hearing without statement of case or reply.

## The treatment of a 'standard' appeal

**6.57** Here we come to more likely territory for IHT practitioners, such as the question: 'is it a farmhouse?' There will be a statement of case, and at that

**6.58** *Compliance*

point the case may be designated as 'complex'. A list of documents must be produced. There may be a case-management hearing but in its absence the case will be listed for hearing. It is likely that many cases that would in the past have gone to the Special Commissioner will follow this route to a hearing.

## The treatment of a 'complex' appeal

**6.58** These will be rare. They will be treated like standard cases, but may enjoy specific directions before any case management hearing or the hearing itself.

## Internal reviews

**6.59** A system of 'internal reviews' by HMRC was introduced to coincide with the Tax Tribunals regime from 1 April 2009. Internal reviews broadly provide an alternative means for taxpayers and HMRC to resolve disputes, rather than a tribunal hearing. If an appeal has been submitted to HMRC and the issue cannot be settled, the taxpayer can notify the appeal to the Tribunal. Alternatively, the taxpayer may ask HMRC to review the point at issue, or HMRC may offer the taxpayer a review (*TMA 1970, s 49A*).

If the taxpayer requests a review, HMRC must respond by stating their original view within 30 days, or possibly a longer period if this is reasonable. If HMRC offer a review, the taxpayer has 30 days in which to accept. Otherwise, HMRC's original view generally stands (*s 49C*).

If a review takes place, HMRC may uphold, vary or cancel their original view of the case, and notify the taxpayer of their conclusion within the following 45 days, or other agreed period (*s 49E*). If HMRC's review is unfavourable, the taxpayer may notify an appeal to the Tribunal within 30 days, or outside this period with the Tribunal's permission.

## Appeal

**6.60** Appeals may be brought out of time with the consent of HMRC if there is reasonable excuse: *s 223*. Equally, the taxpayer may have second thoughts about the grounds for appeal. The Special Commissioners could, under the old rules, allow him to put forward ideas that were not specified in the notice of appeal provided that the omission was neither wilful nor unreasonable and could then decide the matter.

Under the new system, which is designed to be seen to be totally independent of HMRC, it is likely that that facility will continue, but we must wait to see how the new tribunals exercise their powers.

**Example 6.10—Progress of a dispute with HMRC (II)**

[Continuing from **Example 6.9** above]

Following a review of the facts, the executors give up the claim to relief on the farm buildings that were virtually empty but pursue the main claim, relief on the house. It has not yet been sold. A meeting is fixed between HMRC, the Valuation Office, the valuer for the executors and the executors themselves. At that meeting the valuers agree the open market value of the farm house, the value of the buildings in respect of which no relief is claimed, and without prejudice to the dispute also agree the value of the house for the purposes of agricultural relief. They also agree that, if the arrangement for sheep farming really was a partnership rather than a tenancy, there was enough agricultural land to support the claim that the house was a farmhouse; and that, on that basis, the house was of 'character appropriate'. That just leaves one issue to be decided: quite what was the arrangement between the deceased and his neighbour? On that now hangs the entire claim to APR on the house.

One week later, whilst still under the 'old' regime, HMRC issue the Notice of Determination. One week after that the executors appeal, arguing that the deceased was a farmer to the date of his death. The case is designated a 'standard' appeal because it turns entirely on questions of fact; but see below as to the progress of the matter.

# Costs

**6.61** The main concern of taxpayers, apart from the decision itself, is costs. This is currently the subject of informal consultation, to see if the present arrangements work fairly. Following the introduction of the First-tier and Upper Tax Tribunal regime from 1 April 2009, there are provisions for the award of costs in certain specific circumstances. The rules for the First-tier Tribunal (*The Tribunal Procedure (First-tier Tribunal) (Tax Chamber) Rules, SI 2009/273*) provide for costs if (among other circumstances) a party to the appeal (or their representative) has acted unreasonably in bringing, defending or conducting the proceedings. In addition, if a case falls into the 'complex' category, the taxpayer may effectively 'opt out' of costs or expenses by written request to the Tribunal within 28 days (*rule 10*). The Upper Tribunal Rules also make provision for the award of costs following unreasonable behaviour, but do not include an 'opt out' facility.

Under the previous appeals regime *SI 1994/1811, reg 21* provided, in relation to the old tribunals, that a tribunal might award costs against any party to the proceedings including one who has withdrawn his appeal if that party had acted 'wholly unreasonably'. For an example of this rule applied in favour of

**6.62** *Compliance*

the taxpayer, see *Robertson v CIR (No 2)* SpC [2002] SSCD 242 (SpC 3130). The Revenue won, however, against an unreasonable taxpayer in *Phillips v Burrows* SpC [2000] SSCD 112 (SpC 229, 229A).

Costs were an issue in the case of *Wells (Personal Representative of Glowacki (deceased)) v Revenue and customs Commissioners* [2008] STC (SCD) 188, which decided in favour of HMRC that a slightly curiously drafted deed of variation did not have the effect of removing a house from the estate of the deceased by means of a non-chargeable deemed lifetime transfer. In the event, Malcolm Gammie QC as Special Commissioner quashed the determination that was the subject of the appeal but acknowledged, see para 48 of the decision, that the next step would be a further determination, based on his decision in the instant case. He ruled that neither party had acted unreasonably and that he could therefore make no order as to costs.

No order for costs is made without giving that party a chance to make representations. The tribunal can order one party to pay all the costs of the other. If not agreed they are taxed in the county courts like county court costs. There are special rules in Scotland.

The Special Commissioner appeal procedure has in the past been helpful both to HMRC and to the profession. It was very appropriate in deciding how the law should be applied in particular circumstances where the law was unclear. Strictly speaking, the decision of a Special Commissioner bound neither him in a subsequent case nor any other commissioner nor any court. However, the costs of an appeal are such that taxpayers, and no doubt HMRC and the new tribunals, will be guided by previous decisions of the Special Commissioners where the facts of the current case are broadly similar to one that has already been decided.

## Do the changes represent a better way?

**6.62** Classification of cases as 'default paper' or as 'basic' should allow for cheaper decisions. There is virtually no risk that precedents will be set, whether good or doubtful.

HMRC hope that their introduction of the internal review process mentioned above will reduce the number of disputes that go to appeal. The review will be done 'at a distance from caseworkers', something no doubt harder to achieve within the fairly narrow compass of IHT officers. Taxpayers can appeal from what they see as an unsatisfactory review.

**Example 6.11—Progress of a dispute with HMRC (III)**

Returning to the example of John Davis: the executors correspond with HMRC to identify the issues that are relevant to the hearing and, where possible, to agree the facts of the case. The executors obtain a proof of evidence from the neighbour and research the financial transactions between the deceased and the neighbour. It turns out that a diligent junior employee of the accountants had attended a meeting between the deceased and the neighbour some time previously, at which the basis of the farming arrangements was discussed. Prompted by the employee, a contemporaneous note was made of the arrangement, initialled by both parties and the accountant!

This shows that in fact the deceased remained the main decision maker, that he was responsible for various aspects of management of the flock and that the neighbour provided occasional help when required; brawn rather than brains.

By this time, the case has still not been listed under the old rules, so it falls to be considered within the rules for the new tribunal procedure. The tax in issue is not substantial. There is an internal review by the dedicated HMRC review team, whose decision can bind their case workers. After discussion between the executors and HMRC the matter is compromised on terms that require the taxpayer to pay some money, but not as much as tax on the entire farmhouse.

*Chapter 7*

# Trusts: interest in possession

## IHT TREATMENT

### The old law: how an interest in possession was taxed

**7.1** The 'old law' refers to the position before the changes introduced in *FA 2006*.

*IHTA 1984, s 49* treated a person who was entitled to an interest in possession in settled property as if that person was beneficially entitled to the property in which the interest subsisted. This had consequences – particularly on partition of a fund between the tenant for life and the remaindermen – that were difficult to explain to the lay client. One illustration of the difficulty is *Executors of Patch deceased* [2007] SpC 600, which is reviewed at **13.49**. (All statutory references in this chapter are to *IHTA 1984* unless otherwise stated.) The issue of the existence of an interest in possession is frequently litigated.

---

**Example 7.1—Half a house in a trust**

Spouses owned the matrimonial home as tenants in common in equal shares. Each made a will leaving their half share in the house to their children direct and without any kind of restriction on use or alienation, hoping that there would be no interest in possession in the half share, even though the survivor would still be living there. The idea was that the gift might use and be covered by the nil rate band of the first to die. (Note – the benefit of the tax planning has since largely been removed by the new provisions as to the transferable nil rate band – see **Chapter 13** for existing schemes and **Chapter 14** for the position going forward.)

There is no case directly in point. The robust view is that there is no interest in possession in the half house owned by the children. The downside is that main residence relief from CGT is not available on the children's share if the house is later sold at a profit.

---

**7.2** In *IRC v Lloyds Private Banking Ltd* [1998] STC 559, considered further at **15.43**, mother gave her share in the house to daughter but, contrary to the example above, out of natural caution the will contained provisions restricting the daughter from disposing of the half share in the house during father's lifetime. Before the Special Commissioner, the daughter successfully argued that her father did not gain significant advantage from the will because he was now responsible for all the outgoings instead of only half as before. On appeal, the High Court held that father had, during widowhood, enjoyed the exclusive use of mother's half share in the house and therefore had an interest in possession in it, nullifying the tax scheme.

## Interpretation of the law in *Judge v HMRC*

**7.3** In *Judge (personal representatives of Walden deceased) v Revenue and Customs Comrs* [2005] SSCD 863 (SpC 506), the Special Commissioner had to consider a badly drawn will. The case is analysed at **15.32** and is important because it reviews several important and practical issues. The material part of the will gave an interest in a property:

> 'free of tax ... upon trust with the consent in writing of my wife during her lifetime to sell the same with full power to postpone the sale for so long as they shall in their absolute discretion think fit ... and I declare my trustees during the lifetime of my Wife to permit her to have the use and enjoyment of the said property for such period or periods as they shall in their absolute discretion think fit pending postponement of sale she paying the rates taxes and other outgoings and keeping the same in good repair and insured against fire to the full value thereof'.

**7.4** Did this give the widow an interest in possession? She had a substantial economic interest, because she could effectively restrict sale. On her death her executors thought that she did not have an interest in possession. Her interest could have been terminated at any time by the trustees. The property was held on discretionary trusts.

The Commissioner agreed. Had the trustees required the widow to vacate, they could not have sold the house but they could have let it. The Commissioner disregarded the external evidence of the way that the advisers had treated the trust and looked only at the (unsatisfactory) terms of the will, inserting one or two words to complete its sense but giving effect to the intention of the testator as expressed in the terms of the whole will. There was nothing to go on as far as extrinsic evidence of the intentions of the testator was concerned.

**7.5** An 'interest in possession' was defined by adopting the tests in *Gartside v IRC* [1968] AC 553 and in *Pearson v IRC* [1980] STC 318. In *Pearson* it was described as 'a present right to the present enjoyment' of

## 7.5 Trusts: interest in possession

something. More recent cases such as *Woodhall (Woodhall's Representative) v IRC* [2000] SSCD 558 (SpC 261) and *Faulkner (Adams Trustee) v IRC* [2001] SSCD 112 (SpC 278) had shown that a right of occupation could constitute an interest in possession. In the present case the widow's right to occupation could be terminated, so she did not have an interest in possession. The *Judge* case is limited to its facts. In particular it does not tell us whether Statement of Practice 10/79, reviewed below, is good law or anything about the effectiveness of the 'debt or charge' scheme. That scheme is examined in detail at **15.46ff**.

One recent 'finding' of an interest in possession was in *Smith and others v HMRC* [2009] SpC 742, where an account formerly in the name of the late husband of the deceased had been put into the name of a son of the deceased jointly with his mother. This was on the basis (never committed to writing) that mother would receive the interest during her life but that on her death the capital would belong to the son. The reason for this was that the son helped his parents with both time and money. The fund was not included in the estate of mother at death but was later notified to HMRC, who issued Notice of Determination that the executors were liable for IHT on the value. The son was assessed both as executor and as the recipient of the funds. The other executor appealed, partly because he had not received the funds.

The Commissioner found that the account had become settled property before the mother's death, being held for her and for the son in succession within *IHTA 1984, s 43(1)(a)*. As a result, the executors were not liable to tax on the fund itself, so to that extent their appeal succeeded; but the son was liable as trustee. The executors were liable, however, for tax as adjusted for the amount due on the fund itself, ie the increase that resulted from aggregation of the settled fund with the free estate.

Contrast that with the decision in *Davies and Rippon v HMRC* [2009] UKFTT 138 (TC) TC00106, where the existence of an interest in possession was asserted but not proved to the satisfaction of Judith Powell, sitting as judge in the First-tier Tribunal, who brought her usual scholarly approach to the problem. The case is perhaps of greater interest to lawyers and will writers than to tax specialists, but establishes a useful reference point.

Mrs Rhona Goodman, the mother of the appellants, was the widow of Geoffrey Goodman, who had died in 1969. It was argued, following the death of Mrs Goodman, that estate duty surviving spouse relief should apply to certain assets, though HMRC considered that they were part of Mrs Goodman's estate for IHT. The taxpayers argued that, by his conduct, Mr Goodman had, in effect, settled certain property on his wife for life, with remainder to his daughters; alternatively that he and Mrs Goodman had executed mutual wills, with the result that property later inherited by Mrs Goodman from him was fixed with a trust and could not be alienated by her except in accordance with that mutual agreement.

*Trusts: interest in possession* **7.7**

The evidence was that the wills of husband and wife were similar but not identical; that as a widow Mrs Goodman formed a friendship with a Mr Dodd but was concerned to protect her daughters' inheritance; that she did not spend the capital but that she also inherited from Mr Dodd when she survived him.

The judge held that, for the claim to succeed, the appellants must show that the property had been settled and that the surviving souse must not be competent to dispose of it. The burden of proof of a secret trust is on those who assert it; see *re Snowden Deceased* [1979] Ch 528. Past evidence is admissible: see *Blackwell v Blackwell* [1929] HL 318. There must be 'clear and satisfactory evidence' to support mutual wills: see *re Cleaver* [1981] 2 All ER 1018. She considered the arguments as to a secret trust; and as to mutual wills; but found no evidence to support either contention. There was no written trust. All the property was taxable as part of Mrs Goodman's free estate.

## Statement of Practice 10/79

**7.6** Statement of Practice 10/79 has never been tested in court. Put simply, it states that where, pursuant to their powers, trustees of a discretionary trust allow a beneficiary to rent trust property or to have non-exclusive occupation of it, that does not create an interest in possession if full rent is paid or even if the tenancy is for less than full consideration (though that will usually trigger the 'exit' charge). If, in the exercise of a power drawn widely enough, the trustees use that power so as to provide a beneficiary with a permanent home, HMRC will treat that as creating an interest in possession.

In *Judge*, Statement of Practice 10/79 was not in point because the trustees had never done anything. In *IRC v Eversden (exors of Greenstock, decd)* [2002] EWHC 1360 (Ch), [2002] STC 1109 there was an opportunity to rely on SP 10/79 which was not taken by the court. *Eversden*, which is discussed at **5.9**, went in favour of the taxpayer but was nullified by *FA 2003, s 185*, which inserted *sub-s (5A)* into *FA 1986, s 102* (the 'gifts with reservation' legislation).

## Changes under FA 2006

**7.7** *Section 156* of the *Finance Act 2006* introduced *FA 1986, Sch 20*, which changed the IHT treatment of many forms of interests in possession. It had become common, in settlements and even more so in wills, for any life interest to a spouse or civil partner to be subject to overriding powers of appointment. Occasionally, these powers were included for family reasons, such as where, following second marriage, the testator had strong reasons to protect the capital of the fund from the second spouse for the benefit of children of the first marriage. Whilst that might have been unobjectionable, one very common result of the structure was that, during widowhood, the trustees could exercise their powers to terminate the interest in possession and yet allow the

**7.8** *Trusts: interest in possession*

widow(er) to continue to live in trust property whilst not having an interest in possessing it.

Equally, where a rich, divorced old man had married a much younger woman late in life, effectively he could use her as a 'peg life' or 'bridge' for substantial gifts to his children. Whilst he might not have seven years to live, giving her a short-term interest in possession had the effect that the indirect gifts to his children were likely to escape tax: their stepmother would live seven years from the date on which her interest in possession ceased. This is specifically countered by *FA 1986, s 102ZA*, though some doubts have been expressed as to whether that section in fact closes all possible loopholes in this area.

**7.8** With effect from 22 March 2006 many trusts came to be treated like discretionary, or 'relevant property' trusts. Transitional rules were introduced, most of which applied up to 6 April 2008. This chapter does not attempt to do justice to all the issues that have been raised, particularly since some are unresolved, though *Finance Act 2008, s 140* did contain some amending legislation (see at **7.27** below).

# IPDI

**7.9** A gift by will to a life tenant will continue to be taxed under the old rules (*s 49A*). This preserves the old rule, in that the spouse or civil partner exemption will continue to be available to shelter life interests under wills.

The conditions of *s 49A* ('Immediate post-death interest' (IPDI)) are as follows:

(1) The settlement was effected by will or on intestacy.

(2) The tenant for life must become beneficially entitled to the interest in possession on the death of the testator or intestate.

(3) The trusts must not currently be for bereaved minors and the interest is not that of a disabled person.

(4) Condition (3) must have been satisfied at all times since the tenant for life became entitled to the interest in possession.

The concept of the IPDI is retained as part of the overall anti-avoidance scheme of *FA 2006*. Thus, if the trustees use overriding powers to terminate the life interest of the spouse or civil partner and to create ongoing trusts for adult beneficiaries, that will trigger an IHT charge and the funds will then migrate to the IHT regime described in **Chapter 8**. We therefore have a form of 'wait and see'.

*Trusts: interest in possession* **7.9**

The specific target of abuse of 'peg lives' was countered by *FA 1986, s 102ZA*. This treats the termination of an interest in possession as being a 'gift' by the tenant for life, thus bringing the gift with reservation rules into play.

**Example 7.2—House in a nil rate trust**

Sarah's will leaves her house to a discretionary trust of which John is a potential beneficiary. The trustees, within two years of the death, allow him to occupy. That does not automatically give him an interest in possession: it will depend on the facts, as it did in *Judge v HMRC*, reviewed at **7.3–7.5**.

If the trustees appointed assets absolutely, more than three but less than 24 months from the death, *s 144* would treat that as effective from the death; but if they gave, say, John an IPDI only 30 days from the death that would be effective in the same way: there is no three-month waiting period as caused the trouble in *Frankland v IRC* [1997] STC 1450.

If John was living there even before the death, and just never moved out, and the trustees did nothing, they could not be said to have exercised their powers to create an IPDI.

If John was a part owner of the house anyway, how could the trustees throw him out? In such a case, HMRC would look carefully and decide the case on its facts.

Although the common case will be of beneficial ownership of a house that goes into trust under the terms of a will, some property is held within trusts that give a general power of appointment, usually to the tenant for life. The exercise of that power to give an immediate interest in possession can be an IPDI.

**Example 7.3—IPDI by default**

Ursula's will leaves shares in the family property company to her nephew, Tom and the residue of her estate to her niece Yolande for life, with remainder to her great-nieces. Tom promptly disclaims his gift. Yolande's resulting interest is an IPDI.

**Example 7.4—Pilot trust**

Hank set up a pilot trust of £100 for his son for life, remainder to grandchildren. By his will he left his estate to the trust. The fund passing under the will and now held on the trusts is an IPDI: it was in effect settled on death, not when the pilot trust was formed (though if it should ever be relevant, the trust began when the £100 went in).

**7.10**  *Trusts: interest in possession*

## 'Old' interests in possession

**7.10** Questions arise as to whether an interest in possession that existed on or before 22 March 2006 (for short an 'old IIP') remains within *s 49(1)*, ie is treated the way it always was. The issue is whether, by virtue of *s 49(1A)* the old treatment is displaced where the interest in question is one to which the beneficiary becomes entitled after 22 March 2006. Is it a new interest? The problem may gradually cease to be relevant but is best understood by examples.

**Example 7.5—Coming of age**

A trust was set up in 2002 giving Bill, who was born on New Year's Day 1988, the income if he should attain 25. That gift carries the intermediate income. Bill celebrates his adulthood and the beginning of 2006 in suitable style. The trustees, in making their return to 5 April 2006, show that for part of the year the income has been due to Bill. This continues: even when Bill turns 25 in 2013, he has no different interest from what he had on 22 March 2006: there is only one interest.

It follows that, if he had wished, he could have created a 'transitional serial interest' (TSI; see below) before 6 April 2008 (extended to 5 October 2008 by *Finance Act 2008, s 140*) and could even after then give away his interest as a potentially exempt transfer (PET); but why would a young man want to do that?

**Example 7.6—Protected heiress**

A fund is held for Bill's twin, Celia. If she attains 25 the capital is for her benefit, but only for life, with remainder for any children she may have. The trusts give her the intermediate income. *TA 1925, s 31* applies.

Celia has an 'old' IIP already. In 2013 she will still have an old IIP, even though the particular trust provision under which income is paid to her is actually one that becomes operative only then. This would still be the case if the further trusts were in a separate clause in the trust document: Celia has an old IIP.

**Example 7.7—Long delayed enjoyment of the fund**

David was 25 early in 2006 and had an 'old' IIP on 22 March in that year. However, the trust ties up the capital so that, even though David becomes entitled to it at age 40, the trustees can at any time take it away from him by exercising a power of appointment in favour of his younger sister, Emma.

What is his interest after 2021? His original old IIP is, in one sense, replaced by a new but precarious capital interest. The fund is still settled because the trustees could take the capital away. It is a defeasible interest in the capital. *Section 49(1)* still applies: he still has an old IIP.

**Example 7.8—Using the TSI facility but still controlling the capital**

Frances had an 'old' IIP and once the terms of *FA 2006* became clear she agreed to the creation of a TSI on terms that the fund was to be held to pay the income to her daughter Harriet, now 21, until age 35. At 35, Harriet is not to get the capital outright: there are overriding powers that could take the capital away.

Harriet has a TSI now and will still have a TSI once she is 35.

The common thread running through these examples, which are taken from an exchange of questions and answers between STEP/CIOT and HMRC (available via the STEP website: www.step.org/default.aspx?page=955), is that the interests stem from the original trust instrument, not from action taken by the trustees later. The parties are not artificially prolonging the trust beyond what was originally provided.

# DISPOSAL OF INTEREST IN POSSESSION

## The basic rule

**7.11** *Section 51(1)* provides that the disposal of an interest in possession by the person who is entitled to it is not the transfer of money but is treated as the termination of the interest in possession, triggering the provisions of *s 52*. The exception, see *s 51(2)*, is a disposition for the maintenance of a family under *s 11*. In practice, claims that dispositions are covered by *s 11* are rare.

The charging regime under *s 52* imposes tax on capital of the fund in which the interest in possession subsisted. If, for example, the person disposing of the interest was entitled to half the income, it is half the capital that is taxed. If the tenant for life sells his interest for money, the money is then part of his estate and the tax on the fund is reduced by the amount of the money. However, that does not affect the valuation of a reversionary interest in the property.

**Example 7.9—Partition of a life interest fund**

Sally, aged 60, enjoys a life interest under the will of her late husband. On her death the property will pass to her daughter Jane. Given Sally's life expectancy, actuaries determine that the commercial value of her interest is equal to 55%

**7.12** *Trusts: interest in possession*

of the fund. Sally and Jane agree to divide the fund equally between them, Jane paying Sally cash equal to 5% by way of equalisation.

The IHT treatment is not what they might expect. Sally and Jane, having read about *s 10*, thought that this was a transaction at open market value and was not a gift at all. *Section 52*, however, treats the entire fund as belonging to Sally and not just 55% of it. There is therefore a transfer by her of 95% after taking account of what Jane has paid her. This was the point in issue in *Executors of Patch deceased* [2007] SpC 600: see **13.49**.

# Exceptions from charge on disposal

**7.12** There are exceptions from the *s 52* charge. They are examined in more detail when considering the 'true' termination, rather than the deemed termination, of an interest in possession, but are:

- excluded property (see **7.32** and following below);
- exchange of one interest in possession for another;
- reverter to settlor; and
- spouse/civil partner relief.

The new scheme is that many life interests will be treated as interests under discretionary trusts, so *FA 2006, Sch 20, para 15* amended *s 52* so that the charge now applies only in relation to the coming to an end of an interest which is within the new restricted class of favoured life interests, namely:

- an IPDI;
- a disabled person's interest (see **Chapter 8**); or
- a transitional serial interest (see **7.27** and **7.29** below).

Similarly, *FA 2006, Sch 20, para 14* amended *s 53* so that tax is not chargeable under *s 52* where:

- the tenant for life was entitled to the interest before 22 March 2006;
- the life interest was terminated after that day; and
- immediately before the termination of the life interest, the new *s 71A* (bereaved minors) or *s 71D* (18-to-25 trusts) provisions applied to the property in which the interest subsisted.

This is part of the regime that limits favoured life interests to 'simple' life interest for spouses followed by absolute interests for children on attaining the age of 18 or by short-term discretionary trusts that end by age 25. *Schedule*

*Trusts: interest in possession* **7.14**

*20, para 14* made consequential amendments where a person becomes entitled to an interest in settled property on or after 22 March 2006 and the interest is not that of a disabled person and therefore not favoured under the new regime.

*Finance Act 2010* introduced legislation to give effect to the Chancellor's Autumn Statement in 2009 announcing anti-avoidance measures to combat the exploitation of the rules as to excluded property trusts. This is discussed in greater detail at **7.24** below.

## TERMINATION OF INTEREST IN POSSESSION

### The old law

**7.13** *Section 52* provided for a deemed transfer by the tenant for life of the property in which he had an interest in possession. The exceptions from charge on a disposal of an interest in possession have been noted at **7.12**. There are exceptions from charge when an interest in possession comes to an end and:

- the tenant for life becomes absolutely entitled to the property;
- the tenant for life gains some other interest in possession in the property;
- the capital of the fund reverts to the settlor;
- the capital of the fund passes absolutely to the spouse of the settlor; the capital of the fund passes absolutely to the widow or widower of the spouse of the settlor where that settlor has died within two years earlier and the widow or widower is domiciled in the UK.

There are qualifications to these rules in certain specialised circumstances: see *s 53(5)–(8)*.

**7.14** In addition to the general exceptions from the charge on deemed termination there were, under the old law, other exceptions in *s 54*. They mirrored the *s 53* exceptions:

- reversion of the fund to the settlor during the lifetime of the settlor – the value of the fund not to be included as part of the estate of the tenant for life;
- the passing of the fund on the death of the tenant for life to the UK-domiciled spouse of the settlor absolutely – again, leave the capital of the fund out of account;
- the passing of the fund to the UK-domiciled widow or widower of the settlor where the settlor had died less than two years earlier – leave the capital out of account.

**7.15** *Trusts: interest in possession*

These exceptions are subject to qualification in the (somewhat rare) circumstances provided by *s 53(5)* and *(6)*. The even rarer situation of *commorientes* will apply here.

## Reverter to settlor

**7.15** This type of settlement has long been popular in appropriate circumstances. At its simplest, A settled funds on B for life, with remainder to A. There was no IHT charge on B's death if A was still alive, which was logical because the property was returning to its original owner. However, this device was often used in relation to the family home or a share in it. A, married to B, left his share of the house to their child, C, absolutely. Following A's death C would settle the share of the house on B for life, with remainder back to C. Thus, a share in the house might pass down the generations whilst still being occupied by the surviving parent without being taxed on the second death.

This did not always work for CGT. If the house was sold during B's lifetime, any gain might be sheltered by *TCGA 1992, s 225*; but if it was unsold at the time it reverted to C there was no tax-free uplift on B's death because of *TCGA 1992, s 73*. To avoid that situation arising, the settlement was drafted so that it did not end on B's death, but the fund passed to C for life with gifts over and powers of appointment of capital. That sidestepped *s 73* and, instead, *TCGA 1992, s 72* gave the desired uplift.

*Finance Act 2006* spoilt this structure. On B's death a relevant property trust will arise unless, to avoid that, it is arranged that the property is to vest absolutely; and if it does the CGT problem revives. The trustees, with the concurrence of the parties, must do their sums. Which is the greater evil, CGT or IHT? Action must be taken whilst B is still alive or it will be too late. These things cannot always be engineered, but a good solution would be to crystallise the gain whilst it is still sheltered by *s 225*. That would be possible if B was willing to move house, perhaps to more sheltered accommodation or even to a place offering substantial care.

There can be no tax-free uplift on B's death. If the trustees leave the ongoing trusts in place, a sale soon after B's death might be substantially sheltered from CGT by *s 225*. Reverter to settlor cannot apply for IHT because a relevant property trust has arisen, but if the funds are promptly appointed out to C, the IHT charge may be moderate, even nil.

There is still one occasion where an uplift may be achieved. This arises under *s 53(4)*, which provides that there is no *s 52* charge (termination of an interest in possession) if, on that termination, either:

- UK-domiciled spouse or civil partner of the settlor; or
- UK-domiciled widow/former civil partner, if the settlor has died

becomes beneficially entitled to the settled property. In these circumstances the property is still in trust, so it is *s 72* that is in point rather than *s 73*; and *s 72(1)(b)* excludes a chargeable gain.

FA 2006, s 80 changed *para 11(9)* and inserted *sub-paras (11)–(13)* into FA 2004, Sch 15. The situation may not often arise and the new rules are difficult to follow. There is now an exception to the previous more general exception. Consider the following situation, sometimes used in 'non-dom' families; self-settlement.

### Example 7.10—POAT problem?

Jennifer settled property on 1 February 2006 on herself for life. She occupies the trust property. POAT ought not to apply, under the general scheme, because the property is in Jennifer's estate. However *para 11(11)* provides that where at any time:

- the relevant property has ceased to be comprised in a person's estate (which it has here); or
- (s)he has directly or indirectly funded it;

and later the property is aggregated with his estate because (s)he is a tenant for life (which has happened here); *para 11(12)* comes into force.

*Paragraph 11(12)* prevents relevant property from being treated as comprised in the taxpayer's estate for the purposes of the *para 11(1)* or *para 11(2)* exemptions 'at that subsequent time'.

If Jennifer's trust gave her an immediate interest in possession, as was possible before 22 March 2006, there is no problem. If, however, there was a gap, such as a period during which the trust was a discretionary one, a POAT issue would arise by virtue of these sub-paragraphs. Jennifer would then have to think about electing back into GWR to avoid POAT.

No new interest in possession trusts can be created except for disabled persons or in quite specialised circumstances or on death, so maybe the point is academic. Where an election is not made in time, POAT will continue until the property is appointed back to the settlor or its enjoyment is terminated by other means.

One specific, but rarefied, problem arises where a trust owns a company that in turn owns a residence. A POAT election will cause the assets to be treated as part of the taxpayer's estate. It could bring assets within the IHT net where previously the rules as to situs might otherwise have sheltered the assets.

**7.16** *Trusts: interest in possession*

Some of the heat has been taken out of the problem in the situation described in the example of Jennifer above because HMRC say that the words 'at any subsequent time' in *para 11(11)* do not literally mean 'at any later occasion', but something like 'at any later time after value leaves the donor's estate, thereby reducing his estate, but returns to it because property is purchased with that value and the taxpayer has an interest in possession in the property'.

As a result there may be no difficulty where:

- A settled cash on himself before 22 March 2006; or
- B, being a disabled person, did the same after that date,
- and in either case, the trustees:
- bought a house for A (or B, as the case might be) to live in; or
- sold that house and bought another; or
- used some of the proceeds of the house to buy shares, etc.

That leaves only the problem of the discretionary trust that was later appointed onto interest in possession trust. There, an election is the only way to avoid POAT.

### Anti-avoidance rule

**7.16** As will be seen in **Chapter 8**, the creation of a discretionary trust is nearly always a chargeable transfer. Elaborate provisions are included to prevent taxpayers from getting around this charge.

One tactic which the draftsman feared concerns the actions of a taxpayer who had already made substantial chargeable transfers and now wished to set up a further discretionary trust, but realised that this would trigger an immediate IHT charge. The device the draftsman feared was that the settlor would create a short-term interest in possession trust in favour of a person (the 'poor relation') who still had available the nil rate band; and subject to that would provide that the fund was to be held on full discretionary trusts. The object of this would that the new trust would be chargeable to IHT by reference to the poor relation, under the rules described in **Chapter 8**, at much lower rates than otherwise the case.

The language of *ss 54A* and *54B* is obscure, but is designed to frustrate this tactic. *Schedule 20, para 16* introduces changes that give effect to the post-21 March 2006 regime.

### Use of annual exemption

**7.17** The release by the tenant for life of his interest in part of the fund is a potentially exempt transfer. If not used elsewhere, the annual exemption may be set against this transfer, provided that the life tenant notifies the trustees that he wishes to do so. *Section 57(4)* suggests that the notice should be in some special form, but that is misleading. Although there was originally a form its use has been discontinued. All that is required is a letter from the tenant for life to the trustees indicating that the tenant for life has available an annual exemption (or two, as the case may be) and that he wishes to set it or them against the transfer.

## Maintenance funds

**7.18** There are special provisions where, on the termination of an interest in possession, property passes to a maintenance fund. This is a fund connected with the maintenance of heritage property and use of the relief must be very rare. The anti-avoidance measures in *FA 2010*, described at **7.25** below, contain a 'let out' for transfers to maintenance funds.

## The law since 22 March 2006

**7.19** *FA 2006, Sch 20* redefined potentially exempt transfers (PETs) made on or after 22 March 2006 so that lifetime transfers which can be PETs are limited to outright gifts to individuals or gifts into disabled trusts.

This is a fundamental change and effectively all lifetime gifts into trust are chargeable unless within exemptions or reliefs. Disabled trusts are those falling within the definition in *s 89*. As a result, many trust interests that would have been regarded as life interests are now within the discretionary trust tax regime. The death of the tenant for life no longer triggers a charge to IHT because the trust is within the scheme of periodic and exit charges described in **Chapter 8**. The estate of the tenant for life will therefore not include the fund in which he had an interest but which is now treated as discretionary under the new rules. The exceptions are:

- an IPDI;
- a disabled person's interest;
- a transitional serial interest (see **7.27** and **7.29** below).

## Termination of IPDI

**7.20** The termination of a qualifying IPDI is governed by the normal rules for interest in possession. Tax is charged under *s 52* on the whole or any part of the fund affected. The same rule applies to a disabled person's interest or, see **7.27** below, to a transitional serial interest.

**7.21** *Trusts: interest in possession*

There is an exception from the *s 52* charge brought in under the new rules where:

- the interest of a person who was entitled as tenant for life before 22 March 2006 now comes to an end; and
- immediately before it does so, the fund is within the new provisions of *s 71A* (trusts for bereaved minors); or
- the fund is within *s 71D* (18-to-25 trusts); see again *Sch 20, para 13*.

Until 22 March 2006, accumulation and maintenance trusts for children were (perhaps simplistically) treated by practitioners as if they were within the IHT charge for interest in possession trusts. That is certainly no longer the case. Accumulation and maintenance trusts are therefore examined in detail in **Chapter 8**.

## Exceptions from charge under the rules from 22 March 2006

**7.21** The exceptions from charge that were noted at **7.12** are now restricted. They apply only where the interest concerned is a disabled person's interest or a transitional serial interest. A modified version of the exception from charge is now specified by *s 54(2B)*. The value of the fund is left out of account in fixing the value of the estate of the tenant for life where:

- the tenant for life was entitled to the interest in possession on or after 22 March 2006 and dies thereafter; or
- the interest in possession held by the tenant for life was an IPDI; or
- the settlor died before the tenant for life but less than two years before; and
- on the death of the tenant for life the fund passes to the UK-domiciled widow or widower or surviving civil partner of the settlor.

The anti-avoidance rule noted at **7.15** is adapted so that it applies only to a disabled person's interest or a transitional serial interest.

The rules relating to maintenance funds for heritage property are adapted so as to apply only to an IPDI, a disabled person's interest or a transitional serial interest.

## REVERSIONARY AND PURCHASED INTERESTS

### The general rule

**7.22** The basic rule is that a reversionary interest is not part of the estate of the person who holds it because it is treated as part of the estate of the tenant for life. The market value rule in *s 10*, which would normally exclude a transaction from being a transfer of value, does not apply to an acquired reversionary interest. The law has been made a good deal more complicated by anti-avoidance rules introduced by *FA 2010, s 53* and described at **7.24** below.

## The rule in *Melville v IRC* and its aftermath

**7.23** To counter a perceived abuse, *FA 2002* introduced *s 55A* in relation to purchased settlement powers. It applies where a person becomes entitled to a 'settlement power' or the right to exercise a power over a settlement or restrict such a power. The disposition by which the taxpayer acquires that power, for money or money's worth, does not qualify for the market value rule in *s 10*, nor can it be treated as exempt by virtue of spouse relief or the reliefs relating to charities and other gifts for public benefit.

This is an anti-avoidance provision. The use and retention of settlement powers is less common in UK-based trusts than in trusts for certain non-UK domiciliaries, especially US citizens. The legislation arises out of the decision in favour of the taxpayer in *Melville v IRC* [2001] EWCA Civ 1247, [2001] STC 1271. The case turned upon a scheme for a gift of a substantial portfolio of securities. A simple gift would have triggered an unacceptably large capital gains tax charge, whilst the transfer to a discretionary trust would have triggered an exceptionally large IHT charge. The device used was a discretionary trust, enabling the capital gains to be held over; but including a power over the settlement for the benefit of the settlor. This had the effect of devaluing the chargeable transfer, thus mitigating the IHT charge. The scheme was nullified by *s 47A*, which defined 'settlement power', and by *s 55A*, which addressed the scheme itself.

## Purchase of interests in trusts

**7.24** Finance Act 2010, s 52 inserts new s 81A into IHTA 1984 with the intention of preventing perceived abuse of trusts. Where a person:

- transfers property into a trust in which they or a spouse or civil partner has a future interest, as reversioner; or
- buys a reversionary interest,

the new legislation imposes an IHT charge when that future interest comes to an end and the property vests.

The guidance notes to the legislation use the term 'future interest' interchangeably with 'reversionary interest'. When the interest comes to an end and the person becomes actually entitled to the trust interest there is a charge if that person:

### 7.25 *Trusts: interest in possession*

- actually bought the reversionary interest; or
- is the settlor of the trust or the spouse or civil partner of the settlor and becomes entitled to the reversionary interest.

By *s 81A(2)*, the gift of a reversionary interest as defined in *s 81A(1)* is a chargeable transfer, not a PET. These rules are effective as from 9 December 2009, being the date of the Pre-Budget Report when the rules were announced. The rationale for the new legislation is that neither a purchased reversionary interest nor a settlor's reversionary interest in trust property is excluded property. Each forms part of a person's estate; whereas since *FA 2006* an interest in possession does not normally form part of his estate by virtue of *s 5(1A)*. A possible IHT saving could arise on the vesting of an interest in possession because the reversionary interest was no longer held. As a result of the changes it will no longer be possible to avoid an IHT charge by making a gift of a purchased reversionary interest before the interest actually vests. These rules do not apply to those interests in possession which are protected by *FA 2006* and do not form part of the relevant property regime. Thus disabled trusts, for example, are outside the scope of these changes.

## Changes to the tax treatment of interests in possession

**7.25** *Finance Act 2010, s 53* reviews *IHTA 1984, s 3A* which sets out which transfers are potentially exempt and which are chargeable. A purchased interest in possession is, by *FA 2010, s 53*, treated as part of the estate of the person who buys it. Whereas normally under *s 3A* dealings with an interest in possession are potentially exempt, *FA 2010, s 53(2)(a)* changes *IHTA 1984, s 3A* by removing the reference to *IHTA 1984, s 52* and by inserting new *IHTA 1984, s 3A(6A)*. As will be seen from the account that follows, general tax practitioners would do well to steer their clients well clear of purchased trust interests.

The result of the changes is that a transfer of value under *IHTA 1984, s 52* will be potentially exempt except where it arises in respect of an interest that, under the new rules, is treated as part of a person's estate, ie by virtue of *IHTA 1984, s 5(1B)*. Therefore, where such a trust comes to an end and the capital is paid out, the transfer of value is a chargeable one for IHT, not a PET.

*Section 5(1)(a)(ii)* of *IHTA 1984* is also amended so that, where an interest in possession falls within the new definition in *s 5(1B)*, it will be excluded from the general provision that a (new) interest in possession is not treated as part of a person's estate. Thus we now have a new *IHTA 1984, s 5(1B)* with a new category of interests in possession. These are:

- interests that are included as part of a person's estate, being
- those to which a person is entitled;
- who is domiciled in the UK;
- where that person acquired the interest in a transaction at arm's length.

For this purpose 'arm's length' is as defined in *IHTA 1984, s 10*. Thus in future the holder of a purchased interest in possession within *s 5(1B)* is treated as entitled to the property, as under *IHTA 1984, s 49(1A)*, so on death the value of the fund will be aggregated with the free estate.

There is, as a result, a change to *IHTA 1984, s 51(1A)*. That section normally provides that where a person disposes of an interest in possession that is not a transfer of value, though an IHT charge could arise under *IHTA 1984, s 52*. However that does not apply to all interests. It does, by virtue of *FA 2010*, now apply to purchased life interests within *s 5(1B)*.

The regime for IHT charges when an interest in possession comes to an end during the lifetime of a beneficiary is mainly regulated by *s 52(2A)* and *(3A)*. Those charges now apply only to certain interests in possession, but the category of interest to which the charge can apply is now extended to include purchased interests within *s 5(1B)*. The gift of a purchased life interest; or its termination; will trigger a chargeable event for IHT.

The changes go further. There can be relief under *IHTA 1984, s 57A(1A)* in relation to the IHT charge on an interest in possession where, somewhat unusually, the trust property is shifted to a heritage maintenance fund within two years of the death. There are actually very few heritage maintenance funds in existence, so the point is somewhat esoteric, but the relief is now extended to *s 5(1B)* purchased life interests. There is a similar extension by way of an amendment to *IHTA 1984, s 100(1A)* in relation to reconstruction of the share capital of a close company and to slightly similar changes to company capital contemplated by *s 101(1A)*.

*Section 102ZA(1)(b)(ii)* of *FA 1986* legislates on the gift with reservation rules as they apply to the holder of an interest in possession. This provision is changed by *FA 2010, s 53(8)* so as to include purchased life interests within *IHTA 1984, s 5(1B)*.

This complicated anti-avoidance legislation is designed to frustrate the exploitation of the excluded property rules as they apply to trust interests that are not subject to charges to IHT in the UK. The result is that if a non-UK domiciled person sets up a trust of foreign property which includes an interest in possession, that interest is excluded property; but if a stranger buys that interest that purchaser will come within the new regime and will not get any of the benefits of the excluded property regime.

*7.26 Trusts: interest in possession*

## Purchase of interests in offshore trusts

**7.26** The excluded property rules (which are considered below) do not apply where:

- a person is entitled to an interest in possession;
- that person is domiciled in the UK; and
- the trust interest was purchased on or after 5 December 2005 (*s 48(3B)*).

It matters not whether the interest was paid for by the tenant for life or someone else. The purchase may be direct or indirect, as under inheritance from the purchaser. These rules are expanded by *FA 2010, s 53*, amending *IHTA 1984, s 5* to introduce *s 5(1B)* and making amendments where necessary so as to include reference to the new *s 5(1B)*.

## TRANSITIONAL PROVISIONS, 2006–2008

### Transitional serial interests: property other than life policies

**7.27** *Section 49C* set out four conditions under which an interest in possession could benefit from the tax treatment that applied to interests that were in existence before 22 March 2006. However, the rules relate to transactions before 6 October 2008. For a fuller account, readers are referred to earlier editions of this work.

The *s 49C* conditions were:

(1) The trust began before 22 March 2006 and immediately before that date the property was subject to an interest in possession ('the prior interest').

(2) The prior interest came to an end at some time between 22 March 2006 and 5 October 2008.

(3) The beneficiary became entitled to an interest in possession ('the current interest') at the time that the prior interest ended.

(4) This was not the settlement for a disabled person nor for a 'bereaved minor' (see below).

Care had to be taken in creating successive interests, perhaps for children, that the original life tenant was excluded from further benefit, because the termination of an interest in possession after 22 March 2006 could be a gift with reservation, even if the interest in possession arose after that date.

Examples of the facility are as follows.

### Example 7.11—Making the beneficiary wait for the capital

Reginald had a life interest before 2006, and would get the capital at age 30. The trustees doubted his business acumen and exercised their power under *Trustee Act 1925, s 32* to advance the fund onto new trusts which would give Reg the fund only when he attained 50, ie long after April 2008. This is a valid TSI.

### Example 7.12—Spinning out the fund

Susan enjoyed the income of a fund, but on her death the capital passes to her brother Tom absolutely. Tom is wealthy and assigned his interest to another trust, set up earlier, in which his own sons have life interests. Susan's interest was terminated before 5 April 2008, whereupon the fund came to be held on interest in possession trusts for her nephews. They do not have a TSI. Their interest is in another trust.

### Example 7.13—Sharing out the fund

The Goldsworthy fund was invested in stocks and shares and was held for Mike and Jim in equal shares, each having a life interest. The trustees created sub-funds by dividing the portfolio down the middle. That operation did not bring to an end the interest of either Mike or Jim.

One issue that could cause difficulty was deciding when an existing interest had been replaced by a new interest for the same beneficiary. There were many issues of detail to clarify. CIOT and STEP led the process of elucidation of the most difficult areas, of which the examples above are good illustrations, and published the results on their websites.

One particular anomaly, arising where an old IIP was replaced by a new IIP for the same beneficiary, was addressed in *Finance Act 2008, s 140*. This resulted in the rewriting of *s 53(2A)*. The change was retrospective to 22 March 2006 and provided that the exception from an IHT charge under *s 52* on termination of an interest in possession, which could apply if the person became entitled to another interest in the same trust, was available where a person became entitled to a new trust interest only if the new interest was a disabled person's interest or a TSI. That would apply regardless of whether the original interest, which terminated, was an old IIP, or an interest that came into being on or after 22 March 2006.

**7.27** *Trusts: interest in possession*

### Example 7.14—Simple creation of a non-policy TSI

Under the will of her husband Leonard, who died on 1 December 2005, his widow Marian became entitled to the income of the residue of his estate for life, with remainder to their grandchildren for life. The will gave the trustees power to advance capital in favour of any beneficiary who had a life interest. Remainder would pass to great grandchildren insofar as capital had not been advanced to grandchildren in their lifetimes.

Marian was well provided for in other ways and hoped to live at least another seven years. On 17 May 2006, she surrendered her life interest in favour of her grandchildren. Her interest was the 'prior interest'. The new life interests that arise in favour of the grandchildren are 'current interests'. Those current interests fall to be treated as interests in possession under the old rules.

The youngest grandchild, Zac, is now five years old. The treatment of interests in possession as it was before 22 March 2006 could therefore continue for many years. If in due course Zac were to marry, the trustees could, no doubt with his consent, appoint capital to him which he could then give to his wife, enabling them to enjoy a fund equal to twice the nil rate band then in force without risk of an IHT charge on it. Other possibilities may be imagined.

---

Special rules apply where a person becomes entitled to an interest on the death of a spouse or civil partner. They are in *s 49D*. These are the conditions:

- trust in being before 22 March 2006 and just before 22 March 2006, there was a prior life interest;
- the prior interest ends, on the death of its holder on or after 6 October 2008;
- the prior holder was the spouse or civil partner of the present life tenant;
- the present life tenant becomes entitled to the life interest as soon as the prior interest ceases;
- it is not a bereaved minor trust (BMT) (see below) nor a disabled person's interest.

### Example 7.15—Availability of spouse relief

George was already tenant for life of a fund on Budget Day 2006. On his marriage to Celia in September 2007 he gave up an interest in half of the trust fund in her favour, so that she became entitled to an interest in possession. That transfer is covered by spouse exemption. It is a TSI.

In May 2010 George inherited funds from another family trust and decided to give up the remainder of his original life interest in favour of Celia. He surrendered it to her so that she became entitled to the income of the whole of the fund. Although Celia in trust law becomes entitled only to income, the second transfer is outside the transitional rules. It is a 'second bite at the cherry'. It is not an IPDI, being a lifetime settlement. Under the rules from 22 March 2006 it is treated like a discretionary trust, thus a chargeable transfer; and since the fund does not increase Celia's estate it is not covered by spouse relief.

## Addition of funds to existing trusts: special rules for policy trusts

**7.28** The transitional provisions did not generally allow existing interest in possession funds to be augmented. The addition of new assets to an existing trust is treated as the creation of a new settlement. This might simply be the transfer of extra funds by the settlor or an indirect benefit, such as the release by the settlor of a debt owed to him by the trustees.

The one exception relates to insurance policies. The payment of premiums simply to keep an existing policy on foot is not regarded as the creation of a new settlement. In any case, depending on the circumstances, the payment of policy premiums may be exempt within *s 21* (normal expenditure out of income).

**7.29** *Section 49E* provides a special form of TSI for existing, but not new, trusts of insurance policies. It can apply where 'C' has an interest in possession in a policy, 'the present interest', before 22 March 2006 and certain conditions apply:

(1) It is a pre-Budget 2006 trust; before 22 March 2006 the property in the trust was a policy; and C (or perhaps more likely some other person) had a life interest ('the earlier interest').

(2) The earlier interest ended on or after 6 October 2008 ('the earlier interest end-time') on the death of whoever was entitled to it and C became entitled to the interest on one of the following occasions:

- at the earlier interest end-time;
- at the end of an interest in possession occurring on the death of the previous life tenant; or
- when one of a series of interests in possession ends, where the first belonged to someone who became entitled to it at the earlier interest end-time and where each life interest came to an end when the holder of that interest died; or alternatively

**7.30** *Trusts: interest in possession*

- C became entitled to the interest that C now has on one of the following occasions:
    - when a transitional serial interest ends by death; or
    - when the last of several consecutive interests ends and the first of them was a transitional serial interest, each ending by death.

There are two further conditions:

(3) The policy rights were in the trust from 22 March 2006 until C became entitled.

(4) This is neither a bereaved minor's trust nor one for a disabled person.

## Associated operations

**7.30** Insurance policies featured in the case of *Smith v Revenue and Customs Commissioners* [2008] STC 1649, where husband and wife took out 'back-to-back' annuity and life policies with the same insurer in circumstances where the annuity income funded the life policies, which were given away to their children. There was no express reference in any policy to any other, but the total package of documents provided by the insurer made the connection plain. Held, the policies taken together were a transfer of value.

## Bereaved minors and age 18-to-25 trusts

**7.31** The provision of funds for young people is dealt with more fully in **Chapter 8** in the context of the new treatment of accumulation and maintenance trusts. *Section 71C* defines 'bereaved minor' as a person not yet 18 at least one of whose parents has died. This definition is central to the *FA 2006* IHT regime. As a result of strong representations that the age of 18 is too young to manage substantial capital, the original structure of IHT, which would have made the tax treatment of capital much more favourable where the young person became absolutely entitled at 18, is toned down slightly.

By introducing *s 71D* for 'Age 18-to-25 trusts' the government has given trustees a choice. These trusts are considered in detail at **8.7**. It seems likely that many families will accept the burden of the IHT regime for discretionary trusts as the price to be paid for securing the capital in the short to medium term.

Wills can be drafted with flexibility to take advantage of the new rules.

### Example 7.16—'Wait and see how they turn out'

Yolande died leaving funds to her husband Alfred for life (an IPDI) with remainder on discretionary trusts for her children. The trustees appoint the reversionary fund onto trusts that comply with *s 71A*. That will be good enough: the *s 71A* trusts need not actually be set out in the will. What is more, it does not matter that capital might be appointed out to Alfred: whilst he has an IPDI the trusts of the reversion are not tested.

## EXCLUDED PROPERTY TRUSTS

## Reversionary interests

**7.32** These have already been considered at **7.22**. A reversionary interest is excluded property unless (see *s 48(1)*):

- purchased; or
- one to which either the settlor or his spouse is beneficially entitled; or
- an interest expectant on the determination of a lease where that lease is treated as a settlement by virtue of the special rules in *s 43(3)*.

As to purchased reversionary interests, note the anti-avoidance provisions of *FA 2010, s 53* described at **7.24** and **7.25** above.

## Foreign assets

**7.33** The other main category of excluded trust property is described in *s 48(3)* and concerns property situated outside the UK. There are two conditions:

- The property itself, but not a reversionary interest in it, is excluded provided that the settlor was not domiciled in the UK when the settlement was made.
- The rules in *s 6(1)* apply to a reversionary interest in the property, but do not otherwise apply to it.

*Section 6(1)* states: 'Property situated outside the United Kingdom is excluded property if the person beneficially entitled to it is an individual domiciled outside the United Kingdom'. The conditions required for property to be excluded within *s 48(3)* would therefore be satisfied if the present tenant for life was domiciled in the UK, but the remainderman was not so domiciled.

**7.34** *Trusts: interest in possession*

**7.34** The excluded property rules may seem to be something of an anomaly.

---

**Example 7.17—Benefiting from the rule years later**

Anton fled to the UK during the Hungarian uprising in 1956. He had been a successful engineer and on arrival in the UK settled his commercial interests in Hungary and in Switzerland through the medium of a Liechtenstein trust for the benefit of his wife Josefina for life with remainder to their son Maxim for life with gifts over. All this happened at a time when Anton still hoped eventually to return to the country of his birth and when he had been in the UK only three years.

Although Anton remained in the UK for many years after making the settlement, such that he became deemed domiciled here under the '17/20 year' rule in *s 267*, he did not add any funds to the settlement. Although in due course the composition of the trust fund changed and included indirect holdings in companies in the UK, the rules of situs were observed in such a way that at all times the trust property was situated outside of the UK. Anton died before 22 March 2006.

Josefina became deemed domiciled in the UK. On her death it was acknowledged that the fund was excluded property.

Maxim was born in the UK and on reaching late teens made it clear that he adopted the UK as his country of domicile. For IHT purposes, that does not matter. The fund is still outside the IHT regime because of the circumstances of its creation and because there has been no addition to the fund at a time when the settlor was domiciled in the UK.

---

In **Example 7.17**, the tax treatment would be different if Anton had purchased the interest after 5 December 2005 (see *s 48(3B)*).

For years advisers have worried about the precise relationship between the rules as to excluded property and those for gifts with reservation, and with good reason. As the law stands, or seems to stand, a 'non-dom' may set up a trust of offshore assets from which he continues to benefit, by drawing the income. If the excluded property rule takes priority over the gift with reservation rule, the settlor continues to draw an income from property that is not taxed as his estate on death, even though he may meanwhile become deemed domiciled here under the residence rule. The slightest indication of Revenue thinking was the wording of paragraph 14396 of the IHT Manual, which varied from time to time. The present position seems to be that the longstanding position would remain the current view of HMRC unless and until they were to issue advice to the contrary. *Caveat* settlor.

*Trusts: interest in possession* **7.35**

Difficulty could come from a non-fiscal source. By a press release dated 14 October 2009, the European Commission published proposals that, if enacted, would change fundamentally the procedures for inheritance within the EEC. A certificate is proposed that would be recognised internationally as giving rights to succession. This poses fundamental problems for English lawyers, with our concepts of domicile, executors, trusts and testamentary freedom. We want to be certain that lifetime gifts cannot be clawed back to satisfy 'forced heirship' rules. The French will not lightly give up rules that protect children from disinheritance. We in England do not accept 'habitual residence' as determinative of the legal system that should govern inheritance. Yet again, our traditions are on a collision course with the EU so we have indicated that we are unwilling to be bound by the new rules if enacted. However, perhaps we may, over time, become more integrated into Europe: and part of the price might be the surrender of the concept of domicile, which many think has outlived its usefulness. If we lost that, many tax loopholes, much cherished by those to whom they relate, might also be lost.

What should settlors and their trustees do now? *Finance Act 2008, ss 24* and *25* and *Sch 7*, introduced a much sharper regime for the taxation of non-UK domiciled taxpayers, cutting down the favourable remittance basis, but that mainly affects income tax and CGT rather than IHT. The law is in a state of flux: thus we have cases on residence that declare the law as it applied to past situations but perhaps not to what we have now. HMRC6 ('Residence, Domicile and the Remittance Basis') sets out new guidance for income tax and CGT, replacing Booklet IR20. The taxpayer recently lost in *Genovese v HMRC* [2009] SpC 741, having tried to avoid UK residence even though he had worked in London from 1998 and had rented in London on one-year tenancies from then until he purchased a home here in 2002. The Commissioner noted that he had lived here with his family and worked for the same employer; his residence here was 'habitual' under the common law and it was not necessary to apply IR20. The appellant was resident 'in' the year of assessment 2001/02.

The residence of trustees for CGT was reviewed in *Smallwood and another v HMRC* [2009] EWHC 777 (Ch). The case turned on exactly where the trust was resident when gains were made; on the facts, that was Mauritius, which had sole taxing rights under the double taxation agreement then in force. The appeal by Mr Smallwood and the trustees was allowed in the High Court.

The rules affect IHT through the test for 'deemed domicile' in *s 267(1)(b)*, which turns on residence: *Finance Act 2008, Sch 7* adjusted the 'day counting' rules.

# Loss of excluded property status: the s 80 problem

**7.35**    *Section 80* ('Initial interest if settlor or spouse or civil partner') imposes a primary fiction on all trusts set up since 27 March 1974, namely that

## 7.35 Trusts: interest in possession

where a settlor or his spouse is entitled to an interest in possession in property as soon as it is within the trust, that property is not treated as joining the trust fund for the purposes of IHT regime for discretionary trusts. Its joinder is postponed. However, once the interests of the settlor or spouse come to an end, as where the property moves from interest in possession to discretionary trusts, it is at that point treated as joining a separate trust, made by the person who last had an interest in possession. 'Spouse' means spouse, widow, widower of a settlor (*s 80(2)*) and will now include a surviving civil partner.

**Example 7.18—Trigger of discretionary trust regime**

On 6 June 1979 Geoff, domiciled in England and Wales, settled £150,000 on trust for his wife Maud for life, with remainder on discretionary trusts for his children and grandchildren. Maud enjoyed the income until 23 May 2004, when she disclaimed her interest with the intention that her family should benefit. At that point the fund was worth £700,000. There is an immediately chargeable lifetime transfer by Maud of £700,000. That would also be the result if the disclaimer took place after 22 March 2006.

**Example 7.19—Side-stepping the discretionary trust regime**

The facts are as in **Example 7.18** above, only instead of a simple disclaimer the change is effected, not by Maud but by the trustees (on 23 May 2004) under a power in the deed. They appoint funds onto new life interest trusts for the children and onto A&M trusts for the grandchildren. This time no discretionary trust arises, so there is no immediate chargeable transfer. It is a PET by Maud. However, see below as to the effect where the event falls under the 'new' regime.

Under the post-*Finance Act 2006* regime, *s 80(4)* has the effect that, where the trigger event under *s 80(1)* happens on or after 22 March 2006, it will apply, not to the coming to an end of an interest in possession, as hitherto, but on the occasion of the ending of any 'postponing interest', by which is meant any type of interest in possession, even (see *s 80(4)(b)*), an IPDI or a disabled person's interest. This will severely cut down the freedom of trustees of offshore trusts for erstwhile non-UK domiciliaries to keep the fund outside the IHT net.

**Example 7.20—The effect on an excluded property trust**

The facts are as in **Example 7.18** except that: Geoff was domiciled in New Zealand in 1979; the disclaimer of Maud's interest occurred on 23 May 2010; and by this time both Geoff and Maud are deemed to be domiciled in the UK. The fund loses its excluded property status, because it is retested as a transfer made on 23 May 2010 by Maud.

Thus, by stealth, the advantage of excluded property trusts will, for many families, disappear. Certainly all trustees of excluded property trusts must regularly consider their position.

## INSURANCE POLICY TRUSTS

### Existing policy trusts

**7.36** The scheme for trusts as finally enacted in *Finance Act 2006* imposes on financial advisers a duty to understand the taxation of trusts and to be able to explain it. *Section 46A* now deals with existing life interest policy trusts. The conditions are:

- the settlement and the life policy both existed before 22 March 2006;
- premiums are payable, or there is a variation of the policy which is permitted by the new rules, some time on or after 22 March 2006;
- there were pre-existing settlement rights, now defined as a 'transitionally protected interest';
- by virtue of continued payment of premiums or of a variation of the policy, rights under the policy become settled as part of the transitionally protected interest; and
- the only variations to the policy are those allowed by the legislation in 2006.

For the purposes of the legislation a variation is 'allowed' only where it takes place by operation of the exercise of rights that existed before 22 March 2006. A 'transitionally-protected interest' means only a pre-existing life interest or a transitional serial interest. Where all of these conditions are satisfied, the payment of any more premiums on the policy is a transfer of value made by the individual who pays it and the transfer of value at that time is a PET.

### Transitional provisions

**7.37** The same treatment will apply in an existing situation where the policy is not held on life interest trusts but on A&M trusts. The relevant legislation is *s 46B*. It follows the pattern of *s 46A*, so the conditions are as follows:

- the settlement and the policy must have existed before 22 March 2006;
- a premium is paid on the policy after that date;
- rights under the policy were settled on A&M trusts before 22 March 2006; and

**7.38** *Trusts: interest in possession*

- further rights (ie those attaching to the next premium) become settled after 22 March 2006 and there is a variation on or after that date of the policy so as to increase the benefits or extend the term of the insurance, but that variation is an 'allowed one'.

Where the conditions are satisfied, A&M provisions may continue notwithstanding the general changes to A&M trusts introduced by *Finance Act 2006*. The payment of a further premium is treated as a PET. For the purposes of policies subject to A&M trusts a variation is 'allowed' only where it represents the exercise of pre-existing rights under the policy.

**7.38** There is a further level of protection of pre-existing policy trusts. This protects the eventual release of funds. The conditions are:

- pre-existing settlements and life policies;
- premiums paid or allowed variation on or after 22 March 2006 where the trusts fall within the 'new' *s 71A* (bereaved minors) or *s 71D* (18-to-25) trusts which were previously A&M trusts and which became *s 71A* or *s 71D* trusts; and
- a further premium was paid, the policy was varied in an allowed manner so as to increase or extend the benefits but only by exercise of pre-existing rights.

These rules apply to property in an 18-to-25 trust only where that property was previously in an A&M settlement and migrated to *s 71D* whilst still in the same settlement. If the settlements are bereaved minor trusts then the transitional provisions apply only where they migrate from A&M trusts under the terms of *FA 2006* or where they would have been in 18-to-25 trusts, but cease to be held on those trusts because the trustees decided to modify the rights so as to comply with the restrictions for bereaved minors: in other words, they let the grandchildren have the money early, ie at 18 rather than at the preferred age of 25.

## New trusts

**7.39** 'New' insurance policy trusts, even if expressed to be interest in possession trusts, are treated for IHT like discretionary trusts and will become subject to the regime of entry charges, periodic charges and exit charges. This regime is described in the next chapter.

## Pensions

**7.40** The IHT treatment of pensions before 22 March 2006 was that benefits might be settled under a discretionary trust. The death benefits were

*Trusts: interest in possession* **7.40**

not relevant property, during the lifetime of the policyholder by virtue of *s 58(1)(d)*, whether the pension was a regulated one or one within *ICTA 1988, s 615* (a '*s 615* scheme').

Equally, under *FA 2004, Sch 29*, the death benefit was 'a defined lump sum benefit' if paid out within two years of death, see *para 13(c)*; or 'an uncrystallised lump sum death benefit' if paid out within the same period: see *para 15(1)(c)*. The language of the pensions simplification legislation is itself anything but simple but the effect was that the tax treatment for discretionary trusts did not apply, if the lump sum, of either kind, was payable at the discretion of the trustees and the funds were distributed within two years of the death. If the funds were paid by the pension scheme trustees to a second trust, IHT became chargeable when the second trust released the benefits but subject to the two-year rule. Where the life tenant was the former spouse or civil partner, the IHT treatment reflected that and usually the funds were released so as to take advantage of that exemption.

The tax treatment following *FA 2006* is that where the funds are transferred at the discretion of the pension scheme trustees to a second trust, that trust will be treated as a discretionary one and the fund may therefore be subject to an exit charge on distribution, with the normal rules described in **Chapter 8** to apply the proportionate fraction. One particular difficulty may be in establishing whether the funds are released by the pension trustees to the second trust at their discretion, or whether effectively they have no choice.

There was a slight relaxation in *Finance Act 2007*. Lump sums, whether arising under regulated schemes or *s 615* schemes, will not come within the IHT rules for relevant property trusts if distributed within two years of the earlier of:

- the day on which the death was known to the trustees or those in charge of the scheme; or

- the day on which they could first be expected to have known of the death.

The taxation of pension savings was revisited in *Finance Act 2008, s 91* and *Sch 28*. These changes are considered in the context of 'lifetime planning' in **Chapter 12**.

For a long time there has been a difficulty for the owners of pension rights in deciding, on approaching retirement, whether or not to accept the annuity rates currently on offer; or to go into drawdown; or to carry on working. The last option might be in the hope of restoring the value of the fund to what it had been before the credit crunch; or the Gulf of Mexico spill; or whatever is the reason of the day for depressed values. *Section 3(3)* imposes a charge to IHT where, by failure to exercise the right to draw the pension, the taxpayer

**7.41** *Trusts: interest in possession*

brings about a situation where, on his death soon afterwards, the fund would otherwise pass free of IHT to close relatives.

The dilemma was well illustrated in *Fryer and others (PRs of Arnold Deceased v HMRC* [2010] UKFTT 87 (TC) 00398. Mrs Arnold could draw her pension on 8 September 2002, her sixtieth birthday. She was at that time diagnosed with a condition likely to prove terminal. Although she received details of the pension choices open to her, she did nothing. She died in September 2009. The First-tier Tribunal held that Mrs Arnold deliberately omitted, at her sixtieth birthday and thereafter until her death, to exercise her pension rights. Her estate in her lifetime lost the value of those rights, so there was a transfer of value within *s 3(3)*. The value transferred was the loss to the estate, ie the value of the right to opt to take the benefits. A hypothetical purchaser of those rights would opt to take the lump sum plus a guaranteed annuity for ten years; taking into account Mrs Arnold's health: all of that to be discounted 25%.

Practitioners have long worried about this issue: when do you test the failure to exercise the right to take the pension? The most difficult outcome of the *Arnold* case is to answer this question 'anytime until death', with the result that, since such a time must fall within two years of death, all future failures to draw pensions will be caught. You must, it seems, begin to draw the pension before death; or risk its exposure to IHT later. That, if correct, is harsh.

## Life policies

**7.41** There is no change to the treatment of discretionary trusts of life policies. Where the trusts are A&M trusts, care should be taken to note the identity of the beneficiaries as at 6 April 2008 because after that date a variation can bring the fund within the discretionary regime. As was noted at **7.28** above, there should be little difficulty with existing trusts. The main problems will concern new policies, especially those where the premiums are substantial. **Chapter 6** outlined the relaxation of the reporting requirements for new discretionary trusts. Once the policy trusts are in being, the usual regime described in the next chapter will apply.

It is of course part of the nature of a life policy, especially one of term assurance, that its value reflects the state of health of the life assured. As will be seen in **Chapter 8** the charging regime of discretionary trusts requires valuation of the fund on the eve of the tenth anniversary. If at that date the life assured is seriously ill the value of the trust may exceed the nil rate band. The same could apply if death occurred just before a tenth anniversary. In relation to particular schemes, such as discounted gift schemes and loan trusts it will be necessary to go back to first principles and establish the exact nature of the rights under the policy and under the trusts before applying the charging provisions.

*Trusts: interest in possession* **7.42**

# A sting in the tail

**7.42** Finally, there is an anomaly of which both trustees and beneficiaries should take note. The issue of burden and incidence of tax was discussed at the beginning of **Chapter 6**. On death, liability for IHT is, see *s 200(1)*, on:

- the personal representatives, for the free estate;
- the trustees, for trust property;
- any person in whom the property is vested, whether beneficially or not, or who has an interest in possession; or
- anyone for whose benefit a trust fund is held.

*Section 201* deals further with trust property and *s 201(1)(b)* makes a person liable for tax if he is entitled to an interest in possession.

These rules do not sit easily with the principle that many new life tenants will not be treated as entitled to the capital. Although they may have an interest in possession for the purposes of trust law and even for CGT, it will for IHT be taxed as the interest of a beneficiary of a discretionary trust. Why treat them differently from 'true' discretionary trust beneficiaries? It seems unfair. HMRC do not really defend the situation: they have commented:

> 'Although an IIP holder whose interest arose before 22 March 2006 has been regarded as owning the underlying property for inheritance tax purposes, in reality he has only ever owned a limited interest. The FA 2006 changes do not alter the IIP owner's real position.'

This seems to recognise the anomaly but does not redress it.

*Chapter 8*

# Relevant property trusts

## TYPES OF DISCRETIONARY OR RELEVANT PROPERTY TRUSTS

### Full relevant property trusts: history of the legislation

**8.1** This book is mainly about IHT, but where trusts are concerned IHT and CGT will often interact. Although at one time it was relatively easy to hold over gains on transfers into and out of trusts, this facility has been eroded, most recently in two ways:

- by the *FA 2003* changes restricting holdover in connection with settlor-interested trusts and trusts of residences; and

- by *FA 2004* rules introducing *TCGA 1992, s 169B* in relation to trusts for minors which are treated as settlor-interested following *FA 2006*, so that in effect there can be no holdover on gifts to children by way of trust. This cuts down the relief that was previously available on transfers of business property under *TCGA 1992, s 165* and of property in general under *TCGA 1992, s 260*.

Where a trust did not fall foul of the 'settlor interested' rules holdover was still possible. The effect of the *FA 2006* changes to IHT that treat more trusts as discretionary was to make holdover relief more available: see **8.6**. By *FA 2008*, some of the restrictions on settlor-interested UK-resident trusts were removed, because there was until the June 2010 Budget proposals a single rate of tax, at 18%. The restoration of a second, higher CGT rate at 28% may involve reintroduction of the settlor-interested rules formerly contained in *TCGA 1992, s 77*.

### The individual as the taxable entity

**8.2** The preferred unit of taxation for IHT is the individual and the size of his or her estate. Thus an outright transfer from one individual to another is taxed on a simpler, if not necessarily more favourable, basis than a transfer which reduces the estate of one person without at the same time increasing the estate of any other. The distinction between potentially exempt transfers and chargeable transfers was examined in **Chapter 1**. The effect of *IHTA 1984, ss 3* and *3A* is that the transfer of funds to a relevant property trust is a chargeable transfer. (Note, all statutory references in this chapter are to *IHTA 1984*, unless otherwise stated.) The amount of the transfer will initially be set against the transferor's unused nil rate band. Any excess will be chargeable initially at the lifetime rate and, in the event of the death of the transferor in three years, at the unabated death rate.

## How relevant property trusts work

**8.3** The normal, straightforward type of relevant property trust will provide for a perpetuity period, which until recently was usually 80 years and (until recently) an accumulation period, usually 21 years. The main effect of *Perpetuities and Accumulations Act 2009*, which came into force on 6 April 2010, is that the only perpetuity period becomes 125 years and the accumulation period will be dispensed with. However, it may be some time before all lawyers get up to speed with their drafting and move over to the new regime.

The settlor transfers assets to the trustees, who then have complete freedom to decide which of the beneficiaries is to receive anything from the trust, whether it be capital, income or the use of an asset.

Commonly the settlor will give the trustees (of whom he may be one) a letter of wishes. An example is included as Form A at the end of this chapter. The letter of wishes is not binding on the trustees. It is a subsidiary document. Significant debate surrounds the issue of whether such a letter is actually a trust document: clearly, it is of interest to all beneficiaries and to tax-gatherers in any jurisdiction.

Although many jurisdictions specifically protect such documents from prying eyes, there is some authority for the view that, if the disclosed principal trust document is so blandly or opaquely drawn that it is meaningless without the letter of wishes, that letter must be a trust document and as such belongs to the beneficiaries as a body, so they can, in fact, demand to see it. The view is advanced in some quarters that disclosure might be forced under the *Data Protection Act 1998*, but most practitioners disagree. The Data Commissioner has not made a ruling on the point. Certainly, most trustees will be guided by it and may find it useful in resisting repeated claims from one beneficiary in particular to preferential treatment. Good trustees can 'stand up to' the beneficiaries and preserve their independence.

A relevant property trust comes to an end by effluxion of time unless the trustees take earlier action. Normally, the trust deed will provide that, in default

**8.4** *Relevant property trusts*

of exercise of their discretion, the fund will at the end of the trust period be held for a particular person absolutely. However, the trustees can bring the trust to an end earlier simply by distributing all the funds in their hands.

## CGT and relevant property trusts

**8.4** Apart from the IHT effect, relevant property trusts enjoy some CGT benefits. *TCGA 1992, s 260* provides that gains may be held over, both on transfers into relevant property trusts and transfers out.

---

**Example 8.1—Tax charges on setting up a trust**

Alice owns a small parade of shops with flats above which she inherited from her husband many years earlier and which have risen substantially in value since then. She wishes to benefit her grandchildren Bella, Catherine and David. The present value of the parade of shops is £700,000. Alice would like to give away the residential part of the property, which is troublesome, but keep the shops. The flats are together worth £300,000, the shops £350,000 (Note: valued separately, the flats and shops are worth less than their combined value of £700,000).

Alice transfers the flats to a relevant property trust. Although they themselves are worth £300,000 the reduction in Alice's estate is £400,000. That is the value of the transfer. Alice has available her nil rate band for 2010/11 of £325,000 and the annual exemption for this year and last. Deducting the nil rate band and the allowances leaves in charge to tax £69,000, which at 20% triggers an IHT charge of £13,800.

Although the transfer to the trustees is a disposal for CGT, Alice may avoid paying that tax herself by electing to hold over the gain, so that it becomes the responsibility of the trustees as and when they dispose of the property. That might be by sale or by transfer out to the beneficiaries. If the transfer out was a chargeable transfer (which in all normal circumstances it would be) the trustees could themselves hold over the gain, so that it became the problem of the beneficiaries. If there are several of them, the fragmentation of the gain and the rates of tax charged on individuals may make this a good move.

---

## Old accumulation and maintenance trusts

**8.5** These trusts no longer exist in their original form, having become interest in possession trusts or relevant property trusts, according to the circumstances prevailing when *Finance Act 2006* came into force. Virtually all A&M trusts, whether established in lifetime or by will, became relevant property trusts. All new trusts, with very few exceptions, are relevant property trusts. The exceptions are:

- disabled trusts;
- trusts for bereaved minors;
- age 18-to-25 trusts; and
- IPDI trusts.

The regime of A&M trusts under *s 71* was terminated with effect from 6 April 2008, except as still provided for bereaved minors under *s 71A* and 18-to-25 trusts under *s 71D*.

## Bereaved Minors' Trusts (BMTs)

**8.6** The essential features of a BMT are:

- It can arise only on death.
- It may arise on intestacy or under deed of variation or by way of appointment under *s 144*.
- The only possible beneficiary is a minor child of the testator. A grandchild is not a child for this purpose. There is some provision for substitution of beneficiaries, but only under the rules of intestacy and not under the terms of a will.
- There is no need for an interest in possession in the income. It may be accumulated. However, the capital and all accumulations of income must vest at 18. It is not possible to exercise discretion between one beneficiary and another. Effectively, it is sub-funded for each beneficiary from the outset (though not in the full sense of that term).
- Holdover relief is available for CGT purposes, as with any other relevant property trust (*TCGA 1992, s 260(2)(da)*).
- There must be no general power of advancement and in particular no power to make a 'settled advance'. This means that whilst *s 71A(4)(a)* allows the statutory power of advancement under *Trustee Act 1925, s 32*, effectively there may be no material extension of the powers in the *Trustee Act 1925*. Merely removing 50% restriction from *s 32* is acceptable.

---

**Example 8.2—The test of a BMT**

Fred died intestate, survived by two children under the age of 18. If both reach the age of 18 they become absolutely entitled under the general intestacy rules and the BMT requirements are satisfied.

**8.6** *Relevant property trusts*

In the unlikely event that one of them married and died in childbirth before obtaining majority, the intestacy rules would provide that the grandchild became entitled and again entitled it to capital at age 18. The BMT rules would be satisfied.

Curiously, if Fred had made a will that provided for his children at age 18 but with substitution clauses, that would not comply with the requirements of BMT and the funds would be treated as held on relevant property trusts.

---

**Example 8.3—Further tests of a BMT**

On her death, Celia leaves her house to her daughter Jessica absolutely on reaching 18 but, if Jessica does not reach 18, to Celia's brother David, who is over 18. The usual clause extending powers of advancement under *TA 1925, s 32* was not included in the will. As a result, the gift is a BMT. The substituted beneficiary is an adult and the other requirements are satisfied.

However, if Celia had instead specified that the house was to go to her daughter at 21, that would have breached the BMT requirements and the result would be a relevant property trust. Returning to the original scenario in this example, shortly before the daughter is 18 the trustees decide that she is too young to have control of the house. They use the statutory power of advancement and move half of the value of the house onto interest in possession trusts. That goes beyond what HMRC approve, not being an appointment 'to the like effect' as *s 32*. What 'to the like effect' means can be seen only from Statement of Practice E7, in the context of protective trusts: it is all we currently have to go on. The appointment therefore triggers the special charge on an A&M trust (or indeed a BMT) under *s 70*: see **8.67** below.

If the will had included the usual clause extending *s 32* to the whole of the fund, that would have been 'to the like effect' and there would have been no BMT from the outset.

---

**Example 8.4—Wording to create a BMT or 18-to-25 trust**

Beverley's will left property 'to such of my children as reach 18 and if more than one in equal shares'. One of her children, Alice, survived her but tragically died of leukaemia at 17. Alice's share passed to her siblings at 18.

HMRC consider that this does not prejudice the shares, which can be treated sibling by sibling. The same treatment would result for 18-to-25 trust purposes.

## 18-to-25 trusts: overview

**8.7** Broadly, the flexibility of vesting age, deferring it to as late as 25, comes at a tax cost. If the beneficiary gets the capital at 18 there is no IHT charge on the fund during its currency or on vesting. If the vesting age is no greater than 25, there will be no IHT charge before 18, so that is the (only) advantage over a fully discretionary trust, but the fund will then enter the IHT regime, suffering periodic and exit charges. The benefit of the 'appropriate fraction', as described at **8.12** below, has the effect that the exit charge will not exceed 4.2% and may well be very much less. If the capital does not vest until, say, 28, the trust is fully within the IHT rules for relevant property trusts for the whole of its life.

These rules apply to existing trusts and to new will trusts. No new lifetime trust can benefit: it will be a relevant property trust from the outset. However, an immediate life interest trust under a will may qualify as an IPDI and, if it does, it will be within the 'old' regime.

## The conditions for 18-to-25 trusts

**8.8** The conditions for an 18-to-25 trust are:

- property held on trust for someone under 25;
- a parent of that person has died;
- the trust is in a will of the parent who has died, or is under the Criminal Injuries Compensation Scheme and meets the 'subsection 6' conditions (see below);
- the 'subsection 6' conditions are, first, that the beneficiary will, by 25 or sooner, get the capital and all income arising and all accumulated income; and, second, that effectively there has been sub-funding so that this fund has never been available to anyone else.

The 18-to-25 rules do not apply to other categories of trust property, such as that in bereaved minor's trusts, existing interest in possession trusts, IPDIs or disabled trusts. A difficulty had been noted where a trust was subject to the *Trustee Act 1925, s 32* (powers of advancement). The problem is resolved by *IHTA 1984, s 71D(7)*.

## Particular points of difficulty affecting BMTs and 18-to-25 trusts

**8.9** HMRC guidance has emerged on three troublesome issues:

**8.10** *Relevant property trusts*

- who is meant by 'the bereaved minor' (or 'B' in the legislation);
- how the legislation deals with the class closing rules; and
- the treatment of settled powers of advancement.

In *s 71A* 'the bereaved minor' can mean all the beneficiaries in the class who are alive and under age when the trust takes effect. This will assist in the common form of bequest to all children who reach 18 in shares appointed by the trustees, where the power of appointment is limited to prevent augmentation or depletion of a share of a child over 18. As a result the fund could be paid out in unequal shares; but age 18 is an effective cut-off point for the further exercise of the power of appointment to that child. Any further 'favouritism' is limited to the children under 18.

---

**Example 8.5—Rich uncle intervening**

Henry died young, leaving his estate to such of his sons, Charles and Trevor and his daughter Alice as should survive him and attain 18, but with power of appointment among them. To begin with, the trustees treated all three children the same; but Henry's brother Iain then died, leaving all his estate to his nephews and nothing to Alice. At this point all are still under 18. To even up the score, the trustees now want (revocably) to allocate a nominal 1% of the fund each to Charles and Trevor, the rest to Alice.

This will not prejudice the BMT status of the interests. Charles and Trevor could still, up to age 18, benefit if the power in favour of Alice were to be revoked, because they are still 'B' for the purpose of the legislation.

---

The mere existence of a power of advancement does not prevent a BMT or 18-to-25 trust from existing: it is the exercise of that power in such a way as to defer the vesting of capital that will cause a relevant property trust to arise.

Settled powers of appointment do not, by their mere existence, take a trust out of the BMT or 18-to-25 regimes. It is the exercise of such powers that will trigger relevant property trusts. If the fund goes out at age 18, there is no IHT charge.

# Tax on 18-to-25 trusts

**8.10** The tax charge on an 18-to-25 trust is set out in *s 71E*. It will not apply if the beneficiary takes at 18, or dies under that age, or if the trust property becomes subject to the rules for a bereaved minor's trust before the beneficiary becomes 18 (ie where the trustees vary it so that it will vest at 18) or the fund is used for the beneficiary before he is 18 or as soon as he is 18. This allows the

*Relevant property trusts* **8.11**

trustees to bring an otherwise non-compliant trust within the rules to escape IHT. In all other cases the charge will apply when the fund leaves the trust or the trustees enter into a depreciatory transaction. There is no tax charge on a depreciatory transaction if at arm's length or if it is the grant of an agricultural tenancy within *s 16*.

The tax itself is calculated under *s 71E* where property comes out of the trust, either to the beneficiary absolutely or for his benefit after the beneficiary is 18; or he dies. The legislation uses a formula multiplying the 'chargeable amount' by 'the relevant fraction' and by the 'settlement rate'. To find the settlement rate the trustees must establish a notional transfer similar to that described later in this chapter in relation to periodic and exit charges.

## Chargeable amount

**8.11** This is the reduction in the value of the trust fund as a result of the transfer. Alternatively, where the IHT is to be paid out of the remaining fund rather than out of the asset released, it is the grossed-up amount.

**Example 8.6—Simple release**

Cyril set up an A&M trust that is now governed by the 'new' rules. It holds £240,000 for Cyril's eight grandchildren, hence £30,000 for each. Rachel, 22, needs money to reduce her student loan, so the trustees pay her £11,000 on the basis that she will pay any IHT due. The chargeable amount is £11,000.

**Example 8.7—Net release**

Continuing the above example, Rachel's brother has bought a car to celebrate his 21st birthday and now wants to insure it. He needs £1,275 and has no money to pay the tax that may be due. There is no income available to distribute and the payment must come from capital. Assuming that the settlement rate is 2% and that the appropriate fraction, see below, is 12/40, the tax would be at the rate of 2% × 30% × 12/40, thus 0.18%. Thus a transfer of £1,277.30 would attract a tax charge:

£1,277.30 × 2% × 30% × 12/40 = £2.30, leaving a net £1,275.00.

**Example 8.8—Fall in value of the fund**

Dimitri's fund holds only shares in the family investment property company. His son Alexei was 18 some four years ago and is joining the board of directors,

**8.12** *Relevant property trusts*

so the trustees want him to have some shares. Owing to the different values of holdings, the fall in value of the fund is in fact greater than the value of the shares themselves. It is that greater value that is the transfer for IHT purposes (but not for CGT purposes).

## Relevant fraction

**8.12** This varies according to the time from when the beneficiary was 18 to the date of the chargeable event, reckoned in complete quarters. The fraction is 30% of x/40 where x is the number of complete quarters.

**Example 8.9—Fractions, timing and risk**

This was illustrated in the example of Rachel's brother, who suffered tax based on the fraction 12/40. Rachel herself is 22: if she is in fact only two months short of her 23rd birthday, the fraction applicable to her is 15/40.

Suppose that an A&M trust was established on 1 March 1998 and 'migrates' to the relevant property regime on 5 April 2008. The ten-year charge appropriate for a relevant property trust would have fallen on 1 March 2008, but the new regime did not at that date apply to this trust. The trustees want to terminate the trust as soon as they safely may, but there are large gains and a simple appointment out would trigger CGT. How soon can they appoint and hold over the gains, relying on *TCGA 1992, s 260*?

The bold answer is 'as soon as they like', on the basis that any appointment that is a chargeable transfer qualifies as a chargeable transfer within *s 260(2) (a)*. A transfer from a trust that was at inception within the nil rate band, and has not been added to, is chargeable to IHT at 0% but is still a chargeable transfer, so we know that it is possible to hold over a gain even where there is no positive IHT charge. What is the difference between that and an appointment which attracts no IHT for a different reason, namely that it is within the first period of three months during which the relevant property regime applies?

The 'exit' charge is calculated under *s 65*, but there is no charge, see *s 65(4)*, if the appointment is made in a quarter beginning with the commencement or with the ten-year anniversary of the trust. *Section 65(1)*, which imposes the charge, is disapplied, so though the result for IHT is the same in economic terms as a charge at 0%, the event is not within the requirements for holdover. The trustees should wait.

How long? Until 1 June, or even longer? A 'quarter' is defined by *s 63* as any period of three months, so it can begin on any day, not a 'quarter day' as such.

*Relevant property trusts* **8.14**

This trust entered the relevant property regime on 6 April pursuant to *Finance Act 2006, Sch 20, para 3*. *Section 69(2)(b)* provides for the situation where, as here, property was in a trust before the ten-year anniversary; but was not then relevant property; and has since become relevant property. The tax in such a situation is charged at the 'appropriate fraction' of the rate, ie x/40 where x is the number of complete quarters from the last ten-year anniversary up to the date of the appointment; see *s 69(4)*. What about the period from 6 April 2008 to 1 June 2008? That is not three months; but *s 68(3)(b)* treats a part-quarter as a full one. On that basis the trustees can safely distribute after 1 June and hold over the gain.

Most trustees and many advisers will play safe and let a further, clear, full quarter elapse, so as to avoid the complexities of this legislation. The IHT charge may be very small compared with the CGT in issue.

## Settlement rate

**8.13** This is the effective rate, ie the tax expressed as a fraction of the notional chargeable transfer. It can be found only after other calculations have been performed. Although the multi-step calculation is difficult to grasp, it can be performed by using the form IHT100 with the working sheet IHT100 (WS) and the guide IHT113. Find these at search2.hmrc.gov.uk/kbroker/hmrc/forms/viewform.jsp?formId=3337 with the event forms and supplementary pages.

## The notional transfer

**8.14** As with relevant property trusts generally, this is an amalgam of elements:

- the original value of the trust;
- the value of any related trust; and
- the value of any property added to the trust just after it joined the fund and before the event now being taxed.

---

**Example 8.10—The notional transfer**

Sean, who had available one annual exemption, divided £400,000 between two trusts that he set up the same day, 6 April 2009: one for his daughter Megan for life and the other for Megan's children. On 16 June 2010, having made no other gifts but fearful of a rise in CGT, he put quoted shares worth £26,500 into a trust.

**8.15**  *Relevant property trusts*

|  | £ |
|---|---:|
| Transfer to A&M trust | 200,000 |
| Less half of annual exemption | (1,500) |
|  | 198,500 |
| Transfer to related trust as above | 198,500 |
| Original notional transfer | 397,000 |
| Addition |  |
|  | 26,500 |
| Less annual exemption | (3,000) |
|  | 23,500 |
| Revised notional transfer | 420,500 |

## Life interest trusts

**8.15** Sometimes a change in tax law proves particularly difficult for practitioners and their clients to grasp. A classic example is the treatment of gifts under estate duty, where taper relief applied to reduce the gift itself and not merely the tax on it. The rules changed under IHT. Over 30 years later, people still fail to grasp that such gifts are now set initially against the nil rate band and that taper relief applies only to the tax and not to the gift. In the same way there will be, for many practitioners and their clients, a fundamental difficulty in understanding that a newly created life interest trust, treated as such for many purposes, such as:

- matrimonial proceedings; or
- the taxation of income; or
- the taxation of gains where main residence may be in point;

is not treated like an old, 'estate' interest in possession trust for IHT purposes but is treated as a relevant property trust. The difficulty may be compounded by anti-avoidance legislation, which often employs the concept of a double negative: see for example the changes introduced by *FA 2010, ss 52* and *53*, noted at **7.24**.

Except where an interest in possession trust is a disabled trust, a BMT, an 18-to-25 or an IPDI it will now fall within the relevant property trust regime unless saved by the existing or transitional rules. In this chapter the name 'life interest trust' is used rather than 'interest in possession trust' to denote a trust in which a beneficiary has a right to income but which for IHT purposes is treated as a

*Relevant property trusts* **8.16**

relevant property trust under the new rules. The conditions for an IPDI were set out in **Chapter 7**.

In future, virtually all life interest trusts established during the lifetime of the settlor will be treated as relevant property trusts. Their creation is a chargeable transfer. The trust will be subject to the periodic charge described at **8.38** and following and the proportionate charge described at **8.26** and following below. Contrary to the traditional treatment of interest in possession trusts, there will (except in relation to purchased interests and reversions of settlor-interested trusts) be no aggregation of the capital of a life interest trust with the estate of the life tenant. There will, for CGT, be some holdover relief.

---

**Example 8.11—Lifetime transfer failing to comply with new rules**

Henry, who has made no previous chargeable transfers and has not used his allowances, settles £331,000 on trust for his wife for life with remainder to their children at 25. The trust is dated 6 May 2010.

This cannot be an IPDI because it is a lifetime settlement. The result is that it must be treated as a relevant property trust. That in turn means that Henry's wife is not deemed to be the owner of the trust fund as would have been the case under the old rules. As a result, relief is not available. Fortunately, after taking account of the two annual exemptions available, the amount of the settlement is within the nil rate band, so its creation does not trigger an IHT charge. However, Henry must keep good records for the future in case he decides to make any other settlements later.

---

# THE RELEVANT PROPERTY IHT REGIME

## The range of charges

**8.16** There are three main occasions of charge on a relevant property trust:

- Entry charges:
    - On creation: use event form IHT100a.
    - On any addition to the fund, other than an exempt addition such as one within *s 21* (normal expenditure out of income): use event form IHT100a.
- Exit charges:
    - Before the first ten-year anniversary: use event form IHT100c.
    - Between ten-year anniversaries: use event form IHT100c.

**8.17** *Relevant property trusts*

- Ten-year charges:
    - Use event form IHT100d.

Other charges to IHT can apply, when for example:

- an interest in possession comes to an end and a relevant property trust arises; or
- a special charge arises, for example on a heritage fund; or
- woodland that was previously exempt is felled; or
- a chargeable event arises on a pension that has been 'alternatively secured'; or
- a purchased reversionary interest vests;

but these are all outside the scope of this chapter.

# TRANSFERS INTO TRUST: THE ENTRY CHARGE

## Simple cases

### Commencement

**8.17** It is important for many of the calculations of IHT on relevant property trusts to know when they began, but that will not always be easy to state. The legislation is brief: 'references to the commencement of a settlement are references to the time when property first becomes comprised in it'. This rule is not subject to *de minimis*, so the setting up of a pilot trust with £100 will be the commencement even though the main funds are not added until, say, a death many years later. This becomes highly relevant to old A&M trusts in respect of which it will now be necessary to fix anniversaries for IHT charges: see **Example 8.9**.

A slightly different rule applies where a trust is initially 'favoured' in some way but becomes a relevant property trust later. In such a case the property is treated, see *s 80(1)*, as joining a new settlement when the first, favoured, interest ends. There is a transfer by the person holding the interest in possession at the time of change. The general rule is that this does not affect the commencement date of the trust. Difficult questions arise where there has been more than one settlor and property has been added at various times. The general rule for the practitioner must be to recommend a new trust for each major transfer of property: the initial cost will be recouped in savings later.

*Relevant property trusts* **8.17**

### Example 8.12—Small family trust

Hubert set up a trust with £100 on 7 July 2002, and the same day made a will leaving to it £300,000. He died on 3 February 2005. A review of the trust in the light of *Finance Act 2006* showed that, in the particular circumstances, unless appointments were made promptly half would be held on relevant property trusts from 6 April 2008 onwards.

The trustees thought the risk of dissipation of the fund by young beneficiaries was much greater than possible IHT charges. They knew that the nil rate band would soon increase, so they did nothing before 5 April 2008 and nothing was paid out. The first ten-year charge will fall due on 7 July 2012 (but tax will in fact be calculated by reference to only part of the ten-year period).

### Example 8.13—Migration of a trust to relevant property regime

Iain was, by 21 March 2006, still tenant for life of a trust established by him on 8 March 1985. On 16 June 2010 the trustees at his request terminated his interest and relevant property trusts arose for his grandchildren. The capital of the fund is treated as passing to a new trust on 16 June 2010 and the event is a chargeable transfer by Iain, but the next ten-year anniversary will be on 8 March 2015, not in June 2020.

An example was given at **Example 8.1** of the setting up of a relevant property trust by Alice and of the calculation of IHT on that occasion. The initial charge on establishing a settlement is relevant in later computations but at this stage is quite straightforward. Potentially exempt transfers are at this stage ignored because they may fall out of account. The annual exemption is set against the first transfer in time in any given tax year: see *s 19(3)(b)*. Where there are no previous chargeable transfers the nil rate band is applied to the gift and the excess taxed at 20%. The only complicating issue is to observe whether the gift is gross, here meaning that the recipient will pay any IHT on it, or net, in which case the donor will pay the extra tax after grossing-up.

### Example 8.14—Simple gross gift

On 13 April 2010 Sandra settles investment properties worth £370,000 on relevant property trusts. The previous tax year, she used her annual allowance but she has made no other gifts. She tells the trustees that they must pay any IHT due.

**8.18**  *Relevant property trusts*

|  | £ |
|---|---:|
| Value transferred | 370,000 |
| Exemption 2010/11 | 3,000 |
|  | 367,000 |
| Nil rate band 2010/11 | 325,000 |
| Excess | 42,000 |
| IHT @ 20% | 8,400 |

## Grossing-up

**8.18** If the donor agrees to pay the tax, that tax is established by grossing-up, that is by finding the size of transfer which, after paying tax on it, results in the net gift. On lifetime transfers the grossing-up fraction is one-quarter; transfers on death are grossed-up with the fraction two-thirds. In calculating the tax any previous chargeable transfers must be taken into account.

### Example 8.15—Net gift following previous chargeable transfer

Tanya on 4 April 2010 gives trustees £280,000 cash to hold on relevant property trusts just like a trust she made the previous year of £100,000. She has used her annual allowance in each year. The gift is to be 'tax free'.

|  |  | £ |
|---|---:|---:|
| Value transferred |  | 280,000 |
| No annual exemption |  |  |
| Nil rate band 2009/10 | 325,000 |  |
| Less: previous chargeable transfer | 100,000 |  |
| Remaining nil rate band |  | (225,000) |
| Net transfer |  | 55,000 |
| Gross-up: £55,000 × 1/4: IHT |  | 13,750 |

**8.19** Although the tax charged on the first making of a lifetime transfer is at the lifetime rates, that is subject to review if death occurs within three years. However, the review may not eventually increase the charge: it depends on the circumstances. There is no refund of tax.

### Example 8.16—Death within three years of a small chargeable transfer

Una died on 5 April 2010. She had made a relevant property trust on 10 April 2007 of £340,000 gross. She had used her annual exemption but had made no prior chargeable transfers. When the trust was set up, the entry charge was:

*Relevant property trusts* **8.20**

|  | £ |
|---|---|
| Value transferred | 340,000 |
| Nil rate band 2007/08 | (300,000) |
| Excess | 40,000 |
| Tax @ 20% | 8,000 |

Death occurs within three years, so apply the 'death' rate as required by *s 7(4)*:

| Value transferred | 340,000 |
|---|---|
| Nil rate band 2009/10 | (325,000) |
|  | 15,000 |
| Tax @ 40% | 6,000 |
| Deduct tax already paid | 8,000 |
| Additional tax charge | NIL |

**8.20** Where the figures are larger, it is much more likely that death within three years will trigger a charge to additional tax.

**Example 8.17—Death within three years of a large chargeable transfer**

Victor died on 17 May 2010 and having made a relevant property trust on 30 May 2007 of £750,000 gross. He had used his annual exemptions. On setting up the trust, the tax charge was:

|  | £ |
|---|---|
| Value transferred | 750,000 |
| Nil rate band 2007/08 | (300,000) |
| Excess | 450,000 |
| Tax at 20% | 90,000 |

Death occurs within three years. Apply the death rate, at the rates then in force.

|  | £ |
|---|---|
| Value transferred | 750,000 |
| Nil rate band 2010/11 | (325,000) |
|  | 425,000 |
| Tax @ 40% | 170,000 |
| Less tax paid earlier | (90,000) |
| Balance now payable | 80,000 |

### 8.21 *Relevant property trusts*

**8.21** The final factor that can affect the entry charge is the existence of prior transfers which, though potentially exempt when made, become chargeable because death occurs within seven years.

**Example 8.18—Review of earlier tax charge and re-computation at death rates**

Willie, who died on 17 April 2010, always used his annual exemption and had made a number of lifetime gifts, thus:

|  | £ |
|---|---|
| 5 April 2002: cash to his daughter (outright) | 150,000 |
| 1 January 2006: cash to A&M trust for his grandchildren | 160,000 |
| 3 May 2007: investment property to a relevant property trust | 305,000 |

No IHT was paid on the cash gifts, being PETs.

Tax was paid on setting up the relevant property trust:

|  | £ |
|---|---|
| Value transferred | 305,000 |
| Nil rate 2007/08 | (300,000) |
| Excess | 5,000 |
| Tax at 20% | 1,000 |

On death it becomes clear that the gift in 2002 was more than seven years earlier but that the PET in 2006 is chargeable. The nil rate band otherwise available is first used towards this gift, so there is tax on the A&M trust itself, but tax is recalculated on the 2007 transfer.

|  | £ | £ |
|---|---|---|
| Value transferred |  | 305,000 |
| Nil rate band 2007/08 | 300,000 |  |
| Less: used for A&M trust | 160,000 |  |
|  |  | (140,000) |
| Balance |  | 165,000 |
| Tax at 20% (but see below) | 33,000 |  |
| Less paid earlier | (1,000) |  |
| Payable now in respect of original event (subject as below) | 32,000 |  |

Death has occurred within three years. Charge death rate.

|  | £ | £ |
|---|---|---|
| Value transferred |  | 305,000 |
| Nil rate band 2010/11 | 325,000 |  |
| Less: used for A&M trust | (160,000) |  |
|  |  | (165,000) |
| Excess |  | 140,000 |
| Tax at 40% | 56,000 |  |
| Less: paid originally | (1,000) |  |
| Less: payable at lifetime rates | (32,000) |  |
| Payable now |  | 23,000 |

Strictly, in the above example it was not necessary to recalculate the tax at the lifetime rates to establish the further burden of tax but circumstances may be imagined where, because of periodic changes in the rates, each step in the calculation is necessary.

## Migrations from the pre-2006 regime: the general position

**8.22** The policy behind *FA 2006* was to bring within the IHT regime for tax on relevant property trusts various trusts that previously were outside it, such as interest in possession trusts subject to overriding powers and A&M trusts where capital did not vest until age 25. The position of interest in possession trusts is protected until the present interest in possession expires (or even longer in a transitional serial interest). On the termination of those interests there will be an IHT charge if the property remains in the settlement, whether it then falls to be held on relevant property trusts or not.

By *s 51(1A)*, the disposal of a post-22 March 2006 interest in possession is a transfer of value unless the interest is an IPDI, a disabled person's interest or a TSI. By *s 51(1B)*, the disposal of a pre-22 March 2006 interest in possession is a transfer of value unless immediately before that disposal the trust as a whole complies with the requirements of *s 71A* trusts for bereaved minors: in other words, that on the disposal the trust will become the property of minors at the age of 18.

## Migration of interest in possession trusts to the relevant property trust tax regime

**8.23** *Section 52* provides the general rule that there is a charge to tax on the coming to an end of an interest in possession, but with the qualification that, where the interest is sold, the proceeds of sale are set against the value that would otherwise be taxed. *Section 52(2A)* provides that in relation to

**8.24** *Relevant property trusts*

'new' interests in possession, *s 52(1)* and *(2)* apply only where the interest being terminated is an IPDI, or a disabled person's interest, or a TSI. The same applies to depreciatory transactions.

*Section 53(1A)* provides for an exception from the general charge to tax on the fund under *s 52* in relation to an 'old' interest in possession which continues after 22 March 2006 where, by the time it ends, the requirements of a BMT or an 18-to-25 trust are met. The structure that results is that the termination of an interest in possession that existed before 22 March 2006 is still to be treated under the old rules. If on that termination relevant property trusts arise, it is a chargeable transfer. If on that termination the fund becomes part of the estate of another person under the old rules, it is a PET. On the other hand, the termination of an interest in possession which has only come into being after 22 March 2006 will be a chargeable transfer unless it is brought within the exceptional regime for a TSI or a BMT.

## Migration of A&M trusts to the relevant property trust tax regime

**8.24** The beneficial IHT treatment described at **8.5** was terminated with effect from 22 March 2006. Any beneficiary who had already obtained an interest in possession can happily continue to benefit from the old treatment.

However, a person who by accident of date of birth had not achieved an interest in possession by 22 March 2006, would be treated as a beneficiary of a relevant property trust, making his interest subject to periodic and proportionate charges. This could cause significant disadvantage as between one beneficiary and another. The provisions have been softened a little, giving trustees a choice in the matter.

**Example 8.19—No election by the trustees**

Hannah had four grandchildren for whom, in 2003, she set up an A&M trust. It was in simple form and the children became entitled to income at the age of 18, because the *Trustee Act 1925, s 31* had not been amended, and to capital at age 25 rather than a mere interest in possession. The trustees either were unaware of the right to elect into the 'at 18' regime or considered it unwise for family reasons.

By 22 March 2006 the eldest grandchild, Isaac, was 25, and received his capital. He is out of the picture.

Jessica was aged 24 on Budget Day 2006. She therefore became entitled to the capital the following year. She was already entitled to income and did not

*Relevant property trusts* **8.26**

suffer an IHT charge on her fund when she became entitled. Conversely, there was no holdover for CGT purposes.

Karen became 18 in December 2007. Because she had not yet obtained an interest in possession under the basic rule, her fund was treated as being in a relevant property trust, but no IHT charge was imposed by *FA 2006* on this change of status. However, the original freedom from IHT exit charges was lost. She suffers tax on the 18-to-25 basis.

Lucy was not 18 until some time after 5 April 2008. Her interest is in a relevant property trust which is subject to ten-year and exit charges.

**8.25** The transitional provisions were set out in *s 71(1A)* and *FA 2006, Sch 20, para 3*. If the terms of the trust were changed so that the age for vesting capital was reduced to 18, its A&M status could be preserved. The time for this has now passed but the following illustration may be relevant to unfinished cases.

**Example 8.20—Action by the trustees**

In the above example, the share of Lucy could have been kept within the old rules until she reached 18 by changing the terms of the trust.

There was actually no exit charge when Karen became entitled to the capital because of the transitional provisions of *FA 2006, Sch 20, para 3(3)*. The reason is one of timing of charges. The periodic charge is calculated by reference to ten-year anniversaries from the commencement. Under the transitional provisions the capital was not treated as being within a relevant property trust until 6 April 2008. Capital that vested before that date therefore escaped the charge. Interests in possession that arose after that date did so within the context of a relevant property trust; they were not an occasion of charge.

# THE PROPORTIONATE OR 'EXIT' CHARGE DURING THE FIRST TEN YEARS

## General considerations and the procedure

**8.26** The taxation of relevant property trusts could have been made very much simpler by applying a single tax rate to all such trusts, regardless of size. Instead, in attempting to tax settlements that are larger, or that are derived from a larger estate, more heavily than smaller ones, rules of extreme complexity have been devised. A fund that is within the nil rate band and remains so is

**8.27** *Relevant property trusts*

infinitely easier to manage than a larger fund. The rate of tax is stipulated in *s 68(1)*, referring to:

- 'the appropriate fraction' of
- 'the effective rate' applied to
- the type of transfer identified in *s 68(4)*, but as varied by
- *s 68(6)* in relation to old trusts.

'Why bother, if they'll do the sums for you?' Perseverance is required, perhaps especially from lawyers not accustomed to multi-step computations, in order to grasp the principles. Given the willingness of HMRC to help with the calculation, few lawyers will waste time on this exercise, but that attitude does leave them unable to check the accuracy of any assessment, which is hardly a professional way of working. Among the professional organisations, both the Chartered Institute of Taxation and the Society of Trust and Estate Practitioners now require new members to show some competence in dealing with the subject.

**8.27** Where the fund is larger than the nil rate band but the circumstances are simple, the computation is still manageable. Virtually no help can be gained from the legislation, which is contained in *ss 64–69* and which tries to express the charge without the use of formulae or examples. It is therefore nearly always simpler to download form IHT100 and the related forms IHT100d and IHT100 (WS) and follow the steps in those forms. Commendably, the similar calculation required for an 18-to-25 trust, set out in *s 71F*, does use a formula and is slightly easier to follow.

In a simple case the settlor will not have added any funds to the trust after first establishing it. However it is distressingly common for this 'rule' to be breached, see **Example 8.29** below, which makes the calculations more complicated.

Further complications arise where the relevant property trust is also used as the vehicle for holding family assets which are the subject of interest in possession trusts: see **Example 8.24** below. Following the changes in *FA 2006*, this is perhaps likely to be less of a problem because it will no longer be possible to create new lifetime interest in possession trusts.

The information gathered in completing IHT100 and IHT100d is then used to calculate the charge.

## Establishing the 'hypothetical transfer'

**8.28** The first step in the calculation is merely to satisfy a hypothesis required by *s 68(4)* as the means of achieving a graduated tax burden. The

*Relevant property trusts* **8.29**

purpose may become clearer as the several examples are worked through. Elements of the hypothesis include (see *s 68(4)(b)*):

- the transfer itself;
- others made on the same day; and
- funds added later.
- The following notes relate only to settlements established after 26 March 1974, thus avoiding the complexities of *s 68(6)*.

### Example 8.21—The hypothetical transfer: simplest version

Alfred had used his annual exemptions and the other exemptions to the full but had made no chargeable transfers until 7 October 2009, when he put a small investment property, worth £260,000, into relevant property trust for his grandchildren.

The hypothetical transfer comprises:

|  | £ |
|---|---|
| • value of property in trust at commencement | 260,000 |
| • value of property in any related settlement | NIL |
| • value of any added property | NIL |
|  | 260,000 |

This is within the nil rate band then in force so, as will be seen, no IHT will be payable on transfer out of the fund during the first ten years of its life.

**8.29** The transfer is of all the property, even though reliefs may apply: remember that no tax is actually being paid at this stage, so the taxpayer is not losing out. A 'related settlement' is, see *s 62*, one made on the same day by the same settlor, except where one is for charity and is unlimited in time.

### Example 8.22—The hypothetical transfer: related settlement and business property

Bernard transferred a block of property to a new relevant property trust on 8 October 2009. It comprised a factory occupied by Bernard's family company and some terraced cottages adjoining. The factory was worth £200,000, the cottages £150,000. The same day Bernard settled £50,000 cash on a separate relevant property trust.

The hypothetical transfer comprises:

**8.30**   *Relevant property trusts*

|  | £ |
|---|---|
| • value of the property in trust at commencement | 350,000 |
| • value of property in related settlement | 50,000 |
| • value of any added property | NIL |
|  | 400,000 |

The first point for the newcomer to this subject to note is what seems to be an anomaly. Although BPR at 50% is available, viz £100,000 on the factory, that relief is ignored when (and only when) calculating the hypothetical transfer.

**8.30**   Can the trustees deduct, from the value of the fund, the tax that they had to pay?

### Example 8.23—The hypothetical transfer: allowance for tax debt

Celia owned a block of flats worth £300,000 and settled it on 9 October 2009 on terms that the trustees would pay any IHT. She had made one chargeable transfer of £50,000 earlier that year, not connected with the trust, against which had been set the annual exemptions for that and the previous year.

The IHT on the transfer is by reference to:

|  | £ |
|---|---|
| • the transfer itself | 300,000 |
| • the earlier 'unconnected' transfer | 50,000 |
|  | 350,000 |
| less: nil rate band 2009/10 | (325,000) |
| chargeable excess | 25,000 |
| 20% of excess (the 'entry' charge): | 5,000 |

The hypothetical transfer comprises:

|  | £ |
|---|---|
| • value of property in trust at commencement | 300,000 |
| • less the entry charge | (5,000) |
|  | 295,000 |
| • value of property in related settlement | NIL |
| • value of any added property | NIL |
|  | 295,000 |

There is no statutory authority for the deduction, but it seems to fit the scheme. Note that at this point we need not consider the prior chargeable transfer; that will be relevant later but is not a component of this stage of the calculation: it is not included in the elements set out in *s 68(5)*.

**8.31** Again, where (in the case of trusts established before 22 March 2006) part of the new trust fund was not to be held on relevant property trusts, logic suggests that that value should be excluded, but it is not. Since 22 March 2006 the entire fund will normally be a relevant property trust, so this particular issue will disappear, but it is retained for the time being.

### Example 8.24—The hypothetical transfer: mixed (but not exempt) settlement

On 1 October 2005, Dennis set up a trust of which half the fund is for his niece for life whilst the remainder is held on relevant property trusts. There are no other complications. The fund is £340,000.

The hypothetical transfer comprises:

|   | £ |
|---|---|
| • value of property in trust at commencement | 340,000 |
| • value of property in related settlement | NIL |
| • value of any added property | NIL |
|   | 340,000 |

Just because half the fund was a PET does not change the hypothetical transfer.

### Example 8.25—Trust migrating to the relevant property regime under the new rules

Doreen had made some chargeable transfers totalling £75,000 in 1994 and created two settlements on 7 July 1995. The first was of £200,000 for her son Eric for life. The second was of £150,000 on A&M trusts for her grandchildren. By virtue of *FA 2006* the A&M trust migrated to the relevant property regime on 6 April 2008. The first ten-year charge will fall due on 7 July 2015.

The hypothetical transfer comprises:

| • Value of property in trust at commencement | 150,000 |
|---|---|
| • Value of property in related settlement | 200,000 |
| • Value of any added property | NIL |
|   | 350,000 |

**8.32** *Relevant property trusts*

**8.32** Related settlements can greatly affect the rate. This will be relevant in relation to A&M trusts that migrate to the IHT regime under *FA 2006*, where we must look at the share that is caught by the new rules in the context of the trust as a whole. See also the way the rule can work, below.

### Example 8.26—The hypothetical transfer: death same day as settlement

Eric made a relevant property trust of £200,000 on 11 November 2009 and died later that day, leaving an estate of £500,000 all on relevant property trusts. No exemptions were available on death.

The hypothetical transfer comprises:

|  |  | £ |
|---|---|---|
| • | value of the fund at commencement | 200,000 |
| • | value of property in related transfer | 500,000 |
| • | value of any added property | NIL |
|  |  | 700,000 |

**8.33** An exemption is treated differently from a relief. Whereas reliefs do not affect the hypothetical transfer, exemptions do, as seen in the next example.

### Example 8.27—The hypothetical transfer: death same-day as settlement

Frances made a lifetime trust of £100,000 on 12 November 2009 having by her will left £100,000 on trust for her local church, £200,000 to her husband and the residue on discretionary trusts. She died on 12 November 2009. The residue amounted to £150,000.

The hypothetical transfer comprises:

|  |  | £ |
|---|---|---|
| • | value of the fund at commencement | 100,000 |
| • | value of property in related settlement | 150,000 |
| • | value of any added property | NIL |
|  |  | 250,000 |

**8.34** Where funds are left on trust for a charity 'without limit of time' there is, as noted earlier, no aggregation: see *s 62(2)*.

## Example 8.28—The hypothetical transfer: exempt share of the trust

On 13 November 2009 Gina put £400,000 in trust as to half for her husband Gregory for life and as to the remainder on relevant property trusts. There were no other complications.

The hypothetical transfer comprises:

|  | £ |
|---|---|
| • value of relevant property fund at commencement | 200,000 |
| • value of property in related transfer | NIL |
| • value of any added property | NIL |
|  | 200,000 |

Contrast this situation with the example of Dennis above.

**8.35** Curiously, even where an asset is added to the trust and later distributed, it affects the calculation. For valuation purposes it would seem that each asset is valued in isolation.

## Example 8.29—Extra funds for a while

On 14 November 2008 Henry settled a property worth £300,000 on relevant property trusts. On 6 April 2009 he added £100,000 cash, of which £75,000 was released at Christmas 2009. The trustees paid the appropriate exit charge at that time. This calculation, like the others in this section, concerns only the hypothetical transfer by reference to a further release of funds, deemed to be made on, say, 3 March 2010.

The hypothetical transfer comprises:

|  | £ |
|---|---|
| • value of relevant property fund at commencement | 300,000 |
| • value of property in related transfer | NIL |
| • value of added property | 100,000 |
|  | 400,000 |

## Example 8.30—Failed PET coming to light

Celia (**Example 8.23**) died on 20 May 2010. It turns out that she had made a potentially exempt transfer of £100,000 after exemptions on 8 August 2004.

### 8.36 *Relevant property trusts*

The PET 'fails' and becomes chargeable by reason of death within seven years. The calculation of the entry charge on her transfer into trust on 9 October 2009 is revised.

The IHT entry charge on the transfer, to calculate the hypothetical rate for the later exit charge, is now:

|  |  | £ |
|---|---|---|
| • | the transfer itself | 300,000 |
| • | the newly discovered transfer | 100,000 |
| • | the earlier transfer | 50,000 |
|  |  | 450,000 |
| • | less: nil rate band (2009/10) | 325,000 |
| • | Chargeable excess | 125,000 |
| • | 20% of excess | 25,000 |

All of this tax relates to the establishment of the trust, because the earlier transfers go against the nil rate band.

The hypothetical transfer comprises:

|  |  | £ |
|---|---|---|
| • | value of property in trust at commencement | 300,000 |
| • | less IHT liability of trustees | (25,000) |
|  |  | 275,000 |
| • | value of property in related settlement | NIL |
| • | value of any added property | NIL |
|  |  | 275,000 |

## Calculating the 'effective rate'

**8.36** Even though the preceding sums are a tax computation, they are but a step to establishing the final calculation, and again the procedure may seem misleading. The taxpayer or his agent must now calculate tax on the hypothetical transfer: piling Pelion upon Ossa, one fiction after another.

This is *not real tax*.

The purpose of this particular set of sums is to fix the charge on assets leaving a relevant property trust. The rate of tax used is the rate in force at the time of the transfer, not at the time that the trust was set up. All that this computation achieves is to identify the 'effective rate'.

Even that is not the rate at which tax will be charged: only a proportion will be charged.

Note that the lifetime rate of 20% is used, even where the transfer was on death.

---

**Example 8.31—Tax on the hypothetical transfers assuming that the exit charge applies on 3 March 2010, and the 'effective rate'**

|  | £ |
|---|---|
| **Alfred (Example 8.21):** | NIL |
| **Bernard (Example 8.22):** | |
| Value of hypothetical transfer | 400,000 |
| Nil rate band at the time of the exit charge (2009/10) | (325,000) |
| Notional chargeable transfer | 75,000 |
| Tax @ 20% | 15,000 |
| Effective rate 15,000/400,000 | 3.75% |
| **Celia (original calculation at Example 8.23):** | |
| Value of hypothetical transfer | 295,000 |
| Nil rate band (2009/10) | (325,000) |
| Notional chargeable transfer | NIL |
| Tax @ 20% | NIL |
| Effective rate | 0% |
| **Celia (revised calculation at Example 8.30):** | |
| Value of hypothetical transfer | 275,000 |
| Nil rate band (2009/10) | (325,000) |
| Notional chargeable transfer | NIL |
| Tax @ 20% | NIL |
| Effective rate | 0% |
| **Dennis (Example 8.24):** | |
| Value of hypothetical transfer | 340,000 |
| Nil rate band (2009/10) | (325,000) |
| Notional chargeable transfer | 15,000 |
| Tax @ 20% | 3,000 |
| Effective rate 3,000/340,000 | 0.88% |

8.37   *Relevant property trusts*

**Eric (Example 8.26):**

| | |
|---|---|
| Value of hypothetical transfer | 700,000 |
| Nil rate band (2009/10) | (325,000) |
| Notional chargeable transfer | 375,000 |
| Tax @ 20% | 75,000 |
| Effective rate 75,000/700,000 | 10.71% |

**Frances (Example 8.27):**

| | |
|---|---|
| Value of hypothetical transfer | 250,000 |
| Nil rate band (2009/10) | (325,000) |
| Tax @ 0% | NIL |
| Effective rate | 0% |

**Gina (Example 8.28):**

| | |
|---|---|
| Value of hypothetical transfer | 200,000 |
| Nil rate band (2009/10) | (325,000) |
| Tax at 0% | NIL |
| Effective rate | 0% |

**Henry (Example 8.29):**

| | |
|---|---|
| Value of hypothetical transfer | 400,000 |
| Nil rate band (2009/10) | (325,000) |
| Notional chargeable transfer | 75,000 |
| Tax @ 20% | 15,000 |
| Effective rate 15,000/400,000 | 3.75% |

# Calculating the 'appropriate fraction' and the actual tax charge

**8.37**   Even the 'effective rate' is not the tax rate; but readers are asked to persevere.

Property may not have been subject to relevant property trusts for a full ten years: indeed it cannot have been for the proportionate charge to apply. Each period of ten years is divided into periods of three months. A fraction is calculated of the number of complete quarter-years during which the property has been subject to relevant property trusts. That fraction is applied to the effective rate: see *s 68(2)*.

Apply these principles:

- *Section 68(2)*: work out the number of complete successive quarters from the commencement of the trust to the exit date, here called 'x'.

*Relevant property trusts* **8.37**

- *Section 68(3)*: look for anomalies, such as a period during which the property was not subject to relevant property trusts; or when the property was in a different trust, here called 'y'.
- Calculate the period of anomaly and exclude it from the earlier calculation, ie x − y.
- Assess accumulations of income, disregarding income that has not been formally accumulated but simply not yet distributed (see Statement of Practice 8/86).
- Apportion the capital distribution that triggers the exit charge across the property that represents it.
- If part now distributed was always subject to discretion, and thus never anomalous, tax it by the fraction x/40. *But*
- If, and to the extent that, an anomaly applies to part, apply the fraction (x − y)/40 to that part, then tax it.
- Charge tax on the property at 30% of the effective rate, reduced by the x/40 or (x − y)/40 fraction, as appropriate.
- With regard to periods of anomaly, where x − y = 0, but x is at least 1, tax at 30% of the effective rate multiplied by 1/40.

---

**Example 8.32—(Continued from the previous scenarios)—in each case there is a distribution of £25,000 cash on 3 March 2010**

For several examples the period from the various dates in October 2009 to March 2010 is only five full months, so one complete quarter, as required by s 68(2); from mid November 2009 to March 2010 is likewise only one full quarter. £25,000 × 1/40 × 30% = £187.50 to be multiplied by the effective rate in each case.

Doreen's example is omitted because it illustrates a slightly different point.

The example of Dennis relates to an earlier year, so there are 13 quarters. For his trust, the calculation is £25,000 × 17/40 × 30% = £3,187.50 to be multiplied by the effective rate.

Admittedly, a distribution of £25,000 may seem modest but the calculations below show how small is the IHT charge where the fund has been subject to a discretion for only a short time.

Alfred's trust (**Example 8.21**): effective rate of 0%: no charge
Bernard's trust (**Example 8.22**): Rate 3.75%, charge £7.03
Celia's trust, on the revised figures (**Example 8.30**): Rate now 0%, so no charge

**8.38** *Relevant property trusts*

Dennis' trust (**Example 8.24**): Rate 0.88%, charge £28.05
Eric's trust (**Example 8.26**): Rate 10.71%, charge £20.08
Frances' trust (**Example 8.27**): rate 0%, so no charge
Gina's trust (**Example 8.28**): rate also 0%
Henry's trust (**Example 8.29**): rate 3.75 % as Bernard's trust, charge £7.03.

## THE PERIODIC OR 'TEN-YEAR' CHARGE

### Simple cases: first ten-year anniversary

**8.38**

**Example 8.33—Reporting the charge**

Sarah, domiciled in the UK and remaining so throughout, establishes a relevant property trust for her adult children and her grandchildren of an amount which, at the time of settlement, is about three-quarters of the nil rate band. There are no related settlements. The fund is invested by the UK trustees on a fairly conservative basis. Ten years later it has grown in value but is still within the nil rate band. In that period there have been distributions of income but not of capital. Although there is a duty on the trustees to complete IHT100 in respect of the ten-year charge if the fund exceeds 80% of the nil rate band (see the *Inheritance Tax (Delivery of Accounts) (Excepted Settlements) Regulations) 2008, reg 4*), there will be no tax to pay.

So as to comply with *s 64* and to the tax fund under *ss 66* and *67* IHT100 will, when completed, show the value of the fund on the eve of the tenth anniversary after taking account of any exemptions or reliefs (note that the annual exemption does not apply). The fund is divided, as would be the case with an estate on death, between assets on which tax must be paid immediately and those where the instalment option applies.

**8.39** Form IHT100d identifies the date (see commentary at **8.16** above) on which property became subject to relevant property trusts and its value at the ten-year anniversary, again providing where appropriate for the instalment option. The form then puts the settlement into its gift context. In a simple case the transferor will have made no previous chargeable transfers in the seven years ending before the settlement was established and will have made no other settlements on the same day as the one which is the subject of the calculation.

Rather like the procedure for the exit charge, the ten-year charge involves a multi-stage calculation. It is again necessary to establish the 'hypothetical chargeable transfer' but the component parts are different. The rate of charge at one ten-year anniversary determines the rate of exit charges from then until the next ten-year anniversary. The tax rate is established by calculating tax on the hypothetical transfer and applying it to the amount on which tax is charged, producing the 'effective rate'. One particular difficulty is the need to put the settlement in the context of other gifts.

## Establishing the 'hypothetical transfer'

**8.40** Special rules apply, see *s 68(6)*, where the settlement commenced before 27 March 1974. The rules are mentioned here, but are not included in any of the illustrations in order to keep the subject as simple as possible. Taxpayers or their advisers dealing with old relevant property trusts are referred to the (fairly difficult) legislation in *s 68(6)* and to commentaries on it.

For all other settlements we must first find and then add together the following (see *s 66(4)*):

- the transfer value for the periodic charge;
- the value of funds not subject to discretion;
- the value of property in related settlements.

### The transfer value

**8.41** This is the value that will form the basis of the actual tax computation, once the hypothetical transfer and the effective rate have been calculated. It is the value of that part of the property in the settlement immediately before the ten-year anniversary which is subject to discretion. In the calculations that follow this is called 'the discretionary trust fund'.

### Other funds within the trust

**8.42** Next, calculate the value of property that is not subject to any discretion, and has never been subject to relevant property trusts, but which is within the main settlement. The value is taken immediately after that property joined the trust. In the computations in this section this is called the 'sub-fund'.

### Related settlements

**8.43** A related settlement is one which commenced on the same day as the main settlement and has the same settlor. A charitable trust is not a related settlement. In this section this property is known as 'the related fund'.

**8.44** *Relevant property trusts*

When calculating the *discretionary trust fund*, do not include excluded property (see *s 58(1)(f)*) or property passing to charitable and similar trusts. Include, in relation to the discretionary trust fund, favoured property qualifying for BPR or APR only at its value as relieved.

When calculating the *related fund*, use the historic value but do not adjust for APR or BPR: see for example IHTM42165 for the official view.

When calculating the *sub-fund*, bring into account property that has always been either exempt or otherwise excluded from charge or property held on permanent charitable trusts.

**8.44** However, there is one category of property that is not taken into account in the hypothetical transfer. This is property in the settlement that was originally subject to a discretion but then became excluded or exempt without suffering any exit charge. One example would be relevant property that became excluded property where the settlor was domiciled outside the UK; another would be relevant property that became held on permanent charitable trusts. Such property does not fall within the statutory definitions of property that would otherwise comprise the discretionary trust fund or the sub-fund, so ignore it for this purpose.

The following example illustrates the form of computation that may be required, though in many instances only some elements of it will be needed.

---

**Example 8.34—Form of computation of the hypothetical transfer required to calculate the ten-year charge**

Elements:

1   Value of the discretionary trust fund, eg:

- quoted securities
- cash
- unquoted securities
- freehold residential property
- business interests
- business assets
- farming interests

*Less*:

- liabilities set against the fund; and
- value of excluded property

- assets held on charitable trusts
- BPR or APR.

2  Value of the sub-fund

*Less*:

- liabilities set against the fund; and
- value of excluded property
- assets held on charitable trusts.

3  Value of the related fund

Hypothetical transfer = (1 + 2 + 3).

**8.45** The following examples take each element of the computation in turn. The first is a simple situation, such as might often be found in practice.

**Example 8.35—Computation of the hypothetical transfer (ten-year charge)**

Zuleika settled cash of £200,000 (which has never been invested by the trustees) and a holding of shares in an unquoted trading company on 7 February 2000. The shares are now worth £75,000. All the fund is held on relevant property trusts for Zuleika's grandchildren. She made no other settlements that day.

1  Value of 'the discretionary trust fund':

|  | £ |
|---|---|
| Cash | 200,000 |
| unquoted securities | 75,000 |
|  | 275,000 |
| *Less*: |  |
| BPR | (75,000) |
|  | 200,000 |

2  Value of the sub-fund – NIL

3  Value of the related fund – NIL

Hypothetical transfer: 200,000

**8.46** Matters become more complicated where APR or BPR is involved, or where not all the fund is held on relevant property trusts.

**8.47** *Relevant property trusts*

### Example 8.36—Computation of the hypothetical transfer (ten-year charge)

Yolande set up a trust, half for her sister for life and half on relevant property trusts, on 6 February 2000. Into it she put quoted securities, now worth £150,000, a pair of cottages now worth £180,000 and a share of some agricultural pasture worth £20,000. She made no other settlements that day.

| | | £ |
|---|---|---:|
| 1 | Value of the discretionary trust fund: | |
| | value of the whole: | |
| | quoted securities | 150,000 |
| | freehold residential properties | 180,000 |
| | farming interests | 20,000 |
| *Less*: | | |
| | APR | (20,000) |
| | | 330,000 |
| | 50% on relevant property trusts: | 165,000 |
| 2 | Value of the sub-fund (as above) | 165,000 |
| 3 | Value of the related fund | NIL |
| Hypothetical transfer | | 330,000 |

**8.47** Related trusts are not all that common: *Rysaffe Trustee Co (CI) Ltd v IRC* [2002] EWHC 1114 (Ch); [2002] STC 872 and on appeal [2003] EWCA Civ 356, [2003] STC 536 is an example of a situation where everything very nearly went badly wrong for advisers who wanted to avoid the computational rules. Where related trusts exist, the hypothetical transfer is greater.

### Example 8.37—Computation of the hypothetical transfer (ten-year charge):

Xanthippe's trust was created on 5 February 2000 and now holds unquoted shares in a trading company worth £1,000,000, the premises from which the company trades worth £860,000 and cash of £100,000. Xanthippe settled £100,000 on other trusts the same day. BPR is available at 100% on the shares but at only 50% on the building.

| | | £ |
|---|---|---:|
| 1 | Value of the discretionary trust fund: | |
| | Cash | 100,000 |
| | unquoted securities | 1,000,000 |
| | business assets | 860,000 |
| | | 1,960,000 |

*Less*:

|  |  |  |
|---|---|---|
|  | BPR (at 100% and at 50%) | 1,430,000 |
|  |  | 530,000 |
| 2 | Value of the sub-fund | NIL |
| 3 | Value of the related fund | 100,000 |
| Hypothetical transfer |  | 630,000 |

**8.48** Excluded property is a complication but does not increase the size of the transfer.

### Example 8.38—Computation of the hypothetical transfer (ten-year charge)

Waltraut, not domiciled in the UK, on 4 February 1998 settled a German Weingut worth £400,000, cash now amounting to £600,000 and a house in England worth £150,000 on relevant property trusts. She made no other settlements that day.

| 1 | Value of the discretionary trust fund: | £ |
|---|---|---|
|  | Cash | 600,000 |
|  | Freehold residential property | 150,000 |
|  | Other property interests (the vineyard) | 400,000 |
|  |  | 1,150,000 |

*Less*:

|  |  |  |
|---|---|---|
| Value of excluded property |  | 400,000 |
|  |  | 750,000 |
| 2 | Value of the sub-fund | NIL |
| 3 | Value of the related fund | NIL |
| Hypothetical transfer |  | 750,000 |

Note: BPR (unlike APR, which until *Finance Act 2009* was restricted to the UK, Channel Islands and Isle of Man, and woodland relief, which until the same legislation was restricted to the UK) is international, so might have been available in respect of the vineyard anyway.

### Example 8.39—Computation of the hypothetical transfer (ten-year charge)

Vera, on 3 February 2000, made two settlements. One was partly discretionary, with half on interest in possession trusts, but the tenant for life died in 2004, after which all the fund was discretionary. That is the trust now being considered. In

**8.49** *Relevant property trusts*

2003, the trustees transferred £20,000 to a separate account for the life tenant as a capital advance. The fund is a share portfolio worth £360,000. The other fund was £50,000 at the outset.

| | | £ |
|---|---|---:|
| 1 | Value of the discretionary trust fund: | |
| | Quoted securities | 360,000 |
| 2 | Value of the sub-fund | 20,000 |
| 3 | Value of the related fund | 50,000 |
| | Hypothetical transfer | 430,000 |

## Previous transfers

**8.49** Again, this computation is not straightforward. It involves considering five possibilities:

- increases in the settlement;
- transfers before the settlement was set up;
- bringing additions to the fund into account;
- assembling the total figure for the transfers; and
- bringing failed PETs into account.

### Additions to the fund

**8.50** The statutory authority for this part of the computation is *s 67(1)*. The legislation requires the taxpayer to show whether there have been chargeable transfers, after the settlement began and before the ten-year anniversary, as a result of which the value of any property in the settlement is increased, whether or not that property is subject to relevant property trusts.

The taxpayer may disregard a transfer that was not primarily intended to increase the value of the settlement and did not in fact increase the value of the trust property by more than 5% of its value immediately before transfer (*s 67(2)*). An exempt transfer is ignored, whether it is exempt by virtue of the small expenditure or annual exemptions or is made out of income within *s 21*. This is important where, for example, the settlor pays annual premiums on an insurance policy that is held by the trust.

### Transfers by the settlor in the seven years before the trust

**8.51** The statutory authority here is *s 66(5)(a)*. Before 18 March 1986, the relevant period was ten years. Advisers may care to speculate on whether under the present government a period greater than seven years may be reinstated. The total is required of any chargeable transfers by the settlor, ie to any person.

## Transfers preceding additions to the fund

**8.52** If there have been any additions to the fund, the history of transfers by the settlor in the seven years before each addition must be examined. If there have been any chargeable transfers by the settlor in any such period of seven years, ending on the day of the addition to the fund, the amount is excluded except in so far as it has already been brought into account in the computation of the hypothetical transfers.

## Assembling the totals

**8.53** Where a settlement commenced before 27 March 1974 there is no aggregate total to carry forward except in respect of additions to the fund. For all other settlements, such as are illustrated in the examples in this chapter, the following rules apply. Again, if the settlement began before 27 March 1974 and there have been some additions to the fund, the total of these additions is added to the total of the transfers in the seven years that immediately precede them.

For all other settlements, the computation depends entirely on whether there have been any additions to the fund. In the simple case where there have been no such additions the relevant sum is the total of the transfers by the settlor in the seven years before the trust began. Where there have been additions to the fund, two calculations are needed. The first is the sum just identified, the transfers by the settlor in the seven years before the trust. The second is the total of the transfers that precede the additions to the fund. The figure to be taken is the greater of the two (*s 67(3)*).

## Bringing failed PETs into account

**8.54** Where the settlor of a relevant property trust also makes potentially exempt transfers and dies within seven years of those transfers, they become chargeable. As a result, they can complicate the calculation of tax on the relevant property trust. Thus:

- If the death of the settlor occurs after the ten-year anniversary and it appears that he has made additions to the fund before that anniversary, and has died within seven years of those additions, the history of his gift before the additions must be re-examined.

- If in the seven years before the additions to the relevant property trust there was a PET which has failed, that failed PET must be brought into account in the calculations described above.

### 8.54 *Relevant property trusts*

This can have the effect of increasing the aggregate of the transfer by the settlor which will feed through to a higher ultimate tax liability. In the example below, the 'aggregate transfer' is the extra value to be brought into the tax computation.

**Example 8.40—Calculating the aggregate transfer: previous transfers**

Ulrich set up a relevant property trust of £300,000 (gross) on 2 February 2005. He had made two earlier gifts: of £56,000 to his daughter on 17 August 2003 and of £12,000 to his son on 20 May 2004. He died on 31 January 2010 without having added any funds to the settlement.

The cash gifts, originally PETs, become chargeable:

|  | £ |
|---|---|
| 17 August 2003 (net of annual exemptions for 2003/04 and 2002/03) | 50,000 |
| 20 May 2004 (net of exemption 2004/05) | 9,000 |
|  | 59,000 |
| The aggregated transfer is calculated: |  |
| Additions to the fund | NIL |
| Transfers seven years before the trust | 59,000 |
| Aggregate transfer: | 59,000 |

**Example 8.41—Calculating the aggregate transfer: addition to a trust**

Tom, who made no previous gifts, settled £100,000 on relevant property trusts on 1 February 2000. On 10 August 2000 he gave his son £30,000. On 4 April 2001 he added £200,000 to the trust. He died within seven years of the gift to his son, so the PET became chargeable:

|  | £ |
|---|---|
| Gift 10 August 2000 | 30,000 |
| Less exemption (2000/01) | 3,000 |
|  | 27,000 |
| The aggregate transfer is calculated: |  |
| Additions to the fund 4 April 2001 | 200,000 |
| No exemptions available |  |
| Transfers preceding addition to the fund | 27,000 |
|  | 227,000 |
| Transfers in seven years before the trust: | NIL |
| Aggregate transfer | 227,000 |

Note: this type of transfer may in certain circumstances be adjusted in accordance with *s 67(4)(b)* and *s 67(5)*. Those sections apply only to trusts created before 27 March 1974 and as was noted at **8.28** above, most of this chapter concentrates on trusts formed after that date to keep matters (relatively) simple. The section brings into account transfers in the seven years before the chargeable transfer but disregards any value already subject to an exit charge.

## Distributions from the trust: special cases

**8.55** Yet again, there are rules to calculate the total distributions. First add together the amounts on which there were exit charges during the first ten years of the life of the trust. Do not include within this computation distributions where property ceased to be relevant property but the transfer was exempt.

Next, review each occasion when property that was in the settlement at the ten-year anniversary had ceased to be subject to a discretion, so that there was an exit charge at that point. The kind of situation where this could arise is where funds were taken from the relevant property trust and set aside for a beneficiary to provide him with an income and that beneficiary died before the ten-year anniversary. Equally, it could apply under the old rules where funds were appointed onto A&M trusts in favour of a beneficiary who then died. In a case like this, the total of distributions which is the subject of this part of the calculation must be reduced. The amount of the reduction is whichever is the lower of:

- the amount on which the exit tax was charged; or
- the value of the relevant fund on which the ten-year charge would otherwise be levied.

**8.56** The purpose of this rule is to prevent double-counting of the same property.

The next aspect of the calculation is particularly rarefied. If the trustees have purchased heritage property and have obtained conditional exemption for it, the price paid for the heritage property must be included in the aggregate now being calculated as if it were subject to an exit charge.

## Calculating the 'effective rate'

**8.57** All the narrative above has been preparation of a hypothetical transfer so as to establish one component of the tax charge, the 'effective rate'. The notional transfer is:

- one made by a transferor immediately before the ten-year anniversary;

**8.57** *Relevant property trusts*

- who had in the previous seven years made other chargeable transfers that were equal in value to the aggregate brought forward from the earlier calculations in **8.49**; and taking account of
- the distributions calculated by reference to **8.55**.

The result of the calculation is most easily seen in an example such as the one that follows.

**Example 8.42—The effective rate**

Sam made a relevant property trust of £250,000 on 31 January 2000, having always used his annual exemptions and having made a chargeable transfer to another trust of £50,000 a year before. He did not add any funds to either trust, nor make any other PETs before his death on 3 February 2007. We are now (somewhat belatedly) concerned with the periodic charge on the fund at 31 January 2010.

The fund in the 2000 trust includes investments now worth £700,000 of which £100,000 are in unquoted trading companies, acquired more than two years before January 2010. No part of the fund has been appointed onto interest in possession trusts, nor is any of it excluded property. £70,000 of capital was distributed in December 2007.

*Computation of the hypothetical transfer*

|  | £ |
|---|---|
| Value of the discretionary trust fund | 700,000 |
| Less: BPR | (100,000) |
|  | 600,000 |
| Value of sub-fund | NIL |
| Value of related fund | NIL |
| *Hypothetical transfer:* | 600,000 |
| **Review of other transfers** |  |
| Previous chargeable transfer | 50,000 |
| Additions | NIL |
| Transfers before addition | NIL |
| Distributions | 70,000 |
| Add hypothetical transfer | 600,000 |
| *Notional transfer:* | 720,000 |
| Nil rate band at 31 January 2010 | (325,000) |
| Excess | 395,000 |
| Notional tax @ 20% | 79,000 |
| Effective rate 79,000/720,000 | 10.97% |

## Calculating the actual tax

**8.58** Yet again, the taxpayer must review the history of the trust. It might be thought that it was enough merely for the trustees to maintain proper accounts of capital and income (though many trustees will not even do as much as that, until forced to review the situation by the need to complete tax returns). In addition to knowing which part of the fund is capital and which is income, for IHT purposes the trustees must also know which part at any one time was subject to their discretion and which was not.

Equally, the trustees must take a view on the subject of income. The view of HMRC is that any income that is accumulated is to be treated as comprised in the settlement from the date that the accumulation occurred: see Statement of Practice 8/86. But SP 8/86 also notes that undistributed and unaccumulated income should not be treated as a taxable trust asset. There is a fine distinction between income of a previous year that has simply not been distributed and income that has, by some action of the trustees or by virtue of the terms of the trust instrument, become accumulated at some interval after it was received by the trustees.

**8.59** Fortunately, this is a somewhat rarefied area of the law where HMRC practice appears to be to accept any reasonable computation put forward by the trustees that can be justified by the record of their actions. For the purposes of this discussion of the taxation of relevant property trusts, it is assumed that any cash held by the trustees at the ten-year anniversary represents undistributed income rather than accumulations of income.

Supposing that the question of income can be readily disposed of, there remains the issue whether capital has been subject to the discretion of the trustees throughout the whole ten years or whether, for example, it was added to the settlement after the ten-year period began. In relation to each 'chunk' of capital affected, it becomes necessary to calculate the appropriate fraction substantially in the way that was described at **8.37**. The result is to apply the tax charge only for the period during which the property was subject to discretion.

The effective rate is then applied to 30% of the fund, unreduced if it has been subject to discretion for the whole ten years and reduced by the appropriate fraction otherwise.

---

**Example 8.43—The tax charge**

Continuation of the **Example 8.42** of Sam's 2000 trust.

All the property in the trust at 31 January 2010 has been subject to the discretion of the trustees since the trust began.

**8.59** *Relevant property trusts*

|  | £ |
|---|---|
| Value of the fund on 31 January 2010: | 600,000 |
| Effective rate 10.97% | |
| Tax: £600,000 × 30/100 × 10.97%: | 19,746.00 |

**Example 8.44—The tax charge where funds have been added to the trust**

Refer to the example of Tom (see **Example 8.41** above). Part of the fund has not been in the trust for ten years. The fund is now worth £600,000 of which £200,000 can be identified with the original capital and £400,000 with the funds added later. All income has been distributed, but none of the capital.

*Calculate the hypothetical transfer*

|  | £ |
|---|---|
| Value of the discretionary trust fund | 600,000 |
| Value of the sub-fund | NIL |
| Value of related fund | NIL |
| Hypothetical transfer | 600,000 |
| *Review of other transfers* | |
| Previous chargeable transfers | NIL |
| Aggregate transfer as previously calculated (see earlier example) | 227,000 |
| Deduct the value attributable to property now in the fund (*s 67(3)(b)* read with *s 66(4)*) | 200,000 |
|  | 27,000 |
| *Notional transfer*: | 627,000 |
| Nil rate band, 1 February 2010 | (325,000) |
| Excess | 302,000 |
| Notional tax: 20% | 60,400 |
| Effective rate: 60,400/627,000: | 9.63% |
| Charge on the initial fund | |
| £200,000 × 30/100 × 9.63% | 5,778 |
| Charge on the added fund | |
| Held subject to discretion from 4 April 2001 to 1 February 2010: 35 complete quarters. | |
| Fraction is therefore 35/40 | |
| £400,000 × 35/40 × 30/100 × 9.63% | 10,111.50 |
| Total tax charge on the fund | 15,889.50 |

*Relevant property trusts* **8.59**

**Example 8.45—Ten-year charge where there has been a distribution**

Brian, who had made no earlier gifts, set up Brian's discretionary trust on 19 November 1999 with cash of £255,000 gross, the trustees paying any IHT entry charge. No more funds have been added. There have been payments out of income to grandchildren, using the tax pool and generating tax-free income in their hands because the payments were covered by their personal allowances.

On 10 June 2005, the trustees advanced £60,000 to Sally to help her buy a flat.

At 18 November 2009 the trustees held:

|  | £ |
| --- | --- |
| Quoted stocks and shares | 200,000 |
| Dividends (ex-dividend) | 1,000 |
| Government stock | 50,000 |
| Unquoted shares | 50,000 |
| Dividends held by brokers | 5,000 |
| Property, let | 175,000 |
| Cash | 30,000 |
| Gross fund | 511,000 |

The trustees had wisely arranged before the anniversary for valuations to be made. Their cost, at £275, was due at the valuation date. There was also income tax due on rental income of £400. The dividends held by the brokers are not relevant property unless appropriated to capital, which they have not been, because the trustees have pursued a policy of making regular distributions. Similarly, of the cash, £13,000 is actually income that is undistributed within Statement of Practice 8/86. The unquoted shares are in a company that used to trade, but now concentrates on property investment, so the trustees decide not to claim business relief.

A significant problem in dealing with the IHT liability on relevant property trusts is relating the text of the statute to the calculation and to the return itself. In this example, reference is made to the various box numbers, in the hope that that will help in following the calculation. The fund is shown on the supplemental forms thus:

*D32, stocks and shares*;

SS1 total values £200,000 and 1,000 dividends (to boxes E1 and E5 in form IHT100);

SS2 total value £50,000 (to box E2);

**8.59 Relevant property trusts**

Unquoted shares £50,000 (to box F10).

*D36, land etc:*

Value shown £175,000 (to box F1).

*IHT100, the Account:*

Event form IHT100d will be appropriate, see below. After details of Brian's tax reference and that of the trust, the only supplementary pages used are as shown above plus perhaps D40. Cash is shown net of the undistributed income at £17,000 (box E8). The assets not qualifying for instalment relief are, gross, £268,000 (box E15) and after offset of the liabilities of £675 are £267,325. There are no exemptions, so the total appears at box E19. There are no liabilities to set against the instalment option property so the total at box F17 is £225,000.

Thus we have:

|     |                                | £       |
| --- | ------------------------------ | ------- |
| (a) | Non-instalment option property: |         |
|     | Stocks and shares:             | 200,000 |
|     | Dividends                      | 1,000   |
|     | Gilts                          | 50,000  |
|     | Cash                           | 17,000  |
| *Less liabilities*: |                |         |
|     | Valuation fee                  | 275     |
|     | Tax due                        | 400     |
|     | Sub-total (E19)                | 267,325 |
| (b) | Instalment option property     |         |
|     | Unquoted shares                | 50,000  |
|     | Land                           | 175,000 |
|     | Subtotal (F17)                 | 225,000 |

*Event form IHT100d:*

A proportionate charge has arisen in the preceding ten years: Sally's £60,000, all of which was taxable (Q1.5). Brian had made no prior chargeable transfers and had added no funds to the trust. Nothing went into the trust that was not subject to the discretion of the trustees, so IHT100d is fairly straightforward to complete.

*Relevant property trusts* **8.60**

*Inheritance tax worksheet IHT100 (WS):*

There is no requirement to fill this in: as already noted, HMRC will do the calculation, but that leaves the adviser vulnerable. In this example, the totals brought across from the main account (£267,325 + £225,000) yield a value for tax of £492,325 (box WSB7). In this (simple!) case the only extra item at this point is Sally's £60,000 (box WSB15) bringing the taxable total to £552,325 (box R12) against which may be set the nil rate band as at 19 November 2009 of £325,000 to leave tax (for the purpose only of calculating the effective rate) on £227,325 at 20% of £45,465 (box R16) which is not adjusted for Sally's £60,000 and therefore enters the fraction (45,465/492,325) × 30% to produce an effective rate of 2.77% (box R24).

That rate, applied to the non-instalment assets of £267,325, yields tax of £7,404.90 (box TX41) and on the other assets,£225,000 of £6,232.50 (box TX48) to which must be added any interest now due; the detail can be calculated using the structure set out in boxes IT1 to IT9 of IHT100 (WS), but by now the reader must be tiring of this example, so the detail of that calculation, and its division between the different categories of property, is ignored for the present purpose.

The tax amounts to (£7,404.90 + £6,232.50): £13,637.40, which is a light burden for a fund of over £500,000 to bear. Since the restriction on tax entering the tax pool under *ITA 2007, s 497* limits the ability of the trustees to pay out income, unless they are willing to incur a 'tax pool adjustment', they may decide to pay the IHT from the accumulated income.

To summarise:

- Fund of personal property: £267,325
- Real property: £225,000
- Taxable fund: £492,325
- Distributions: £60,000
- Tax rate charged: 2.77%
- Tax on personal estate: £7,404.90 (plus interest)
- Tax on the land: £6,232.50 (plus interest)

# Later ten-year anniversaries

**8.60** The legislation at *s 64* provides for an IHT charge in relation to any ten-year anniversary without distinction between the first and others. It is, see *s 66*, charged at 30% of the effective rate on the chargeable transfer as

**8.61** *Relevant property trusts*

described in *s 66(3)*. The result is that the effective rate that was established for the purposes of the first ten-year charge stays with the trust. It is that rate which is used on later ten-year anniversaries unless there has been any addition to the trust.

Additions of property are covered by *s 67* except where within the *de minimis* 5% rule of *s 67(2)(b)* or where there was no intention to increase the value of the fund, within *s 67(2)(a)*. This can arise on, for example, the waiver by the settlor of a dividend which indirectly benefits the trust.

## THE IMPACT OF APR AND BPR

### Effect at commencement

**8.61** Relevant property trusts benefit from APR and BPR so that, when it comes to applying tax to a transfer, the amount of that transfer is reduced by the relief. However, as was seen in the example of Bernard (**Example 8.22**), the hypothetical transfer established for use when calculating the exit charge in the first ten years does not take account of APR or BPR whereas, once the trust is established and the transfer to be considered is at the tenth anniversary or later, APR or BPR can reduce the size of the hypothetical transfer.

Relief is claimed by reference to the ownership of the trustees because, of course, no beneficiary of a relevant property trust is deemed to be the owner of the trust assets. The situation that will give rise to difficulty is of an interest in possession trust that is, by virtue of *FA 2006*, treated as a relevant property trust, with the result that the life tenant is not the person by whom eligibility to APR or BPR is claimed.

### Control

**8.62** Control of a company can be relevant to BPR. Now that an unquoted shareholding of any size can qualify for 100% relief, control is mainly important in claiming relief under *s 105(1)(d)* in relation to land or other business assets used by the relevant company, or under *s 122* in relation to farming companies, where control is essential for the relief to be available at all: see *s 122(1)(b)*. 'Control' of a company for IHT purposes is generally determined according to the specific provisions in *s 269*.

There is a difficult point in deciding whether trustees of a settlement have control of a company only by reference to the shares in that particular settlement or whether other settlements may be taken into account. This was one of the issues considered in *Rysaffe Trustee Co (CI) Ltd v IRC* [2003] EWCA Civ 356, [2003] STC 536.

*Relevant property trusts* **8.63**

## Reduction in the tax charge

**8.63** If a relevant property trust holds business or agricultural property, the exit charge on the trust may be reduced. If the occasion of the charge is the release of property which itself qualifies for relief, this will reduce the value on which the tax is charged but will not as such reduce the rate of tax.

**Example 8.46—Release of farmland**

Sean's relevant property trust holds farmland eligible for APR at 100%. The entire farm is worth £1,500,000 and the records of the settlement show that the effective tax rate at the previous ten-year anniversary was 4%.

The trustees transfer one-third by value of the farm to a beneficiary *in specie*. It turns out that the remaining two-thirds of the farm is not devalued by this release, so the amount of the transfer, applying 'estate before less estate after' principles, is £500,000. The exit charge is applied to this value, but APR reduces the value to NIL and completely avoids the IHT charge.

One capricious element of APR and BPR is its effective cut-off date. If the conditions for relief are satisfied at the time of the chargeable transfer in general terms it does not matter that thereafter the transferee is not entitled to relief. In the example just shown, the beneficiary could immediately sell the farm. There would be no tax charge on the trustees. If the beneficiary were to die thereafter his estate would not include any property qualifying for relief but for two years after acquiring the property that relief would not have been available anyway.

If the parties realise from the outset that it is likely that the relevant asset will be sold, it is better for it to be distributed *in specie* than for the trustees to make the sale.

**Example 8.47—Distribution of cash**

Daniel's relevant property trust, at the tenth anniversary, comprised cash of £1,512,000. It is assumed that that anniversary occurred after 5 April 2010 and that there are no other complicating factors. The nil rate band of £325,000 is available, leaving £1,187,000 in charge to tax. The tax charge at 6% is £71,220 and the effective rate 4.71%.

Just over six months later the trustees distribute cash of £500,000. The amount of the transfer is reduced by the appropriate fraction 38/40, ie £475,000 and the charge applies to the balance of £25,000. This suffers tax at 4.71%: £1,177.50.

*8.64 Relevant property trusts*

## Reduction in the rate of tax

**8.64** The availability of APR or BPR can reduce the overall tax burden, not only by reference to specific releases of property but to the overall context of the settlement. The rate of a periodic charge on a relevant property trust can be reduced as a result of the fact that the amount on which the charge is imposed is itself reduced by BPR or APR. The result will be that on any exit charge in the next ten years there will be a reduction whether or not the distribution that triggers the exit charge is of property that qualifies for APR or BPR.

Clearly, where the subject matter of the distribution itself qualifies for 100% relief, there will be no need for any calculations.

## Clawback

**8.65** The clawback rules, which are one of the more difficult features of the APR and BPR regime, can affect trusts the creation of which were originally PETs and which have become relevant property trusts by the effect of *FA 2006*, but cannot affect trusts that were always relevant property trusts. This is because *ss 113A* and *124A* each refer to value transferred by a PET.

Supposing that a settlor has transferred property that qualified for relief (after 17 March 1986 but before 22 March 2006) in circumstances where APR or BPR applied, and has died within seven years of the transfer. Clawback may apply if the trustees, who are the transferee for the purposes of the clawback rules, no longer own the property that was given to them that qualified for the relief. This will have a double effect;

- the trustees will suffer IHT on the original transfer to them, except in so far as it was within the nil rate band; and
- there will be an increase in the calculations of transfers that have already been set out in this chapter.

## Acquisition of relievable property

**8.66** It is just as useful for trustees of a relevant property trust to acquire property that qualifies for APR or for BPR as it is for individuals in their later years. If trustees have invested the entire fund in assets that qualify for APR or BPR and have satisfied the period of ownership (two years or seven years) appropriate for the type of property, the fund will escape the ten-year charge and on distributions will also escape the periodic charge.

# THE SPECIAL CHARGE UNDER SECTION 70

## Background to the special charge

**8.67** It was considered expedient for several situations for the legislation to include a special rate of charge which arises outside the usual regime for ten-year and periodic charges. Initially, the trigger for this was the situation where property was settled for charitable purposes only until the end of some specific period. Since that period could be quite long, the rate of charge is expressed as a percentage which increases with the passage of time and which can relate to a period of 50 years or more.

## The rate of charge

**8.68** The charge is fixed by reference to the 'relevant period' which is usually a period that begins with the later of: the day on which the property came within *s 70*; or 13 March 1975; and ends with the day before the event that triggers the charge. The rate of tax is:

| | |
|---|---|
| • For each of the first 40 complete successive quarters | 0.25% |
| • For the next 40 quarters | 0.20% |
| • For the next 40 quarters | 0.15% |
| • For the next 40 quarters | 0.10% |
| • For the next 40 quarters | 0.05% |

If the property was excluded property at any time during the period under consideration, then the period of one quarter during which it was excluded property is excluded from the calculation of the relevant period (*s 70(7)*).

**8.69** The calculation is built up by applying the percentages set out above to the relevant period. For the first ten years, assuming that none of the property is excluded property, the rate, when expressed as a percentage, is the same as the period expressed as whole years and quarters. For other periods the following rate will apply:

| | |
|---|---|
| • 15 years | 14% |
| • 20 years | 18% |
| • 25 years | 21% |
| • 30 years | 24% |
| • 35 years | 26% |
| • 40 years | 28% |

**8.70** *Relevant property trusts*

- 45 years                                          29%
- 50 years or more                                  30%

Actually, these rates are in many instances higher than the normal rates of charge, but the fact that they can be calculated without the multi-step computations set out earlier in this chapter may be some compensation. There is however no election available to the taxpayer: the regime under *s 70* applies whenever the legislation states that it applies and not otherwise.

### Variations on the rate of charge

**8.70** Where a trust includes property qualifying for BPR or APR that relief can apply to mitigate the charge under *s 70*. There are also special provisions where property was previously in a maintenance fund for heritage property. Those special provisions are of limited application and the reader is referred to specialist works on the subject.

### When the special charge will apply following FA 2006

**8.71** At **Example 8.3**, the example of Celia showed that trustees could use the statutory power of advancement. That triggered the special charge under *s 70*. It was always the case for A&M settlements that *s 70* would apply where property in an A&M settlement left it otherwise than in accordance with the main provisions of that section or where the trustees entered into a depreciatory transaction. Such occasions were rare and the application of *s 70*, as a result, probably little known to general practitioners.

The position changed following *FA 2006*. *Section 71B* now applies where settled property ceases to qualify as being held for a bereaved minor under *s 71A*. Tax will not be charged where the property leaves the trust because:

- the bereaved minor becomes 18;
- or dies; or the property is applied for his benefit.

Similarly, although there is a general regime which has been described in this chapter for the charge under *s 71E* on 18-to-25 trusts, there is a residual basis of charge under *s 71G* which applies the rates in *s 70* where, see *s 71G(1)(b)*, tax does not fall to be calculated under the system set out in *s 71F*.

### Letter of wishes

**8.72** Often the settlor will wish to be a trustee as well. He may also wish to guide the trustees as to how to exercise their discretion. Some would go

## Relevant property trusts  8.72

further still and must be restrained by their advisers. There follow examples of the kind of letter that might be appropriate in connection with lifetime settlements, discretionary will trusts both of the nil rate band and of residue, as was common before the introduction of the transferable nil rate band that is described fully in **Chapter 14**.

All too often, the family used the fund, by default, for the benefit of the surviving spouse, even mandating income to him or her. Such conduct would play directly into the hands of HMRC, allowing them to argue that the widow(er) enjoyed an interest in possession, destroying all of the adviser's good work. There is a trap here for those who now release funds to the surviving spouse in the mistaken belief that this will retrospectively put them in the position of being able to claim two nil rate bands on the second death: except where that release is sheltered by *s 144*, disaster will ensue.

Sometimes a will contains precatory words and occasionally even, in effect, the text of a letter of wishes. This is bad practice: it denies the testator any flexibility later, and the words used may come back to haunt the draftsman; see for example *s 143*.

**Example 8.48—Letters of wishes**

Note: Form A is a (somewhat bigoted) example for a standard lifetime settlement. Form B (or something like it) is still often seen, dating back to the 'pre-*Finance Act 2008*' situation (ie prior to the introduction of the transferable nil rate band facility), such as an existing will; and Form C is more appropriate for a recently drawn will.

*Form A*

This letter is confidential to my Trustees and is not the property of the beneficiaries.

In the Trust Deed that I have made today I have created a discretionary trust for my immediate family. I am one of the trustees but this letter is intended to guide my trustees after I am no longer a trustee for any reason. The trustees can at their discretion at any time share out the trust fund, either capital or income, between my daughter Susan and my sons Peter and John, with provision for grandchildren. My thinking in setting up the trust was as follows.

Susan is not working at present and her husband will only with difficulty afford to cover their household bills, so I would like the trustees to provide for Susan and her family occasional 'extras', even luxuries such as holidays. They cannot afford private education but I would be happy to see money set aside for when their children go to university.

**8.72** *Relevant property trusts*

Peter is no better at managing money at the age of 40 than he was as a child. The trustees should only in exceptional circumstances release capital to him. Far better to make an allowance to his dear and long-suffering wife Sally, who I know will use it for the family's benefit.

John is too level-headed and successful to need much help from the trust but should not be penalised on that account. His children deserve a good start in life so the trustees should be willing to help, even with golf or flying lessons if that is what they want.

Of course, this is only a guide. The trustees must exercise their discretion as they see fit according to the circumstances prevailing at the time.

Dated this        day of June 2010

Signed. . . . . . . . . . . . . . . . .

*Form B*

In my Will dated 2007 I have created a discretionary trust of 'the nil rate sum' for my immediate family. Apart from that, my Will gives my son Peter my interest in the family company and gives the rest of my estate to my wife Maureen for life. After Maureen's death, the trustees can at their discretion share out the rest of my estate between my daughter Sarah and Philip, with a provision for grandchildren. None of us can know exactly what assets we shall have at the date of our death, but my thinking in preparing the Will this way was as follows.

I want Maureen to be well provided for but I appreciate that if I leave the whole of my estate to her I have effectively 'thrown away' the nil rate band. I therefore hope that the Trustees of the nil rate sum, whilst always having an eye to what Maureen needs, will try to avoid the situation where Maureen is regarded as effectively the only beneficiary of the discretionary trust. It will be wise to encourage Maureen to use up some of her own resources first, to reduce her estate, before the trustees come to her aid.

As to my personal effects, for example, which are part of the nil rate sum, if I still own the yacht at the date of my death, I would like Sarah to have it, if she would like it, whilst Peter and his growing family might like the Volvo estate. Otherwise I hope that Sarah and Peter will agree between themselves if they would like any of my personal possessions.

Apart from that, my gift to Peter recognises that he has given his life to working for the family business. Giving him my interest in the business will, I hope, give him some security. It is also my hope that he will effectively receive that benefit tax free, so that it would not form part of the nil rate sum.

*Relevant property trusts* **8.72**

It would therefore be my wish that the Trustees, in deciding whom to benefit when exercising their discretion over the nil rate sum, should first compensate Sarah and her family to even up the benefit between my two children.

I do not think that there will be a substantial balance of residue over and above the nil rate band after taking account of the gift of the business. However, if there is, again I would like the Trustees to compensate Sarah if, in terms of value, she has received less than Peter.

The Trustees have a complete discretion over the nil rate sum and over the residue of my estate. I leave it to them to exercise that discretion as they think best in the circumstances that arise. This letter is only intended as a guide to my thinking in making my Will.

Dated this         day of 2007

Signed. . . . . . . . . . . . . . . .

[Testator]

*Form C*

In my Will dated [Date] 2008 I have created a discretionary trust of 'the nil rate sum' for my immediate family. Apart from that, my Will gives my son Peter my interest in the family company and gives the rest of my estate to my wife Maureen for life. After Maureen's death, the trustees can at their discretion share out the rest of my estate between my daughter Sarah and Philip, with a provision for grandchildren. None of us can know exactly what assets we shall have at the date of our death, but my thinking in preparing the Will this way was as follows.

I want Maureen to be well provided for and I appreciate that as far as I leave my estate to her I am preserving the nil rate band for use on her eventual death. I therefore hope that the Trustees of the nil rate sum, will always have an eye to what Maureen needs and in particular will consider, before the expiry of two years from my death, whether to release capital to Maureen.

As to my personal effects, which are part of the nil rate sum, Maureen should have anything she wants and needs but if I still own the yacht at the date of my death, I would like Sarah to have it, if she would like it, whilst Peter and his growing family might like the Volvo estate.

Apart from that, my gift to Peter recognises that he has given his life to working for the family business. Giving him my interest in the business will, I hope, allow him some security. It is also my hope that after business relief he will effectively receive that benefit tax free, so that it will not form part of the nil rate sum.

**8.72** *Relevant property trusts*

It would therefore be my wish that the Trustees, in deciding whom to benefit when exercising their discretion over the nil rate sum, should first compensate Sarah and her family to even up the benefit between my two children.

I do not think that there will be a substantial balance of residue over and above the nil rate band after taking account of the gift of the business. However, if there is, again I would like the Trustees to compensate Sarah if, in terms of value, she has received less than Peter.

The Trustees have a complete discretion over the nil rate sum and over the residue of my estate. I leave it to them to exercise that discretion as they think best in the circumstances that arise. This letter is only intended as a guide to my thinking in making my Will.

Dated this          [day] of          [month] 2009

Signed. . . . . . . . . . . . . . . .

[Testator]

*Chapter 9*

# Exemptions and excluded property

## INTRODUCTION

**9.1** IHT exemptions can be divided into three categories, those that only apply on death, those that apply on lifetime transfers only and those that can apply during lifetime or on death, here called 'general' exemptions. A PET is not an exempt transfer, but may become one seven years after the gift is made (see **Chapter 2**). Some exemptions apply to lifetime transfers and death.

## Lifetime exemptions etc

**9.2** *Lifetime* exemptions only apply to lifetime transfers and they are examined in more detail below. These are (all references are to *IHTA 1984*, unless otherwise stated):

- potentially exempt transfers (*s 3A*; see **Chapter 2**);
- annual exemption for gifts not exceeding £3,000 in any tax year (*s 19*);
- small gifts in any tax year up to a total of £250 per donee (*s 20*);
- normal expenditure out of income with no upper limit, if certain conditions are satisfied (*s 21*; see **Chapter 1**);
- wedding or civil partnership gifts within certain limits (*s 22*).

## Dispositions that are not transfers of value

**9.3** Certain dispositions do not constitute transfers of value if certain conditions are satisfied, including the following (see **9.12**):

- dispositions for maintenance of family (*s 11*);
- dispositions allowable for income tax or conferring retirement benefit (*s 12*);
- dispositions by close companies for the benefit of employees (*s 13*).

**9.4** *Exemptions and excluded property*

## General exemptions

**9.4** *General* exemptions, ie those which apply to both lifetime and death transfers are as follows:

- gifts between spouses or civil partners (*s 18*);
- gifts to UK-based charities (*s 23*);
- gifts to qualifying Parliamentary political parties (*s 24*);
- gifts to registered housing associations (*s 24A*);
- gifts for national purposes (eg The National Gallery, National Museums and the National Trust) (*s 25*);
- transfers to maintenance funds for historic buildings, where HMRC so direct upon making a claim (*s 27*);
- transfers of shares or securities by an individual to an employee trust, subject to certain conditions (*s 28*);
- transfers of national heritage property may be exempt from IHT where certain conditions are satisfied, ie 'conditionally exempt transfers' (*ss 30–35*).

## Death exemptions

**9.5** *Death* exemptions: There are three exemptions which are only available on transfers on death:

- death on active service exemption (*s 154*);
- decorations for valour, if never transferred for consideration in money or money's worth (ESC F20);
- wartime compensation payments.

## Excluded property

**9.6** *Excluded property* is property which has been specifically excluded from IHT (see *s 6*). Following *s 3(2)* transfers of value do not take into account the value of any excluded property. Excluded property is also not included in a person's estate following *s 5(1)*. In determining whether property is 'excluded property', one not only has to look at the situs of the property and the domicile of the transferor, but also at the type of property transferred. Excluded property comprises two main types of property:

*Exemptions and excluded property* **9.7**

(a) non-UK situs property beneficially owned by a non-UK domiciled individual; and

(b) non-UK situs property settled in a trust made at the time when the settlor is a non-UK domiciled individual.

It is important not to confuse exempt property with excluded property. While 'excluded property' will not form part of a person's estate for inheritance tax purposes, the application of exemptions depends very much on the recipient of any transfer of value. Note however the amendment in *s 5(1B)* introduced by *FA 2010, s 53* in respect of purchased trust interests..

## LIFETIME EXEMPTIONS

### Annual exemption

**9.7** Transfers of value during the lifetime of a person up to a total of £3,000 per tax year are exempt from IHT (*s 19(1)*).

- Where the annual exemption is not used in any one tax year it can be rolled forward for one year only.

- Where a gift exceeds the £3,000 limit, the excess must:
    - if the gifts were made on different days, be attributed, so far as possible, to a later rather than an earlier transfer; and
    - if the gifts were made on the same day, be attributed to them in proportion to the values transferred by them.

Where a transfer is a PET, in the first instance the annual exemption is left out of account. However if the donor dies within seven years of making the gift, the gift becomes a chargeable transfer. If two transfers are made on different days in the same tax year, the annual exemption is first applied to the earlier transfer. It does not matter whether the transfers are PETs or chargeable transfers when made (IHTM14143).

---

**Example 9.1—Annual exemptions and PETs**

Mrs Smith died on 30 April 2010, having made the following gifts to her daughter:

|  | £ |
| --- | --- |
| 1 June 2008 | 2,500 |
| 6 April 2009 | 1,500 |
| 15 April 2010 | 4,000 |

**9.8** *Exemptions and excluded property*

| | £ |
|---|---|
| IHT position of lifetime gifts on death | |
| 1 June 2008 gift: | 2,500 |
| Deduct 2008/2009 exemption | 3,000 |
| Chargeable transfer on death | NIL |
| | |
| £500 can be carried forward | |
| 6 April 2009 gift | 1,500 |
| *Deduct* 2009/2010 exemption | 3,000 |
| Chargeable transfer on death | NIL |

Only £1,500 can be carried forward. The annual exemption for the current tax year must be used before any unused annual exemption brought forward from the previous year (IHTM14144). The £500 unused exemption from the previous year can only be used during the 2009/10 year. It cannot be carried forward.

| | £ |
|---|---|
| 15 April 2010 gift | 4,000 |
| *Deduct* 2010/2011 exemption | 3,000 |
| *Deduct* unused 2009/2010 exemption | 1,500 |
| Chargeable transfer on death | NIL |

## Small gifts exemption

**9.8** The small gifts exemption under *s 20* covers transfers of value to any one person up to a total of £250 per tax year. The gift can consist of settled property and it may include free use of property. This exemption applies to any number of gifts up to £250 to separate persons, but it cannot be used to cover part of a larger gift.

This exemption can be used in addition to the annual exemption of £3,000, as long as the gift of £250 is made to a separate person. The current rule also means that where the only transfer of value made is an outright gift of £3,250, the small gifts exemption cannot be used on the excess over £3,000 (assuming no carry-forward of the annual exemption from a previous year). Therefore, £250 will be chargeable to IHT.

## Normal expenditure out of income exemption

**9.9** Under *s 21* a lifetime transfer is exempt from IHT if it can be shown that:

*Exemptions and excluded property* **9.10**

- it was made as part of the normal expenditure of the transferor; and
- it was made out of his income; and
- after allowing for all transfers of value forming part of his normal expenditure, the transferor was left with sufficient income to maintain his usual standard of living.

Generally, HMRC Inheritance Tax will judge each case on its facts, therefore evidence to support a claim for this exemption is essential. The case *Bennett v IRC* [1995] STC 54 considered *s 21* in detail and the court identified several points to consider:

- 'Normal expenditure' means expenditure that was part of the settled pattern of expenditure adopted by the donor.
- A 'settled pattern' can be shown from the expenditure of the donor over a period of time *or* by showing that the donor has assumed a commitment, *or* adopted a firm resolution, in relation to future expenditure *and* has then made gifts in accordance with that commitment. One payment will be viewed as sufficient if clear evidence can be shown to support the claim that regular payments were intended.
- There is no fixed minimum period to establish the relief.
- Where there is no formal commitment or resolution, it may be necessary to show a series of payments.
- There can be some variation in the pattern, but to claim the relief it must be shown that the donor intended a pattern to exist and remain for a period of time.
- The amount of the transfer does not have to be fixed; the amount may be fixed by a formula such as a percentage of earnings or a figure such as 'what is left after paying all my outgoings'.
- Tax planning does not disqualify the expenditure; in contrast, if the taxpayer entered into a series of payments after taking advice, it may support his claim.

**9.10** Details of income and expenditure have to be listed to support a claim for this exemption on supporting schedule IHT403 to Form IHT400 (formerly D3a as added to Form IHT200). It is seen as good practice, if someone wishes to rely on this relief, to prepare a short document which explains that the donor has surplus income and that he therefore intends to make regular gifts out of income. See **Chapter 6** as to duty of care.

A premium on a life insurance on the donor's life paid directly or indirectly by the donor will not qualify under the 'normal expenditure out of income' exemption if at any time an annuity was purchased on the donor' life, unless it

**9.11** *Exemptions and excluded property*

can be shown that the purchase of the annuity and the making or varying of the insurance were not associated operations (see *s 21(2)*).

As long as the above conditions are satisfied, the donor can pass funds to a donee limited only to the extent of the donor's available surplus income (IHTM14231–14251).

However in the case of *McDowall & Others (McDowall Executors) v CIR* [2004] STC SCD 22 it was held that a power of attorney does not give the attorney an authority to make gifts out of income.

Gifts in consideration of marriage/civil partnership exemption

**9.11** Gifts in consideration of marriage are exempt from IHT on the value transferred up to the following limits (*s 22*):

- £5,000 by a parent of either party to the marriage/civil partnership. Each of four parents can give £5,000 (a total of £20,000) to the couple.
- £2,500 by one party to the marriage/civil partnership to the other or by a grandparent or remoter ancestor.
- £1,000 in any other case.

The gift must be made before, or contemporaneously with, the marriage/civil partnership. If it is made after the marriage/civil partnership it must be made in satisfaction of a prior legal obligation. If the marriage does not occur, the donor must have the right to recover the gift, otherwise a charge to IHT may occur.

The exemption applies to gifts to an illegitimate child, an adopted child and a stepchild.

This exemption can be used to settle property on trust, but only if the beneficiaries of the trust are limited to the couple, any issue and the spouses of such issue (*s 22(4)*).

# DISPOSITIONS WHICH ARE NOT TRANSFERS OF VALUE

## Disposition for maintenance of family

**9.12** A disposition for the maintenance of family is not a transfer of value and it is therefore exempt from IHT (*s 11*). HMRC's view is that this exemption is limited to lifetime transfers only, so it is uncertain whether payments to the recipient would be covered under this exemption if the payer dies. The following payments are excluded from IHT:

*Exemptions and excluded property* **9.12**

- By one party to the marriage for the maintenance of the other party.

- By one party to a marriage for the maintenance, education or training of a child of either party. This includes stepchildren and adopted children. The maintenance can continue beyond 18 years, if the child is in full-time education.

- The provisions extend to the maintenance of an illegitimate child and to the maintenance of other people's children until they reach the age of 18 years.

- The exemption also covers reasonable provision made for the care or maintenance of a dependent relative who is incapacitated by old age or infirmity from maintaining himself. Mothers and mothers-in-law who are widowed or separated are always dependent relatives for this exemption. This has been confirmed in the case of *R McKelvey (personal representative of D V McKelvey) v HMRC* [2008] SSCD 944 (SpC 694), where a terminally ill daughter transferred properties to provide for her elderly mother.

Unfortunately, 'maintenance' has not been defined and, until the *McKelvey* case, it was uncertain whether the transfer of capital assets (ie the former matrimonial home), would be covered by this exemption. As the above case illustrates, it can also be difficult in practice to quantify what constitutes 'reasonable provision' for care or maintenance, as this will often be a question of judgement.

HMRC also exempt dispositions allowable for income tax or dispositions which provide retirement benefits for employees and their dependants payable under an approved pension arrangement, ie an occupational pension or, from April 2006, a registered pension scheme (*s 12*).

*Section 13* exempts dispositions of property to trustees in favour of employees of close companies.

---

### Example 9.2—Disposition of family

Susan, a young mother of two children, is terminally ill. Her main asset is the family home, which she inherited from her parents and a small share portfolio. Both assets substantially push her above the available nil rate band. The previous year she divorced Simon, who now lives in rented accommodation.

Her main concern is to provide for her two children who would be forced to leave the family home if IHT were to become payable. By relying on *s 11*, she could transfer her assets to the children during her lifetime. As this will not be a transfer of value, the transfer will not become chargeable to IHT on her death.

**9.13** *Exemptions and excluded property*

## Allocation of exemptions and interaction with reliefs

**9.13** Where a transfer qualifies for any of the exemptions considered above, the question often arises how to apply these exemptions and how they interact with other reliefs.

First, there is the question of how business and agricultural reliefs (see **Chapter 11**) fit in with the exempt transfer rules such as those relating to the annual exemptions. This can best be illustrated by an example.

---

**Example 9.3—Annual exemption and business property relief**

Mr Miller dies on 30 April 2010, having transferred a tenanted agricultural property, which qualifies for 50% relief, to his son in January 2008.

|  | £ |
|---|---|
| 1 January 2008 gift: | 100,000 |
| *Deduct* |  |
| 50% APR | 50,000 |
| Unused 2007/2008 exemption | 3,000 |
| Chargeable transfer | 47,000 |

APR and BPR are applied first and the annual exemption is then used to reduce the remaining chargeable transfer.

---

**9.14** As indicated at **9.7**, there is an HMRC practice as to the allocation of exemptions where more than one of the exemptions considered above are involved (see IHTM14143). Where tax is payable, if two transfers are made on different days in the same tax years, the exemption ought to apply first to the earlier transfer. If two transfers are made on the same day, apportion the exemption between them.

---

**Example 9.4—HMRC's Inheritance Tax Manual, at IHTM14143**

On the same day T makes transfers of £4,000 and £8,000. Total value transferred is £12,000.

£4,000/£12,000 × £3,000 = £1,000 exemption on the £4,000 transfer

£8,000/£12,000 × £3,000 = £2,000 exemption on the £8,000 transfer

---

**9.15** Where a number of different exemptions apply, the order of applying the transfers is as follows:

- normal expenditure out of income;
- marriage gifts;
- £3,000 annual exemption.

This provides the transferor with the opportunity for some forward planning to use the exemptions in the most efficient manner. Should the transferor wish to allocate the exemptions in a different order, HMRC will consider the matter accordingly.

## GENERAL EXEMPTIONS

### Spouse or civil partnership exemption

**9.16** Transfers of value between UK-domiciled spouses/civil partners are exempt from inheritance tax (*s 18*):

- where property becomes comprised in the transferee's estate, by the amount by which the transferor's estate is diminished; or
- in any other case (eg payment by the transferor of his spouse's/civil partner's debt) by the amount by which the transferee's estate is increased.

The spouse/civil partner exemption for IHT applies when property is held on trust for the transferee spouse/civil partner under an 'immediate post-death interest' (see **Chapter 7**). However, following changes introduced in *FA 2006*, the exemption does not apply to the lifetime creation of an interest in possession in favour of spouses or civil partners from 22 March 2006, as such transfers do not become comprised in that individual's estate.

The spouse/civil partner exemption is qualified where the transfer passes under a testamentary or other disposition, usually a will, and:

- the disposition takes effect on the termination, after the transfer, of any interest or period; or
- the disposition is conditional on the happening of some event that is not satisfied, or does not take place, within 12 months after the transfer (*s 18(3)*).

**9.17** *Finance Act 2005* introduced the concept 'civil partnership' with the aim of granting equal rights to same-sex couples. A 'civil partnership' is one that exists by virtue of the *Civil Partnership Act 2004*. The spouse exemption applies to same-sex couples who have entered into a 'civil partnership'. By contrast, in *Holland (Exor of Holland Deceased) v IRC* [2003] STC (SCD) 43,

## 9.18 *Exemptions and excluded property*

the Special Commissioner decided that a couple who had lived as husband and wife for 31 years did not qualify for the spouse exemption.

In the more recent case of *Burden v United Kingdom* [2008] STC 1305, it was decided that the spouse/civil partner exemption does not extend to co-habiting siblings.

If, immediately before the transfer, the transferor but not the transferor's spouse, is domiciled in the UK the spouse exemption is limited to a cumulative total of £55,000, without grossing-up for tax (*s 18(2)*). If a lifetime transfer to a non-domiciled spouse exceeds £55,000, the excess will be treated as a PET and may become chargeable if the transferor dies within seven years.

*Finance Act 2008* introduced provisions which enable the survivor of a married couple or civil partnership to inherit the unused proportion of the nil rate band of the first to die (*s 8A*). See **Chapter 14**.

---

**Example 9.5—Spouse exemption and domicile**

Mr Jones, who is UK domiciled, dies on 30 April 2010. In 2002, he married Lucia Benedetti, who is Italian and moved to the UK following the marriage. Mr Jones' estate was valued at £1m and his will left all his estate to his spouse:

IHT position on Mr Jones' death

|  | £ |
|---|---:|
| Estate | 1,000,000 |
| Less: nil rate band | 325,000 |
| Less: limited spouse exemption | 55,000 |
| Net estate | 620,000 |
| IHT @ 40% | 248,000 |

---

# Gifts to UK-based charities

**9.18** Gifts to charity are exempt from IHT (*s 23*). This exemption has been limited to gifts to UK-based charities. Following *Finance Act 2002*, the definition of 'charity' has been extended and now includes community amateur sports clubs, if they are registered and open to the whole community, are organised on an amateur basis and have as their main purpose the provision of facilities for, and the promotion of participation in, one or more eligible sports.

By *s 23(6)*, the property that is the subject matter of the transfer must actually become the property of the charity, or must be held for charitable purposes.

*Exemptions and excluded property* **9.20**

Where the value transferred (ie the loss to the transferor's estate as a result of the disposition), exceeds the value of the gift in the hands of the charity, the exemption extends to the whole value transferred (see Statement of Practice E13).

**9.19** *Section 23(2)* includes various restrictions to this exemption to prevent the abuse of charitable relief. The relief is not given, if the testamentary or other disposition by which it is given:

- takes place after any other transfer of value has had effect for any interest or period; or
- is conditional on something that does happen for 12 months after the transfer; or
- is defeasible, ie can be taken away from the charity after the gift for any reason.

Another restriction has been imposed in *s 23(4)* where the donor of the property wishes to continue living in the property after he has given it to the charity. The general rule is that the exemption does not apply if the donor, his or her spouse or a person connected to the donor has the right to possession of the property or to occupy the whole or part of the land rent free or at a rent that is below the market value.

A transfer that has not been defeated 12 months after it is to have taken effect and that, after that time, is indefeasible, is treated as charitable and secures the exemption.

*Finance Act 2010* has extended UK charity relief to certain EU organisations and community amateur sports clubs in the EU and the European Economic Area countries of Norway and Iceland, following a judgment in the European Court of Justice in January 2009. HMRC have promised to publish a list of such approved charities, however at the date of publication the list is still outstanding.

The government further announced that the consultation aimed at improving the gift aid system is to continue with charity sector representatives by way of the ongoing gift aid forum.

# Gifts to political parties

**9.20** All gifts made to qualifying political parties are exempt from IHT (*s 24*). A political party qualifies for the exemption if, at the last general election preceding the transfer of value:

- two members of that party were elected to the House of Commons; or

**9.21** *Exemptions and excluded property*

- one member of that party was elected to the House of Commons and not less than 150,000 votes were given to candidates who were members of that party.

Restrictions are the same as applied to charitable gifts.

## Gifts to housing associations

**9.21** Under *s 24A*, transfers of value to registered social landlords, as defined by the *Housing Associations Act 1985* or *Housing Act 1996* or *Housing (Northern Ireland) Order 1981 (SI 1981/156) (NI 3)* are exempt to the extent that the value transferred is attributable to land in the UK.

Again, the restrictions are the same as applied to charitable gifts.

## Gifts for national purposes

**9.22** Gifts to certain national bodies are exempt from IHT (*s 25*). The list of national bodies can be found in *Sch 3* and includes, among others, the National Gallery, the British Museum and any university.

Again, the restrictions are the same as applied to charitable gifts.

## Transfers to maintenance funds for historic buildings

**9.23** Transfers into settlements for the maintenance, repair or preservation of historic buildings and assets of outstanding scenic, historic or scientific interest are, subject to certain conditions, exempt (*ss 30–35A, Sch 3*). There is a two-year time limit from transfer to bring the claim, which can be extended by HMRC concession.

## Transfers of shares or securities by an individual to an employee trust

**9.24** Following *s 28*, subject to certain conditions, transfers to trusts for the benefit of employees of a company without interests in possession are exempt from IHT and will escape ten-yearly IHT charges (*s 58(1)*). Such transfers can be made by individuals, close companies and settlements.

The trusts of the settlement must fit the requirements of *s 86(1)*. The conditions are that the settled property is held on trusts, which, either indefinitely, or until the end of a period, do not permit that property to be applied otherwise than for the benefit of:

*Exemptions and excluded property* **9.26**

- people of a class that is defined by reference to employment in a particular trade or profession; or
- people of a class defined by employment by, or holding an office with a particular body carrying on a trade, profession or undertaking; or
- people of a class by reference to marriage to, or a relationship to, or dependence on people of a class defined above; or
- other charitable purposes.

In addition, *s 28(1)(b)* determines that the exemption only applies if all or most of the people working for that body can benefit, or if the trusts fit a profit-sharing scheme that has already been approved by HMRC under *ICTA 1988, Sch 9*, or for trusts which are approved share incentive plans within *ITEPA 2003, Sch 2* (*s 86(3)*).

**9.25** *Section 28(2)* imposes a number of additional restrictions, which are as follows:

- the trustees must hold at least half the shares in the company; and
- the trustees must have a majority of votes in the company; and
- there must be no provisions that effect the company or its management or its shares or securities under which this power of ownership or of voting can be brought to an end without the consent of the trustees.

Finally, no participator (ie someone who owns at least 5% of any class of the shares comprised in its issued share capital and on winding-up of the company is entitled to 5% or more of its assets) may benefit from the trust.

# DEATH EXEMPTION

## Death in service

**9.26** Following *s 154*, no IHT is payable on the death of a person whilst on active service against an enemy or other service of a warlike nature. The Defence Council or the Secretary of State must certify that the person concerned:

- died from a wound that was inflicted when that person was on active service; or
- died from an accident that occurred during such service; or
- died from a disease contracted when the person was on that service.

**9.27**  *Exemptions and excluded property*

Where a disease was contracted at some previous time, but it was aggravated during active military service and therefore death was brought on more quickly, the exemption also applies.

This exemption was invoked in the case of *Executors of 4th Duke of Westminster (otherwise Barty-King) v Ministry of Defence* QB [1978] STC 218 where the 4th Duke of Westminster died of cancer many years after his war wound. Although there was no direct causal connection between the war wound and the cause of his death, the exemption was successfully invoked.

All that is required is to find a 'reasonable link' which may have caused the death. For example a limp following a war injury may have caused a fall which resulted in death.

## Wartime compensation payments

**9.27**  This relief was originally only available to recipients of the £10,000 payment for Japanese prisoners of war, but has now been extended to a range of payments to victims of wrongs suffered during World War II. A list of qualifying payments can be found in Extra Statutory Concession F20.

The amount of compensation received is assumed to be included in the deceased's assets. In effect, for any recipient of relevant compensation payments, the nil rate band for IHT is increased by the amount of compensation received.

## EXCLUDED PROPERTY

**9.28**  No transfer of 'excluded property' is chargeable to IHT following *ss 3(2)* and *5(1)*. The main categories of 'excluded property' are listed in *s 6* and are mentioned below.

## Property situated outside the UK

**9.29**  Property situated outside the UK is excluded property if the person entitled to it is an individual who is domiciled outside the UK for the purposes of IHT, under *s 6*. For the definition of domicile, see **Chapter 1**.

Settled property that is situated outside the UK is 'excluded property' if the settlor was domiciled outside the UK when the settlement was made (*s 48(3)*).

Following *s 82*, if the settlor retains an interest in possession either for himself or his spouse, and a discretionary trust arises on the termination of that interest, an additional test is imposed on the determination of the interest in possession.

*Exemptions and excluded property* **9.30**

It will be necessary to ascertain where the settlor and his spouse are domiciled when their interests end and the discretionary trust arises.

**Example 9.6—Settlement of excluded property**

Hans, a German national, settles shares in a German company on a life interest trust for his wife Gemma in 1992. Both Hans and Gemma are domiciled in Germany. At the date of settlement, the shares are excluded property, being property situated outside the UK and settled by a non-UK domiciliary. However, the trust document determines that on the ending of Gemma's life interest, the trust assets should be resettled on discretionary trusts for Hans' grandchildren. It will therefore be necessary to revisit the settlement, when Gemma's interest ends (it ends in 2011).

Hans and Gemma decided that they prefer the English climate and moved to Suffolk in 1994. When Gemma's life interest ends in 2011, both Hans and Gemma are deemed UK domiciled for IHT. The German shares therefore will not qualify as 'excluded property' when Gemma's interest ends and a charge to IHT will occur, if the shares are valued above the nil rate band at that time.

If the trustees had used their power of appointment to resettle those same shares on discretionary trust prior to Hans and Gemma becoming deemed domiciled, the shares would have remained 'excluded property' and the settlement would have escaped the relevant property regime.

# Property that is excluded or exempt despite being situated in the UK

## Government securities

**9.30** Following *s 6(2)* exempt government securities are excluded property if they are in the beneficial ownership of a person who satisfies the conditions for exemption attached to the stock. The exemption depends on the qualifying person having beneficial ownership and not the mere legal title.

Settled exempt government securities are excluded property if a person neither domiciled nor ordinarily resident in the UK is entitled to a qualifying interest in possession in the settlement. 'Qualifying interest in possession' means an interest in possession to which an individual is beneficially entitled, or an interest in possession to which a company is beneficially entitled as a result of the commercial purchase of the interest in certain circumstances. If an annuitant (or other person entitled to part only of the income of the settled property) domiciled and resident abroad dies, or if his interest terminates at a

**9.31** *Exemptions and excluded property*

time when the settled property is exempt government securities, the relevant 'slice' of the property is excluded property.

Settled exempt government securities not subject to a qualifying interest in possession will only be excluded property if the trustees can demonstrate that all known persons for whose benefit the settled property, or income from it, has been or might be applied, or who are or might become beneficially entitled to an interest in possession in it, are persons who satisfied or satisfy the exemption conditions for the beneficial owner of the securities.

These conditions are, for most exempt stock, that the beneficial owner is domiciled and ordinarily resident outside the UK, but in the case of some recently issued stock the requirement is only that the beneficial owner is ordinarily resident outside the UK.

## Holdings in an authorised unit trust and shares in an open-ended investment company

**9.31** A holding in an authorised unit trust and a share in an open-ended investment company are excluded property if, in either case the person beneficially entitled to it is an individual who, for the purposes of IHT, is domiciled outside the UK, in relation to transfers of value or other events occurring after 15 October 2002 (see *s 6(1A)*).

An authorised unit trust is a scheme authorised as such under the *Financial Services and Markets Act 2000, s 243*.

An open-ended investment company is such a company within the meaning of the *Financial Services and Markets Act 2000, s 236* and which is incorporated in the UK.

## Certain property owned by persons domiciled in the Channel Islands or Isle of Man

**9.32** Some types of national savings contracts are excluded property if the beneficial owner is domiciled in the Channel Islands or Isle of Man. 'Domicile', for this purpose, has its ordinary meaning, and not the extended meaning given to it for certain IHT purposes. The consequence will be that no IHT is payable on the death of the owner, or on any lifetime transfer of the savings. The savings contracts in question are (see *s 6(3)*):

- war savings certificates;
- national savings certificates (including Ulster savings certificates but not national savings income bonds);

*Exemptions and excluded property* **9.36**

- premium savings bonds;
- deposits with the National Savings Bank or with a trustee savings bank;
- certified contractual savings schemes within the meaning of *ITTOIA 2005, s 703(1)* (ie, SAYE schemes).

## Visiting forces

**9.33** *Section 6(4)* allows limited reliefs from IHT for visiting forces and the staff of allied headquarters. The reliefs fall into two categories. First, certain items of property belonging to visiting forces and staff are excluded property. Secondly, certain periods of residence in the UK are disregarded for IHT purposes. Details can be found in *s 155(1)* and are beyond the scope of this book.

## Overseas pensions

**9.34** Following *s 153*, some categories of foreign pensions relating to service in certain foreign colonial territories or relating to service for the government of an overseas territory are excluded property. The rule applies on death only and has the effect that the pension is left out of account in determining the value of a person's estate immediately before his death. The effect is that no IHT will be payable on the death of the pensioner, wherever he is domiciled and whatever the nature of his entitlement (eg a repayment of contributions due to the deceased's estate).

## Non-sterling bank accounts

**9.35** *FA 1982, s 96* introduced a statutory exemption from capital transfer tax in relation to qualifying foreign currency bank accounts held by non-residents. The exemption is now provided by *IHTA 1984, s 157* and is only available on death.

A 'foreign currency account' is any account other than one denominated in sterling.

A 'qualifying' foreign currency account is a foreign currency account with the Post Office, the Bank of England, an institution authorised under the *Banking Act 1987*, a relevant European institution, or an international organisation of which the UK is a member which is designated as a bank by Treasury order.

## Foreign works of art

**9.36** By ESC F7, as modified by Ministerial Statement dated 25 February 2003, there will be no liability to IHT on a work of art normally kept overseas

**9.37**  *Exemptions and excluded property*

and beneficially owned by a foreign domiciliary, if it is situated in the UK at the date of death and was brought to the UK solely for the purposes of public exhibition, cleaning or restoration, or if it would otherwise have left the UK to be kept overseas but is retained in the UK solely for these purposes. The concession also applies to waive the periodic charge to tax if the work of art is comprised in settled property in which there is no interest in possession.

## Property owned by diplomatic agents

**9.37** The *Diplomatic Privileges Act 1964, s 2(1)* gives the force of law to Articles of the *Vienna Convention on Diplomatic Relations*. Article 34 of the *Convention* provides that a diplomatic agent is exempt from all taxes with certain exceptions. These exceptions include dues and taxes on private immovable property situated in the territory of the receiving state, dues and taxes on private income having its source in the receiving state and capital taxes on investments made in commercial undertakings in the receiving state.

It would seem therefore that tax will not be chargeable on any transfer *inter vivos* by a diplomatic agent of property situated in the UK, but that it will in strictness be leviable on his death on his immovable property situated here, and on any movable property unless its presence in this country can be attributed solely to the deceased's presence as a member of a mission. Thus, his personal chattels would be exempt, and (presumably) his personal current bank account, but (probably) not any investment capital assets.

## Reversionary interests

**9.38** Following *s 48(1)* a reversionary interest is excluded property unless:

- it has at any time been acquired, either by the person entitled to it or by a person previously entitled to it, for a consideration in money or money's worth; or

- it is one to which the settlor or his spouse is or has been beneficially entitled; or

- it is an interest expectant on the determination of a lease of property which is for life or lives, or for a period ascertainable only by reference to a death and not granted for a full consideration in money or money's worth.

Provided that the above conditions are satisfied, the situs of the trust property, and the domicile of the settlor and reversioner, are irrelevant.

In addition, even if those conditions are not satisfied, a reversionary interest is excluded property if the interest, as distinct from the fund in which it subsists,

*Exemptions and excluded property* **9.39**

is situated outside the UK and the person who owns the reversion, whether or not it has been acquired by purchase, is domiciled outside the UK.

**9.39** *Section 48* was amended by *Finance Act 2006*, which inserted *s 48(3B)*. This provides that where property situated outside the UK is excluded property, such property will not continue to be excluded if a UK-domiciled individual purchases an interest in possession in the excluded property for consideration in money or money's worth after 5 December 2005. This in effect is an anti-avoidance measure against 'deathbed' arrangements to prevent UK-domiciled individuals with a limited life expectancy (eg elderly or infirmed individuals) purchasing excluded property shortly before death.

**Example 9.7—Reversionary interest (I)**

A fund consisting entirely of non-UK situs property is held on trust for A for life, remainder to B. B dies.

There is no charge to IHT on B's death. The domicile of the settlor and B's domicile are irrelevant.

**Example 9.8—Reversionary interest (II)**

A fund consisting entirely of non-UK situs assets is held on trust for A for life, remainder to B. B has sold his interest to X. X dies.

IHT is payable on the value of the reversion as part of X's estate, as the condition in *s 48(1)(a)* has been breached.

The fund will escape a charge to IHT if, following *s 48(3)* the settlor was a non-UK domiciliary, X was domiciled abroad at the date of his death and the reversion can be regarded as excluded property under *s 6(1)* (ie the trust is non-UK resident).

**Example 9.9—Reversionary interest (III)**

A fund is held on trust for A for life, remainder to B. The fund contains (*inter alia*) reversions purchased by the trustees as investments. A dies.

There is a charge to IHT on A's death except in so far as it consists of excluded property. If the settlor was domiciled outside the UK when the settlement was made, the reversions should be excluded property if (but only if) they are situated abroad.

*Chapter 10*

# Reliefs – General

## INTRODUCTION

**10.1** In addition to the reliefs listed in **Chapter 9** and business property relief and agricultural property relief detailed in **Chapter 11** there are a number of other reliefs which can reduce a charge to IHT (see also **1.21**) (all statutory references in this chapter are to *IHTA 1984*, unless otherwise stated):

- Taper relief is available on both chargeable lifetime transfers and potentially exempt transfers made more than three years before death (*s 7*) (see **1.21**).

- Quick succession relief provides relief against two charges to IHT where there was more than one chargeable transfer within a five-year period (*s 141*) (see outline in **3.23**).

- Property valued on death as 'related property' (see **3.18**) may qualify for relief if it is sold within three years of death at less than that valuation (*s 161*).

- Relief is available when the market value of property transferred within seven years before death is lower at the date of death than at the time of the chargeable transfer (*ss 131–140*).

- Relief is available if quoted securities are sold within 12 months of death for less than their probate value (*ss 178*ff), and if land is sold within four years of death for less than its probate value (*ss 190*ff).

- Where the transferor is liable to IHT charges on the same assets in two jurisdictions, double tax relief may be available in certain circumstances.

- 'The *Inheritance Tax (Double Charges Relief) Regulations 1987 (SI 1987/1130)* and the *Inheritance Tax (Double Charges Relief) Regulations 2005 (SI 2005/3441)* prevent a person being charged to IHT twice on the same property in certain circumstances.

- An election can be made which enables the IHT chargeable on death in respect of growing timber and underwood to be deferred until sale (*ss 125–130*).

*Reliefs – General* **10.3**

- Heritage property relief is a 'conditional exemption' which may be available on transfers of national heritage property if certain conditions are met (*s 30*).

These reliefs are covered in detail below.

## TAPER RELIEF

**10.2** IHT on all lifetime transfers (PETs and chargeable lifetime transfers) made within seven years before death may be subject to taper relief if the lifetime transfer was made more than three years before death, thereby reducing a potential charge to IHT. The taper relief rates are as follows (*s 7(4)*):

**Table 10.1—Taper relief rates**

| Transfer: | | |
|---|---|---|
| | 3–4 years before death: rate reduced to: | 80% |
| | 4–5 years before death: | 60% |
| | 5–6 years before death: | 40% |
| | 6–7 years before death: | 20% |

IHT at full death rates is calculated at the time of death on any PETs made within seven years prior to death, subject to the availability of taper relief. The value of the transfer stays the same for taper relief purposes, but the full rate(s) of IHT charged are reduced by taper relief.

**10.3** Tax on chargeable lifetime transfers is calculated at lifetime rates. If the transferor dies within seven years, the tax is recomputed at full death rates, subject to taper relief where the death is more than three years after the gift, but using the rates in force at the date of death.

However, if IHT on a chargeable lifetime transfer is recalculated on death with taper relief and produces a lower tax figure than the tax originally calculated at lifetime rates, no IHT repayments will result from the application of taper relief (*s 7(5)*).

**Example 10.1—Taper relief on PETs made within seven years of death**

In September 2004 Alice made a gift of £110,000 to her son Alistair. In October 2004 she made a gift of £110,000 to her daughter Jennifer. Alice subsequently decided to give her second son James £115,000 in November 2004 and in December 2006 she gave her youngest daughter Eleanor £110,000.

## 10.3 Reliefs – General

In June 2010 Alice dies, so all four PETs become chargeable transfers. No annual exemptions are available, as Alice used them each Christmas to make gifts to the grandchildren.

Alistair's and Jennifer's gifts escape a charge to IHT, as they are within the nil rate band of £325,000. The IHT payable by James and Eleanor will be calculated as follows:

|  | £ |
|---|---:|
| *James's gift* | 115,000 |
| Available nil rate band 2010/11 (£325,000 – £220,000) | 105,000 |
| Taxable gift | 10,000 |
| Tax charge @ 40% | 4,000 |
| Taper to 40% | 1,600 |
| James' IHT liability therefore will be £1,600 | |
| *Eleanor's gift* | 110,000 |
| The nil rate band has been used up, therefore available NRB | 0 |
| Taxable gift | 110,000 |
| Tax charge @ 40% | 44,000 |
| Taper to 80% | 35,200 |
| Eleanor's IHT liability therefore will be £35,200 | |

### Example 10.2—Taper relief on chargeable lifetime transfers made within seven years of death

Alice's husband Felix made a potentially exempt transfer of £200,000 to his daughter Jennifer in July 2005. He made a transfer to a discretionary trust of £500,000 in September 2006 and IHT at the lifetime rate of 20% was paid on this chargeable transfer. Felix died in August 2010 having made no other lifetime transfers. No annual exemptions are available, as Felix used these to make annual gifts to his grandchildren.

The IHT on the transfer to the discretionary trust payable during Felix's life is calculated as follows:

|  | £ |
|---|---:|
| Gift to discretionary trust | 500,000 |
| *Deduct*: | |
| Nil rate band 2006/07 | 285,000 |
|  | 215,000 |
| IHT payable at the lifetime rate of 20% | 43,000 |

Following Felix's death the PET to Jennifer in July 2005 will become chargeable. This will use up any available annual exemptions and part of the nil rate band. The additional IHT on the chargeable lifetime transfer to the discretionary trust is calculated as follows. The IHT on the trust at death rates is:

(£500,000 − (£325,000 − £200,000)) × 40% = £150,000.

This is now subject to taper relief at the rate of 80%.

£150,000 × 80% = £120,000

From this must be deducted the lifetime IHT payment of £43,000 to arrive at additional IHT of £77,000 payable as a result of Felix's death.

## QUICK SUCCESSION RELIEF

**10.4** Quick succession relief (QSR) provides relief against two charges to IHT where there was more than one chargeable transfer within a five-year period (*s 141*).

QSR is given on death, where the value of a person's estate was increased by a chargeable transfer made within the previous five years. The previous chargeable transfer may have been made *inter vivos*, or on death. The property subject to the first chargeable transfer does not have to be part of the deceased's estate for the relief to apply, ie it may have been given away by the deceased, but still form part of the deceased's estate for IHT as a chargeable PET.

**10.5** In relation to settled property, the relief is only available where the later transfer is of settled property and the transferor had an interest in possession in the property under the pre-*Finance Act 2006* rules. In relation to settlements the relief can be granted on death and *inter vivos* transfers.

QSR reduces the tax payable on the later transfer and the formula to calculate the relief can be found in *s 141(3)*. In essence it is calculated as follows:

$$\text{Percentage} \times \frac{\text{(Gross chargeable} - \text{Tax on FT)}}{\text{Gross chargeable FT}} \times \text{Tax on FT}$$

FT = First transfer

The percentages for the periods between transfers are as follows:

- 100% if the period beginning with the date of the first transfer and ending with the date of the later transfer does not exceed one year.

## 10.5 Reliefs – General

- 80% if it exceeds one year, but does not exceed two years.
- 60% if it exceeds two years, but does not exceed three years.
- 40% if it exceeds three years, but does not exceed four years.
- 20% if it exceeds four years.

---

**Example 10.3—QSR in action**

On 1 July 2007 Anna's father Fred gifted Anna £40,000 (his favourite son Freddie having received a gift of £400,000 earlier in the year). Anna's father died shortly afterwards and Anna paid IHT of £16,000 on the failed otentially exempt transfer received from her father.

Anna's mother died on 15 June 2008 and Anna was entitled to an interest in possession in her mother's estate. Her mother had a net estate of £450,000 on which IHT of £55,200 ((£450,000 – £312,000) × 40%) was paid.

On 1 June 2010 Anna dies leaving assets valued at £500,000. Her life interest in her mother's estate passes to her brother James and is valued at £275,000.

| *IHT on Anna's estate (before QSR)*: | £ |
|---|---|
| Free estate | 500,000 |
| Settled property | 275,000 |
| Anna's estate | 775,000 |
| *Deduct* | |
| Nil rate band (2010/11) | 325,000 |
| Taxable estate | 450,000 |
| IHT payable @ 40% | 180,000 |

**Quick succession relief**

The PET from Fred was made more than two years but less than three years before Anna's death and therefore quick succession relief of 60% applies.

$$60\% \times \frac{(40{,}000 - £16{,}000)}{£40{,}000} \times £16{,}000 = £5{,}760$$

Anna's mother died more than one year but less than two years before Anna's death and therefore quick succession relief of 80% applies.

$$80\% \times \frac{(£450{,}000 - £55{,}200)}{£450{,}000} \times £55{,}200 = £38{,}743$$

*Reliefs – General* **10.7**

**Tax payable on Anna's death**

|  |  | £ |
|---|---|---:|
| IHT on Anna's estate |  | 180,000 |
| *Deduct* |  |  |
|  | Quick succession relief on PET from Fred | 5,760 |
|  | Quick succession relief on life interest | 38,743 |
| Total IHT payable |  | 135,497 |

# RELATED PROPERTY RELIEF

**10.6** If property was valued on death as 'related property' under *s 161* (see **3.18** as to the valuation of 'related property') and is sold within three years at less than that valuation, a claim can be made to substitute that valuation with the value it would have been had it not been determined together with the related property or the other property in the estate (*s 176*). The following conditions must be complied with for the relief to apply (*s 176(3)*):

- the vendors are the persons in whom the property vested immediately after the death, or are the personal representatives of the deceased;

- the sale is at arm's length, for a price freely negotiated, and is separate from any sale of related property;

- no vendor (or any person having an interest in the sale proceeds) is, or is connected with, any purchaser (or any person having an interest in the purchase); and

- neither the vendors nor anyone having an interest in the sale proceeds obtain, in connection with the sale, a right to acquire the property sold or any interest in or created out of it.

**10.7** Where the relevant property consists of shares in or securities of a close company, the relief is not available if, at any time between the death and the qualifying sale, the value of the shares or securities is reduced by more than 5% as a result of an alteration in the company's share or loan capital or in any rights attaching to shares in or securities of the company (*s 176(5)*). This provision was introduced as an anti-avoidance measure.

The relief is given only if claimed, and the claim must be made within the six-year time limit as provided in *s 241* (reduced to four years with effect from 1 April 2011 (*SI 2010/867, reg 2*)).

The two examples below illustrate related property relief.

## 10.7 Reliefs – General

### Example 10.4—Related property relief (I)

Husband owns land worth £15,000 and his wife owns adjoining land worth £25,000.

The combined value is £80,000.

The related property value of the husband's land is calculated as follows:

$$\frac{15,000}{15,000 + 25,000} \times £80,000 = £30,000$$

The above calculation was made to ascertain the value of the husband's land following his death. The husband's property is sold for £20,000 within three years of his death, so a claim can be made to substitute the value of £30,000 with £15,000.

---

### Example 10.5—Related property relief (II)

On the husband's death on 31 October 2010, the share capital of a private company was held as follows:

Issued share capital – 10,000 shares

| | | |
|---|---:|---:|
| Husband | 4,000 | 40% |
| Wife | 4,000 | 40% |
| Others (employees) | 2,000 | 20% |
| | 10,000 | 100% |

The value of an 80% holding is £80,000, while the value of a 40% holding is £24,000. In his will, the husband left his 4,000 shares to his daughter.

The related property rules apply to aggregate the shares of:

| | |
|---|---|
| Husband | 4,000 |
| Wife | 4,000 |
| Related property | 8,000 shares |
| Chargeable transfer on legacy to daughter | |
| IHT value of 8,000 shares (80%) | £80,000 |
| IHT value attributed to legacy of husband's shares | $\frac{4,000}{8,000} \times £80,000 = £40,000$ |

If the 4,000 shares are sold within three years of the husband's death for less than £40,000, a claim can be made to substitute the value of £40,000 with £24,000 to reclaim some of the IHT paid.

## TRANSFERS WITHIN SEVEN YEARS BEFORE DEATH

## The relief

**10.8** Where market conditions have changed following a PET or a chargeable transfer and the value of the property transferred is less at the time of the transferor's death (or on a prior sale by the transferee or his spouse) than at the time of his gift, relief is available in certain circumstances when computing the IHT or additional IHT, so that the tax or additional tax is charged on the reduced value (*s 131*).

The relief is available in the following circumstances:

- tax or additional tax is chargeable on the value transferred by a chargeable transfer or a potentially exempt transfer because of the transferor's death within seven years of the transfer; and

- all or part of the value transferred is attributable to the value of property which, at the date of the death, remains the property of the transferee or of his spouse, or has before the date of the death been sold by the transferee or his spouse by a qualifying sale.

**10.9** For the purposes of the relief, it is important that:

- any transaction was an arm's length transaction for a price freely negotiable at the time of the sale; and

- the vendor (or any person having an interest in the proceeds of the sale) is not the same as or connected with the purchaser (or any person having an interest in the purchase); and

- no provision is made, in or in connection with the agreement for the sale, that the vendor (or any person having an interest in the proceeds of sale) is to have any right to acquire some or all of the property sold or some interest in or created out of it.

In order to avoid giving too much relief, there is a special rule for calculating the relief where the property also qualifies for business or agricultural relief. In this case the market values of the transferred property on the two dates that are compared to establish the reduction in value must be taken as reduced by the percentage appropriate to any available business or agricultural relief.

**10.10** *Reliefs – General*

**10.10** When valuing property transferred in order to ascertain whether relief should become available, no account should be taken of the related property under *IHTA, s 161* or property passing under another title with which it was originally valued (IHTM09752).

In the case of a transfer that was immediately chargeable at lifetime rates, the relief does not give rise to a repayment or remission of the tax that has already become payable during the transferor's life.

The relief also does not apply where the property has before the death been given away by the transferee or his spouse.

## Wasting assets

**10.11** The relief is not available if the transferred property is tangible movable property which is a wasting asset, such as a motor car (*s 132*). An asset is a wasting asset if immediately before the chargeable transfer it had a predictable useful life not exceeding 50 years having regard to the purpose for which it was used by the transferor.

Plant and machinery is always regarded as a wasting asset unless it is incorporated in the structure of the building, in which case it is immovable property.

## 'Fall in value' relief

**10.12** Relief will only be given in respect of a fall in the value of shares or securities because of adverse market conditions. Therefore, if the value of the shares fell subsequent to capital payments, calls and corporate reorganisations, the relief will not be available. This prevents the relief being available if the value of the shares has been reduced deliberately by making capital payments by the company to its shareholders.

---

**Example 10.6—Fall in value of property and shares**

Mr Jones died on 8 June 2010. He made two PETs which are now chargeable to IHT. On 1 July 2007 he gifted a property, valued at £500,000, to his daughter Alice. On 1 July 2008 he passed his shares in ABC plc to his son Thomas. The shares were valued at £250,000.

Unfortunately, both investments have fallen in value since the PETs were made. When the assets were revalued on Mr Jones's death, it transpires that the property is only worth £450,000 and the shares are worth £125,000.

IHT payable on the PETs that are now chargeable is calculated as follows:

|  |  | £ |
|---|---|---|
| PET of property to Alice |  | 500,000 |
| *Deduct* |  |  |
| 2 annual exemptions |  | 6,000 |
| Fall in value |  | 50,000 |
|  |  | 444,000 |
| *Deduct*: Nil rate band (2010/11) |  | 325,000 |
| Chargeable to IHT |  | 119,000 |
| PET of shares to Thomas |  | 250,000 |
| *Deduct* |  |  |
| 1 annual exemption |  | 3,000 |
| Fall in value |  | 125,000 |
| Chargeable to IHT |  | 122,000 |
| Total value of PETs |  | 241,000 |
| IHT payable | (£241,000 @ 40%) | 96,400 |
| *Apportionment of tax*: |  |  |
| PET of property to Alice | $96,400 \times \dfrac{119,000}{241,000} =$ | £47,600 |
| PET of shares to Thomas | $96,400 \times \dfrac{122,000}{241,000} =$ | £48,800 |

The overall IHT saving in this example is £70,000. The relief can be extremely valuable in times when house prices and/or share prices fall.

## Setting aside PETs

**10.13** In exceptional circumstances PETs may be set aside, as was the case in *Griffiths (Deceased): Ogden & Anor v Trustees of the RHS Griffiths 2003 Settlement & Others* [2008] STC 2008. Mr Griffiths made gifts in April 2003 and February 2004. However later in 2004 he was diagnosed with terminal cancer and died in April 2005 as a result of which both PETs failed. The High Court decided that the later gift was to be set aside on the grounds of mistake. Lewison J said that 'The operative mistake must, in my judgment, be a mistake which existed at the time when the transaction was entered into.'

Strangely, HMRC did not contest this case, especially as the tax at stake was in excess of £1m. In cases where the deceased died unexpectedly after having made substantial PETs it may be worthwhile considering whether they can be set aside, but it is uncertain whether the lenient approach in *Griffiths* will be repeated.

## 10.14 Reliefs – General

In *Pitt & Anor v Holt & Anor* [2010] EWHC 45 (Ch) the second defendant was HMRC, taking an interest in opposing the reliance of the receiver under the Mental Health Act 1983 on the *Hastings-Bass* principle. Mrs Pitt made a settlement on behalf of her husband but in so doing failed to take IHT into account and later regretted her action. The second claimant was the husband's executor. The court held that the *Hastings-Bass* principle need not apply only to trustees: a receiver was in a similar position to a trustee, and exercised a fiduciary power. The critical point here was that it was for Mrs Pitt to decide whether or not it was in the interest of her late husband for her to pass his property to the trustees. The case fell squarely within the tests imposed in *Mettoy Pension Trustee v Evans* [1990] 1 WLR 1587 and in *Sieff v Fox* [2005] 1 WLR 3811. The transfer would be set aside.

## POST-DEATH RELIEFS

### Post-death relief: shares (ss 178–189)

**10.14** When 'qualifying investments' (quoted shares and securities, holdings in an authorised unit trust and shares in a common investment fund (ie funds managed by the Public Trustee)) are sold within 12 months after death for less than their probate valuation on death, the personal representative, or anyone else who is liable to pay the IHT on the shares, may claim a repayment for IHT. The shares or securities must be listed on the Stock Exchange, so the relief does not apply to private company shares. Incidental costs of sale cannot be deducted.

All the investments sold within 12 months after death have to be taken into account, when the relief is claimed. Therefore, where investments have fallen in value since date of death, and where the relief would affect the amount of IHT payable, a personal representative should review the estate portfolio in good time before the 12-month period expires and:

- consider selling within 12 months of the death all holdings of quoted shares and holdings in authorised unit trusts and shares in any common investment fund ('qualifying investments') which have dropped in value since the death;

- keep qualifying investments which have risen in value since the death.

**10.15** The relief is also available for shares, which are cancelled without replacement within 12 months of death, when the deemed sale value will be a nominal consideration of £1 at the date of cancellation. If shares are suspended within 12 months of death and remain suspended on the first anniversary of death, relief can be claimed on a deemed sale of the suspended investment at the value immediately before the first anniversary.

*Reliefs – General* **10.16**

If during the 12-month period, the personal representative purchases qualifying investments, the original loss on sale relief is reduced proportionately. The reduction on the original relief is calculated as follows (*s 180(1)*):

$$\frac{\text{Value of reinvestment}}{\text{Sales proceeds}} \times \text{Original reduction in value}$$

**10.16** The probate value of each of the investments sold will have to be adjusted both for inheritance tax and capital gains tax to the gross sale proceeds, plus the relevant proportion in the fall in value.

---

**Example 10.7—Sale of shares by PRs**

Anna Williams died on 31 January 2009 leaving a substantial share portfolio to her nephews and nieces. A number of shares have fallen in value and the PRs decided to sell those shares and to claim the relief.

The probate value of the shares sold was £100,000, while the sale proceeds were only £25,000.

The executors purchased a new holding in A plc for £15,000 on 31 March 2009.

The estate included shares in B plc, which had a probate value of £1,000, but they were cancelled on 1 April 2009.

The shares in C plc, which had a probate value of £2,500, were suspended on 1 December 2009. On 31 January 2010 these shares were still suspended with an estimated value of £99.

|  |  | £ |
|---|---|---|
| Value of investments at probate value: |  |  |
|  | Shares which have fallen in value | 100,000 |
|  | B plc | 1,000 |
|  | C plc | 2,500 |
|  | Probate value | 103,500 |
| Sales proceeds |  |  |
|  | Shares which have fallen in value | 25,000 |
|  | B plc (deemed value of £1) | 1 |
|  | C plc (estimated value of £99) | 99 |
|  | Sales proceeds | 25,100 |
| Reduction in estate's value |  | 78,400 |

**10.17** *Reliefs – General*

Therefore, the executors would initially be able to claim a reduction of £78,400.

However, after the purchase of the shares in A plc, the 'reduction in the estate's value' will be restricted as follows:

$$\frac{15,000}{25,100} \times £78,400 = £46,853$$

The total relief claimed will be £31,547 (£78,400 – £46,853).

## Post-death relief: land (ss 190–198)

**10.17** Similar to the relief on quoted securities, where an 'interest in land' is sold within three years of death, a claim can be made by the personal representatives to substitute the sale value with the probate value. *Section 197A* introduced a restriction for sale in that the election is not available for sales in the fourth year, if the sale value would exceed the probate value.

Following *Jones (Ball's Administrators) v IRC* [1997] STC 358, exchange of contracts does not qualify as a sale for this relief.

No claim can be made if:

- the sale value differs from the value on death by less than the lower of £1,000 and 5% of the value on death (*s 191(2)*);
- the sale is by a personal representative or trustee to the following:
    - a person, who, at any time between death and sale, has been beneficially entitled to, or has an interest in possession in, property comprising the interest sold, or
    - the spouse, child or remoter descendant of such a person, or
    - a trustee of a settlement under which such a person has an interest in possession in property comprising the interest sold;
- the vendor obtains a right in connection with the sale to acquire the interest sold or any other interest in the same land (*s 191(3)*).

**10.18** If an estate comprises a number of interests in land, the loss relief claim cannot be made until four months have elapsed from the date of sale of the last interest in land, as there is the possibility of further purchases of land. If an estate only has one interest in land, the relief is available and HMRC Inheritance Tax will make a provisional payment of tax, but HMRC will not issue a certificate of discharge until the expiry of the statutory four-month time limit.

Expenses of sale, ie estate agent fees or legal fees cannot be deducted.

*Reliefs – General* **10.18**

### Example 10.8—Sale of land interests by PRs

Peter's estate (he died on 31 January 2007) leaves four parcels of land.

The probate value of the land is as follows:

|  | £ |
|---|---|
| Blackacre | 100,000 |
| Whiteacre | 150,000 |
| Greenacre | 300,000 |
| Peter's home | 500,000 |
|  | 1,050,000 |

In the four years since Peter's death, his executors sell all his interests in the above land. On 5 May 2009, a compulsory purchase order was made to purchase Peter's home to build a by-pass. The acquisition of Peter's home is finalised on 15 February 2011 and the executors receive £400,000. (Again expenses of sale cannot be deducted):

|  | £ |
|---|---|
| Blackacre sold 1 July 2007 | 99,100 |
| Whiteacre sold 15 December 2009 | 125,000 |
| Greenacre sold 1 February 2010 | 300,100 |
| Peter's home | 400,000 |
|  | 924,200 |

### The claim

The sale of Blackacre is disregarded in the claim, as the loss on sale (£900) is less than 5% of £100,000 (£5,000) and is lower than £1,000.

Greenacre will be disregarded because it is sold in the fourth year since Peter's death and the sale proceeds are larger than the probate value.

The loss on Peter's property following the compulsory purchase order however can be included in the claim, as the compulsory purchase order was made within three years of Peter's death, although it was finalised more than four years after his death.

The overall allowable reduction therefore is £125,000 (£25,000 for Whiteacre and £100,000 for Peter's home).

## 10.19 Reliefs – General

If the executors purchase further interests in land within a period beginning with the death and ending four months after the date of the last sale, the available relief has to be reduced. Unlike for the relief on quoted securities, one has to revisit each interest to recalculate the relief, which is complex and beyond the scope of this book.

# DOUBLE TAXATION RELIEF

## Introduction

**10.19** Double taxation of gifts and inheritances can arise in a number of ways, and knowledge of the relevant provisions will become more relevant given the increase in the ownership of foreign property and the number of UK-domiciled persons moving abroad.

Below are a few examples where double charges to IHT may arise:

- A UK-domiciled person who makes a gift of a foreign asset may be liable to a foreign gift tax on the disposal and may also be liable to IHT in the UK either immediately if it is a chargeable transfer or, if the gift is a potentially exempt transfer, on his death within seven years.

- A person not domiciled in the UK may be liable to IHT in the UK, as well as gift tax or inheritance tax in his own country, if he dies while owning assets situated in the UK.

- A UK-domiciled person moving abroad with the intention of living there permanently remains UK domiciled for at least three years (*s 267(1)*), and therefore remains subject to IHT on his estate wherever it is situated. Should he die during that period he may be liable both to IHT in the UK and to foreign estate tax in his country of residence.

- Similarly, a non-UK domiciled individual who has been resident in the UK for at least 17 of the last 20 tax years and who goes to live abroad permanently may be deemed to be domiciled in the UK for up to three years following his departure. Should he die during this period, his estate may be liable both to IHT in the UK and IHT in his country of residence.

**10.20** Where IHT is chargeable in the UK and a similar tax is charged by another country on the same property, relief may be available in two ways:

- under the specific terms of a double tax agreement between UK and that country, following *s 158*; or

- under the unilateral double tax relief provisions in the UK legislation under *s 159*.

*Reliefs – General* **10.23**

## Double taxation agreements

**10.21** The following countries have entered into double taxation agreements with the UK:

France (*SI 1963/1319*);

- India (*SI 1956/998*);
- Italy (*SI 1968/304*);
- Ireland (*SI 1978/1107*);
- the Netherlands (*SI 1980/706 and SI 1996/730*);
- Pakistan (*SI 1957/1522*);
- South Africa (*SI 1979/576*);
- Sweden (*SI 1981/840* and S*I 1989/986*);
- Switzerland (*SI 1957/426* and *SI 1994/3214*); and
- USA (*SI 1979/1454*).

Under these treaties, the country in which the transferor was domiciled is generally entitled to tax his whole estate. The other country is usually restricted to tax the property situated in that country, for example, land and buildings. Relief is then available on the double taxation of the same property.

Care ought to be taken, as some double tax agreements override the deemed domicile rules in *s 267* (see **1.3**).

## Unilateral relief by UK

**10.22** In the absence of double tax agreements, relief may be obtained by means of a credit for the foreign tax charged against the UK inheritance tax. This relief may also be important in cases where it is greater than the relief obtained under a double taxation agreement (*s 159*).

Unfortunately, in cases where the overseas tax suffered exceeded the UK liability before relief, no IHT will be payable in the UK, but the excess would not be repayable.

## DOUBLE CHARGES RELIEF

**10.23** The *Inheritance Tax (Double Charges Relief) Regulations (SI 1987/1130)* prevent a person being charged IHT twice on the same property in various circumstances, where the event or transfer occurred after 17 March 1986.

**10.24** *Reliefs – General*

Double charges relief applies in the following circumstances:

- where someone has made a lifetime transfer which following his death is a chargeable transfer and he has subsequently been given back the property comprised in the transfer (eg under the will of the donee) and he still owns the property on his death; or

- where someone has made a gift with reservation where the original gift was or turns out to be a chargeable transfer and the property comprised in the gift is also charged to IHT as property subject to a reservation; or

- where someone has died owing a debt which is wholly or partly non-deductible under *FA 1986, s 103* and has made a lifetime transfer to the person to whom the debt was owed which was or turns out to be chargeable.

The *Inheritance Tax (Double Charges Relief) Regulations* are complicated, partly because of the extensive use of cross-references. The *Schedule* to the Regulations therefore includes helpful examples of how they are supposed to operate.

# WOODLANDS RELIEF

## The relief

**10.24** An election can be made which enables the IHT chargeable on death in respect of growing timber and underwood to be deferred until sale. The relief is only available on death and does not extend to the IHT in respect of the land upon which the trees are growing.

Following *s 125(1)* certain conditions need to apply for woodlands relief to be available:

- the woodland must be based in the UK or, following *FA 2009*, elsewhere in the EEA; and

- the woodland does not qualify for agricultural property relief under *s 115(2)*. The District Valuer will be able to advise on this point; and

- the deceased must have owned the land throughout the five years up to his death or have acquired the land otherwise than for consideration in money or moneys worth, ie through inheritance or gift; and

- an election for relief must be made in writing to HMRC within two years of the death or such longer time as they may allow.

The relief is given by leaving the value of the timber out of account in determining the value transferred on death. The value of the timber is then not taxed until the timber, or any interest in it, is disposed of.

## Calculation of IHT on disposals of trees or underwood

**10.25** Where woodlands relief has been given on death, if the whole or any part of the trees or underwood is disposed of, IHT is charged on the following amounts:

- if the disposal is a sale for full consideration in money or money's worth, on the net proceeds of the sale; and
- in any other case, on the net value, at the time of the disposal, of the trees or underwood.

The IHT is chargeable at the rate or rates at which it would have been chargeable on the death if that amount, and any amount on which IHT was previously chargeable in relation to the death, had been included in the value transferred on the death, and the amount on which the IHT is chargeable had formed the highest part of that value.

References to the net proceeds of sale or the net value of any trees or underwood are references to the proceeds of sale or value after deduction of any expenses allowable in *s 130(2)*.

---

**Example 10.9—Sale of timber following woodlands relief claim**

Alice died in June 2009 leaving a net estate of £1,000,000, which included woodlands worth £500,000, of which £200,000 related to the land on which they stood (the value of the timber is £300,000). Her nil rate band was not available. Alice left her estate to her son Benedict, who elected for woodlands relief. In August 2011, Benedict sold timber from the woodlands for £500,000, incurring costs for felling of £100,000, sales commission of £10,000, and replanting expenses of £75,000.

The IHT chargeable on the death of Alice was £280,000 (Alice's taxable estate was £700,000 (ie £1,000,000 less value of the timber £300,000)). On the sale of the timber by Benedict, further IHT becomes payable as follows:

| | |
|---|---|
| Gross proceeds of sale | £500,000 |
| *Deduct*: Expenses incurred in disposal: | |
| Felling | £100,000 |
| Sales commission | £10,000 |
| Expenses incurred in replanting | £75,000 |
| | £185,000 |
| Net proceeds of sale | £315,000 |
| The IHT chargeable on the disposal is calculated: | |
| IHT on £315,000 @ 40% | £126,000 |

**10.26** *Reliefs – General*

## Planning

**10.26** Woodlands relief is generally less attractive than BPR, as it only postpones an IHT liability. Therefore, if the woodlands are managed on a commercial basis and if the other conditions for BPR are satisfied (see **Chapter 11**), one should apply for BPR rather than woodlands relief.

If BPR is not available it may, in certain circumstances, still be a difficult choice whether to make an election for woodlands relief or not:

- Where the woodland passes under the will to a spouse or to a charity, an election will not be appropriate, as the woodland will be exempt for IHT purposes in any event.

- If someone dies leaving a life interest in woodland to an elderly relative, whose estate (excluding the woodland) is just below the nil rate band, and there is little chance of a disposal during the elderly relative's lifetime, it may be better to defer the payment of IHT to avoid a charge to IHT.

- On the other hand, if someone dies leaving newly planted woodlands with a low value to a minor beneficiary, and the IHT rate is low (or nil) it would be better to pay a small amount of tax (or no tax), rather than elect and chance a much larger charge especially if the woodland is expected to increase in value.

In most cases, therefore, it is necessary to weigh the cash-flow advantages of an election and the possibility of avoiding the payment of tax altogether, against the possibility of having to pay a much larger amount of tax at the deceased's top tax rate on a greatly enhanced value at some future date.

## HERITAGE PROPERTY

**10.27** On certain conditions transfers of national heritage property (eg works of art, print or scientific objects) can be exempted from IHT (*s 30*). This conditional exemption applies to transfers of value made in lifetime and on death as well as to settled property. The conditional exemption cannot be claimed in relation to a potentially exempt transfer, unless and until the transferor dies within seven years of the transfer and it becomes a chargeable transfer.

The relief works as follows:

- An application for conditional exemption is made to HMRC within two years of the transfer, or within two years of death of the transferor.

- HMRC designate the property as 'heritage property' under *s 31*.

*Reliefs – General* **10.30**

- An undertaking has to be given by a person HMRC consider appropriate, usually the transferor or personal representative.

- Death, disposal or a breach of the undertaking can be a chargeable event giving rise to a claim for IHT (*s 32*) (IHTM04115).

**10.28** The following objects can be 'designated' as 'heritage property' within the conditional exemption:

(a) any relevant object which appears to HMRC to be pre-eminent for its national, scientific, historic or artistic interest;

(b) any collection or group of relevant objects which, taken as a whole, appears to HMRC to be pre-eminent for its national, scientific, historic or artistic interest;

(c) any land which in the opinion of HMRC is of outstanding scenic or historic or scientific interest;

(d) any building for the preservation of which special steps should in the opinion of HMRC be taken by reason of its outstanding historic or architectural interest;

(e) any area of land which in the opinion of HMRC is essential for the protection of the character and amenities of such a building;

(f) any object which in the opinion of HMRC is historically associated with such a building as is mentioned in paragraph (d) above.

**10.29** In addition to the designation by HMRC, it is necessary for an undertaking to be given by the transferee – that is, the intended beneficial owner. Where the property will be subject to a trust, the trustee is also required to give the undertaking. With regard to pictures, prints, books, manuscripts, works of art, scientific collections and other things not producing income, the requisite undertaking is that, until the person beneficially entitled to the property dies or the property is disposed of, whether by sale or gift or otherwise:

- the property will be kept permanently in the UK and will not leave it temporarily except for a purpose and a period approved by HMRC; and

- steps will be taken for the preservation of the property and for securing reasonable access to the public, as agreed between HMRC and the person giving the undertaking.

**10.30** The requirement of access to the public can give rise to considerable expense and difficulty where the objects are kept in a private house or flat. Where an undertaking is given after 30 July 1998, the steps agreed for securing reasonable access to the public must ensure that the access that is secured is not confined to an appointment-only basis. Although this only applies to post-*FA*

**10.30** *Reliefs – General*

*1998* undertakings, it should be noted that *FA 1998* also introduces provision for pre-*FA 1998* undertakings to be varied so that there is public access without prior appointment.

This is a specialised topic and the general practitioner is referred to specialist books on the subject and in particular to the decision of the Special Commissioner in the case of *Re an application to vary the undertakings of A; Re an application to vary the undertakings of B* [2004] SpC 439; [2005] STC (SCD) 103.

Chapter 11

# Business property relief and agricultural property relief

## SCOPE OF BUSINESS PROPERTY RELIEF

### Unincorporated businesses

**11.1** *IHTA 1984, s 105(1)(a)* appeared for a long time to allow relief to be claimed only on a 'business or an interest in a business'. Later parts of *s 105* suggested that this meant an unincorporated business and that it is the business itself rather than the underlying assets. That broad statement of the law has been qualified by the recent case of *HMRC v Trustees of the Nelson Dance Family Settlement*: [2009] EWHC 71 (Ch) see **11.7** below.

*Section 105(3)* excludes investment-type businesses. Property management itself may be a business, but only where the business is the supply of the service of management rather than the management of assets belonging to the business: see *Clark and Southern (Clark's executors) v HMRC* [2005] SpC 502; [2005] SSCD 823. Farming is a business, but where it consists only of managing land so as to produce a crop of grass, that is an investment-type business: see *McCall and Keenan v Revenue and Customs Commissioners* [2009] NICA 12 examined in greater detail at **11.14**.

Businesses of authors, painters, sculptors, musicians, and the like attract special treatment, because it is arguable that the income from copyright is not the business itself, but income from an investment. IHTM25153 requires Inspectors to refer such cases to Technical Group for guidance. Where the ongoing business is the exploitation of existing work it may be possible to show that it outlives the originator, as where executors go to great lengths to ensure that a musician's catalogue is regularly performed, thus enhancing the flow of royalties to the estate.

Difficulties arise because an enterprise may be a business for the purposes of income tax, or even of capital gains tax, and yet not qualify for BPR. In particular, lettings of holiday cottages are treated restrictively. Owning one holiday cottage, which is used by the family for the most popular weeks of

**11.2** *Business property relief and agricultural property relief*

the year and is otherwise occupied by friends on a 'break-even' basis, is not a business for relief. Owning and managing a seasonal holiday caravan park, providing for short lets and offering catering, entertainment and other services will qualify for relief.

The business must be carried on for gain; s *103(3)*. (All statutory references in this chapter are to *IHTA 1984* unless otherwise stated.) Thus passive management of a collection of classic cars, which are only occasionally exhibited or used for films etc, where revenue barely covers storage and insurance, will not qualify for BPR.

**11.2** Until the decision in the *Nelson Dance* case it was widely thought that an interest in a business did not include a 'mere asset': see **11.7** below. A business may still exist even where a trade, even the principal trade, has been sold: see *Brown's Executors v IRC* [1996] STC (SCD) 277. The interest of a partner is an interest in the business unless and until the partner retires (see *Beckman v IRC* [2000] SSCD 59), whereupon the value of that partnership interest becomes a mere loan to the business that attracts no relief.

The position in relation to Lloyd's underwriters is complicated but may be summarised by the general principle that the assets that are actually at risk will qualify for BPR, whereas assets that secure a guarantee but far exceed in value the amount needed to support that guarantee will not so qualify. See, for example, *IRC v Mallender (Drury-Lowe's Executors)* [2001] STC 514 and in relation to the treatment of losses see *Hardcastle (Vernede's Executors) v IRC* [2000] STC (SCD) 532.

**11.3** Limited liability partnerships (LLPs) are provided for by *s 267A*, introduced by the *Limited Liability Partnerships Act 2000* with affect from 6 April 2001. Thus:

- Property belonging to the partnership is treated as the property of its members.
- Property occupied or used by the limited liability partnership is treated as occupied or used by the members.
- Business carried on by the limited liability partnership is treated as carried on in partnership by the members.
- An incorporation of the limited liability partnership is treated in the same way as formation of partnership, and changes are treated as they would be for a partnership.
- A transfer of value made by a limited liability partnership is treated as a transfer by its members.

- A transfer of value to a limited liability partnership is treated as a transfer to the members of the partnership.

A Jersey LLP may be a partnership or a company: we do not know (see *R v IRC ex p Bishopp* [1999] STC 531). However, HMRC appear inclined to treat them as 'opaque' (see *Tax Bulletin* Issue 83 (June 2006)), which is more in the nature of a body corporate than a partnership.

In the past, if a family wanted to test the availability of BPR before entering into planning transactions, there was no help from HMRC, who were not resourced for that purpose. For instance, if an estate is spouse-exempt, no IHT is payable regardless of the nature of the assets, so HMRC will not consider the relief: see IHT Newsletter 25 August 2006. This put taxpayers and their advisers on the spot.

**Example 11.1—Frustrated appropriation or variation**

At her death in May 2009 Samantha's estate was left as to cash equal to the nil rate band to her children with residue to her husband, Peregrine. She had made no lifetime gifts. The estate included (unquoted) shares in a business which had originally specialised in the provision of sunbeds, massage and other lifestyle services. Over the years, profits were reinvested in premises and latterly there has been some repositioning of the business, with the result that part is franchised and many of the outlets are now occupied on short leases. The bulk of the profits now come in the form of rents and franchise fees, very little from hands-on work. The 'wholly or mainly' test is worrying the family: see **11.10** below.

If BPR is available, Peregrine would be happy to see the shares, now worth not more than £700,000, allocated to the children instead of the cash; but if not, he will take them and make gifts over time, hoping to live seven years. Well within the two-year period required by *s 142*, half the shares are allocated to the children pursuant to a deed of variation, which is lodged on the basis that, if BPR is unavailable, IHT has become due: in effect asking for a ruling in circumstances where, if there is no BPR the tax in issue will at worst be only £10,000 (40% of the excess in value of the shares over the nil rate band).

HMRC will probably not be drawn into considering the relief. The tax in issue, after the exercise of valuation, is marginal. Instead they may seek to read the variation back into the will: they may take the view that what is given is the nil rate band and that the excess is, in effect, a gift from Peregrine; and that they will examine the issue of relief on his death. The family must nail their colours to the mast and decide whether or not to transfer the rest of the company's shares to the children.

## 11.3 Business property relief and agricultural property relief

A limited form of help by way of clearance is now available in situations of genuine difficulty. The procedure is described by HMRC on their website (www.hmrc.gov.uk/cap/clearanceiht.htm) and requires an application, preferably by e-mail, with supporting information. The checklist supplied involves the following:

- particulars of the applicant;
- IHT reference, if any;
- details of the business, including UTR or company registration number;
- details of interest in the business held;
- contact details;
- what the application is about;
- why the transaction arises;
- description of the proposed transaction;
- what HMRC are being asked to clear;
- likely date of the transaction;
- contingencies involved;
- how important tax is to the transaction;
- the reason for doing the deal this way;
- other related clearances;
- the commercial importance of the issue to the business;
- two years' business accounts;
- the legislation in point;
- the doubt as to the application of the legislation, with reference to published guidance and case law;
- legal advice obtained that the taxpayer is willing to disclose;
- details of previous HMRC advice.

The description of the service suggests that it is only for cases of genuine difficulty and that it is no substitute for a thorough study of the law and of guidance as to its application. However it is the experience of the writers that applications, properly made, are dealt with promptly and give the family much valued certainty. Some practitioners may find the completion of the application for clearance a useful basis for advising and that, having thought the issues through, it may not be necessary to seek clearance.

## Interests in companies

**11.4** The chief category of property qualifying for BPR, see *s 105(1)(bb)*, is 'any unquoted shares in a company'. Other categories are mentioned below. 'Shares' means any kind of share. This can include a preference share, but tax planners should take care to draft the company documents in such a way that the share has all the attributes of a share and is not really a loan to the company dressed up as a share. There is no case directly in point. The drafting must be robust.

'Unquoted' has a specialised meaning, see *s 105(1ZA)*, which in relation to UK companies will usually mean not quoted on the full list of the London Stock Exchange, but note the comment below as to other exchanges. This has given rise, in the light of *FA 2006*, to considerable investor interest in small companies.

With effect from 19 July 2007, *Income Tax Act 2007, s 1005* was amended so as to allow HMRC to designate as a 'recognised stock exchange' any investment exchange that the Financial Services Authority designates as a 'recognised investment exchange'. This power was exercised, for example, in relation to part, but not all, of the market formerly known as OFEX, now PLUS. The result is confusing: some shares on PLUS qualify for BPR, while others do not.

**Example 11.2—Diversified investments**

Richard dabbled in stock market investments. On his death on 20 May 2010 his estate included holdings in the following companies:

Microsoft

IBM

Nokia

Café Direct

Churchill China

Adnams

Of these, the first three holdings are of shares listed on a 'recognised stock exchange'. Unless the holding is large, giving control, it cannot qualify for BPR.

The other three holdings may all qualify for the relief. Café Direct is traded only on ETHEX, a matched bargain exchange. Churchill China is only on the

**11.5** *Business property relief and agricultural property relief*

Alternative Investment Market (AIM). Adnams is only on the part of PLUS that is not a recognised exchange.

Provided these last three companies are not simply investment companies; and subject to the point mentioned below; their shares may qualify for BPR because they are not 'listed', even though prices for them are quoted regularly in the financial press. Note that where a company, say a mining enterprise, seems to qualify because its shares are traded on AIM, and it is also listed on another foreign stock exchange, BPR will not be available if that other exchange is a 'recognised' one.

**11.5** Shares or securities in a quoted company will qualify for relief where they together comprise a controlling holding: see *s 105(1)(cc)*. Unquoted securities of a company which give the transferor control of it, either by themselves or with other securities, qualify for relief under *s 105(1)(b)*.

In every case, the securities must have been held by the transferor for two years under *s 106* or must qualify for a holding period by virtue of the replacement provisions of *s 107* or the succession provisions of *s 108* or the provisions as to successive transfers in *s 109*.

# Trading assets

**11.6** Relief is available under *s 105(1)(d)* and *(e)* on business assets that are not in themselves an interest in the business. The categories of asset include land or buildings, machinery or plant. These assets will qualify for relief according to the basis of ownership. Relief is available as follows:

- assets used for the business of a company controlled by the transferor;
- assets used by a partnership of which the transferor was a member;
- assets used for a business carried on by the transferor but owned by a trust in which he had an interest in possession.

The last of these categories, exemplified by *Fetherstonaugh v IRC* [1984] STC 261, will be of less importance in future as the number of interest in possession trusts that are still treated as such declines because of the *FA 2006* rules.

The distinction between relief on a company or business and relief on the assets themselves is important in two ways. First, relief on trading assets is at 50% only. Second, relief on trading assets is available only where the asset is still held at the time of transfer and is not at that date subject to any binding contract for sale. Where, however, the claim is made in respect of the business rather than its assets, it does not matter that a particular asset may be in the course of sale at the time of transfer because that does not necessarily bring the business itself to an end: the principle illustrated in the *Brown* case mentioned above.

**11.7** It was long the accepted interpretation of the legislation that relief was allowed by *s 106(1)(a)* only in respect of an interest in a business, rather than an asset of that business. The decision in *Trustees of Nelson Dance Family Settlement v Revenue and Customs Commissioners* [2009] EWHC 71 (Ch) has caused us all to rethink. Mr Dance, a farmer, transferred land to a settlement. Agricultural relief was not in issue: the taxpayer wanted business relief, because the land had development value. HMRC denied relief on the basis that what Mr Dance transferred was not an interest in his farming business but a 'mere asset'.

The taxpayer successfully argued that we must look, not at the asset transferred, but at the transfer of value and apply the 'loss to the estate' principle. The estate of Mr Dance was reduced by the transfer: what was reduced was the value of his farming business; he had been in farming for many years; so the transfer of value fell to be reduced by business relief.

At first instance the Special Commissioner could see a distinction between those cases, such as spouse relief, where the recipient is important, and the present situation, where the basis of relief is the transfer, not the underlying asset, commenting (at para 16):

'All these form part of an overall scheme. Everything turns on the loss in value to the donor's estate, rather than what is given or how the loss to the estate arises, except where the identity of the recipient is crucial to a particular exemption.'

HMRC appealed to the High Court. The reference in the legislation to the value of business property implied that the transfer must be of business property, not merely business assets.

Sales J dismissed the appeal. It was enough that a possible and proper characterisation of the attribution of the value transferred was that it was attributable to the value of a business but did not require an exclusive type of characterisation, so it did not matter that the attribution could be to the value of the land transferred, as long as it could be said that the attribution could also be to the value of a business. That interpretation was simple and certain. It also fitted well with *s 110* and with the 'loss to donor 'principle in *s 103*.

Does this mean that any transfer of a mere asset now attracts relief? No: for example, such an asset owned jointly by sisters, one of whom does not trade, may not attract relief. It has been said in BPR cases that a sole trader is in a special position; in effect, he 'is' the business and he may make no distinction

**11.8** *Business property relief and agricultural property relief*

between those assets he trades with and others: he may not actually show all assets in his balance sheet and yet be using them for his business. To rely in the new rule established, taxpayers must study the case report and bring themselves precisely within its facts.

To determine whether a particular asset is a business or a 'mere asset' we may therefore still have to refer to the line of old cases that used to be relevant to the old CGT retirement relief, then fell into disuse but which may now enjoy a revival of interest in applying CGT entrepreneurs' relief, for example *McGregor (Inspector of Taxes) v Adcock* [1977] STC 206; *Mannion (Inspector of Taxes) v Johnston* [1988] STC 758; *Atkinson v Dancer* [1988] STC 758 and *Pepper (Inspector of Taxes) v Daffurn* [1993] STC 466.

Timing is important in relation to gifts of shares and assets in family businesses.

**Example 11.3—Getting it wrong**

Jason owned 60% of Fleece Ltd, the family business, his sons Artemis and Theseus each owning 20%. Fleece Ltd traded from an industrial estate which Jason also owned. Jason wished to keep the parts of the trading estate that were let to third parties but was tiring of the risks of business itself and wanted to hand over the company and its factory premises to his sons.

He had intended all this as a celebration of his retirement on reaching the age of 80, but as things turned out the lawyers were slow in dealing with the transfer of the land and it took place some weeks after the actual handover celebrations concerning the company itself.

The transfer of the shares qualified for BPR, but the later transfer of the factory premises did not, because by then Jason was no longer a shareholder in the company. Artemis and Theseus were therefore on risk of a liability to IHT until Jason had survived the gift by seven years. Understandably, they required the lawyers to pay them compensation equal to the cost of insuring Jason's life for that period in a sum sufficient to pay the IHT at risk.

# Rate of relief

**11.8**    BPR is allowed at 100% on the following categories of property:

- business;
- interest in a business;
- unquoted securities of a company giving control;
- unquoted shares.

Relief is available at 50% only in connection with the following categories of property:

- control holding of quoted company;
- land, building, machinery or plant used for a business of a company controlled by the transferor or a partnership of which it was a member;
- similar trading assets used for a business carried on by the transferor but owned by a trust in which he had a life interest.

## CONDITIONS

### Period of ownership

**11.9** Property will not qualify for BPR unless owned throughout the two years immediately preceding the transfer; see *s 106*. It may however be treated as satisfying that condition (see *s 107*) where it replaces other property that would have qualified for BPR.

There is scope for a gap in ownership. *Section 107(1)(a)* requires the property held at the time of transfer and the property which it replaces to have been owned by the transferor for at least two of the five years before the transfer. The property concerned must qualify for BPR in all respects other than the period of ownership. There is generally no scope for 'trading up' within this rule. Capital reconstruction can be disregarded so as to 'look through' a period of ownership.

**Example 11.4—Business angel**

Returning to the example of Richard, it appears that Richard had held the shares in Café Direct for only 18 months. However, the money that he used to buy the shares came from the sale, only two months before, of shares in Genus plc which, at the relevant time, was (though as it happens is no longer) quoted on the Alternative Investment Market, and from Thwaites plc, an OFEX company. The records of those companies show that they were unquoted trading companies throughout the relevant time. As a result, BPR is available on the shares in Café Direct, even though they have not yet been owned for two years.

This does illustrate that investors who hope to secure BPR by investing in unquoted shares must be vigilant: companies migrate from smaller exchanges to larger as they develop, and it is only rarely (see eg Bernard Matthews plc) that they move the other way. Small companies are vulnerable to takeovers, forcing the investor to seek new 'BPRable' opportunities, but few will complain if the price is right.

**11.9** *Business property relief and agricultural property relief*

**Example 11.5—Capital changes**

Jason, in the example above, had formed Fleece Ltd from a family partnership comprising himself and his sons. They had been trading together for a number of years before the incorporation. At the time of the share transfer, Jason had only held the shares for one year but his period of ownership of an interest in the partnership counts so as to satisfy the test in *s 106*.

The period of ownership was the main issue in *The Executors of Mrs Mary Dugan-Chapman & Anor v Revenue and Customs Commissioners* [2008] SpC 666. It had been hoped by the taxpayer that the use of a rights issue to capitalise a loan might effectively sidestep the two-year ownership rule by deeming the shares acquired to be, in effect, part of an existing shareholding which had been owned for the requisite period. This relied on the reorganisation provisions of *Taxation of Chargeable Gains Act 1992, s 126* when read with *s 107(4)*. The case turned on its own, very special, facts, the description of which occupies 31 paragraphs of the report. Actions taken under extreme time pressures did not, it was held, achieve the effect that had been hoped for.

The general principles that practitioners may draw from the case are long established:

- get the paperwork right;
- keep only one (correct) record of the transaction, not two conflicting notes; and
- *get on with it.*

The parties had considered tax planning. The elderly shareholder then seemed to recover her health and at the instigation of her family there was delay. A few precious weeks were lost, leaving everything to be done in a rush just before Christmas when her health deteriorated. In the end, the transactions were construed, not as a rights issue, but as a cash subscription for shares, with the result that on the shareholder's death days later she had not satisfied the requirements of *s 106*.

The aftermath of that decision returned to the High Court as *Vinton and others v Fladgate Fielder* [2010] EWHC 904 (Ch) where the daughters of Mrs Dugan-Chapman sued the solicitors for damages to recover the IHT that became payable and the costs of the unsuccessful tax appeal. The solicitors applied to have the claim struck out as 'fanciful'. The court considered the pleadings and evidence and refused to strike out the claim, so the case continues.

Even if a rights issue is properly undertaken, there should be a commercial need for cash, since otherwise the money subscribed for the new shares will be an excepted asset within *s 112* (see **11.22** below). The directors should record the need for funds for the purposes of the business of the company.

## Not investment business

### Background

**11.10** This is an area of great practical difficulty for advisers. A young business may comprise trading assets, intangible assets and may be burdened with substantial debt. A mature business may hold the undistributed profits earned over many years which have been reinvested in 'safe' assets such as property, because the tax burden on distributions was unacceptably high. The problem comes in two forms: at its most extreme, relief is denied on the entire company because it is no longer trading. In a more moderate form, relief is restricted under the rules as to excepted assets considered below.

Relief is excluded by *s 105(3)* where the business of the trading entity, whether incorporated or not, 'consists wholly or mainly of one or more of the following, that is to say, dealing in securities, stocks or shares, land or buildings, or making or holding investments'. Relatively few cases arise on simple land dealing. Equally, the directors of pure investment companies recognise that a claim to relief would be hopeless. The disputes arise where the accounts of the company show some trading activity and the receipt of some rental income.

### Cases concerning lettings

**11.11** For background reading, see the following cases and specialist works on the subject:

- *Martin (Moore's Executors) v IRC* [1995] STC (SCD) 5 and *Burkinyoung (Burkinyoung's Executors) v IRC* [1995] STC (SCD) 29 both concerned businesses that were primarily making an income from lettings.
- See also the caravan park cases *of Hall (Hall's Executors) v IRC* [1997] STC (SCD) 126; *Powell v IRC* [1997] STC (SCD) 181; *Furness v IRC* [1999] STC (SCD) 232; *Weston (Weston's Executors) v IRC* [2000] STC 1064 and *IRC v George* [2003] EWCA Civ 1763, [2004] STC 147.

### Landed estates

**11.12** Until recently, the leading case was *Farmer (Farmer's Executors) v IRC* [1999] STC (SCD) 321, which considered an estate where the best of the income came from lettings or licence fees but the main capital value was in the farmland, farmhouse and farm buildings. After detailed consideration relief

**11.13** *Business property relief and agricultural property relief*

was allowed on the basis there was a business of running a landed estate. That case concerned a substantial acreage; what the decided cases do not tell us is how small an estate may qualify for BPR on this principle. There are doubtless many landholdings in the range of five to 50 acres where a Tax Tribunal decision would be welcome clarification of the law.

The *Farmer* case was followed recently in the Scottish case of *Brander (Representative of Earl of Balfour deceased) v HMRC* [2009] TC 00069. In *Balfour* two issues arose: whether the requirements of *s 107* as to replacement property were satisfied (they were); and whether the business failed the 'wholly or mainly' test of *s 105(3)*. It was held that the lowland landed estate in question fully satisfied the tests for BPR: in particular the late Earl, in managing the tenancies of estate cottages, had selected tenants who could be of service to the estate rather than always going for the highest available rent, so the running of residential property was integrated into the overall business purpose of managing the estate.

## Inter-company loans

**11.13** A case of specialist interest is *Phillips & others (Phillips' executors) v HMRC* [2006] SpC 555; [2006] SSCD 639. An unquoted company lent money to related family businesses. HMRC denied BPR under *s 105(3)*. An appeal to the Special Commissioner succeeded, on the basis that the company was the 'banking arm' for in-house transactions. Few would treat money-lending as a mere investment activity. The company was making loans, not investing in them, so BPR was allowed.

This is an interesting case for advisers. Commonly an elderly entrepreneur will be happy to give up the cut and thrust of daily commerce to his children but will still be happy to support their activities by providing finance, even though that may involve him in significant commercial risk. Relief will, of course, depend on the facts of each case.

## The business of providing a crop of grass

**11.14** Regularly, cases come before the courts or tribunals where the report shows that the issue has been considered with great care and the decision is particularly helpful in establishing general principles, if not always giving the result the taxpayers might hope for. It is probably no coincidence that several such cases have been argued by William Massey QC (the successful advocate in the *Nelson Dance* case mentioned above). He represented the taxpayers in *McCall and Keenan v Revenue and Customs Commissioners* [2009] NICA 12, where a parcel of land had an agricultural value, at the date of death, of £165,000 but a market value of £5,800,000. It was therefore important for the

## Business property relief and agricultural property relief  11.14

executors to show that there was, at the date of death, a business qualifying for BPR rather than an agricultural interest.

The evidence showed (just) that the son-in-law of the deceased had spent time looking after the land, which lay on the edge of a town. The work involved walking the land, repairing the fencing, cleaning drinking troughs, clearing the drainage systems of mud and leaves, cutting and spraying weeds. For these purposes, the son-in-law had a tractor and reaper and a knapsack sprayer. He probably worked no more than 100 hours per year. Some work was contracted out. The grazier fertilised the fields.

At first instance the Commissioner reviewed the authorities, including several mentioned above and in particular the *indicia* noted by Gibson J in *Customs and Excise Commissioners v Lord Fisher* [1981] STC 238. He concluded that the son-in-law's activity of tending the land 'was, just, enough to constitute a business .... The letting of the land was earnestly pursued, the work of tending the land was modest but serious, the letting and tending were pursued with some continuity, the income was not insubstantial, the letting was conducted in a regular manner although the use of [the son-in-law's] time was something which is not a feature of an ordinary business, and the letting of land for profit is a common business. To my mind the *Lord Fisher indicia* point towards a business.'

However, the taxpayers' case fell, both at first instance and on appeal, because the business consisted wholly or mainly of holding investments, within *s 105(3)*. After a detailed consideration of the nature of farming arrangements under the law of Northern Ireland which may not be of general application the Commissioner held that:

> 'The test to be applied is that of an intelligent businessman, not a land lawyer. Such a person would be concerned with the use to which the asset was put. The deceased was making the land available, not to make a living on it but from it; the management activities related to letting the land; it was unlike "hotel accommodation for cattle" as suggested by Mr Massey; nor was it like a "pick your own" fruit farm after months of weeding, fertilising spraying and pruning, customers are licensed to enter to take the produce and pay by the pound for what they take away; in the business of letting the fields there was less preparatory work, the fields were let for the accommodation of the cattle as well as for the grazing, and the rent was paid by the acre rather than by the ton of grass eaten.'

The Court of Appeal in Northern Ireland agreed. The Commissioner had properly understood the law. The test was that of the intelligent businessman, who would look at the use to which the land was put. A landowner who derives income from land or a building will be treated as having a business of holding an investment even though he may carry out incidental work to obtain the income.

**11.15** *Business property relief and agricultural property relief*

Here, the activities of the son-in-law were in the nature of maintenance work to achieve a successful letting. The use of the land by graziers was exclusive, so the owner could not use the land for any purpose that interfered with the grazing. The appeal was dismissed.

## Holiday lettings

**11.15** Care is needed when dealing with holiday lettings. HMRC guidance originally indicated that BPR would normally be allowed if the lettings were short term (eg weekly or fortnightly) and there was substantial involvement with the holidaymakers both on and off the premises. This applied even if the lettings were for only part of the year.

However, HMRC's guidance (IHTM25278) was amended in late 2008, and at the time of writing states: 'Recent advice from Solicitor's Office has caused us to reconsider our approach and it may well be that some cases that might have previously qualified should not have done so. In particular we will be looking more closely at the *level and type of services, rather than who provided them*' (emphasis added). The guidance goes on to indicate that cases involving claims for business property relief on holiday lettings should be referred to HMRC's Technical Team (litigation).

Although the 2010 Budget proposals deal with furnished holiday lettings and announce a consultation the likely outcome of which will be to increase how much a property must be let to qualify, the present information, for example Questions and Answers published on 22 June 2010, appears to relate to treatment for taxes other than IHT: the reference to relief for gifts of business assets is in the context of CGT, not IHT.

## Small company group

**11.16** A strict examination of *s 105(4)(b)*, with its emphasis on holding 'companies' rather than 'assets' suggests that where a holding company has no trade of its own but holds only:

- shares in a trading subsidiary; and
- the premises from which that company trades,

the shares in the top company fail the test for BPR. What is the holding company 'wholly or mainly' doing? The problem would not arise if there were a trade on the top company, but here there is none. Suppose that the trade is of little value relative to the value of the premises: does that make a difference? Would it be wise to set up a second subsidiary, just to hold the premises?

It might be. However, we must look at the situation in the round: if the group as a whole trades, and the land is held only to facilitate the trade, there should be no problem. HMRC appear to take that view, though of course each case will turn on its own facts.

## VALUATION, EXCEPTED ASSETS

**11.17** If the property is of the type identified at **11.22** as qualifying for 100% relief it might seem that valuation is not an important issue. Sometimes, that will be the case but where there are excepted assets it is still necessary to undertake the full valuation exercise to establish the relief.

### Shares

**11.18** The vast majority of claims to BPR on shares will be on unquoted shares and related securities. The general principles of valuation of assets that are subject to restrictions will apply, as seen for example in *IRC v Crossman* [1936] 1 All ER 762. In practice there may be a conflict between arguments that were raised in valuing company shares for CGT purposes, especially as at March 1982 where the taxpayer may want to value high, and the value that may apply for probate, particularly where there is some restriction on relief and the taxpayer is valuing low.

Difficulties arise, as in *I C McArthur's Executors v HMRC* [2008] SpC 700, where 'clever' structures are used. There the main shareholder lent money to companies on terms that linked the loans to options to purchase other shares. On his death, HMRC required the valuation of the loans to reflect the value of the options. Although the executors argued that the options had little or no value, the Special Commissioner disagreed. There was evidence, in the form of 'writs' of the debtor, that there were loans and conversion rights. The unit of valuation was the loan plus the relevant conversion rights.

**11.19** The level of information that would be available to a purchase of shares and many of the other general principles of valuation were considered in *Caton's Administrators v Couch* [1995] STC (SCD) 34. There the Special Commissioner had to decide: how much unpublished information would be available to a purchaser; the value of the shares on the date of Mr Caton's death; and whether professional costs including the appeal itself might be allowable in computing the chargeable gain. The Commissioner concluded that the purchaser of a small block of shares would not normally expect to receive as much information as a larger investor. He would get no more than published information or what he could find out without questioning the directors.

**11.20** *Business property relief and agricultural property relief*

**11.20** Family companies can involve competing factions and that competition can affect the value of the shares. These principles were examined in detail in *Hawkings-Byass v Sassen (Inspector of Taxes)* [1996] STC (SCD) 319 and in *Denekamp v Pearce (Inspector of Taxes)* [1998] STC 1120. A dispute in *CVC/ Opportunity Equity Partners Ltd v Almeida* [2002] UKPC 16, forced the Privy Council to consider the valuation basis where a company in the nature of a limited partnership had expelled one of the partners. The court decided that in such a case the majority may exclude the minority only if they buy them out at a fair price. The continuing shareholders had to pay the expelled partner a value on a going concern basis without discount. For a contrary view, see *Phoenix Office Supplies v Larvin* [2002] EWCA Civ 1740, [2003] 1 BCLC 76, where a discount did apply.

The determining factor seems to be that there must actually be someone in the market who has a special reason for buying the shares. The valuer should consider whether there is, in the circumstances of the company, another shareholder who is prepared to offer full market value without discount. Arguably some discount will always be appropriate: see the decision in *Re Courthorpe* KB 1928 7 ATC 538. Although there has from time to time been comment to establish a rule of thumb (see for example *Taxation*, 17 June 1997 p 322), there is no hard and fast rule and the value must be negotiated each time.

# Net value

**11.21** One clear rule is established by *s 110*, though it seems to apply only to unincorporated businesses: see the reference to 'a business or an interest in a business'. The value of the business is the net value. As a result all liabilities incurred 'for the purpose of business' are set against the value of the company assets, whether or not secured on them. This rule also applies to unincorporated businesses. There is a distinction between debts incurred 'for the purposes of the business' and liabilities that are incurred in acquiring the business itself.

---

**Example 11.6—Net value**

Charles sets up in business as a solicitor. Having no previous capital, the premises and equipment are rented. At the end of his second year of trade, Charles very fairly recognises the value of some of his work in progress that has not been billed out because it related to work done partly by him and partly by assistants. However, there is no money to pay the tax, so the firm goes into overdraft. On a valuation of the business at that date the overdraft would be netted off against the value of the work in progress.

David gives up his job as a solicitor and buys a will-writing business. Having no capital, he negotiates a loan from his bank, secured on his house, to buy a franchise interest, comprising a fireproof safe, a collection of 500 wills and a software package of precedents. On a later valuation of the business for BPR, the loan secured against the house is not deducted from the value of the business, because it was a loan incurred to buy the business rather than for running the business.

Charles wants to retire and agrees to sell his business to David, who takes out a further loan. On a valuation of David's business some time later, the second loan probably would be deducted from the value because the purchase of Charles's business could be seen as a mere extension of the existing business so that the cost of finance was for the purposes of the business that David already owned.

Subject to the rule just illustrated, there is a general rule that debt lies against the asset on which it is secured. Clearly, moving a debt can affect relief, especially APR, where the rule in *s 110* has no parallel. Since this is a 'snapshot' test, moving the debt only days before death can save significant tax.

# Excepted assets

**11.22** *Section 112* requires a double valuation exercise. First, the value of the business is calculated under general principles. It is then recalculated without taking account of the value of 'excepted assets', ie those that are neither used wholly or mainly for the purposes of the business nor required at the time of transfer for future use.

Slightly different rules apply to incorporated and unincorporated businesses. For companies it has been argued robustly that *s 112* will seldom apply because the business of a company is indivisible and therefore, if the asset contributes to the overall business success of the company, its value ought not to be excluded when calculating BPR. If the business is not incorporated, this argument does not apply and it becomes easier for HMRC to exclude an asset from relief.

**11.23** In any event, there are specific exceptions to the 'robust' argument. The first is cash. In *Barclays Bank Trust Co v IRC* [1998] STC (SCD) 125 it was held that surplus cash did not qualify for the relief. In that case a substantial cash balance was still unused many years after the valuation date. The court held that, in the circumstances, cash was not 'required' for future use for business purposes within *s 112(2)(b)*. Recent reluctance of high street banks to lend will have persuaded owners of small businesses to hoard cash to see them through the recession. It is understood that HMRC acknowledge that greater levels of prudence may currently be appropriate in terms of liquidity retained in the business when considering the tests for *s 112*.

**11.24** *Business property relief and agricultural property relief*

The second exception is that an asset that is not used for business purposes at all, such as a holiday flat used exclusively by the family of the majority shareholder, falls squarely within *s 112*. A more borderline issue is whether certain 'passive' assets are excluded. For example, surplus funds for the company invested in quoted securities will probably not be excluded assets if they are moderate in value compared with the capital of the company as a whole. It is more difficult where, perhaps over a number of years, surplus profits have been invested in building up a portfolio of freehold investment properties. After a time, the existence of substantial or non-trading assets can threaten the whole claim to BPR under the rule already noted relating to 'wholly or mainly holding investments' in *s 105(3)*.

It might have seemed, from initial review of the facts in *Executors of Marquess of Hertford v IRC* [2004] SpC 00444, that the rules as to excepted assets might be in point. HMRC wished to disallow BPR on the value of that part of Ragley Hall which was not open to the public, thus cutting down a claim to BPR on the value of the business of opening the house to the public which had been the subject of a lifetime gift. However, it was successfully argued that the whole of the house was an asset of the business. Visitors saw the whole of the outside and most of the interior and the entire building was thus an integral part of the business. *Section 112(4)* was not in point because that concerned a building that would, but for relief, qualify for no BPR at all.

The placing of assets within a company group can be significant in claiming relief. The interaction of *ss 105(4)* and *111* has the effect that it may be best, in appropriate circumstances, for the 'working' freeholds of a group to sit with the top company and for any properties that are more in the nature of investments to be spread around the group.

## SCOPE OF AGRICULTURAL PROPERTY RELIEF

### Agricultural property

**11.24** One basic distinction between BPR and APR is that the exclusion (subject to the *Nelson Dance* case) from BPR of a 'mere asset' has no parallel in APR. Essentially, APR is on 'mere assets' but of particular categories. They are as follows:

- agricultural land;
- pasture;
- woodland occupied with agricultural land or pasture where occupation ancillary;
- buildings used for intensive stock or fish rearing where occupied with agricultural land or pasture and occupation ancillary;

- farm cottages and their land of a character appropriate;
- farm buildings and their land of a character appropriate;
- farm houses and their land of a character appropriate;
- stud farms;
- land in habitat schemes;
- a 'look through' provision to the assets of farming companies.

**11.25** In practice, problems arise through lack of scale of the farming enterprise. Fields may have been sold off and the operation scaled down as the farmer gets older. Nothing in the legislation as such requires the farming operation to be profitable, which is just as well in the present economic climate for farming. Many will argue that the mere growing of crops is now not enough to support a farming enterprise and that viability can be achieved only with a combination of growing of crops and/or of stock and the use of various rural initiatives and the exploitation of grant schemes. The difficulties arise where the main, if not the only, source of income is the entitlement to Single Farm Payment and where, in reliance on that scheme, the farmer has sold all his farm machinery and other equipment. In such a situation, farm buildings may have become redundant. They will lose APR, being no longer 'occupied for the purposes of agriculture' within *s 117*.

**11.26** Property may be of the appropriate type, but may fail to qualify for APR because of the particular requirements of *s 115* when read with the ownership requirements of s 117 that the land be occupied for the purposes of agriculture. For example, woodland may qualify if it adjoins meadow land and if it provides shade for 'meat' animals grazing nearby, but an isolated coppice which is effectively used only for shooting will not qualify because its occupation is not ancillary to that of agricultural land. Equally, as demonstrated in *Williams (Williams Personal Representative) v HMRC* [2005] SSCD 782; [2005] SpC 500, a building used for the intensive rearing of poultry does not qualify for APR where it stands on small landholding only, dominating it because its use is not 'ancillary' to the land on which it stands.

The occupation test gives rise to other problems, particularly in connection with cottages and houses.

---

### Example 11.7—Loss of relief on farmhouse

Geoffrey farmed for many years. His house was the nerve centre of the business. It adjoined a traditional range of farm buildings, some of which over the years had been adapted to allow the storage of modern farming equipment. It had been a small mixed farm, but over the years Geoffrey sold his stock and let some of the buildings as stabling and two of the fields as

**11.27** *Business property relief and agricultural property relief*

paddock. Eventually, he scrapped the redundant farm machinery and sold the rest. He entered into an informal letting agreement with his neighbour for the rest of the land.

On Geoffrey's death relief is available on the land let to the neighbour for farming, but not on the paddocks because they are not occupied for the purposes of agriculture. The horses are not 'meat' animals, but family pets. No relief is allowed on the farmhouse because it is no longer the nerve centre of a farming business. It had become no more than the house where a retired farmer lived until the date of his death.

## Farmhouses

**11.27** Several developments have made this a difficult area of law. With the exception of a heritage house open to the public, there is virtually no other form of residence that can escape a charge to IHT, making it very popular for taxpayers to claim that their residence should be treated as a farmhouse. Farmhouses are often well situated, having slightly more seclusion than normal residential properties, so they can command a 'charm' premium. That seems certainly to have been true in the *McKenna* case, considered at **11.34** below. There are fewer working farms than formerly, so the likelihood that the occupier of a farmhouse makes his living from the adjoining land is much less than it was even 50 years ago. Much greater use is now made of farming contractors than formerly and a farmer may live some distance from the field where his business is carried on.

**11.28** The combination of all these factors results in a situation where arguably the basis for the original relief has gone. If income from farming activities consists partly or even mainly of the Single Farm Payment there is now really no particular link between the house where the farmer lives and the land in respect of which the payment is earned. Some of these tensions are well reflected in the observations, admittedly *obiter*, of the Lands Tribunal in *Antrobus (No 2)* [2006] RVR 138, as was recognised in the *McKenna* case. Certainly practitioners are seeing regular challenge by HMRC to APR claims on farmhouses because there is really no viable business to be run from the house in question; and for this purpose HMRC also rely heavily on the *McCall* case to disregard a 'farming' business that consists only of owning land that is subject to grazing licences.

*Section 115(2)* allows APR on 'such cottages, farm buildings and farmhouses, together with the land occupied with them, as are of a character appropriate to the property'. This tends to show that the relief can apply not only to the house, but also to its garden and that for the relief to be available there must be 'the property' and there must be some link between the farmhouse and 'the property'.

## Farming business? What farming business?

**11.29** Nothing in the legislation actually states that there must be a viable farming business. An unpublished decision of the Special Commissioners in 1994 stated that 'whether or not one can make a living from a given acreage of land cannot be determinative of the question whether a building is a farmhouse'. However, no relief is given on any agricultural property absent its occupation for the purposes of agriculture as required by *s 116*.

A claim to APR on a dwelling will therefore never get off the ground unless there is at least some recognisable farming activity. See, for example, *Dixon v IRC* SpC 297 [2002] SSCD 53 concerning a cottage, its garden and orchard of which the total area was 0.6 acres and the gross cash turnover (ignoring bartering arrangements) was £70 per year. It was held that the activities were consistent with the use of the property as a residence and garden, not for agriculture. The property was primarily a cottage with garden and orchard. APR was refused.

It was, for a long time, HMRC's practice to enquire closely into claims for APR on houses worth £250,000 or more and where the land holding is 100 acres or less, but the value limit has been eroded. Now the approach seems to be to deny relief on any farmhouse where the farm land does not seem extensive enough to support a viable business; but where values are moderate such cases may not reach the courts.

**11.30** There may in the past have been a farming business, but it may no longer relate to the dwelling. Thus, in *Rosser v IRC* SpC 368, [2003] SSCD 311, the relevant dwelling had for many years been a farmhouse for 41 acres comprising agricultural land, the house itself and a barn. Fatally, as it turned out, the deceased and her husband gave 39 acres of land to their daughter, who was married to a farmer and who then farmed that land with other land. That effectively 'demoted' the retained residence from its status of a farmhouse to that of a retirement home.

There is a restricted argument resulting from the decision of the Court of Appeal in *Starke (Brown's Executors) v IRC* [1996] 1 All ER 622. There the farmhouse had become separated in ownership from the adjoining farmland, which was owned through the medium of a company. Argument there turned on a technicality, so the decision in *Starke* will not always decide the matter. In summary, a claim to APR on a dwelling will always be dependent upon first proving that there is a farming business and, as will be seen below, that the house is the place from which that business is run.

Unoccupied farmhouses cause problems: see the review at **11.37** below of *Harrold v IRC* [1996] STC (SCD) 195 and of *Atkinson v HMRC* [2010] UKFTT 108 (TC) TC00420.

**11.31** *Business property relief and agricultural property relief*

## 'Character appropriate'

**11.31** There are many houses that look like farmhouses, but fail the test as to 'character appropriate' because they are disproportionate in size or quality to the farming business that allegedly supports them. The legislation originally included a category of dwelling that qualified for relief –mansion houses. The removal of that category has strengthened the HMRC argument that grand houses should not qualify for APR. The test is whether the property is in substance a fine house surrounded by land, in which case APR will be hard to justify, or is a land holding that happens to contain a house, where the chances of APR will be better.

**11.32** In *Higginson's Executors v IRC* [2002] STC (SCD) 483, a property was set in a landed estate of 134 acres, of which only 63 were agricultural land. The gardens extended to three acres and there were 68 acres of woodland and wetland. This was a special property and, although it had for years been occupied as a farmhouse for some time before the death of the owner, the farmland had been let and the woodland and wetland were made areas of nature conservation. The estate was not economically viable and was sold for £1,150,000, a price described from a farming perspective as being 'an appalling investment in terms of yield', being well beyond farmers' means.

### Antrobus

**11.33** In *Lloyds TSB (Personal representative of Antrobus) v IRC* [2002] STC (SCD) 468 (*Antrobus (No 1)*) Cookhill Priory, which was enjoyed with 126 acres of freehold land plus 6.5 acres of tenanted land, had been occupied by the Antrobus family since 1907. The original nunnery had been founded in 1260. The six-bedroom house dated to the mid-sixteenth century with an extension in 1765 and was altered in 1785, in the Georgian period and in 1910. Father farmed the land until 1942. His widow died in 1959. Miss Antrobus occupied 124 acres and acquired the property from relatives in 1959, then farming it until her death. She was definitely a farmer. It was agreed that the land and buildings were agricultural property but the claim in respect of two let houses and Cookhill Priory was disputed. Doctor Brice summarised the relevant questions to be answered in relation to any claim for APR on a farmhouse. That list was updated in the *McKenna* case, considered below.

### McKenna

**11.34** *Arnander (Executors of McKenna Deceased) v HMRC* [2006] SpC 00565 is a valuable and very thorough examination of the issues outlined above, to which this summary cannot do justice.

Rosteague House, Cornwall, overlooked the sea. It was in poor condition but nevertheless listed Grade II* and 'at the very top end of the size of a

## Business property relief and agricultural property relief  11.34

farmhouse', even in the context of many fine examples in the district. It stood in 187 acres which included 52 acres of coastal slope and over a mile of sea frontage. It went back in part to 1597, according to contemporary maps. It was very substantial, with impressive gardens. There were farm buildings.

The farming history could be traced back to 1365, though recently it had been conducted by agents and through contract-farming arrangements. The woodland area was extended with the help of a planting grant. The farm buildings were little used as such, but did house garden implements.

The owner spent perhaps an hour a day on farm work until illness prevented him. The estate was sold, but not as a farm, for £3,050,000. Later evidence showed that urgent repairs would cost the purchaser nearly £200,000.

Against that background, Dr Brice found as follows:

- It was not a farmhouse. She quoted with approval the decision in *Rosser v IRC*. She approached the views of the Lands Tribunal in *Antrobus No 2* 'with some caution' as *obiter*, but held that the principle that 'the farmer of the land is the person who farms it on a day-to-day basis rather than the person who is in overall control of the agricultural business conducted on the land is a helpful principle'. After a review of all the cases she derived the following principles:

    - A farmhouse is a dwelling for the farmer from which the farm is managed.

    - The farmer is the person who farms on a day-to-day basis, not the manager.

    - The purpose, not the status, of occupation is what matters.

    - If the premises are extravagantly large, then even though occupied for the purpose of agriculture they may have become something more grand.

    - Each case turns on its own facts, judged by ordinary ideas of what is appropriate in size, content and layout, taken in context with the buildings and the land.

    Based on this, Dr Brice found that the actual farming was not done from the house, which was too grand for the much-reduced farming operations carried on.

- It was not of a 'character appropriate' anyway. After referring to the *Antrobus* principles and to *Higginson* Dr Brice reviewed the elements as follows:

    - There were many fine farmhouses in Cornwall, some quite large and with very pleasant gardens.

**11.35** *Business property relief and agricultural property relief*

- Rosteague House was large and despite its condition had 'an interior of grace and charm'.
- The farm buildings were not really used as such.
- There was not enough land.
- A layman would think of it as a large country house; it was in effect marketed as such.
- On sale, 65% of the price realised was for the house, part for tenanted properties and only 12% for the agricultural land. It would not attract commercial farmers needing to make a living from the land.

- It was not occupied for the purposes of agriculture. Neither Mr McKenna, nor Lady McKenna had been able to farm actively during the relevant two-year period.
- Most of the farm buildings were not occupied for the purposes of agriculture. One was a dung stead, latterly used in connection with livery, but livery of horses is not an agricultural purpose. On the facts, however, some were used for agriculture.

It will take time to assimilate the decision before advising on fine houses in future, but it makes a claim for a 'lifestyle' farmer in respect of a charming country house that much harder to pursue.

## Farm buildings

**11.35** It was noted earlier that farm buildings do not automatically qualify for APR by virtue of their use. Such buildings must be ancillary to the main land holding. This was confirmed in *Williams (Williams Personal Representative) v HMRC* [2005] SSCD 782; [2005] SpC 500.

# CONDITIONS FOR APR

## Period of ownership or occupation

**11.36** *Section 117* denies APR unless property complies with one of two conditions. The first condition is occupation by the transferor for the purposes of agriculture throughout the period of two years ending with the date of transfer. This can lead to slightly surprising results.

---

### Example 11.8—Deathbed purchase

James and Phillip were brought up on their father's farm and eventually inherited it from him. James lived on in the family house whilst his brother moved into the bungalow which had been his father's home in retirement. For a time they tried to run the farm between them, but there were differences of temperament and the land holding was not really big enough to support them both. They agreed to partition the land between them. James thereafter owned the main farmhouse and half the land and rented the remainder of the land from his brother.

Some years later James was forced to sell part of his land to the Highways Authority, generating substantial cash. Though no longer in good health he continued to farm the remaining land, including his brother's land. He used the compensation to buy out his brother's land. He died only days after the transaction was completed.

APR will be allowed in respect of the whole acreage, including land that had only been in James's estate for a matter of days before his death.

---

**11.37** The second and alternative qualification for APR under *s 117* is that the property was owned by the transferor throughout the seven years ending with the date of transfer and throughout that period was occupied for the purposes of agriculture. It does not matter, for this second test, whether the land was occupied by the owner or by some other person. Qualification for APR under the second test is most likely to be in relation to bare land rather than a farmhouse because of the arguments already noted in relation to farmhouses. However, this can be a very useful relief.

---

**Example 11.9—Small let farm**

Olwen's family had always been farmers. The holdings were small hillside properties, the main occupation sheep farming. Olwen's uncle eventually moved out of his 90-acre property, letting it on a commercial basis – house, land and farm buildings – to a neighbour. By his will he left the property to Olwen who thereafter drew the rents and still owned the property at the date of her own death more than seven years after inheriting it.

Relief will be allowed on the land and on the house (at its tenanted value) because the entire holding has been occupied for the purposes of agriculture throughout the qualifying period.

---

Note **Example 11.7** above of Geoffrey's loss of APR on his house because land was tenanted.

The need for actual occupation has been tested in two 'farmhouse' cases. The first, *Harrold v IRC* [1996] STC (SCD) 195, was a 'clawback' case arising on death within seven years of a gift. A building that in all respects satisfied the

**11.38** *Business property relief and agricultural property relief*

farmhouse tests nevertheless failed because it had not, at the relevant time, been renovated to habitable standard. It was not occupied for agriculture because it was not occupied at all.

By contrast in *Atkinson and another v HMRC* [2010] UKFTT 108 (TC) TC00420 the bungalow had been occupied, as part of a larger unit, by a farming partnership but at the date of death the farmer, a partner in the business, was in a nursing home. Evidence showed that he still took an interest in farm business. The occupation was not merely by the farmer but by the partnership. The farmer's possessions were left there; no-one else moved in. It was 'occupation for the purposes of agriculture in the relevant sense because the bungalow was still used to accommodate the diminishing needs of the senior partner'.

## Successions

**11.38** When farming property passes on death, the person inheriting it is treated as owning it from the date of death and, if he later occupies the property as having occupied it from the date of death whether he did or not; *s 120(1)(a)*. Where inheritance is between spouses or civil partners the person inheriting the farming property is also credited with the period of occupation of the previous owner.

**Example 11.10—Keeping it in the family**

Sarah ran a small stud farm and equestrian centre with arable land and pasture. Her lifelong companion Margaret helped with the horses. As soon as they were able to do so they formalised their relationship by registration as a civil partnership. Sarah left the property to Margaret on her death. Margaret herself died within only 18 months of inheriting the property, leaving it to her niece.

APR, if allowable on the farming enterprise at all, is allowable just as much on the death of Margaret as it had been on that of Sarah.

## Replacements

**11.39** There is not much turnover in farm property. When people sell farmland they tend to get out of farming altogether. Nevertheless, *s 118* preserves entitlement to APR where a person who previously owned agricultural property exchanges it directly or indirectly for other agricultural property and occupies one property or the other for the purposes of agriculture for periods which together comprise at least two years within the five years ending with the date of transfer. This is in substitution for the two-year occupation condition in *s 117(A)*.

**11.40** There is a corresponding provision by which replacement property may qualify for the purposes of *s 117(B)*. Where agricultural property is replaced, the test is satisfied if the new property and the old were held for periods together comprising at least seven years in the last ten prior to transfer and were occupied by someone for the purposes of agriculture.

It should be noted that *s 118* does not generally allow for 'trading up'. The relief is restricted to the extent that the new property replaced the old.

---

**Example 11.11—Trading up**

Quentin's farm was small and inconvenient but he put up with it for many years until he came into some money from an inheritance. He then sold the farm for £400,000, purchasing a slightly larger and much more convenient property for £600,000. There was then a general downturn in the value of all farms.

On his death soon afterwards, when the new farm was worth only £550,000, relief was allowed only on £366,667, being the (two-thirds) proportion of the value of the new farm that was referable to the earlier holding; see *s 118(3)*.

---

## The valuation of the transfer

**11.41** All agricultural property must be valued twice for IHT. Under the general rule in *s 160* the taxpayer must show the price the property might reasonably be expected to fetch on the open market at the time of transfer. That means the gross open market value, not some vaguely discounted 'probate' value. It also means, where several parcels of land are concerned, the value would be achieved by offering the land in the lots which, within reason, would be likely to yield the best value.

This issue is examined in detail in *Ellesmere (Earl) v IRC* [1918] 2 KB 735 and *Buccleuch (Duke) v IRC* [1967] 1 AC 506. More recently, when considering two interests in the same parcel of land in *Gray (surviving executor of Lady Fox) v IRC* [1994] STC 360, discussed in greater detail below, the Lands Tribunal considered that the 'natural unit' for sale would be to offer both the land itself and a partnership interest in it as the same item, on the basis that the hypothetical vendor must be regarded as having done whatever was reasonably necessary to get the best price including taking separate properties, or separate interests in property, and selling them together.

**11.42** The open market value will however take account of the existence of any tenancy and the tenancy itself may have a value. In *Baird's Executors v IRC* [1991] 1 EGLR 201 George Baird had given up the tenancy of an agricultural holding in favour of his daughter-in-law and his grandson. The tenancy had

**11.43** *Business property relief and agricultural property relief*

first been granted in 1921 and the transfer was in December 1977. The landlord consented. Mr Baird died in 1985. The gift of the tenancy was a chargeable transfer under the rules in *Finance Act 1975* and the Lands Tribunal had to decide whether the 'rump' of the lease had any value.

Held, it could and did. The District Valuer's figure was 25% of vacant possession value, having regard to what the landlord might pay to get the land back, what a tenant might pay in a sale and leaseback, the sort of figure paid to a tenant on compulsory purchase of land and on prevailing rents of other similar land. The case, being brought in Scotland, was particularly concerned with *s 177*, which provides that in certain circumstances value of a lease may be left out of account.

**11.43** In the *Lady Fox* case, the Court of Appeal reviewed the decision of the Lands Tribunal. Lady Fox owned an agricultural estate farmed by a partnership which had an agricultural tenancy. She was entitled to 92.5% of the partnership profits and on her death the Inland Revenue (as they then were) assessed CTT on the basis that her interests in the land and her partnership share could be valued together. The vacant possession of the land would be discounted in a number of ways. The result of that argument was to produce a much higher valuation figure than would apply to the land if disregarding the partnership share.

The Lands Tribunal had originally decided that the assets should be valued separately, but had considered what the value would be if the assets were taken together, in accordance with the method that was approved by the Court of Appeal. Taking open market vacant possession value, the District Valuer deducted the amount that the partners other than Lady Fox would accept to sell their share of the tenancy. He took a percentage of the difference between a vacant possession of value and tenancy value and discounted it to compensate for risk and delay in obtaining vacant possession.

The Tribunal, applying the rules as required by the Court of Appeal, felt that there was no guarantee that the minority partners would accept the particular sum suggested by the District Valuer and would have been willing to accept a slightly larger discount for the uncertainty, but there was no evidence from the taxpayer on that point.

**11.44** Every valuation of agricultural land will turn on its own facts. Where there is in existence an 'old' tenancy, ie one established before 1 September 1995, agricultural relief will be allowed at 50% only except where Extra-statutory Concession F17 applies. This will allow relief at 100% where possession of the land is obtainable within 24 months or where, notwithstanding the terms of any tenancy, land is valued at an amount broadly equivalent to the vacant possession value. That can arise where the tenant is a company and where the transferor controls the company. This may seem slightly anomalous.

## Example 11.12—ESC F17 in action

David owned 52% of the shares in Hanley Farms Ltd, having given 24 shares each to his sons Eric and Fred. The company had the tenancy of Old Hanley Farm, which was owned by David. Late in life David remarried. His wife, Geraldine, is very much younger than he and more interested in fashion than in farming. Her tenacious personality resulted in the transfer of half of Old Hanley Farm into her name, subject to the existing lease.

By his will David left his shares in Hanley Farms Ltd to Geraldine for life with remainder to Eric and Fred. As it turned out Geraldine was the only proving executor and trustee of the will. Following the death Geraldine was advised of ESC F17 and claimed that the farm should therefore be valued at open market value and that relief should be available at 100%. The Concession conveniently ignores the fact that a surrender of the lease by the company, which lies in Geraldine's power by virtue of her controlling shareholding, would be action oppressive of the minority because it would take away value from the holdings of Eric and Fred.

## The value for relief

**11.45** The second valuation of agricultural land is required by *s 115(3)* and is 'the value which would be the value of the property if the property were subject to a perpetual covenant prohibiting its use otherwise than as agricultural property'. In short, for farmhouses this now probably means 70% of open market value unless particular circumstances dictate otherwise, as will be seen from the discussion below of the leading case, referred to many times in this chapter, of *Lloyds TSB Private Banking plc (personal representative of Rosemary Antrobus deceased) v Twiddy* (IRCT) [2005] DET/47/2004 (*'Antrobus Number 2'*).

## Example 11.13—Farmhouse in East Norfolk

Lower Bylaugh Farm comprises a four-bedroomed detached house with single garage standing in a quarter of an acre adjoining a range of modern farm buildings. The farm itself is 175 acres of arable land. The journey time from the farm to Liverpool Street station is slightly over three hours, allowing for the distressed state of certain country roads. It is five miles to the nearest petrol station and seven miles to the nearest regular public transport network. Although the land is very productive the scenery is featureless and could have inspired Noel Coward's well-known description of the county in *Private Lives*.

The existence or absence of an agricultural restriction would make little difference to the value of the property. It has no particular aesthetic charm

**11.46** *Business property relief and agricultural property relief*

and is so far from any centre of employment or of education that it would be of little interest to any purchaser who still had to earn a living or had teenage children. In the circumstances, the agricultural value of the property must be almost the same as the open market value.

### Example 11.14—Farmhouse in Dedham Vale

Although not actually a building that was in existence in John Constable's time, Valley Farm is set in landscape that the painter might still (just) recognise, but for the electricity pylons. Although not listed, the property retains many original features and is set in small but well-managed gardens as part of a holding of 50 acres all of which, as it happens, are managed by a farm contractor. The journey time to Liverpool Street from Manningtree Station is just under one hour and the station itself is only 12 minutes away. There are excellent shopping and restaurant facilities, schools (and nightclubs) within 15 miles.

The land is not enough to support a farming family, but that is irrelevant. Only those who, even in these troubled times, are still earning seven-figure bonuses in the City of London need consider showing any interest in the property, which commands a premium by virtue of its situation, the ease with which it can be managed and what was described in *Higginson's Executors v IRC* [2002] STC (SCD) 483 as 'a case where the property has a value greater than ordinary, not because of development potential but rather because of what I might call "vanity value" on account of its site, style or the like'. The agricultural value of the farmhouse is perhaps only 55% of its full market value.

**11.46** For a time HMRC attempted to establish a rule of thumb that the agricultural value of a farmhouse was 70% of its open market value. Many tax liabilities were settled on that basis until the decision of the Lands Tribunal in *Re Antrobus (No 2)*. The background to this case was the decision, noted at **11.45** above, that the house in question, Cookhill Priory, was a farmhouse. The decision of the Lands Tribunal must be read carefully. It is only a decision on value, though the Tribunal did consider certain wider issues in order to arrive at their decision. The open market value of the farmhouse and gardens was £608,475. HMRC, applying the 70% 'rule' argued that agricultural relief should be available on only £425,932.50. In the end the tribunal fixed the agricultural value at that figure.

**11.47** The case was very fully argued. The taxpayer wanted relief on the entire value by arguing that some purchasers actually welcome a restriction on the use of property because it keeps other people away. However, these may not be 'true' farmers but 'lifestyle' farmers who have perhaps made money in some other occupation and can therefore afford to pay a premium for the seclusion of an agricultural property. There was evidence that offers had been made for Cookhill Priory of £935,000 and eventually £1,035,000. The Valuation Office argued for a discount of 30% because the terms of *s 115(3)* are even more restrictive than a 'planning tie'. This is because a planning tie can eventually be lifted, whereas the effect of *s 115(3)* is permanent. No true agricultural purchaser would overpay for a house because as a farmer he would have to buy land to go with it. The over bid for the farmhouse, with a small area of land adjoining it, from non-farming residential purchasers should be excluded since that over bid or excess would depend on matters such as location, setting, views etc which did not impact on the viability of a farming operation.

**11.48** To arrive at their decision, the Lands Tribunal considered what a farmhouse actually was and decided that 'a farmhouse is the chief dwelling house attached to a farm, the house in which the farmer of the land lived'. They went further to define the farmer as 'the person who lives in the farmhouse in order to farm the land comprised in the farm and who farms the land on a day-to-day basis'. Based on that, the Tribunal was able to ignore the premium price that would be paid by a 'lifestyle' farmer. It had already been established that lifestyle farmers were a substantial part of the market for this type of property, so if they were excluded the value of the property fell to only 70% of the open market value.

Here, as in many other aspects of APR, practitioners should take note of HMRC's updated guidance on APR (www.hmrc.gov.uk/manuals/ihtmanual/ IHTM24000.htm) on the basis, as with all such guidance, that whilst it represents only an HMRC view, and is not actually law, to take a line that is inconsistent with it puts the adviser on a collision course with HMRC that may end only before the First-tier Tribunal, and perhaps not even there.

# LOSS OF BPR AND APR

**11.49** Neither BPR nor APR is available where the subject matter of the transfer is itself already subject to a binding contract for sale at the time of the transfer: see *s 113* for BPR and *s 124* for APR. In that sense there is a loss of relief, in that the owner of the property can no longer claim the relief on a transfer made after the contract has been entered into.

The provisions cause difficulty, especially in partnership situations where it may be suggested that there is, by virtue of the terms of a partnership deed, a binding contract under which surviving partners can and must buy in the share of the deceased partner. If all else fails, look carefully to see if there has been a partnership change effected, not by deed, but by conduct. If there has, argue that it is now a partnership at will only and drive a coach and horses through the old partnership deed. Alternatively, look for help to Statement of Practice12/80 and perhaps at IHTM25292 for HMRC's view.

**11.49**  *Business property relief and agricultural property relief*

Another instance of the loss of relief is some change in the nature of the asset during the period of ownership of the transferor, as where an unquoted trading company goes public and lists on a recognised stock exchange. Again there is loss of BPR, in the sense that on a subsequent transfer it will no longer be available, where a controlling shareholder who owns property used by an unquoted trading company reduces his shareholding with the result that the conditions for BPR on the other assets are lost. As has been noted, there can be loss of APR on a farmhouse where it ceases to be the nerve centre of a true farming business.

However, all these are instances, not so much of loss of relief that has been granted, but of situations where relief would previously have been available and is not now. This section is concerned with clawback of relief under *ss 113A* and *124A*. Although there is a separate code for BPR and APR, their wording is so similar that they are taken together with commentary.

Relief, whether BPR or APR, may be lost where, following a transfer which would otherwise qualify for relief, certain conditions are not satisfied. The relief that would otherwise have sheltered the transfer from tax is clawed back. Clawback applies where the potentially exempt transfer is made within seven years of the death of the transferor and the PET fails. It operates by applying the concept of a 'notional transfer' made by the donee of the property immediately before the death of the transferor or, if earlier, of the transferee. On the occasion that triggers clawback, the notional transfer tests the continued availability of the relief that was originally granted. If the conditions for relief are not satisfied it will be clawed back.

The conditions are:

- that the original property was owned by the transferee throughout the period beginning with the date of the chargeable transfer and ending with the death of the transferor; and
- that, subject to one exception, in relation to a notional transfer of value made by the transferee immediately before the death, the property would qualify for relief but for satisfaction of the requirement as to ownership or occupation.

---

**Example 11.15—Clawback**

Olive gives Renee a 30% holding of unquoted shares which qualify for BPR. Olive dies within seven years, so the PET fails. Tax becomes chargeable on the gift. If Renee still holds the shares, all is well and BPR will shelter the gift but if Renee has in the meantime sold the shares no BPR will be available.

Albert gives Denise a 15% holding in an unquoted trading company which later becomes listed on the London Stock Exchange. The shares qualify for

*Business property relief and agricultural property relief* **11.51**

BPR at the date of the gift but, even though Denise may in fact keep them and may still be holding them at the time of Albert's death within seven years, there will be no BPR because on the notional transfer at that date by Denise conditions for relief are no longer satisfied (*s 113A(3A)(b)*).

There are rules for substitution of property in the BPR and APR codes: these were considered by the Revenue in RI 95, to which reference should be made.

## Computation of the tax

**11.50** Where a gift of business property is a failed PET and clawback applies, this affects the history of chargeable transfers by the donor.

Where the transfer that originally benefited from APR or BPR was a chargeable one, clawback operates to charge extra tax on the original gift on the basis that no relief is available. In this circumstance there is no change to the history of chargeable transfers by the donor, because the value before relief of the property has not changed.

Special rules apply to shares or securities which were unquoted and qualified for BPR both at the time of gift and at the time of death. It does not matter that the shares may qualify for relief by reference to a different subsection of *s 105*. Provided that they so qualify by reference to the donee, that is good enough.

### Example 11.16—Different classes of share

Sidney controls a quoted company and gives a small minority holding of shares in it to his son Alfred, those shares qualifying for relief at 50% under *s 105(1)(cc)*.

Alfred keeps the shares and is still holding them when Sidney dies only two years later. No relief would normally be available in respect of a minority holding in a quoted company. Although the gift was of quoted shares within *s 113A(3A)(a)*, rather than within *s 113A(3A)(b)*, that brings into play *s 113A(3)(b)* so that, in relation to the transfer that Alfred is deemed to make, it is not necessary to satisfy the earlier test.

Alfred therefore, in effect, manages to keep the original claim to BPR at 50% on shares in a quoted company and suffers no clawback. The distinction between different classes of interest in a company used to be more important where the relief was not always 100%.

**11.51** One major area of difficulty used to concern gifts into trust. For the purposes of the clawback rules, the donee of the property is the trustee, not the

**11.52** *Business property relief and agricultural property relief*

beneficiary. Under the rules in force prior to *Finance Act 2006*, a transfer to a trust other than a discretionary trust could be a PET and could therefore come within *s 113A(1)* or *s 124A(1)*, so clawback could apply.

If the trustee appointed the property to a beneficiary before seven years had elapsed from the gift and if the donor died within seven years of the gift there was a risk of clawback that the trustee could have avoided simply by not making the appointment. That option was not available where, for example, the trust was an A&M settlement prior to Budget 2006, as will be seen in the second of the examples below.

### Example 11.17—Land for a young farmer

Percy settles farmland on discretionary trusts for his nephews and nieces. At the time of the transfer all the requirements for APR are satisfied. Five years later in the exercise of their discretion the trustees appoint part of the land to a nephew, who then farms. The following year Percy dies.

Clawback is not in point, because the creation of the trust was a chargeable transfer at the time: that was when it mattered whether APR was available. It does not matter that the trustee no longer holds the fields that were appointed out to the nephew. There is no clawback of the relief in respect of the original gift.

### Example 11.18

Dawn set up an A&M settlement for her grandchildren and on 3 March 2001 transferred to the trustees shares in her trading company, Roller Doors Ltd. At the time of the gift the eldest beneficiary is 15. The *Trustee Act 1925, s 31* has not been excluded. The powers of the trustees to accumulate have been limited, with the result that three years later the eldest beneficiary, on attaining 18, becomes entitled to an interest in possession in part of the fund. All the other beneficiaries are much younger.

On Dawn's death three years later, six years from the original settlement, the notional transfer by the trustees is examined. At that point the trustees still hold all the shares but, in relation to the eldest beneficiary, the shares are now treated by virtue of *s 49* (prior to the amendments in *FA 2006*) as being part of the estate of the eldest beneficiary. To that extent the trustee no longer holds them and relief in respect of that part of the fund is clawed back. There is no clawback of the relief of the remainder of the fund because the trustee still holds it.

**11.52** Over the years there have been difficulties with clawback because of changes in the definition of 'quoted' affecting shares on the old Unlisted

*Business property relief and agricultural property relief* **11.53**

Securities Market. They are now treated as unquoted for the purposes of clawback throughout the period from the date of transfer to the date of the notional transfer. The effect of a change in 1996 is to avoid clawback where it might otherwise have applied. Note, however, that if a company listed on AIM acquired a second listing, perhaps on a major foreign and 'recognised' stock exchange, it would lose its favoured BPR status and clawback could apply.

## Comparison of PETs and chargeable transfers and the treatment for clawback

**11.53** The following checklist may help to assess the effect on the transfer of business or agricultural property (Ch T = chargeable transfer).

|  | *PET Treatment* | *Ch T Treatment* |
| --- | --- | --- |
| Immediate charge to IHT? | No: a PET | Only on value as reduced by relief |
| Death within seven years of transfer: assets retained by donee | No IHT: full relief | No IHT: full relief |
| Death within seven years of transfer where clawback applies: effect on the transfer itself | IHT charge, subject to availability of nil rate band. Charge is on the full amount of the transfer. | IHT charge, subject to availability of nil rate band. Charge is on the full amount of the transfer. |
| Death within seven years of transfer where clawback applies: effect on aggregation with later transfers eg on death | Full value is aggregated | The value is nil so there is an advantage here in making the transfer by Ch T |
| Transferor lives seven years from gift and no benefit has been reserved | No IHT: transfer has become exempt | No IHT: transfer falls out of cumulation |

305

*Chapter 12*

# Lifetime planning

## USE ALL THE RELIEFS

### Lifetime reliefs

**12.1** The taxation of lifetime transfers was discussed in **Chapter 2**. The main exemptions and exclusions were described in **Chapter 9** and the reliefs of general application in **Chapter 10**. There is, naturally, some overlap between this chapter and **Chapter 14**, relating to the nil rate band. The cardinal rule for IHT planning, if not of all tax planning, is first to use all of the reliefs that the legislation provides.

*Finance Act 2006* restricted the scope for lifetime giving, making it more urgent for taxpayers with substantial estates to consider their options and to exercise them. However, several factors tend to restrict use of lifetime gifts, all of which contribute to difficulties for taxpayers later in life. They can be seen from the following extended example (all statutory references are to *IHTA 1984*, unless otherwise stated).

---

**Example 12.1—Ian, Prudence and family: background**

Ian worked for many years in local government and is now in his early sixties. He took early retirement, which has provided him with a useful pension pot that he will soon draw. He now works from home, providing consultancy services to his former employer and to other local authorities (in connection with leaking drains). He was first married to Sarah. They had a daughter, Samantha, now a chartered accountant, and a son, Jonathan, who is employed by the NHS. Ian and Sarah were divorced many years ago. Ian eventually achieved a clean break settlement. He now lives with Prudence. Their only son, Ben, is a student.

Prudence came out of her own divorce with some savings, now worth £100,000. Ian has no worthwhile savings apart from his pension, but he does own the house in which they live, worth £700,000.

Ian gets on fairly well with Sam and Jon. Sam's biological clock is ticking and she and her husband would really like to start a family but their

*Lifetime planning* **12.1**

present mortgage is such that they really both need to work to fund it. Jon is in rented accommodation and finding it difficult to get onto the property ladder. Prudence does not really object to the idea that Ian might make some provision for the children of his first marriage provided, of course, that Ben's interests are protected. Ben is prudent save in the matter of that essential aid to concentration, a red sports car, on which he could spend any money that lay around anywhere.

### Example 12.2—Ian, Prudence and family: existing wills etc

Prudence's will leaves her estate to Ben. Ian's will leaves the house to Prudence for life with remainder to Sam, Jon and Ben in equal shares. Ian has nominated Prudence as the main beneficiary of his pension if he dies before drawing it. His will leaves the residue of his estate, which would include the value, if any, of his consultancy, to Prudence.

If Prudence died first, there would be no IHT on her estate, which would pass to Ben free of tax. It is, however, assumed that Ian dies first, in the year 2012/13 when the (single) nil rate band is still £325,000. His pension provision was nominated to Prudence many years ago and falls outside his estate. The consultancy is worth £20,000, comprising the benefit of work in progress and some other realisable assets: these are all genuine trading assets and 100% BPR is available in respect of them. By then, the house is assumed to be worth £775,000. No gifts have been made, the nil rate band of £325,000 is set against the value of the house, leaving in charge £450,000 and giving rise to a tax charge at 40% of £180,000.

Although Prudence would have the benefit of a reduced pension, and could use her own savings to pay part of the IHT, she might decide that the house must be sold and ask the trustees to buy something more modest. If she were to die shortly thereafter, the estate to be considered would be her own capital of £100,000, the money realised from the consultancy plus the net value of the remaining trust fund, say £595,000 ignoring expenses. The IHT bill, if she died within a year of Ian's death, would reflect the benefit of quick succession relief.

### Example 12.3—Ian, Prudence and family: what might have been: marriage and downsizing

If Ian and Pru had taken tax advice, things might have been rather different. Although they were living together they were not married. The only real bar to their marriage was the emotional scar left on Ian by his protracted and very messy divorce. If he and Pru married, spouse relief could be available on the first death of either of them.

## 12.1   Lifetime planning

Second, following Ian's retirement there is no real need for them to continue to live in the London commuter belt. Ian's consultancy is not worth a significant amount: besides, drains leak all over the country so he could work from home anywhere. It therefore makes sense for Ian to sell the house and to buy something that is quite big enough for him and Prudence (and for Ben when he needs to detox from student life). They find a suburban property in East Anglia, which they purchase in their joint names as tenants in common for £250,000.

**Example 12.4—Ian, Prudence and family: gifts and wills**

That leaves Ian with cash of £450,000 and increases Pru's estate to £225,000. Ian gives £50,000 each to Samantha and Jon. Ben has found a property in the university town where he is studying (with off-street parking) that could be bought for £150,000. Ian therefore gives Ben £50,000 as a deposit on the house.

Ben establishes that, even in the present market, with a substantial deposit a 'student/buy to let' mortgage is on offer at quite favourable terms with an introductory period at a competitive low fixed rate for the next two years, with an alternative rate pegged to LIBOR. Having obtained confirmation of the rates available in the open market, he then borrows £100,000 from Ian on terms that are quite good for Ian but actually give Ben a significantly better interest rate than he could have secured elsewhere, so there is no reservation of benefit in the transaction.

Ben has student friends who will rent two-thirds of the property. The rent will be almost enough to pay the interest to Ian.

That leaves Ian with £200,000. He invests £150,000 on the advice of a stockbroker friend in blue-chip securities outside the oil sector. The last £50,000 is invested in a small AIM company providing services to local authorities in a commercial field that Ian happens to know about and which he thinks is reasonably safe.

Pru changes her will. She now leaves £100,000 to Ben outright, then leaves the balance of the nil rate band on discretionary trusts for Ben, Jon, Sam and Ian. She leaves the residue of her estate to Ian absolutely. Ian makes a will leaving the AIM shares and the nil rate band on discretionary trusts for his children and Pru. He gives his executors power not to call in the mortgage on Ben's property. He leaves the residue of his estate to Pru for life with power to advance capital for her with remainder to his children and provides that the gift of the nil rate band need not be satisfied by the immediate payment of cash. Instead, his half of the house may be charged with payment of the gift of the nil rate band.

*Lifetime planning* **12.1**

**Example 12.5—The tax effect**

Broadly, the effect of these arrangements is to make full use of the nil rate band, as was the case under the previous part of the illustration, but this time there is no crippling IHT charge on Ian's death. If Pru were to die first the gift to Ben would be tax-free and, because her estate is now larger, she is able to use more of the nil rate band than before. The saving is 40% of £125,000: £50,000 of tax.

On the assumption that Ian dies first during 2012/13 and that the nil rate band is pegged meanwhile, his estate is as follows:

|  | £ | £ |
|---|---|---|
| Half share in house |  | 125,000 |
| Quoted shares |  | 150,000 |
| Unquoted shares |  | 50,000 |
| Consultancy |  | 20,000 |
| Loan |  | 100,000 |
| Sub total |  | 445,000 |
| Recent gifts (£150,000 less £6,000 exempt) |  | 144,000 |
| Estate before reliefs |  | 589,000 |
| Deduct |  |  |
| BPR on shares | 50,000 |  |
| BPR on consultancy | 20,000 | 70,000 |
| Estate after reliefs |  | 519,000 |

The estate suffers no IHT, being exempt or relieved. Distribution is as follows:

| | |
|---|---|
| Gross estate for distribution as above | 589,000 |
| Deduct balance of nil rate band (see below) | 231,000 |
| Residuary fund (below) | 358,000 |
| Spouse relief | 358,000 |

The nil rate band is £325,000. From it are deducted the three gifts to the children, less two annual exemptions. The nil rate fund is the balance of £181,000 plus the (tax-free) shares, £50,000: £231,000. Residue is therefore £358,000. The trust of the nil rate band includes the AIM shares, but not the consultancy.

The specific gift avoids the difficulties of *s 39A*: for more detail see **3.27**, **Example 3.3** and **13.25**. There is no formal need for an IOU in respect of the cash balance of the nil rate band of £181,000: the trustees will simply maintain two funds of residue, one of which is subject to the discretionary trusts and one

## 12.2 Lifetime planning

of which is subject to the simple life interest for Pru. Her life interest is an IPDI and therefore qualifies for spouse relief.

### Example 12.6—Incidental benefits for the family

The result of this arrangement is that Sam can reduce her mortgage and think about starting a family. Jon can put a deposit down on a property. Ben has secure accommodation whilst he is a student and, if he sells at a profit after he graduates, main residence relief will be available on the whole of the gain. In the meantime he can claim rent-a-room relief.

The family as a whole will benefit from BPR on the eventual disposal of the consultancy and on the investment in the AIM company. If the AIM company does no more than hold its value the saving after two years will be tax of £20,000 (though that saving only lasts if shares are still owned by Ian at the date of his death and if at that date the company is still an unquoted company).

Pru's position is more secure. She now owns half of the house she lives in and has a life interest in the other half. If she wanted to move, main residence relief should be available both to her and to the trustees. She has the income from the quoted securities and from Ben's mortgage. If Ben sells his house well when he graduates, he will have a substantial deposit and should find it easy to borrow in the open market, releasing £100,000 to the trustees.

If Pru finds that she does not need all of the income from the trust fund, she has one or two choices available to her. She may simply authorise the trustees to pay away to the family any income in so far as it exceeds a certain sum that she needs to live on. That would be entirely within the rule in *Bennett v IRC* [1995] STC 54 and the payments would quickly gain relief under *s 21*. Alternatively, she may release part of her life interest, allowing the children to become absolutely entitled. That would be a PET against which, if she gave notice to the trustees, she could set her annual exemption under *s 57*.

This example shows how the 'old' rules, ie those in force before transferable nil rate bands, can be used to good effect in a 'double family' situation, such as is very common nowadays.

## The Child Trust Fund

**12.2** This initiative was an early casualty of the coalition government following its election in 2010, but government contributions will be reduced and then stopped. What is not yet clear is whether, as a savings vehicle that

*Lifetime planning* **12.3**

has actually benefited 'middle England' far more than any other sector of society, the tax structure will be retained. Apart from trusts for the disabled it is now the only form of lifetime trust fund favoured by the government. It offers substantial scope for saving income tax, capital gains tax and IHT. Although the amounts may seem modest the effects of full use of the allowance and of accumulation of income may be greater than is generally realised.

This is a UK-based gross roll-up fund. Normally, a parent achieves no advantage from a settlement on his unmarried minor child. Normally, any income of such a settlement is assessable on him. The CTF avoids this difficulty. The parent, or indeed any family member, can add £100 per month to the fund without the tax penalties that would otherwise apply. The limit of £1,200 per year is calculated by reference to the child's birthday, not the tax year.

---

**Example 12.7—Generous but forgetful grandfather**

Robert's children had blessed him with several grandchildren, some born after 31 August 2002. On 1 May 2007, to celebrate his eightieth birthday he gave each of his grandchildren £500. For each of the younger children this was promptly added to the CTF that the parent had taken out. In late March 2008, having read about the CTF, Robert quickly sent £1,000 to the parent of each younger grandchild, to catch the end of the tax year.

For any grandchild whose birthday falls in May or, say, June, only £700 of the new gift may be added to their CTF because the previous £500 falls in the same birth year as the recent gift. If the others can show that the earlier gift went into the CTF in their previous birth year, the whole £1,000 may now be added.

In each case, if the pattern continues, it may be possible to argue that the gifts from part of Robert's normal expenditure are within *IHTA 1984, s 21*.

---

**12.3** There is no way of deferring the enjoyment of the fund beyond the age of 18, but that is really the only drawback of the scheme. As was noted in the Parliamentary debates on the Finance Bill 2006, many people at age 18 are just starting a university education and will need money. The accumulation of the contributions alone, ignoring any money from the government, generates a fund at age 18 of £21,600. If the fund and its accumulations of income are well invested, the eventual sum available could be considerably more.

In the past, secondary school education has often been funded by grandparents through A&M trusts. The facility of doing that is cut down significantly by *FA 2006*. If, therefore, the burden, for those who choose it, of funding secondary education falls more heavily on parents than on grandparents, the grandparents could use the CTF to help with the cost of further education.

**12.4** *Lifetime planning*

# BPR and APR

**12.4** The rate of BPR and APR has not always been as much as 100%. The coalition government must raise tax where it can. The 'emergency' Budget on 22 June 2010 came too soon for a considered change to tax policy, but any LibDem input is likely to target those who are 'asset rich' even if, as so often, they are 'cash poor'. APR, with its emphasis on assets rather than on hands-on business involvement (farmhouses excepted), may seem a softer target than BPR. Farming families might do well to take land in hand and, if they can, to reduce their reliance on contractors.

**12.5** The difficulty for families will be that the assets that qualify for BPR are those that involve some element of risk. Sometimes such assets are held more for the possibility of capital growth than for income. As a result, an elderly estate owner may wish to keep the assets that are safe and that yield a good income, whilst disposing of other assets. If IHT mitigation is the only consideration, the estate owner should probably do the opposite. If at his death his estate comprises entirely assets that qualify for APR or BPR there will be no IHT to pay except in so far as lifetime gifts, originally PETs, become chargeable. The exceptions are those gifts that by their very nature prejudice subsequent claims to relief. See the example 'Getting it wrong' at **Example 11.3** and of loss of relief on farmhouse at **Example 11.7**.

Another factor that will often influence the subject matter of gifts is the availability, or lack of it, of hold-over relief for CGT purposes. *TCGA 1992, s 165* offers fairly wide scope for holdover relief of business assets and is extended.

There is always someone who would like the benefit of a relief without necessarily 'meriting' it, in the sense of falling within the policy of the relief. One illustration of this approach is as follows.

---

**Example 12.8—Recycling business property into investments**

Alan invested in unquoted shares, gradually building up a portfolio worth £800,000 in which all the holdings had been held for at least two years. He then transferred them all to a trust under the rules in force before *Finance Act 2006*, such that the transfer was a PET that might be subject to clawback of BPR if he died within seven years. None of the companies had a secondary listing on any recognised stock exchange, so the transfer attracted 100% relief, but subject for the next seven years to the clawback rule in *s 113A*.

The trustees were wary of such investments, fearing lack of liquidity and risk generally. They realised that a clawback charge could apply in the event of Alan's death, if they no longer held assets that qualified for 100% BPR, so they took out term insurance. Having done that, they sold all the shares and bought gilts and investment properties to stabilise the portfolio.

## OUTRIGHT GIFTS

### True outright gifts

**12.6** The attitude of members of Parliament to the correct age at which young people should inherit has been noted elsewhere, with reference to serving in the armed forces overseas. Many people of moderate wealth will accept the present regime and will suffer the tax on discretionary trusts as the price to be paid for preserving family property from dissipation as a result of vesting at age 18.

The advantages of outright gifts are:

- simplicity;
- cheapness, in terms of legal fees saved;
- the transfer is a PET;
- holdover relief from CGT may be available under *TCGA 1992, s 165*, avoiding the complexities of *TCGA 1992, s 169B* that arise on gifts to settlor interested settlements.

The trouble with simplicity is its transparency. Many a potential donor seems to want something more complicated, as if that confers tax advantages. No formal deed is necessary to make a gift of cash: let the donor just write out a cheque and, mindful of the rule in *Curnock (Curnock's Personal Representative) v IRC* [2003] STC (SCD) 283, do it soon enough that it can be encashed before death. A gift of shares in a plc held in certificated form requires no more than a stock transfer, again delivered timeously to avoid the rule in *Rose, Re, Rose v IRC* [1952] 1 All ER 1217. For a gift of land to an adult, a transfer is enough; if in Scotland, the date of the disposition is the effective date, not the later date of registration (*Marquess of Linlithgow and Earl of Hopetoun v HMRC* [2010] CSIH 19). A car or a valuable chattel may be given by simple delivery.

Many of these transactions generate little in professional fees but are effective none the less. If reliance is to be placed on *s 21* relief, what is needed is not so much a formal deed as a record of the intention to make regular gifts and its execution over a period of years. Just do it.

### Unwise gifts

**12.7** A gift is perceived as being unwise where family assets as a result can be at risk of claim in matrimonial proceedings or at the suit of creditors. Apart

**12.8** *Lifetime planning*

from that, gifts may be unwise where they prejudice APR or BPR. This was illustrated in the **Example 11.3** of Jason where the transferor no longer had control of the company at the time of a gift of an asset used by that company.

If readers of the actual report will forgive the pun, it is 'starkly' illustrated in the case of *Rosser v IRC* SpC 368, [2003] SSCD 311, discussed at **11.30**. It is also illustrated by the considerations that have just been described above in relation to the choice of asset to give away.

**12.8** There are other circumstances where a gift may prove to have been unwise. The example of Willie in **Example 8.18** shows how gifts may be taxable in the context of a discretionary trust. Certainly, if an outright gift has been made nearly seven years ago and the transferor is considering establishing a trust now, which will be treated as a discretionary one under the rules in *FA 2006*, it makes sense to allow the seven years from the earlier gift to run off so that it does not affect the calculation of the hypothetical transfer, see the example of Celia at **Example 8.3** where a failed PET came to light.

There is also a slightly specialised situation where a gift can prove to have been unwise.

---

**Example 12.9—A gift that should not have been made**

Henry, whose late wife had used her nil rate band in full, settled £400,000 on discretionary trusts on 18 June 2002. On 22 July 2007, he gave his daughter Jennifer a cheque for £160,000. When he died on 30 June 2010 his estate was £500,000 and had the benefit neither of APR nor BPR. The chargeable transfer to the discretionary trust was more than seven years before the death and therefore itself fell out of aggregation with the estate at death.

The PET was less than three years before the death and outside the scope of taper relief. IHT on the PET is calculated by reference to the situation on the day that it was made. On that date the cumulative total of transfers was £400,000, so IHT on the failed PET is based on £560,000. The nil rate band is that on death, £325,000, leaving all of the £160,000 in charge at 40%, tax therefore £64,000.

The estate for probate purposes includes the £500,000. The failed PET of £160,000 must be taken into account. After allowing for the nil rate band in force at the date of death of £325,000, the tax is £134,000 (ie £500,000 − (£325,000 − £160,000) × 40%). This liability is in addition to the IHT on the failed PET.

The situation could have been better if the gift had not been made and instead there had been equivalent provision by will. Assuming that the £160,000 had not been spent and that none of the income from it was saved, the estate at death might then have been £660,000. The tax on that would be £134,000. There would have been no failed PET and therefore no tax charge on it.

The moral of the story is that someone who has made a substantial chargeable transfer must weigh up quite carefully the advantages of early giving and the risk that a charge on his estate may apply by virtue of *s 7(1)*.

---

For a time, it seemed that if a taxpayer (or if we are honest, his adviser) made a mistaken gift, there was some scope for 'putting the toothpaste back in the tube' by relying on the principle in *Hastings-Bass Deceased, Hastings v CIR* [1974] 2 All ER 193. If, say, trustees had mistakenly appointed out funds on the wrong day, they could apply to have the deed set aside on the ground that they had not appreciated the full effect of the document when entering into it. Thus, Abacus Trust Co were twice before the courts, once with NSPCC and again with Barr, to seek help.

In *Sieff v Fox* [2005] WLR 3811 Lloyd LJ reformulated the Hastings-Bass principle as it relates to exercise by trustees of their discretion. The court will interfere '… if it is clear that [the trustees] would not have acted as they did had they not failed to take into account considerations which they ought to have … or taken into account considerations which they ought not …' He also observed that it might help the court if HMRC did not always decline the invitation to take part when such matters were litigated.

In *Tax Bulletin* 83 (June 2006), HMRC indicated that they would in future consider joining in litigation if much tax is in issue. They feel that where, as in *Abacus Trust Co (Isle of Man) Ltd v NSPCC* [2001] STC 1344, the trustee takes tax advice but fails correctly to implement it, there should be no relief. That would (though of course the *Bulletin* does not use such language) effectively blow many such cases out of the water. A mistake as to the intended tax effect of a document is unlikely to be the subject of rectification by the court (see *Allnutt and Another v Wilding and Others* [2007] EWCA Civ 412).

The most recent illustration of the principle, and an example of the joinder of HMRC, is *Pitt v Holt* [2010] EWHC 45 (Ch) considered at **10.13**. The court there applied the principle to a person acting in a fiduciary capacity making a voluntary transfer to a trust and later regretting it.

It may be possible successfully to apply to the court to have a gift set aside on the grounds of mistake in certain circumstances. In *Ogden v Trustees of the RHS Griffiths 2003 Settlement and others* [2008] EWHC 188 (Ch), Mr Griffiths made gifts in 2003, and a further gift in February 2004. In autumn 2004, he was diagnosed with lung cancer, and he died in April 2005. The executors argued that the transfers had been made under a mistake by the deceased as to the state of his health, ie that there was a real chance he would survive for seven years.

**12.9** *Lifetime planning*

The court refused to set aside the transactions in 2003, as they were made when the deceased had not had lung cancer, so he had made no mistake about the state of his health. However, the deceased had been suffering from lung cancer by the time of the third transaction in February 2004. Had he known that he was suffering from lung cancer, he would not have acted as he did. Accordingly, the court held that transaction to be voidable.

For further comment on this issue, see the CGT case of *Futter and Futter v HMRC* [2010] EWHC 449 (Ch) where the taxpayer mistakenly sought to set losses against a stockpiled gains charge despite the (somewhat obscure) wording of *TCGA, 1992, s 2(4)* which prevents that. The rule in *Hastings-Bass* is not, the judge held, based on the law of mistake but on the validity of exercise of discretionary powers after giving due weight to all relevant factors. The principle existed, not to relieve advisers from the consequences of their mistakes, but to ensure that beneficiaries do not suffer by an invalid exercise of trustees' powers. The deeds of appointment were set aside as invalid. It is understood that this decision may be appealed.

## More subtle schemes

**12.9** The steady rise in house prices (until recently) has forced planners to explore ways of sheltering the home from IHT. At its least aggressive, this may involve the gift of a share in the home to a child who continues to live there and is likely to remain permanently – a state of affairs suffered by increasing numbers of parents as their offspring return from college with a qualification, but without a job.

If the sale is to an unconnected third party, pre-owned asset tax (POAT) will not be a problem, though it will otherwise be, unless the transaction took place before 7 March 2005, or (which is rather contrived) the consideration is not for money or readily convertible into money (*SI 2005/724, reg 5*).

More adventurous is the creation of a lease, followed by the sale of the freehold reversion and a gift of the proceeds of that sale. This level of planning must carry a health warning and must be carefully executed.

A variant of this idea is the sale of a share in the house followed by gift of the proceeds, but again it will have to be to a stranger, or not for cash, to avoid POAT.

Boldest of all is:

- the sale of the house (or perhaps an investment property) to a spouse;
- the price is satisfied by a debt; and
- the debt is given away (eg to adult children).

It is argued that there is no gift with reservation, because:

- a sale is not a gift;
- the deduction should be allowable, unless *FA 1986, s 103* happens to be an issue; there will be SDLT to pay, but no POAT, because it is an excluded transaction.

It is understood that, at the time of writing, HMRC are looking closely at such arrangements, with a view to possible litigation. Advisers who attempt this type of structure and their clients must not complain, as Dawn Primarolo once put it, if on any failure they get their fingers burnt.

## DISABLED TRUSTS

**12.10** The coalition government probably does not wish the tax treatment of trusts to be unfair on vulnerable members of society, including specifically the disabled. Disabled trusts escaped some of the changes in *FA 2006*.

There has long been a code for disabled trusts, which has been little used because it is slightly inflexible and many of the advantages could be achieved through normal discretionary trusts. There is little evidence that enactment of *FA 2006* has encouraged the creation of disabled trusts.

## The statutory requirements

**12.11** *Section 89* applies to settled property which has been transferred into a trust after 9 March 1981. The requirements of the trusts are simple:

- there is no interest in possession in the trust fund during the life of a disabled person; and
- at least half of the settled property which is applied, during the lifetime of the disabled person, must be applied for his benefit.

Under *s 89*, the disabled person is treated as being entitled to an interest in possession, even though the trusts may be discretionary. In brief, that has the effect that there can be a charge on the fund on the death of the disabled person and, on the other hand, that no holdover relief is available for capital gains tax on transfer to or from the trust if the disabled person is the settlor such that the trust is settlor-interested.

**12.12** A disabled person is someone:

- incapable of administering his property or managing his affairs by reason of mental disorder with the meaning of the *Mental Health Act 1983*; or

**12.13** *Lifetime planning*

- receiving attendance allowance under the *Social Security Contributions and Benefits Act 1992 (SSCBA 1992), s 64* or the equivalent provision for Northern Ireland; or
- receiving disability living allowance under *SSCBA 1992, s 71* at the middle or the highest rate of entitlement to the care component, or the equivalent provision for Northern Ireland; or who (see *s 89(5)*, with effect from 22 March 2006), when property was transferred into a settlement, would have been receiving attendance allowance or disability allowance but for technical disentitlement where that person was undergoing treatment for renal failure in a hospital, or was provided with certain accommodation; or
- who (see *s 89(6)*, with effect from 22 March 2006) can satisfy HMRC that, at the time property was transferred into a settlement, he would have been entitled to receive attendance allowance if he had met the residence conditions or if regulations under *SSCBA 1992, s 67(1)* or *67(2)* had been ignored; or
- who (see again *s 89(6)*), can satisfy HMRC that, at the time property went into trust, he would have received disability living allowance at the middle or highest rate if he had met the residence conditions.

## Self-settlement under FA 2006

**12.13** Treatment of all lifetime settlements as discretionary trusts, in accordance with the general thrust of *FA 2006*, could have penalised the disabled. There is provision for those people who wish, whilst still in control of their affairs, to make settlements to protect assets against a future time when they might not be able to look after themselves. In particular, such arrangements can be useful at the early onset of Alzheimer's disease. *Section 89A* provides for a person suffering from a condition expected to lead to disability (in the legislation referred to as 'A'). The conditions are as follows:

- A was entitled to the property before settling it.
- A satisfies HMRC that at the time of making the settlement he had a condition that was likely to lead to his disability such that he would later be a disabled person within the original definition in *s 89(4)*, or that he would become entitled to attendance allowance or disability living allowance in accordance with the descriptions set out earlier in this chapter; and
- the property is held on discretionary trust which comply with two conditions namely:
    - Condition 1: if any of the trusts property is used during A's life, it is used for the benefit of A (HMRC have explained that this refers

to the application of settled property, meaning property held on the disabled trusts); and

- Condition 2: any power to bring the trusts to an end during A's lifetime is so framed that, if the power to end the trusts is exercised during A's life, further sub conditions will apply namely:

    (a) the fund will be held absolutely for A or for some other person; or

    (b) when the trusts end there will still be the interest of a disabled person within *s 89B(1)(a)* or *s 89B(1)(c)*.

(HMRC have explained that these conditions apply where the original disabled trusts are brought to an end.)

**12.14** Broadly, *s 89B(1)(a)* is an interest in possession in favour of the disabled person and *s 89B(1)(c)* is an interest in possession in settled property to which the disabled person is entitled and was so entitled on or after 22 March 2006.

Where these conditions are met, the person making the settlement is treated as beneficially entitled to an interest in possession in the settled property, so there is no immediate IHT charge on the settlement. There is a saving provision in relation to compliance with attendance allowance and the like under which we may assume that A will meet the conditions as to residence under the relevant legislation and that that legislation will not be changed. This applies where the basis of claim to the relief is that A suffered from a condition that was likely to lead to his being entitled to either attendance allowance or to disability living allowance.

There are further saving provisions relating to the terms of the trust document itself. In deciding whether a trust actually complies with all the requirements of *s 89A*, we may ignore powers in the trust deed to give directions as to the settled property where those powers are exercisable jointly by the people who, between them, are entitled to the whole of the fund. We are also entitled to ignore anything that could result from the exercise of such a power.

**12.15** A 'disabled person's interest' means, see *s 89B*, any one of the following:

- an interest in possession under *s 89(2)*;
- an interest in possession where the person is treated as being entitled to under the self-settlement rules in *s 89A(4)*;
- an interest in possession that the person is entitled to, not falling within the two previous categories, where property was transferred into a settlement on or after 22 March 2006;

**12.16** *Lifetime planning*

- an interest in possession in settled property, not falling within the first two categories just set out, where the following five sub-conditions are met, namely:
    - A is a settlor;
    - A was entitled to the property before settling it;
    - A satisfies HMRC that his condition could deteriorate and lead to disability as already described;
    - property was settled on or after 22 March 2006; and
    - under its terms, the trust fund is so held that, if any property is applied during the lifetime of A, it goes to the benefit of A.

**12.16** As can be seen from the third category above, which is *s 89B(1)(c)*, a disabled person who becomes entitled, after 22 March 2006, to trust property that had already been settled some time before, is treated favourably, as if the trust assets were part of the estate of the disabled person. That creates a 'level playing field' between existing and new provisions for disabled people.

## PROTECTED GIFTS WITHOUT TRUSTS

### Pensions for grandchildren

**12.17** Notwithstanding the rules for age 18-to-25 trusts, many taxpayers who wish to provide for young members of the family will insist on a late vesting age and will not wish the fund to be subject to the complications that are set out in **Chapter 8**.

One possibility is opened up by the liberalisation of the pensions regime. Quite simply, assuming that no other pension provision has been made for the grandchild, the grandparent can set aside limited contributions to a pension policy for a grandchild, knowing that the fund cannot be touched for very many years. The paperwork with many of the recognised investment houses and investment trusts is simple and the fees moderate. Pensions (of moderate size) are favoured by the government and, although there is no recovery of tax on dividend income within the fund, freedom from repayable income tax and from capital gains tax will combine to help the fund to grow. If the premiums are, as would be likely, paid on a regular basis it may be possible for the grandparents (or their executors) to claim relief for all of the gifts under *s 21*.

### Pensions for young children

**12.18** Generally, apart from the Child Trust Fund described above, there is little scope for parents, rather than grandparents, to make tax-efficient

*Lifetime planning* **12.21**

provision for their children under the age of 18. The normal rules in the *Income Tax (Trading and Other Income) Act 2005, s 624* and following, especially *ITTOIA, s 629*, prevent the arrangement from achieving any saving of income tax. For many years gains of trustees for children enjoyed the same low rate as individuals. The redefinition of 'settlor interested' for the purposes of CGT briefly had the effect of substituting the settlor's top tax rate. However *TCGA 1992, s 77* which imposed that rule, was no longer needed following the 18% rate of CGT and was repealed. The introduction of the 28% rate for all trusts has removed some of the attraction of trusts for young people.

However, parents, like grandparents, may within overall limits contribute to pension policies for children, which fall outside the trust regime and achieve useful long-term savings. Care should be taken not to try to take this too far, by using 'family pension pots' to try to slide assets down the generations free of IHT: that possibility has been foreseen by the legislation. Given the uncertainty that must now affect existing CTF investments, many may prefer pensions as the vehicle for saving for children.

## Options

**12.19**   This is a contentious area and one that a general practitioner should not enter without specialist advice. The clear intent of the government, when introducing *FA 2006*, was to deprive the benefit of gift relief as a PET to anything other than an outright gift. However, many taxpayers find it very difficult to bring themselves to making outright gifts, for a variety of reasons. Where the donor wishes to retain some benefit from the gift, such as the income, the result is clear. It is a gift with reservation within *FA 1986, s 102* and following. It is thus ineffective as a means of saving IHT.

**12.20**   More subtly, a donor may not wish actually to receive any benefit himself from the thing given away, but may wish to restrict the dispositive powers of the donee. This could apply either to shares in a family company of which the donor was still an active working director or to land, part of the family farm and still farmed by the donor. Many taxpayers who have worked hard to assemble capital are reluctant to risk its dissipation by their children, whether through the financial inexperience or waywardness, financial or marital, of the donees.

**12.21**   One structure that may be imagined is that of a gift which, sooner or later, is followed by the grant by the donee of an option to the donor that would allow the donor to repurchase the asset either at its market value or at some predetermined value if certain circumstances were to arise. There is probably little abuse where the option can be exercised only at full market value, because the donee exchanges the original subject matter of the gift for full value and no economic benefit passes back to the donor. The situation is more difficult

**12.22** *Lifetime planning*

where the option price is determined at the outset or where it becomes clear from a course of dealing between the parties that the donor would never have made the original gift unless the donee had already agreed in principle to enter into the option.

Given the very wide interpretation of the expression 'to the entire exclusion of the donor and of any benefit to him by contract or otherwise' as set out in RI 55, it is likely that a 'gift plus option' arrangement might be challenged under *FA 1986, s 102*. Planners should also bear in mind the decision in the *Smith* case, noted in **Chapter 7**, on the issue of associated operations.

## Family limited partnerships

**12.22** For a time practitioners explored the idea of a partnership within the family in which younger members could enjoy a share but subject to carefully drawn limitations to ensure that they never actually got to enjoy the money unless and until their elders approved. It is fair to say that this structure is not for everyone. Chief among the problems has been investment, where the received wisdom is that the partner who manages the family money will need help from managers who are FSA-registered. The cost of a dedicated adviser will put the arrangement out of the reach of most families and in any case reasonably wealthy families are often headed by an entrepreneur who would like to control the entity anyway. However, over time it may become possible to devise a form of partnership that does actually work and can be created and run at moderate cost.

## TRADITIONAL PROTECTED GIFTS

## Existing interest in possession trusts and the TSI facility

**12.23** Following the enactment of *FA 2006*, trustees should have reviewed the interests of beneficiaries, identifying those interests that were interests in possession on 21 March 2006 and retaining the old IHT treatment where that was beneficial. Trustees should also have considered the possibility of replacing existing interests in possession with Transitional Serial Interests as described at **7.27** and in the example of Marian and her surrender of the life interest.

The facility expired on 5 October 2008, although a limited TSI facility still exists in respect of spouses and civil partners, and in respect of life insurance contracts (*IHTA 1984, ss 49D, 49E*).

## A&M settlements as part of the relevant property regime

**12.24** For many trustees, the main issue will now be extraction of value from the trust with the benefit of holdover relief from CGT.

*Lifetime planning* **12.26**

## Policy trusts

**12.25** These were examined in **Chapter 7**. *Section 46A* deals only with life interest policy trusts that already existed on 22 March 2006, by and large preserving their status. Trustees of policies, perhaps more than those holding any other property, tend to take a relaxed view of their duties. They may not even know that they are appointed or that the policy is a trust with requirements as to compliance like any other. It is therefore possible that such trustees may have taken no action at all following the enactment of *FA 2006* and in particular will not have tried to vary the existing rights under the policies. In many cases, the best advice may have been to 'leave well alone'. As was noted at **7.41**, where the existing trusts are on an A&M basis it will have been important, as for any other 'ex-A&M trust', to see who the beneficiaries were and whether the trust should have been varied so as to accelerate vesting age. In one sense, it is still not too late to take action; such trusts have only recently entered the relevant property regime and the IHT charge on exit will not yet be significant, though the incidental costs of release may be.

There is one major conceptual difficulty for clients taking out policies and writing them in trust. Where the premiums are paid on a regular basis the donor may seek exemption under *s 19* or *s 21* (but not under *s 20* which refers to outright gifts only). An exempt transfer is not a chargeable one. It follows that the gift of a policy written in trust will often be outside the complications of **Chapter 8**. Previously, it was important to take care not to breach the limits described at **6.4** for reporting lifetime transfers, but the higher limits under the Regulations described in **Chapter 6** largely remove this worry.

Generally, chargeable event gains are assessable on the settlor, though HMRC have taken advice which leads them to regard the beneficiary as assessable if the trust is a bare one, even where the trustees do actually have some duties to perform: see Business Brief 51/08. For 2007/08 onwards it is the beneficiary of a 'true' bare trust who should declare chargeable event gains 'rather than the settlor'; but the Brief does point out that the settlor, if a parent, is still 'potentially' taxable on policy gains. To avoid the possibility of double taxation, which is not referred to in the Brief but not in terms excluded, many families may decide that it will be best for policies to be settled by grandparents rather than by parents.

## Discounted gift schemes

**12.26** These arrangements became more popular after *FA 2006*. A capital redemption bond is put in trust. It leaves the estate of the settlor. There is an immediate discount, calculated by reference to the liability to make repayments, according to the sex, age and health, etc of the settlor. Withdrawals of 5% may be taken. The balance of the investment is a chargeable transfer for IHT. There

**12.26** *Lifetime planning*

are two separate interests, thus avoiding reservation of benefit; the settlor has no access to the balance of the investment. The key issue is the value of what is given away.

HMRC have considered discounted gift schemes, see the technical note posted to their website dated 1 May 2007 (www.hmrc.gov.uk/cto/dgs-tech-note.pdf). For a clear insight into the way that HMRC view such schemes, see IHTM20401 to 20635, which contain not only a description of the schemes but also a 'checklist' of schemes in common use. It is considered that the taking out of the plan and the making of the gift are linked, as was found by the Special Commissioner in the similar, but slightly different scheme employed in *Smith v Revenue and Customs Commissioners* [2008] STC 1649.

The issue was fully explored in *HMRC v Bower and another (Executors of Bower Deceased)* [2009] STC 510. The deceased took out a life annuity in 2002, being then 90. She paid £73,000. The policy was issued to trustees of a settlement that she had created. She reserved rights to an annuity of 5%. She died within five months. That being within three years of the gift of the balance of the rights under the policy, there was a chargeable transfer of the amount of the gift. It was agreed that the gift was £73,000 less the value of the retained rights; but HMRC considered the value of the rights was negligible: £250, so the gift was of £72,750.

This contrasted with the insurance certificate, valuing the rights at £7,800, so the executors appealed to the Special Commissioner, who valued them at £4,200. That figure was arrived at by discounting the figure of £7,800 by one-third and by a further £1,000 for legal costs. HMRC appealed successfully to the High Court, which held that the Commissioner, in the absence of evidence, had gone too far in deciding the value.

Thus where the settlor is, by age or for any other reason uninsurable at the date of gift, the value of the retained rights will be nominal and virtually all the bond will be the gift. That will be true, see below, whenever the settlor is 90 or over. The May 2007 note explains the HMRC attitude to joint settlements and the apportionment of any discount. In the past, valuation was seldom necessary but that has changed now that the settlement is a chargeable transfer. The old procedure of lumping both discounts together is no longer appropriate. Instead, the discount must be calculated for each settlor in turn. In HMRC Brief 65/08, dated 31 December 2008, it was announced that the valuation rate of interest for discounted gift schemes, ie the discount rate (which the Commissioner had not felt able to use in *Bower*) would be reduced from 6.75% to 5.25% pa with effect from 1 February 2009. In HMRC Brief 21/09, issued after the High Court ruling in *Bower*, HMRC understandably reaffirmed their view of the valuation basis where the settlor is uninsurable or is (actually or for underwriting purposes) 90 or over at the transaction date. Only a nominal value will be attributed to the retained rights. Nothing in the legislation allows any withdrawals actually taken between the date of the gift and the death to be taken into account and set against the sum invested in the scheme. Cases that were held pending the judgment will now be processed.

## Flexible reversion trusts

**12.27** There is a constant desire among donors, which the life assurance industry tries to satisfy, to eat one's cake and still have it; to make an effective gift but to retain some 'comeback' if circumstances change. One such structure is the 'flexible reversion trust'. It is actually a settlement of a string of single premium endowment policies, but for clarity imagine a consignment of several cases of wine the contents of which will mature individually in successive years. The settlement of them, say for grandchildren, is a chargeable transfer, so best limited to the available nil rate band. The settlor retains the right, at maturity, to the proceeds (if he is still alive) but this is not treated by HMRC as the reservation of a benefit; nor is any payment to the settlor of those proceeds subject to an exit charge.

The trustees have wide powers, including the power to give one of the policies *before* maturity to beneficiaries (opening one of the bottles) or the power to defer maturity (laying the bottle down for a further period). As (it is hoped) the policy increases in value with time, that increase belongs to the trust, not the settlor. Although this is an insurance scheme, it is not limited to investment in life policies, so could admit some flexibility, though doubtless not actually into wine. It appears to have achieved a successful 'shearing' of the right to receive the maturity proceeds, not given away, from all the other rights under the policies: something possible with an insurance product but much harder to achieve with any other asset.

## Lifetime gifts into trusts since FA 2006

**12.28** Trusts, except disabled trusts, set up by life transfers after 22 March 2006 are relevant property trusts and their creation is a chargeable transfer, unless exempt. This will probably have two effects. The taxpayer of substantial means may in the past have been willing to delay making gifts on the basis that a large gift made into an interest in possession trust or an A&M trust would have been potentially exempt and, if he survived it by seven years, substantial value could be transferred whilst retaining safeguards over the capital.

**12.29** *FA 2006* has curtailed that facility. Transferors will probably not wish to pay IHT on the establishing of lifetime trusts and will not want the complications of grossing-up. Many will therefore limit their generosity to settlements that are within the nil rate band. This will lend urgency to the situation because seven years must elapse after the making of a nil rate band discretionary trust before another one can be made that will not be 'tainted' by

**12.30** *Lifetime planning*

the existence of the prior trust, leading to the complications that are described in **Chapter 8**. The message to wealthy estate owners is therefore: 'get on with it'.

**12.30** The second effect of the rule that virtually all new lifetime trusts are chargeable will be that, below a certain level, many taxpayers will decide that the complexities of a discretionary trust are simply not worthwhile even though the burden of IHT on a nil rate band trust for the first ten years is nil and, as has been seen in **Chapter 8**, the burden of tax on quite a substantial trust is only moderate. It is therefore likely that fewer small trusts will be set up because their administrative costs will be unacceptable.

Chapter 13

# Wills and estate planning

## THE NIL RATE BAND

### Nil rate band discretionary trust

**13.1** It was for many years common for the public to avoid straightforward mirror wills by which spouses (or civil partners) left everything to each other with remainder to children. Before the introduction of the right to transfer the nil rate band, such simple wills were inefficient because they failed to use the nil rate band of the first of the spouses or partners to die. Instead a more complicated structure was used, seldom fully understood by those implementing it and, it must be said, not always by those recommending it. This was inefficient in a different way, imposing significant extra work on taxpayers, on the one hand; and on HMRC, because of the multiplicity of forms to be processed that yielded little or no tax (unless the taxpayer committed some procedural error, which it was the tiresome duty of HMRC to spot and to penalise). All this became largely unnecessary by virtue of *FA 2008, s 10* and *Sch 4*, which are fully discussed in the next chapter.

### The old 'debt or charge' scheme

**13.2** The solution commonly devised before the transferable nil rate band was a gift of the nil rate band to trustees coupled with a provision that that gift need not be satisfied by immediate payment, but might be satisfied either (and there were significant differences of approach here):

- by taking a charge over other assets in the estate; or
- by accepting a promise of payment from the surviving spouse or civil partner.

The difficulty was that few families really understood the structure (for examples in related fields, see *Wolff v Wolff and Wolff* [2004] STC 1633, in which the claimants were forced to apply to the court to set aside a reversionary lease scheme on the grounds that they had made a mistake as to the legal effect

**13.3** *Wills and estate planning*

of the arrangement. See also, more recently, *Bhatt v Bhatt and others* [2009] EWHC 734 (Ch), as to the difficulties for 'ordinary' people in engaging in tax planning). To work well, the scheme needed the executors to take certain action at certain times: many cases are now coming to light where this was not done, or was skimped.

The effect of *Finance Act 1986, s 103* ('Treatment of certain debts and incumbrances') on the scheme was even less well understood. It was litigated in *Phizackerley v IRC* [2007] SpC 00591, where the Special Commissioner had to decide whether deduction of the liability under the scheme was prevented by *FA 1986, s 103*. He noted that *s 103* prevents the deduction of the debt where, and to the extent that, the consideration given for the debt or incumbrance consists of 'property derived from the Deceased' and held that:

- On the face of it, the half share in the house in issue was indeed derived from the deceased. It was the subject matter of a disposition made by the deceased.
- The debt incurred by the deceased in favour of the trustees of the nil rate band was not deductible.

The Special Commissioner dismissed the taxpayer's appeal.

**13.3**    James Kessler QC argued that the use of the 'charge' structure (which was not used in *Phizackerley*) offered a complete defence because the debt is not 'incurred by him [the deceased]' within *FA 1986, s 103(1)*. That argument is attractively simple, but there can be a problem on 'trading down' later: see **13.5** below.

## Give the spouse a life interest

**13.4**    If, instead of receiving the residue outright, the surviving spouse receives only an IPDI with residue passing to the children, there is no deduction of the nil rate band from the estate of the surviving spouse that can fall foul of *s 103*. The liability operates to reduce the value of the aggregable trust fund of residue, rather than the estate of the second spouse to die. It is therefore not 'a liability consisting of a debt incurred by him or an encumbrance created by a disposition made by him' within *s 103(1)*.

## Is the debt or charge scheme any use, now?

**13.5**    The decision in *Phizackerley* did not totally invalidate the debt or charge scheme. The structure should not be entered into where the family would benefit more from the provisions of a transferable nil rate band, as will usually be the case. It will fail if the parties behave as if the nil rate

## Wills and estate planning  13.6

band fund was always, and would remain, at the disposal of the surviving spouse. The surviving spouse must understand that the value comprised in the discretionary trust *is not his/her money*. There must always be the risk, from the point of view of the surviving spouse, that the trustees could at any time call in the loan.

Where, in relation to an existing scheme, the surviving spouse later decides to 'trade down' in property terms, the trustees must consider calling in their debt, and should encourage the surviving spouse to use his or her own resources to purchase and refurnish the replacement property. They may give assurances that the fund will not be dissipated, but should not compromise their discretion. This may also help to shield the family fund from the burden of nursing home fees. The surviving spouse should come to the trustees for help only when those resources are used up.

Note that if *s 103* had originally been a problem that was obviated by the imposition of a charge before assent to the surviving spouse, the sale of that property and the purchase of a new one with some help from the trustees throws the surviving spouse back into the *Phizackerley* situation: another reason to favour the use of an IPDI instead. Alternatively, the discretionary trustees could, instead of making a loan, join in as purchasers. Provided that two years had elapsed from the death, to prevent any relating back to the death, the trustees could then give the surviving spouse a formal right to occupy the share of the house that they had bought. It would not be aggregable with the free estate on the second death, but main residence relief would be secured.

## Avoiding *Phizackerley*: proof of contribution to the house by the spouse

**13.6**   Where it is for any reason appropriate to retain a pre-*FA 2008* form of will, and *Phizackerley* issues arise, it must be increasingly common that, at some time during a marriage, particularly in the early years, both husband and wife will earn and pool those earnings. Most wives will be able to claim, as a matter of simple mathematics and disregarding the attitudes of the courts on divorce, that they have made a contribution to the cost of the house and that the purchase of the house in joint names does not lead to the automatic conclusion that '*the funds must have been provided by the Deceased*'. The facts of *Phizackerley* can be distinguished where families can show that:

- both husband and wife worked at various times during the marriage;
- both directly or indirectly contributed to the cost of one home after another; and
- the family home that is in their joint ownership at the time of the death of the first of them to die is truly owned by them equally.

## 13.6 Wills and estate planning

A serious issue to address is that *Finance Act 1986, s 103* contains no time limit. The debt which the executors seek to deduct from the estate of the second spouse to die is (see *s 103(1)*):

> 'subject to abatement to an extent proportionate to the value of any of the consideration for the debt or encumbrance which consisted of
>
> (a) property derived from the deceased; or
>
> (b) consideration (not being property derived from the deceased) given by any person who was at any time entitled to, or amongst whose resources there was at any time included, any property derived from the deceased.'

It matters not how long ago the gift was made. It could still be caught.

How will all this be proved? Some executors will be reluctant to carry out an expensive enquiry into transactions long ago. Some beneficiaries will resent the cost of that enquiry, as in: *re Sir Malcolm Arnold Deceased, Day v Harris and others* (2010, unreported). Beware of breaching the duty of care in delivering accounts under *IHTA 1984, s 216*. If there is any clear link between the debt which is to be deducted from the estate of the surviving spouse and a gift made, however long ago, by that spouse to the first spouse to die, *Phizackerley* can apply. This case increases the burden on executors and their advisers, and the risk of a penalty for failure to make proper enquiries. Students of the approach to penalties that resulted from the merger of the Inland Revenue and HM Customs and Excise will naturally hope that the failures in this area can be put down to 'mistake'.

---

### Example 13.1—'Battles long ago'

Seamus and Kathleen's stormy marriage survived mainly through a religious conviction that persuaded Kathleen to put up with more than many would have tolerated. Seamus was successful in the building trade but there had been a time when his business was 'close to the wire' in financial terms.

On one such occasion, when Kathleen had almost decided to leave, Seamus transferred to her several plots of land and the house in which they were then living, but made it clear that she should regard herself as no more than trustee of the value for him. Later, when the financial threat had abated, she did return the plots but, on the advice of her daughter, she kept her name on the deeds of the house, where she lived until her death.

In such a case it would be appropriate for the executors to enquire closely into all the transactions, even (to misquote Wordsworth) long ago, because for emotional reasons the family members might very well remember them. In any case, the deeds may still be in existence, though that is less likely if the family has moved house since.

## The effect of *Phizackerley* on existing wills

**13.7** The enactment of *FA 2008* will trigger the rewriting of many wills. Those left untouched can be 'mended' by prompt exercise of the power of appointment to create an IPDI, so as to nullify the structure and achieve a transferable nil rate band. Subject to that, where there has been no gift of an interest in the house (which will usually be the relevant asset), it may not be necessary to change anything purely in the light of the decision in *Phizackerley*. If there has ever been a substantial gift, existing structures should be reviewed. The problem arises only where the donor spouse is the second to die: so in the common case of value transferred in lifetime by husband to wife, where she survives him, there is no problem.

## Procedural difficulties with existing structures

**13.8** For the pre-*FA 2008* structures that remain, there may be difficulties of execution. Where, for example, the will has not been properly drawn and infant beneficiaries have interests in residue there can be difficulty in correcting the errors. Where there is a gift of the nil rate band, but no corresponding provision that that gift may be satisfied by an IOU it is not possible, by simple deed of variation, to put matters right. Any deed of variation, to be effective, must alter the *dispositions* of the estate of the testator, so the inclusion of the desired clauses must effectively ride on the back of another variation.

Even supposing the paperwork all to be correct, further difficulties arise both as to the intention of the parties and execution of the structure. The problem with intention is that, if the surviving spouse from the outset refuses to acknowledge that the debt is inevitably repayable and if the trustees go along with that, there is effectively a 'sham' because the parties have rejected the thinking behind the scheme. However, if the family are 'stuck' with an old will, there might almost be an advantage in suggesting that 'we never really meant/understood it' to get out of an old debt/charge scheme and into a transferable nil rate band situation.

At a less acute level, there may be simply inaccuracies or lapses which cause the scheme to fail. On the eventual death of the second spouse or civil partner it may be impossible to prove that appropriate formalities were put in place to recognise the debt. There may be no evidence that the trustees ever at any time considered calling it in. The trustees must recognise the realities of what is happening. They are lending an amount equal to the value, in many parts of England, of a three or four-bedroom detached house. Trustees would not

**13.9** *Wills and estate planning*

normally lend that amount of money without taking security. Trustees must therefore consider whether or not to take security. If they fail to do so they should have a reason for their failure.

There is certainly a risk that people will fall between two stools: the old structure fails for want of proper execution but it has been partly effective to use the nil rate band so that it is not transferable. The difficulty for advisers is that the ongoing trust may be administered by the family who may not remember all the advice given when it was set up; or it may not be possible to show that such advice was given; and yet if the scheme fails at the second death people may be quick to claim that the original adviser was at fault. Ideally, the adviser should call each scheme in for a 'health check' but that would be difficult to organise and the family might resent the cost. Perhaps the only practical solution is a mailshot to all affected clients explaining the issues and inviting trustees in for a brief, free health check. That might be the occasion of getting new work from the family that could offset the cost of the review.

## Practical issues arising out of existing debt or charge scheme structures

### Choice of trustees

**13.9** The choice of trustees is important. They should not be subject to the control of the surviving spouse. It is therefore helpful, but by no means essential, for one of the trustees to be independent. The trustees should have due regard for the requirements of the arrangement and should meet at reasonable intervals to consider whether or not to call in the debt. If left indefinitely, it can become statute barred. As far as the surviving spouse is concerned, there must always be a *frisson* of uncertainty that the trustees could call in the debt. Certainly, if the surviving spouse decides to move house the original loan should be repaid in full and the surviving spouse should then approach the trustees to ask for a fresh loan of such amount as is needed to finance the new purchase.

### Liquidity

**13.10** The next issue is the extent to which liquidity in the estate of the first to die should have been applied towards satisfying the gift of the nil rate band. Although there is no case precisely in point, it lends reality to the whole structure if the executors apply available securities and other savings in part satisfaction of the nil rate band so that the debt or charge is only for such sum as cannot be satisfied from the available liquid assets. That may be unpopular with the surviving spouse.

## Interest and index linking

**13.11** Interest may, but need not, be charged on the debt. In many instances the charging of interest will be neutral. Receipt of interest by the trustees of the nil rate band will attract income tax at 50%, whilst reducing the estate of the surviving spouse and thus saving IHT at 40%. At that point, therefore, the exercise seems not to be worthwhile. If, however, there are many beneficiaries of the nil rate band who, perhaps because they are young, do not pay income tax, there will be a saving because after expenses the trustees can make distributions of income to the non-taxpaying beneficiaries who will recover some or all of the tax thus paid.

Occasionally, the nil rate band is index linked. On final resolution of matters it is certainly arguable that the extra money so received is essentially payment, by reference to time, for the use of money and is therefore interest receivable at the time of repayment of the loan, even though it is calculated by reference to inflation or a house price index. Others argue to the contrary: there is no decided case directly in point, and perhaps the sums involved are too small to litigate about. Well-drawn wills allow the trustees to waive their rights as to index-linking or the charging of interest.

## DEFERRAL OF TAX USING SPOUSE RELIEF

## Background

**13.12** In its most simple form, this planning is acceptable and allowed for by the legislation.

---

**Example 13.2—Post-war nuclear family**

John was born in 1912, Susan in 1915. They married when he was home on leave in 1940 and had two sons, born in 1941 and 1945. Returning to civilian life he became an engineer. She was a teacher. By 1980 they were both enjoying a happy retirement and spending time with their grandchildren when John's smoking finally caught up with him and it became clear that he would not live much longer. His will provided for legacies for his grandchildren but left the bulk of his estate to Susan.

She was widowed in 1982, then aged only 67 and in good health. On John's death she inherited from him free of IHT, sold the family home, traded down and made substantial gifts to her sons, hoping to live seven years so that the gifts would be free of tax. In the event Susan did survive until 1990. The gifts made soon after John's death fell out of account and her nil rate band, together with John's, was available to Susan's executors.

---

**13.13** *Wills and estate planning*

**13.13** The scheme of deferral of tax in the above example has worked substantially in the way that legislation intended, saving the family from an immediate IHT charge on the death of John. However, many circumstances arose prior to *FA 2006* where the relief was claimed in circumstances less acceptable to the government.

---

**Example 13.3—William's life and loves**

William was born in 1912. His first wife, Mary was born in 1915. They married in 1940 and had two children, one born later that year and another born in 1943. Mary died in 1955, leaving William to bring up the boys, then aged 15 and 12, just when his building business was reaching a very busy stage of its development. His secretary Rachel helped bring up the boys and William and Rachel had a daughter born in 1960. By 1995 the stresses of running a family business had taken their toll on William, who had become so difficult to live with that Rachel had left him.

Whilst on holiday in Thailand he met and married Anja, then aged 32. By now, the construction business had developed substantially into a property investment business and was run by the younger of William's sons with some help from his daughter. Anja's gifts lay more in looking after William and in building up a fine collection of personal jewellery than in household or financial management. In fairness to his children William wanted to provide substantially for them rather than Anja, so he made a will leaving the nil rate sum equally between his children and giving the residue of his estate to Anja on life interest trusts but with a power for the trustees to revoke those trusts at any time, with remainder to his children.

William died in 2000. There was no IHT on his death, because by then Anja had acquired a UK domicile of choice, so the residue of the estate qualified for unrestricted spouse relief. Anja then however indicated that she would like to return to Thailand. That suited the trustees well, because they had never intended that she should enjoy an interest in possession in the whole of the substantial estate for very long. Being unable, because of local laws, to own property in Thailand direct, the trustees entered a structure that allowed the purchase of a property in Thailand for the benefit of Anja for life with remainder as before, then shortly afterwards terminated the life interest. It was anticipated that Anja would live at least seven years. The cost of insuring against the possibility of her death within that period was moderate and was paid by the trustees. At the same time they terminated Anja's formal interest in possession in the structure that provided her with a home, but without forcing her to leave.

The result, under the law as it then stood, was that although Anja was living in trust property she was doing so on a mere licence from the trustees. Although the termination of her interest in possession was a potentially exempt transfer

*Wills and estate planning* **13.16**

it happened independently of her wishes and it was not therefore a 'gift' by her. Thus, the fact that she continued to benefit from the property that had previously been in her estate was not a reservation of benefit because she had not made a gift.

## Counteraction of perceived abuse

**13.14** The device described in the example of William above was specifically counteracted by *FA 1986, s 102ZA*. The success of the device, as noted in the example, rested on the fact that the continued enjoyment of trust property after termination of an interest in possession in it was not reservation out of a gift because the gift had not been made by the former tenant for life. The government considered that the abuse was sufficiently serious that it should be brought to an end in two ways. As part of a general attack on trusts there was initially provision that denied spouse relief wherever there was an ongoing trust (except for minors) following the death of the spouse.

**13.15** As was noted in **Chapter 7**, those proposals were in part withdrawn but the more specific provisions of *FA 1986, s 102ZA* remain. The operative section is *FA 1986, s 102ZA(2)*, which provides that, on the ending of an interest in possession, an individual is treated as if he had disposed by way of gift of property in which the interest in possession previously subsisted. That may be enough to bring the GWR code into play. The provision applies where:

- an individual enjoys an interest in possession in settled property; and
- that individual became entitled to the interest before 22 March 2006 or became entitled to the interest in possession after that date but the interest is an IPDI, a disabled persons interest or a TSI.

In other words it is one of the remaining categories of interest in possession that still falls to be taxed under the 'old' rules and is not treated as a relevant property trust.

**13.16** The property that is deemed by the section to be given is described as 'the no-longer-possessed property'. This is any property in which there was an interest in possession, except such part of the fund as the life tenant actually retains and in which he or she does still have an interest in possession. Thus, if the fund is £100,000 and the trustees terminate the interest in three-quarters of it, the no-longer-possessed property is £75,000 because the remainder is still subject to the interest in possession.

Consequential amendments to *FA 1986, s 102* apply where there has been a termination of a life interest, now treated as being by way of gift under *FA 1986, s 102ZA*, but the property remains in the settlement. The new provision

**13.16** *Wills and estate planning*

treats the property that is the subject of the deemed gift as consisting of the property that remains in the settlement except insofar as the trust fund does not consist of any asset in which there was an interest in possession that has been terminated by the gift.

There is an anti-avoidance provision to provide that the property in the deemed gift includes derived property, even including property derived from a loan made by the former tenant for life to the trustees. Accumulations of income are also treated as being derived from property. All of this operates to increase the size of the gift in respect of which an interest in possession may apply.

### Example 13.4—Failure to revise a will

Alec, a widower aged 80, had sons Brian, 45 and Charles 40 when he married Denise, a sprightly 72-year-old. He wanted to provide adequately for Denise, but substantially for Brian and Charles. He made a will leaving the nil rate band to Brian and Charles between them and residue on terminable interests in possession for Denise with remainder to Brian and Charles. His estate comprised a substantial house and investments not qualifying for reliefs. The plan had been to use Denise as a 'peg life' to get substantial value down to Brian and Charles free of inheritance tax.

Alec died on 1 February 2006 when the house in his name was worth £1.5 million and the residue of his estate after debts amounted to £3,275,000. The trust fund was therefore £4.5 million (ie the total net estate, less the nil rate band of £275,000). The trustees, then of course unaware of the impending terms of the Finance Bill 2006, terminated the interest in possession of Denise in the house but allowed her to go on living there. They also advanced £1 million of residue each to Brian and Charles.

*FA 1986, s 102ZA* treats the termination of the interest in possession in the house as a gift by Denise. The house is still in the trust. The interest in possession for Denise came into existence before 22 March 2006. The GWR code therefore applies so that, in the event of the death of Denise, the value of the house will be taxed as part of her estate. There is however no reservation of benefit out of the £2 million released to Brian and Charles. Those transfers are treated as PETs by Denise in the normal way. If she lives seven years those gifts will fall out of account.

The tax planning has therefore partially succeeded. Depending on her state of health, Denise may survive the transfers to her stepsons by seven years so that those gifts fall out of account. It had however been hoped that the structure would effectively take the house out of the IHT net by way of gift whilst allowing Denise to go on living there. That part of the tax planning is frustrated by the new legislation.

## Later IHT charge on a 'wait and see' basis

**13.17** The prevalence of second marriages and of children who are 'his, hers, and ours' has resulted in a proliferation of wills that attempt to do justice to the reasonable expectations of the constituent parts of a 'put-together family'. Each party to a second marriage may bring family and assets and may wish to benefit existing family alongside the issue of the union.

As originally drafted, the amendments in the Finance Bill 2006 were very strict. Any ongoing trust interests were taxed in such a way that spouse relief could very easily be lost. As revised, *s 49A* allows greater flexibility. Thus, parties to a second marriage may wish to give each other an interest in possession in the residue of estate with discretionary trusts thereafter so that the fund can be used according to the needs of the various beneficiaries at the time.

As noted in **Chapter 7**, an IPDI exists where a will trust provides for the tenant for life; and not for bereaved minors or for a disabled person; and the interest in possession exists continuously from the death. The termination of that interest in possession on the occasion where discretionary trusts arise is a chargeable transfer. The ongoing trusts are then taxed under the regime described in **Chapter 8**. If full flexibility is what the family want, they can have it, but at a price. All of this must also be considered in the light of the *FA 2008* provisions as to transferability of the nil rate band.

## Trusts for bereaved minors

**13.18** Having reviewed the tax charges that would otherwise apply, in future many taxpayers may decide to 'grumble and give in'. If they provide that shares that pass to children or grandchildren vest absolutely at 18, including accumulations of income, they will achieve the simplest tax treatment that is now available and there will be no ongoing IHT trust charges. If taxpayers want more flexibility, it must be paid for.

## 18-to-25 trusts

**13.19** Many families will want the slightly greater flexibility of a vesting age of 25. The maximum IHT cost of that arrangement, over and above the IHT charge on death, will be 4.2% as described in **Chapter 8**. In fact, as noted in that section, the actual ongoing IHT charge may be less than that.

### Early life interest trusts

**13.20** One possibility that in appropriate circumstances may give testators what they want is the creation by will of an immediate life interest in favour

**13.21** *Wills and estate planning*

of a young beneficiary. An IPDI is now less restricted than formerly following the changes to the draft of *IHTA 1984, s 49A*. There is therefore scope for a long life interest (all subsequent statutory references are to *IHTA 1984*, unless otherwise stated).

---

**Example 13.5—Dynastic wills**

Fred's three sons George, Henry and Ian are all married and doing quite well financially. The grandchildren are respectively John, 9, Ken, 7, Lucy, 8, Mary, 6, Nancy, 5 and Olive, 3 (and it seems that there will be no more). It is hoped that they will attend good schools and go on to further education. Fred is widowed and does not need to provide for his sons. His will therefore divides the residue of his estate into six shares, held respectively for each of his grandchildren for life with wide powers of advancement of capital to each tenant for life (but not to any of the others) and with remainder to great-grandchildren with gifts over.

None of the grandchildren is disabled. The provisions of *s 71A* do not apply because those rules apply to children as opposed to grandchildren, and in any event the grandchildren will not automatically become entitled to capital at age 18. 'Condition 3' of *s 49A* is therefore satisfied and each of the interests in possession is an IPDI. If the trustees advance capital to any of the grandchildren to help fund secondary or tertiary education that is neutral for IHT because each already has an interest in possession so there is no change in the estate of any of them.

If any of the grandchildren marries, spouse relief may become available to exempt a transfer that would otherwise become taxable on the termination of an interest in possession by an advance to the spouse or to the life tenant for the benefit of the spouse. The structure gives Fred's family considerable flexibility for years to come.

---

# BPR, APR AND WOODLANDS RELIEF

## Placing the relievable property

**13.21** Gifts by will to spouses and civil partners are still exempt in 'uncomplicated' structures notwithstanding *FA 2006*. There is therefore overlap of property relief and exemption. This is wasteful but may be unavoidable.

---

**Example 13.6—Simple farming situation**

Cedric inherited the family farm years ago and on his death its 150 acres were worth £450,000 and the house itself £400,000. Savings built up when farming

*Wills and estate planning* **13.21**

was better have been eroded but still stand at £200,000. His wife Mary owns some adjoining land worth £50,000 which has always been occupied with the farm and savings of £300,000. They have two daughters. Cedric's will leaves the house and land to Mary and the cash to the daughters.

On his death in November 2009 there is no IHT because the gifts to the daughters are within the nil rate band (then £325,000), and the gift to Mary is exempt.

On Mary's death in May 2010, her estate comprises the house, land totalling £500,000 and savings, now reduced to £285,000. The nil rate band available is approximately 138.46% of the current figure of £325,000 ie £450,000, because 38.46% of the band was unused on Cedric's death and is thus still available (it is actually the same amount as was unused because the nil rate band is frozen but the calculation is set out to illustrate the principle). Although Mary's death occurs only shortly after that of Cedric, APR is allowed on the farming assets under the succession provisions of *s 120*. Applying the valuation principles of *Antrobus (No 2)* [2002] STC (SCD) 468, APR on the farmhouse is restricted (ie to 70% of £400,000), so £120,000 of the value is chargeable, but even when added to her cash savings of £285,000, the resulting inheritance for Mary's daughters is within the nil rate band. The result is that the daughters inherit entirely tax free.

---

**Example 13.7—Wastage of exemption and the scope for 'double dipping'**

The facts are the same as in the previous example, only some of the figures are larger. The house is worth £600,000, Cedric's savings are £400,000 and Mary has her own farmland worth £50,000 as before but her savings amount to £475,000. If the will provisions are the same, there is an IHT charge (in 2009/10) on Cedric's death on the amount by which his cash gift to his daughters exceeds the nil rate band, (£400,000 – £325,000) ie 75,000 × 40%: £30,000. Mary's estate, on death soon after that of Cedric, is £1,575,000.

There are other problems. Farmland worth £450,000 belonging to Cedric has been enjoyed with a house valued at £600,000. Questions arise as to whether such a valuable property is indeed a farmhouse and whether, to a working farmer, the purchase of the landholding as a whole for £1,050,000 might represent 'an appalling investment in terms of yield' within the rule in *Higginson v CIR*. APR may be denied on the house on the basis that the entity as a whole is really 'a house with land' rather than a farm. Matters will be eased if Mary's own land is included, though it is of relatively little value and there may be little connection between it and the farmhouse, which could present a problem.

Assuming that that problem can be overcome, APR on the house will be restricted to £420,000 (70% of £600,000), leaving £180,000 in charge. The

**13.22** *Wills and estate planning*

daughters therefore inherit the house, the land which should qualify entirely for APR and a further £475,000 of cash: a chargeable estate of £655,000. (The gift to them from their father's estate exhausted the nil rate band, so there is no transferable nil rate band.) Value of £330,000 after Mary's nil rate band (£325,000 in 2010/11) is taxable at 40%, attracting IHT of £132,000.

## Alternative structures to save tax by 'double dipping'

**13.22** There may have been some wastage of relief in the above example. Nothing much could be done if Mary died within two years of Cedric but, if she had been in good health at the time of his death and had survived by two years or so, tax could have been saved by reordering his will. Cedric could have given his daughters the farmland, which it may be remembered was worth £450,000, and the nil rate band. That would have allowed them, on the rates in force when he died, to inherit value amounting to £775,000 tax free. Mary's estate would then comprise the farmhouse, her own land and cash of £550,000, being the £475,000 that she already had plus cash from Cedric's estate of (£400,000 less the nil rate band, leaving) £75,000.

Mary could have used part of the cash to buy the farmland from her daughters. Only if she lived two years from Cedric's death would APR again be available to her (because she would not be within *s 120*). On her death, assuming that she lived two years, her estate would comprise the farmhouse, the land and cash of £100,000 or as much of it as she still had left after two more years of farming. There would still be the argument as to whether the house was a farmhouse, but assuming that the executors were successful most of its value would be relieved, leaving (on the assumptions already made) £180,000 in charge. Mary's chargeable estate would therefore amount to £280,000.

The nil rate band (where there is no augmentation by transfer) is £325,000 for the time being. The daughters should have no tax to pay. However, as noted above, this arrangement works only where Mary lives long enough after the purchase of the relievable assets to qualify for APR in her own right under *s 117*. Depending on ages and other factors, many will hope that we may return to index-linking of the nil rate band, which would increase the eventual nil rate band available and preserve the freedom for the surviving spouse to control assets in the meantime.

## Woodlands relief

**13.23** Woodlands relief is available on death only. Calculation of the relief can be complicated and, where it is possible to show that there is commercial occupation of the woodlands, it may be simpler and more effective to claim BPR. There is, for example, provision for 50% reduction in value under *s 127*,

## Wills and estate planning 13.24

but this is rare and the practitioner is referred to specialist books on the subject. One situation in which will planning can exploit woodlands relief is illustrated below.

---

### Example 13.8—Peg life

Ralph owns very valuable woods. The trees are of a quality and age that are very attractive to the market. Even timber of lesser quality now sells well to those who can no longer afford to heat their homes with oil. Ralph is not in good health but has an impecunious sister, Freda, who might well outlive him. Ralph leaves the woodland to Freda, who does not have a substantial chargeable estate and who, having no family of her own, is likely by her will to leave all of her estate to Ralph's children.

On Ralph's death an election is made to leave the value of the timber out of account on the basis that it will be chargeable on any later disposal by Freda. If Freda does dispose of the timber that will trigger an IHT charge against which can be set her nil rate band, but if she retains the woodland until her own death the charge (at 0%) on that death will frank the IHT charge on Ralph's death. Death is not an 'associated operation'.

---

It may be assumed, as a rule of thumb, that timber grows annually by around 4%. That is an incentive only to fell it when the price is good: in times of surplus, one simply waits for a better price on a larger volume of stock.

**13.24** The more normal situation will be one in which the beneficiary of woodland which is ripe for felling will want to draw the cash. In this case a different arrangement may be appropriate.

---

### Example 13.9—No deferral of taxable event

Steve owned woodlands similar to those of Ralph and recently had the land clear-felled and replanted. He leaves the woodland by will to his grandson. On his death woodlands relief is not claimed. The value of the timber at that time is negligible because the trees are still young and the cost of looking after them is greater than any economic benefit from the landholding.

There is no point in making an election for woodlands relief because when the deferred tax comes to be payable, it is hoped not until many years later, the woodlands may have increased considerably in value.

Although there might be some merit in electing for woodlands relief so as to relieve the value on the transfer to the grandson, on balance it will be better if residue can carry the moderate tax cost.

---

**13.25** *Wills and estate planning*

## The problems of s 39A

**13.25** The interaction of exempt transfers with business and agricultural property relief is examined at **3.27**. An inexpertly drawn will can easily lead to the complications of tax that are described at **3.28** and **3.29**. There is a single transfer on death to both chargeable and exempt beneficiaries. An estate that includes business or agricultural property may be likened, on allocation of reliefs, to a Victoria sponge cake (or for younger readers Vienetta ice cream). Any slice of the cake or of the ice cream contains jam (or chocolate as the case may be), which is wasted on an exempt beneficiary such as spouse, civil partner or charity. That delicacy, ie the BPR or APR in the case of the estate, should have been reserved for the children or other chargeable beneficiaries.

The computations required under *s 39A* are more complicated than that analogy might suggest and the reader is referred to specialist books on the topic. For the general practitioner the answer is simply to take care to avoid gifts of chargeable property that will trigger the rules as to grossing-up. If a chargeable specific gift is made of an asset that qualifies for relief, that will fix the availability of the relief.

---

**Example 13.10—A will that should be varied**

Kenneth has made no chargeable transfers or PETs in the last seven years. His estate comprises:

| | |
|---|---|
| Business property with 50% BPR | £650,000 |
| Quoted shares | £370,000 |
| House | £325,000 |

His existing will leaves the house and the business assets to his widow Linda and the investments to his daughter Melanie. The gifts to Melanie slightly exceed the current nil rate band, triggering a modest charge to IHT.

On present tax rates, his will should be varied in his lifetime or by deed after his death. Quite apart from considerations of transferable nil rate band, Melanie should receive the business assets and the remainder of the estate should go to Linda. After relief at 50% the chargeable transfer is just slightly less than it was before, giving a small IHT saving; but more to the point the actual value that has passed to Melanie is now nearly double what it would have been.

The nil rate band is still available on Linda's death and there will be an overall saving on the second death. As with the example of Mary above, the transfer of the business property direct to Melanie leaves open the possibility that Linda might use some of the liquidity to buy business property back from Melanie in the hope that Linda will live two years from the purchase. That will effectively use the BPR twice, if Linda lives two years from the purchase.

*Wills and estate planning* **13.27**

**13.26** Where the spouse is young, attractive, wealthy in his or her own right – or perhaps all three – some consideration must be given to the possibility of remarriage. That will affect IHT planning and may encourage the first spouse to die at least to use the nil rate band to protect any existing children from disinheritance. It is in such situations that the debt/charge scheme may still be attractive, or that a gift of the nil rate band to or in trust for the children will be wholly appropriate. After all, if the young spouse does remarry there can be only one transferable nil rate band on eventual death, so perhaps best to use the elder spouse's nil rate band now.

## Not seeing the wood for the trees

**13.27** In family situations and in the drafting of wills it is easy for the practitioner to be distracted by the various considerations, as can be seen in the following extended example.

---

### Example 13.11—Will-drafting traps

Melissa and Wendy lived together but were not of the generation who would consider making themselves civil partners. Melissa owned the house which, though modest, enjoyed a wide road frontage. Wendy was her companion. Melissa also held stocks and shares worth £400,000 including £100,000 worth as a minority holding in her cousin's unquoted trading company.

Melissa instructed her solicitor that in the event of her death she would want Wendy to be able to continue to live in the house for as long as she wanted and to have a 'cushion' of money to tide her over. That provision ought to be tax free. Apart from that, Melissa wanted her estate as far as possible to go in equal shares to three charities and two cousins.

The first consideration for the draftsman will be to avoid the problems of *Re Benham*. This is explained at **3.37**. However, there is a second issue, s *39A*, to be addressed by the will. It would also be unwise simply to give Wendy the right to continue to live in the house for life and a legacy tax free of such sum (not exceeding a stated maximum) as the executors might think necessary for her care. The reasons are as follows:

- The first is the rule in *Judge (personal representatives of Walden deceased) v Revenue and Customs Comrs* [2005] SSCD 863 (SpC 506), referred to at **7.3** and **15.32** et seq. Practitioners may consider that the decision in that case could have gone either way, in the light of the general rule of HMRC as expressed in Statement of Practice 10/79. The fact that one ill-drawn will did not create an interest in possession in a residence does not mean that SP 10/79 will never be invoked in future. There is therefore a risk that provision tax free of Melissa's house for Wendy

- to occupy for the rest of her life creates an interest in possession and, depending on the value, that gift alone could exhaust the nil rate band, particularly if the wide frontage of the property concerned constitutes access to back land and has considerable value. Supposing therefore that provision of the home for Melissa exceeds the nil rate band, grossing-up will be necessary.
- The second problem follows from the first. The further provision of the 'cushion' tax free will also require grossing-up and, applying the principles of *s 39A*, that gift will be seen as coming from the rest of the estate, including the part represented by the value of the unquoted shares which qualify for 100% BPR.
- Finally, the lack of a specific gift of the shares causes some of the BPR on them to be wasted on the charitable beneficiaries of residue.

A better drawn will would make a specific gift of the shares to the chargeable beneficiaries, perhaps especially the cousin who actually runs the company. That would secure BPR in full.

If it is known from the outset that part of the garden has development value, the provision for Melissa should be restricted to the residence itself excluding the garden, so as to minimise the amount by which that chargeable gift exceeds the nil rate band. Great care should be taken in drafting the clause relating to the house so as to show that the right of Wendy to live there can be terminated at any time by the trustees so that she does not have an interest in possession.

An alternative would have been a lifetime gift by Melissa of a share in the house to Wendy, effectively giving Wendy a right of occupation by virtue of her share in the house. The retained share in the house could then have been given to the charities outright. They would not have been able to sell the share of the house until Wendy moved out; but they would not have received any benefit from the house until Wendy's death anyway. That arrangement would have given charitable exemption on the value of the retained share in the house.

## EXEMPT GIFTS ON DEATH

### Charities

**13.28** Practitioners are regularly lobbied by charities to encourage clients to give in their wills. In the light of *RSPCA v Sharp* [2010] WTLR 855 some will writers may be discouraged from leaving residue, or a share of it, to charities, for fear that the charity may in some way 'make trouble' for the family, as (in the view of the judge) happened there. That is an issue to discuss carefully with the testator.

## Wills and estate planning 13.30

The issue in *Cancer Research Campaign v Ernest Brown & Co (a firm)* [1997] STC 1425 concerned the failure of a lawyer to take advantage of the relief. The facts are important enough to quote in detail.

Mr Berry died on 11 December 1986 leaving the residue of his estate to his sister Phoebe. They owned a house jointly which passed to Phoebe by survivorship. The rest of his estate amounted to some £170,000 from which were paid legacies of £30,000. About five months after her brother's death Phoebe visited Mr Palfreyman, a legal executive and executor of her brother's will, to make her own will. By then no application had been made for a grant of probate of the brother's will, but it was assumed that Mr Palfreyman knew how much Phoebe would inherit.

**13.29** She left virtually all her estate to seven charities. Details of the interview are scant because Mr Palfreyman himself died before the case came to trial. There was no record of any discussion between Phoebe and Mr Palfreyman of the possibility of a deed of variation. It was therefore not possible to say whether Phoebe lived so modestly that she did not need the cash inheritance from her brother. Phoebe then died, having included Mr Palfreyman as an executor. Phoebe's will was not proved until June 1989; that of her brother not until October 1992. Phoebe's estate was thus swollen by the 'unnecessary' inheritance from her brother, which could have been diverted to the charities.

The charities were concerned that Phoebe, had she been so advised, could have varied her brother's will to provide direct benefit to the charities, taking advantage of *s 142*, with the result that IHT could have been saved. The last date on which an effective variation could have taken place was 10 December 1988, but at that time the charities did not even know of their entitlement. They only learned of it from the probate agents, Smee and Ford, on 23 June 1989, by which time it was too late. IHT on the brother's estate was about £203,000, but was not paid until 7 October 1992. The figure included substantial interest and penalties.

**13.30** Held, the solicitors had no duty to advise Phoebe on the possibilities of saving IHT in relation to her estate; nor any duty to advise on tax mitigation when administering the estate of her brother. Further, there was no duty to communicate the tax-mitigation possibilities of a deed of variation to the residuary legatees. The solicitors were obliged to administer the estate properly, but were under no obligation to advise the charitable legatees of the potential legacy.

Practitioners may think, given the whole circumstances, including the long time that it took to administer the estates of Phoebe and of her brother, that the solicitors did well to escape liability. Certainly, in drafting wills and in administering estates the practitioner should always be aware of the interests of the charities and the possibilities of exemption.

**13.31** *Wills and estate planning*

**13.31** Note the limitation on charitable relief in *s 23(2)*. There is no relief where the charitable disposition takes effect only on the termination of an interest or period after the transfer of value, or where it depends on a condition which is not satisfied within 12 months, or where it is defeasible.

**Example 13.12—Non-exempt charitable gifts**

Samantha's will leaves £100,000 on trust for her brother Robert for life with remainder to the Children's Society. The gift is not exempt on the death of Samantha, but the fund will be exempt on Robert's death.

## Heritage relief

**13.32** The relief is valuable but rare. For detailed analysis the reader is referred to specialist works on the subject. The gift of heritage property by will is unlikely of itself to take account of heritage relief except to the extent that property is transferred to a maintenance fund under *s 27*. Mainly, therefore, the way in which a will takes account of the existence of heritage relief will be in avoiding dispositions that force or encourage the sale of property in respect of which an undertaking has already been given, because such a forced sale would breach any undertaking that had already been given under *s 31* or earlier legislation in force.

It is a particular feature of heritage relief that property may have benefited many years ago from the relief at a time when capital taxation was much higher. Care must be taken not to trigger the clawback of relief that had been given on an earlier occasion. The difficulty for the owner of conditional exempt property is in knowing who is actually the relevant person for the purposes of undertaking it at any time. This is because the rules work in such a way that the identity of the 'relevant person' changes according to a retrospective test. There are three rules set out in *s 33(5)*, as follows:

**Rule 1: Simple cases**

**13.33** Where there has been only one conditionally exempt transfer of the heritage property before the chargeable event, the relevant person is the one who made the transfer.

**Rule 2: Two or more conditional transfers, one going back 30 years**

**13.34** In these cases it is necessary to consider the ownership of the property for the period of 30 years leading up to the chargeable event. Where the most recent transfer of that property was more than 30 years ago, the person who made that transfer is the relevant person. Where there have been several transfers, and one of them took place in the last 30 years, that transferor is the relevant person.

**Rule 3: Two or more recent conditional transfers**

**13.35** Suppose that there have been two or more transfers in the last 30 years. HMRC may choose whichever of the transferors they please as the relevant person. The reason for this is to prevent avoidance of tax by channelling heritage property through those members of the family who have few other assets in the hope of ensuring that, where there is a chargeable event, the tax charged will be as low as possible.

These rules make life very difficult for executors and trustees. They may have to keep sums back in the administration of an estate against the possibility of clawback of tax on breach of undertaking. They will not necessarily know how much will be involved. Two cases on the subject may offer some guidance: *Bedford (Duke), Re, Russell v Bedford* [1960] 3 All ER 756 and *Re Scott* [1916] 2 Ch 268.

**13.36** Claims to heritage relief must be made within two years of the date of transfer (see *s 30(3BA)*), 'or ... such longer period as the board may allow'. HMRC have discretion to allow a longer time than two years and will consider a late claim on its merits. The difficulty for the practitioner is that the property that might be the subject of a claim might also by its very nature qualify for, say, APR, a protective claim should be made.

---

**Example 13.13—Fine house, part of an estate**

Algernon inherited from his father the Lyhart estate comprising Lyhart House and 700 acres of mixed farm land, some of it woodland, some of it good arable and some pasture. Lyhart House itself is substantial, with 16 bedrooms, several fine reception rooms and many original features from its construction in 1760. It is Grade II* listed. The property was requisitioned and used as a hospital during World War II but Algernon's father kept many of the old furnishings. These have been stored in an attic because they did not suit the taste of Algernon's wife, Tracey.

Algernon worked as a conveyancing solicitor in a nearby town and entered into a contracting agreement with a national farming company for the management of the land. Such paperwork as there is in relation to the contract farming was dealt with by Algernon from an office maintained in the house.

On Algernon's death a claim was made for APR on the land and on the house but was resisted by HMRC in respect of the house in reliance on the comments, admittedly *obiter*, in *Antrobus (No 2)*, as confirmed in *McKenna*.

**13.37** *Wills and estate planning*

Algernon's executors firmly resist the suggestion that *Antrobus (No 2)* is determinative of what constitutes a farmhouse, but mindful of the decision in *McKenna* and as a back-up plan if APR should be refused, Tracey reviews the possibility of reinstating some of the original furnishings from store to improve the chances that a claim to heritage relief might succeed, accepting that the cost of that relief will be that she must make proposals as to maintenance and preservation of the asset, for public access and for publicising the arrangements for public access. The protective claim is lodged within two years of the death to start the protracted process of claiming relief.

## POLICY TRUSTS

**13.37** These were discussed in **Chapter 7**. Apart from bare trusts, which give no flexibility as to choice of beneficiary or vesting age, trusts entered into after 22 March 2006 will generally be treated as discretionary. Their creation will be a chargeable transfer, though the value of a new policy under which regular premiums are paid is likely to be not merely within the nil rate band, but also within the annual exemption. The payment of further premiums on the policy is likely to be exempt under *s 21*. If the policy is a single premium bond, the transfer will usually be of its value at the time of gift. If substantial, that triggers the compliance issues discussed in **Chapter 6**.

The tax charge on such trusts therefore arises principally when, at the occasion of a ten-year anniversary, the policy value exceeds the nil rate band; or on an exit charge when the value of the fund exceeds that band. There is a valuation rule, see *s 167*, which can apply to a policy, but it is limited in scope. Usually, the value will be the market value rather than the total of premiums paid.

In the past, it was commonplace for a financial adviser quite correctly not only to sell a policy but to arrange for it to be written in trust. Given the complexity of the regime for taxing discretionary trusts financial advisers may be less keen to undertake the full explanation of trust documents and their tax consequences that is likely to be necessary in future. Each structure must be analysed for its efficacy: it seems that discounted gift trusts in particular may be less viable than they once were.

## POST-DEATH VARIATIONS

**13.38** *Section 142* permits families and their advisers to be 'wise after the event'. Subject to various safeguards it is possible to rewrite a will or to put in place provisions akin to a will where a person has died intestate. The document need not be a deed, only 'an instrument in writing'. It must be signed by anyone who would have benefited but for the changes brought about by the deed. A difficulty therefore arises if the beneficiaries of the will to be changed or under intestacy are minors.

## Variations where there are minor beneficiaries

**13.39** Two courses are open. The first is to apply to the court for an order permitting the variation to take place on the ground that it is in the interests of the infant beneficiaries. The simpler course, which is not objected to by HMRC, is to frame any variation in such a way that it does clearly benefit younger members of the family.

### Example 13.14—No need for an application to the court

Ian, a widower, left his estate in four equal shares, one for each of his three sons and the last for his grandchildren equally per capita. One of the sons does not need his inheritance and wishes his share to pass immediately to his children. There is no need for any of the children to sign the resulting deed of variation. None of them gives anything up. There is no need for any application to the court.

### Example 13.15—Avoiding an application to the court

Michael, who was widowed and who remarried late in life, made a will that carves out the nil rate band to be held on discretionary trusts with residue to his widow for life with remainder in four shares, one to each of his sons and the fourth to his grandchildren equally per capita. The will does not contain the 'debt or charge' provisions and for family reasons it is now desired to incorporate them.

As was noted in **Chapter 3**, it is not possible simply to incorporate the requisite clauses by deed of variation. The parties therefore wish to enter into a deed that will comply with *s 142*. They agree to vary the terms of the will. The gift of residue is changed so that each son receives 20% only and the grandchildren receive 40% between them.

Although there will be no benefit to the grandchildren during the lifetime of their 'step-grandmother', it is nevertheless clear from the face of the deed that the grandchildren, who are themselves too young to sign the deed, are better off by virtue of the deed than they would have been under the will. It is therefore not necessary to seek the approval of the court to the variation.

## Posthumous severance

**13.40** *Section 142* permits a variation of the dispositions of the property comprised in the estate of the deceased 'whether affected by will, under the

**13.41** *Wills and estate planning*

law relating to intestacy or otherwise'. The words 'or otherwise' have been taken to include dispositions that take effect by operation of law, such as survivorship to joint property. Accordingly, it is possible by deed of variation posthumously to sever the joint tenancy in any property (for IHT purposes, at least) so that the share belonging to the deceased can pass under the will as varied rather than direct to the other joint owner. This is often essential where it is proposed to put in place the debt or charge scheme by deed of variation.

## 'Only one bite at the cherry'

**13.41** A disposition that has been varied by deed of variation may not be further varied: see *Russell v IRC* [1988] STC195. The issue was discussed in *Law Society's Gazette* 22 May 1985, noting that the Revenue had taken further advice on the interpretation of *s 142* and had indicated that:

- an election which is validly made is irrevocable;
- an instrument will not fall within *s 142* if it further redirects any item or any part of an item that has already been redirected under an earlier instrument; and
- to avoid any uncertainty, variations covering a number of items should ideally be made in one instrument.

There must be no consideration for entering into a deed of variation, see *s 142(3)*, other than consideration consisting of the making in respect of another of the dispositions of a variation or disclaimer to which that subsection applies.

## Abuse

**13.42** Deeds of variation, like so many other documents, are open to abuse.

---

**Example 13.16—Trying it on**

By his will Henry left his estate to his son Ian absolutely. By deed of variation Ian changed the will so that it provided for Joan, the wife of Henry and the mother of Ian.

Careful reading of the deed showed that Joan's address was different from Henry's. Enquiries revealed that they had been separated for many years and that Joan was amply provided for. Further enquiries and the threat of the exercise of a power to call for documents under *s 219A* elicited from Ian the admission, fully documented in the solicitor's papers, that it was understood from the outset that Joan would release anything that she inherited from her husband's estate to Ian by way of gift.

Whilst a transfer from Henry to Joan would have been sheltered by spouse relief, since nothing in *s 18* requires spouses or civil partners to be living together, relief under *s 142* was denied on the basis that Joan gave Ian consideration within *s 142(3)*.

## Disclaimers

**13.43** A disclaimer has been described as a 'blunt instrument'. By *s 142(1) (b)* it has the effect of redirecting inheritance to another party though, apart from entering into the disclaimer in the first place, the original beneficiary has no control over the destination of the property disclaimed. Relief is not available under *s 142* in respect of a disclaimer if consideration has been given for it.

A disclaimer failed to achieve its purpose in *Lau (executor of Lau Deceased) v HMRC* [2009] SpC 740. The husband had left his son £665,000 free of IHT. There were other legacies to other children. Residue was left to his (second) wife. The son disclaimed his legacy; £3,800,000 was transferred to the widow; she transferred £1,000,000 to the son; correspondence showed that this was part of a plan to save IHT. HMRC refused to allow *s 142* to apply because of the direct link between the disclaimer and the later payment. It was held on appeal that the evidence showed a direct link. The evidence of the widow was 'utterly unpersuasive'. The appeal was dismissed.

## Formalities of post-death variations

**13.44** Since 31 July 2002, notice of any deed of variation need not now be given to HMRC, except where IHT is thereby increased, but relief will not be given by *s 142* unless the variation contains a statement, made by all the relevant persons, that they intend the relief to apply.

## Statement of variation

**13.45** The following will be enough:

'The parties to this variation intend that the provisions of section 142(2) [and where appropriate and section 62(6) Taxation of Chargeable Gains Act 1992] shall apply.'

The relevant persons are those making the instrument and, where extra taxes are payable by virtue of the variation, the personal representatives.

**13.46** *Wills and estate planning*

## Footnote: the *Glowacki* case

**13.46** A case which is special to its own facts is *Wells (Personal representatives of Glowacki deceased) v HMRC* [2008] STC (SCD) 188. A deed of variation was entered into which purported to deem a gift of a house to have been made immediately before death; but if the deed did not have the intended effect, the variation was to have no effect, giving the family a second chance of a variation by avoiding the *Russell* rule noted above.

HMRC determined that the effect of the deed was to set the benefit of the nil rate band against the value of the house in priority to the gift in the will of the nil rate band. The personal representatives appealed, arguing that *IHTA 1984, s 17(a)*, which provides that a qualifying deed of variation is not a transfer of value, had the effect of taking the house out of the estate before death, so £230,000 could pass under the gift of the nil rate band.

Held, *IHTA 1984, ss 4* and *17* did not work that way. *IHTA 1984, s 142* could not remove property from the estate to take it outside *s 4*. Any variation under *s 17* was of the dispositions on death only. The variation therefore failed. HMRC had decided the effect of the deed and had taxed accordingly. That was wrong: they should have decided whether *s 142* could be used in the way attempted; and should then have decided whether the deed remained in force as a result; which it did not, so part of the determination was quashed.

## Alternative post-death relief: ss 143 and 144

**13.47** There are two alternatives to the relief under *s 142*. By *s 143*, there is limited relief where the will sets out a wish that property be transferred by a legatee to other persons and the legatee does, within two years, carry out those wishes.

An attempt to push this rule to the limit was illustrated in the case of *Harding (executors of Loveday) v IRC* [1997] STC (SCD) 321. The will contained a discretionary trust for the widow and children. The executors appointed a fund to the widow. The Revenue argued that this was not an exempt transfer, being outside the terms of *s 144*. The executors appealed, wishing the appointment to be treated as a transfer under *s 143*. The Special Commissioner decided against the executors for three reasons: a legatee could include a trustee, but here the trustees were not legatees within *s 143*; an appointment of property was different from a transfer of it, so outside what *s 143* contemplated; and there was no evidence that the appointment was what the deceased had wanted, thus failing the requirement expressed in *s 143*.

In practice, a gift to a spouse that is quickly followed by an ongoing gift to a non-exempt beneficiary may well be challenged by HMRC.

*Wills and estate planning* **13.49**

A further form of relief applies under *s 144* to discretionary trusts established by a will. If trustees of a discretionary will trust exercise their discretion within two years of the death *s 144* applies so as to treat the release of funds or other transactions by the trustees as if they had been made by the testator.

**13.48** However, the position is slightly more complicated than this summary might suggest, as the advisers found to their cost of *Frankland v IRC* [1997] STC 1450. Commonly, a will may establish a discretionary trust for the close family of the testator, including the surviving spouse. The idea is that, following the death and perhaps following establishment of reliefs such as APR and BPR, the executors will be able to decide on the relative needs of various members of the family and will be able to make appropriate provision. It was common in such situations, particularly where the surviving spouse was young and likely to live many years, to appoint funds to the surviving spouse in the hope that he or she could be used as a 'peg life'.

However, the mechanics of *s 144(1)(a)* refer to an event which, but for the relief, would trigger an IHT charge, being either the ten-year anniversary charge under *s 64* or the fixed rate under *s 79*; or which would be subject to an exit charge except for certain special reliefs. The effect was therefore that an appointment by the trustees which would not under any circumstances have triggered an exit or periodic charge did not fall within *s 144(1)*.

The proportionate charge, which is described in **Chapter 8**, does not apply during the first period of three months from the creation of settlement. As a result, an appointment made within the first three months of death does not benefit from relief under *s 144*. That, most unfortunately, had the result, in *Frankland v IRC* [1997] STC 1450, that an appointment that could otherwise have saved significant tax triggered a very substantial tax charge.

## Other forms of post-death restructuring

**13.49** Apart from deeds of variation the parties may feel that they want to reorganise beneficial interests under a will, as happened in *Executors of Patch deceased* [2007] SpC 600, where the deceased had left his estate to his wife for life with remainder to his children. The fund was mainly shares, and it was agreed that the widow should have one-third (represented by the house) and the children two-thirds. Under a deed of partition, not a deed of variation, the widow assigned her interest in the fund, other than the house, to the children. They in return assigned their interest in the house to her. She agreed to pay them £25,000 each within 30 days and to pay more later.

Only five months later, the widow died, not in fact having made the payments. Her executors sent HMRC details of the deed and of the widow's estate. Tax

**13.50** *Wills and estate planning*

was levied on the value of the house; but later HMRC sought to tax also the value of the trust fund that had passed to the children because the arrangement had effectively achieved a transfer of value, taxable under *s 52(1)*, which was within seven years of death. The executors appealed, on two grounds: there was no transfer of value, because the money had never been paid over, and they had made full disclosure anyway.

Not so, held the Special Commissioner. The assignments were not conditional on the payment. There was a division of the fund, which was a transfer. The value that was deemed to have left the estate of the widow under the partition should have been included in the account of the estate. Further, there had not been full disclosure: although the deed itself was disclosed, the executors had not included in the account the value of the lifetime transfer, so HMRC were entirely right to claim the tax.

## 'Mending' discretionary trusts after FA 2006

**13.50** The effect of *FA 2006* is to treat certain will trusts as discretionary that would not previously have been so treated. Amendments have been made to *s 144* so that estates caught by *FA 2006* may escape the full IHT charging regime if distributions are made of trust funds into one of the asset holding vehicles that is still acceptable under the new regime.

Where *s 144(2)* now applies, tax is not to be charged on the basis of the original discretionary trust. In each case in which *s 144(2)* is in point tax is charged as if the will had provided that the fund should be held, not on the terms of the will but on the terms of the varied disposition. Whereas *s 144(1)* previously could apply only to a discretionary trust it can now, by virtue of *s 144(1A)*, apply to a conventional discretionary trust and to an interest in possession that is neither an IPDI nor a disabled person's interest.

**13.51** Where the necessary conditions are satisfied *s 144(4)* provides that tax is to be charged as if the will had provided for the property to be held as it will be held by virtue of the actions of the trustees described below. Where that happens, the fund escapes the discretionary trust charging regime.

The conditions for this are as follows:

- Death on or after 22 March 2006.

- Property in the estate of the deceased settled by will.

- Within two years of death (but before there has subsisted, in relation to the property, either an IPDI or a disabled persons interest), there is a trust event. The event concerned is one by which the property in the estate comes to be held on favoured trusts ie:

- an IPDI; or
- a BMT; or
- an 18-to-25 trust.

Effectively, by this amendment to *s 144*, trustees will be able to bring will trusts into line with the regime now favoured by the government.

*Chapter 14*

# Transferable nil rate bands

## BACKGROUND

**14.1** Estate planning for many married couples and civil partnerships was simplified following changes introduced in *Finance Act 2008*, which allow a claim for all or part of an unused nil rate band on the death of a spouse or civil partner to be transferred to a surviving spouse or civil partner who dies on or after 9 October 2007 (*IHTA 1984, ss 8A–8C;* all references in this chapter are to *IHTA 1984*, unless otherwise stated). The rules apply in the same way whether the survivor leaves a will, or dies intestate.

The facility to make claims for the transfer of unused nil rate band remains very useful despite the nil rate band being frozen at its 2009/10 level of £325,000 for the tax years 2010/11 to 2014/15 inclusive (*FA 2010, s 8*), even though the nil rate band for 2010/11 was initially set at £350,000 in *FA 2007*.

Prior to the introduction of transferable nil rate bands, it was generally important to ensure that the estates of spouses or civil partners were sufficient to utilise their available IHT thresholds (or 'nil rate bands') if possible, and that optimum use was made of the nil rate band on the first death. If each spouse or civil partner owned sufficient assets to constitute their nil rate bands, the estates of each individual could be sheltered from IHT up to an amount equal to the nil rate band multiplied by the 40% 'death rate'.

However, as indicated at **1.20**, there is a complete exemption (in *s 18*) for transfers between UK-domiciled spouses or civil partners during lifetime and on death (although if the transferor spouse or civil partner is UK domiciled but the transferee is foreign domiciled, the exemption is restricted to a cumulative total of £55,000). Thus, if a deceased spouse or civil partner leaves their entire estate to the surviving spouse, then (unless the recipient spouse or civil partner is non-UK domiciled), the legacy will normally be wholly exempt from IHT. However, the estate of the survivor increases accordingly.

Prior to the *Finance Act 2008* changes, exempt legacies between spouses or civil partners often resulted in a higher IHT liability on the second death, and a higher IHT liability overall. Therefore IHT planning for married couples or civil partners typically involved ensuring that an amount up to the available nil rate band was left to non-exempt legatees (eg children), or (say) to a family discretionary trust in which the surviving spouse was included among the class of beneficiaries. This planning was relatively straightforward and simple to implement if each spouse or civil partner owned sufficient 'liquid' assets (eg cash, shares or other investments) to constitute their nil rate bands. However, lifetime transfers between spouses or civil partners were often necessary to achieve this result on death. In some cases, the only asset of any substantial value would be an interest in the family home. This resulted in relatively complicated and artificial arrangements involving an interest in the family home to constitute the nil rate band, such as 'debt' or 'charge' schemes (see **Chapter 15**).

Transferable nil rate band claims cannot be made by co-habiting couples who are not legally married or civil partners (see *Executor of Holland deceased v IRC* [2003] SpC 350), or by family members who occupy the same property, such as siblings (see *Burden and another v United Kingdom* [2008] All ER (D) 391 (Apr)).

Whilst nil rate band legacies to chargeable (non-exempt) beneficiaries on the first spouse or civil partner to die will undoubtedly be less common or popular following the transferable nil rate band facility, there may be circumstances in which such legacies are necessary or preferred, such as in terms of making provision for offspring. In addition, aside from IHT considerations there may be other reasons why an interest in the home may be left on trust (eg due to concerns about care fees or divorce). However, the transferable nil rate band has undoubtedly made IHT planning simpler for many spouses or civil partners, compared with the position prior to 9 October 2007.

HMRC published guidance on the transferable nil rate band provisions contained in the Inheritance Tax Manual at IHTM43000 onwards, and reference is made to some of this guidance below.

# OUTLINE OF THE RULES

**14.2** The transferable nil rate band legislation forms new *ss 8A–8C*, and amends *s 151BA*, with consequential changes to *ss 239, 242* and *272*. The provisions broadly allow claims for the transfer of a spouse's or civil partner's unused nil rate band to a surviving spouse or civil partner who dies on or after 9 October 2007. Therefore, if both spouses or civil partners died before 9 October 2007, it is not possible to take advantage of the transferable nil rate band facility.

The amount that can be transferred is based on a percentage of the deceased's nil rate band. That percentage (which cannot exceed 100) represents the nil rate band (or, where there was more than one former spouse or civil partner, bands) not used on any previous occasion, taking into account lifetime transfers made

**14.3** *Transferable nil rate bands*

within seven years before death, and is applied to the nil rate band in operation on the death of the surviving spouse (*s 8A*).

A claim to transfer unused nil rate band must be made by the survivor's personal representatives, within two years from the end of the month in which the survivor dies, or (if later) within three months of the personal representatives first acting as such. However, HMRC may allow a longer period at their discretion. In the absence of a claim by the personal representatives, a late claim may be made by any person liable to IHT on the survivor's death, subject to HMRC's agreement (*s 8B*).

There are potentially complicated rules for dealing with the transfer of the nil rate band and the calculation of IHT when certain IHT and capital transfer tax deferred charges (ie on heritage assts and woodlands) are triggered, where the deferred IHT is calculated by reference to the earlier deceased spouse. There are also rules to determine the amount of nil rate band to be applied in calculating IHT where a dependant who inherits an alternatively secured pension fund dies or ceases to be a dependant (*s 8C*).

## CALCULATING THE UNUSED NIL RATE BAND

**14.3** The provisions allowing for the transfer of unused nil rate band between spouses and civil partners apply if someone dies leaving a surviving spouse or civil partner, and there is some unused nil rate band on the deceased's death (*s 8A(1)*). It does not matter if the unused nil rate band arises because no assets were owned on death. The rules for calculating the unused nil rate band apply a formula approach (*s 8A(2)*). However, in essence there is 'unused' nil rate band to the extent that the spouse or civil partner's chargeable estate on death was less than their available nil rate band.

On the death of the surviving spouse or civil partner, their available nil rate band is increased by a percentage. The legislation provides a formula for calculating that percentage (*s 8A(4)*). The terminology and formulae used in the legislation for the basic calculation of the transferable nil rate band is reproduced below, but is broadly the amount of the deceased's unused nil rate band, divided by the available nil rate band available upon the deceased spouse's or civil partner's death.

*Unused nil rate band on death (s 8A(2))*:

M > VT, where –

- M is the maximum amount that could be transferred by a chargeable transfer made on the person's death if it were to be wholly chargeable to tax at the rate of 0%; and

*Transferable nil rate bands* **14.3**

- VT is the value actually transferred by the chargeable transfer so made (or nil, if applicable).

*The percentage increase in the survivor's nil rate band maximum* (NB this is subject to an overriding maximum of 100% (*s 8A(5)*), and to the 'clawback' rules (*s 8C*) in respect of heritage property and woodlands relief):

$$\left(\frac{E}{NRBMD}\right) \times 100$$

Where –

- E is the amount by which M is greater than VT in the case of the deceased person; and
- NRBMD is the nil rate band maximum at the time of the deceased person's death.

In HMRC's view, the percentage should be taken to four decimal places, if necessary (IHTM43020).

---

**Example 14.1—Practical effect of a nil rate band transfer**

Adam died on 31 March 2010. His chargeable death estate amounted to £145,000, and he had made no lifetime gifts. His wife Bertha died on 1 November 2010 with a chargeable estate of £400,000 and having made no lifetime gifts.

Adam's unused nil rate band available on Bertha's death is calculated as follows:

Unused nil rate band (M > VT) (*s 8A(2)*):

£325,000 (M, being the nil rate band maximum for 2009/10) – £145,000 (VT, being the chargeable death estate) = £180,000

Percentage increase $\left(\frac{E}{NRBMD}\right) \times 100$ (*s 8A(3)*):

Where E is Adam's unused nil rate band, and NRBMD is the nil rate band on Adam's death:

$$\frac{£180,000}{£325,000} \times 100 = 55.3846\%$$

On Bertha's death, 55.3846% of unused nil rate band (£325,000 for 2010/11) in respect of Adam can be added to her own:

£325,000 × 55.3846% = £180,000

**14.4** *Transferable nil rate bands*

The combination of Adam's unused nil rate band (£180,000) and Bertha's nil rate band (£325,000) is sufficient to cover Bertha's chargeable estate of £400,000. No IHT is therefore payable on her death.

**14.4** However, the amount of unused nil rate band that can be claimed on the survivor's death is subject to the following potential restrictions:

- The estate of the earlier spouse or civil partner to die made a claim to transfer unused nil rate band from a previous deceased spouse or civil partner. The estate of the surviving spouse or civil partner may only claim a maximum of the nil rate band then in force (*s 8A(5)*).

- There is an overriding limit of one additional nil rate band, based on the rate applicable on the survivor's death. This restriction could apply if, for example, a surviving spouse was married more than once, and his or her deceased spouses did not use up their nil rate bands on death. The survivor's estate can claim in respect of both previous spouses, but the nil rate band of the survivor's estate can only be increased by 100%, or one additional nil rate band (*s 8A(6)*).

- As indicated at **14.2**, the nil rate band of the deceased spouse or civil partner may be subject to adjustment in respect of certain deferred charges (*s 8A(3)*) (see **14.8** below).

**Example 14.2—Maximum claim**

Colin and Delia had been married for many years, until Delia sadly died on 31 January 1998. By her will, Delia left £50,000 to their only daughter Joanne, with residue to Colin.

Colin subsequently found friendship and love in Elizabeth, and they were married in 2002. Elizabeth died on 1 May 2008, leaving £150,000 to her nieces and nephews, with residue to Colin.

Colin finally passed away on 31 March 2011, leaving a chargeable estate of £800,000 to Joanne.

Delia's unused nil rate band amounted to £165,000, ie £215,000 (the nil rate band maximum for 1997/98), less the chargeable legacy of £50,000. The percentage nil rate band unused was 76.7442%.

Elizabeth's unused nil rate band amounted to £162,000, ie £312,000 (the nil rate band maximum for 2008/09), less chargeable legacies of £150,000. The percentage unused nil rate band was 51.9231%.

On Colin's death, the unused nil rate band percentage from his two marriages amounts to 128.6673% (ie 76.7442% for Delia and 51.9231% for Elizabeth).

However, the maximum percentage that can be claimed by Colin's estate is 100%. A claim is therefore made to add 100% of £325,000 (the nil rate band maximum for 2010/11) to Colin's own nil rate band of £325,000. The combined nil rate bands therefore amount to £650,000.

The IHT payable in respect of Colin's estate is as follows:

£800,000 − £650,000 = £150,000 × 40% = £60,000

## TRANSFER CLAIMS

**14.5** Transfers of unused nil rate band on the death of a spouse or civil partner must be claimed (*s 8A(3)*). The rules for such claims are in *s 8B*.

In practice, the claim is made on Schedule IHT402 ('Claim to transfer unused nil rate band') by the personal representative of the surviving spouse or civil partner within a permitted period, but HMRC may allow a longer period. The 'permitted period' is (see *s 8B(3)*) two years from the end of the month in which the survivor dies or, if later, three months from the date on which the personal representatives first act as such. If no claim has been made by the personal representatives, a claim can be made by any other person who is liable to IHT on the survivor's death. The legislation permits late claims at HMRC's discretion (*s 8B(1)(b)*).

HMRC may admit claims submitted late due to reasons beyond the claimant's control on a discretionary basis. Possible circumstances may include the following (see IHTM43009):

- if there is a dispute over the estate, which must be resolved before the personal representatives can be identified;
- unforeseen postal disruptions resulting in the loss or delay of a claim;
- the loss of records supporting a claim due to fire, flood or theft, where the records could not be replaced in time for a claim within the permitted period;
- serious illness of the claimant (or possibly a close relative or partner, depending on the circumstances);
- the death of a close relative or partner shortly before the end of the permitted period, where necessary steps had already been taken to make the claim on time;
- the claimant can show that they were not aware (and could not reasonably have been aware) of their entitlement to make a claim.

**14.6** *Transferable nil rate bands*

Schedule IHT402 is available via the HMRC website: (www.hmrc.gov.uk/inheritancetax/iht402.pdf).

The nil rate band in force upon the spouse or civil partner's death can be found on form IHT210A (www.hmrc.gov.uk/cto/iht210a_1.pdf). However, the form only lists the nil rate bands in operation from 15 March 1988. A list of thresholds applicable for earlier years can be obtained via HMRC's website (www.hmrc.gov.uk/rates/iht-thresholds.htm).

HMRC's IHT & Trusts Newsletter (August 2008) included the following comments about claims by agents to transfer unused nil rate bands on behalf of their clients, which are worth noting:

'One disappointing feature since the introduction of these new provisions is the very high initial failure rate by agents to provide the supporting details we ask for. The IHT216 claim form lists the documents that we want to see to support the claim for relief, and in only 20 per cent of cases submitted by agents are all the requested documents provided. This is in stark contrast to claims made by unrepresented taxpayers who manage to provide all the documents at the first time of asking.'

**14.6** The failure to make a claim on an earlier death could have an unfortunate knock-on effect on the amount of nil rate band that may subsequently be claimed. However, the legislation provides for some possible relief. For example, when a surviving spouse ('C') dies and C's personal representatives discover that no claim was made on the deceased spouse's ('B') death in respect of an earlier spouse's death ('A'), a claim is allowed in respect of the A's death as well as B's death, if the original IHT position of A is unaffected (*s 8B(2)*).

Once a claim is made it can be withdrawn, but no later than one month after the end of the permitted claim period (*s 8B(4)*).

**14.7** Claims for the transfer of unused IHT nil rate bands between spouses and civil partners apply 'for the purposes of the charge to tax on the death of the survivor' (*s 8A(3)*). A transfer could therefore reduce IHT on the survivor's free estate, together with any gifts with reservation of benefit property included in the estate, and the value of property subject to a qualifying interest in possession. It can also reduce the additional tax on a chargeable lifetime transfer, and the tax on a failed PET.

However, surviving spouses or civil partners should not try to claim an extra nil rate band on a chargeable lifetime transfer, such as to a discretionary trust. The deceased's nil rate band is not available in that event, and an unexpected IHT liability could therefore arise. Of course, should the surviving spouse or civil partner die within seven years, an extra nil rate band may then be available.

*Transferable nil rate bands* **14.8**

However, the rules do not provide for the refund of any lifetime IHT paid, in which case the transferred nil rate band effectively provides relief at only 20%, as opposed to 40%.

---

**Example 14.3—Lifetime transfers and the death estate**

Ken died in May 2002, leaving his entire estate to his wife Susan. In June 2008, Susan added £200,000 to a discretionary trust for her adult children. She had originally established the trust in October 2003, by settling an investment property worth £200,000. She used her annual exemptions elsewhere each year. Susan died in December 2010, leaving her estate of £400,000 to her children.

*June 2008 – IHT on lifetime transfer to discretionary trust*

The value transferred of £200,000, when added to the earlier chargeable transfer of £200,000, exceeded Susan's nil rate band for 2008/09 of £312,000 (note that it is not possible to add Ken's unused nil rate band for this lifetime transfer) by £88,000. The IHT payable is £88,000 × 20% = £17,600.

*December 2010 – Susan's death*

Susan's estate amounted to £400,000. Her remaining nil rate band, after taking into account the gift of £200,000 in June 2008 (NB the earlier gift of £200,000 in October 2003 is not taken into account for the purpose of this calculation, as it was made more than seven years previously) is £125,000 (ie £325,000 less £200,000). A claim is made for Ken's unused nil rate band percentage of 100%, giving Susan's estate an additional nil rate band of £325,000.

The total nil rate band of £450,000 is sufficient to cover Susan's death estate, so no IHT is due. However, the lifetime IHT in June 2008 cannot be repaid.

---

# CLAWBACK OF NIL RATE BAND

**14.8** It may become necessary, in relation to heritage relief and woodland relief, to look back to an earlier death to establish the tax charge. As may be imagined, the availability of the nil rate band can affect that tax charge. *Section 8C* takes account of this, by providing rules dealing with the interaction of the nil rate band and the calculation of IHT where a heritage or woodland deferred IHT or capital transfer tax charge applies.

The clawback provisions apply if there was unused nil rate band on the death of a spouse or civil partner, and after the person's death a deferred tax charge

### 14.9 Transferable nil rate bands

arises on heritage assets or woodlands, by reference to the deceased spouse's or civil partner's estates (*s 8C(1)*).

## Clawback whilst surviving spouse still alive

**14.9** If the event triggering the change happens before the death of the surviving spouse, it becomes necessary to recalculate the available (or used) nil rate band.

To apply the legislation, first find the nil rate band for the first spouse to die (defined as 'NRBMD' in *s 8A(4)*).

Next, find the current nil rate band, ie that in force at the time of the event triggering the charge (defined by *s 8C(2)* as 'NRBME').

Next, establish 'E': this is the excess of the nil rate band over the chargeable transfer at the first death: effectively the unused nil rate band.

Finally (for this stage of the computation) calculate 'TA': this is the amount on which the clawback is charged.

Then apply the fraction $\left(\dfrac{E}{NRBMD} - \dfrac{TA}{NRBME}\right) \times 100$

The result represents the percentage of the nil rate band in respect of which a claim may be made.

---

**Example 14.4—Heritage property**

Edwina owned a painting by a well-known artist, which was the subject of an undertaking (under *s 30*) upon her death in January 2009. That undertaking was breached in November 2010 when the general public were no longer allowed reasonable access to the painting, triggering an IHT charge (under *s 32*). The painting was worth £200,000.

Edwina had made no chargeable lifetime transfers. In her will, she left £10,000 to her cleaner Mavis, and the residue of her estate (apart from the painting) to her husband Frederick.

Nil rate band, January 2009 (NRBMD):   £312,000
Nil rate band, November 2010 (NRBME):   £325,000
Unused nil rate band, January 2009
(applying the formula in s 8A(2) and (4) (E)):   £302,000
M = £312,000

VT = £10,000
E = (M − VT) = £302,000
TA: £200,000

Computation:
$$\left(\frac{£302{,}000}{£312{,}000} - \frac{£200{,}000}{£325{,}000}\right) \times 100$$

$(0.9679 - 0.6154) \times 100$

= 35.2500% of the nil rate band available for transfer to Frederick's estate on his death.

If there is more than one breach of undertaking, or where for example there are several woodland clawback charges, the nil rate band that may be transferred is reduced by the proportion of the nil rate band clawed back by all the deferred charges, ie by the aggregate of TA/NRBME in respect of each triggering event (*s 8C(3)*).

## Clawback after the second death

**14.10** If a deferred charge is triggered after the nil rate band has been transferred, *s 8C(4)* reduces the nil rate band of the first spouse to die. The mechanics of the adjustment are set out in *s 8C(5)*.

The nil rate band of the first to die of the spouses or civil partners is first adjusted by applying *Sch 2* (the uprating provisions that give the benefit of any reduction in the tax that applies because the nil rate band has been increased over time). That uprated nil rate band is then potentially both increased and decreased. The increase can apply where the first spouse to die might himself have more than one nil rate band available, perhaps being a widower. The reduction is the amount of any increase in that band by virtue of the nil band transfer rules. A worked example is included in the Inheritance Tax Manual (see IHTM43046).

### Example 14.5—Practical effect of a clawback

Jonathan was first married to Katherine, who left her estate to Jonathan when she died in May 1995. Katherine had not used any of her nil rate band.

In January 2001, Jonathan married Lucy.

On Jonathan's death in January 2011, he left Lucy his estate, apart from a legacy of £100,000 to his favourite nephew Percy. Jonathan's family's heritage property was sold for £150,000 by Lucy's executors shortly after her death in March 2012, thereby triggering a clawback charge under *s 32*.

**14.11** *Transferable nil rate bands*

The nil rate band in May 1995 was £154,000. None of it was used.

The nil rate band in January 2011 was £325,000. The total nil rate band available to Jonathan's executor is (£325,000 – £100,000 = £225,000 + £325,000) = £550,000.

The nil rate band at Lucy's death in March 2012 is £325,000. The clawback charge is on £150,000. The reduction (under *s 8C(5)*) is of the increase in the nil rate band from Jonathan's death to that of Lucy: Nil (ie £325,000 – £325,000).

Jonathan's executor has available an increased nil rate band of (£550,000 – £0 – £150,000): £400,000.

NB: If a Scottish law claim to 'legitim' is made after a claim to transfer unused nil rate band following the death of the second parent, HMRC may adjust the claim in respect of the unused nil band accordingly (*s 147(10)*).

## Unexhausted ASP funds

**14.11** The background to the rules is the IHT charge that arises (under *s 151B*) on that part of an alternatively secured pension (ASP) fund which has not been used in benefits for the fund member and his dependants. In broad terms, the unexhausted fund is treated as the 'top slice' of the member's estate for IHT purposes. *Section 151BA(5)* uprates the nil rate band that is to be applied. The provisions were modified in *FA 2008*, by the introduction of *ss 151BA(6), (7)*.

Once again, a formula first requires the taxpayer to establish certain values:

E (as before) is the unused excess nil rate band available; and

NRBM is the nil rate band in force when the member died.

The formula is $100 - \left(\dfrac{E}{NRBM}\right) \times 100$

This produces 'the used up percentage', ie the fraction by which the nil rate band otherwise available to the member is to be reduced.

**Example 14.6—Pension funds and the clawback**

Martha died in May 2010, when the nil rate band was £325,000. She made no lifetime gifts but left £75,000 to her sister and the rest of her estate, including her pension rights, to her husband Norman. He did not draw the entire pension.

*Transferable nil rate bands* **14.12**

He had no dependants. The unexhausted portion of the pension fund, at his death on 2 February 2011, was £150,000.

For Martha's estate:

E = £250,000 (ie £325,000 − £75,000);

NRBM = £325,000; and

The 'used up percentage' is 100 − ((£250,000/£325,000) × 100), ie 100% − 76.9231% = 23.0769%.

This is the part of Martha's nil rate band that has been used. A full worked example where the deceased's estate includes funds in an ASP is included in the Inheritance Tax Manual at IHTM43048 to IHTM43050.

**14.12** The position becomes more complicated where the pension fund is still not exhausted by the death of the second person benefiting from it. This follows from *s 151BA(8)–(12)*, which was also introduced in *Finance Act 2008*. First, the situation is addressed where there has been an IHT charge on an ASP fund by reference to the first spouse or civil partner to die. This change will affect the person's nil rate band and restrict the amount available for transfer later: it is 'appropriately reduced' (under *s 151BA(9)*) where the chargeable event occurred after the death of the surviving spouse.

If, however, the surviving spouse is still alive when the chargeable event happens, tax is charged when the survivor dies by adjusting the member's transferable nil rate band using a formula (see *s 151BA(12)*), which compares the 'adjusted excess' with the 'adjusted nil rate band maximum', expressed as a percentage.

Where the charge arises after both spouses have died, each may have used part of his or her nil rate band, so there may be less available to meet the IHT charge under *s 151B* (see *s 151BA(9)*, as augmented by the definitions set out in *s 151BA(10)*).

Where the charge arises whilst the surviving spouse is still alive, the formula in *s 151BA(12)* applies. This restricts the nil rate band available later. AE, the adjusted excess, deducts from the maximum nil rate band the value transferred by chargeable transfers after calculating the taxable amount and after adjusting the nil rate band itself: ANRBM. ANRBM is the nil rate band, adjusted for ASP charges under *s 151B*. HMRC's Inheritance Tax Manual includes a worked example of the calculations (see IHTM43052).

Inevitably, there is always a risk that tax charges will be missed. Most taxpayers tend to think that the capital of pension funds is in some way exempt from IHT.

**14.13** *Transferable nil rate bands*

The new rules as to transferable nil rate bands, when affected by ASP fund charges, can reopen settled cases.

## IHT clearance certificates

**14.13** A 'certificate of discharge' (or clearance certificate) confirms HMRC's satisfaction that all the IHT due in a particular case has been (or will be) paid (*s 239*).

However, the clearance certificate issued by HMRC will not guarantee freedom from IHT charges where the amount of the nil rate band that was transferred must be adjusted, such as by the clawback effect of ASP charges. *Section 239* is qualified accordingly with effect from 9 October 2007, so that if too little IHT has been paid because of adjustment to the nil rate band, those persons who are accountable remain liable to pay the balance (*s 239(4)(aa)*).

## Penalties

**14.14** The penalty regime for inaccuracies in tax returns (in *FA 2007, Sch 24*) was extended for IHT purposes (by *FA 2008, Sch 40*) in respect of events and periods from 1 April 2009, where the filing date is 1 April 2010 or later (although if information or a document is produced under *s 256* ('Regulations about accounts, etc') from 1 April 2009, the tax period must begin on or after that date). It provides for tax-geared penalties of between 0% and 100%, broadly depending on a person's behaviour and the level of disclosure to HMRC.

The circumstances in which a penalty could be imposed potentially includes (for example) an overstated claim for the transfer of unused nil rate band, resulting in an IHT underpayment. Penalties can be imposed on the person making the return, and on another person who deliberately supplies false information resulting in an incorrect return (or who withholds information with the same intention) (*FA 2007, Sch 24 paras 1–1A*). As to compliance and penalties generally, see **Chapter 6**.

For periods prior to the introduction of the above penalty regime for inaccuracies for IHT purposes (see below), a person liable for the tax who fraudulently or negligently supplies an incorrect account, information or document to HMRC is liable to a penalty (*s 247(1)*). The maximum penalty is 100% of the tax potentially lost (ie broadly the difference between the amount of tax correctly payable, and the amount of tax payable based on the incorrect return etc). Such penalties could apply to a wide range of people including someone other than the person in default (under *s 247(2)*) if incorrect information was supplied in connection with a claim to transfer unused nil rate band. The rules were amended from 21 July 2008 to apply to an incorrect IHT return delivered in respect of the first death from that date (see IHTM43061).

Personal representatives of the surviving spouse or civil partner must therefore be mindful of the potential risk, and exercise due diligence when claiming unused nil rate band from an earlier death.

## Valuations

**14.15** The 'value ascertained' capital gains tax rule in *TCGA 1992, s 274* ('Value determined for inheritance tax'), under which values ascertained for IHT purposes apply for capital gains tax purposes, was amended in *Finance Act 2008* as a consequence of the introduction of the transferable nil rate band, from 6 April 2008. The effect is that an asset valuation for the purposes of calculating the amount of transferable nil rate band (as opposed to calculating the amount of any IHT on death) cannot be applied for CGT purposes as well.

## DEATHS BEFORE 25 JULY 1986

**14.16** IHT was introduced in 1986. However, the transferable nil rate band provisions are adapted in cases where an earlier spouse died before 25 July 1986, and the surviving spouse died on or after 9 October 2007. *Finance Act 2008* adapted *s 8A* accordingly, so that the rules apply for capital transfer tax purposes where the spouse died between 1 January 1985 and 24 July 1986, or between 13 March 1975 and 31 December 1984, as appropriate (*FA 2008, Sch 4 para 10(2), (3)*).

Similarly, the transferable nil rate band provisions are adapted for estate duty purposes where the spouse died between 16 April 1969 and 12 March 1975, or before 16 April 1969, as appropriate (*FA 2008, Sch 4 para 10(4), (5)*).

For deaths before 13 November 1974, if property was left to a spouse, an estate duty charge would have arisen. If the estate was large enough for duty to be paid, the equivalent of the nil rate band would have been exhausted, so that there would be nothing left to transfer.

---

**Example 14.7—Elderly testatrix**

Sarah is now nearly 90. She has a bungalow worth £250,000 and savings of £350,000. She married Frank in 1959 but he died in November 1971 intestate. Frank's personal estate was negligible but he and Sarah did own their house jointly, so it passed by survivorship to Sarah. Frank's share was then worth £2,500 at a time when the estate duty tax-free band was £12,500.

There was no spouse exemption in November 1971: relief limited to £15,000 was introduced on 22 March 1972. That limitation was lifted on 11 November 1974. Sarah's inheritance of the share of the house therefore used 20% of the

**14.17** *Transferable nil rate bands*

then equivalent of the nil rate band, so 80% was unused and is still available for transfer.

Against Sarah's estate of £600,000 her executors may set 180% of the current nil rate band, ie £585,000, leaving £15,000 to suffer an IHT charge at 40% of £6,000.

---

The 'clawback' provisions dealing with the interaction of the transferable nil rate band and IHT or capital transfer tax charges in respect of heritage relief and woodland relief (see **14.8**) are also adapted accordingly, where the surviving spouse died on or after 9 October 2007 and the earlier spouse died between 13 March 1975 and 24 July 1986, or between 1 January 1985 and 24 July 1986, or between 7 April 1976 and 31 December 1984, or between 13 March 1975 and 6 April 1976, so that the clawback rules in *s 8C* apply to the appropriate capital transfer tax legislation (*FA 2008, Sch 4 para 11*).

As to ascertaining the nil rate band for earlier years, see **14.5** above.

# PRACTICAL ISSUES

## Record keeping

**14.17** The transferability of unused nil rate band comes at an administrative cost in terms of keeping records and documents. Some discipline will be required on the part of surviving spouses or civil partners and their personal representatives, in terms of obtaining, keeping and maintaining records in respect of the earlier spouse or civil partner to die and their estate.

Practical issues may arise in terms of the valuation of assets and the availability of IHT reliefs. For example, the present policy of HMRC Inheritance Tax seems to be not to check claims for 100% business property relief (BPR) or agricultural property relief (APR) where there is no immediate IHT liability, such as where personal representatives claim relief on an individual's death and no IHT liability would arise on the death regardless of the availability of BPR or APR, due to the deceased's available nil rate band. However, such an issue will now be relevant in determining the unused nil rate band available to the surviving spouse or civil partner. This may result in HMRC Inheritance Tax testing the availability of BPR or APR following the second death.

One important self-help procedure will be for widows, widowers and surviving civil partners to make and keep a record of the extent to which their late spouses or civil partners had used the nil rate band. The case of Sarah at **Example 14.7** shows that it may be difficult to produce values many years later. IHT practitioners should also encourage their clients to keep good records. A simple form, along the lines of the following, might be placed with the survivor's will. Enterprising practitioners may like to produce a form of 'aide memoire', perhaps embellished with the firm's logo, as a marketing exercise.

### Example 14.8—Record of use of the nil rate band for IHT purposes

The following record is designed to establish how much of the nil rate band was used by a former spouse. In it, the terms 'married' and 'widowed' include being a member of a registered civil partnership and still being such a member when the civil partner died.

#### Part 1: Your relationship to the deceased person(s)

1. Have you been married?
2. If so, how many times?
3. Did your marriage end only on the death of your spouse?
4. If so, state the date your spouse died.
5. If you have been widowed more than once, state the date that each spouse died.

#### Part 2: Details of transfers and of the nil rate band available

6. If you know it, state the amount of the nil rate band when your spouse died (or when each spouse died).
7. Do you have a copy of the will that your spouse made?
8. Was that will, if any, varied within two years of death? If so, do you have a copy?
9. Did your spouse leave all his or her estate to you?
10. If not, state the value given by your late spouse to others, and specify if any was left exempt (for example, to charity).
11. Did your spouse make gifts to others in the seven years before death?
12. If so, state the amount given and to whom (again noting any gifts that were exempt for any reason).

## Documents to support a claim

**14.18** In addition to keeping a record of material events, the deceased spouse's or civil partner's personal representatives should provide certain documents in support of their claim to transfer the available unused nil rate band, when submitting form IHT400 on the death of the surviving spouse or civil partner.

**14.19** *Transferable nil rate bands*

Schedule IHT402 ('Claim to transfer unused nil rate band') sets out the photocopied documents which must accompany the claim:

- copy of the grant of representation (Confirmation in Scotland) to the estate of the spouse or civil partner (or, if no grant has been taken out, a copy of the death certificate);
- if the spouse or civil partner left a will, a copy of it;
- if a deed of variation or other similar document was executed to change the people who inherited the estate of the spouse or civil partner, a copy of it.

In addition, the personal representatives of the deceased spouse or civil partner should typically keep the following information in a safe place, or provide for the survivor to keep in a safe place, to help establish the unused nil rate band available on their death:

- a copy of the HMRC return (form IHT205 or IHT400; in Scotland, forms C1 and C5);
- a copy of the deceased's will (if any);
- a copy of any documents (eg a deed of variation) executed after the death of the first spouse or civil partner, that changes who benefits from their estate;
- any valuation(s) of assets that pass under will or intestacy other than to the surviving spouse or civil partner; and/or
- any evidence to support the availability of relief (such as APR or BPR) where the relievable assets pass to someone other than to the surviving spouse or civil partner.

In the case of jointly owned assets, and in certain other cases (eg assets of the deceased's 'estate' interests in possession, lifetime gifts within seven years before death, 'gift with reservation' (GWR) assets and (if aged over 75) any alternatively secured pension from which the deceased received a pension), surviving spouses or civil partners (or their personal representatives) will need to obtain whatever relevant information and documentation is available in support of nil rate band claims (eg details of the assets concerned, and any evidence of their values).

**14.19** Particularly in cases where the earlier spouse or civil partner died some time ago, there may be gaps in the information and documentation available. The survivor may have been unaware of the importance of keeping them, or documents may have been lost, stolen or accidentally destroyed. HMRC have previously pointed out that certain documents are obtainable from public records bodies (eg copies of wills, grants of representation or confirmation from the Court Service, or copies of death or marriage (or civil partnership) certificates from the General Register Office). The documents do not need to be originals, or official copies; certified copies will suffice (HMRC IHT & Trusts Newsletter, April 2008).

However, the full details to make a claim may still be incomplete (eg such as assets subject to the GWR rules, as mentioned above). In those circumstances, the survivor's personal representatives will need to complete the claim form to the best of their knowledge and ability, attaching whatever documents are available, and explaining to HMRC Inheritance Tax the reason for any omission.

It will clearly be preferable if personal representatives of the earlier spouse or civil partner can undertake the preparatory work for a possible future claim on the survivor's death, such as by packaging together the required information and documents and passing them to the survivor.

# PLANNING ISSUES

## Should the nil rate band be used on the first death?

**14.20** As mentioned earlier in this chapter, the changes introduced in *Finance Act 2008* to allow for claims to transfer the unused nil rate band were backdated to cases where the surviving spouse or civil partner died on or after 9 October 2007.

IHT was previously charged on an ascending scale, which encouraged the equalisation of estates between husband and wife. However, since 15 March 1988 the position has been simpler. After the nil rate band (£325,000 in 2010/11) has been used, there is only one single rate of 40% on death (half of that, 20%, for lifetime chargeable transfers).

Thus, as a general rule, there is no advantage for IHT purposes in equalising estates as between husband and wife or civil partners. Following the introduction of the transferable nil rate band, it is no longer necessary for the nil rate band to be used on the death of the first spouse or civil partner, due to the possibility of transferring the unused proportion of a nil rate band to the estate of the surviving spouse or civil partner.

**14.21** The thinking behind utilising the nil rate band on the first death was to leave it to chargeable beneficiaries. However, many testators really wanted the primary benefit to go to the surviving spouse or civil partner, so the trustees of a discretionary nil rate band trust were encouraged to regard the surviving spouse as the primary beneficiary, with the deceased spouse or civil partner

**14.22** *Transferable nil rate bands*

typically leaving a sum equivalent to the upper limit of the nil rate band upon a discretionary trust so that the surviving spouse could have the benefit of the fund and at the same time the nil rate band could be utilised and not wasted. Distributions could be made in favour of the surviving spouse in case of need; and if they were of capital any exit charge under the discretionary trust regime in the first ten years would be by reference to the nil rate band on the testator's death.

Much of that thinking was rendered obsolete by the introduction of the transferable nil rate band. In most cases, the emphasis will be on *not* using the nil rate band on the first death, in the hope that the transferable band will be larger on the second death, when it will really be needed. However, some individuals will prefer to 'bank' the nil rate band, rather than rely on its availability on the survivor's death. In addition, there are still special circumstances where a will should contain a nil rate band trust, as will be seen below.

Particular care should be taken over '28-day' survivorship clauses, especially where one spouse has most of the estate and the other very little. This is because the effect of not passing value to the spouse could be to pass (chargeable) value to the next generation on the first death that exceeded the nil rate band which, had it been channelled through the estate of the (short) surviving spouse, might have benefited from that survivor's unused nil rate band. Do the sums before drafting the will.

**14.22** If it is appropriate to use the nil rate band as described above, it is worth noting that the nil rate band can normally be expected to increase annually by reference to the retail prices index (*s 8*). The limit for 2009/10 was increased from £312,000 to £325,000, and for 2010/11 was originally set at £350,000 by *FA 2007, s 4*. However, the IHT threshold for 2010/11 was subsequently restored to its 2009/10 level of £325,000 (*FA 2010, s 8*). In addition, as mentioned at **14.1**, the nil rate band was effectively frozen at £325,000 for the tax years 2011/12 to 2014/15 inclusive. In practice, the testator's will is often drafted to ensure that the gift matches the ceiling of the nil rate band when he dies.

The gift in the will should therefore be of an amount equivalent to the upper limit of the IHT nil rate band in force at the time of the testator's death under *Sch 1*, as amended in accordance with the indexation provisions of *s 8*, if applicable. Such a formula, while most useful for cash gifts, cannot of course operate in the same straightforward way in the case of specific legacies of assets, particularly where business or agricultural reliefs are involved and changes in values may occur.

**14.23** For those taxpayers who had previously considered IHT planning in respect of their wills, such as the inclusion of a nil rate band discretionary trust on the first death, there are several arguments for doing nothing at all. For example, discretionary will trusts can still be helpful in the following cases:

- where there is property qualifying for business or agricultural property relief; or
- to shelter property from care fees; or
- for asset protection purposes, such as in the event of a future marriage breakdown; or
- if an asset is likely to appreciate in value faster than the nil rate band.

In some cases, even if a discretionary will trust is no longer considered to be desirable, it may be possible to reverse its effects for IHT purposes. This can be achieved during lifetime through a codicil to revoke the nil rate band transfer, or possibly following death by means of a deed of appointment, as illustrated in the example below.

### Example 14.9—Appointment from nil rate band trust

Oliver and Patricia, who have been married for many years, made wills in 2005 that incorporate nil rate band discretionary trusts.

There is scope (under *s 144*) for the trustees of a discretionary trust to appoint funds or assets to beneficiaries within two years of the death. To avoid the difficulty that was shown in the case of *Frankland v IRC* [1997] STC 1450 (see **13.48**), the trustees should not normally take any action until three months have elapsed from the date of death. Between the fourth and the twenty-fourth month, however, a distribution from the discretionary trust will take effect as if it had been a gift under the terms of the will and not a distribution from the trust.

Therefore, there is no need to change the will. On the death of the first to die of husband and wife, the trustees simply wait three months and appoint the whole of the nil rate band to the surviving spouse. There is no need to wait three months if the effect of the deed of appointment is to create an 'immediate post-death interest' (see **7.9**); only if the interest created is an absolute one.

If the will of the surviving spouse is drafted in common form, the provision as to the nil rate band will not apply because it has been excluded where the surviving spouse is not married at the date of death. In this scenario, therefore, all that is needed is a deed of appointment by the trustees of the nil rate band set up by the will of the first spouse to die.

**14.24** However, family conflict or indolence can delay the application for a grant of probate. Things can get left. If one of the executors is a professional person, he will probably be negligent if he fails to do what is right for the family in terms of IHT. If the executors are all family members and if they miss the various deadlines, they could be worse off than if they had simpler wills.

**14.25** *Transferable nil rate bands*

**14.25** The family home, and the use of an interest in the family home to constitute the nil rate band, are discussed in **Chapter 15**.

'Debt' or 'charge' arrangements (see **15.46**) are relatively complicated and difficult for taxpayers to understand. In addition, where there is an *FA 1986, s 103* problem, as illustrated by the *Phizackerley* case (see **15.47**) it can be difficult for advisers to explain the scheme to clients. Many people may have been slightly uncomfortable with the complexity of wills containing nil rate band discretionary trusts and they may feel much happier with simple new wills even though that will involve paying a new fee to have them prepared.

If both spouses or civil partners died before 9 October 2007, it will not be possible to make use of the transferable nil rate band provisions. Similarly, if one spouse or civil partner died some time ago, it may be too late to take advantage of the rules.

---

**Example 14.10—Too late for action**

Quentin died in 2005, leaving a widow, Rose. Quentin's will had a nil rate band discretionary trust. In this situation, nothing can (or should) be done. By putting in place a nil rate band discretionary trust, Quentin has used his nil rate band.

Due to the time which has elapsed since his death, it is now too late to make any changes relying on the 'two-year rule' in *s 144*. It is also too late to consider a deed of variation because, to be effective, it also had to be made within two years of death to claim relief under *s 142*.

---

Therefore, the only nil rate band available to Rose in the above example (unless she remarries and survives her second husband!) is the single nil rate band. It would be totally wrong for the family to assume that 'we just don't need that silly scheme now' and to appoint all the funds in the discretionary trust to the widow. That would just increase her estate without giving her back her late husband's nil rate band. This is an area that will be examined closely by HMRC: they are fully aware of the family's dilemma.

If a spouse or civil partner died recently, perhaps with a pre-9 October 2007 will in place, it may be possible in some cases to re-assess earlier estate planning with hindsight.

---

**Example 14.11—Estate planning updated**

Stanley made a will including a nil rate band discretionary trust for the benefit of his close family, with residue to his wife Tracy. The main asset was their house, worth £700,000, which was held by them as tenants in common in equal shares. Stanley had savings of £200,000. He died on 30 September 2010, having made no chargeable lifetime gifts.

Tracy and her daughter Ursula agreed that Tracy would sell the family home and move to a less expensive property closer to Ursula. The house would now sell for £800,000. Stanley's nil rate band of £325,000 was to be satisfied with his savings of £200,000, plus a further £125,000 from the house sale.

Tracy subsequently realised that she would not need any of the nil rate band, and preferred that, following the house sale, all of the money be released to Ursula. The family met with their adviser in May 2011 to consider whether to take advantage of the transferable nil rate band provisions (which had been introduced after Stanley's will was drafted). They decided that since they were still within two years of Stanley's death, they should effectively rewrite his will so that all Stanley's estate went to Tracy. That way, the whole of Stanley's nil rate band would be available on Tracy's death.

Any assets already transferred to Ursula would not now be from the discretionary trust, but would be treated as a gift by Tracy. If Tracy lived seven years, those gifts would fall out of account. Apart from that, if the will was varied, the sale of the house could all be treated as a sale by Tracy, and the whole of the gain would be tax free. They decided that it would be worthwhile rewriting Stanley's will so that his nil rate band was unused on his death.

## Earlier marriages or civil partnerships

**14.26** The starting point in a claim to transfer unused nil rate band is that the spouses or civil partners were married to each other at the time of the earlier death. It does not matter if, for example, a surviving spouse later remarried (although the surviving spouse's personal representatives can only claim one extra nil rate band) and was subsequently divorced.

If the surviving spouse remarries and dies before their new spouse, the unused nil rate band of the earlier spouse to die from the first marriage may be claimed by the survivor's personal representatives. The surviving spouse from the later marriage may subsequently be able to claim unused nil rate band from the remarried spouse if appropriate, subject to the overriding maximum of 100% of the nil rate band applicable on the last survivor's death.

If an individual has survived more than one marriage or civil partnership, his personal representatives may be able to claim additional nil rate band from more than one estate, subject to the aforementioned maximum. A separate claim form is required in respect of each estate. It is important to remember that unused nil rate band is not available for chargeable lifetime transfers by

**14.27** *Transferable nil rate bands*

the survivor, although it may be available when calculating the IHT position in the event of the survivor's death within seven years of making that transfer.

Remarried spouses or civil partners who have already accrued an extra nil rate band from an earlier marriage or civil partnership should consider chargeable legacies (eg a discretionary trust) in their wills, as opposed to leaving everything to their later spouse. The former course of action could result in three nil rate bands being utilised upon the last surviving spouse's death (ie the nil rate band of the deceased spouse from the earlier marriage, the remarried spouse and the last surviving spouse). The latter course of action could result in the complete loss of the nil rate band from their earlier marriage.

## Cohabiting couples

**14.27** In certain circumstances, up to four nil rate bands may be available. This could happen if, for example, a co-habiting couple who had each been married before left their respective estates to chargeable legatees such as adult children (or to the survivor), in order to utilise both their own nil rate band and the transferred nil rate band of their deceased spouse.

However, following marriage their overall IHT position could dramatically worsen.

---

**Example 14.12—The effect of marrying**

Vera, widowed with one daughter, had inherited from her husband all his modest estate. Her house was now worth £550,000. She had also accumulated investments worth £75,000.

William was retired. He had also inherited all of his late wife's estate and intended to leave his entire estate worth £600,000 to their son and daughter.

Vera and William decided to set up home together, living in Vera's house and letting out William's house. They consulted a tax adviser about getting married and leaving their estates to each other. Their adviser pointed out that leaving their estates to each other would not only result in the nil rate band of either William or Vera being wasted on the first death, but also the unused nil rate band of the spouse from their first marriage.

Marrying each other may well create a further unused nil rate band on the first of William or Vera to die, but it could not be transferred to the survivor, whose maximum nil rate entitlement had already been reached. The deceased spouse's additional nil rate band entitlement from their first marriage could not be transferred either.

---

However, if Vera and William did marry in the above example, consideration could be given to including a legacy to chargeable beneficiaries (eg to adult children or a discretionary will trust) on the first death, sufficient to use the deceased's nil rate band plus the transferred nil rate band from that person's first marriage.

## Business or agricultural property

**14.28** As discussed elsewhere in this chapter, discretionary trusts are a relatively common feature of wills drafted before the introduction of the transferable nil rate band, as they represented a possible means of using the nil rate band of the first spouse or civil partner to die.

A discretionary will trust may still be a useful vehicle to hold assets that are within the nil rate band, if their value is wholly or partly reduced for IHT purposes by business or agricultural property reliefs. Alternatively, a legacy of assets qualifying for 100% business or agricultural property to non-exempt beneficiaries on the first death should similarly result in the deceased's unused nil rate band being available for later transfer.

The effect of those reliefs is very important. Where relief is at 100% the benefit on top of the nil rate band is unlimited. With relief at 50%, for 2010/11 the nil rate band can cover a transfer of £650,000. As a general principle, because of this multiplying effect, business and agricultural property should be given to chargeable parties rather than to the surviving spouse, to prevent it being wasted.

**Example 14.13—'Doubling up' BPR**

Yogi's will left his nil rate band on discretionary trust for the benefit of his children, and the residue to his wife Zoe. They had both always taken a keen interest in the family company's business. After Yogi's death, Zoe encouraged the executors to allocate all Yogi's shares, attracting 100% BPR, to the nil rate discretionary will trust. The shares were worth £500,000. Zoe received those parts of the estate that did not qualify for any relief, together with substantial cash from insurance policies.

Zoe used the cash to buy the shares from the trustees. That gave the trustees far more, in real terms, than the nil rate band, so effectively the children received more than Yogi could have given in simple cash terms. If Zoe lives two years from her purchase of the shares, BPR will again be available. Meanwhile, there is control over the children's inheritance.

In the case of a partially exempt estate (ie because the spouse or civil partner exemption in *s 18* applies) the gift should be of the business or agricultural

**14.29** *Transferable nil rate bands*

property itself. It is not sufficient merely to create a specific pecuniary legacy payable out of the business or agricultural property. In the latter situation, relief is denied on the value of the pecuniary legacy and therefore (at least in part) lost (*s 39A(6)*).

## Care fees considerations

**14.29** Many couples are more concerned about the likely burden of care fees than about IHT. Care fee considerations are outside the scope of this book. However, in very broad terms a discretionary trust, properly run, is expensive (especially as compliance procedures such as anti-money laundering rules in the UK become more detailed and complex) but can shelter from care fees the estate of the first spouse, who is often cared for by the spouse who survives, but who thereafter also needs care.

Alternatively, a simple 'immediate post-death interest' settlement would protect the capital, and might be cheaper to run.

## OTHER ISSUES

**14.30** The estate duty surviving spouse exemption (*Sch 6, para* 2) is unaffected by the introduction of a transferable nil rate band. Taxpayers should generally do nothing to disturb that very useful situation, which confers freedom from both IHT and capital gains tax.

**14.31** An 'immediate post-death' interest (see **Chapter 7**) in favour of the surviving spouse or civil partner may be a suitable option if, for example, asset protection is a concern. Such a legacy is subject to the spouse or civil partner exemption, resulting in the deceased's unused nil rate band being available on the survivor's death.

**14.32** Practitioners should note the effect of *s 143* ('Compliance with testator's request') (see **13.47**) and take care to avoid accidental use of the 'first' nil rate band where, for example, the surviving spouse trades down after the first death and shares out the contents of the old home.

**14.33** As indicated at **14.23** above, a nil rate band relevant property trust may still be considered desirable for various reasons, despite the facility to transfer unused nil rate band. However, some care is required in respect of wills drafted before the introduction of the transferable nil rate band provisions, and also when drafting new wills that incorporate such trusts of the nil rate band.

For example, if the will of a surviving spouse or civil partner leaves a sum 'that is equal to an amount that will not give rise to an IHT charge' on a relevant

## Transferable nil rate bands  14.33

property trust, in HMRC's view that amount will include nil rate band that has been transferred. The effect when calculating an exit charge before the first ten-year anniversary of the trust is that there will be a positive rate of tax under *s 68(1)*, and an IHT liability arises on the exit (IHTM43065).

The inclusion of the transferred nil rate band from the first death with the survivor's own nil rate band legacy could also adversely affect charities, eg if the surviving spouse wished to leave a nil rate band legacy to family members, with the residuary estate after the nil rate band legacy to be left to a charity.

Such difficulties could be prevented by limiting the nil rate band legacy on the survivor's death by reference to the nil rate band in force at the date of death, rather than by reference to, say, 'such an amount that does not give rise to an IHT charge'.

Chapter 15

# The family home

## INTRODUCTION

**15.1** The family home (a term used in this chapter to include a property owned and occupied by husband and wife, or civil partners) is probably the most significant asset in the estates of most individuals, and often the most valuable in monetary terms. Escalating property prices over a number of years resulted in the value of an increasing number of family homes exceeding the IHT nil rate band, which did not rise in step with property prices.

This chapter considers some IHT planning ideas involving the family home. It must be remembered that transactions undertaken to save IHT must be considered 'in the round' taking into account any legal implications, as well as the possible implications for other taxes and/or possibly means-tested state benefits.

## Duty of care in connection with tax

**15.2** A warning for tax advisers on this note was provided in *Hurlingham Estates Ltd v Wilde & Partners* [1997] STC 627. In that case, it was held that a professional (a reasonably competent conveyancer and commercial lawyer) owed a duty to his client to advise on the tax implications of the transaction unless his retainer was limited, or unless it was apparent that advice was not needed by the client.

Apart from the direct duty to a client just described, an adviser may owe a duty of care to other people affected by the transaction. In *White v Jones* [1995] 2 AC 207, the House of Lords held that solicitors owed a duty of care to the intended beneficiary of a testator: in assuming responsibility to the client, the solicitor also became responsible to the intended beneficiary. The court wanted to do practical justice in a situation where the only person who might have a valid claim (the testator) would have suffered no loss and the only person who suffered a loss (the disappointed beneficiary) would have no claim.

**15.3** The principle in *White v Jones* can apply even to lifetime transactions. In *Hughes v Richards (t/a Colin Richards & Co)* [2004] EWCA Civ 266, two parents and their children sued the accountant to the parents in respect of tax and investment advice that failed to produce the promised benefits. The accountant said that the children were not his clients and he owed them no duty of care. He therefore wanted to strike out their claim, but the Court of Appeal refused. The court did have some doubt as to whether the children were owed a duty of care, but that was based on the fact that at that point the parents were still alive and could therefore sue for the same loss.

The rule in *White v Jones* was adopted in *Gorham v British Telecommunications plc* [2000] 4 All ER 867. An insurance company was held to have owed a duty of care to the intended beneficiaries of a policy taken out by its customer when it advised him. The duty was owed to the intended beneficiaries to advise the customer with reasonable skill and care. The reason was that the customer sought the advice not only for his own interests but also for the interests of his dependants if he should die before them, so that a duty was owed not to give negligent advice to the customer which would adversely affect the interest of the dependants.

**15.4** Although there may be a duty of care, the client or third parties will not succeed unless the particular loss suffered falls within the duties of the adviser. In *Cancer Research Campaign v Ernest Brown & Co (a firm)* [1997] STC 1425, a solicitor was sued in connection with the administration of an estate. Tax could have been saved if the solicitor had recommended a deed of variation, but the solicitor successfully claimed that he was instructed merely to draw up a will in accordance with what the deceased wanted (which he had done) and that it was not within his instructions to advise the testatrix on how best to minimise tax for the advantage of (charitable) beneficiaries.

Professional negligence issues also potentially apply to a firm's directors and employees. Employed professional staff may perhaps believe that they are not at risk, on the basis that they are not principals or partners. However, an employee can be sued jointly or severally with the employer by the client. In *Merrett v Babb* [2001] EWCA Civ 214, Mr Babb was a surveyor and valuer, who was employed as branch manager for a firm of surveyors and valuers. Mr Babb prepared and signed a valuation report on behalf of his firm, following instructions by a building society in respect of a mortgage application. The principal of the firm of surveyors and valuers which employed Mr Babb was subsequently made bankrupt, and the firm ceased business. The firm's professional insurance was cancelled without run-off cover. The court held that the valuation report had failed adequately to report on cracks in the building, and that the failure to recommend further investigation was negligent. However, it is perhaps worth noting that the appellant in this case signed the original valuation report in his personal capacity, and therefore assumed personal responsibility for it.

## 15.5 *The family home*

**15.5** In *Vinton and others v Fladgate Fielder and another* [2010] EWHC 904 (Ch), a family sued their advisers in respect of a botched IHT planning scheme, described at **11.9**. They sued as the personal representatives of Mrs Dugan-Chapman; as the prospective executors; and as the residuary beneficiaries under her will. They wanted to recover the tax lost (which ran into hundreds of thousands of pounds) and the costs of the unsuccessful tax appeal (which themselves amounted to £106,394).

The solicitors applied to have the claim struck out as not showing reasonable grounds for a claim; or alternatively that the claim had no real prospect of success. The lawyers argued that they had been engaged only to deal with a capital-raising project for the family company, not to advise on tax; and that their liability was to the deceased, not to her estate, nor to her personal representatives, nor to the beneficiaries.

The court considered the decisions in *Carr Glyn v Frearsons* [1999] Ch 326, *Daniels v Thompson* [2004] EWCA Civ 307 and *Richards v Hughes* [2004] EWCA Civ 266. It held that in so far as the claims lay in contract, there was a serious claim on which to adjudicate. It was clear that tax was a significant consideration in the proposed transaction on which advice was sought. In so far as the claims lay in tort, ie relied on allegations of negligence, it was inappropriate to strike them out: the claims were not fanciful. Although the law did not at present give the family a clear claim, Peter Gibson LJ had noted in *Richards v Hughes* that the implications of the decision in *White v Jones* were to be explored case by case. Thus the Court of Appeal might wish to develop the principles in *Carr Glyn v Frearsons* such that failure to protect the estate of the deceased from an unnecessary liability to IHT was a proper subject of a claim in negligence.

The problem for an adviser is the level of expertise that he holds himself out as having and the extent to which, in his agreement with his client, he is able to limit his liability. It begins to look as if any family member who is disadvantaged by bad tax advice, even if not given to him direct but to a third party, may have a claim against the adviser. Clients are getting more and more sophisticated. Articles in financial pages of the weekend press alert the public to tax issues and commonly used structures for tax mitigation. The four schemes described in this section were all the subject of considerable discussion in the serious press and the fourth one, the 'IOU scheme' was also described in detail on the Internet by Motley Fool. All this creates a public which is aware of tax and which has very high expectations of its advisers.

The issue of considering other taxes when undertaking IHT planning involving the family home (and generally) has become even more relevant since the introduction of the 'pre-owned asset' (POA) income tax charge from 6 April

2005 (see **Chapter 16**), which is primarily aimed at what the government apparently regarded as unacceptable IHT avoidance.

A detailed consideration of those IHT avoidance schemes which apparently provoked the POA regime is outside the scope of this chapter. However, the main types of scheme used in the past involving the family home are summarised below.

## Reversionary lease schemes

**15.6** The intention of 'reversionary lease schemes' is broadly to allow the home owner to make a gift of an interest in the property to reduce his IHT estate, whilst continuing to occupy and without being subject to the 'gifts with reservation' (GWR) rules (see **Chapter 5**). This popular planning arrangement typically involved the donor retaining the property freehold, but granting a deferred long lease as a gift, under which the right of the lessee to occupy is deferred (eg for 20 years).

The scheme was generally considered to be effective before 9 March 1999, although the position became less certain following legislative changes from that date. As indicated at **5.13**, HMRC's guidance states the view (at IHTM14360) that reversionary lease schemes effected from 9 March 1999 are subject to the GWR rules, on the basis that the donor's occupation of the freehold (even if held more than seven years before the creation of the lease) is nevertheless considered to be a 'significant right in relation to the land' for GWR purposes (*FA 1986, s 102A(3)*). However, HMRC's subsequent 'Income Tax and Pre-Owned Assets Guidance' (www.hmrc.gov.uk/poa/poa_guidance5.htm#9) states that HMRC's view has changed, and that if the freehold interest was acquired more than seven years before the gift, continued occupation by the donor would not be a 'significant right', and that *s 102A* cannot apply to the gift due to the seven-year exclusion in *s 102A(5)*.

Those reversionary lease schemes which are considered to be effective for IHT purposes are nevertheless subject to a potential income tax liability from 2005/06 under the POA regime (*FA 2004, Sch 15, paras 3(2), (4)*), unless the donor elects out of the income tax charge and into the GWR rules for IHT purposes.

## Lease carve-out schemes

**15.7** Lease carve-out arrangements were highlighted in *Ingram (Executors of Lady Ingram's Estate) v IRC* [1997] STC 1234 (see **5.11**), in which a carve-out scheme in relation to the late Lady Ingram's main residence was upheld by the House of Lords.

## 15.8 The family home

'*Ingram* schemes' involving lease carve outs were generally blocked from 9 March 1999 by changes to the GWR rules (*FA 1986, s 102A*), but as with reversionary leases, any carve-out schemes before that date and still in existence appear to be effective for IHT purposes. However, like reversionary lease schemes, pre-9 March 1999 Ingram schemes are also subject to an income tax charge under the POA rules, unless an election is made to the contrary.

*Ingram* schemes could still operate over 14 years. The GWR rules concerning interests in land (see **5.10**) state that a right or interest over land is not 'significant' for GWR purposes if it was granted or acquired before the seven-year period ending with the date of the gift (*FA 1986, s 102A(5)*). This exception could therefore apply if there was a gap of at least seven years between the creation of the lease and the gift of the freehold reversion. The gift would still be a PET, which would require the donor to survive a further seven years after making it. However, HMRC apparently consider that *Ingram* schemes effected from 9 March 1999 are still caught by the GWR rules if the lease is not for full consideration (IHTM14360).

*Ingram* schemes caught by the GWR rules are not subject to a POA income tax charge. However, those schemes not subject to the GWR rules (eg if effected before 9 March 1999) are not excluded from a POA charge, and therefore such arrangements are subject to those income tax rules.

## 'Eversden schemes'

**15.8** In *IRC v Eversden (exors of Greenstock, decd)* [2003] EWCA Civ 668, [2003] STC 822, the Court of Appeal upheld the effectiveness against the GWR rules of an arrangement whereby property was initially placed into an interest in possession trust for the spouse, followed by a discretionary trust in which the beneficiaries included the settlor and spouse. Accordingly, changes to the GWR rules were introduced in 2003 to block '*Eversden* schemes' (*FA 1986, 102(5A)*), affecting settlements created from 20 June 2003 (see **5.9**).

For schemes involving the family home, a POA income tax charge is excluded for so long as the spouse or civil partner continues to have an interest in possession in the trust (*FA 2004, Sch 15, para 10(1)(c)*). However, this exclusion is unlikely to apply in practice, because the initial interest in possession of the property is normally terminated during the life of the spouse or civil partner. *Eversden* schemes of the family home effected before 20 June 2003 are generally considered to be subject to income tax under the POA rules, whereas schemes effected from that date are subject to the GWR rules and therefore fall outside a POA charge.

## 'Lifetime debt' or 'double trust' arrangements ('IOU schemes')

**15.9**

### Example 15.1—'IOU scheme'

There are different names and variants of debt and trust arrangements ('IOU' or 'double trust' schemes), which were more popular prior to the introduction of stamp duty land tax from 1 December 2003. However, an example of a typical scheme would be one in which an individual (call him Jake) sold his house for £1 million in February 2006, to a trust in which he has a life interest (Trust 1). Note that the transaction would be liable to stamp duty land tax. The trustees gave Jake an IOU for the purchase price, which Jake gifted to a second trust for the benefit of his adult children (Trust 2). He remains in occupation of the property. The outstanding debt owed to Trust 2 reduces the value of the house in Trust 1 in Jake's estate for IHT purposes.

HMRC do not accept that all types of double trust arrangements achieve their desired IHT objective. In particular, if the loan to Trust 2 is repayable on demand, HMRC's view is that there is a GWR until the trustees call in the loan. (NB: it should be noted that the GWR is in the loan, as opposed to the house.)

On the other hand, if the terms of the loan provide that the debt is only repayable after the death of the life tenant (ie Jake), HMRC generally consider that such schemes are not caught by the GWR rules in respect of the property. It is therefore important to check the terms of IOU arrangements carefully. Even if the arrangement works for IHT purposes in respect of the property, a POA income tax charge can still apply to the property, with a GWR in respect of the loan, unless the loan is written off or appointed back to the donor, or unless an election is made for the POA rules not to apply at all. See HMRC's 'Income Tax and Pre-Owned Assets Guidance' at section 5 (www.hmrc.gov.uk/poa/poa_guidance5.htm#11).

**15.10** In the above example, the value of Jake's life interest forms part of his estate for IHT purposes (note that this IHT treatment does not generally apply to interests in possession created from 22 March 2006: see **Chapter 7**), less the outstanding debt owed to the trustees of the children's trust. Assuming HMRC accept that the scheme is effective for IHT purposes and that the GWR rules do not apply, as indicated above, a POA income tax liability potentially arises to the extent that the value of the property exceeds the value of the debt (*FA 2004, Sch 15, para 11(4)*), unless Jake elects out of POA and into IHT.

The *Charge to Income Tax by Reference to Enjoyment of Property Previously Owned Regulations 2005 (SI 2005/724)* provide relief from a double IHT charge for taxpayers who elect into the GWR regime after making lifetime

**15.11** *The family home*

double trust home loan arrangements, where the individual dies after 5 April 2005 and within seven years of making the original gift. The *Inheritance Tax (Double Charges Relief) Regulations 2005 (SI 2005/3441)* also provide relief from the double IHT charge that may arise for taxpayers who decide to end double trust arrangements, ie where the loan is written off, waived or released (so that the value of the house forms part of their estate again) and the individual dies after 5 April 2005 and within seven years of gifting the loan.

## Ownership

**15.11** The property may be owned in an individual's sole name (eg husband, wife or civil partner), or as joint tenants, or as tenants in common (different rules apply in Scotland; see **4.18**).

- On the death of a 'joint tenant', the survivor takes the entire interest absolutely by operation of law. Therefore, it is not possible (subject to severance, which HMRC currently accept can be effected for IHT purposes through a deed of variation) to leave an interest in jointly tenanted property to a third party, because this interest accrues automatically to the surviving joint tenant.

- By contrast, ownership as 'tenants in common' gives each spouse a separate (typically equal) share of the property, which can be left by will or disposed of during lifetime. This is frequently found to be the most satisfactory form of ownership from both an IHT planning and practical point of view.

If the property is held by husband and wife (or civil partners) as joint tenants and the parties wish to sever the joint tenancy so that they become tenants in common instead, a simple form of severance notice should suffice. This notice should be given during lifetime because a joint tenancy cannot be severed by will (although a deed of variation can result in the tenancy being treated as such for IHT purposes). It is preferable for a severance to be agreed and signed by both parties.

A sample notice of severance is provided below.

---

**Example 15.2—Notice of severance**

NOTICE OF SEVERANCE

TO: [Name of joint tenant (1)] of [full address]

FROM: [Name of joint tenant (2)] of [full address]

I HEREBY GIVE YOU NOTICE severing our joint tenancy in equity of and in [full address of property] ('the property') now held by yourself and myself as joint tenants at law and in equity. The property shall henceforth be held by yourself and myself as tenants in common in equity in ['equal' or relevant percentage] shares.

THIS NOTICE REQUIRES that you acknowledge and indicate your acceptance to this Notice by signing the Notice where indicated below.

SIGNED BY ............................

DATED............................

I HEREBY ACKNOWLEDGE AND ACCEPT this Notice of Severance in respect of the aforementioned property

SIGNED BY............................

DATED............................

**15.12** The notice itself is valid as soon as it has been signed by one joint owner and acknowledged by the other. However, this is a transaction between two people, one of whom will probably have died by the time it becomes necessary to look at the issue. Husband and wife (or civil partners) might sign the notice at the time of signing wills and might not realise that it is important to keep the notice of severance in a safe place so that it can be produced later on to show how the property is held. If the title to the property is unregistered (very rare these days), the notice of severance should be placed with the original deeds. These will often be held by the building society that financed the purchase. Normally, the title will be registered: if so, the notice of severance should be lodged with HM Land Registry to bring the register of title up to date. That way, there will be clear evidence later on when it is needed.

# LIFETIME PLANNING

## Equity release

**15.13** A straightforward form of lifetime IHT planning involves releasing equity in the property, as opposed to making a direct gift of an interest in the property. The following possibilities could be considered:

## Mortgage or loan

**15.14** A loan or mortgage secured on the property will reduce its net value for IHT purposes. The funds borrowed could be gifted to non-exempt beneficiaries

**15.15** *The family home*

such as adult children (ie a PET) or into trust from which the settlor is excluded as a beneficiary (the latter normally being a chargeable lifetime transfer since 22 March 2006).

Such planning should be best suited to individuals whose life expectancy is restricted by old age or infirmity, as a commercial loan or mortgage will bear interest. However, the donor would normally need to survive at least seven years for the gifted proceeds to escape IHT consequences on death. Decreasing term assurance could be considered to cover any IHT liability (with the donees paying the premiums). If life expectancy is more than two years but less than seven years, consideration could be given to investing the loan proceeds in shares eligible for 100% business property relief (see **Chapter 11**), and leaving those shares by will to the intended (non-exempt) beneficiaries. The relief applies to shares in unquoted trading companies, and also shares in trading companies listed on the Alternative Investment Market (AIM), or traded on OFEX (IHTM18337). However, by their nature such investments are often high risk.

If the property is (say) a farmhouse eligible for agricultural property relief, the loan should preferably be secured on other assets, which do not qualify for agricultural or other forms of IHT relief.

### 'Trading down'

**15.15** Selling the family home and moving to a smaller, less expensive house represents an alternative form of equity release. The surplus funds generated could be dealt with as outlined at **15.14** above. Although unpopular with clients, this arrangement has side benefits:

- It may reduce imbalance in asset allocation: far too many families have too much capital tied up in the family home, so its sale can release liquidity that enhances the lifestyle of the elderly.

- A smaller property may be cheaper to run, releasing further freedom to save tax by gifts out of income under *s 21*.

- Tax is payable in hard cash, albeit by instalments where property is concerned. The reallocation of resources to increase liquidity can make the estate much easier to administer after the death.

### Commercial sale

**15.16** The house owner may wish to sell the whole of the property or an interest in it, so as to enhance his standard of living. A commercial sale is not a transfer of value for IHT purposes if it can be shown that there was no intention to confer a gratuitous benefit on any person, and *either* it was an arm's-length

*The family home* **15.16**

transaction between unconnected persons, or that the transaction was on arm's-length terms (*IHTA 1984, s 10*).

Particularly in the case of sales between family members, independent property valuations should be obtained by both parties, to rebut any presumption by HMRC that a gratuitous benefit has been conferred.

For POA income tax purposes, the disposal of property is an 'excluded transaction' if it is a disposal by an individual of his whole interest in the property 'except for any right expressly reserved by him over the property either by an arm's-length transaction or by a transaction such as might be expected to be made at arm's length between unconnected persons' (*FA 2004, Sch 15, para 10(1)(a)*).

POA regulations also allow for partial arm's-length type equity releases (the *Charge to Income Tax by Reference to Enjoyment of Property Previously Owned Regulations 2005, SI 2005/724, reg 5*). This exemption applies to transactions between unconnected persons. It also applies to any disposals between connected persons on arm's-length terms before 7 March 2005, or to disposals from that date if the consideration was not in money or readily convertible assets.

The latter exemption may assist in cases where an elderly or infirm parent gives an interest in their home to adult offspring in return for the provision of care in the property on an ongoing basis. This is confirmed in HMRC's POA guidance ('Land – equitable interests'), which states the following (see www.hmrc.gov.uk/poa/poa_guidance5.htm#1):

> '... we would need information about how the essential elements of the transaction had been arrived at. We do recognise that there is a substantial body of case law dealing with the circumstances in which an interest in a house is acquired in consequence of a person acting to his detriment. The Ministerial Statement had these sorts of situations in mind and we would interpret Regulation 5 accordingly. In particular, we accept that the requirement that "the disposal was by a transaction such as might be expected to be made at arm's length between persons not connected with each other" would be interpreted with such cases in mind. Where the parties had sought separate advice and acted upon it or had obtained a court order confirming the property entitlement, that would reinforce the claim that the conditions were satisfied. But we would not expect parties to such an arrangement to have done this. We recognise that detriment that the acquirer can demonstrate he has suffered can provide consideration for the acquisition of the interest and prevent the transaction from being gratuitous.'

It is also worth noting that, in the case of dependent relatives, an IHT exemption applies to the extent that a disposition represents a 'reasonable provision' for his care or maintenance. In *McKelvey (Personal Representative of McKelvey*

**15.17** *The family home*

*Deceased) v Revenue and Customs Commissioners)* [2008] SpC 694 the deceased (D) was a spinster who lived with her widowed mother (M), who was 85 years old, blind and in poor health. D was diagnosed with terminal cancer, and in 2003 gave away two houses that she owned to M. D died in 2005, and M died in 2007. HMRC sought to charge IHT on the value of D's gift of the houses to M of £169,000. D's executor appealed, on the grounds that the gifts were exempt transfers within *IHTA 1984, s 11(3)* as a disposition being a reasonable provision for the care and maintenance of a dependent relative. The executor contended that D gave the houses to M so that they could be sold to pay for nursing care.

The executor's appeal was allowed in part. The Special Commissioner held that it was reasonable for D to assume that M would need residential nursing care. The difficulty in this case was in determining what was 'reasonably required' for this purpose. The Commissioner concluded that 'reasonable provision at the time the transfers were made amounted in all to £140,500'. This amount qualified for exemption under *s 11*, with the balance of £28,500 being a chargeable transfer (*s 3A(4)*).

## Gifting the family home

**15.17** Lifetime planning involving the family home often includes gifting an interest in the property, or sometimes the property as a whole. Of course, such a gift is a disposal for CGT purposes at market value, although private residence relief will normally be available (*TCGA 1992, s 222*). It is possible that the donor(s) may wish to move out of the family home (eg into a residential nursing home or, for example, purchase a smaller property if they can afford to do so). In either case, the 'gifts with reservation' (GWR) anti-avoidance rules (see **Chapter 5**) must be safely negotiated for IHT purposes.

The GWR provisions can apply (*inter alia*) if an individual makes a gift of property (from 18 March 1986) which is not enjoyed to the entire exclusion, or virtually the entire exclusion, of the donor (*FA 1986, s 102(1)(b)*). As there is no definition of 'virtually the entire exclusion' in the IHT legislation, HMRC published guidance on its view of the expression in Revenue Interpretation 55 (see **5.28**), which interprets it to include visits to stay at the house for certain limited periods, normal social visits, certain short-term stays (eg due to convalescence following medical treatment) and domestic visits (eg babysitting the donee's children). However, care should be taken to ensure that stays or visits to the house do not escalate beyond the *de minimis* limits and into a GWR charge. Examples given in Revenue Interpretation 55 of situations in which those limits are exceeded include:

- a house in which the donor then stays most weekends, or for a month or more each year; and

- a house with a library in which the donor continues to keep his own books, or which the donor uses on a regular basis, for example because it is necessary for his work.

However, a GWR charge is avoided if the donor pays a market rent for any periods of occupation (eg a gift of the property to the children, followed by a leaseback at a full commercial rent throughout the period of occupation). An exception to the GWR rules applies if full consideration is paid in money or money's worth for occupying the land *(FA 1986, Sch 20, para 6(1)(a))*. Independent advice should be obtained, together with separate professional valuations to establish a full market rent. For the recipient, the payment of rent and/or a lease premium has potential income tax implications. In addition, the stamp duty land tax position of the lease must be considered. A subsequent sale of the property will also have capital gains tax implications in respect of any increase in value of the property.

## Gifting a share of the home

### Joint occupation

**15.18** The gift of an 'undivided share of an interest in land' (from 9 March 1999) can give rise to a GWR charge *(FA 1986, s 102B(1)*; see **5.14**), subject to certain 'let-outs' considered below. This joint occupation rule takes precedence over other GWR provisions *(FA 1986, s 102C(6))*.

### Example 15.3—Gift to family member

Freda, who is an elderly widowed parent, gifts a share in the house (say 50%) to her adult unmarried daughter, Gertrude. Both live together in the house until Freda's death.

What is the GWR position?

**15.19** The basic principle is that the GWR rules apply to the gift of an undivided share in land, except in three cases:

- The donor does not occupy the land *(FA 1986, s 102B(3)(a))*. This would appear to allow a non-occupying donor to receive their share of rent and profit from the property without constituting a GWR, but does not assist Freda in the above example.

- If the donor's occupation is for full consideration in money or money's worth *(s 102B(3)(b))*. Whilst the parent's payment of rent to the daughter could reduce the eventual IHT liability on the parent's estate, it is often

**15.20** *The family home*

difficult to establish a market rent in these circumstances, and to ensure that the amount paid continues to reflect a market rent. In any event, the income tax implications for the daughter of receiving rental income are likely to make this option seem unattractive.

- Both donor and donee occupy the land, and the donor receives no benefit (other than a negligible one) provided by or at the expense of the donee in connection with the gift (*s 102B(4)*).

The third exception above appears to be based on a statement made by the Minister of State for the Treasury in 1986 (see below), although the above legislation did not take effect until 9 March 1999.

### Hansard Statement

'It may be that my Hon. Friend's intention concerns the common case where someone gives away an individual share in land, typically a house, which is then occupied by all the joint owners including the donor. For example, elderly parents may make unconditional gifts of undivided shares in their house to their children and the parents and children occupy the property as their family home, each owner bearing his or her share of the running costs. In those circumstances, the parents' occupation or enjoyment of the part of the house that they have given away is in return for similar enjoyment of the children of the other part of the property. Thus the donors' occupation is for a full consideration.

Accordingly, I assure my Hon. Friend that the gift with reservation rules will not be applied to an unconditional gift of an undivided share in land merely because the property is occupied by all the joint owners or tenants in common, including the donor.'

**15.20** The scope of the 'shared occupation' rule in *FA 1986, s 102B(4)* is potentially wider than the example given in the Hansard statement indicates. For instance, the legislation deals with land in general, not necessarily the family home. In addition, the requirement that the donor must not receive any connected benefit (other than a negligible one) does not necessarily mean that household running costs must be shared proportionately. The donor may wish to continue paying all the running costs, or the 'lion's share' of them. Otherwise, the difficulty arises in establishing how much the donee can safely pay, without the donor falling foul of the GWR rules.

In the above, example, Freda gifted a 50% share of the house to her daughter. However, *FA 1986, s 102B* does not contain a requirement to gift an equal share. The donor may therefore wish to consider giving away more than a 50% interest. However, HMRC could contend that if two individuals occupy a property jointly, the most that can be given away is 50%. In addition, the

*The family home* **15.23**

Inheritance Tax Manual at IHTM14332 (which provides a number of examples involving joint property) includes the following health warning:

'The joint property examples are on the basis that the joint owners take the property in equal shares. Refer any case in which the transferor takes less than an equal share to Technical Group.'

The value of Freda's share of the house may be subject to a discount on her death of between 10–15%, subject to the Land Tribunal's agreement. The higher percentage potentially applies if the other co-owner continues to occupy the property (see **4.20**).

**15.21** It should be noted that the above GWR exception applies while the property is occupied jointly. What would happen then if, for example, the daughter left home to get married? A GWR could be avoided by the mother paying a full market rent for her continued occupation in respect of her daughter's share. In addition, it should be borne in mind that the above exception applies to the gift of an interest in land, not the whole.

For income tax purposes, there is an exemption from a POA charge in joint occupation circumstances in which *FA 1986, s 102B(4)* would apply (*FA 2004, Sch 15, para 11(5)(c)*).

## Changes in circumstances

**15.22** Consider the following example:

---

**Example 15.4—Infirmity of donor**

George gifted his house ('Blackacre') to his adult son Harold in April 2005, which Harold occupied as his home. In May 2010, George (who did not previously have any major health problems) suffered a serious heart attack, which left him needing constant care. After George's release from hospital, he had to move back to Blackacre where Harold looked after him, until George sadly died shortly afterwards.

---

**15.23** There is a special relieving provision to prevent an unfortunate GWR charge arising following such an unexpected and sad change in circumstances. The donor's occupation of the gifted land is disregarded if (as in the above example) the donee is a relative of the donor or his spouse (or civil partner), and certain conditions are satisfied (*FA 1986, s 102C(3); Sch 20, para 6(1)(b)*); see **5.15**, ie:

- the occupation results from an unforeseen change in the donor's circumstances (ie the GWR exception would not apply in the above

**15.24** *The family home*

example if George had a long history of ill health, and he made the gift when it seemed likely that he would need looking after);

- the donor has become unable to maintain himself through old age, infirmity or otherwise; and
- the occupation represents reasonable provision by the donee for the donor's care and maintenance.

In the case of serious illness where the donor cannot maintain himself, HMRC accept that occupation represents reasonable provision for his care and maintenance (IHTM14342), although this exception would only be available until the donor sufficiently recovered. For POA income tax purposes, there is also an exemption from charge if the above conditions are satisfied (*FA 2004, Sch 15, para 11(5)(d)*).

## Statutory settlements

**15.24** In some cases, a lifetime gift can result in a statutory settlement for IHT purposes, eg a leasehold interest for life for less than full consideration (*IHTA 1984, s 43(3)*). The same applies if property is 'held in trust for persons in succession or for any persons subject to a contingency' (*IHTA 1984, s 43(2)(a)*).

For example, the lifetime gift of a share in the family home between spouses or civil partners subject to provisions in their wills that the property may not be sold without the survivor's consent could result in HMRC arguing that there is an interest in possession of the deceased's interest if left to the children on the first death. See also **15.40** below, and *IRC v Lloyds Private Banking Ltd* [1998] STC 559 (at **15.43**) in particular.

## WILL PLANNING

### Will or intestacy?

**15.25** Spouses or civil partners who occupy the family home as 'tenants in common' (see **15.11**) should make provision in their wills concerning their shares in the property. The rules of intestacy (see **3.1**) do not give a surviving spouse or civil partner an automatic right to the deceased's interest in the family home. Property owned as joint tenants passes by survivorship. Therefore, if the owners wish to leave their interests on death other than to each other, the joint tenancy should be severed during their lifetimes, and suitable provision made in their wills.

It may be possible for an instrument of variation to redirect joint property to give effect to the survivor's continued occupation (assuming that those who

*The family home* **15.27**

would otherwise benefit agree), and also effectively to sever the joint tenancy if appropriate. The IHT provisions (*IHTA 1984, s 142*, 'Alteration of dispositions taking effect on death') apply to dispositions which are '... effected by will, under the law relating to intestacy, *or otherwise*' (emphasis added). The latter disposition would seem to cover property passing by survivorship, if the notice of variation so provides. This is a point that HMRC appear to accept (IHTM35092). (NB: all subsequent statutory references in this chapter are to *IHTA 1984*, unless otherwise stated.)

However, it would surely be easier, and would provide greater certainty, to deal with this issue in the wills of both spouses (or civil partners) during their lifetimes. The wills should be reviewed at regular intervals to ensure that they reflect current wishes, and to protect against unforeseen changes in circumstances.

## Using the nil rate band

**15.26** Prior to changes introduced in *Finance Act 2008*, it was important for married couples or civil partnerships to ensure that optimum use was made of the available IHT threshold (or 'nil rate band') on the first death (see **Chapter 13**). If a deceased spouse (or civil partner) leaves their entire estate to the surviving spouse, then (unless the recipient spouse is non-UK domiciled), the legacy will normally be wholly exempt from IHT (*s 18*). However, the estate of the survivor increases accordingly. This could result in a potentially higher IHT liability on the second death, and a higher IHT liability overall. If each spouse (or civil partner) owned sufficient assets to constitute their nil rate bands, a non-exempt legacy on the first death could have saved IHT of an amount up to the nil rate band multiplied by the 40% 'death rate'.

A common IHT planning technique before the *Finance Act 2008* changes was therefore to ensure that an amount up to the available nil rate band was left to (say) the children directly, or possibly by way of a 'nil rate band discretionary trust' in which the surviving spouse could be included among the class of beneficiaries. This planning was relatively straightforward and simple to implement if each spouse (or civil partner) owned sufficient 'liquid' assets to constitute their nil rate bands, such as cash, shares and securities. However, very often the only asset of any substantial value would be an interest in the family home.

## Transferable nil rate bands

**15.27** Estate planning for married couples or civil partnerships was simplified in many cases by the introduction of transferable nil rate bands from 9 October 2007 (*ss 8A–8C*). The provisions broadly allow claims for the transfer of a spouse's or civil partner's unused nil rate band to surviving

**15.28** *The family home*

spouses or civil partners who die on or after 9 October 2007. The amount that can be transferred is based on the unused percentage of the deceased's nil rate band. That percentage is applied to the nil rate band in operation on the death of the survivor. See **Chapter 14** for further information.

From an IHT planning perspective, it is therefore no longer necessary for spouses and civil partners to utilise the nil rate band on the first death, such as by providing for the transfer of an interest in the family home to non-exempt beneficiaries (although if both spouses or civil partners died before 9 October 2007, it is not possible to take advantage of the transferable nil rate band).

Whilst nil rate band legacies of interests in the family home to discretionary trusts or other chargeable beneficiaries on the first spouse or civil partner to die will undoubtedly be less common or popular due to the transferable nil rate band, there may be circumstances in which such legacies are necessary or preferred, such as where the property occupants are unmarried (see *Burden v United Kingdom* [2008] All ER (D) 391 (Apr)), or to make provision for offspring. In addition, aside from IHT considerations there may be other reasons why an interest in the home may be left on trust, eg due to concerns about care fees or divorce.

## Ownership by first spouse (or civil partner) to die

**15.28** NB: See **15.26** above and **Chapter 14** regarding the transferable nil rate band for spouses and civil partners from 9 October 2007. The commentary below deals with situations in which it is not possible, or not preferred, to leave an outright legacy of the family home to the surviving spouse or civil partner on the first death for the purpose of claiming the deceased's unused nil rate band on the death of the surviving spouse or civil partner.

If one spouse or civil partner owns the entire family home and dies first, an interest in it could be left to a chargeable party (eg a daughter), whilst enabling the surviving spouse or civil partner to occupy by leaving an interest. Their respective shares may depend upon the value of the family home, and the proportionate interest necessary to constitute the nil rate band (assuming that the deceased owned insufficient assets to do so otherwise).

For example, the surviving spouse or civil partner may receive (say) a 25% tenant in common share, with 75% to the daughter (the latter interest being worth up to the available nil rate band). The survivor would then be able to occupy the whole by virtue of their 25% interest as a tenant in common. There must be no restriction on the daughter occupying the house as co-owner, as this would give the survivor an interest in possession in the whole, with the result that the same IHT liability would arise as if the house had been given to them outright, unless the interest terminates more than seven years before the individual's death (ie the termination being a deemed PET). The survivor's occupation could be made informal (eg by way of a non-enforceable licence). However, legal issues arise, such as 'security of tenure'. Can the daughter (assuming that she lives elsewhere) be trusted not to sell her interest? Even if she can be trusted, her interest is not secure from creditors and others.

Alternatively, the will of the deceased spouse or civil partner may create a trust of the family home (see below).

## Life interest trust

**15.29** For life interests created before 22 March 2006, a beneficiary with an interest in possession in settled property is treated as owning the underlying trust assets. This treatment continues to apply to certain life interests created from that date, such as those created by will or on intestacy. Subject to this and certain other exceptions (see **Chapter 7**), interests in possession created on or after 22 March 2006 are subject to the same IHT treatment as discretionary trusts (see **Chapter 8**).

If the first spouse or civil partner to die has already used the nil rate band (eg by making chargeable lifetime gifts) the deceased's will could establish a life interest trust of the whole home in favour of the survivor. From 22 March 2006, such an interest created by will (or under the laws of intestacy) is an 'immediate post-death interest' (*s 49A*), which qualifies for the spouse (or civil partner) exemption (*s 18*). Alternatively, the deceased's will could establish a life interest in an appropriate share of the house to the surviving spouse, with the remaining interest to non-exempt beneficiaries (eg the children), in order to utilise the nil rate band, if available.

**15.30** The trustees could subsequently decide to appoint a share of the life interest to (say) the children, the trust remaining subject to wide overriding powers of appointment. The survivor could remain in occupation, albeit on a non-exclusive basis, as the children must not be barred from occupying the home as well. On the survivor's death, the interest which falls to be taken into account for IHT purposes is the relevant proportion of the interest remaining (*s 50(5)*).

There is no GWR if the survivor is a co-owner, and as such is legally entitled to occupy the whole. Otherwise, prior to 22 March 2006 the termination of a life interest is not a disposal by way of gift (*FA 1986, s 102(1)*). However, from that date, the lifetime termination of an interest in possession can be treated as a gift for GWR purposes (*FA 1986, s 102ZA*). An IHT charge could therefore arise if an individual continues to derive a benefit from the property after it has been given away or the interest has been terminated. See **Chapter 13**.

**15.31** *The family home*

What if the surviving spouse or civil partner is a trustee? HMRC generally accept that the appointment of a donor, spouse or civil partner as a trustee is not of itself a GWR. The spouse or civil partner holds the property in a fiduciary capacity only, and is required to deal with it in accordance with their fiduciary duties as a trustee. The same applies if the donor, spouse or civil partner is entitled to payment for their services as trustee, if the trust deed allows and provided the remuneration is not excessive (IHTM14394). Nevertheless, it may be considered safer if the survivor is not a trustee.

For capital gains tax purposes, private residence exemption should be available (eg if the property is sold during the survivor's lifetime) if he is 'entitled to occupy it under the terms of the settlement' (*TCGA 1992, s 225*).

It is important that the trust is properly administered and that the decisions of the trustees are made independently and in the best interests of the beneficiary, to reduce the possibility of a challenge by HMRC that the trust is a 'sham'. This point is discussed further at **15.52**. The same comment applies to trusts in general.

## Discretionary trust

**15.31** A discretionary trust is one in which the beneficiaries normally have no interest in possession of the settled property, because the discretionary nature of the trust means that they have no absolute entitlement to trust income or assets.

However, the trustees of a discretionary trust can exercise their powers under the trust deed in favour of a beneficiary in such a way that an interest in possession is created. The IHT treatment of such an interest in possession broadly depends on whether it is deemed to arise before 22 March 2006 or since that date, subject to certain exceptions (see **15.29** above).

## Statement of Practice 10/79 and the *Judge* case

**15.32** HMRC Statement of Practice 10/79 ('Power of trustees to allow a beneficiary to occupy a dwelling house') states that if the trust deed allows '... an exclusive or joint residence ... for a definite or indefinite period ... with the intention of providing a particular beneficiary with a permanent home, HMRC will normally regard the exercise of the power as creating an interest in possession'. In addition, a lease for life for less than full consideration is treated as an interest in possession (*s 43(3)*).

The correctness of SP 10/79 was called into question in *Judge (Personal representatives of Walden deceased) v Revenue and Customs Comrs* [2005]

## The family home  15.34

SSCD 863, in which it was held that the beneficiary under a will trust had no right to occupy the property, but that the trustees had absolute discretion (not a duty) to allow her to occupy.

In the *Judge* case, Mr and Mrs Walden lived at 30 Perrymead Street in London. Mr Walden owned the property. He made a will. Clause 3 of that will, which dealt with the matrimonial home, included the following provision:

> 'AND I DECLARE my Trustees during the lifetime of my Wife to permit her to have the use and enjoyment of the said property for such period or periods as they shall in their absolute discretion think fit pending postponement of sale she paying the rates taxes and other outgoings and keeping the same in good repair and insured against fire to the full value thereof … '

**15.33** Mr Walden subsequently died. His personal representatives concluded that the effect of Clause 3 of Mr Walden's will was to give Mrs Walden an interest in possession in the property. The IHT account submitted to Capital Taxes (as it then was) for Mr Walden's estate was completed on that basis. A claim for the IHT spouse exemption was made on the value of Perrymead Street, which was shown as £625,000. This resulted in no IHT being paid on Mr Walden's estate, because his other estate assets were covered by the nil rate band.

Mrs Walden died a few years later. Her personal representatives submitted an IHT account to Capital Taxes, but the account did not mention the Perrymead Street property. This was presumably on the footing that Mr Walden's will established a discretionary trust, so that the property was not part of Mrs Walden's estate. The Revenue issued a determination on the basis that Mrs Walden had an interest in possession in the property, and the personal representatives appealed to the Special Commissioner.

The Special Commissioner said that a right of occupation can be an interest in possession. However, a proper construction of the will was crucial to the decision whether an interest in possession had been created. The Commissioner had to interpret Mr Walden's will. Where Clause 3 referred to 'for such period or periods as they shall in their absolute discretion think fit' the Commissioner considered that those words were clear and unambiguous. They gave Mrs Walden no right to occupy Perrymead Street, but gave the trustees an absolute discretion to allow Mrs Walden to occupy it. There was no duty to allow her to occupy the property. Therefore, Mrs Walden did not have an interest in possession. The personal representatives' appeal was allowed.

## Points to note

**15.34** It should be remembered that gifts to discretionary trusts are immediately chargeable transfers (although special treatment can apply to

**15.35** *The family home*

discretionary trusts created by will (*s 144*; see **Chapter 13**)). In the *Judge* case, Mr Walden's will created a discretionary trust with an asset worth £625,000 at the time of his death, ie well in excess of the nil rate band at the time. However, no IHT was paid because the personal representatives assumed (incorrectly as it turned out) that Mrs Walden had an interest in possession in the house. The Special Commissioner's decision effectively meant that no IHT was payable on the property from Mrs Walden's estate, but was payable on Mr Walden's earlier death.

**15.35** If an interest in the property is left outright to the surviving spouse (or civil partner) and the other interest is owned by a discretionary trust, there is an argument that the survivor should not be treated as having an interest in possession in it on the basis that she is entitled to occupy by reason of the interest they own, ie as a tenant in common has a right to occupy the entire house (*Bull v Bull* [1955] 1 QB 234). However, HMRC may challenge this analysis, particularly if the discretionary trust gives the survivor exclusive rights of occupation.

**15.36** The *Trusts of Land and Appointment of Trustees Act 1996* provides for a trust of land, giving a statutory right of occupation of the family home to the surviving spouse or civil partner. The provisions confer on any 'beneficiary who is beneficially entitled to an interest in possession in land subject to a trust of land' a right of occupation if certain conditions are satisfied (*TLATA 1996, s 12*). That right is not absolute – note the term 'interest in possession' does not necessarily confer the same meaning as for IHT purposes, although HMRC may contend that it does – and is subject to restriction (*TLATA 1996, s 13*). However, the trustees cannot exercise their powers to exclude or restrict occupation by a person who is in occupation of land from continuing to do so, unless consent is given or the approval of the court is obtained (*TLATA 1996, s 13(7)*).

**15.37** In the case of a surviving tenant in common, some doubt has been expressed whether (s)he obtains an interest in possession in the whole property on the other's death. This is because *TLATA 1996, s 12* only gives rights of occupation to trust beneficiaries if the property (as opposed to a share in it) is held in trust (*TLATA 1996, s 22(1)*). Does *TLATA 1996, s 13(7)* effectively give the survivor a right to possess the whole property? Or is any right to occupy non-exclusive, so that the trustees may require a proportionate rent to be paid (indicating that there is not an interest in possession in the whole)?

If a half-share in the property was settled under the deceased's will, it is possible to interpret *s 22(1)* as meaning that the trust beneficiaries have no right under *s 12*, so that *s 13* does not need to be considered. This would therefore seem to give the surviving spouse or partner the immediate right to possession under *s 12*. However, the position is not free from doubt, and

*The family home* **15.38**

ideally requires litigation to clarify the matter, or at least some guidance on HMRC's view.

The application of *TLATA 1996* also casts doubt over the availability of only or main residence relief for the trustees under *TCGA 1992, s 225* on a disposal of their interest in the family home, on the basis that the surviving spouse occupied the property by reason of their rights as joint beneficial owner, rather than under the terms of the settlement as required for CGT relief purposes. However, in *Drafting Trusts and Will Trusts: A Modern Approach* (9th edn, Sweet & Maxwell) by James Kessler QC and Leon Sartin, the authors express the view that if the testator's interest in the property is appropriated to a nil rate band discretionary trust two years or more after the testator's death (ie to avoid the surviving spouse acquiring an 'immediate post-death interest', which would form part of the individual's estate) and the surviving spouse (who is not a disabled person for IHT purposes on the testator's death) is subsequently given an interest in possession in the trust's share, only or main residence relief should be available to the trustees when the property is eventually sold. The beneficiary would have an interest in possession in the trust's share of land (as required by *TLATA 1996, s 12*), and the relief in *TCGA 1992, s 225* does not require that the beneficiary is only entitled to occupy it by virtue of an entitlement under the settlement.

The arrangement described above is a simpler and potentially more convenient alternative way of dealing with a nil rate band trust than the 'debt' or 'charge' arrangements described at **15.46** below.

**15.38** Consideration needs to be given to Statement of Practice 10/79 (see above), which indicates that if the trustees have powers to allow the creation of an exclusive occupation and that power is exercised with the intention of providing a particular beneficiary with a permanent home, HMRC will normally regard the exercise of that power as creating an interest in possession. However, notwithstanding SP 10/79 and depending on the circumstances, it would seem (following the *Judge* case) that trustees of a discretionary trust could claim private residence relief for CGT purposes, without the beneficiary occupying the property being considered to have an interest in possession for IHT purposes.

HMRC provided guidance on interests in possession and SP 10/79 in November 2007, in response to queries raised by STEP and CIOT. HMRC's response included the following salient points:

- The circumstances in which HMRC would *not* regard the trustees as having exercised their power to give a beneficiary an exclusive right of occupation (ie so as not to create an interest in possession) are 'rare', but might include instances where there was no evidence of (or significant doubt as to) the intentions of the trustees.

**15.39** *The family home*

- An SP 10/79 interest in possession generally arises if there is evidence that the trustees have knowingly exercised their powers so as to give a beneficiary exclusive occupation of the property.

- If the trustees have intended to grant a beneficiary the right to occupy a specific, named property owned by the trust, the beneficiary's interest in possession would end when the property was sold.

The above guidance ('Schedule 20 – SP 10/79 and Transitional Serial Interests') can be accessed via the STEP website (www.step.org/default.aspx?page=967).

**15.39** A CGT advantage of leaving a share in the family home to trustees (as opposed to a direct legacy to a family member who does not live there) is the potential availability of private residence relief on a subsequent disposal of the property. The relief applies if, during the trustees' period of ownership, a beneficiary is 'a person entitled under the terms of the settlement' to occupy the property as their only or main residence, and does so occupy it (*TCGA 1992, s 225*). The relief is available to trustees of both interest in possession and discretionary trusts (*Sansom v Peay* [1976] STC 494).

## Appointing an interest in possession

**15.40** Prior to *Finance Act 2006*, a potential pitfall in HMRC successfully contending that the surviving spouse or civil partner had an interest in possession within Statement of Practice 10/79 in respect of the property interest held by the trustees of the discretionary trust was that the survivor fell to be treated as beneficially entitled to that property interest, which would therefore form part of their estate for IHT purposes.

However, following *Finance Act 2006*, it does not normally matter if HMRC successfully argue that SP 10/79 applies, or if the trustees appoint an actual interest in possession to the surviving spouse or civil partner, provided that the interest does not arise within two years of death (or the survivor is not disabled, as defined for IHT purposes). This is because the provisions dealing with discretionary will trusts (*s 144*; see **Chapter 13**) broadly allow appointments of trust assets within two years following death to be effectively read back into the will. An interest in possession to the surviving spouse or civil partner on death would therefore fall to be treated as an 'immediate post-death interest' (see **Chapter 7**), subject to the spouse or civil partner exemption, resulting in the potential wastage of the deceased's nil rate band (although the transferable nil rate band facility could possibly assist in that case).

To avoid this treatment, the safest course of action for the trustees to consider would therefore be to wait until at least two years have expired following the first death if practical, before appointing an interest in the family home to the survivor.

## Joint ownership (tenants in common)

**15.41** If the family home is jointly owned (ie as tenants in common) the deceased spouse or civil partner may, for example, leave their share to their adult children, to make use of his available nil rate band. The surviving spouse or civil partner may continue to occupy by reason of their own beneficial share in the home.

## Interest in possession for survivor

**15.42** An interest in possession created by will in favour of the surviving spouse or civil partner is generally subject to the spouse IHT exemption (*s 18*).

If the nil rate band has already been used elsewhere, it may be that the deceased's estate is left on a 'flexible life interest trust' in which the trustees are given wide, overriding powers of appointment. Those powers may enable the trustees either to appoint property in whole or part to the survivor absolutely, and/or to terminate the life interest in whole or part and appoint the property to other beneficiaries under the will (eg children or grandchildren). As to the IHT treatment of interest in possession trusts generally, see **Chapter 7**.

Following the *Finance Act 2006*, the lifetime termination of an interest in possession, after which the former interest holder continues to occupy 'the no-longer possessed property', can constitute a gift for GWR purposes (see **Chapter 13**).

Even without a formal interest in possession trust, as indicated the terms of the will can create an effective interest in possession for the deceased. Such an interest in possession could be caused inadvertently.

**15.43** In *IRC v Lloyds Private Banking Ltd* [1998] STC 559, an interest in possession was held to exist where a wife left her share in the matrimonial home, by her will upon the following terms:

'(1) While my husband remains alive and desires to reside in the property and keeps the same in good repair and insured comprehensively to its full value with Insurers approved by my Trustees and pays and indemnifies my Trustees against all rates, taxes and other outgoings in respect of the property my Trustee shall not make any objection to such residence and shall not disturb or restrict it in any way and shall not take any steps to enforce the trust for sale on which the property is held or to realise my share therein or to obtain any rent or profit from the property.

(2) On the death of my said Husband ... I devise and bequeath the said property ... to my Daughter ... absolutely.'

**15.44** *The family home*

The High Court considered that the above clause in the wife's will was a dispositive provision, which conferred on the husband a determinable life interest in the half-share in the property. This created a settlement (within the meaning of *s 43(2)*) by which an interest in possession had been conferred on the husband. Accordingly, on his death IHT was charged on the basis that his estate included an interest in the entire property. This decision has been applied in other cases (*Woodhall v IRC* [2000] STC (SCD) 558, and *Faulkner (Adams' Trustee) v IRC* [2001] SSCD 112 (SpC 278)).

However, contrast those cases with the decision in the *Judge* case (see **15.32** above), in which the Special Commissioner held that the surviving spouse did not have an interest in possession of a residence because the deceased spouse's trustees had absolute discretion as to whether to permit her to occupy the property for any period, notwithstanding that a sale of the property required the consent of the surviving spouse.

### 'Nil rate band' discretionary trusts

**15.44** An alternative to such a legacy of the first spouse or civil partner to die (eg the husband) is to gift the nil rate band in his will for chargeable beneficiaries through the use of a 'nil rate band discretionary trust'. The residue of his estate (ie in particular the home) is left to the widow. Such trusts are discussed in greater detail in **Chapter 13**.

**15.45** It must be remembered that nil rate band discretionary trusts of an interest in the family home involve both tax law and property law considerations. The latter is outside the scope of this book. However, property law and tax law principles may diverge. For example, although HMRC will accept that a purported severance of a joint tenancy is a deed of variation for IHT purposes under *s 142*, it has no effect for general property law purposes. The joint tenant will normally obtain absolute ownership of the whole property on the death of the other owner.

The Land Registry's Practice Guide 70 'Nil rate band discretionary trusts' (www.landreg.gov.uk/publications/?pubtype=309), which is aimed at solicitors, licensed conveyancers and other legal advisers, outlines some of the property law and land registration issues surrounding the creation of such trusts. However, general guidance of this nature cannot be a substitute for specific legal advice, as appropriate.

### 'Debt' or 'charge' schemes

**15.46** As indicated at **15.27** above, following the introduction of a transferable nil rate band between spouses and civil partners from 9 October 2007, in most cases it will no longer be necessary (or desirable) for married

*The family home* **15.48**

couples or civil partners to leave an interest in the family home to the survivor on the first death. Previously, if the home was the main asset in the estate, a relatively well-known IHT planning arrangement was for a nil rate band gift to be satisfied either by a *debt* or *charge* on the property in favour of the trustees of the nil rate band discretionary trust (see **Chapter 13**).

Such arrangements may still be a feature of many wills drafted before 9 October 2007 in particular, in which the will of the deceased spouse or civil partner may give the trustees the power to make loans or to charge over the house, and on favourable terms (say) for the widow (eg an interest-free loan, capital payments deferred). However, the debt should preferably be repayable on demand to the trustees, to reduce the possibility of an argument by HMRC that the survivor has an interest in possession.

The charge should generally be a deduction from the widow's estate on her death, with her ownership allowing for continued occupation of the house during lifetime. However, in the case of a debt arrangement, a deduction may be restricted or denied if the widow made lifetime gifts to the husband. A loan is not deductible from an estate to the extent that the loan was property derived from the deceased, ie the widow (*FA 1986, s 103(1)(a)*).

**15.47** For example, suppose that a widower, who had previously owned the family home, made a lifetime gift of a half share to his wife. The wife subsequently died, and her will created a nil rate band discretionary trust. The husband receives his wife's interest in the family home, and incurs a debt to the trust. HMRC are likely to contend that the widower's debt is disallowable for IHT purposes under *FA 1986, s 103*.

These were broadly the facts in *Phizackerley (Personal representative of Phizackerley, deceased) v Revenue and Customs Comrs* [2007] SpC 591, where HMRC's disallowance of an 'IOU' as a liability of the surviving spouse's estate was upheld by the Special Commissioner. Such a challenge could be avoided by using charge arrangements instead, where the charge is made by the personal representatives. The home should be part of the residuary estate. This would allow the personal representatives to appropriate the home to the widow, subject to a charge. The identity of the personal representatives and the trustees of the discretionary will trust should not be identical (particularly as to the first named), and the surviving spouse or civil partner should preferably not be a personal representative.

**15.48** The charge method may also avoid stamp duty land tax (SDLT). HMRC originally published guidance on stamp duty land tax and nil rate band discretionary trusts on their website. This information is now contained in their Stamp Duty Land Tax Manual (at SDLTM04045), which contrasts debt and charge arrangements and their SDLT consequences (see below).

**15.49** *The family home*

*HMRC guidance: Charge scheme – SDLT liability*

'Land is transferred to the surviving spouse or civil partner and the spouse or civil partner charges the property with payment of the amount of the pecuniary legacy. The NRB trustees accept this charge in satisfaction of the pecuniary legacy.

The charge is money's worth and so is chargeable consideration for Stamp Duty Land Tax purposes.'

*HMRC guidance: Charge scheme – no SDLT liability*

'The personal representatives charge land with the payment of the pecuniary legacy. The personal representatives and NRB trustees also agree that the trustees have no right to enforce payment of the amount of the legacy personally against the owner of the land for the time being. The NRB trustees accept this charge in satisfaction of the legacy. The property is transferred to the surviving spouse or civil partner subject to the charge.

There is no chargeable consideration for Stamp Duty Land Tax purpose provided that there is no change in the rights or liabilities of any person in relation to the debt secured by the charge.'

**15.49** By contrast, HMRC's view is that SDLT is payable if the surviving spouse or civil partner (or the personal representatives) creates the debt – as it is then arguable that the land is transferred for consideration, ie the 'promise' to pay (see below).

*HMRC guidance: Debt scheme – SDLT liability*

'The NRB trustees accept the surviving spouse's or civil partner's promise to pay in satisfaction of the pecuniary legacy and in consideration of that promise land is transferred to the surviving spouse or civil partner.

The promise to pay is chargeable consideration for Stamp Duty Land Tax purposes.'

'The NRB trustees accept the personal representatives' promise to pay in satisfaction of the pecuniary legacy and land is transferred to the surviving spouse or civil partner in consideration of the spouse accepting liability for the promise.

The acceptance of liability for the promise is chargeable consideration for Stamp Duty Land Tax purposes. The amount of chargeable consideration is the amount promised, not exceeding the market value of the land transferred.'

**15.50** SDLT is a tax on 'land transactions', which is defined as 'any acquisition of a chargeable interest' (*FA 2003, s 43(1)*). A detailed discussion of SDLT is outside the scope of this book. However, in Appendix 4 of *Drafting Trusts and Will Trusts: a Modern Approach* (9th edn, Sweet & Maxwell by

*The family home* **15.51**

James Kessler QC and Leon Sartin), the authors advance the view that an SDLT liability should not normally arise on debt schemes. This is broadly on the footing that the execution of the survivor's undertaking to pay the debt does not involve the acquisition of a 'chargeable interest'. Further, there is considered to be no SDLT on the assent of the land interest to the survivor, as an SDLT charge arises on 'chargeable consideration' (as defined in *FA 2003, Sch 4, para 1*), and the survivor's undertaking is not 'consideration' for acquiring the land. Whilst an SDLT charge arises in the above examples if the transfer is in fact in consideration of the spouse's promise to pay the nil rate band sum, the undertaking and assent do not need to be structured in this way.

Nevertheless, the charge route may be considered preferable to the debt route, on the basis of HMRC's confirmation that no SDLT charge arises if the documentation is in accordance with the precise wording of their statement above.

Some debt schemes are drafted on the basis that the spouse undertakes to pay the trustees an 'indexed-linked nil-rate sum', ie a nil rate sum increased by the retail price index. Charge schemes may be drafted on the basis that executors charge property with payment of the index-linked nil rate sum. The question arises whether the trustees are chargeable to tax on the indexation element when that amount is paid. The authors of the above book advance the view that there is no tax on the payment of the indexed-linked sum, and the benefit of a debt or charge is not a deeply discounted security for income tax purposes, or a debt on a security for CGT purposes.

However, a drafter unfamiliar with the tax rules could inadvertently create a debt on which interest accrues (liable to income tax if the interest is paid), or a deeply discounted security (liable to income tax on disposal), or a debt on a security (liable to CGT on disposal). Care and an understanding of the tax issues involved are therefore important.

**15.51** For pre-owned assets income tax purposes, HMRC accept that no charge arises in respect of nil rate band discretionary trusts of a debt. The HMRC online guidance on pre-owned assets (www.hmrc.gov.uk/poa/poa_ guidance5.htm#10) states the following:

Land – death scheme involving a loan

'Mr and Mrs S own a house in equal shares as tenants in common. Under the Will of Mr S, assets not exceeding the 'nil-rate band' for inheritance tax pass into a discretionary trust, of which Mrs S is one of the potential beneficiaries. The remainder of his estate passes to Mrs S. Following the death of Mr S in June 2005 his executors transferred his half-share of the property to Mrs S and, in return, she executed a loan agreement equivalent to the value of the half-share. No inheritance tax is payable.

**15.52** *The family home*

The income tax charge under this schedule will not apply here. As Mrs S did not own her husband's share at the relevant time and did not dispose of it the disposal conditions in paragraph 3(2) do not apply. If she did not provide Mr S with any of the consideration given by him for the purchase of his half-share the contribution condition in paragraph 3(3) will not apply either. Even if she had provided him with some or all of the consideration the condition will still not apply as it would have been an excluded transaction under paragraph 10(2)(a). In the final scenario, however, the debt would not be allowable for inheritance tax on the death of Mrs S by virtue of section 103 Finance Act 1986.'

## Warning: 'sham' trusts

**15.52** It is important that the trustees of nil rate band discretionary trusts (and trustees in general) act and properly perform their duties as such. Care should be taken to protect against accusations of a 'sham'.

It is not sufficient just to have a well-drafted trust deed. The trustees must be active rather than passive, and be seen to consider and (if appropriate) exercise their discretions and not just leave the survivor in indefinite, favourable occupation of the property. The trustees should meet regularly (eg twice a year) and carefully minute their decisions (eg whether to take a charge as opposed to a debt, as to the charging of interest, whether repayment of the loan should be requested etc).

If the trustees merely 'sit on their hands' the whole arrangement can be challenged by HMRC, or it may be argued that the widow has an interest in possession in the trust property.

*Chapter 16*

# Pre-owned assets

## INTRODUCTION

**16.1** The *Finance Act 2004* (*s 84* and *Sch 15*) introduced a charge to tax which draws on a combination of income tax and inheritance tax rules.

Ever since the introduction of the gift with reservation (GWR) rules in 1986 (see **Chapter 5**), tax advisers have been devising schemes by which individuals could make gifts of property without being caught by the reservation of benefit rules, while at the same time continuing to enjoy the property given away. The pre-owned assets (POAT) legislation has primarily targeted artificial inheritance tax avoidance schemes, as outlined below, but some more 'innocent' arrangements are also now caught. The schemes (see **5.10**ff for an illustration of the various schemes) initially targeted are as follows:

- Lease carve-out schemes (*Ingram* schemes) following the case *of Ingram (Executors of Lady Ingram's Estate) v IRC* [2000] 1 AC 293.

- Settlements on interest in possession trusts (*Eversden* schemes) following the case of *IRC v Eversden (executors of Greenstock, decd)* [2003] EWCA Civ 668, [2003] STC 822.

- Reversionary lease schemes.

- 'Double trust' or 'Lifetime debt' schemes.

The coalition government is considering introducing a General Anti-avoidance Rule (GAAR). This tends to appeal more to politicians, the public and to general legal practitioners than it does to specialists, because it allows any areas of doubt to be resolved in favour of HMRC. The Institute of Chartered Accountants in Scotland did, however, recognise that a GAAR might help if accompanied by repeal of specific anti-avoidance rules. It would certainly make life easier for rank and file advisers whose clients were not 'sailing close to the wind' and who just wanted to comply with the tax rules. The public recognise that we need tax to fund essential services and are less sympathetic to 'clever' schemes than formerly. When a GAAR was considered in 1999 it foundered in part because of the need for a clearance procedure. The number

**16.2** *Pre-owned assets*

and scope of such procedures has since increased, particularly where IHT reliefs are concerned. Vince Cable MP, writing on the issue recently, included a clearance procedure in his proposals for a GAAR.

A GAAR could facilitate the repeal of POAT. That said, the POAT rules described in this chapter do seem to have worked. The writers know of no recorded cases on the legislation – a fair indicator of the clarity of its drafting. Equally, it is very rare indeed to see entries on personal tax returns relating to the tax, suggesting that:

- people have unscrambled offensive transactions; or
- the values involved are covered by the *de minimis* rules; or
- people do not realise that the transactions that were entered into offend the rules; or more likely
- the transactions entered into did not achieve their tax object and were caught by the gift with reservation rules.

Perhaps it is too early to assess the impact of the POAT rules, which will be seen more clearly when taxpayers die who had in their lifetimes tried to circumvent the GWR rules.

**16.2** The pre-owned asset tax is not a charge to inheritance tax. The regime imposes an income tax charge on the use of capital based on:

- the benefit an individual enjoys from the occupation of land or the possession or use of chattels which they once owned, or which they assisted other persons to acquire; and
- their deemed power to enjoy intangible property in certain settlor-interested settlements.

The pre-owned asset tax can be charged on the use of:

- land;
- chattels; and
- intangible assets.

The legislation provides that certain transactions are excluded (see **16.18** below) and there are a number of exemptions (see **16.19**ff below). It also gives the option to elect out of the pre-owned assets charge arising (as discussed in **16.28**ff below). All references in this chapter are to *FA 2004*, unless otherwise stated.

HMRC, on their website (www.hmrc.gov.uk/poa) provide useful guidance on how the pre-owned asset charge is assessed.

## THE PRE-OWNED ASSETS CHARGE ON LAND

**16.3**   A charge to income tax may arise when an individual:

- occupies any land, whether alone or together with other persons; and
- either the 'disposal condition' or the 'contribution condition' is met in respect of that land (*Sch 15, para 3(1)*).

Unfortunately, the term 'occupation' is not defined within the legislation. HMRC's Technical Guidance provides the following, rather vague, explanation (see: www.hmrc.gov.uk/poa/poa_guidance4.htm#7):

> 'In this context "occupation" is construed quite widely. For example, the chargeable person would be regarded as in occupation not only if they were resident in the relevant property but also if they used it for storage or had sole possession of the means of access and used the property from time to time. The chargeable person would not be regarded as occupying a property from which they receive rental payments from the person(s) actually in occupation.'

Each case is likely to be decided on the facts and the particular circumstances relating to it. However, in line with HMRC's Interpretation of inheritance tax and gifts with reservation (RI 55 (November 1993)) – the list of examples which excludes the pre-owned assets charge on a *de minimis* basis can be found in **5.28**.

**16.4**   Examples of more significant use of the property which may bring the chargeable person within the scope of *Sch 15, para 3* are as follows:

- a house in which the chargeable person stays most weekends or for more than a month each year;
- a second home or holiday home which the chargeable person and the owner both then use on an occasional basis;
- a house with a library in which the chargeable person continues to keep their own books, or which they use on a regular basis, for example because it is necessary for their work.

An exemption from a pre-owned assets charge may apply if the property in question is treated for inheritance tax purposes as being subject to the gift with reservation rules (see **16.21**).

**16.5**   In addition to the 'occupation' condition, the 'disposal condition' or the 'contribution condition' has to be satisfied for the pre-owned asset charge to apply.

The 'disposal condition' (in *para 3(2)*) in relation to any land is that:

**16.6** *Pre-owned assets*

- at any time after 17 March 1986 the individual owned an interest in the relevant land; or
- in other property, the proceeds of the disposal of which were (directly or indirectly) applied by another person towards the acquisition of an interest in the relevant land; and
- the individual has disposed of all, or part of, his interest in the relevant land or the other property, otherwise than by an excluded transaction (see **16.18** below).

**16.6** The 'contribution condition' (in *para 3(3)*) in relation to any land is that:

- at any time after 17 March 1986 the individual has directly or indirectly provided, otherwise than by an excluded transaction, any of the consideration given by another person for the acquisition of:
  - an interest in the relevant land; or
  - an interest in any other property the proceeds of the disposal of which were (directly or indirectly) applied by another person towards the acquisition of an interest in the relevant land.

HMRC confirm in the above guidance (www.hmrc.gov.uk/poa/poa_guidance1.htm#121) that the contribution condition is not met where a lender resides in property purchased by another with money loaned to him by the lender (even if the loan was interest free), as the outstanding debt remains part of the lender's estate for IHT.

Whether the pre-owned asset charge applies can best be illustrated by a number of examples. Some of the examples below, while prima facie being caught by the charge, may escape a charge to income tax due to one of the exemptions listed at **16.19**ff below.

---

**Example 16.1—Father moves in with donee son**

Mr Jones gives one of his three properties to his son. After later having been widowed, Mr Jones moves in to live with his son. While the disposal condition is met, Mr Jones is likely to escape a charge to income tax as (by virtue of *para 11(5)(a)*) the property will be subject to a gift of reservation for inheritance tax purposes. For exemptions, see **16.19**ff.

---

**Example 16.2—Sale followed by occupation**

Mrs Smith required funds to renovate her property. She considered a number of commercial options but then decided to sell 50% of the property to her son for £100,000. The market value of the 50% share is £300,000. Mrs Smith continues to live in the house.

Again, the disposal condition is met and Mrs Smith may face an income tax charge as she will have reserved a benefit in two-thirds of the half share which is likely to escape a charge to income tax as this share will be subject to the gift with reservation rules.

### Example 16.3—Link with property broken

Mrs Williams owned a number of investments which she gave to her daughter, who subsequently sold them and used the proceeds to extend her existing house, adding a 'granny flat' in which Mrs Williams now lives.

Neither the disposal condition nor the contribution condition is satisfied, because the proceeds of the sale of the shares were applied by the daughter in improving her existing property and not in acquiring an interest in land.

### Example 16.4—Funding of residence

In 2005, Mr Smith gave his son £300,000, and in 2010 he used this money to buy a house where Mr Smith now lives with him.

The contribution condition is met and Mr Smith may face a tax charge.

### Example 16.5—Change of circumstances

Mr White decided to move to Spain and after he sold his property in England, he gave his daughter £200,000, and she used this money to purchase a property. Mr White now finds that the heat in Spain in summer is too much for his health and he therefore stays with his daughter for three months of each year.

The contribution condition is met during each period of occupation and it will be a question of fact whether he will be seen to be in occupation during the remaining nine months. If, for example, he has a room set aside for him for the rest of the year, he will be seen as in occupation for the whole year and Mr White's occupation may be subject to income tax.

# THE PRE-OWNED ASSETS CHARGE ON CHATTELS

**16.7** The pre-owned assets charge on chattels (*Sch 15, para* 6) is similar to that on land. Therefore, a charge to income tax may arise on an individual where:

**16.8** *Pre-owned assets*

- the individual is in 'possession' of, or has the 'use' of, a chattel, whether alone or together with other persons; and
- either the 'disposal condition' or the 'contribution condition' is met in respect of the chattel.

**16.8** The terms 'possession' and 'use' are not defined in *FA 2004* and HMRC's Technical Guidance is vague (www.hmrc.gov.uk/poa/poa_guidance4.htm#5):

'Similar considerations apply to the possession or use of previously owned chattels when the application of paragraph 6 is contemplated. Very limited or occasional use of the chattel in question will not incur an income tax charge under this schedule.'

'For example, a car used to give occasional lifts (ie less than three times a month) to the chargeable person will not be liable to the charge. But if the chargeable person is taken to work every day in the car it is likely an income tax charge will be incurred.'

**16.9** The expression 'chattel' is defined for the purpose of *Sch 15* (at *para 1*) and includes any tangible movable property other than money.

The 'disposal condition' (in *para 6(2)*) in relation to any chattels is that:

- at any time after 17 March 1986 the individual owned the chattel; or
- any other property, the proceeds of the disposal of which were (directly or indirectly) applied by another person towards the acquisition of the chattel; and
- the individual has disposed of all, or part of, the chattel or the other property, otherwise than by an excluded transaction (see **16.18** below).

**16.10** The 'contribution condition' (in *para 6(3)*) in relation to any chattel is that at any time after 17 March 1986 the individual has directly or indirectly provided, otherwise than by an excluded transaction, any of the consideration given by another person for the acquisition of:

– the chattel; or
– an interest in any other property the proceeds of the disposal of which were (directly or indirectly) applied by another person towards the acquisition of the chattel.

**16.11** Some of the examples below, while prima facie being caught by the charge, may escape a charge to income tax due to one of the exemptions listed at **16.19**ff below.

### Example 16.6—Retained painting

Mr Smith gives a valuable painting to his daughter, but he keeps the painting hanging on display in his own house for safekeeping and to meet insurance requirements.

The disposal condition is met, but (by virtue of *para 11(5)(a)*) Mr Smith is likely to escape an income tax charge, as the gift is subject to the gift with reservation rules.

### Example 16.7—Costly storage arrangements

Mrs Jones gifted a flat to her son. He sold it in 2005 for £500,000. He purchased another flat for £350,000 and with the remaining £150,000 he purchased several pieces of art. The son is now working abroad and let his flat. All his possessions are in storage apart from the valuable paintings, which are temporarily displayed in his mother's house. As the mother is 'enjoying' the chattels, she may now face an income tax charge.

### Example 16.8—Shared campervan

Mr Williams gave his daughter cash of £100,000, which, in 2004, she used towards the purchase price of a £50,000 motor home. Mr Williams borrows the motor home for long holidays.

The contribution condition is met during each period of its use and Mr Williams may face a tax charge.

## PRE-OWNED ASSETS CHARGE ON INTANGIBLE PROPERTY COMPRISED IN SETTLOR-INTERESTED SETTLEMENTS

**16.12** The pre-owned assets charge on intangible property (*Sch 15, para* 8) is drafted in different terms from the charges on land and chattels.

The charge arises, when all the following elements exist:

- a person has settled any property (not necessarily intangible property); and
- the terms of the settlement, as they affect any property comprised in the settlement, are such that any income arising from the property would be treated by virtue of *ITTOIA 2005, s 624* as settlor-interested; and

**16.13**  *Pre-owned assets*

- such income would be so treated even if *ITTOIA 2005, s 625(1)* ('Settlor's retained interest') did not include any reference to the spouse/civil partner of the settlor; and
- that property includes any intangible property which is or represents property which the chargeable person settled, or added to the settlement, after 17 March 1986.

For the pre-owned assets charge on intangible property to apply, it is only necessary that the above elements exist. There is no need for the individual to benefit from the intangible property in question, and no need for that intangible property to produce any actual income.

A charge under *para 8* is not triggered where *ITTOIA 2005, s 624* only applies because the settlor's spouse rather than the settlor has retained an interest within *s 625*. However if, for example, the settlor sets up a trust where his wife receives the income but he can benefit if she dies, an income tax charge may potentially apply subject to any relevant exemptions.

The expression 'intangible property' is defined for the purposes of *Sch 15* (at *para 1*) as meaning any property other than chattels or interests in land. Therefore most investments are caught, and it also includes money. The pre-owned assets charge on intangible property does not apply to any land or chattels included in a settlement.

None of the 'excluded transactions' provisions (see **16.18**) apply in relation to intangible property, but all of the exemptions (see **16.19**ff) potentially apply.

## SCOPE OF THE PRE-OWNED ASSETS LEGISLATION

**16.13** The pre-owned assets legislation is drafted in much wider terms than the gift with reservation (GWR) rules (see **Chapter 5**). For example, for inheritance tax purposes, an absolute gift of cash is not subject to the GWR rules. In contrast, for pre-owned assets purposes, tracing through cash is permissible when determining whether proceeds on disposal have been applied or consideration has been provided in respect of land or chattels, for a period of up to seven years *(Sch 15, para 10(2)(c))*.

The use of the expression 'directly or indirectly' in the contribution condition extends the scope of this provision to cover circumstances where an individual routes a gift indirectly through a third party. However, it is considered that a contribution can only be traced through a third party where that party is obliged, or expected to pass this gift on.

### Example 16.9—No trace of the money

A grandfather gifts £300,000 to each of his two sons. One of the sons is well off and decides to pass his share to his daughter, who subsequently buys a property with these funds. The grandfather, who in the interim was widowed, moves into the property with his granddaughter.

Although the gift of £300,000 was used in purchasing the property, the grandfather is likely to escape a charge to income tax. However, if there was an agreement or understanding between the grandfather and his son, that he would pass the gift of money on to his daughter, the contribution condition is likely to be met and the grandfather may face a charge to tax.

## CALCULATION OF TAX CHARGE IN RELATION TO LAND

**16.14** In relation to land, income tax will be charged on the 'rental value' less the amount of certain allowable payments made by the taxpayer in respect of their occupation of the relevant land. The 'appropriate rental value' is based on a hypothetical letting from year to year where the tenant undertakes to pay all taxes, rates and charges usually paid by a tenant, and the landlord undertakes to pay for repairs, insurance and any other necessary maintenance. Where the taxpayer occupies the property for less than a year, the rental value is applied pro rata and the income tax charge is adjusted accordingly.

HMRC's Technical Guidance does not indicate whether (and, if so, how) the appropriate rental value may be reduced to reflect any limitations or restrictions on the taxpayer's occupation of the land. For example, where the relevant land is a holiday home that is available for occupation by the taxpayer and by other persons and occasional use is made of it by the taxpayer and by others, it is unclear what adjustments can be made to the appropriate rental value to reflect any periods of non-use or shared use by the taxpayer.

The 'appropriate rental value' is defined as such proportion of the rental value (R) as is found by the following formula (*Sch 15, para 4*):

$$R \times \frac{DV}{V}$$

R is the rental value of the relevant land for the taxable period;

V is the value of the relevant land at the valuation date; and

DV can assume a variety of different values, as follows:

**16.15**  *Pre-owned assets*

- where the disposal condition is met and the taxpayer owned an interest in the relevant land, DV is the value at the valuation date of the interest in the relevant land disposed of by the taxpayer; or
- where the disposal condition is met and the taxpayer owned an interest in replaced property, DV is such part of the value of the relevant land at the valuation date as can reasonably be attributed to the property originally disposed of by the taxpayer;
- where the contribution condition is met, DV is such part of the value of the relevant land at the valuation date as can reasonably be attributed to the consideration provided by the taxpayer.

In calculating the chargeable amount, certain payments made in respect of the occupation of the land may be deducted. These are payments which, in pursuance of any legal obligation, are made by the taxpayer to the owner of the land in respect of the occupation by the chargeable person.

**Example 16.10—Moving in with daughter**

Mr Jones gives his daughter £500,000 to purchase a property. He subsequently moves in and now lives there with his daughter. He has use of the whole house. He pays his daughter £50 per week to cover expenses. The contribution condition has been met and (subject to any exclusions or exemptions, which are discussed below) the question now arises how to assess the 'appropriate rental value'. The value of the house is £600,000. The rental value is £18,000. The payments made by Mr Jones do not qualify for deduction as they are not made in relation to rental payments and also are not made under a legal obligation.

If Mr Jones had paid the £50 each week as rental payments following a legal obligation, they would be deductible from the rental value.

Mr Jones will pay income tax on £18,000 at his marginal tax rate. Therefore, if he is a 40% taxpayer, the pre-owned asset charge will cost him £7,200 per annum.

In contrast, if the house had included a self-contained annexe and he only occasionally visited the main house, eg for Sunday lunch, the income tax charge would have been assessed on the 'appropriate rental value' of the annexe rather than the whole house.

# CALCULATION OF TAX CHARGE IN RELATION TO CHATTELS

**16.15**   In relation to chattels, income tax will be charged on the 'appropriate amount' less the amount of certain allowable payments made by the taxpayer in respect of his possession or use of the chattel.

## Pre-owned assets  16.15

In contrast to the pre-owned assets charge on land, which is based on rental value, the charge on a chattel is based on the notional amount of interest that would be payable for the taxable period if interest were payable at the 'prescribed rate' on an amount equal to the value of the chattel at the valuation date. Therefore, the fact that the donor is paying a market rent for the use of the chattel, does not necessarily prevent a charge to income tax.

The 'prescribed rate' of interest is set by regulations and is equal to 'the official rate of interest' as defined for the purposes of taxable benefits on taxable cheap loans (see the *Charge to Income Tax by Reference to Enjoyment of Property Previously Owned Regulations (SI 2005/724), reg 3*). The official rate of interest is defined by *ITEPA 2003, s 181*. On 1 March 2009 it decreased from 6.25% to 4.75%, and it decreased again to 4% from 6 April 2010.

The 'appropriate amount' is found by multiplying the prescribed interest (N) for the taxable period by the fraction as follows (*Sch 15, para 7*):

$$N \times \frac{DV}{V}$$

N is the notional interest for the taxable period, at the prescribed rate, on the value of the chattel at the valuation date;

V is the value of the chattel at the valuation date; and

DV can assume a variety of different values, as follows:

- where the disposal condition is met and the taxpayer owned an interest in the chattel, DV is the value at the valuation date of the interest in the chattel disposed of by the taxpayer; or
- where the disposal condition is met and the taxpayer owned an interest in replaced property, DV is such part of the value of the chattel at the valuation date as can reasonably be attributed to the property originally disposed of by the taxpayer;
- where the contribution condition is met, DV is such part of the value of the chattel at the valuation date as can reasonably be attributed to the consideration provided by the taxpayer.

In calculating the chargeable amount, certain payments made in respect of the possession or use of the chattel may be deducted. These are payments which, in pursuance of any legal obligation, are made by the taxpayer to the owner of the chattel in respect of the possession or use of the chattel by the chargeable person (*Sch 15, para 7(1)*).

**16.16** *Pre-owned assets*

**Example 16.11—Gift and leaseback**

Patrick disposed of a painting to his daughter, but he keeps it hanging on display in his own house for safekeeping and to meet insurance requirements. Following a legal agreement with his daughter, he pays her 2% of the value of the painting in respect of its enjoyment; this price is based on an arm's-length valuation, and is designed to avoid a gift with reservation for inheritance tax. The father also pays the insurance premium based on 1% of the value. The painting is valued at £1 million.

As the prescribed rate of interest is 4%, Patrick will be caught by the pre-owned asset charge, subject to any exclusions or exemptions from charge, which are considered below. The payment of 2% of the value of the painting to his daughter is deductible, however the insurance premium does not qualify as a deduction, as it is not paid under a legal obligation.

The taxable amount is £40,000 (4% of £1 million) less £20,000 paid by the father for his enjoyment of the painting, leaving a net taxable amount of £20,000.

*Note*: this example is based on an example published in HMRC Guidance Notes at Section 2 (www.hmrc.gov.uk/poa/poa_guidance2.htm#21). One would expect the full consideration exemption (see **16.23**) to apply, but the Guidance Note states:

> 'Note that the charge is computed differently from land and while any rental payments made by the owner will reduce the amount on which he is chargeable, the fact that he pays a market rent for their use, does not prevent an income tax charge arising.'

# CALCULATION OF TAX CHARGE IN RELATION TO INTANGIBLE PROPERTY

**16.16** In relation to intangible property, the 'chargeable amount' is broadly as follows (*Sch 15, para 9*):

N minus T

N    Is the 'prescribed interest'
T    Is the 'tax allowance'

The 'prescribed interest' is the amount of interest that would be payable for the taxable period if interest were payable at the prescribed rate on an amount equal to the value of the relevant property at the valuation date. The 'prescribed rate' is set by regulations and is equal to 'the official rate of interest' as defined

*Pre-owned assets* **16.17**

for the purposes of taxable benefits on taxable cheap loans, and was reduced from 4.75% to 4% with effect from 6 April 2010.

The 'tax allowance' is the amount of any income tax or capital gains tax payable by the taxpayer in respect of the taxable period by virtue of any of a number of specified provisions, so far as the tax is attributable to the relevant property. The provisions in question are *ITTOIA 2005, ss 461, 624, ITA 2007, ss 720–730,* and *TCGA 1992, ss 77* (although this section was repealed from 2008/09), *86.*

In contrast to the computation of the pre-owned assets charges relating to land and chattels, there is no provision for the deduction of any allowable payments made by the taxpayer in respect of his enjoyment or potential enjoyment of the intangible property.

**Example 16.12—Pre-owned assets charge on intangibles**

(The following example is contained in HMRC's guidance notes at: www.hmrc.gov.uk/poa/poa_guidance2.htm)

Mr A is the UK resident and domiciled settlor of a non-resident settlor-interested settlement. (You should assume that Mr A has not reserved a benefit in the settled property. Nor does he have an interest in possession in the trust and he is therefore subject to the pre-owned asset charge).

The settlement comprises 'intangible' property of cash and shares with a value of £1.5 million at the valuation date. In the tax year 2005/06 the trustees receive income of £60,000 which is chargeable to income tax on Mr A under *ITTOIA 2005, s 624*. A further £150,000 capital gains are realised which are deemed to be Mr A's gains by virtue of *TCGA 1992, s 86*.

In these circumstances £24,000 income tax is payable on the £60,000 and £60,000 in CGT on the gain of £150,000. The tax allowance (T) against the potential *Sch 15* charge is therefore £84,000. The chargeable amount (N) under *Sch 15* is 5% (the prescribed rate in 2005/06) of £1,500,000 = £75,000. Since the tax allowance is greater than the chargeable amount, a charge under *Sch 15* will not arise.

# VALUATION PROBLEMS

**16.17** For the purposes of the pre-owned asset charge, the value of any property is broadly the price which the property might reasonably be expected to fetch if sold in the open market at that time (*Sch 15, para 15*); this reflects the 'market value' provision for inheritance tax purposes (*IHTA 1984, s 160*).

**16.18** *Pre-owned assets*

In relation to any land, chattel or intangible property, the 'valuation date' is prescribed by regulations (*Charge to Income Tax by Reference to Enjoyment of Property Previously Owned Regulations, SI 2005/724*) and is 6 April in the relevant year of assessment or, if later, the first day of the 'taxable period'. The regulations dispense with annual valuations but instead require a new valuation on the 'five-year anniversary' of the previous valuation.

A new valuation may be required when the value of the retained benefit is reduced, for example, because the taxpayer moved into a smaller property.

The fifth anniversary of the implementation of POAT charge passed on 6 April 2010, therefore taxpayers who have been subject to POAT will need to obtain relevant capital or rental values as of 6 April 2010. If any adjustments to the payment of income tax need to be made, the deadline will be 31 January 2012.

# EXCLUDED TRANSACTIONS

**16.18** The concept of excluded transactions has no application to intangible property. The provisions only serve to exclude certain transactions in relation to land and chattels from the income tax charge.

*Schedule 15, para 10* includes different provisions for the 'disposal' condition and 'contribution' condition in relation to interest in possession trusts for the spouse/civil partner, as outlined below:

- Disposals of entire interests to unconnected third parties at arm's length are excluded transactions.
- Disposals of entire interests to connected parties at arm's length are excluded transactions, if the transaction is such as might be expected at arm's length between unconnected parties.
- An inter-spouse/civil partner disposal remains an excluded transaction in relation to the original donor, even if it is followed by an onward disposal to a third party.
- A disposal by virtue of which the property became settled property in which his spouse/civil partner or former spouse/civil partner is beneficially entitled to an interest in possession, and that interest in possession has not come to an end *except* on the death of the spouse/civil partner or former spouse/civil partner. In relation to the disposal condition, it is stipulated that the disposal has to be a gift, while under the contribution condition it is only required that the property become settled on acquisition.
- A disposition falling within the inheritance tax exemption available in respect of dispositions for the maintenance of family members (*IHTA 1984, s 11*).

- The provision by a person of consideration for another's acquisition of land or chattels is an excluded transaction if it constituted an outright gift of money by the individual to the other person and was made at least seven years before the earliest date on which either the individual occupies the land or, in the case of chattels, the individual is in possession of, or has the use of the chattel.

- It is an outright gift to an individual and is wholly exempt by virtue of either the inheritance tax annual exemption (*s 19*) or the inheritance tax small gifts exemption (*s 20*).

Note that there is no exclusion from the pre-owned assets regime for gifts that are exempt from inheritance tax under the provisions relating to normal expenditure gifts out of income, or gifts in consideration of marriage.

**Example 16.13—Daughter moves in**

In 2008, Mr Miller sold his daughter a 50% share in his property at market value, and she moved in permanently to live with him. They share the running costs equally. Subject to possible exemptions which will be considered later, the disposal condition is met. However, as Mr Miller only sold a 50% interest in his property, it is not an excluded transaction.

If he had sold all his interest, the transaction would have been excluded from the pre-owned asset charge. However, see below the full consideration exemption in **16.23** and reference to the gift with reservation exemption following *Finance Act 1986, s 102B(4)* (see **16.22**).

As to the equity release exemption and its limitations, see **16.24**.

**Example 16.14—Mother moves in later**

In 1995, Mrs Smith gave her daughter £500,000, which the daughter uses to purchase a property. In 2005, the mother moves into the property.

As Mrs Smith's commencement of her occupation occurred more than seven years after the gift was made, this will be an excluded transaction.

# EXEMPTIONS

**16.19** There are a number of exemptions (in *Sch 15, paras 11, 12* and *13*) from the pre-owned assets charge otherwise arising on land, chattels or intangible property:

**16.20** *Pre-owned assets*

- exemption for property that is in the taxpayer's estate for inheritance tax purposes;
- exemption for property that is deemed to be in the taxpayer's estate under the gift with reservation of benefit (GWR) provisions;
- property that escapes the GWR provisions by virtue of certain specified inheritance tax exemptions or reliefs;
- property covered by certain equity release arrangements defined in regulations; and
- certain *de minimis* amounts.

## Exemption for property in the taxpayer's estate

**16.20** There is no pre-owned assets charge on land, chattels or intangible property where the taxpayer's estate for inheritance tax purposes includes the following (*Sch 15, para 11(1)*):

- the relevant property; or
- other property which derives its value from the relevant property and whose value, so far as attributable to the relevant property, is not substantially less than the relevant property.

This exemption recognises that the pre-owned assets charge should not penalise taxpayers in respect of their enjoyment of property that is still included in their estate for inheritance tax purposes.

## Exemption where the gift with reservation rules apply

**16.21** There is no pre-owned assets charge on land, chattels or intangible property where the 'gift with reservation' (GWR) provisions apply for IHT (see *Sch 15, para 11(5)*), or would apply but for certain specified provisions, to:

- the relevant property; or
- other property which derives its value from the relevant property and whose value, so far as attributable to the relevant property, is not substantially less than the relevant property.

This exemption for property that falls within the GWR provisions is fundamental to the concept of the pre-owned assets charge, and recognises that the charge should not penalise taxpayers in respect of their enjoyment of property that is still deemed to be included in their estate under the GWR provisions, or would be deemed to be so included but for certain specific inheritance tax exemptions.

*Pre-owned assets* **16.22**

**16.22** See **Chapter 5** for discussion on when property is subject to the GWR rules. The GWR exemption from the pre-owned assets charge extends to property subject to the GWR rules, and property that would have been subject to the GWR rules but for certain specified provisions contained in *Sch 15, para 11(5)*:

- Any of the exemptions in *FA 1986, s 102(5)(d)–(i)*, which cover certain cases where disposal by way of gift is an exempt transfer for inheritance tax purposes. This includes gifts to charities, gifts to political parties, gifts to housing associations, gifts for national purposes, maintenance funds for historic buildings and employee trusts (see **Chapter 9**).

- *FA 1986, s 102B(4)*, which deals with gifts with reservation (share of interest in land). This relief from inheritance tax was introduced with effect from 9 March 1999; it applies where an individual disposes by way of gift of an undivided share of an interest in land, which is then occupied by donor and donee without the donor receiving any benefit, other than a negligible one, provided by or at the expense of the donee for some reason connected with the gift.

- *FA 1986, s 102C(3)* provides that in applying *FA 1986, ss 102A* and *102B*, no account is to be taken of a donor's occupation of land in circumstances where that occupation would be disregarded in accordance with *FA 1986, Sch 20, para 6(1)(b)*. It allows occupation by the donor to be disregarded where:

    – it arises from an unforeseen change in circumstances; and

    – it arises when the donor has become unable to maintain himself through old age, infirmity or otherwise; and

    – it represents reasonable provision by the donee for the care and maintenance of the donor; and

    – the donee is a relative of the donor or his spouse/civil partner.

**Example 16.15—Illness intervening (see Example 16.1)**

Mr Jones gives his son £300,000 to purchase a property. After having been widowed, Mr Jones moves in to live with his son. The contribution condition is met and Mr Jones may face a charge to income tax.

Assuming Mr Jones moves in because he became unable to maintain himself through age or infirmity and the occupation represents reasonable provision by his son for his father's care and maintenance, Mr Jones will escape a charge to income tax, as well as an inheritance tax charge under the GWR rules. This is provided by *Sch 15, para 11(5)(d)* and *FA 1986, s 102C(3)*.

**16.23** *Pre-owned assets*

## Full consideration exemption

**16.23** It follows from the interpretation of *Sch 15, para 11(5)(d)* that the pre-owned assets rules import the 'full consideration' exemption from the GWR rules. This applies for inheritance tax in certain circumstances where the property in question would be subject to the GWR rules but for the payment of full consideration in money or money's worth for the actual occupation of land or enjoyment of an incorporeal right over land, or for the actual possession of chattels.

HMRC's Technical Guidance (www.hmrc.gov.uk/poa/poa_guidance4.htm#5) states:

> 'If the chargeable person's occupation of the relevant land, or enjoyment of the relevant chattel, is for full consideration in money or money's worth, ie a full market rent is paid by them for their continued occupation/enjoyment, their occupation/enjoyment is not a reservation of benefit for inheritance tax purposes *(para 6(1)(a) Sch 20 Finance Act 1986)*. This treatment is extended to the income tax charge under this schedule by virtue of *paragraph 11(5)(d)*. Any arrangement or transaction entered into on or after 18 March 1986 where the chargeable person pays full consideration for their enjoyment or occupation of the relevant asset will not be subject to the income tax charge.'

This guidance seems to be at odds with the example given in the same Notes (under section 2.2; see **Example 16.11**).

HMRC's Technical Guidance continues:

> 'If the consideration paid by the chargeable person is less than full consideration, or if they initially pay a full consideration but, over time, this falls below market rates, the asset in question will be treated as subject to a reservation of benefit from the date the chargeable person ceased to pay full consideration. There will be no income tax charge under this schedule provided that the provisions of paragraph 11(5)(a) apply.'

Care therefore needs to be taken to ensure that the amount of consideration paid by the chargeable person is reviewed on a regular basis.

---

**Example 16.16—Gift and full rent**

Jane gifted one of her properties to her son. She subsequently moves in, but she pays her son a full market rent in respect of her occupation.

The disposal condition is met, but Jane will be exempt from a pre-owned assets charge because she pays full consideration for the occupation of the property.

## Equity release exemption

**16.24** Following concerns whether equity release schemes were affected by the pre-owned asset charge, the Treasury used its power to confer further exemptions by regulations (*Charge to Income Tax by Reference to Enjoyment of Property Previously Owned Regulations (SI 2005/724)*).

Under this exemption, the pre-owned assets charging provisions on land and chattels do not apply to a person in relation to a disposal of *part* of an interest in any property if:

- the disposal was by a transaction made at arm's length with a person not connected with him; or

- the disposal was by a transaction such as might be expected to be made at arm's length between persons not connected with each other and the disposal was for a consideration not in money or in the form of readily convertible assets; or

- the disposal was made before 7 March 2005 (*SI 2005/724, reg 5*).

Note that this exemption applies to transactions between unconnected persons. It also applies to any disposals on arm's-length terms before 7 March 2005, or disposals from that date in the limited circumstances described above. Sadly, despite representations, the treatment for unconnected parties is not extended to similar transactions within the family, even if on full commercial terms.

## *De minimis* exemption

**16.25** An individual will not be chargeable to pre-owned assets in a year of assessment if the aggregate of the amounts specified below in respect of that year do not exceed £5,000 (*Sch 15, para 13*). Those amounts are:

- the appropriate rental value in relation to land (see **16.14** above);
- the appropriate amount in relation to chattels (see **16.15** above); and
- the chargeable amount in relation to intangible assets (see **16.16** above).

Note that the amounts to be included in respect of land and chattels are not the chargeable amounts; instead, they are the sums arrived at before deducting any eligible payments made in respect of occupation, possession or use. A person therefore cannot avoid the tax charge by paying an annual rent to bring himself below the £5,000 limit.

**16.26** The *de minimis* exemption is available to each individual, and therefore applies independently to husband and wife. When the pre-owned

**16.27** *Pre-owned assets*

assets provisions were introduced, the then Paymaster General, Dawn Primarolo, explained the effect of the exemption as follows:

> 'With regard to the £5,000 ... I would call it a cliff edge effect: essentially, if the value is £5,001, taxation would be paid on the whole £5,001, not just on the £1 excess.'

**Example 16.17—Over the limit**

Alice gave her daughter £500,000, which she used towards the purchase of a property and towards the purchase of a painting that is displayed in her property. Alice now lives in the property with her daughter, and pays her £50 per week as rent under a legal agreement. The contribution condition applies in respect of the relevant land and the chattel. The appropriate rental value of the land amounts to £5,000, and the appropriate amount in respect of the painting amounts to £1,000.

The aggregate of the amounts is £6,000 which exceeds the *de minimis* exemption of £5,000, therefore Alice must pay the pre-owned assets tax charge. The fact that she pays an annual rent of £2,600 will not help her to bring herself within the *de minimis* exception.

## RESIDENCE AND/OR DOMICILE OF TAXPAYER

**16.27** The pre-owned asset charge does not apply in relation to any person for any year of assessment during which he or she is not resident in the UK for the purposes of income tax (*Sch 15, para 12*).

Where a person is resident, but not domiciled, in the UK the pre-owned asset charge does not apply to him unless the land, chattel or intangible property in respect of which the charge arises is situated in the UK.

The deemed domicile rules of *s 267* (see **Chapter 1**) have seemingly been imported for the purposes of the income tax charge on pre-owned assets. Whilst not specifically stated in the legislation, a person is regarded as domiciled in the UK if he or she would be treated as such under *IHTA 1984*.

## 'OPTING OUT' OF THE PRE-OWNED ASSETS CHARGE

**16.28** An individual taxpayer facing the pre-owned asset charge has a right to elect that *Sch 15* shall not apply to him during the 'initial year' and subsequent years of assessment by reference to that property or any other property for which it has been substituted (*Sch 15, paras 21–23*).

The opt-out election treats the property as though it were subject to a reservation under the gift with reservation rules, even though there had been no gift. The opt-out provisions dispense with the requirement for there to have been a gift; an election simply invokes the GWR rules as though there had been a gift.

An election to opt out of the pre-owned assets charge in respect of land, chattels, or intangible property, must be made in the prescribed manner. HMRC's Technical Guidance (www.hmrc.gov.uk/poa/poa_guidance3.htm#32) states that the election must be made on form IHT500. The relevant filing date for the 'opt-out' is 31 January in the year of assessment immediately following the 'initial year' when the pre-owned asset charge arises. The *Finance Act 2007* relaxed this deadline, so that from 21 March 2007 elections can be accepted at HMRC's discretion that would otherwise be late (*Sch 15, para 23(3)*, as amended).

HMRC will accept a late election in certain circumstances. Examples of what they may accept as 'reasonable' excuses are:

- the election is lost or delayed in the post;
- loss of the chargeable person's financial records or relevant papers;
- serious illness;
- bereavement.

**16.29** The pre-owned assets legislation, as originally enacted, created a possibility that, where a valid opt-out election is made and the taxpayer dies within the next seven years, there might be two inheritance tax charges on the same underlying asset value. The government recognised this as a particular risk for taxpayers using 'double trust' schemes, and the regulations introduced a new relief from inheritance tax in such circumstances. The relief ensures that tax is due on only one of these components, whichever gives the larger tax liability (the *Inheritance Tax (Double Charges) Regulations 2005 (SI 2005/3441)*: see HMRC's Technical Guidance at www.hmrc.gov.uk/poa/poa_guidance4.htm#9).

Whether or not to opt out of the pre-owned assets regime in respect of particular property will depend upon the facts in each case, in particular the financial position and life expectancy of the taxpayer. If the taxpayer is elderly with a relatively low life expectancy, he may decide to pay the pre-owned assets charge rather than elect for a full 40% inheritance tax charge on death.

# REMEDIAL ACTION IN RELATION TO EXISTING ARRANGEMENTS

**16.30** It is unlikely that clients will enter into new arrangements that fall foul of the POAT rules. Any who were caught by those rules in relation to existing

**16.30** *Pre-owned assets*

structures should long since have taken advice and, if appropriate, remedial action to avoid payment of the pre-owned asset charge. The available options depend on the clients' circumstances and the type of scheme they entered into, but in essence they are as follows:

- Pay the pre-owned asset charge. This will depend upon a number of factors including the age and life expectancy of the chargeable person and any potential inheritance tax, capital gains tax and income tax charges which may become payable when opting for one of the alternatives.

- Pay rent in respect of the occupation of the land or the use of the chattel. As such rent payments have to be paid out of taxed income and are likely also to be taxed in the hands of the recipient, this option may not be very attractive.

- Opt into the gift of reservation legislation, which will make the previous arrangement ineffective for IHT planning, while at the same time, the property will continue to be subject to capital gains tax in the hands of the donee, as there will no uplift in the value of the asset on the donor's death.

- Unwind the arrangements and pass the property or chattel back to the donor. The taxation consequences (including IHT, CGT and in some cases stamp duty land tax) may be prohibitive and each case requires careful consideration. As the donee (whether this may be an individual or in many cases trustees) has to consent to the 'unravelling', this alternative may not be feasible.

- End the benefit, ie cease occupation of the property in question or enjoyment of the chattel. Especially in relation to property this often is not practical as the donor may not have sufficient funds to purchase alternative accommodation.

One feature that may work in favour of the taxpayer is stability in the value of property, both in terms of capital and rental value. Many schemes relating to the family home that were later caught by the POAT were sold to families of moderate wealth. The schemes were often short-term in nature, being entered into by elderly home owners, so might run their course before the quinquennial review of the value of occupation. The review was mentioned at **16.17** and is required by the *Charge to Income Tax by Reference to Enjoyment of Property Previously Owned Regulations 2005, SI 2005/724, para 4*. Often the value of occupation initially fell below £10,000 and was therefore potentially covered by the *de minimis* charge, if there were two estate owners. With the recent fall in property prices many may find that they are still within the exemption.

**Example 16.18—Property subject to the 'Ingram' scheme**

Mr Moore entered into an *Ingram* scheme in January 1999. The value of the property was £500,000. Mr Moore retained the leasehold, valued at £200,000

*Pre-owned assets* **16.30**

in January 1999 and the freehold (valued at £275,000) was passed into an accumulation and maintenance trust for the benefit of his grandchildren.

House prices increased in the interim and, on 6 April 2005, the value of the freehold interest subject to the lease was £450,000; the leasehold interest also was valued at £450,000. The market value of the freehold interest in possession (ie assuming that it is not subject to the lease carve-out) is £1 million.

The market rent is £500 per week (£26,000 per annum).

Following the introduction of the pre-owned assets regime, Mr Moore had a number of options. Mr Moore's financial and personal circumstances had to be considered carefully. For example, if his life expectancy is low, it may be preferable to pay the pre-owned asset charge rather than choosing one of the alternatives. His options were as follows:

1. *Pay the income tax charge*

As Mr Moore retained the leasehold the appropriate rental value is calculated as follows:

$$\text{Market rent} \times \frac{\text{Value of freehold as of 6 April 2005}}{\text{Value of freehold (without lease)}}$$

$$£26,000 \times \frac{£450,000}{£1,000,000} = £11,700$$

As Mr Moore is a 40% taxpayer, he will suffer an annual income tax charge of £4,680.

The leasehold will remain in Mr Moore's estate for IHT and on his death his estate will face an IHT charge of £180,000 (£450,000 @ 40%), assuming that his nil rate band has been used elsewhere.

If the trustees, after Mr Moore's death, decide to sell the property, they will incur a substantial charge to CGT, as the base cost is only £275,000 and the freehold over time will increase in value with the diminishing term of the lease.

2. *Pay a market rent to the trustees of the A&M settlement*

The payment of the market rent has to be made subject to a legal obligation and will cost Mr Moore £26,000 per annum. At that level, from 6 April 2010 the trustees of the A&M settlement will have to pay tax of £13,000 (£26,000 @ 50%) (for earlier tax years, the tax charge would be at 40%, ie £10,400).

**16.30** *Pre-owned assets*

Alternatively, the rent could be paid to the trustees following a deed of covenant which would avoid a charge to income tax payable by the trustees under *ITTOIA 2005, s 727*.

The IHT and CGT considerations outlined in option 1 will also have to be considered.

This option has to be considered carefully, as Mr Moore may not have sufficient funds to continue paying rent until his death or until he moves out of the property.

3.  *Elect for the property to be charged to IHT*

Mr Moore could opt into the reservation of benefit rules and elect to have the property charged to IHT as an asset of his estate. Assuming that the nil rate band has been exhausted, an IHT charge of £400,000 (£1,000,000 @ 40%) will arise on his death.

In addition to the IHT charge, the trustees of the A&M settlement will suffer a charge to CGT if they decide to sell the property after Mr Moore's death (see option 1 above).

Mr Moore is outside the time limit for an election. In practice, HMRC have discretion (from 21 March 2007) to consider any election that should have been made (by 31 January 2007) to see whether there may be a reasonable excuse for the delay (see **16.28** above).

4.  *Unscramble the scheme*

If the trustees of the A&M settlement agree to unscramble the scheme, they will face a substantial charge to CGT once the freehold passes back to Mr Moore.

The property then will form part of his estate for IHT with a potential charge of £400,000 (£1,000,000 @ 40%).

5.  *End the benefit*

Mr Moore could consider moving out of the property, but this will only be a viable option if he has sufficient funds to purchase or rent another property. Any rent received on the property will have to be taxed and, for CGT and IHT considerations, the problems outlined in option 1 remain.

# Index

*[All references are to paragraph number]*

## A

**Acceptance of property in lieu**
  payment of tax, and 6.35
**Accounts and returns**
  *see also* **Returns**
  introduction 6.2
  lifetime transfers 6.4
**Accumulation and maintenance trusts**
  *see also* **Age 18-to-25 trusts**
  *see also* **Bereaved minors trusts**
  *see also* **Relevant property trusts**
  generally 8.5
  legislative changes 8.5
  migration to new regime 8.24–8.25
  potentially exempt transfers, and 2.8
  protected gifts, and 12.24
**Active service, death on**
  generally 9.5
  introduction 1.20
**Administration expenses**
  liabilities on death, and 3.15
**Age 18-to-25 trusts**
  *see also* **Bereaved minors trusts**
  *see also* **Relevant property trusts**
  chargeable amount 8.11
  conditions 8.8
  deemed potentially exempt transfers, and 2.11
  estate planning, and 13.19
  generally 8.7
  interest in possession trusts, and 7.31
  introduction 8.5
  notional transfer 8.14
  post-death variations, and 13.50–13.51
  problem areas 8.9
  relevant fraction 8.12
  settlement rate 8.13
  spouse exemption, and 13.19
  taxation 8.10
**Agricultural property**
  transferable nil rate band, and 14.28
**Agricultural property relief**
  'agricultural property' 11.24–11.26
  calculation of tax, and 11.50–11.52

**Agricultural property relief** – *contd*
  'character appropriate' 11.31–11.34
  comparison of PETs and chargeable transfers 11.53
  conditions
    occupation or ownership period 11.36–11.37
    replacements 11.39–11.40
    successions 11.38
    valuation of transfer 11.41–11.44
    value for relief 11.45–11.48
  double dipping, and 13.22
  estate on death, and 3.3
  estate planning, and 13.21–13.27
  exemptions and exceptions, and 9.13
  farm buildings 11.35
  farmhouses 11.27–11.28
  farming business 11.29–11.30
  lifetime planning 12.4–12.5
  loss of 11.49
  'mere assets', and 11.24
  ownership period 11.36–11.37
  relevant property trusts, and 8.61–8.66
  replacements 11.39–11.40
  scope
    'agricultural property' 11.24–11.26
    'character appropriate' 11.31–11.34
    farm buildings 11.35
    farmhouses 11.27–11.28
    farming business 11.29–11.30
    types of asset 11.24
  settled gifts, and 5.23
  successions 11.38
  transfer on death, and 3.27
  types of asset 11.24
  valuation of transfer 11.41–11.44
  value for relief 11.45–11.48
**Allocation of burden of tax**
  transfer on death, and 3.35–3.36
**Alternatively secured pension (ASP) funds**
  transferable nil rate band, and 14.11–14.12

*Index*

**Annual exemption**
  estate on death, and 3.4
  exempt property, and 1.20
  generally 9.7
  lifetime transfers, and 2.3
**Annuities**
  accounts and returns, and 6.22
  exempt property, and 1.20
**Anti-avoidance**
  estate on death, and 3.10
  general rule (GAAR) 16.1
  interest in possession trusts, and
    generally 7.10
    termination 7.16
**Appeals**
  'basic' appeal 6.56
  categories 6.54
  'complex' appeal 6.58
  costs 6.61
  'default paper' model 6.55
  generally 6.60
  internal reviews, and 6.59
  overview 6.62
  'standard' appeal 6.57
**Asset valuations**
  'ascertained', 4.30
  bank accounts 4.19
  debts 4.28
  discounted gifts schemes, 4.13
  'estate concept' 4.3
  gifts with reservation 4.27
  guarantees, and 4.31
  household goods 4.29
  introduction 4.1
  joint property
    generally 4.18
    land 4.20–4.24
    money accounts 4.19
  land 4.20–4.24
  liabilities, and 4.31
  life policies
    'back-to-back' arrangements 4.12
    lifetime transfers 4.10
    transfers on death 4.11
  lifetime transfers, and
    generally 2.17
    PETS 2.18
    transfers by close companies 2.19
  'loss to estate' principle 4.2
  open market value 4.1

**Asset valuations** – *contd*
  personal effects 4.29
  quoted shares and securities 4.14
  related property rule
    application 4.5–4.7
    generally 4.4
    relief 4.8
  settled property 4.25
  specific asset rules 4.9
  transfers on death, and
    generally 3.17
    related property 3.18
  unit trusts 4.15
  unquoted shares and securities 4.16–4.17
**Associated operations**
  lifetime transfers, and 2.21–2.22
**Authorised unit trusts**
  generally 9.31
  introduction 1.18
  valuation of assets, and 4.15

**B**

**'Back-to-back' arrangements**
  life policies, and 4.12
**Bank accounts**
  valuation of assets, and 4.19
**Bare trusts**
  generally 6.16
**Bereaved minors trusts**
  *see also* **Age 18-to-25 trusts**
  *see also* **Relevant property trusts**
  conditions 8.6
  estate planning, and 13.18
  generally 8.6
  interest in possession trusts, and 7.31
  introduction 8.5
  post-death variations, and 13.50–13.51
  problem areas 8.9
  spouse exemption, and 13.18
**Business property**
  transferable nil rate band, and 14.28
**Business property relief**
  calculation of tax, and 11.50–11.52
  comparison of PETs and chargeable transfers 11.53
  conditions
    not an investment business 11.10–11.16
    ownership period 11.9

*Index*

**Business property relief** – *contd*
  crops of grass 11.14
  double dipping, and 13.22
  estate on death, and 3.3
  estate planning, and 13.21–13.27
  excepted assets 11.22–11.23
  exemptions and exceptions, and 9.13
  holiday lettings 11.15
  inter-company loans 11.13
  'interest in a business' 11.1–11.2
  landed estates 11.12
  lifetime planning 12.4–12.5
  limited liability partnerships, and 11.3
  loss of 11.49
  'mere assets', and 11.2
  net value 11.21
  'not an investment business'
    background 11.10
    cases concerning lettings 11.11
    crops of grass 11.14
    holiday lettings 11.15
    inter-company loans 11.13
    landed estates 11.12
    small company group 11.16
  ownership period 11.9
  quoted shares in a company 11.5
  rate 11.8
  relevant property trusts, and 8.61–8.66
  scope
    'interest in a business' 11.1–11.2
    limited liability partnerships 11.3
    'mere assets' 11.2
    quoted shares in a company 11.5
    rate of relief 11.8
    shares in a company 11.4–11.5
    trading assets 11.6–11.7
  settled gifts, and 5.23
  shares in a company
    generally 11.4–11.5
    valuation 11.18–11.20
  small company group 11.16
  trading assets 11.6–11.7
  transfer on death, and 3.27
  unincorporated business, and 11.1–11.3
  unquoted shares in a company
    11.4–11.5
  valuation
    net value 11.21
    introduction 11.17
    shares 11.18–11.20

**C**

**Calculation of tax**
  lifetime transfers, and 2.23–2.24
  transfer on death, and
    death estate 3.21
    double tax relief 3.24
    general 3.19
    lifetime transfers 3.20
    quick succession relief 3.23
    transferable nil rate band, 3.22
**Capital gains tax**
  relevant property trusts, and 8.4
**Capital transfer tax**
  generally 1.1
**Care fees**
  transferable nil rate band, and 14.29
**Cash options**
  estate on death, and 3.5
**Chargeable transfers**
  death, on 1.17
  generally 1.9
  lifetime transfers 1.16
  lifetime transfers, and
    generally 2.14–2.16
    introduction 1.16
  relevant property trusts, and 8.2
**Charitable gifts**
  accounts and returns, and 6.19
  estate planning, and 13.28–13.31
  exempt property, and 1.20
  generally 9.18–9.19
  gifts with reservation, and 5.25
  lifetime transfers, and 2.3
**Chattel gifts**
  gifts with reservation, and 5.4
**Child Trust Fund**
  generally 12.2–12.3
**Civil partners, transfers between**
  exempt property, and 1.20
  gifts with reservation, and 5.25
  lifetime transfers, and 2.3
**Civil partnership exemption**
  generally 9.16–9.17
**Clawback of nil rate band**
  alternatively secured pension funds
    14.11–14.12
  clearance certificates 14.13
  introduction 14.8
  penalties 14.14
  second death, after 14.10

*Index*

**Clawback of nil rate band** – *contd*
  surviving spouse still alive, whilst 14.9
  valuations 14.15
**Clearance certificates**
  transferable nil rate band, and 14.13
**Close companies**
  lifetime transfers, and
    generally 2.14
    valuation 2.19
  transfers of value, and 1.27–1.28
**Cohabiting couple**
  transferable nil rate band, and 14.27
**Commorientes**
  transfer on death, and 3.7–3.8
**Compliance**
  acceptance of property in lieu 6.35
  accounts
    introduction 6.2
    lifetime transfers 6.4
  annuities 6.22
  appeals
    'basic' appeal 6.56
    categories 6.54
    'complex' appeal 6.58
    costs 6.61
    'default paper' model 6.55
    generally 6.60
    internal reviews, and 6.59
    overview 6.62
    'standard' appeal 6.57
  bare trusts 6.16
  charitable gifts 6.19
  costs 6.61
  determinations
    form of notice 6.53–6.54
    procedure 6.52
  development value of land 6.21
  direct payment scheme 6.34
  estimates 6.15
  excepted estates and settlements
    bare trusts 6.16
    charitable gifts 6.19
    small estates 6.18
    small foreign estates 6.20
    spouse exemption 6.19
    transfers on death 6.17–6.20
  excepted settlements, 6.8
  excepted terminations, 6.7

**Compliance** – *contd*
  excepted transfers
    generally, 6.6
    introduction, 6.5
  exempt transfers 6.7
  fixed-value fund 6.7
  incidence of tax 6.1
  Inland Revenue charge 6.32
  instalment payments
    generally 6.28
    interest 6.30
    loss of option 6.31
    section 228 shares 6.29
  interest
    generally 6.46
    instalment payments 6.30
  internal reviews, and 6.59
  joint property 6.23
  liability for tax 6.1
  lifetime transfers
    accounts 6.3
    due date 6.27
    payment of tax 6.25–6.27
    reporting after death 6.11
  nil rate band 6.7
  normal expenditure out of income 6.12–6.13
  payment of tax
    acceptance of property in lieu 6.35
    death, on 6.33
    direct payment scheme 6.34
    Inland Revenue charge 6.32
    instalments, by 6.28–6.31
    introduction 6.24
    lifetime transfers 6.25–6.27
  penalties
    degrees of culpability 6.37
    disclosure, and 6.39
    failure to file 6.43
    incorrect returns 6.44–6.45
    introduction 6.36
    late filing 6.50
    late payment 6.49
    levels 6.38
    mitigation of 30% penalties 6.40
    mitigation of 70% penalties 6.41
    mitigation of 100% penalties 6.42
    new approach 6.36
    reductions for disclosure 6.39
    suspension 6.47

**Compliance** – *contd*
  personal effects 6.14
  potentially exempt transfers 6.4
  recent developments 6.2–6.3
  record keeping 6.49
  returns
    estimates 6.15
    introduction 6.2
    lifetime transfers 6.11
    normal expenditure out of income
      6.12–6.13
    personal effects 6.14
    potentially exempt transfers 6.4
    transfers on death 6.4
  small estates 6.18
  small foreign estates 6.20
  small transfers 6.7
  spouse exemption 6.19
  suspension of penalties 6.47
  transfers on death
    charitable gifts 6.19
    generally 6.17–6.20
    payment of tax 6.33
    returns 6.4
    small estates 6.18
    small foreign estates 6.20
    spouse exemption 6.19
  variable value funds 6.7
**Conditionally exempt transfers**
  lifetime transfers, and 2.3
**Consideration of marriage, gifts in**
  estate on death, and 3.4
  exempt property, and 1.20
  gifts with reservation, and 5.25
  lifetime transfers, and 2.3
**Costs**
  determinations and appeals, and
    6.61
**Crops of grass**
  business property relief, and
    11.14
**Cumulation**
  generally 1.10

**D**
**De minimis exceptions**
  gifts with reservation, and 5.28
  pre-owned assets charge, and
    16.25–16.26

**Death, IHT on**
  asset valuations
    generally 3.17
    related property 3.18
  calculation of tax
    death estate 3.21
    double tax relief 3.24
    general 3.19
    lifetime transfers 3.20
    quick succession relief 3.23
    transferable nil rate band, 3.22
  chargeable and exempt estate
    agricultural property relief, and 3.27
    allocation of burden of tax 3.35–3.36
    business property relief, and 3.27
    division of residuary estate between
      exempt and chargeable gifts
      3.37–3.38
    grossing up 3.29–3.34
    introduction 3.25
    partly exempt gifts 3.28
    terminology 3.26
  chargeable transfers, and 1.17
  commorientes 3.7–3.8
  double tax relief 3.24
  estate on death
    calculation of tax, and 3.21
    commorientes 3.7–3.8
    exemptions and exclusions 3.4–3.5
    general 3.2–3.3
    survivorship 3.7–3.8
    woodlands relief 3.6
  estate planning
    agricultural property relief
      13.21–13.27
    business property relief 13.21–13.27
    charitable gifts 13.28–13.31
    deferral of tax 13.12–13.20
    heritage relief 13.32–13.36
    nil rate band 13.1–13.11
    policy trusts 13.37
    post-death variations 13.38–13.51
    spouse exemption 13.12–13.20
    woodlands relief 13.23–13.24
  exemptions and exclusions
    death on active service 9.26
    generally 3.4–3.5
    summary 9.5
    war compensation 9.27
  general 3.2–3.3

*Index*

**Death, IHT on** – *contd*
  grossing up
    double 3.33–3.34
    introduction 3.29
    single 3.30–3.32
  introduction 3.1
  liabilities
    amount 3.13–3.16
    funeral expenses 3.14
    general 3.9–3.11
    guarantee debts 3.12
    Schedule IHT419 3.16
    valuation 3.13–3.16
  post-death variations
    abuse, and 13.42
    alternative relief 13.47–13.49
    child beneficiaries 13.39
    disclaimers 13.43
    formalities 13.44
    further variations, and 13.41
    Glowacki case, 13.46
    introduction 13.38
    post-22 March 2006 relevant
      property trusts 13.50–13.51
    posthumous severance 13.40
    statement of variation 13.45
  quick succession relief 3.23
  rates of tax, and 1.11
  survivorship 3.7–3.8
  transferable nil rate band, 3.22
  woodlands relief 3.6
**'Debt or charge' scheme**
  background 13.2
  charge scheme 13.3
  choice of trustees 13.9
  existing wills, and 13.7
  family home, and 15.46–15.51
  future reform 13.5–13.6
  gift of life interest to spouse 13.4
  index-linking 13.11
  interest 13.11
  liquidity 13.10
  practical issues
    choice of trustees 13.9
    index-linking 13.11
    liquidity 13.10
    trustees 13.9
  procedural difficulties, 13.8
  transferable nil rate band, and 14.1
  trustees 13.9

**Debts**
  valuation of assets, and 4.28
**Decorations for valour**
  excluded property, and 1.19
**Deeds of partition**
  generally 13.49
**Deeds of variation**
  *see* **Post-death variations**
**Deemed PETs**
  *see also* **Potentially exempt transfers**
  age 18-to-25 trusts 2.11
  from 22 March 2006 2.11
  introduction 2.9
  prior to 22 March 2006 2.10
  transitional serial interest 2.11
**Determinations**
  form of notice 6.53–6.54
  procedure 6.52
**Development value of land**
  accounts and returns, and 6.21
**Diplomatic agents, property owned by**
  excluded property, and 9.37
**Direct payment scheme**
  payment of tax, and 6.34
**Disabled person's interest**
  estate on death, and 3.2
**Disabled trusts**
  deemed potentially exempt transfers, and 2.8
  government policy 12.10
  relevant property trusts, and 8.5
  requirements 12.11–12.12
  self-settlement 12.13–12.16
**Discounted gift schemes**
  protected gifts, and 12.26
**Discretionary trusts**
  accumulation and maintenance trusts
    generally 8.5
    legislative changes 8.5
    migration to new regime 8.24–8.25
  age 18-to-25 trusts
    chargeable amount 8.11
    conditions 8.8
    generally 8.7
    introduction 8.5
    notional transfer 8.14
    problem areas 8.9
    relevant fraction 8.12
    settlement rate 8.13
    taxation 8.10

**Discretionary trusts** – *contd*
background 8.1
bereaved minors trusts
  conditions 8.6
  generally 8.6
  introduction 8.5
  problem areas 8.9
capital gains tax, and 8.4
chargeable transfers, and 8.2
deemed potentially exempt transfers, and 2.14
disabled trusts 8.5
effluxion of time, and 8.3
entry charge
  introduction 8.16
  migration from old regime 8.23–8.25
  simple cases 8.17–8.22
exit charge
  'appropriate fraction' 8.37
  'effective rate' 8.36
  general considerations 8.26–8.27
  'hypothetical transfer' 8.28–8.35
  introduction 8.16
  tax charge 8.37
family home, and
  generally 15.31
  points to note 15.34–15.39
  Statement of Practice 15.32–15.33
identifying the taxable entity 8.2
IPDI trusts 8.5
legislative background 8.1
letter of wishes, and
  generally 8.72
  introduction 8.3
life interest trusts
  generally 8.15
operation 8.3
periodic charge
  additions to fund 8.50
  'effective rate' 8.57
  distributions from trust 8.55–8.56
  failed PETs 8.54
  general considerations 8.38–8.39
  'hypothetical transfer' 8.40–8.48
  later anniversaries, and 8.60
  previous transfers 8.49–8.54
  related settlements 8.43–8.48
  tax charge 8.58–8.59
  transfer of value 8.41

**Discretionary trusts** – *contd*
property reliefs, and 8.61–8.66
proportionate charge
  'appropriate fraction' 8.37
  'effective rate' 8.36
  general considerations 8.26–8.27
  'hypothetical transfer' 8.28–8.35
  tax charge 8.37
special charge
  application 8.71
  background 8.67
  rate 8.68–8.69
  variations on rate 8.70
ten-year charge
  additions to fund 8.50
  'effective rate' 8.57
  distributions from trust 8.55–8.56
  failed PETs 8.54
  general considerations 8.38–8.39
  'hypothetical transfer' 8.40–8.48
  later anniversaries, and 8.60
  previous transfers 8.49–8.54
  related settlements 8.43–8.48
  tax charge 8.58–8.59
  transfer of value 8.41
termination 8.3
transfer into trust, and
  migration from old regime 8.23–8.25
  simple cases 8.17–8.22
types 8.1–8.15
**Dispositions for maintenance of family**
generally 9.12
introduction 9.3
**Domicile**
choice, of 1.5
deemed 1.7–1.8
dependence, of 1.6
introduction 1.3
origin, of 1.4
pre-owned assets charge, and 16.27
'3 year rule' 1.7
'17 out of 20 rule' 1.7
**Double charges relief**
generally 10.23
**Double dipping**
generally 13.22
**Double tax agreements**
domicile, and 1.8
generally 10.21

*Index*

**Double taxation relief**
double taxation agreements 10.21
generally 10.19–10.20
gifts with reservation, and 5.36–5.37
introduction 1.24
transfer on death, and 3.24
Treaty relief 1.25
unilateral relief 1.26, 10.22
**'Double trust' arrangements**
family home, and 15.9–15.10
pre-owned assets, and 16.1
**Duty of care**
family home, and 15.2–15.5

**E**

**Effluxion of time**
relevant property trusts, and 8.3
**Employee trusts**
exempt property, and 1.20
generally 9.24–9.25
gifts with reservation, and 5.25
lifetime transfers, and 2.3
**Entry charge**
*see also* **Relevant property trusts**
introduction 8.16
migration from old regime 8.23–8.25
simple cases 8.17–8.22
**Equity release**
commercial sale 15.16
introduction 15.13
loan or mortgage 15.14
pre-owned assets charge, and 16.24
'trading down' 15.15
**Estate agency fees**
liabilities on death, and 3.15
**'Estate concept'**
valuation of assets, and 4.3
**Estate duty**
generally 1.1
**Estate on death**
calculation of tax, and 3.21
commorientes 3.7–3.8
exemptions and exclusions 3.4–3.5
general 3.2–3.3
survivorship 3.7–3.8
woodlands relief 3.6
**Estate planning**
aged 18-to-25 trusts 13.19
agricultural property relief 13.21–13.27

**Estate planning** – *contd*
bereaved minors trusts 13.18
business property relief 13.21–13.27
charitable gifts 13.28–13.31
'debt or charge' scheme
background 13.2
charge scheme 13.3
choice of trustees 13.9
existing wills, and 13.7
future reform 13.5–13.6
gift of life interest to spouse 13.4
index-linking 13.11
interest 13.11
liquidity 13.10
procedural difficulties 13.8
deferral of tax
aged 18-to-25 trusts 13.19
background 13.12–13.13
bereaved minors trusts 13.18
counteraction to perceived abuse 13.14–13.16
life interest trusts 13.20
'wait and see' charge 13.17
family home, and
introduction 15.25
joint ownership 15.41–15.51
nil rate band 15.26
ownership by first spouse to die 15.27–15.39
heritage relief 13.32–13.36
life interest trusts 13.20
nil rate band discretionary trust
debt or charge scheme 13.2–13.11
generally 13.1
policy trusts 13.37
post-death variations
abuse, and 13.42
alternative relief 13.47–13.49
child beneficiaries 13.39
disclaimers 13.43
formalities 13.44
further variations, and 13.41
Glowacki case, 13.46
introduction 13.38
post-22 March 2006 relevant property trusts 13.50–13.51
posthumous severance 13.40
statement of variation 13.45

442

*Index*

**Estate planning** – *contd*
  spouse exemption
    aged 18-to-25 trusts 13.19
    background 13.12–13.13
    bereaved minors trusts 13.18
    counteraction to perceived abuse 13.14–13.16
    life interest trusts 13.20
    'wait and see' charge 13.17
  woodlands relief 13.23–13.24
**Estimates**
  generally 6.15
**'Eversden' schemes**
  family home, and 15.8
  gifts with reservation, and 5.9
**Excluded property**
  authorised unit trust holdings 9.31
  categories 9.28
  decorations for valour 1.18
  diplomatic agents, property owned by 9.37
  foreign property 9.29
  foreign works of art 9.36
  generally 9.6
  government securities 9.30
  introduction 1.18
  National Savings certificates and deposits 1.18
  non-sterling bank accounts 9.35
  OEIC holdings 9.31
  overseas pensions 9.34
  Premium bonds 1.18
  property owned by persons domiciled in Channel Islands or Isle of Man 9.32
  reversionary interests 9.38–9.39
  settled property
    foreign property 1.18
    generally 1.19
  visiting forces 9.33
  war savings certificates 1.18
**Exemptions and exceptions**
  *see also* **Excluded property**
  accounts and returns, and
    charitable gifts 6.19
    small estates 6.18
    small foreign estates 6.20
    spouse exemption 6.19
    transfers on death 6.17–6.20
  active service 9.5

**Exemptions and exceptions** – *contd*
  agricultural property relief, and 9.13
  annual exemption 9.7
  business property relief, and 9.13
  charitable gifts 9.18–9.19
  civil partnership exemption 9.16–9.17
  dispositions for maintenance of family
    generally 9.12
    introduction 9.3
  employee trusts 9.24–9.25
  family maintenance 9.12
  general exemptions
    charitable gifts 9.18–9.19
    civil partnership exemption 9.16–9.17
    employee trusts 9.24–9.25
    housing associations, gifts to 9.21
    maintenance funds 9.23
    national purposes, gifts for 9.22
    political gifts 9.20
    spouse exemption 9.16–9.17
    summary 9.4
  gifts with reservation, and
    de minimis 5.28
    full consideration 5.29–5.30
    general 5.25–5.27
    gifts made before 18 March 1986 5.24
    instruments of variation 5.31
    non-UK assets of non-UK domiciliary 5.32–5.35
  historic buildings, maintenance funds for 9.23
  housing associations, gifts to 9.21
  introduction 9.1
  lifetime transfers, and
    allocation of exemptions 9.13–9.15
    annual exemption 9.7
    dispositions for maintenance of family 9.12
    family maintenance 9.12
    generally 2.2–2.4
    interaction with reliefs 9.13–9.15
    marriage gifts 9.11
    normal expenditure out of income 9.9–9.10
    small gifts 9.8
    summary 9.2
    wedding gifts 9.11
  maintenance funds 9.23

## Index

**Exemptions and exceptions** – *contd*
  marriage gifts 9.11
  national heritage property 9.4
  national purposes, gifts for 9.22
  normal expenditure out of income
    9.9–9.10
  political gifts 9.20
  pre-owned assets charge, and
    de minimis 16.25–16.26
    equity release 16.24
    full consideration 16.23
    GWR rule apply 16.21–16.22
    introduction 16.19
    property in taxpayer's estate 16.20
  small gifts 9.8
  spouse exemption 9.16–9.17
  summary 1.20
  transfers of value, and 1.14
  transfers on death, and
    death on active service 9.26
    generally 3.4–3.5
    summary 9.5
    war compensation 9.27
  war compensation claims 9.27
  wedding gifts 9.11
**Exit charge**
  *see also* **Relevant property trusts**
  'appropriate fraction' 8.37
  'effective rate' 8.36
  general considerations 8.26–8.27
  'hypothetical transfer' 8.28–8.35
  tax charge 8.37

### F

**Failure to file**
  penalties, and 6.43
**'Fall in value' relief**
  generally 10.12
**Family home**
  advisers' duty of care 15.2–15.5
  'debt or charge' schemes 15.46–15.51
  discretionary trusts
    generally 15.31
    points to note 15.34–15.39
    Statement of Practice 15.32–15.33
  'double trust' arrangements
    15.9–15.10
  equity release
    commercial sale 15.16
    introduction 15.13

**Family home** – *contd*
  equity release – *contd*
    loan or mortgage 15.14
    'trading down' 15.15
  estate planning
    introduction 15.25
    joint ownership 15.41–15.51
    nil rate band 15.26
    ownership by first spouse to die
      15.27–15.39
  'Eversden' schemes 15.8
  gift of share of interest
    change of circumstances
      15.22–15.23
    joint occupation 15.18–15.21
    statutory settlements 15.24
  gift of whole of interest 15.17
  interest in possession for survivor
    15.42–15.43
  introduction 15.1
  IOU schemes 15.9–15.10
  joint ownership
    'debt or charge' schemes
      15.46–15.51
    interest in possession for survivor
      15.42–15.43
    introduction 15.41
    nil rate band relevant property trusts
      15.44—15.45
    'sham' trusts 15.52
  lease carve-out schemes 15.7
  life interest trust 15.28–15.30
  'lifetime debt' arrangements
    15.9–15.10
  lifetime planning
    equity release 15.13–15.16
    gift of share 15.18–15.24
    outright gift 15.17
  nil rate band
    relevant property trusts 15.44–15.45
    use 15.26
  notices of severance 15.11–15.12
  outright gift 15.17
  ownership
    first spouse to die, by 15.27–15.39
    generally 15.11–15.12
  ownership by first spouse to die
    discretionary trust 15.31–15.39
    generally 15.27
    life interest trust 15.28–15.30

**Family home** – *contd*
  relevant property trusts
    generally 15.31
    points to note 15.34–15.39
    Statement of Practice 15.32–15.33
  reversionary lease schemes 15.6
  'sham' trusts 15.52
  tenancies in common
    'debt or charge' schemes
      15.46–15.51
    interest in possession for survivor
      15.42–15.43
    introduction 15.41
    nil rate band relevant property trusts
      15.44—15.45
    'sham' trusts 15.52
  'trading down' 15.15
**Family limited partnerships**
  protected gifts without trusts, and 12.22
**Family maintenance**
  exempt lifetime transfers, and 2.4
  transfers of value, and 1.14
**Farming**
  *see* **Agricultural property relief**
**Flexible reversion trusts**
  protected gifts, and 12.27
**Foreign currency bank accounts**
  exempt property, and 9.35
  transfers on death, and 3.5
**Foreign property**
  excluded property, and
    generally 9.29
    introduction 1.18
  interest in possession trusts, and
    7.33–7.34
**Foreign works of art**
  excluded property, and 9.36
**Free estate**
  estate on death, and 3.2
**Funds for historic buildings**
  exempt property, and 1.20
  generally 9.23
  gifts with reservation, and 5.25
  lifetime transfers, and 2.3
**Funeral expenses**
  liabilities at death, and 3.14

**G**
**Gaming debts**
  estate on death, and 3.10

**General anti-avoidance rule (GAAR)**
  generally 16.1
**Gifts**
  exempt property, and
  share of interest in family home, of
    change of circumstances
      15.22–15.23
    joint occupation 15.18–15.21
    statutory settlements 15.24
  transfers of value, and 1.14
  whole of interest in family home, of
    15.17
**Gifts with reservation (GWR)**
  agricultural property relief 5.23
  business property relief 5.23
  chattel gifts 5.4
  de minimis exceptions 5.28
  double tax relief 5.36–5.37
  effect of rules 5.7–5.8
  estate on death, and 3.3
  Eversden schemes 5.9
  exceptions and exclusions
    de minimis 5.28
    full consideration 5.29–5.30
    general 5.25–5.27
    gifts made before 18 March 1986
      5.24
    instruments of variation 5.31
    non-UK assets of non-UK
      domiciliary 5.32–5.35
  'gift' 5.6
  gifts made before 18 March 1986
    5.24
  Ingram schemes 5.11
  instruments of variation 5.31
  insurance policies 5.22
  interest in possession trusts 5.19
  interests in land rules
    Ingram schemes 5.11
    introduction 5.10
    other issues 5.15
    reversionary lease schemes 5.13
    share of interest in land 5.14
    statutory rules 5.12
  interest in possession trusts 5.19
  introduction 5.1–5.2
  lifetime transfers, and 2.20
  non-UK assets of non-UK domiciliary
    5.32–5.35

*Index*

**Gifts with reservation (GWR)** – *contd*
pre-owned assets charge, and
  generally 16.21–16.22
  introduction 5.3
'property' 5.6
relevant period 5.5
reversionary lease schemes 5.13
scope of rules 5.4–5.6
settled gifts, and
  agricultural property relief 5.23
  business property relief 5.23
  insurance policies 5.22
  interest in possession trusts 5.19
  introduction 5.18
  settlor as trustee 5.21
  tracing 5.20
share of interest in land 5.14
'shearing' arrangements 5.38
spouse exemption, and
  Eversden schemes 5.9
  generally 5.25
tracing rules
  generally 5.16–5.17
  settled gifts 5.20
valuation of assets, and 4.27
**Government securities**
generally 9.30
introduction 1.18
**Grossing up**
double 3.33–3.34
generally 1.13
introduction 3.29
single 3.30–3.32
**Guarantees**
liabilities at death, and 3.12
valuation of liabilities, and 4.31

**H**

**Heritage property**
estate planning, and 13.32–13.36
generally 10.27–10.30
transferable nil rate band, and 14.8
**Historic buildings, funds for**
exempt property, and 1.20
generally 9.23
gifts with reservation, and 5.25
lifetime transfers, and 2.3
**Holiday lettings**
business property relief, and 11.15

**Household goods**
valuation of assets, and 4.29
**Housing associations, gifts to**
exempt property, and 1.20
generally 9.21
gifts with reservation, and 5.25
lifetime transfers, and 2.3

**I**

**Immediate post-death interest (IPDI)**
estate on death, and 3.2
generally 7.9
relevant property trusts, and 8.5
termination 7.20
transferable nil rate band, and 14.31
**Incidence of tax**
generally 6.1
**Incorrect returns**
penalties, and 6.44–6.45
**Index-linking**
'debt or charge' scheme, and 13.11
joint ownership of family home, and, 15.50
**Ingram schemes**
interests in land rules, and 5.11
**Inland Revenue charge**
generally 6.32
**Instalment payments**
generally 6.28
interest 6.30
loss of option 6.31
section 228 shares 6.29
**Instruments of variation**
gifts with reservation, and 5.31
**Insurance policies**
interest in possession trusts, and
  existing trusts 7.36
  life policies 7.41
  new trusts 7.39
  pensions 7.40
  transitional provisions 7.37–7.38
  transitionally protected interests 7.36
settled gifts, and 5.22
**Intangible property comprised in settlor**
calculation 16.16
generally 16.12
**Inter-company loans**
business property relief, and 11.13

# Index

**Inter-spouse transfers**
  exempt property, and 1.20
  gifts with reservation, and 5.25
**Interest**
  'debt or charge' scheme, and 13.11
  generally 6.46
  instalment payments 6.30
**Interest in a business**
  business property relief, and 11.1–11.2
**Interest in possession trusts**
  *see also* **No interest in possession trusts**
  age 18-to-25 trusts, and 7.31
  anti-avoidance 7.10
  bereaved minors trusts, and 7.31
  burden of tax, and 7.42
  case law developments 7.3–7.5
  definition 7.5
  disposal
    exceptions from charge 7.12
    general rule 7.11
  estate on death, and 3.2
  excluded property trusts
    foreign assets 7.33–7.34
    loss of status 7.35
    reversionary interests 7.32
  family home, and 15.42–15.43
  gifts with reservation, and 5.19
  immediate post-death interests (IPDI)
    generally 7.9
    termination 7.20
  incidence of tax 7.42
  insurance policy trusts
    existing trusts 7.36
    life policies 7.41
    new trusts 7.39
    pensions 7.40
    transitional provisions 7.37–7.38
    transitionally protected interests 7.36
  introduction
    case law developments 7.3–7.5
    old law 7.1–7.2
    Statement of Practice 7.6
    statutory changes 7.7–7.10
  life policies 7.41
  offshore trusts 7.26
  old law 7.1–7.2
  pensions 7.40
  policy trusts 7.28–7.30

**Interest in possession trusts** – *contd*
  pre-owned assets, and 16.1
  protected gifts, and 12.23
  reversionary and purchased interests
    changes to tax treatment of IIP 7.25
    general rule 7.22
    offshore trusts 7.26
    purchase of interests in trusts 7.24
    rule in *Melville v IRC* 7.23
  Statement of Practice (10/79) 7.6
  statutory changes
    background 7.7
    outline 7.8–7.10
  termination
    anti-avoidance 7.16
    exceptions from charge 7.21
    immediate post death interests, of 7.20
    law from 22 March 2006 7.19
    maintenance funds 7.18
    old law 7.13–7.14
    revertor to settlor 7.15
    use of annual exemption 7.17
  transfers on death, and 3.2
  transitional provisions 7.27–7.31
  transitional serial interests 7.27
  transitionally protected interests 7.36
**Interests in land rules**
  Ingram schemes 5.11
  introduction 5.10
  other issues 5.15
  reversionary lease schemes 5.13
  share of interest in land 5.14
  statutory rules 5.1
**Intestate estates**
  order of distribution 3.1
**IOU schemes**
  family home, and 15.9–15.10
**IPDI trusts**
  estate on death, and 3.2
  generally 7.9
  relevant property trusts, and 8.5
  termination 7.20

## J

**Joint ownership of family home**
  'debt or charge' schemes 15.46–15.51
  index-linked nil rate sums, 15.50
  interest in possession for survivor 15.42–15.43

## Index

**Joint ownership of family home** – *contd*
  introduction 15.41
  nil rate band relevant property trusts 15.44—15.45
  'sham' trusts 15.52
**Joint property**
  accounts and returns, and 6.23
  valuation of assets, and
    generally 4.18
    land 4.20–4.24
    money accounts 4.19

### L

**Land**
  post-death relief, and 10.17–10.18
  pre-owned assets charge, and
    calculation 16.14
    generally 16.3–16.6
  valuation of assets, and 4.20–4.24
**Landed estates**
  business property relief, and 11.12
**Lease carve-out schemes**
  family home, and 15.7
  pre-owned assets, and 16.1
**Letter of wishes**
  *see also* **Relevant property trusts**
  generally 8.72
  introduction 8.3
**Liabilities on death**
  amount 3.13–3.16
  funeral expenses 3.14
  general 3.9–3.11
  guarantee debts 3.12
  Schedule IHT419 3.16
  valuation 3.13–3.16
**Liability for tax**
  generally 6.1
**Liability of individuals**
  generally 1.2
**Life insurance policies**
  deemed potentially exempt transfers, and 2.5
  interest in possession trusts, and 7.41
  protected gifts, and 12.25
  settled gifts, and 5.22
  valuation of assets, and
    'back-to-back' arrangements 4.12–4.13
    lifetime transfers 4.10
    transfers on death 4.11

**Life interest trusts**
  *see also* **Relevant property trusts**
  estate planning, and 13.20
  family home, and 15.28–15.30
  generally 8.15
**'Lifetime debt' arrangements**
  family home, and 15.9–15.10
  pre-owned assets, and 16.1
**Lifetime planning**
  accumulation and maintenance trusts 12.24
  agricultural property relief 12.4–12.5
  business property relief 12.4–12.5
  Child Trust Fund 12.2–12.3
  disabled trusts
    government policy 12.10
    requirements 12.11–12.12
    self-settlement 12.13–12.16
  discounted gift schemes 12.26
  discretionary trusts 12.28–12.30
  family home, and
    equity release 15.13–15.16
    gift of share 15.18–15.24
    outright gift 15.17
  family limited partnerships, 12.22
  flexible reversion trusts, 12.27
  interest in possession trusts 12.23
  life policy trusts 12.25
  options 12.19–12.21
  outright gifts
    generally 12.6
    subtle schemes 12.9
    unwise gifts 12.7–12.8
  pensions
    children, for 12.18
    grandchildren, for 12.17
  policy trusts 12.25
  post-22 March 2006 trusts 12.28–12.30
  protected gifts
    accumulation and maintenance trusts 12.24
    discounted gift schemes 12.26
    flexible reversion trusts, 12.27
    relevant property trusts 12.28–12.30
    interest in possession trusts 12.23
    life policy trusts 12.25
    options 12.19–12.21
    pensions for children 12.18
    pensions for grandchildren 12.17

448

*Index*

**Lifetime planning** – *contd*
  protected gifts – *contd*
    policy trusts 12.25
    post-22 March 2006 trusts 12.28–12.30
    transitional serial interests 12.23
    relevant property trusts 12.28–12.30
    unwise gifts 12.7–12.8
    use of reliefs 12.1
**Lifetime transfers**
  accounts 6.3
  accumulation and maintenance trusts 2.8
  age 18-to-25 trusts 2.11
  associated operations 2.21–2.22
  calculation of tax 2.23–2.24
  chargeable transfers
    generally 2.14–2.16
    introduction 1.16
  close companies, by
    generally 2.14
    valuation 2.19
  deemed PETs
    age 18-to-25 trusts 2.11
    from 22 March 2006 2.11
    introduction 2.9
    prior to 22 March 2006 2.10
    transitional serial interest 2.11
  disabled trusts, gifts to 2.8
  discretionary trusts 2.14
  due date for payment 6.27
  exempt transfers
    interaction with reliefs 9.13–9.15
    marriage gifts 9.11
    normal expenditure out of income 9.9–9.10
    small gifts 9.8
    summary 9.2
    wedding gifts 9.11
  gifts with reservation 2.20
  introduction 2.1
  life insurance polices, and 2.5
  payment of tax 6.25–6.27
  planning
    agricultural property relief 12.4–12.5
    business property relief 12.4–12.5
    Child Trust Fund 12.2–12.3
    disabled trusts 12.10–12.16
    outright gifts 12.6–12.9

**Lifetime transfers** – *contd*
  planning – *contd*
    protected gifts 12.17–12.30
    unwise gifts 12.7–12.8
    use of reliefs 12.1
  potentially exempt transfers
    accumulation and maintenance trusts 2.8
    deemed PETs 2.9–2.12
    definition 2.5–2.8
    disabled trusts, gifts to 2.8
    from 22 March 2006 2.7
    implications 2.13
    introduction 2.1
    life insurance polices, and 2.5
    prior to 22 March 2006 2.6
    scope 2.5–2.8
    valuation 2.18
  rates of tax
    generally 2.23
    introduction 1.11
  relevant property trusts 2.14
  reporting requirements
    after death 6.11
    generally 2.25
  taper relief 2.24
  valuation
    generally 2.17
    PETS 2.18
    transfers by close companies 2.19
**Limited liability partnerships**
  business property relief, and 11.3
**'Loss to estate' principle**
  valuation of assets, and 4.2

**M**

**Maintenance funds for historic buildings**
  exempt property, and 1.20
  generally 9.23
  gifts with reservation, and 5.25
  lifetime transfers, and 2.3
**Marriage gifts**
  estate on death, and 3.4
  exempt property, and 1.20
  generally 9.11
  gifts with reservation, and 5.25
  lifetime transfers, and 2.3
**Medals for valour**
  excluded property, and 1.19

*Index*

## N

**National heritage transfers**
generally 9.4
introduction 2.3
**National purposes, gifts for**
exempt property, and 1.20
generally 9.22
gifts with reservation, and 5.25
lifetime transfers, and 2.3
**National Savings Bank deposits**
excluded property, and 1.18
**National Savings Certificates**
excluded property, and 1.18
**Net value**
business property relief, and 11.21
**Nil rate band**
cumulation, and 1.10
debt or charge scheme
background 13.2
charge scheme 13.3
choice of trustees 13.9
existing wills, and 13.7
future reform 13.5–13.6
gift of life interest to spouse 13.4
index-linking 13.11
interest 13.11
liquidity 13.10
procedural difficulties 13.8
family home, and
relevant property trusts 15.44–15.45
use 15.26
generally 13.1
**Non-domiciled individuals**
gifts with reservation, and 5.32–5.35
liability 1.2
**Non-sterling bank accounts**
generally 9.35
introduction 1.18
**Non-UK assets of non-UK domiciliary**
gifts with reservation, and 5.32–5.35
**Normal expenditure out of income**
claims 6.12–6.13
estate on death, and 3.4
exempt property, and 1.20
generally 9.9–9.10
lifetime transfers, and 2.3
**Notices of severance**
family home, and 15.11–15.12

## O

**Offshore trusts**
interest in possession trusts, and 7.26
**Open-ended investment company investments**
generally 9.31
introduction 1.18
**Open market value**
valuation of assets, and 4.1
**Options**
protected gifts, and 12.19–12.21
**Outright gifts**
family home, and 15.17
generally 12.6
subtle schemes 12.9
unwise gifts 12.7–12.8
**Overseas pensions**
estate on death, and 3.5
excluded property, and 9.34
**Ownership of family home**
first spouse to die, by 15.27–15.39
discretionary trust 15.31–15.39
generally 15.27
life interest trust 15.28–15.30
generally 15.11–15.12

## P

**Partly exempt gifts**
transfer on death, and 3.28
**Payment of tax**
acceptance of property in lieu 6.35
death, on 6.33
direct payment scheme 6.34
Inland Revenue charge 6.32
instalments, by
generally 6.28
interest 6.30
loss of option 6.31
section 228 shares 6.29
introduction 6.24
lifetime transfers 6.25–6.27
**Penalties**
degrees of culpability, 6.37
disclosure, and, 6.39
failure to file 6.43
incorrect returns 6.44–6.45
introduction, 6.36
late filing 6.50
late payment 6.49
levels, 6.38

**Penalties** – *contd*
  mitigation of 30% penalties, 6.40
  mitigation of 70% penalties, 6.41
  mitigation of 100% penalties, 6.42
  new approach, 6.36
  reductions for disclosure, 6.39
  suspension, 6.47
  transferable nil rate band, and 14.14
**Pension schemes**
  children, for 12.18
  estate on death, and 3.5
  grandchildren, for 12.17
  interest in possession trusts, and 7.40
**Periodic charge**
  *see also* **Relevant property trusts**
  additions to fund 8.50
  'effective rate' 8.57
  distributions from trust 8.55–8.56
  failed PETs 8.54
  general considerations 8.38–8.39
  'hypothetical transfer' 8.40–8.48
  later anniversaries, and 8.60
  previous transfers 8.49–8.54
  related settlements 8.43–8.48
  tax charge 8.58–8.59
  transfer of value 8.41
**Personal effects**
  generally 6.14
  valuation of assets, and 4.29
**Personal pension schemes**
  estate on death, and 3.5
  exempt property, and 1.20
**Policy trusts**
  estate planning, and 13.37
  interest in possession trusts, and 7.28–7.30
  protected gifts, and 12.25
**Political gifts**
  exempt property, and 1.20
  generally 9.20
  gifts with reservation, and 5.25
  lifetime transfers, and 2.3
**Post-death variations**
  abuse, and 13.42
  alternative relief 13.47–13.49
  child beneficiaries 13.39
  deed of partition 13.49
  disclaimers 13.43
  formalities 13.44

**Post-death variations** – *contd*
  further variations, and 13.41
  Glowacki case, 13.46
  introduction 13.38
  post-22 March 2006 relevant property trusts 13.50–13.51
  posthumous severance 13.40
  statement of variation 13.45
**Potentially exempt transfers (PETs)**
  accounts and returns, and 6.4
  accumulation and maintenance trusts 2.8
  deemed PETs
    age 18-to-25 trusts 2.11
    from 22 March 2006 2.11
    introduction 2.9
    prior to 22 March 2006 2.10
    transitional serial interest 2.11
  definition 2.5–2.8
  disabled trusts, gifts to 2.8
  from 22 March 2006 2.7
  generally 1.15
  implications 2.13
  introduction 2.1
  life insurance polices, and 2.5
  prior to 22 March 2006 2.6
  scope 2.5–2.8
  setting aside 10.13
  valuation 2.18
**Pre-owned assets charge**
  chattels, on
    calculation 16.15
    generally 16.7–16.11
  domicile of taxpayer 16.27
  excluded transactions 16.18
  exemptions
    de minimis 16.25–16.26
    equity release 16.24
    full consideration 16.23
    GWR rule apply 16.21–16.22
    introduction 16.19
    property in taxpayer's estate 16.20
  family home, and 15.5
  gifts with reservation, and 5.3
  intangible property comprised in settlor, on
    calculation 16.16
    generally 16.12
    introduction 16.1–16.2

*Index*

**Pre-owned assets charge** – *contd*
  land, on
    calculation 16.14
    generally 16.3–16.6
    opting out 16.28–16.29
    remedial action to existing
      arrangements 16.30
    residence of taxpayer 16.27
    scope of legislation 16.13
    valuation 16.17
**Premium savings bonds**
  generally 1.18
  introduction 1.18
**Probate fees**
  liabilities on death, and 3.15
**Professional fees**
  liabilities on death, and 3.15
**Professional negligence**
  family home, and 15.2–15.5
**Proportionate charge**
  *see also* **Relevant property trusts**
  'appropriate fraction' 8.37
  'effective rate' 8.36
  general considerations 8.26–8.27
  'hypothetical transfer' 8.28–8.35
  tax charge 8.37
**Protected gifts**
  accumulation and maintenance trusts 12.24
  discounted gift schemes 12.26
  interest in possession trusts 12.23
  life policy trusts 12.25
  options 12.19–12.21
  pensions for children 12.18
  pensions for grandchildren 12.17
  policy trusts 12.25
  post-22 March 2006 trusts 12.28–12.30
  relevant property trusts 12.28–12.30
  transitional serial interests 12.23
**Public benefit, gifts for**
  exempt property, and 1.20
  gifts with reservation, and 5.25

**Q**
**Quick succession relief**
  generally 10.4–10.5
  introduction 1.23
  overview 10.1
  transfer on death, and 3.23

**Quoted shares and securities**
  business property relief, and 11.5
  valuation of assets, and 4.14

**R**
**Rates of tax**
  death 1.12
  grossing-up 1.13
  lifetime transfers 1.11
  lifetime transfers, and
    generally 2.23
    introduction 1.11
  transfer on death, and 1.11
**Record keeping**
  generally 6.49
  transferable nil rate band, and 14.17
**Related property relief**
  generally 10.6–10.7
  introduction 4.8
  overview 10.1
**Related property rule**
  application 4.5–4.7
  generally 4.4
  introduction 3.18
  relief 4.8
**Relevant property trusts**
  accumulation and maintenance trusts
    generally 8.5
    legislative changes 8.5
    migration to new regime 8.24–8.25
  age 18-to-25 trusts
    chargeable amount 8.11
    conditions 8.8
    generally 8.7
    introduction 8.5
    notional transfer 8.14
    problem areas 8.9
    relevant fraction 8.12
    settlement rate 8.13
    taxation 8.10
  background 8.1
  bereaved minors trusts
    conditions 8.6
    generally 8.6
    introduction 8.5
    problem areas 8.9
  capital gains tax, and 8.4
  chargeable transfers, and 8.2
  deemed potentially exempt transfers, and 2.14

452

## Index

**Relevant property trusts** – *contd*
disabled trusts 8.5
effluxion of time, and 8.3
entry charge
  introduction 8.16
  migration from old regime 8.23–8.25
  simple cases 8.17–8.22
exit charge
  'appropriate fraction' 8.37
  'effective rate' 8.36
  general considerations 8.26–8.27
  'hypothetical transfer' 8.28–8.35
  introduction 8.16
  tax charge 8.37
family home, and
  generally 15.31
  points to note 15.34–15.39
  Statement of Practice 15.32–15.33
identifying the taxable entity 8.2
IPDI trusts 8.5
legislative background 8.1
letter of wishes, and
  generally 8.72
  introduction 8.3
life interest trusts 8.15
operation 8.3
periodic charge
  additions to fund 8.50
  'effective rate' 8.57
  distributions from trust 8.55–8.56
  failed PETs 8.54
  general considerations 8.38–8.39
  'hypothetical transfer' 8.40–8.48
  later anniversaries, and 8.60
  previous transfers 8.49–8.54
  related settlements 8.43–8.48
  tax charge 8.58–8.59
  transfer of value 8.41
property reliefs, and 8.61–8.66
proportionate charge
  'appropriate fraction' 8.37
  'effective rate' 8.36
  general considerations 8.26–8.27
  'hypothetical transfer' 8.28–8.35
  tax charge 8.37
special charge
  application 8.71
  background 8.67
  rate 8.68–8.69
  variations on rate 8.70

**Relevant property trusts** – *contd*
ten-year charge
  additions to fund 8.50
  'effective rate' 8.57
  distributions from trust 8.55–8.56
  failed PETs 8.54
  general considerations 8.38–8.39
  'hypothetical transfer' 8.40–8.48
  later anniversaries, and 8.60
  previous transfers 8.49–8.54
  related settlements 8.43–8.48
  tax charge 8.58–8.59
  transfer of value 8.41
termination 8.3
transfer into trust, and
  migration from old regime 8.23–8.25
  simple cases 8.17–8.22
types 8.1–8.15
**Reliefs**
agricultural property relief
  *and see* **Agricultural property relief**
  conditions 11.36–11.48
  lifetime planning 12.4–12.5
  loss of 11.49–11.52
  scope 11.24–11.35
business property relief
  *and see* **Business property relief**
  conditions 11.9–11.16
  excepted assets 11.22–11.23
  lifetime planning 12.4–12.5
  loss of 11.49–11.52
  scope 11.1–11.8
  valuation 11.17–11.21
Child Trust Fund 12.2–12.3
disabled trusts
  government policy 12.10
  requirements 12.11–12.12
  self-settlement 12.13–12.16
double charges relief 10.23
double taxation relief
  double taxation agreements 10.21
  generally 10.19–10.20
  introduction 1.24
  Treaty relief 1.25
  unilateral relief 1.26, 10.22
'fall in value' relief 10.12

## Index

**Reliefs** – *contd*
gifts
  outright gifts 12.6
  protected gifts 12.17–12.30
  unwise gifts 12.7–12.8
heritage property 10.27–10.30
introduction 10.1
land 10.17–10.18
lifetime planning
  agricultural property relief 12.4–12.5
  business property relief 12.4–12.5
  Child Trust Fund 12.2–12.3
  disabled trusts 12.10–12.16
  outright gifts 12.6–12.9
  protected gifts 12.17–12.30
  unwise gifts 12.7–12.8
  use of reliefs 12.1
outright gifts
  generally 12.6
  subtle schemes 12.9
  unwise gifts 12.7–12.8
post-death reliefs
  land 10.17–10.18
  shares 10.14–10.16
protected gifts
  accumulation and maintenance trusts 12.24
  discounted gift schemes 12.26
  interest in possession trusts 12.23
  life policy trusts 12.25
  options 12.19–12.21
  pensions for children 12.18
  pensions for grandchildren 12.17
  policy trusts 12.25
  post-22 March 2006 trusts 12.28–12.30
  relevant property trusts 12.28–12.30
  transitional serial interests 12.23
quick succession relief
  generally 10.4–10.5
  introduction 1.23
  overview 10.1
related property relief
  generally 10.6–10.7
  introduction 4.8
  overview 10.1
setting aside PETs 10.13
shares 10.14–10.16

**Reliefs** – *contd*
taper relief
  generally 10.2–10.3
  introduction 1.21–1.22
  overview 10.1
transfers within seven years before death
  'fall in value' relief 10.12
  generally 10.8–10.10
  setting aside PETs 10.13
  wasting assets 10.11
wasting assets, and 10.11
woodlands relief
  disposal of trees or underwood 10.25
  generally 10.24
  planning 10.26
**Reporting requirements**
lifetime transfers, and 2.25
**Residence**
*see also* **Domicile**
pre-owned assets charge, and 16.27
**Retirement annuity contracts**
estate on death, and 3.5
exempt property, and 1.20
**Returns**
estimates 6.15
excepted estates and settlements, and
  charitable gifts 6.19
  small estates 6.18
  small foreign estates 6.20
  spouse exemption 6.19
  transfers on death 6.17–6.20
introduction 6.2
lifetime transfers 6.11
normal expenditure out of income 6.12–6.13
penalties
  failure to file 6.43
  incorrect returns 6.44–6.45
personal effects 6.14
potentially exempt transfers 6.4
transfers on death 6.4
**Reversionary interests**
changes to tax treatment of IIP 7.25
excluded property, and
  generally 9.38–9.39
  introduction 1.18
general rule 7.22
offshore trusts 7.26

*Index*

**Reversionary interests** – *contd*
purchase of interests in trusts 7.24
rule in *Melville v IRC* 7.23
**Reversionary lease schemes**
family home, and 15.6
interests in land rules, and 5.13
pre-owned assets, and 16.1

**S**

**Settled life policies**
generally 8.17
**Settled property**
estate on death, and 3.2
excluded property, and
generally 1.19
introduction 1.18
gifts with reservation, and
agricultural property relief 5.23
business property relief 5.23
insurance policies 5.22
interest in possession trusts 5.19
introduction 5.18
settlor as trustee 5.21
tracing 5.20
interest in possession
*and see* **Interest in possession**
case law developments 7.3–7.5
disposal 7.11–7.12
excluded property trusts 7.32–7.35
insurance policy trusts 7.36–7.41
old law 7.1–7.2
purchased interests 7.22–7.26
reversionary interests 7.22–7.26
Statement of Practice 7.6
statutory changes 7.7–7.10
termination 7.13–7.21
transitional provisions 7.27–7.31
no interest in possession
*and see* **No interest in possession**
exit charge 8.26–8.37
periodic charge 8.38–8.60
property reliefs, and 8.61–8.66
proportionate charge 8.26–8.37
special charge 8.67–8.71
ten-year charge 8.38–8.60
transfer into trust 8.17–8.25
types of relevant property trusts 8.1–8.15

**Settled property** – *contd*
trusts
interest in possession 7.1–7.41
non-interest in possession 8.1–8.71
valuation of assets, and 4.25
**Settlors**
settled gifts, and 5.21
**'Sham' trusts**
family home, and 15.52
**Share transfers to employee trusts**
exempt property, and 1.20
generally 9.24–9.25
gifts with reservation, and 5.25
lifetime transfers, and 2.3
**Shares**
post-death relief, and 10.14–10.16
**'Shearing' arrangements**
gifts with reservation, and 5.38
**Small company group**
business property relief, and 11.16
**Small estates**
accounts and returns, and 6.18
**Small foreign estates**
accounts and returns, and 6.20
**Small gifts**
estate on death, and 3.4
exempt property, and 1.20
generally 9.8
gifts with reservation, and 5.25
lifetime transfers, and 2.3
**Special (s 70) charge**
*see also* **Relevant property trusts**
application 8.71
background 8.67
rate 8.68–8.69
variations on rate 8.70
**Spouse exemption**
accounts and returns, and 6.19
estate planning, and
aged 18-to-25 trusts 13.19
background 13.12–13.13
bereaved minors trusts 13.18
counteraction to perceived abuse 13.14–13.16
life interest trusts 13.20
'wait and see' charge 13.17
exempt property, and 1.20
generally 9.16–9.17

455

*Index*

**Spouse exemption** – *contd*
  gifts with reservation, and
    Eversden schemes 5.9
  generally 5.25
  lifetime transfers, and 2.3
  transferable nil rate band, and 14.30
**Statements of Practice**
  interest in possession trusts, and 7.6
**Superannuation funds**
  estate on death, and 3.5
**Survivorship**
  commorientes, and 3.7–3.8

**T**

**Taper relief**
  generally 10.2–10.3
  introduction 1.21–1.22
  overview 10.1
  lifetime transfers, and 2.24
**Ten-year charge**
  *see also* **Relevant property trusts**
  additions to fund 8.50
  'effective rate' 8.57
  distributions from trust 8.55–8.56
  failed PETs 8.54
  general considerations 8.38–8.39
  'hypothetical transfer' 8.40–8.48
  later anniversaries, and 8.60
  previous transfers 8.49–8.54
  related settlements 8.43–8.48
  tax charge 8.58–8.59
  transfer of value 8.41
**Tenancies in common**
  'debt or charge' schemes 15.46–15.51
  interest in possession for survivor
    15.42–15.43
  introduction 15.41
  nil rate band relevant property trusts
    15.44—15.45
  'sham' trusts 15.52
**Threshold**
  *and see* **Nil rate band**
  cumulation, and 1.10
**Tracing rules**
  generally 5.16–5.17
  settled gifts 5.20
**Trading assets**
  business property relief, and 11.6–11.7
**'Trading down'**
  family home, and 15.15

**Transferable nil rate bands**
  alternative pension funds, and
    14.11–14.12
  background 14.1
  calculation of tax on transfer on death,
    and 3.22
  calculation of unused nil rate band
    14.3
  clawback of nil rate band
    alternative pension funds
      14.11–14.12
    clearance certificates 14.13
    introduction 14.8
    penalties 14.14
    second death, after 14.10
    surviving spouse still alive, whilst
      14.9
    valuations 14.15
  clearance certificates 14.13
  deaths before 25 July 1986, and
    14.86
  'debt or charge' schemes, and 14.1
  heritage assets 14.8
  immediate post-death interest, and
    14.31
  outline of rules 14.2
  penalties 14.14
  planning issues
    agricultural property 14.28
    business property 14.28
    care fees, 14.29
    cohabiting couple 14.27
    earlier marriages or civil
      partnerships 14.26
    use of nil rate band on first death
      14.20–14.25
  record keeping 14.17
  supporting documentation,
    14.18–14.19
  surviving spouse exemption, and
    14.30
  transfer claims 14.5–14.7
  unexhausted ASP funds 14.11
  use of nil rate band on first death
    14.20
  valuations 14.15
  woodlands 14.8
**Transfers of value**
  close companies, by 1.27–1.28
  generally 1.14

*Index*

**Transfers on death**
  accounts and returns, and
    charitable gifts 6.19
    generally 6.17
    small estates 6.18
    small foreign estates 6.20
    spouse exemption 6.19
  asset valuations
    generally 3.17
    related property 3.18
  calculation of tax
    death estate 3.21
    double tax relief 3.24
    general 3.19
    lifetime transfers 3.20
    quick succession relief 3.23
    transferable nil rate band, 3.22
  chargeable and exempt estate
    agricultural property relief, and 3.27
    allocation of burden of tax 3.35–3.36
    business property relief, and 3.27
    division of residuary estate between
        exempt and chargeable gifts
        3.37–3.38
    grossing up 3.29–3.34
    introduction 3.25
    partly exempt gifts 3.28
    terminology 3.26
  chargeable transfers, and 1.17
  commorientes 3.7–3.8
  double tax relief 3.24
  estate on death
    calculation of tax, and 3.21
    commorientes 3.7–3.8
    exemptions and exclusions 3.4–3.5
    general 3.2–3.3
    survivorship 3.7–3.8
    woodlands relief 3.6
  estate planning
    agricultural property relief
      13.21–13.27
    business property relief 13.21–13.27
    charitable gifts 13.28–13.31
    deferral of tax 13.12–13.20
    heritage relief 13.32–13.36
    nil rate band 13.1–13.11
    policy trusts 13.37
    post-death variations 13.38–13.51
    spouse exemption 13.12–13.20
    woodlands relief 13.23–13.24

**Transfers on death** – *contd*
  exemptions and exclusions
    death on active service 9.26
    generally 3.4–3.5
    summary 9.5
    war compensation 9.27
  general 3.2–3.3
  grossing up
    double 3.33–3.34
    introduction 3.29
    single 3.30–3.32
  introduction 3.1
  liabilities
    amount 3.13–3.16
    funeral expenses 3.14
    general 3.9–3.11
    guarantee debts 3.12
    Schedule IHT419 3.16
    valuation 3.13–3.16
  payment of tax 6.33
  post-death variations
    abuse, and 13.42
    alternative relief 13.47–13.49
    child beneficiaries 13.39
    disclaimers 13.43
    formalities 13.44
    further variations, and 13.41
    Glowacki case, 13.46
    introduction 13.38
    post-22 March 2006 relevant
        property trusts 13.50–13.51
    posthumous severance 13.40
    statement of variation 13.45
  quick succession relief 3.23
  rates of tax, and 1.11
  returns 6.4
  survivorship 3.7–3.8
  transferable nil rate band, 3.22
  woodlands relief 3.6

**Transfers within seven years before death**
  'fall in value' relief 10.12
  generally 10.8–10.10
  setting aside PETs 10.13
  wasting assets 10.11

**Transitional serial interests**
  deemed PETs, and 2.11
  estate on death, and 3.2
  generally 7.27
  protected gifts, and 12.23

*Index*

**Transitionally protected interests**
generally 7.36
**Trusts**
interest in possession
*and see* **Interest in possession**
case law developments 7.3–7.5
disposal 7.11–7.12
excluded property trusts 7.32–7.35
insurance policy trusts 7.36–7.41
old law 7.1–7.2
purchased interests 7.22–7.26
reversionary interests 7.22–7.26
Statement of Practice 7.6
statutory changes 7.7–7.10
termination 7.13–7.21
transitional provisions 7.27–7.31
no interest in possession
*and see* **No interest in possession**
exit charge 8.26–8.37
periodic charge 8.38–8.60
property reliefs, and 8.61–8.66
proportionate charge 8.26–8.37
special charge 8.67–8.71
ten-year charge 8.38–8.60
transfer into trust 8.17–8.25
types of relevant property trusts 8.1–8.15

**U**

**UK-domiciled individuals**
liability 1.2
**Unit trusts**
generally 9.31
introduction 1.18
valuation of assets, and 4.15
**Unincorporated business**
business property relief, and 11.1–11.3
**Unquoted shares and securities**
business property relief, and 11.4–11.5
valuation of assets, and 4.16–4.17

**V**

**Valuation**
*and see* **Valuation of assets**
agricultural property relief, and
transfer 11.41–11.44
value for relief 11.45–11.48

**Valuation** – *contd*
business property relief, and
net value 11.21
introduction 11.17
shares 11.18–11.20
liabilities at death, and 3.13–3.16
pre-owned assets charge, and 16.17
transferable nil rate band, and 14.15
**Valuation of assets**
'ascertained', 4.30
bank accounts 4.19
debts 4.28
discounted gifts schemes, 4.13
'estate concept' 4.3
gifts with reservation 4.27
guarantees, and 4.31
household goods 4.29
introduction 4.1
joint property
generally 4.18
land 4.20–4.24
money accounts 4.19
land 4.20–4.24
liabilities, and 4.31
life policies
'back-to-back' arrangements 4.12
lifetime transfers 4.10
transfers on death 4.11
lifetime transfers, and
generally 2.17
PETS 2.18
transfers by close companies 2.19
'loss to estate' principle 4.2
open market value 4.1
personal effects 4.29
quoted shares and securities 4.14
related property rule
application 4.5–4.7
generally 4.4
relief 4.8
settled property 4.25
specific asset rules 4.9
transfers on death, and
generally 3.17
related property 3.18
unit trusts 4.15
unquoted shares and securities 4.16–4.17
**Valuation of liabilities**
guarantees 4.31

*Index*

**Visiting forces**
excluded property, and 9.33

**W**

**Waivers of remuneration**
transfers of value, and 1.14
**War compensation claims**
generally 9.27
introduction 1.18
**War savings certificates**
excluded property, and 1.18
**Wasting assets**
reliefs, and 10.11
**Wedding gifts**
estate on death, and 3.4

**Wedding gifts** – *contd*
exempt property, and 1.20
generally 9.11
gifts with reservation, and 5.25
lifetime transfers, and 2.3
**Woodlands**
transferable nil rate band, and 14.8
**Woodlands relief**
disposal of trees or underwood 10.25
double dipping, and 13.22
estate planning, and 13.23–13.24
generally 10.24
introduction 3.6
planning 10.26